A Woman Is Responsible for Everything

JEWISH WOMEN IN EARLY
MODERN EUROPE

DEBRA KAPLAN AND
ELISHEVA CARLEBACH

PRINCETON UNIVERSITY PRESS
PRINCETON & OXFORD

Copyright © 2025 by Princeton University Press

Princeton University Press is committed to the protection of copyright and the intellectual property our authors entrust to us. Copyright promotes the progress and integrity of knowledge created by humans. By engaging with an authorized copy of this work, you are supporting creators and the global exchange of ideas. As it is protected by copyright, any intentions to reproduce, distribute any part of the work in any form for any purpose require permission; permission requests should be sent to permissions@press.princeton.edu. Ingestion of any IP for any AI purposes is strictly prohibited.

Published by Princeton University Press
41 William Street, Princeton, New Jersey 08540
99 Banbury Road, Oxford OX2 6JX

press.princeton.edu

All Rights Reserved

Debra Kaplan and Elisheva Carlebach assert equal authorship rights in all aspects of this book.

Library of Congress Control Number: 2025930664

ISBN 9780691268613
ISBN (e-book) 9780691268637

British Library Cataloging-in-Publication Data is available

Editorial: Fred Appel, James Collier
Production Editorial: Elizabeth Byrd
Jacket: Kathryn Stevens
Production: Erin Suydam
Publicity: William Pagdatoon (US), Kathryn Stevens (UK)
Copyeditor: Sherry Howard Salois

Jacket image: Friedrich Campe, *Der Samstug (Saturday)*, c. 1800, hand-colored engraving. Skirball Cultural Center, Los Angeles.

Printed in the United States of America

10 9 8 7 6 5 4 3 2 1

CONTENTS

	Introduction	1
1	Life in the Kehillah	20
2	Sacred Societies: Women's Hevrot	47
3	Honor and Shame, Center and Periphery	74
4	Jewish Women and Print Culture	100
5	Ordinary and Literary Writing	126
6	Dynamic Households	152
7	Economic Agents	186
8	Material Worlds	222
9	Last Words	252
10	Bodies and Souls	274
11	Custom and Ritual	306
	Conclusion	338

Acknowledgments 343
Glossary 347
Notes 349
Selected Bibliography 403

Illustration Credits 435

Index 441

Color plates follow pages 136 and 312

A WOMAN IS RESPONSIBLE
FOR EVERYTHING

Introduction

RECHLE DRACH did not get much sleep, occupied as she was with work, family, and pious deeds in her native Frankfurt. "In all seasons, during the night as if it were day, in darkness and in light, she was called by women sitting on the birthing stools, and they chased after her to go hither and thither. Nevertheless, she arrived early and stayed late in the synagogue."[1] Learned in medical remedies, she purchased ointments and balms with her own earnings, providing care to her neighbors. A member of the women's burial society, she sat at the side of the ill, tending also to the purification of women's bodies when they passed on. Her hands were never at rest; "from the beginning to the end of the year, she behaved piously, sewing prayer shawls for men, shrouds, and blankets" for the wealthy and poor alike.[2] Mother to Moshe and Serle and grandmother to eight grandchildren, she was also wife to Ber, a wealthy member of the community who served for some time as the charity officer; as his wife, Rechle would have distributed goods, food, and financial support to the poor alongside him.[3] Ber served the community in a formal capacity, as did Rechle's father Abraham, who had represented Frankfurt Jewry before the emperor in the mid-seventeenth century.[4] Rechle's responsibilities in her community were informal yet crucial. The Jews in Frankfurt's Judengasse depended on Rechle, whose tireless presence in neighbors' homes and in the synagogue aided them from childbed to deathbed on cold and warm nights (see plate 1).

Rechle is one of thousands of Jewish women whose names and stories have been preserved in Jewish communal archives. Long ignored because they held no official position in the Jewish community, their untold stories, presented in this book, are truly hiding in plain sight. Rechle was honored in the communal memorial book and praised on her tombstone. Her family life can be reconstructed through burial registers, communal records, tombstones, and German court cases. One only has to look to find them. Women like Rechle lived in a traditional and heavily gendered society, but they were active and enterprising participants in every aspect of communal life. Communal records typically referred to households as headed by men. Reading through sources such as those documenting Rechle's life, however, demonstrates that married women, beyond running their households and actively partnering in family businesses, were indispensable to the functioning of their communities. These women were *ba'alot bayit* (female heads of household; sing. *ba'alat bayit*), without whom our knowledge of the Jewish community is incomplete. Their stories, and the stories of other women, are presented here for the first time (see plate 2).

The period historians call early modern (ca. 1500–1800) witnessed critical transformations that shaped the world as we know it. Advances in seafaring technology permitted travel to new realms, while the printing press and the Renaissance broadened men's and women's intellectual and cultural horizons. The Protestant Reformation permanently altered Europe's religious landscape, as in its wake, European cities and towns adopted different Christian confessions. In the wake of expulsions and migrations, Jews in Europe at this time often resettled in different geographic areas. In small villages and in the recently founded ghettos in German- and Italian-speaking realms, Jews contended with new demographic constellations and their impact on communal dynamics.

Three driving forces in the early modern period facilitated the increased participation of women in communal life. First, during this period, Jewish communities flourished and developed, and the community as an organized entity had greater power than ever before.[5] Second, along with the community's greater institutional development came an increase in communal recordkeeping, which created an archive of documents that preserved the rhythms of men's and women's daily lives. Third was the advent of print, the concomitant rise in female literacy, and its stimulating impact on women's reading and writing. Not only did these three forces facilitate the enterprising roles that women undertook, but they also created new bodies of written sources that render these women more visible than in any previous period in history. This book traces women's lives and deeds through their own words and through the new body of communal regulations and records in which they are ubiquitous.

The Kehillah

The early modern European *kehillah* (Jewish community; pl. *kehillot*) was a purposeful and highly organized establishment. Unlike modern times, when "Jewish community" can refer to a loose association of individuals around a synagogue or civic center, in premodern times, the kehillah was a formal entity through which Jews could interact with state authorities. This organization was the mechanism through which Jews collected and paid taxes, as well as the means for their interactions with the local, regional, and imperial Christian authorities. The early modern period in Europe was one of state building. As states and rulers consolidated their powers, they developed more intense administration and bureaucracies. The Jewish community, which interacted with these leaders, evolved similarly. Formal mechanisms for membership, administration, and recordkeeping were established, and new official societies (such as charitable funds and confraternities) were founded within kehillot.

Jewish communities were governed by *parnassim* (lay leaders), men who were elected out of the body of official communal members, known as *ba'ale bayit* (male heads of household; sing. *ba'al bayit*), a term parallel to German *Haushaber* or *Hauswirt/en*).[6] The right to communal membership, known as *hezkat kahal*, was awarded only to households with enough means to pay taxes; other factors also limited the right of official membership and the policies governing its inheritance by the next generation. Thus, some Jewish communities were physically restrained from expanding beyond ghetto walls, while others were limited by quotas restricting the number of Jewish households. Typically, the elected leadership of the community, known as the *kahal*, came from the highest socioeconomic echelon of community members.

The lay leaders set internal communal policy, collected taxes and charity, and interfaced with the Christian authorities. It was they who hired religious and communal functionaries, such as rabbis, cantors, and scribes, who were often not official members of the community. The parnassim were more influential than ever before in this age of expanded communal agency and administration. Moreover, the early modern period marks the first time that Jewish-generated records were deliberately produced and preserved by the non-rabbinic elite.

The ba'al bayit was the pivotal figure in the records of early modern European Jews, often designated by the acronym *b"b*. The denominating of heads of household as male in most community records, combined with the fact that civic and rabbinic practice barred women from participating in the political life of communities, obscures the fundamental role that women played in every aspect of the formation, sustenance, and continuity of households.[7] Yet as Rivkah Tiktiner wrote in the late sixteenth century, "A woman is responsible for everything: for her husband, for her children, and for her servants."[8] Our research shows that Rivkah has greatly understated the case. As the case of Rechle and myriad other women in our sources prove, women were central to the functioning of Jewish communities. The entire class of ba'alot bayit emerges as a highly visible group from the pages of our sources, enabling us to trace for the first time a detailed picture of their economic, communal, familial, and spiritual lives. We have uncovered the roles of thousands of women who appear in the records but whom historians have mostly ignored.

The Communal Archive

When the daughter of Zekel Weiss wished to marry R. Yudel, the parnassim, together with the tax collectors of Altona, refused to permit the couple to draft premarital contracts until the bride paid 540 Mark that she owed to the collectors.[9] This decision, inscribed in the logbooks of a communal scribe, was linked to other records in the communal archive. Tax and charity records would have indicated that the bride owed money to the community. Until she paid, she would not be issued the slip of paper provided to couples who had received a green light to wed. Once she paid, the records would be updated. This web of records was often indexed and cross-referenced, creating a communal archive for each and every Jewish community (unlike the random collection generated by *genizot*). Furthermore, because these records were intended to be consulted by the lay leaders who composed them, the names and details of men and women were not anonymized as they were in rabbinic responsa.

The highly developed administration of early modern communities generated a wealth and variety of records and documents, some of which were new to this period and others of which had existed previously in a more scattered form rather than in a deliberate collection. Of primary importance in the communal archive was the *pinkas* (logbook) of the community that detailed the important decisions of the parnassim, including elections, appointments, and daily administration. Written in a mix of Hebrew and Yiddish (and sometimes with a smattering of local languages), these logbooks, which could be hundreds of folios long, include not only tax payments, regulations, and developments that affected all community members but individual requests and cases as well. In addition to the pinkas kahal, every communal official maintained a separate pinkas detailing administrative work performed on behalf of the community. Scribes, charity officials, tax collectors, *mohalim* (ritual circumcisers), and court judges copiously inscribed the details of how they fulfilled their duties, often on a daily or weekly basis. It is rare to find a page in these logbooks that does not mention a woman. The installments in which men and women paid their taxes, the donations they pledged, and the petitions of individual community members, from maidservant to mistress, are all preserved in detail. Women appeared before lay leaders and local courts of justice and tenaciously fought for their interests; the pinkassim tell of their familial disputes, economic enterprises, and living arrangements. Although male officials created almost all communal records, some records were generated by women. Administrators of women's sacred and charitable sororities kept financial and administrative records, and midwives kept records of the babies they had delivered.

The community also maintained copies of many wills dictated by men and women to ensure that the lay leaders complied with the last wishes of its members. Some women used their wills to distribute income to favored offspring or to settle scores for real or perceived injustices that their families had inflicted upon them. Others acted magnanimously and made sure to include relatives and servants in the distributions of their earthly goods. Wealthy ba'alot bayit often owned extensive property, encumbered in complicated ways, with loans and debts outstanding and a greater interest of the state in the estate. Their wills tended to be copied by more than one party. Jews often made one notarized copy for purposes of the state and another in a Jewish language that prioritized spiritual care of the soul, at least formulaically, over the distribution of earthly property.

Another genre within the communal archive that highlights women's daily participation in and contribution to the kehillah is the *Memorbuch* (communal memorial book), in which women such as Rechle Drach were commemorated. Common in communities small and large, from Metz in the west to Moravia in the east, these volumes preserved the names of deceased male and female community members, which were then recited as part of the Shabbat liturgy. By the seventeenth and eighteenth centuries, the entries for individuals included an often impressive list of pious deeds the deceased had performed in life. Along with the epitaphs in Jewish cemeteries, these capture the defining characteristics of the spiritual lives of individual ba'alot bayit and their daughters, from young girls to wizened women.

Regulations

Jewish communal archives also included *takkanot*, detailed regulations of areas of life that had not been subject to such rules earlier or had not been subject in this detailed way. The expansion of small states' policing ever more aspects of their subjects' lives began in German lands in the sixteenth century and intensified greatly after the Thirty Years' War in the mid-seventeenth century.[10] In Protestant states, the elimination of the Catholic Church allowed the secular princes to extend their control of the moral lives of their subjects into areas that previously had not been the domain of the state.[11] The reliance on the existing infrastructure of corporate entities to carry out new goals of administration from above, a characteristic of this period, can be applied as well to much of the regulation instituted and enforced in Jewish communities, which internalized these developments. Communities typically read their takkanot aloud in the synagogue to inform community members about newly executed ordinances and their enforcement. Lay leaders would congregate to legislate a matter, craft a takkanah, and duly record it. The text was then often read aloud in the synagogue, which was sometimes followed by a written record of the text as it had been announced.

Through the regulation of areas of life previously left to custom, the informal became formal, and private acts became matters of public concern. This was a sea change for all affected but for women in particular because their presumed sphere had been the domestic and private, and, therefore, their daily activities had often slipped under the radar of public law. Much ink has been spilled on the question of how closely the public-private distinction maps onto a gendered binary. Strict differentiation is unsustainable, as European women were never locked behind closed doors (with the exception of nuns in convents), and rigid conceptions of domestic versus public did not run along gendered lines in many respects. Yet, there were some significant areas of congruence. These areas of previously unregulated space came under the gaze of the law that impacted women disproportionately. Supervision over many types of foods provide an example of this. Everything to do with the slaughter, preparation, and sale of meat came under both the religious and civil oversight of the Jewish community. The Worms regulations of 1684 warned that the sale of meat, milk, cheese, wine, and liquor would be strictly monitored and overseen by the community.[12] Other communities issued statutes concerning baked goods, types of fish and poultry that could be eaten, the consumption of coffee, and the like. In many communities, food that had not been granted the communal seal of approval "was to be considered nonkosher."[13] Although the import, production, or sales of these items may have been primarily in the hands of men, Jewish women were mainly responsible for the retail purchase, preparation, and consumption in the home. Women who failed to follow the regulations could be harshly punished. In one instance in the protocols of the Ashkenazi community of Amsterdam from 1758, Hendele bat Abraham was accused of obtaining meat from a non-Jewish butcher, feeding it to her family, and selling the meat to others. Wishing to make an example of her, the parnassim sentenced her (with the complicity of the non-Jewish government) to six months of imprisonment in the Spinhuis (where criminally charged women were subjected to forced labor and horrible conditions), followed by eternal banishment from the city.[14]

As formal control of daily life increased, aspects of Jewish women's lives that previously had not been subject to regulation came under its scope. The profusion of communal recordkeeping reveals so many aspects of the daily lives of women and men. The entire range of sumptuary laws was weighted toward restricting the dress of women.[15] These rules were often so detailed that it seems Jewish women may have been consulted in composing them. Even regulations that attempted to impose severe limitations on leisure activities promoting the commingling of young men and women could be heavily gendered. An ordinance against playing games of chance issued in Altona-Hamburg was gender-neutral until it addressed specific concerns about crossing gendered boundary lines, at which point it reads: "A [married] woman or virgin should not play with a householder or single man, all the more so if he is a gentile. A woman should not play [games of chance, even on days when permitted] after the afternoon prayer, upon pain of fine."[16] The lay leaders could easily have formulated the ordinance with the onus falling on the males, but they did not do so. The burden of observing separation between sexes fell onto the women alone.

Between the sixteenth and the eighteenth centuries, the sheer number of takkanot affecting women's lives (and thereby revealing details about them) increased substantially. The takkanot from Friedberg in 1664, for example, contained 228 regulations; of these, seven concerned women alone, while another twenty-three explicitly referred to both men and women. Similarly, the 1674 takkanot from Frankfurt am Main included six takkanot that singularly addressed women.[17] About a century later, the number of takkanot addressing women increased. The 1769 takkanot from Metz included twenty-two regulations (out of 125) that were aimed explicitly at women, while those issued in Fürth in 1770 included eighty takkanot out of 515 that concerned women's lives.[18]

Print

Along with the structured community, and with the recording and archiving impulse in the early modern period, print was the third driving force that enveloped women in literate culture, drawing them more deeply into communal life and rendering them more visible than in the past. Not long after the advent of the printing press, books designed specifically for female Jewish readers were printed. These included all types of works, from Bible translations and commentaries to prayer books and translations of popular tales. The availability of an ever-increasing body of texts in print, regardless of whether they were marketed primarily to women, motivated more women to learn to read or to expand upon a small range of texts they were already reading. Chava Turniansky has argued persuasively that the expansion of print to include Yiddish language materials of many genres greatly extended the access of children, women, and average men to all types of texts. Yiddish was the spoken language of Jews across the Ashkenazi diaspora, and the nearly universal teaching of Hebrew letters allowed most men and women to slip into reading Yiddish with natural ease.[19] The availability of texts in early modern Jewish culture intersected with the lives of women, resulting in consequences far beyond the world of books and literature. It allowed women to become far more knowledgeable about current events, Jewish lore and customs, their own bodies, and the material world around them. Women read and absorbed news reports and travel memoirs, advice for medical conditions, and household management matters. It allowed them to read business contracts and legal documents, write letters, and draw up wills in far greater numbers than ever before. Rabbanit Knendel corresponded with Frankfurt's parnassim in 1766 about her husband's estate, using his letters to reconstruct the taxes that they owed and any refund they were due after he had relinquished his communal membership. It was Knendel who pored over the family records, corresponded with the lay leaders, and signed the agreement that was later recorded in the pinkas kahal.[20]

This is not to say that these were the first Jewish women in the circle of literacy. There are multiple examples of Jewish women from rabbinic and lay households throughout the earlier periods who both read and wrote. Visual and textual evidence from central Europe and northern Italy show that during the fifteenth century, book ownership and literate participation in Jewish life increased for women. But there can be no question that print completely changed the cultural landscape. The increasing amount of available printed materials in the vernacular allowed a greater number of women to build literacy. While some elite women were able to read Hebrew, the Yiddish printed books allowed women from different classes to access a wealth of texts and ideas. The readership for these texts even extended to women who could not read but who might listen to the texts as someone else read them aloud, a common pastime in early modern Europe.[21] Literacy and writing were not just about books and documents. What we witness in the early modern period is the written word becoming the primary platform for the business of life itself.

Genres

When Hindel, owner of a *birkat ha-mazon* (Grace after Meals) manuscript, recorded the births of her seven children between 1729 and 1741 on blank pages between sections, she exemplified the intensifying bond between regular Jews and written material.[22] Her inscriptions capture the cycle of owning books, reading, and writing, which is critical to the increased visibility of early modern Jewish women. Valued by women as well as men, casual writing is just one of the many sources we draw upon in this book. Beyond records generated by the officials of the community in the course of their work, we based our book on written and visual depictions of Jewish women going about the course of their daily lives, and we strove to obtain as much material as possible from the pens of our subjects themselves. We were continually surprised by the wealth of sources available in plain sight that had never been used to form a picture of the lives of Jewish women in the past. The literate output of well-born classes was complemented by the private jottings of "everywoman." Recipes, laundry lists, and personal letters are just a few examples of the troves of riches we have found to illuminate the lives we trace here. Throughout the book, we have included visual sources and material objects as another form of evidence about the lives of the Jewish women we discuss. These should not be understood as literal representations of a particular woman from a specific locale. The artists and creators of these illustrations allow us to imagine the women in their own settings. The sheer number of images that we found depicting Jewish women, which far exceeds what we could include in this book, speaks to their presence in so many aspects of Jewish life that have largely been ignored.

While not all the types of sources we discuss here were unique to the early modern era, each acquired a new intensity or valence in this period. We can begin with personal letters, a genre that reaches back to antiquity. Both the form—greeting, body, closing—and the substance—family, business, emotions—date to the very beginning of letter writing. In this period, as in the medieval, Jewish women in good standing had their own signet rings with which to seal their letters or sign their documents. Several aspects were new in the early modern period. The first was the proliferation of literacy and writing. More men and women who earlier had had no access to these skills now had rudimentary training. Even if a woman could only dictate a letter to another writer, she could be reasonably certain the recipient would find someone to read it to her as well. In the early modern period, people collected letters and used them as the basis for model letter collections, some of them printed, allowing us to read entire exchanges from centuries ago. Regardless of how they came to be preserved, women's personal letters allow us to peer into intimate aspects of their lives. Similarly, a collection of last wills and testaments contained the rich and complex estates and emotions of wealthy widows as well as the will of a Jewish maidservant.

Other women have left us more literary writing about their own lives. Most famous is the seventeenth-century Yiddish memoir of Glikl "of Hameln."[23] A new English translation of Glikl has recently been published, and the memoir has garnered more scholarship than has been written for any other early modern Jewish woman. While we make ample use of it throughout this book, our intention was not to center on any specific woman but to highlight the lives of hundreds and thousands of other women who have left partial stories of their lives embedded in wills, letters, ethical works, and other genres.

Religious works of all types proliferated in this period. Some of them, such as *sifre minhagim* (books of customs), not only prescribed how certain ceremonies should be conducted but also described the actual participation of men and women in particular times and locales. Books of Jewish customs, often with illustrations, proliferated in this period, and some, like that of Juspe Schammes, sexton of Worms, paid particular attention to the gatherings, practices, and even songs of women in his particular community. *Tkhines* (informal prayers offered by women on various occasions, sometimes written or collected by women) circulated more widely than ever before, spurred on by numerous printings. They allow us a unique window into the points in women's lives that were not marked by official prayer services. Generations of Jewish women felt the need to utter some form of religious expression on occasions, such as childbirth or milestones in their children's lives, for which no formal prayers existed in the regular *siddur* (prayer book; pl. *siddurim*). *Lider* (collections of popular tunes; sing. *lid*) codified some of the comic, tragic, and religious songs that women sang at various occasions on their own. We listen for the funereal dirges women sang as they performed the final purification of the dead, as well as for the songs they sang for a bride as she prepared for her wedding. Our period abounded in small books filled with blessings, Grace after Meals, bedtime prayers, and special services for Shabbat, crafted individually for particular women or printed for the masses of women to buy.

Many of them highlighted the three "women's *mitzvot*" (commandments) in particular, and their illustrations depicted women performing the practice while simultaneously instructing others as to how it was done.

Two of the genres we draw on allow us to hear the voices and observe the practices of women through a scrim: *she'elot u-teshuvot* (responsa) of rabbis and the depictions of Jewish practices by Christian observers. Christian scholars, sometimes former Jews, issued compendia on Jewish life, to varying degrees of accuracy. Some hired artists to illustrate from life the Jewish rituals and lifeways they described in their works. These grant us some rare visual attestations to women's spaces and practices for which we have no other visual record. Rabbis had been authoring responsa for a millennium, but the genre was reshaped and reconfigured in particular ways in the early modern period. Women never authored rabbinic responsa, but a woman often initiated the exchange by approaching a man to write/present her query. Many areas of family life, particularly the sexual life of a married couple, menstruation, infertility, and divorce, fell under rabbinic jurisdiction, as did every manner of commercial dispute and inheritance case. Women brought their cases before rabbinical judicial venues, and the rabbinic authors sometimes preserved their voices verbatim as they presented their arguments. There were no hard boundaries between genres. It was a sixteenth-century rabbinic responsum that preserved the earliest Yiddish love letter, in its original language, between illicit lovers. Among the foremost rabbinic figures in western Europe to build the authority of the community as the framework for Jewish life was Rabbi Yair Hayim Bacharach. His works raised the profile of the learned women who contributed to his own life. In their introductions and sometimes in their memoirs, rabbis like Bacharach, Pinhas Katzenellenbogen, and Judah Mehler wrote of the lives of the women around them, many of whom attained scholarly achievement that was rarely documented in any other source.

Beautifully illuminated manuscripts written for women reflected their homes, furnishings, and lifestyles. Inventories taken by communal officials upon death showed the way women's possessions, including their intimate garments, were handled and tallied. In addition to texts of all types, artifacts and textiles from the early modern period have allowed us to fill in some of the missing pieces of women's lives. From the Torah binders and *parokhot* (decorative textile coverings) that women sewed to the hats they wore and the thimbles that protected their fingers, three-dimensional objects that have survived time and destruction allow us to feel and visualize what we otherwise would know only through words. The visual illustrations in so many of the sources add another dimension. Literacy intersected with material culture in the bronze pots with women's names engraved upon them in Hebrew and in the samplers sewn by Jewish girls. We can hear about a bed as the foundation of a woman's furnishings brought into her marriage, but seeing how beds were constructed to provide privacy or babies' cribs built to rock them to sleep adds another layer to our work of the retrieval of the past. Far from being an age in which the silence of the sources forces us to resort to creative ways to reconstruct a narrative of women's lives, the early modern period is one for which we have found an overwhelming treasury of materials.

That said, all primary sources must be used with caution and cannot be read naively. Entries in memorial books and epitaphs on tombstones emphasize the positive attributes that society values; they omit the negative or irritating aspects of a person's life. Regulations, laws, and custom books are mainly prescriptive sources; they reflect a society's ideals. Christian reports about Jewish life could be biased. Court cases present carefully crafted narratives. Material artifacts that survive provide only a small hint of the circumstances under which families dwelled, dressed, and ate. Entries in pinkassim reflect the interests of the lay leaders—they did not aspire to provide a comprehensive chronicle of daily life. Nevertheless, by putting all these sources in conversation with one another, we can draw a fuller and richer picture of women's activities and roles. Collectively, they allow us a transformational evaluation of Jewish women's lives in early modern Europe.

Historiography

As a work of history, this book is at least fifty years late. Women's history in the larger sphere of historical discourse is so well established as to be somewhat passé; contemporary scholars view society through more inclusive lenses.[24] Several historiographic turns brought the field to where it stands today. In terms of class, the daily lives of ordinary people became central to historians through pioneering movements such as the French *Annales* school, German *Alltagsgeschichte*, and the work of social historians more generally. Scholars have also embraced a more sophisticated view of society by analyzing culture through the lens of gender and through the categories of masculinity and femininity.[25] While general historiography has embraced a more complex view of history, including the high and the low, and men as well as women, since the 1960s and 1970s, scholars of Jewish history have been late to that party.

The study of Jews and Judaism, with some exceptions, continued to favor intellectual and religious history. Liturgical, philosophical, and legal texts formed the basis of the study of the Jewish past, and these tended to omit the lives of women altogether or include them only as subjects. The first professional writers of Jewish history (the German-Jewish *Wissenschaft* school) focused on texts, ideas, and political developments. This is true for both the broader historiography of the Jews and that which focused on the early modern period in particular. A long tradition centered on a canon that had erased women from the record and rendered them invisible still prevailed over the course of the nineteenth century and the first three quarters of the twentieth.

To be sure, there were exceptions. In some cases, historians focused on institutions that could not exclude women's lives completely, such as Jacob Katz's essay, "Marriage and Sexual Life at the Close of the Middle Ages," which originally appeared in *Zion* in 1944–45,[26] and histories of court Jews and salon hosts.[27] Katz's work of historical sociology, which relied almost completely on prescriptive sources, was nevertheless pathbreaking in its time; like his *Tradition and Crisis*, it was concerned primarily with the larger contours of institutions rather than with the individual lives within them.[28] Certain individual women, such as Glikl of Hameln, Sara Copia Sullam, and Doña Gracia Nasi, merited attention from historians, but they were depicted as exceptional rather than presented within the context of other Jewish women's lives.[29]

In the past generation, historians have begun to rectify this omission of Jewish women from the historical record. We build on the precedent of many works from the past few decades that highlight medieval and modern Jewish women. Judith Baskin and Elisheva Baumgarten have paved the way by writing comparative histories of Jewish and Christian women in the Middle Ages. Baumgarten has also extensively compared men's and women's pious practices and, together with her students, explored their roles in everyday life.[30] Avraham Grossman has mined prescriptive rabbinic sources to survey women's place in medieval Jewish society. Eve Krakowski stands out among historians of the medieval genizah world for her pioneering work on Jewish adolescent girls.[31] Claudia Ulbrich's rich comparative work on the Jewish and Christian women of the small village of Steinbiedersdorf and Federica Francesconi's recent work on Modena are model comparative approaches to early modern Jewish women's history in local settings. Local social histories published in German, among them the scholarship of Martha Keil, Rotraud Ries, Barbara Staudinger, and Sabine Ullmann, also have noted the importance of women's roles. Other scholars have furthered our understanding of Jewish women in the early modern period: Renée Levine Melammed focused on early modern Iberian *conversas*, Howard Adelman, Elliot Horowitz, and Stefanie Siegmund on Italian Jewish women, and Moshe Rosman on the Jewish women of Eastern Europe.[32] None of these provides a robust overall accounting of early modern Jewish women within the framework of the Jewish community. Historians such as Shmuel Feiner for the eighteenth century and Paula Hyman, Deborah Hertz, and Marion Kaplan for the nineteenth century illustrate our argument from a different vantage point. As Jewish women lost the kehillah structure and entered mainstream society, their ties to the deep knowledge of Jewish sources and strong connection to the Jewish community became attenuated.

The dominant view remained that the early modern period was one of stasis rather than change in the lives of most Jewish women. This view justified the neglect of Jewish women among historians so that writers of authoritative surveys could move on to "more important" matters. This posture was summed up by one of the leading historians of early modern Jewish history in the past decades, David Ruderman: "With respect to women's life and popular culture, we are not yet in a position to weigh either factor as primary in defining the early modern experience for Jews. This is partly a function of the state of the scholarship in these fields which is still in its infancy. It also stems from the fact that the changing statuses of women and of nonelite culture appear to be highly more significant in the centuries that follow our period."[33] We disagree with the assumption that any entity that maintained continuity over time deserves to be relegated to the dustbin of history. Jewish women's lives were an integral part of "the early modern experience for Jews." After all, they formed roughly half the Jewish people, and we cannot make any statements about "the Jews" without taking both halves into account. Women upheld the pillars of Jewish communal life and much of its culture as intensively as men did throughout the early modern period.

As we argue throughout this book, moreover, many of the cultural changes to which Ruderman pointed in his indispensable survey of the early modern period, among them the proliferation of print and the ascendance of the kehillah, significantly impacted the lives of both men and women, often in gendered ways that must be considered. We, therefore, disagree with arguments that we can be satisfied with studying the history of women of any premodern period as a stand-in for another as if nothing changed over time.[34] None of the works making such statements take advantage of, or even acknowledge, the rich stores of internal sources for western Ashkenazi women in early modern Europe, which stand in sharp contrast to the Middle Ages, a period for which many medievalists must coax history out of relative silence.[35] The very existence of a ramified Jewish recordkeeping culture in the early modern period is one of the marked characteristics that distinguish this period from its predecessor and successor.

While the state or its political precursors formed the context for understanding Jewish legal and political status, the kehillah formed the framework within which Jewish life unfolded in the early modern period. It generated an unprecedented wealth of sources, rendering thousands of ordinary and some exceptional women visible. These sources highlight the intense participation of women in the framework of Jewish communal life, bolstered by new access to knowledge and by the increasingly formal administrative structures of the kehillah. We disagree with the widely held perception that the nineteenth century marked a period of greater change in status and is, therefore, a better starting point for studying Jewish women. We argue that more change occurred in the lives of women in the early modern period than in the century that succeeded it.

Early Modern Women

Despite the great strides in scholarship on the history of European women, Jewish women remained marginal to that endeavor and rarely figured within it. Jewish women were not always legible to the historians who engaged in gendered history, despite being the most visible minority in many places where Jews were still allowed to reside or work. Lacking the technical and linguistic expertise to include or even consider Jewish women's lives, historians of early modern women and society have almost entirely neglected Jewish women of this period. Surveys of women's history and primary source anthologies thus mention Jews only fleetingly, if at all.[36] Few scholars have compared Jewish women to their Catholic and Protestant neighbors despite the obvious parallels between the Jewish and Christian women, all of whom lived in highly gendered traditional European societies. Some of the sources that provide rich details of Jewish women's lives speak to the interactions between Jews and their Christian neighbors. These include the German works of Christian Hebraists and the records of the municipal and imperial courts to which Jewish women turned.

The tools and methods modeled by scholars of European Christian women prove invaluable for researching their Jewish neighbors. For decades, scholars of early modern European history have noted how the intellectual debates during the Renaissance and the Reformation deeply affected the social realities of ordinary men and women. Early modern intellectuals conducted vigorous discussions and reexaminations of certitudes about women's biological nature, their position within the family, and their intellectual and spiritual capacities. The Protestant and Catholic Reformations led to concrete changes, with married Protestant couples granted permission to divorce for the first time and Catholics enclosing nuns far more strictly in the convents.[37] Certain differences between Jewish and Christian women stand out immediately. Divorce had always been permitted in Jewish communities, and Jewish women had never resided in convents. Nevertheless, many of the cultural changes that impacted Christian women undeniably affected Jewish women as well, particularly in the realms of household economies and gendered norms. Marriage was the building block of Christian and Jewish communities alike; sexual reputations were far more essential to women's social standing than to men's across faith communities, and male leaders sought to regulate and control many aspects of Jewish and Christian women's lives. Yet, within the patently patriarchal systems of early modern Europe, women expressed their own agency within families or religious communities by working, running a household, and writing.[38] Women of different faiths gained greater access to state institutions, such as courts, and they, too, were affected by technological developments such as print.[39] Early modern Jewish women read and wrote just as their Christian counterparts did; they, too, shaped their communities, albeit in gendered ways.[40] Furthermore, just as convents affected life in political courts, women's sections in synagogues and *mikva'ot* (ritual baths; sing. *mikveh*) were critical sites within Jewish communities and cannot be ignored.[41]

Among its other goals, this book aims to make the lives of Jewish women accessible to those who cannot read Jewish communal sources. While our focus on Jewish women is primarily through various genres of Hebrew and Yiddish sources that were internal to the Jewish community and its members, we are mindful of the broader context of women in early modernity. We note where broadly held concepts of gender rendered Jewish women's lives similar to those of their Catholic and Protestant neighbors, as well as where religion distinguished them more than did gender and class.

A New History

A Woman Is Responsible for Everything presents a dimension in Jewish women's history that historians believed could not be written. There were not enough sources and insufficient justification, they argued. We present the experiences of Ashkenazi Jewish women from circa 1500 through circa 1800 in the context of their families and communities. The women who appear in our sources were residents of open cities, crowded ghettos, and small rural villages in western and central Europe. We discuss Ashkenazi women from Amsterdam in the west to Prague in the east, from as far north as Copenhagen to as far south as northern Italy, itself a flourishing center of Yiddish culture in the sixteenth and early seventeenth centuries. We define the area we include as one that was culturally contiguous, with Yiddish as a lingua franca. It was connected by kinship, communal and rabbinic networks, and similar recordkeeping practices.

Given our claim that the Jewish community framed women's lives in the early modern period, we begin our inquiry with two chapters on the active leadership roles they played within the community and its institutions. Individual women, such as Hindele Gold of Amsterdam, managed ritual baths; Miriam Teomim was one of several women responsible for the women's section in Prague's Pinkas synagogue; Malka headed the hospice for Vienna's poor. In addition, formal sacred sororities provided essential services to the community. Under their auspices, women tended to the sick, clothed and dowered poor brides, and purified the dead. One can hardly imagine a community without women like Rechle Drach, who served her family, neighbors, and community from cradle to grave. Chapter 3 expands our discussion to include Jewish women beyond the prestigious circle of ba'alot bayit. Communal leaders and members honored those they esteemed and shamed those they did not. Records of fines, punishments, court cases, and more provide a glimpse of the women who were pushed to the margins of the kehillah, including female criminals, displaced poor women, and women who gave birth out of wedlock. Though nominally at the periphery, these women were intertwined with the community and, therefore, appear in its records.

We then turn our attention to print, another major factor spurring women's deep involvement in their homes and communities, exploring the rich volumes written for women that, in turn, increased their literacy. Chapters 4 and 5 deal with the cycle of reading and writing. Women maintained books of their household accounts and wrote down their recipes and laundry lists. Women like Rivkah Tiktiner, Bella Perlhefter, and Glikl of Hameln composed literary works; this was the first time in history that so many Jewish women had used the written word for the sake of their posterity.

Ba'alot bayit played essential roles not only within the kehillah but also within their households. Households were the building blocks of the community. In chapter 6, we trace how women's roles within the household shifted from youth to old age and how women navigated those changes. We then turn to women's economic lives in chapter 7, exploring not only their access to property but also the range of professions in which they engaged: Chaile Kaulla became an imperial court agent, Brendlin Schiff a midwife, and Sarel a woman who ran a mail service. The subsequent chapter deals with women's material worlds, including the mundane objects they kept in their kitchens and the sacred objects that adorned their homes, some of which they had fashioned with their own hands. We also include the clothing that they wore every day and on special occasions. We devote a separate chapter to women's wills, which reflect their economic standing, their kinship ties, their donations to communal institutions, their piety, and their connection to the written word. Throughout, we point to the distinctions between wealthy ba'alot bayit and poorer women, from maidservants to obscure vagrants. We also note the differences between the occupations, possessions, and devotions of Jewish women, on the one hand, and their Christian counterparts, on the other.

Our next chapter, chapter 10, analyzes the impact of communal and religious dictates on women's bodies: on their pregnancies, miscarriages, menstrual cycles, and illnesses. Though, as women, they shared much in common with their Christian neighbors, they were bound by Jewish law, which dictated different norms affecting their bodily experiences. The final chapter explores women's extensive participation in Jewish rituals, fueled by their increased access to texts. We demonstrate, through text and rich imagery, that women were active in a wide range of rituals, both at home and in communal spaces, throughout the year and during life cycle celebrations.

We end our analysis at the point when states began to dismantle many aspects of corporate Jewish life, lifting restrictions and centralizing and secularizing recordkeeping. Unlike other historians, who have viewed the nineteenth century as the time in which Jewish women first were able to make a mark on their societies, we stress the essential role of women within the framework of the traditional kehillah.

This is not to say that the Jewish community was not deeply gendered. Although the pinkassim and communal records that form the basis of so much of our research include hundreds, if not thousands, of women, these records reproduced the thoroughly gendered nature of the society itself. For example, men's appellations referred to their rank, but women's often indicated their gender and marital status alone. If a woman were single or widowed, that might be her sole designation. A widow was always denoted by the Hebrew appellation *almanah*, but a widower was seldom referred to by the parallel term, *alman*. The same held true for divorced women and men. Women were sometimes called by their husband's or father's name ("wife of" or "daughter of"). Even when the scribes called a woman by her own name, they prefaced it with the designation *ha-ishah* (the woman), implying that women were beyond a certain universe of discourse composed of men. It is precisely this distancing we seek to subvert.

The culture of early modern recordkeeping, which subordinated women's presence and voices in its production of documents, has led people astray in thinking they had neither a voice nor a place. A close reading across different genres reveals their lives and demonstrates that women were vital to the very functioning of the Jewish community. By showing that women availed themselves of a rich variety of possibilities, we try to show them as they saw and acted rather than as they were reflected in the writings of others, in their own time and in later scholarship. Our goal is not to mine these sources exhaustively but rather to gesture to them to indicate the kinds of knowledge about Jewish women's lives we can retrieve from them. We trust that the pathway we have opened before our readers will inspire many other historians to build upon our initial efforts, to utilize these bodies of sources, and to tell the other half of Jewish history.

1

Life in the Kehillah

RAIZEL, FRAIDEL, Edel, and Ella, four married women from prominent families in the bustling and crowded Prague ghetto, had their names inscribed in the Pinkas synagogue's record book in 1630. Their selection by lottery meant they would serve as the new *gabbetes* (officers; sing. *gabbete*; see glossary for variants) in the synagogue, one of several in the Jewish quarter. The scribe recorded their names alongside those of various male officials. This was not an unusual occurrence. These annual lists of elected male and female officials recur throughout the logbook.[1]

From the historians' perspective, these lists of gabbetes omit much information that we would like to know. The male *gabbay* (pl. *gabbaim*) oversaw the synagogue in the broadest sense: he was responsible for maintaining the building and paying for upkeep and repairs. He also managed both the collection and disbursement of charity that was donated in the sanctuary. The exact role of the female gabbete is not defined, as it would have been obvious and even irrelevant to the scribe who was charged with recording the results of the election. Since there were several gabbetes, sometimes as many as seven per election, it is likely that they shouldered multiple responsibilities. Presumably, they assigned specific gabbetes as respectively responsible for the upper and lower women's galleries in the synagogue.[2] They may have been tasked with ensuring decorum or women's sitting in their assigned seats. Perhaps they guided women through the prayers during the service. The gabbete was, like her male counterpart, responsible for charity donated in the synagogue, as noted on one ornate folio in the synagogue logbook. The record book contained a blessing for "six important and confident women who perform lovingkindness to the worthy and respectable poor and indigent" alongside the elected male synagogue officials.[3]

Despite the uncertainty surrounding the scope of the gabbetes' roles, the recurring lists with their names constitute a modest historical treasure, for they

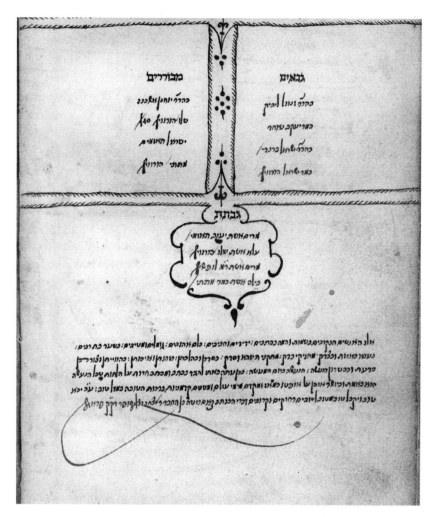

FIG. 1.1. Election of male *gabba'im* and *mevorarim* (top) and female *gabbetes* (center). Logbook of the Pinkas synagogue Prague, 1630.

demonstrate that women were hired and appointed to hold official positions within early modern Jewish communities. Countless regulations across regions point to men's roles in the daily management of the community. These governed the elections of lay leaders, the appointments of rabbis and judges, and the scope of the work performed by numerous male communal officials. Jewish women, by contrast, typically have been excluded from studies of communities and communal leadership. In one example, Salo Baron referred in passing to London's female "keepers of the ritual bath" in a lengthy list of ancillary communal roles.[4] Women could not serve as rabbis, nor could they lead the formal synagogue services. They were not permitted to serve as judges nor to hold any formal administrative offices in the lay leadership.[5] Since women could not hold formal office, the records about their work were typically far less detailed than those that documented the work of male communal officials; sometimes we do not even know their names. Yet a wide variety of communal sources reveals that women performed vital work without which the community could not have functioned. In this chapter, we argue that women served both as salaried official appointees and as volunteers in areas that were crucial to the smooth functioning of a Jewish community.

This chapter explores how women came by public communal roles. Different principles applied to different types of positions, and we classify our examples according to the categories that applied to each role, despite some degree of overlap. First, we discuss female leadership in spaces that were segregated by sex, into which men did not enter. Second, we discuss tasks that were usually performed by women because that type of work was gendered female. Third, we discuss cases in which women served as extensions of the communal leaders for navigating issues involving women's bodies. For reasons of modesty, men could not directly approach them. Finally, we explore the formal and informal power wielded by wives of communal leaders. These four categories include women's paid and unpaid responsibilities within official communal structures. Women of varying means and stations held positions. Many of the formal tasks performed by women required that they maintain their own set of records, as did other functionaries who worked with communal leaders.

In the Synagogue

Women held formal positions within the Jewish community in their own right, particularly as administrators of communal spaces segregated by sex. Men did not enter these spaces when women used them, which led to a need for official female leadership. These spaces were not the primary locus of Jewish synagogue ritual, and, as such, many scholars disregarded them as secondary. The critical and formal roles played by women in such communal spaces have, therefore, not received adequate attention. Communal ordinances and records, however, both recognized and regulated women's leadership in these spaces, including the women's section of the synagogue and the ritual bath.[6]

Early modern synagogues, both large and small, typically included a women's section, as many women attended prayers on a daily basis.[7] The architectural design of the women's section differed from location to location. In some communities, an older medieval structure was still in use, comprising adjacent sanctuaries for men and women in separate but proximate buildings. The women's section connected to the men's section via windows and a narrow door (see plate 3). Newer construction featured women's galleries overlooking the men's synagogue, some with multiple stories of women's galleries, one above the other.[8]

The specific spatial layout of the synagogue determined the degree of women's visual and aural access to the prayers conducted in the men's sanctuary. In some communities, a *firzogerin* or *zogerke* led women in prayer from the women's section of the synagogue. An image of one firzogerin leading women in lamentations recited on the fast of Tishah be-Av can be seen in Paul Christian Kirchner's early-eighteenth-century book about Jewish practices.[9]

Standing at the podium, she leads the other women, who are seated on the floor around her, in the prayers mourning the destruction of the Temple. Yet most textual references to women who led prayers are from the medieval period or from the nineteenth century.[10] Although Yemima Chovav has argued that references to both medieval and modern women who led the prayers point to a continuous and linear practice, we have found almost no textual indications of a firzogerin in the regions we have examined during the early modern period.[11]

The spatial layout of the synagogue likely determined whether it was necessary or even possible to have a woman formally lead the women in prayer. Engaging a female prayer leader was more critical in older construction, in which only a small aperture allowed sound from the men's sanctuary to enter the women's section. In galleries that overlooked the men's sanctuary with multiple windows, by contrast, the women had greater access to the prayers led by the male cantor. Moreover, a female voice from within the women's section might have carried into the men's sanctuary, interfering with the main prayer service.

One tombstone, that of Rivkah bat Shabbetai Horowitz (d. 1597) of Prague, relates that Rivkah "expounded and interpreted the holiday prayer book to the daughters of Israel."[12] It is not clear whether Rivkah led the prayers in one of Prague's synagogues, as Chovav claims, or whether she taught women the meaning of the liturgy. Her later contemporary, the author Rivkah Tiktiner, was referred to in her epitaph as a *darshanit* (public speaker), who "preached day and night to women."[13] Did these sermons occur in the women's section? The genre of texts in which these women's activities were recorded leaves the

FIG. 1.2. *Firzogerin* (standing right) leading women's services in the women's gallery of the synagogue on Tishah be-Av (enlarged detail). Kirchner, *Jüdisches Ceremoniel*, 1726.

details opaque. Neither the tombstones nor the memorial books commemorating women preserved the particulars of their activities, yet they left traces of the prayers and sermons that were recited and heard.

Another manuscript from eighteenth-century Prague also hints at women's prayers, though its specific use is shrouded in mystery. This memorial book includes only the names of women who participated in or donated to the women's burial society; unlike other memorial books, men were not included.[14] Were these names read aloud in one of Prague's women's sections, some of which were connected to the adjacent men's sections only by a small window or recited at a festive meal of the women's burial society? While we cannot pinpoint its specific use, the memorial book nevertheless testifies to women's prayers and communal leadership.

A brief notice in the takkanot of the Jewish community of Friedberg (1664) announced, "Anyone [man] who remains on the street after the *hazzante* rings the bell indicating that everyone must leave, or if she just announces it, if someone does not heed, he must pay a fine.... And if they add to their sin and mock the woman, they will be fined ... [double]."[15] This is the only reference to a figure called "the hazzante" that we have found in communal records. The word denotes in Yiddish a female *hazzan* (cantor), a term that cannot be taken literally, as women could not serve as cantors before the synagogue public in the premodern period. The writers of the takkanot employed a term indicating a female communal appointee whose function they did not fully elucidate, as they took for granted that everyone in the community knew the woman and her tasks. It is unclear if she was the same as a female firzogerin in the synagogue, who led prayers in the women's section. The hazzante in Friedberg was also tasked with clearing the street in front of the women's entrance to the synagogue to minimize mingling of the sexes after prayer services. Or, perhaps, she was doing this for the mikveh, clearing the street so that men would not watch while the women attended.[16] The brief mention serves further notice to us that the community employed many women for various functions necessary to the smooth running of the kehillah and the maintenance of its institutions and standards. But whereas the hazzan appears often in communal records, any female counterparts have generally disappeared.

Female officials also managed and oversaw charitable donations, which often took place in the synagogue, as they alone were in the women's section during services. Not only did women collect money several times a week within the synagogue, but special collections could also be arranged. A seventeenth-century Yiddish supplication from poor women in Jerusalem requested that their European sisters appoint special *gabba'ot* for a fund intended solely to support the poor widows and orphans in Jerusalem.[17] Noting their economic distress, Jerusalem's Ashkenazi Jewish women explained that they were unable to provide funding for dowries, as the general charity was disbursed by men for other causes. Anxious that the funds to be collected reach the women of Jerusalem directly, they turned to women in the diaspora, asking them to institute a special coffer for this purpose. While we do not have any direct evidence that their request was granted, a pinkas from Altona-Hamburg relates that a special coffer for collections among the women was instituted to support the poor of Hebron.[18] In other words, women in western Europe responded positively to pleas from the Holy Land and organized to create designated women's coffers. Although this fund was organized and administered by women at the request of other women, the community instated a male overseer. His oversight would have been limited; all day-to-day responsibilities would have remained in the women's hands because women donated in their synagogue during services.

Communal officials did not always regard kindly women's impromptu collections in the synagogue; at times, they sought to restrict the women's activities. In 1741, the Halberstadt lay leaders issued an ordinance banning women from collecting for any new charities in the women's section unless the collector had a letter granting her permission to do so.[19] While men could not supervise the collection during services, the demand for a letter ensured male supervision of the women's collection. It guaranteed that no additional collections transpired without communal approval and created a channel through which male communal officials could track and control donations made by women.

A takkanah from Metz in 1769 went even further in limiting women's collections without approval: "Since some women have been walking around the women's synagogue with coffers, and they collect money for candles, and for those who are ill on their deathbeds, and the like: Not only is it inherently inappropriate that the women are taking glory for themselves, to go around the synagogue with coffers without permission from the communal leaders, may they be protected by God, they also damage the coffer for the local poor, and the charity fund of the community, may it be protected by God."[20] The ordinance forbade women from collecting charity and imposed a fine on any woman who persisted in doing so. The communal leaders also decreed that any donors who contributed to the women's coffer would be considered as having stolen from the charity fund. Consolidating donations in the hands of the official charity collector was a policy that appeared across communities—and not only in the context of gender. Since the synagogue was a major locus for donations, many Jewish communities insisted that funds be channeled to the official communal charity collector in the synagogue.[21] In this case, the women of Metz were encouraged to continue donating to the main charity fund managed by the male leadership. This passage, however, went beyond the standard insistence on maintaining only one communal fund. By critiquing the women for "taking glory for themselves," the lay leaders interpreted women's unrelenting fundraising for the poor and for synagogue maintenance as inappropriate on gendered grounds.[22] The tension between the communal leaders and women's initiatives points to the specifically gendered aspect of the intense communal regulation of the late seventeenth and eighteenth centuries.

Regulations from eighteenth-century Fürth, a prominent Jewish community near Nuremberg, by contrast, reflect a collaborative dynamic in which husbands and wives worked together to collect, oversee, and distribute charity.

While the husbands were formally appointed, their wives were obligated to perform parallel volunteer work among the women in the community and the spaces where they congregated. The shamash distributed alms to poor men, while his wife did so for poor women. Male administrators collected and managed funds to support the poor, the sick, and Torah study from male donors, while their wives collected and distributed funds donated by the women in the women's section.[23] Women were thus aware of the means of the donors and the needs of the poor. It is also likely that the women were involved in the accounting process, since funds collected from and disbursed among women were included in the careful records that the charity collectors submitted for auditing.[24]

Women's donations included items intended for use in the synagogue, which made their presence felt by all worshippers who viewed and benefited from the treasures women crafted and bequeathed. Several wealthy women donated Torah scrolls to synagogues. These were expensive items, as a scribe was required to copy each letter onto the parchment scroll with utmost precision. In Prague, Sarah, the daughter of Hayim Schmelkes Schammes, donated a Torah scroll with jeweled accessories.[25] The widowed Michla, daughter of R. Yohanan Hanover from Amsterdam, donated a Torah scroll in 1786, along with a pointer and garments for both the Shabbat and weekdays. She specified particular dates on which the scroll was to be used.[26] Months later, another woman, Dinah, the wife of the parnas Mordekhai Levi Emden, also donated a Torah scroll, a pointer, and three garments. She stipulated, however, "that if in her old age, she would become impoverished, that they would return her donation, either in its entirety or in part, so that she might sustain herself."[27] Her concern for her economic well-being in old age expressed her perception of the vulnerability of elderly women, even those of elite status.

Women also donated other implements for the synagogue, as did the widow Sarah, daughter of the parnas Isaac Rintel of Amsterdam, in 1753. Her gift of "a tall and wide splendid silver lamp, beautiful to behold; all who saw it would praise her" was accompanied by a *parokhet* (textile ark covering; pl. *parokhot*).[28] Another unnamed woman donated a sink for use in the women's section of the synagogue in the seventeenth century, echoing the donations made by the Jewish women to the Tabernacle in the Bible.[29]

Women sewed the tapestries used in synagogues, as did Melkhen, daughter of the notable Zanvil Strauss of Frankfurt, who "crafted holy vessels for the synagogue with her own hands."[30] The epitaph of Gütchen, wife of Isaac Ring of Worms, noted her handiwork in sewing parokhot and *mappot* (decorative textile coverings) for the synagogue.[31] Elite women in both larger and smaller communities also fashioned parokhot out of their own dresses, as did Breindel, daughter of the esteemed Joseph of Wallerstein in Bavaria, who "fashioned a parokhet for the synagogue from her garment."[32] Some women sewed these textiles themselves, while others donated fabric from their own wardrobes to fashion something in their memory.[33] Reizl, wife of Zelig Bischitz of Prague, "instructed her husband before her death that he should make a parokhet for the Holy Ark out of one of her garments. When her husband fulfilled her wishes, he added his own money to it for the sake of her soul, and he made a holy parokhet, combining one of her garments with six silver bells."[34] Women also sewed and embroidered numerous holy garments, such as an early seventeenth-century circumcision pillow from southern Germany for ritual use (see plate 4).

Shprinkhen, daughter of the esteemed Isaac of Frankfurt, donated a prayer shawl for the cantor along with other items for use on the holidays; it is not clear whether she sewed the shawl herself or if she commissioned it.[35] Women's nimble fingers fashioned the candles used in the synagogue, as is seen from multiple entries in the Memorbuch from Alzey and Mainz.[36] Takkanot from other communities, unrelated to women per se, discuss using even the smallest bit of leftover wicks and wax, indicating how valuable these gifts were.[37]

Ritual Baths

In 1681, the communal leaders of Altona appointed the widow Pessim, daughter of Abraham Lübeck, and the unnamed wife of Jacob ben Moses Joseph to manage the respective ritual baths in their homes. A new regulation insisted that communal members "immerse their wives specifically in the two aforementioned mikva'ot," a decree that transformed ritual baths in private homes into official communal institutions.[38] While both men and women immersed ritually, the communal mikveh was reserved solely for women's immersions during the nighttime hours; hence, only women could oversee those spaces.[39] Immersion, like other personal behaviors, was increasingly regulated in the early modern period. Communities either constructed or designated an already existing ritual bath as the official communal mikveh. The leaders established fees for immersion, from which the community collected revenue, and appointed overseers over the ritual baths to collect the required sums. Individual community members, usually women, leased the right to manage the ritual bath, dividing the proceeds with the community after deducting their expenses. Pessim and Jacob's wife collected eight Schilling from each woman who immersed (a reduced rate of four Schilling was levied on poorer women). Each month, the women brought the funds from the designated coffer in the mikveh to the parnas of the month, who logged the income and division of revenue in a special account book; unfortunately, these have not survived.

Several years later, the Jewish community of Altona constructed a new communal ritual bath, and the community forbade the use of Pessim and Jacob's private mikva'ot.[40] Yet this by no means ended female supervision of communal mikva'ot. In eighteenth-century Altona and Hamburg, the leaders granted two women the respective leases for the two official ritual baths. Reitzche acquired the lease for the Altona mikveh for five hundred Reichsthaler per year, while the unnamed wife of Shimon rented the mikveh in Hamburg for 2,325 Mark per year.[41] A similar practice was adopted in Amsterdam, where Hindele, the widow of Elia Gold, managed the ritual bath for a three-year period beginning in May 1735. She made quarterly payments to the community, totaling 1,150 Gulden per year.[42] The rate for acquiring such a lease was high, yet presumably, the women had the opportunity to earn a greater sum from their share of the immersion fees.

Even when the leaseholder was male, it was his wife who would collect money from women who came to the ritual bath, as he could not enter the space of the ritual bath to collect money from the women who immersed. Jacob and his wife in Altona operated accordingly, and she was specifically tasked with collecting immersion fees. Similarly, in the small Franconian town of Schnaittach, the ritual bath was located under a trapdoor in the house of the cantor. Communal regulations required him to leave the house whenever a woman came to immerse. A reference to the salary of one of Schnaittach's cantors, R. Yosef, included a percentage of the immersion fees from 1704 to 1705. Yet the entry expounds that "only the wife of R. Yosef is obligated to handle immersing women."[43] Even though a portion of the immersion revenues went to the cantor's salary, only his wife could accompany the immersing woman and collect the fee.

Communal logbooks primarily document the financial arrangements between the community leaders and the leaseholders, which point to the extensive collaboration between them. The leaseholding women collected and handed over the fees from the immersing women to the parnassim either on a monthly basis or several times per year.[44] We assume that women must have maintained records of the income they collected from immersions since they were required to provide a detailed accounting to the parnassim. A precise balance sheet was necessary for a correct and efficient division of the revenue between the community and the leaseholder. The women also played a ritual role, serving as mikveh attendants who ensured that the immersing women acted in accordance with the legal requirements of submerging their bodies completely under the water.[45] Finally, these women were the sole bearers of the knowledge as to who had immersed in which bath. Only they knew whether a woman had complied with the regulations to immerse in a specific mikveh or whether she had paid the requisite fee on time. The leaders of the Amsterdam Sephardi community requested of another community under its supervision in 1728 to "send us, if possible, a declaration in which the bathing ladies [mikveh attendants] will declare which ladies use [the bath], which you have to obtain in the utmost secrecy from the said ladies, and . . . you will send another relation comprising those who do not use the said bath."[46] The communal leaders may have sought to regulate women's immersion, but compliance and enforcement remained in the hands of the women who managed these spaces.

Women worked in these spaces in other capacities as well, as recorded in a proclamation made on Monday, the fourth of Adar, 1731, in the Altona synagogue: "Hear, holy community, hear what is announced in the name of the leaders (*alufim, ketzinim,* and *parnassim*) of our community, may it be preserved by God. Whereas it has been mandated that two women be hired as caretakers for the sick; our communal leaders have enacted that heads of household must hire these women and not others, for weddings, and for bathing, and also when parturients go to the synagogue."[47] This policy was prompted by community members who had violated the existing communal policy by hiring women other than the two officially appointed to this role. Seeking to address this infraction, the leaders insisted that only the two specific community-appointed women could be hired for these jobs and that they were to be paid the mandated fee. The kahal would impose a fine of double the amount for anyone who hired other women. Frustratingly, the announcement does not mention the names of the two official women escorts who accompanied other women through illness and various life cycle celebrations, such as weddings, ritual bathing, and a woman's first postpartum attendance at synagogue. We do not know when they were first hired, what their qualifications were, nor the fee for their services. These details would have been apparent to the men and women listening in the synagogue and were thus not included in the proclamation. What is apparent, however, is that men could not aid women during these intimate times, nor could they accompany them into female spaces, such as a bath or the women's section of the synagogue. While the presence of female escorts was likely not new to this period, the communal designation of two specific women as the sole attendants certainly was novel.[48] By formalizing the women's roles, communal leaders left traces of their work in the written record.

Gendered Labor

Communal spaces required maintenance, which was typically managed by the charity collector, who paid for these expenses from the charity coffer.[49] While he supervised broken windows and the like, women were responsible for cleaning, particularly in the synagogue. Women adapted domestic tasks they performed at home as forms of voluntary piety in communal institutions. Parallel practices can be seen among Christian women, who tended to their parish church by laundering vestments, making candles, and scrubbing candlesticks.[50] In Worms, women vied for these honors at an auction on the festival of Simhat Torah. At the same time that the men sold the honors of being called to the Torah for the upcoming year, the women sold honors that included synagogue maintenance of a more domestic nature: "They [the women] go to their synagogue, and there a youth [a young unmarried man] reads aloud and announces all of the mitzvot of women for the year, and he sells them. And these include sweeping the synagogue, distributing *wimpeln* [swaddling cloths donated after the birth of a son, to be used to bind the Torah scroll] for folding, making wicks and lighting them, drawing water for the ritual washing of hands in the courtyard of the men and women's synagogue."[51]

Maintaining a clean and well-lit prayer space, furnished with clean and organized cloths for the Torah, as well as water for handwashing, was vital for the community. Since sweeping, folding, drawing water, and fashioning candles were part of women's domestic chores, women volunteered to fulfill these responsibilities in the communal sphere. They viewed these tasks as communal honors and bid for the right to perform these duties. The proceeds collected at the auction were reserved for the gabba'ot: "The money from these mitzvot does not go to the hands of the *gabba'e tzedakah* (charity officials); rather, the women retain their money for themselves and appoint two righteous women as their gabba'ot, and they [the gabba'ot] buy wax with [this money], with which they light candles in the women's synagogue all year long."[52] Although women toiled in both the men's and women's sections, the donations collected from their labor remained in the hands of the female charity collectors, funding the lighting in the women's sanctuary.

A similar gendered division of labor is also apparent among charity collectors and their wives, who worked together, as we saw in the above discussion of Fürth. Even outside of the women's section of the synagogue, the wives of charity collectors were obligated to work alongside their husbands: they were responsible for those elements of charitable giving that were domestic and gendered female. In Worms, the charity collectors' wives were explicitly expected to be available at home to provide sustenance to the poor.[53] In Frankfurt, charity collectors' wives washed the secondhand clothing of the deceased that was later given to the poor. They were further instructed not to distribute any clothing or money to the poor without their husbands' knowledge. This last enactment acknowledges the deep involvement of these women in distribution and poor relief, but it reiterates that oversight of the daily enterprise remained at least nominally in the hands of their husbands.[54] The essential tasks of providing the poor with food and clothing, two tasks associated with women's work, fell under the purview of the women.

Women's work was particularly critical in communities in which formal institutions, such as hospices or inns to house travelers, refugees, and the poor, had not yet been founded. There, the home functioned as a locus for additional forms of aid. In seventeenth-century Hamburg, before the community established a *hekdesh* (hospice) to house travelers and the sick, Glikl's grandmother Mata cared for ten refugees from Wilno (Vilna). Insisting that she personally tend to their needs, she then died of plague, having contracted it from the people she attended to in her home. Somewhat ironically, in his treatment of rabbis in Altona-Hamburg-Wandsbek, Eduard Duckesz credits Glikl's *father* with providing the refugees with food and care.[55] Yet, in Glikl's own narrative, Mata is placed at the center. We learn that it was her grandmother who labored and provided care directly to the ill, paying the ultimate price for her piety.

Memorbücher lavish praise on women whose homes "were open for sustenance," acknowledging in this context that they were primarily responsible for food, lodging, and other forms of support that were served and distributed in the home, often to a variety of people. In larger communities, vouchers known as *pletten* were handed out to approved visitors, who often would then be fed by women in their homes.[56] When yeshivah students or poor guests needed to be fed in local homes, the women of the house were the ones who would have seen to their needs. The elderly Mehrle bat Joseph Katz is singled out in the Mainz memorial book for "feeding the poor at her table. She also welcomed guests with a kind and pleasant demeanor, and in particular, scholars of Torah. She always had scholars of Torah at her table."[57] Mehrle's hospitality to students had two dimensions: she supported Torah study but also opened her home to do so, an act that was commendable in its own right.

Women were particularly active in providing for orphans, as orphanages were not founded in most Jewish communities until the nineteenth century. It was only in the second half of the eighteenth century that confraternities charged with caring for orphans were established.[58] Just as Mata tended to the sick refugees in Hamburg in her own home when there was no hekdesh, other women served as the primary daily caregivers of orphans in their own homes. Memorbücher and tombstones point to examples of orphans who were cared for by well-to-do relatives. Gitla, the daughter of Isaac Sheier of Frankfurt, "was mother to and raised her husband's orphaned grandchildren that he had from his first wife."[59] Several sources praise men and women for raising orphans at home, seeing to their needs until they could marry; since the texts focus on the caregivers rather than on the orphans, it is impossible to determine whether the children were relatives or strangers. Most references to the care of orphans are entries for women, as they would have been primarily responsible for feeding and clothing these children. Shinche, the widow of the parnas Avraham Naftali Hirtz Ginzburg of Mainz, "raised several orphans at her table."[60] Not only did these elite women feed and likely house these orphans, but they also provided them with an education and with the financial support necessary to see them married. Breinle, daughter of Avraham Hildesheim of Frankfurt, "raised orphans in her home and at her table, and provided for all of their needs, and raised them to study Torah, until she brought them to the wedding canopy."[61] It is Breinle, rather than her husband, who is credited with marrying off the orphans that she raised and educated, and her actions are visible through genres that focus on individual men and women alike. Even when sources do not credit women, they provided the daily care that raising children demanded. When Mordekhai Gumpel ben Moshe Hadamar of Frankfurt "raised an orphaned girl in his home, and brought her to the marriage canopy (*huppah*) like one of his sons," we can assume that he welcomed her into his household and gave her the financial support she needed to marry, but that the brunt of the daily interaction with the orphan girl fell on his unnamed wife.[62] Such informal adoptions occur often enough in the sources, although the fact that they were noted as a great act of piety shows that they exceeded the norm.

The wealthy Rebecca Sinzheim of Mannheim relates having cared for her sibling's children in her last will and testament: "I nevertheless specifically request and entreat my son R. Leyb, may he live, whom God has granted a good heart from the cradle, that he should establish himself as a father and guardian to my nieces and nephews, that he should take care of them at all times, as much as possible; he should try to help them to the greatest extent possible, as though I were still here."[63] Her husband Hayim is credited on his tombstone with "raising orphans in his home," which may refer to these nieces and nephews.[64] Clearly, when Rebecca was alive, she saw to the children's every need; as such, she beseeched Leyb to continue to care for them "as though I were still here."

Children of the poor were at a greater disadvantage than those who had wealthier relations. Even when men formed societies to raise funds for the care of orphans, very little information about the fate of parentless poor children can be gleaned from the records. An enigmatic reference in a petition from the eighteenth century by the Altona community against that of Hamburg refers to the expenses for the upkeep of six unaccompanied children who were sent to the community. The Altona community complained that their gabbay supported them solely from Altona's treasury when their care should have been a shared expense. In its reply, the Hamburg community wrote, "Had these children been sent to us, we would have been responsible for their upkeep, but as they were sent to you, they are your responsibility, and may the blessing for those who raise orphans fall upon you."[65] This exchange implies that the children were orphans sent to a large community because they lacked support in their hometowns. The writer of the petition did not mention their origin, gender, ages, or the frequency of such occurrences. In most cases, the orphans became integral members of the households. There, they fell under the purview of the ba'alat bayit.

Still other communal institutions similarly involved labor that was gendered as female. Among these was the *Garküche*, an eatery that fed and sometimes lodged travelers and the poor. While a large community might have more than one such eatery, and some Garküchen were private businesses, over time, the community regulated these establishments, as their function overlapped with and was integrated into the communal system of poor relief. In one of the Garküchen in eighteenth-century Frankfurt, expenses were paid for with communal money, whether with vouchers or other funds managed by the charity collectors.[66] Often, though not always, these eateries were managed by women, who cooked food for the Jewish travelers who needed kosher food. In seventeenth-century Frankfurt, a woman named Gutge ran a Garküche, and when a brawl between customers led to a brutal murder, it was she who was interrogated directly by the police.[67] In Metz, too, Matkhe, the wife of Ziskind of Paris, served community members (and possibly others) in her home. A man named Yuzpa spread rumors casting doubt on the *kashrut* in her home. Matkhe appealed to the rabbinical court, staunchly denying these claims. Yuzpa recanted, acknowledging that he had never seen anything amiss in her home and had not eaten there in over ten years. The rabbinical court consulted with other community members who ate in her home, and they willingly testified that she met all required standards. The rabbinical court ruled that Matkhe was in "*hezkat kashrut* [deemed kosher] like all the women of Israel," thereby protecting her reputation and her business.[68]

An itemized list, drafted on a single slip of paper by Mindele, a woman from Darmstadt who ran a Garküche, lists the services that she provided: "Three Jerusalemites drank coffee at my [establishment], and one slept here for two nights . . . on Tuesday, the fifth of Adar [5]535 (1775), two Jerusalemites appeared here and stayed for six days. . . . Rabbi Koppel of Worms came here on Thursday, the third of Sivan 1775, with a youth and stayed here for eight days . . . on Tuesday, the twenty-ninth of Sivan, two foreign guests stayed here for two days."[69] For each entry, the amount she was paid is listed; this was likely submitted as a record to the community, as various rabbis were involved in these visits. Thus, in addition to the responsibilities of cooking for and hosting the lodgers, Mindele kept a detailed log of her business. By a stroke of good fortune, this single sheet remained in the communal archives and reveals the important role that she, and women like her, played within her community.

The Hekdesh (Hospice)

While a Garküche served meals both to the local poor and to a range of travelers, it was the communal hospice that provided lodging to the traveling poor and medical care to the sick. European Christian communities had constructed similar hospitals earlier in the Middle Ages, while Jewish communities established parallel institutions beginning in the fourteenth century.[70] During the early modern period, these hospices developed further and were more highly regulated, especially as laws regarding charity to itinerants were enacted in European cities.[71]

Inside the hospice, men and women were divided either into separate rooms or into different buildings.[72] Both the gendered division of space and the intimate ministrations to the sick demanded that at least one female attendant supervise and care for the female lodgers.[73] (We discuss women's sororities, which played an active role in hospices by the mid-eighteenth century, in a separate chapter.)

In seventeenth-century Frankfurt, a married couple managed the communal hospice, presumably splitting the tasks of caring for men and women between them.[74] In seventeenth-century Altona, poor men and women who received stipends from the community were expected to care for the sick in the event of a plague; the demand that the "worthy" poor labor in exchange for alms was common in Christian communities as well.[75] By the eighteenth century, a formal hekdesh had been established in Altona, supervised by a *hekdeshman*, to whom both male and female attendants reported. The attendants were expected to care for the respective male or female inhabitants in accordance with institutional regulations, and deviation from those norms resulted in punishment.[76] The regulations bound the hekdeshman to uphold standards of cleanliness and care in the hospice, but the myriad tasks required to uphold his duties were undoubtedly shared by the attendants. These included ensuring that each bed was fitted with fresh linen, that a balance of meat and dairy meals were prepared for the inhabitants as contracted, and that the rooms were cleaned on schedule.[77] Women would have undoubtedly shouldered many of the domestic tasks.

Additional responsibilities of hekdesh workers can be gleaned from details of a family of hekdesh attendants from Vienna. Their stories can be pieced together from various mentions over the course of three decades, including several wills and inventories. In 1750, a *Krankenwarter* (attendant for the ill) named Salman passed away at age 77, leaving his widow Malka (Malca) and a daughter, Mindl. Malka later appears in the records as a female hekdesh attendant. In March 1759, she was summoned to testify about the death and effects of Jonas Loew, a widower who had died in the hekdesh, leaving behind two children.[78] Malka knew from which town he had come and details of his personal effects, indicating that even as a female attendant, she was familiar with the men in the hospice.[79] The duties of the woman who cared for the ill in the hekdesh, at least in Vienna, included the responsibility to remember (and possibly to record) the personal details of the sick and to inventory their effects if they died.[80]

A further glimpse into Malka's life opened when her widowed sister, Bella, passed away in the hekdesh on Rossau. In the report on Bella's death, we learn that the widowed Malka served as an attendant to and paid for the expenses and support of her sister, Bella. Although a lock was placed on Bella's effects, another Jewish woman, Minga Berin, in the German record, testified that there was nothing of value in Bella's possessions. Minga was none other than Malka's daughter, Mindl, who, despite not having the official designation of being paid to work in the hekdesh, was called upon to perform some of the duties there, including testifying about her aunt's estate. More significantly, Mindl was married to Beer Jacob (in the German records sometimes called Jacob Beer), named as the attendant in many hekdesh inventories during this time. She was thus the daughter and the wife of hekdesh attendants. Like Malka before him, Beer Jacob was responsible for the effects and last wishes of the residents of the hospice. Beer wrote that when the widow Bella from Trebitsch died poor and intestate in the hekdesh on Rossau after fifteen weeks of being cared for there, he raised the funds for her burial "with my own hands."[81] He also recorded the last wishes of Anna, a widow from Moravia who died in the hekdesh without making a will but had expressed the wish that fifty Gulden that she left to her brother be given to her son.[82] Beer appears in many death records of the poorest to testify to their (lack of) effects left behind, and his word was never questioned. The women of the hekdesh played a similar official role, caring for the poor and the sick and later recording and reporting on what, if anything, they left behind after their deaths. These three generations of Viennese Jewish women were of very limited means, and they cared for those who had even less; the hekdesh women had a place to live and communal employment.

Communal Midwives

Communities hired official midwives to deliver the babies of the poor that were born in the hekdesh, since poor families could not afford to pay for a midwife's services.[83] This support was also extended to foreign poor women who did not reside in one of the larger Jewish communities and had traveled to a nearby hekdesh in order to deliver.[84] One such midwife, Fromet, daughter of Meir Schnapper of Frankfurt, was compared to the biblical midwives Shifra and Pu'ah for "the children she delivered in the hekdesh."[85]

Certain rooms in the Berlin hekdesh were allocated for delivering the babies of the poor, both local and foreign. Beyond the medical care necessary for delivery, the women were provided with food, financial assistance, and linens for four weeks postpartum. The community similarly funded circumcisions of baby boys born in the hospice, including the customary festive meal following the rite. Foreign women were also provided with travel money to move onward after the lying-in period.[86] Over the course of the eighteenth century, pious confraternities dedicated to caring for the sick oversaw some of the activities in the hekdesh; the newly founded women's sororities were responsible for childbirth and postpartum care.[87] The deep entanglement of women's work within broader communal structures is nowhere more apparent than in the care provided to poor women during and after childbirth. The midwives delivered babies and provided care to the parturients; these costs were paid from the general community charity fund; the parturients were housed in the hekdesh overseen by the men's society for the sick; and the stipends were distributed by the women's society, which also oversaw the women's medical care.[88] Though an independent organization in its own right, the women's *hevrah* (sorority) served in this instance as a branch of the community's official operation, through which care could be extended to women in need.

Wealthier women, by contrast, gave birth to their babies at home and hired a *varts froy* or a *warterin* (postpartum nurse) (see plate 5). While these nurses were hired privately, communal leaders nevertheless regulated the conditions of their employment. In 1698, Altona's Jewish community renewed its policy that a varts froy could only be hired by one woman at a time:

> Renewed, 26 Sivan 1698. The *varts vayber* (postpartum attendants) may not hire themselves out to two women at the same time; they must let their clients know whom they have booked to serve the month before and after [the due date], so that a woman can rely on this. If she [the *varts vayb*] violates this, her salary shall go to charity. And if by chance two women give birth at the same time, the right of priority shall go to the one who paid her "maid money" first. And if the woman who hired first gives birth second, she [the varts vayb] must leave the mother who hired her second and go to the one who hired her first.[89]

By fining any nurse who transgressed this policy at the communal level, the leaders inserted themselves into the dynamic between employer and employee. In Fürth, regulations were enacted about who was eligible to serve as a varts froy. The employment of a foreign varts froy whose husband did not accompany her was contingent on her husband's consent, and she was to return home at least once every six weeks for one month.[90] Although the community did not directly employ these postpartum nurses, they nevertheless determined who could be employed as nurses in the community and oversaw and controlled the terms of these women's employment.

By contrast, the community, employing various financial arrangements, directly compensated professional midwives hired to deliver poor Jewish babies. Some, such as Brendlin Schiff of Frankfurt, were paid an annual salary; she was hired in 1656 at the rate of six Reichsthaler per year.[91] Similarly, in

Berlin in 1744, the community issued a stipend to the unnamed midwife because "it is well-known that she served the poor of our community for free."[92] She was paid six times less than the local doctor, who also had his own budget for travel.[93] In 1796, one of Frankfurt's midwives received a weekly salary as well as lodging from the community.[94] Another model of compensation was adopted in eighteenth-century Altona, where the midwife Brenle was compensated one Mark for each baby she delivered in the hekdesh.

Moses, son and husband to two other midwives in Hamburg, referred to the arrangement between Brenle and Altona's lay leaders in a letter; he noted that his deceased mother had been exempted from paying communal taxes in exchange for the labor she provided to the community as a midwife. He requested an extension of that same policy to his wife, who delivered "hundreds of babies ... for which she did not take even one penny."[95] Hamburg's Jewish community deducted 50 percent from the assessment of his worth in exchange for the labor of his wife, Sara.[96] Whether her compensation was structured through tax reductions or salary, the midwife was clearly recognized as a communal employee.

Midwives bore additional responsibilities within the community, as is evident from a series of interactions between Altona's lay leaders and another local midwife, Friedche. In 1767, Friedche reported that Sprintsche, daughter of Aaron Baz, had stated "on the birthing stool" that Hirts, son of Moshe, had fathered her illegitimate child. The paternity suit that ensued was based on Friedche's report to the lay leaders.

The expectation that, as a communal midwife, Friedche would supply information from the birthing mother to the lay leaders was raised again just over two years later when the latter demanded that Friedche reveal the identities of the parents whose illegitimate child she had delivered three weeks earlier. In this case, Friedche refused to divulge the names of both mother and father, and the lay leaders banned her services, only to reinstate them three days later. It is difficult to know who blinked first, the indignant lay leaders or the recalcitrant midwife. Either scenario is possible since each was dependent on the other: the midwife provided a vital service, and the kahal controlled the framework and means of her livelihood. Friedche continued to work in Altona and its hekdesh, but the lay leaders insisted that another woman be present during births alongside the midwife. The communal shamash who recorded this decision does not elaborate beyond this information, but it appears as though the kahal was signaling its distrust of Friedche as an official witness and recorder of the births in the community. Friedche had failed to act as the representative of the lay leadership in the delivery room and failed as a trustworthy "respectable woman." The lay leaders marked her as an unreliable agent by inserting a different woman into the room to perform that function for the kahal. Midwives were prized at least as much for their stature within the community as for their skill in the delivery room, and when either of these aspects was compromised, their positions would suffer.[97]

In Metz, too, the midwife was expected to use her knowledge to aid male officials who were unable to obtain information from pregnant women due to modesty and lack of expertise. In a paternity suit brought before the rabbinical court in the late eighteenth century, a maidservant named Yitle accused her employer's son, Moshe, of promising to marry her and impregnating her. Moshe claimed that while he had considered marrying Yitle, he had decided against it due to flaws in her character and pedigree. Moshe insisted, moreover, that he had never had sexual relations with her. The rabbinical court appointed two upstanding women and midwives to ascertain whether Yitle was indeed pregnant; if so, Moshe would be obligated to take an oath that he had not had relations with her and was not the father of her child. Yitle, however, physically pushed the two women away and refused to be examined; her paternity suit was then dropped.[98] As was the case with Friedche in Altona, the midwives' knowledge of women's anatomy positioned them to assist the rabbis; as communal employees, they were expected to furnish the necessary information.

The desire to identify fathers in paternity suits was not limited to justice for the baby and the mother. Communities were intent on identifying the father to ensure that he would take financial responsibility for the baby, as an orphaned child would be added to the community's already extensive list of welfare recipients. With communal coffers stretched thin, lay leaders even negotiated over the burial costs of illegitimate babies who had died. In one case in Altona-Hamburg-Wandsbek, the illegitimate daughter of a maidservant named Devorah had been left by her mother with local Christians to nurse. When the girl died, the lay leaders of Altona and Wandsbek argued over who was responsible for covering her burial costs despite the fact that the girl's body remained unburied for two days in the hot weather.[99] The role of the midwife in supplying information about paternity could be vital to the community, as it allowed its leaders to assign financial responsibility for living and dead children.

In Metz and Altona, additional women, usually termed *nashim hagunot* or *nashim kesherot* (upstanding women) oversaw the midwives and sometimes served alongside them as liaisons to the communal leaders. These were usually ba'alot bayit in the community whose probity and standing, rather than any expertise, commended them to provide oversight. References to *nashim zekenot* (elderly and knowledgeable women) and to *nashim memunot*, women who had been appointed to answer other women's questions about menstrual purity, also appear in rabbinic responsa. As Jordan Katz has illustrated, these knowledgeable women and communal midwives served as an "extension of the rabbinic gaze," responding to rabbis on Jewish legal questions that required expertise about female anatomy, including paternity, miscarriage, illness, menstruation, or uterine and vaginal bleeding.[100]

When one woman in the sixteenth century saw bloodstains that she believed may have been induced by coughing, she first consulted with "elderly women," to whom she likely showed the stains. They told her that the blood was from a burst vessel, and their opinion was relayed to the rabbi, Isaac miSee, who had been asked to rule on the status of her menstrual purity.[101] In another case in the eighteenth century, a woman who likely suffered from uterine prolapse sent her sister-in-law to Rabbi Aaron Aurich with a swatch of her stained robe. The sister-in-law had even been present at one of the woman's internal examinations. Rabbi Aurich listened both to her and to local elderly women when deciding the matter.[102]

Women's expertise was also critical for cases in which young girls had been injured, sometimes by falling onto a bench or a chair; these injuries left the appearance that the girl was no longer a virgin. In The Hague, parents and witnesses appeared before the lay leaders or the rabbi and testified about the injury. Two knowledgeable women would then examine the girl to confirm the injury. A record called *shetar mukat etz* was then entered into a communal logbook, which documented the injury, ensuring that when the girl married, her virginal status would not be called into question. Eight such cases were brought before communal leaders in The Hague in the eighteenth century, each dealing with girls younger than nine years old.[103] Male communal leaders could not physically examine these girls for reasons of modesty, and they likely lacked the expertise to do so. In a wide range of cases, then, wise women's knowledge was indispensable in the community, in court, and to individual *poskim* (religious legal deciders).

The Rebbetzin

In the fifteenth century, Shondlein, the wife of R. Israel Isserlein of Austria, signed a responsum about menstrual purity. In Yiddish, Shondlein recounted "speaking with my husband" about a query the woman had brought directly to her concerning a stain she had found on her bed linens.[104] This highlights the very real possibility that other rabbis' wives served as conduits between their husbands and women who wished to turn to their rabbi with questions, particularly in cases involving intimate discussions of female anatomy and sexuality. A similar case can be found in the seventeenth century, when Rebbetzin Fromet, the wife of Rabbi Judah Mehler, was thoroughly implicated in the case of an unnamed woman from Koblenz. For almost a full year, the woman had experienced vaginal discharge with red stains, rendering her sexually impermissible to her husband. She was "known to the rabbi's wife, who had spoken to the woman face to face" when Mehler was traveling away from home. Fromet had also corresponded directly with the woman in writing; a copy of her letter was seen by Yaakov ha-Kohen, who was serving as the rabbi in Koblenz and who mentioned Fromet's letter when he turned to Mehler seeking the latter's opinion.[105] Perhaps the woman felt comfortable turning to Fromet, who was not only a woman but a native of Koblenz; regardless, Fromet took a leading role in this case in her husband's absence, conducting both verbal and written exchanges that were later reported to the relevant rabbinical figures.[106]

Rabbis' wives like Fromet and Shondlein partnered with their husbands, and when a rabbi was hired by a community, his wife was awarded the title of *rabbanit* (Hebr.) or *rebbetzin* (Yid.). She would continue to hold this title even after his death, as is evident from a list of taxpayers in Friedberg from 1550. Women who paid taxes were typically widowed heads of households, and two different women, Rabbanit Michlen and Rabbanit Hindchen, appear on the list. Either or both women may have been widows of former rabbis of Friedberg; despite their widowed status, each rebbetzin retained her title.[107] The title was not simply a matter of respect but, rather, a reflection of the position, which entailed various obligations to the community, both formal and informal. The tombstone of Moses Samson Bacharach, rabbi of Worms in the seventeenth century, refers to the forty-one years he had served with his wife, referred to as "the *rabbanit*" and "the *darshanit*."[108] The latter term suggests that she taught Torah, likely to the women of the community.[109] Additional sources confirm that the rabbanit in Worms played a central role in pre-wedding festivities held by women in honor of the bride.[110] The primary role played by the rabbi's wife paralleled the role played by her husband at celebrations held among men for the groom.

The rabbi's wife likewise blessed the youths of Worms on a special Shabbat on which they held a procession into the women's section of the synagogue after Purim.[111] The importance of the rabbanit's formal and informal leadership was recognized by granting her a special seat within the synagogue, just as the rabbi was furnished with a special seat in the men's sanctuary. In Schnaittach, the rabbi sat on the southern side next to the ark; his wife sat on the eastern side of the middle bench. Her seat was clearly marked in the communal seating chart with the word *rabbanit*, highlighting the formal role and status that she was accorded.[112]

Not only did a widowed rabbanit maintain her title, but the community was obliged to provide for her if she remained in the kehillah. Rabbi Aharon Kaidonover's 1667 contract in Frankfurt stipulated that "his wife would not be pushed out of Frankfurt for the duration of her widowhood," a significant promise in the restricted space of the ghetto.[113] In Worms, several residences were built on the stories above the communal dance hall and *kloyz* [study hall; pl. *kloyzen*]. In 1760, one residence was occupied by a rabbi, the other by the rebbetzin of the former rabbi.[114] The higher costs of supporting a married rabbi, which included the possibility of dealing with a widowed rebbetzin, led some smaller communities in the countryside to refrain from hiring a married rabbi, but this was unthinkable in larger and more prominent communities.[115] In larger communities, lay leaders sometimes fulfilled their obligation to the widowed rebbetzin begrudgingly. Since the new rabbi would have brought his own wife as well, lay leaders saw the upkeep of the rabbi's widow as a burden. In 1764, the widowed rabbanit of Altona demanded that the community release the money owed to her under the terms of her wedding contract, leveraging their desire that she leave to pressure them to release funds from her husband's estate:

> Today Friday, 7 Heshvan [1764], I was sent by parnas R. Hirsch Breslau to the [lay leader of that month] to tell him that the rabbanit of the late chief rabbi came to him and said that if the kahal does not provide her with her *ketubbah* [marriage contract] money, she will not depart from here at all. At the least, the kahal must give her a promissory note . . . if the kahal will do this, then she will depart from here, and if not, she will not. The *apotropsim* [custodians of the estate] of the chief rabbi replied that if she does not leave now, she will lose several hundred Reichsthaler, and not only is she diminishing the principle of the estate, but a great expense will accrue to the kahal.[116]

In another heartbreaking example from Altona, a small slip of paper inserted into a court register permits the executors of Rabbi Emden's will to grant his widow, the rabbanit, a stipend of one Reichsthaler per month as a food allowance, so that she would not be abandoned by the heirs to the estate.[117]

Other communities embraced this obligation, sending support to an impoverished rebbetzin even after she had left the community. In 1735, the lay leaders of Amsterdam agreed to support Shatel, the widow of Rabbi Leyb Kalisch, who had moved to Rzeszów in Poland. Shatel had turned to them "in distress," noting her indigence and old age. They decided to send her a yearly sum of fifty Gulden, one Gulden per week, for the rest of her life "so that she could support herself and to honor her husband."[118]

Marriage, Status, and Communal Influence

The rebbetzin was not alone among Jewish women in wielding influence and prestige during her husband's lifetime and after his death. As we saw above, the same was true for the wives of various communal officials who worked alongside their husbands. The wives of parnassim were recognized as sharing in the honor of their husbands' positions.[119] In seventeenth-century Worms, when a parnas was appointed, he took a formal oath on a Bible. "The custom after the oath [was to] visit the parnas and his wife and his relatives, and say to them: 'Congratulations,'" after which the parnas hosted a festive meal for the community members.[120] That the custom dictated formally acknowledging the wife of the parnas and further celebrating at a meal she had undoubtedly supervised and prepared indicates that the honor extended beyond the individual man to include his family and, most prominently, his wife. Hundreds of references across all genres of communal records refer not only to the wives of parnassim but to their widows as such, further indicating that the status associated with serving as a parnas was conferred on both spouses. A later custom from eighteenth-century Metz that privileged the widows of former parnassim demonstrates this clearly. While members of the community were required to enter a lottery to acquire individual *etrogim* (ritual citrons) for Sukkot, current and former parnassim, as well as the widows of former parnassim, were exempted from the lottery.[121] Like the rebbetzin, these ba'alot bayit, although widows, retained a favored status in the community that demonstrates the honor and status accorded to them even after their husbands' deaths.

Ba'alot bayit also shared access to information. The shared space of the home rendered them privy to information that normally would have been reserved for communal officials. A Frankfurt regulation from 1662 insisted that no external parties be present when judges were in session. Judges' meetings took place in the warm room of a house, and all outsiders were to be sent outside the room, "including the wife of the judge."[122] By singling out the judge's wife, the regulation reveals that her presence was otherwise to be expected. While judges' wives were asked to leave to protect the inner workings of the court, one can extrapolate that the wives of other communal officials may have been aware of and perhaps able to influence communal developments. It was not just a matter of overhearing discussions. In the small Franconian village of Schnaittach, a bylaw issued in 1689 decreed that the lay leaders could demand absolute secrecy regarding certain decisions, banning "divulging [these matters] even to their wives and children."[123] We can infer from the bylaw that, ordinarily, wives were deeply aware of the inner workings of the community and the decisions their husbands had made. Indeed, women had access to more than just spoken words. An announcement proclaimed in the Altona synagogue mandated that communal officials return the logbooks they had taken home with them within eight days of the announcement. Special mention was made of the widows and children of former officials, who were also required to return said records, indicating that, at times, these women had access to official communal records.[124] An inventory taken upon the death of a lay leader in late eighteenth-century Altona confirms that the deceased had left records belonging to the community atop his desk, among his other effects.[125]

Women and Communal Records

Both the women employed by the community and those who served as volunteers, like their male counterparts, maintained records of their work. Although many of the women surveyed here would have kept registers, the only ones that have survived from among the materials we surveyed belonged to midwives, who inscribed detailed lists of the babies they delivered. These, along with circumcisers' logbooks, constitute the only birth records we have from early modern Jewish communities.[126] Several pinkassim belonging to midwives are extant, and like the records of circumcisers, they include both personal and communal elements. One pinkas from early-eighteenth-century Amsterdam includes a Yiddish gynecological treatise.[127] It belonged to Roza, a midwife who was licensed in Amsterdam, who also recorded the names of the babies she delivered. For every entry in the register, Roza began with the Jewish date (day of the week, day of the month, Jewish month), in some cases (but not most) followed by the civil date, and after that, the child's sex, always using the words "a son" or "a daughter."[128] Another pinkas from Hamburg records deliveries between 1778 and 1799.[129] These registers could be consulted to determine parentage and status. When an unwed mother delivered a baby, the midwife included this fact in the records. The enduring importance of birth records as proof of identity and status within the community likely led to the preservation of these pinkassim, unlike the financial logbooks of women who maintained ritual baths, which did not survive.

A third written record of another Jewish midwife in the Netherlands (1794–1832) was also preserved. Roza, "wife of Leyzer ben Moshe Yehudah," as she identified herself on the title page, was a midwife in Groningen. Roza highlighted the active role she took as author and scribe of her record book: "I took this book as my possession, and I recorded in it the names of those giving birth (*yoledot*) with the name of the newborn, with the date of the birth, so that it should be a *zikkaron* (remembrance) from the day I began this profession [6 November 1794] and forward." The bolded chronogram (a customizable Hebrew acronym) for the year of writing is "I, the mid-wife."[130] She wrote a literary preface to her register, in both Yiddish and Hebrew, in facing columns on the same title page. Her opening words intersperse textual references to the famous biblical midwives in Egypt, who always came too late to implement Pharaoh's nefarious plan to kill Israelite male newborns. The vitality of Jewish mothers allowed them to give birth before the midwives arrived (see Exod. 1:15–19). Roza prayed that no harm would come to the mothers on the birthstools or to the children about to be born: "Only let them be expelled from the uterus like an egg from a hen."[131] She further maintained a Dutch-language register for the Christian babies she delivered, which sadly has not been preserved.[132]

The words written in Roza's own hand exemplify the intersection between early modern Jewish women and recordkeeping, here in the context of their communal work. Most women involved in communal work maintained records, whether of the sums they collected in synagogues and ritual baths, of the items the poor left behind in the hekdesh after death, or of the babies they delivered in private homes and in the hospice. Although most of their records did not endure, that they maintained registers is evident from the demands of their labor, as documented in other communal logbooks. The women's records transferred information between the female actors, who were active in roles and spaces in which men were not present, and the male lay leaders, who oversaw the community. Moreover, when their records did survive, they also preserved the names, identities, and actions of women like Roza. The detailed writings in the midwives' pinkassim are a precious window into the intense involvement of women in elements of communal life, through which they provided essential services to the kehillah.

2

Sacred Societies

WOMEN'S HEVROT

LEAH YACHT of Mainz, the widow of Meir ben Tevele, was "one of the women in the sacred society of righteous women, [and she tended] to the living and the dead with lovingkindness and true grace, particularly toward the sick."[1] She was renowned for the dedication and care she provided to those who were ill, as "she hastened to help them for Heaven's sake, to feed and listen to them, and to arrange for them all kind of medication. And she herself prepared their beds, to clean them."[2] This description of her piety, inscribed in the communal Memorbuch after her death in 1738, depicted the range of actions a woman in the *hevrah kaddisha* (burial society) might perform on behalf of the sick. Leah Yacht, however, was not just a member of the prestigious sorority in Mainz; she served as one of its leaders and was memorialized as "the mother to all eighteen righteous women [who tended to] the living and the dead."[3] Leah Yacht was not alone: in every community, large and small, women assumed positions of leadership in sororities, most prominently in the burial society. The 1785 tombstone of Rivkah Devorah memorializes her as "*gabbete* (official) of the sorority of righteous women; an elderly and important woman like [the biblical] Abigail."[4] Though the stone was not large enough to engrave her many activities, it afforded public recognition of her leadership role.

It was not until the late seventeenth and, more prominently, through the eighteenth century that rich documentation of women's societies arose in the Ashkenazi realm.[5] The earliest regulations referring to female members were embedded in the logbooks and bylaws of men's societies; by the late eighteenth century, women's societies had their own stand-alone sets of bylaws. Two loose folios in the communal archive in Rendsburg, a small town near Hamburg, provide an extraordinary window into an organized women's association that was essential to communal life. This manuscript of the 1776 Yiddish bylaws of the women's burial society includes members' signatures and a division of the women's duties into several shifts, each of which comprised four women: "The first duty is to stand watch during the night over the sick person; the duty of the next shift is to lay the dead person on the ground on straw. The third shift performs the purification rite, while the following one [attends] to the funeral, and four women must take out or follow the bier to the cemetery, that the dead will be treated properly."[6] While these bylaws were likely written by men, they governed an independent women's burial society that worked in parallel with the men's society. The establishment of formal burial societies and the drafting of their detailed regulations were early modern developments that deeply reflected contemporary culture, in which regulations, structure, and order governed both Jewish and Christian societies in Europe. The detailed ordinances of sororities permit us to reconstruct women's voices and actions, the initiatives they developed, and the enterprises they advanced. Women had fewer arenas within the Jewish community than men where they could express their individuality and piety, marks of good standing in society. Membership in a sorority promoted status and responsibility, recordkeeping and accounting, craftsmanship, and caring—in short, means for women to serve their communities in a formal role, as well as to mark themselves as pious, selfless, and industrious. This chapter examines women's pious sororities, beginning with references to various sororities that are scattered across pinkassim and memorial books, often only in passing. Our main focus will be the women's burial society, for which the textual and material record is remarkably rich, with exquisitely detailed information about women's knowledge and communal responsibilities.

Early Modern Pious Societies

Several Jewish confraternities were established in medieval Spain, and an even greater variety of societies developed in early modern Italy, where pious confraternities were common among Catholics.[7] While Jewish confraternities may have modeled their structure on Christian societies, the content of their rituals rested on older rabbinic teachings as well as the newer influences of Lurianic kabbalah.[8]

Early modern confraternities were organized and modeled on the communities' governance structure, although their membership was not identical to the communal leadership, despite great overlap. Large communities had many *hevrot*, smaller circles or confraternities devoted to study, good works, and allocation of charity. Even small communities had a formal burial society. Male societies elected (or approved) leaders and deputies and voted on new members.[9] In large communities, these were prestigious positions; in some cases, slots were passed down within families who reserved positions for their offspring.[10] Societies collected dues and gave preferential treatment to their members. Some had separate meeting spaces and owned equipment that they could rent or lend when not used for their primary purpose by their members.[11] Like early modern communities, different societies maintained logbooks to keep track of their finances and activities. These hevrot also enacted formal takkanot (regulations) to govern their activities, some of which were copied into the logbook and preserved for posterity.[12]

The first formal confraternity in central Europe was the burial society established in Prague in 1564.[13] By the seventeenth century, men's societies for caring for the sick, ritually preparing the dead, building coffins, digging graves, and burying the dead proliferated across Jewish communities.[14] Formal women's sororities followed suit, providing structure for the care of the sick and the dead, tasks which had previously been performed on an ad hoc basis by individual women. While in the twelfth century, Dolcia of Worms, an elite Jewish woman from the Rhineland, sewed shrouds for the dead, several hundred years later, a formally appointed and recognized group of women cut and sewed shrouds and prepared the dead for burial.[15] In some instances in the sixteenth century, women functioned within men's confraternities and appear as signatories to their bylaws; by the eighteenth century, however, they had formally separate sororities with their own regulations.[16]

Jacob Rader Marcus was the first historian to devote a separate chapter, "Women's Sick Care Societies," to the subject.[17] Marcus noted the prominent position of women's circles in Christian society from the medieval period, in which sisterhoods of women played significant roles in caring for the sick, the dying, and the dead. The role of convents and professional religious women can only partly account for this. The desire to impose order, reflected in so many aspects of communal life, also contributed to the creation of formal women's societies, which replaced the care that individual women had provided to the needy, the sick, and the dead. The rise and concomitant documentation relating to women's societies illustrates the central argument of this book: certain activities of women became both formal and visible only in the early modern period. This is the case for the crystallization of confraternal hierarchies in general, as well as for the documentation that accompanied various aspects of their formation, governance, and other endeavors.

FIG. 2.1. A list of the "pious women who stand ready to serve, united, woman to woman, to perform acts of kindness to Jewish men and women." *Pinkas gemilut hasadim be-kehillat Ferrara*, 1515.

Pious Sororities

Women in various Jewish communities united both in formal associations and in less formal alliances to perform a range of charitable activities. Sometimes, a brief reference in a communal logbook is the only trace left of the confraternity. One such example is a women's society in Altona-Hamburg-Wandsbek for dowering poor brides. While little is known about its organization or its activities, it is mentioned in the community's takkanot from 1698, when the leaders mandated that its finances be governed "as per the takkanot of the kahal and the appointed communal officials."[18] We can glimpse this society through the lens of the communal leaders, who took its existence for granted and attempted to bring it under their control. Another fleeting mention of a women's society for tending to the sick in Frankfurt can be found in a body of regulations for a men's charitable confraternity in Frankfurt in 1786. The rules concerning a prayer quorum in the home of a mourner were said to apply equally to those who were not members of either the men's or the women's societies for sick care.¹⁹ We learn only of the society's existence, no more. In Berlin, the women's burial society, discussed at length below, expanded its operations in 1745 to include poor relief. The women in charge of sewing shrouds and the purification of the dead began to help the ill and the poor in the hekdesh (hospice) as well.²⁰

The existence of still other hevrot emerges from references in the entries of Memorbücher (communal memorial books). While it is not always possible to discern whether an individual woman had performed a pious act, such as visiting the sick, sewing shrouds, or tending to orphans in an official context, some entries explicitly praise women's membership in formal societies. Haylah, daughter of the Jewish notable (*bat he-aluf*) Lezer Strauss of Frankfurt, was remembered for "laboring and toiling to send food to the poor, sick, and downtrodden from the funds of her women's society."²¹ Leah Hindchen of Frankfurt likewise "labored and toiled to send food, drink, and wood from the funds of her women's confraternity to the sick and the poor."²² Though short references penned in nearly identical language do not elucidate details about either organization, women were clearly involved in organized charitable relief. In Metz, several sisterhoods performed pious deeds, among them a society for "pious women"; another sorority for sewing shrouds; and a third, led by Rebecca Hadamard, which sewed twelve dresses each year for poor women.²³

Tangible remnants of another eighteenth-century women's society, *hevrah kaddisha pikuah nefesh* in Amsterdam, can be found in a logbook of the receipts the society issued for contributions. Though damaged, it contains clippings of receipts that would have been cut out of the volume and handed to donors. Each printed receipt includes a receipt number, the handwritten name of the donor, and the months for which she had contributed to the association.²⁴ These contributions may have been monthly membership dues to support the society's work. Although the nature of that work and the organizational structure remain opaque, the small slips of paper from the receipt book reveal a highly organized association. The meticulous set of records and printed receipts maintained by the women mirror the culture of the early modern kehillah and its detailed receipts and record books.

Though the Amsterdam receipt book stands out among our archival finds, there is no reason to assume that other hevrot did not maintain similar documentation. More abundant still than the receipt book from Amsterdam are the various regulations of women's burial societies, which provide a far more detailed understanding of the women's responsibilities, as well as of the organization and administration of the society.

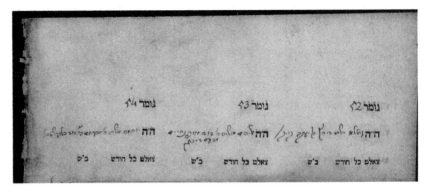

FIG. 2.2. Receipt for two stuiver monthly payment, Amsterdam benevolent sorority, eighteenth century.

Material Texts of Women's Burial Societies

While there is a relative abundance of documentation from men's burial societies and a comparative scarcity from women's societies, we have found regulations for women's burial societies in Berlin, Mainz (in the Rhineland), Prague, and Rendsburg, as well as a wealth of other manuals, material items, and manuscripts from Altona-Hamburg, Amsterdam, Metz, Copenhagen, and Moravia. In Rendsburg, the takkanot of the women's burial society and those of the men's, both from the second half of the eighteenth century, have been preserved. The Rendsburg men's regulations were copied into a logbook, while the women's, as noted above, were recorded on separate sheets of paper, bearing the crease of having been folded and tucked somewhere; it is miraculous that they survived.

That the women's takkanot were written on paper rather than on parchment, as some men's takkanot were, is a further noteworthy distinction as to their place in the community's records.[25] The Mainz takkanot confirm that the women, at least those in leadership positions of the burial society, practiced accurate recordkeeping. When the leadership changed hands, those who stepped down "should render a correct accounting from the previous year, both of income as well as expenses."[26] It was essential to keep track of the appointment of officials, the induction of new members, the receipt of membership fees and fines that the women collected, and the expenses they incurred in buying linen, thread, and other tools. Hevrot collected charity to fund the materials and expenses involved with their activities. Given that the societies for preparing the dead often also cared for the sick, medical and sustenance expenses for the families of the ill could mount very quickly. Every penny raised for charity had to be carefully counted and guarded. While so far we have not found a women's pinkas from the Jewish communities surveyed in this chapter, the *So'ed holim* women's society from Modena in northern Italy maintained a logbook spanning over two centuries, from 1735 to 1943.[27] It is possible that the women's society logbook would have been regarded as less crucial for communal archives than were the records of the male burial society, which included burial information for men and women and was sometimes consulted for other purposes.[28]

Scraps of paper preserved in the back of one Altona pinkas illuminate the way in which every separate expense related to the preparation of the dead was recorded.[29] When the *bahur hashuv*, the respected unmarried young man Hayim, son of the late Eliezer from Zwoleń in the Lublin district of Poland (called in some documents "Hayim Vilner"), lay ill, the Altona Jewish communal authorities hastened to have him record a will.[30] As he left sufficient assets, every expense incurred by the community and the burial society pertaining to his death and burial was tallied and recorded to be deducted from his estate. These expenses were not written into a formal record book. Instead, they were tallied on various slips of paper and, by a random stroke of fortune, preserved within the pages of the community's record of wills and other important documents (titled *Pinkas divre ha-yamim*).[31]

One list noted the amounts that were paid to the bursar of the community, the burial costs according to a tally, the cost of supporting scholars as per the will, the cost of a headstone, and the cost of installing the headstone by the burial society. A second slip of paper contained the breakdown of the final tally for burial costs, excluding those just mentioned, down to the last Schilling: the price of twenty-eight lengths of linen, of shrouds, of a casket, of a guardian over the casket, payment to the burial society, for the bag of soil from the Holy Land, for the sextons of the undertakers' society, for the purification board, and for messenger fees (presumably to notify his family of his death and bequests). All told, the community charged Hayim's estate twenty-five Mark and thirteen Schilling for the charges relating to his death, a significant amount. Another slip served as a receipt to assure that the payment from his estate had been made to a communal leader, Hayim (Hyman) Birgel. These accounts illuminate an important element of confraternities: while they seem to operate within their own ambit, electing officials, observing rituals, and raising and disbursing funds, in fact, they functioned as an integral arm of the community's official structure. In some communities, such as Prague, the men's society provided formal stipends to the poor before holidays, effectively taking on a role that was managed directly by the communal leaders in other communities.[32] These types of arrangements strengthened the status of women's sororities as key elements within the community; they also allow us to understand why precise recordkeeping was so important to all parties, and how it was that in one case, a men's burial society could attempt to limit the functions of a women's society.

The intense scribal and textual culture of the eighteenth century manifested in various other ways that intersect with recordkeeping by pious societies. Many of the documents are designated as copies of original agreements (*he'etek*). The Rendsburg women's takkanot, for example, are labeled as a copy. Even the copy includes certain standard scribal flourishes, such as lightly inking over blank spaces to prevent the insertion of additional clauses. Most of the signatures are copied by the same hand; the originals would have been signed by the many women whose names appear. Despite this, additional clauses were written into the copy, over the strike marks, and later insertions were dated and signed.

The Duties of the Women's Burial Society

The women of the hevrah kaddisha worked in shifts (each termed *mishmar*), performing various tasks from the onset of illness through burial. In some larger communities, more than one women's hevrah divided these tasks between them. The Berlin women's burial society expanded its relief activities in 1745, caring for the poor, the infirm, and the deceased.[33] The same was true in Metz, as Fromet, the widow of Eliya Levi, left money in her will to two women's sororities: one that sewed shrouds and another that performed the purification rite.[34]

The women of the burial societies tended to the female ill both during the day and at night; they alone, rather than men, could do so for reasons of modesty. Regulations from Rendsburg indicate that during the long, dark hours of the winter months, two shifts of women would be assigned to perform this onerous task; the youngest woman on the first shift was charged with waking the members of the next watch.[35] When a woman died, her body was removed from her bed by the members of the sorority and placed on the floor on a matting of straw. Women's great desire to participate in honoring the dead had the potential for disorder as they vied with one another for various tasks. In Mainz, women jostled and squabbled since "each woman from the society wants to help the dead from the bed and lay her on the straw ... the younger women push the older ones."[36] To prevent such unruliness, which was deemed unseemly and disrespectful toward the dead, the sorority adopted a general practice that "in all matters older women [the more experienced members] come one after the other, without any younger woman pushing them."[37]

Once the body was laid on the straw, the burial society prayed for the soul of the deceased. Rebecca Sinzheim, who served on the burial society in Mannheim, not far from Mainz, instructed, "While I am lying between death and burial, I should not be left alone for one second. Only Psalms should be said completely, and I should be well-watched."[38] She further ordered that charity be donated while she was lying on the straw; other women instructed the same between death and burial.[39] Next, the women's society sewed shrouds, which they did for both the male and female dead. The material was to be white linen to symbolize purity.[40]

In the famous Prague cycle image (held in the Jewish Museum in Prague), the men on the left can be seen cutting lengths of material with a large scissor, while the actual sewing of the shaped garments was done by women. To the right, a basket on the ground was used to collect scraps of fabric. Rebecca Sinzheim instructed that the scraps from her shrouds be used to fashion undershirts for needy brides.[41] As the society used many pieces of cloth to wash the dead, it is possible that the larger scraps could have been used for that purpose. An inventory from eighteenth-century Altona accounts for a small piece of linen from the home of the deceased that had been given to the burial society for the purification rite, highlighting how every scrap was valued, accounted for, and recorded.[42]

Although the image depicts the men and women working side by side, this was not the reality in every community. In Prague, where the men's society had its own building adjacent to the cemetery, women sewed in the warm room of the shamash in inclement winter weather. In the summertime, they sewed in the courtyard of the Kloyz synagogue.[43] In Worms, women sewed in the room where the deceased had passed, in the annex off the women's section of the synagogue, or wherever they wished.[44]

Detailed regulations from Mainz stipulating that only women from the society were permitted to sew shrouds allow us to enter and reconstruct the centralized location in which women sewed under the watchful eyes of the gabbete and long-standing members of the society. The shrouds lay on a table, at which women cut and sewed the linen. Oversight was critical, as in the past, "the gravediggers and the men's burial society found something missing

FIG. 2.3. Men and women preparing burial shrouds, burial society Prague, late eighteenth century. See plate 6.

from the shrouds, and they were disturbed and stopped from their duties." The gabbete and more experienced members checked to ensure "that all of the shrouds are sewn properly: nothing is missing or too fitted."[45]

Ideally, shrouds were to be custom prepared for each dead person between the hour of death and the beginning of the purification ritual. This ideal was called for in the takkanot made by the men's society in Prague to control the women's.[46] Juspe Schammes of Worms similarly noted that immediately after someone died, the shamash was to call the women to begin sewing the shroud.[47] In reality, the idea of tailoring each shroud immediately upon a person's death was impractical, especially in a large community where more than one death could occur within a short time. In times of plague or other calamity, when multiple deaths occurred, multiple shrouds would be needed at the same time. If a person died on Shabbat, moreover, sewing could not occur until after Shabbat; if on a holiday, it had to wait until the second day of a holiday if no non-Jew could perform the task. This need spurred the women of Prague to begin to prepare shrouds in advance.

It was only after they had completed sewing the shrouds that the women began the purification rite.[48] Women warmed the water in order to wash the body. In Prague's takkanot, the gabbete was instructed to ensure that no woman who was menstrually impure or expecting the onset of menstruation be involved in this rite.[49] The same instruction was given by Rebecca Sinzheim, who insisted that "women who are not completely pure should stay away from me ... no living creature who is not pure should come anywhere within my proximity" (see plate 7).[50]

After washing and dressing the deceased in her shroud, women placed the dead in the coffin built by the men.[51] The women sewed and filled a bag with dirt to be placed (by the men if for a deceased man) by the women under the deceased's head in the grave. In Worms, if the woman who died had made her own candles, the board on which she did so could be used to construct her coffin.[52] Women of the burial society also made the *keri'ah* (symbolic tear of garments) for a brief time on their own clothing (which they could repair immediately), and they rent the clothing for female mourners of the male or female deceased. Women's societies were also charged with caring for the clothing of the deceased that they had removed.[53] They completed their duties by accompanying the body of the deceased to the burial, a task undertaken by the last shift of women. Jitta bat Mattias Glückstadt, in her will recorded in Altona in 1774, instructed that four women escort her body to the cemetery in a coach.[54] This was also the practice in Rendsburg, where the cemetery was one-and-a-half kilometers away, in Weström̈hnfeld. The regulations initially stipulated that four women escort the deceased to burial, but the policy was later amended to insist that "all the women must go out to the funeral in a wagon. If a person can afford to take their own wagon, they must; if they cannot afford to pay, the sacred society has to pay from its coffer."[55]

We can compare the bylaws of men's and women's societies in Rendsburg, both of which have survived, to determine which tasks were shared by the men's and women's societies and which were differentiated by gender. Almost all of the regulations paralleled one another, with only a few gendered differences. Only Rendsburg's women sewed shrouds, which they did for male and female dead. By contrast, Rendsburg's men constructed coffins and dug graves for all the dead. The men were also responsible for the *minyan* (prayer quorum) required for the recitation of the mourners' prayer, as such a quorum consisted of at least ten men over the age of thirteen, according to Jewish law.[56]

Difficult Death

Even under the best of circumstances, caring for the dead on a regular basis was a difficult task for the living. Under ideal conditions, bedside deaths were carefully curated from the final days of illness. The dying could issue final words of comfort to their families, their last wishes could be recorded by notaries, and the departure of soul from body would be accompanied by prayer

FIG. 2.4. Burial society coach, Hungary, nineteenth century.

and mournful singing. Participants could experience the sanctity, sadness, and stillness of the moment, allowing them to begin the work of preparing the body for its final journey in an elevated frame of mind. Depictions of dying moments in early modern art often show the deceased on white linens in a clean home surrounded by loving family members. The reality was often more difficult: suppurating wounds, excrement and bodily fluids, and ravaged flesh often greeted members of the hevrah kaddisha. The sight and odors of advanced illness aroused instinctive recoil. Bodies of those who had met with a violent end could be bloody, animal-eaten, and partially decomposed. Such difficult emotional labor met all members of a burial society, male and female, on occasion. In 1676, in Metz, for example, fortifications in the city required the removal of the fence around the perimeter of the Jewish cemetery. As a result, "the dead were uprooted from their graves, and the valley was filled with dried bones." Their spiritual angst over the dishonor of the dead was accompanied by practical concerns: the agonizing labor of collecting and reburying the remains of family members whose final rest had been disturbed. The burial society logbook relates that "each and every one of us gathered the bones of his relatives and buried them in an alternate spot, and no one knew where his own grave or the grave of his forefathers was [located]."[57]

Women were not spared even the most excruciating tasks associated with preparing the dead for burial, as the experience of the women who prepared the dead in Metz demonstrates. The pinkas of the Metz burial society contains several entries about the desecration of individual graves, such as the following, from 1712:

> Our souls are grieved, as due to the sins of the living, the dead have been disturbed in their graves. An unthinkable deed [happened] to the aforementioned *Marat* (Mrs.) Shprintz. After she was buried on the above-mentioned Sunday, on the following Monday night, some evil thieves and robbers dug the graves and removed all the clothes of the woman [name unclear], and she remained in her grave naked and with bare head. As we saw, the women took care of her under the instruction of our chief rabbi, the sage R. Avraham, may God protect him: she should be dressed as the other dead are dressed, but with regards to the purification rite, only in the places where she had been dirtied by earth did the women scrub her with cold water with a piece of cloth. And we hope that God puts her to rest in her grave and allows her to sleep in peace until such time as the heavenly spirit descends to arouse the dead.[58]

Another entry from 1724 in the same pinkas describes a similar grave desecration of a woman's grave, and a similar task of the women to restore the body to a dignified state:

> The elderly woman Mrs. Pessle, daughter of R. Eliezer [name unclear], wife of Leyb Grotman, z"l (of blessed memory), died and was buried.... This woman was snatched by gentiles, due to our sins, that is, her grave was disturbed such that it could not be recognized as a grave. The entire hevrah kaddisha of gravediggers went to dig in the yard; they found her coffin upside down: what should have been on top was on bottom, and the woman was down on her face, heaven forfend, and only the top layer of her shrouds [the *pultar*][59] was missing. Our sage and master, the great rabbi Jacob Reischer [Rzeszów], decided that the women who are occupied with

the dead should remove the dirt from her face and put her in her coffin and bury her.[60]

Rabbi Reischer's wife was herself to become a victim; an elderly woman, she was violently murdered in her bed. The task of seeing to her burial would have fallen to the women of the burial society, who had to make sure that all her bloodied bedclothes were included in her coffin and take care of her mutilated body.[61] Such vicious vandalism allows us to see some of the more emotionally difficult aspects of belonging to the burial society. It adds nuance to Glikl's lamentation when she described the dead as "creeping into the dark earth."[62] A line from Rebecca Sinzheim's will is equally telling. Appealing to her sons to respect her instructions, she urged, "Now, my beloved and pious sons, think of your beloved mother. The respect that you showed me during my lifetime [was] toward my corporeal self, which will rot and be given to worms, for all is vanity and emptiness."[63] Her graphic description was not likely rooted in familiar metaphors alone but also in her own experiences as a member of the burial society.

That these episodes were traumatic can be seen from another story told by Glikl about her father's stepdaughter, child of his first wife, whom he adopted and whom Glikl greatly admired. When the stepsister died during her first childbirth,

> Several days after that her grave was robbed and all her shrouds were removed from her. She came in a dream and revealed this. Then they removed her from her grave and found that it was true. The women hurried to sew her new shrouds. While they were sitting and sewing the maidservant comes into the room, saying: "For God's sake, hurry up with your sewing, can't you see that the dead woman is sitting among you?" But the women saw nothing. When they were done, they gave the dead her shroud. So she never returned during all her days [!] and remained in her [eternal] rest.[64]

The story underscores women's fears of being left naked in their graves and the popular belief that they could not rest comfortably in their eternity until their proper attire was restored to them. As the Mainz takkanot explained, the rationale for overseeing the proper sewing of the necessary garments was to ensure that "the dead do not, Heaven forbid, come to disgrace."[65]

Emotionally difficult work was not always due to acts of violence by criminals. Occasionally, people were trapped on the road by bad weather and froze to death. Glikl described one journey in which she feared that her children would die of exposure.[66] The Metz Memorbuch notes that Elche, wife of

Shmiel, "travelled from Boulay on a wagon loaded with wheat, on top [she had to sit on top because the wagon itself was filled with wheat]. The wagon driver found her dead on the wagon, and she was buried on Tuesday, Purim Katan [14 Adar I], 1731. That night, there had been a great frost, and that is why he found her dead. May her soul be bound up in eternal life."[67] Death from exposure to extreme cold was common enough that Shmuel Halevi, in his responsa *Nahalat shivah*, ruled, "Someone who died on the road because of freezing weather and snow, one removes his clothes and performs the purification rite and dresses him in shrouds, as he suffered no wounds, and no blood left him."[68]

The scribe of the Metz burial society logbook lamented another incident: the terrible day when a stampede in the women's section crushed six women to death as they tried to escape down a narrow staircase. They were all praying on a Shabbat and festival in the prime of their lives. Two of them were said to be "extremely young," and one of those was pregnant. The burial society record notes that although they were buried in a common grave, they each received the full purification rites for the dead, as was customary.[69] The emotional labor of preparing the bodies of these friends and neighbors, whose lives had been snuffed out in moments, turning a festive day into a cause for mourning, was part of the heartbreak of being a member of the burial society.

While such tasks may have been borne by the men's societies as well, there is one category associated with women alone: deaths of mothers and children in childbirth or during the early days of parturition. In many communities, it was customary to refrain from washing and purifying the bodies of women who had died in childbirth; they were buried in the soiled and bloody garments in which they had died. Belief that the soul exited the body via the blood made it essential that any item containing an individual's blood be buried alongside her. This principle was universally applied to murder victims, whose bodies were not purified ritually and who were buried in the clothing in which they had been killed.[70] While not all early modern rabbis agreed that these guidelines should be extended to women who died in childbirth, the takkanot and customs of several burial societies indicate that it was nevertheless the practice in multiple communities.[71]

In seventeenth-century Worms, the custom was to refrain from purifying the body of a woman who had died in childbirth.[72] She was dressed in a white robe (possibly over the clothing in which she had died); next, a white skirt, often one she had worn in her lifetime, was placed atop the white shrouds.[73] R. Loewe Kirchheim, author of a custom book from Worms, noted that a coat of pitch was added to the woman's coffin "so that the blood flowing from her

[body] does not seep into the grave."[74] This description evokes the difficulty of dressing in shrouds a woman whose body was covered in blood immediately after she had given birth. The burden was both physical and emotional, as most of the women in the society were mothers themselves.[75]

The prescriptive manual *Sha'ar Shimon* mandated a similar practice, noting in particular that any part of a bed that had been soaked in a woman's blood was to be buried with her, as were her shoes and stockings, should they have become soiled.[76] In those communities in which the normal purification rites were performed for women who had died in childbirth, the women would wash the blood off the deceased woman, purify her ritually, and dress her in shrouds. They would then layer the soiled clothes in which the woman had died over her shrouds and cover her with a sheet.[77]

An additional heart-wrenching aspect of the burial society's work was tending to a baby who had died alongside her mother. While male babies would have been tended to (and circumcised before burial) by the men's society, female babies would have been washed and prepared by the women's hevrah.[78] In Worms, the baby was buried in the coffin beside the mother's feet. In Altona-Hamburg in the eighteenth century, the practice was even more detailed. If the baby died before its mother, it was placed in a small box that was positioned atop the mother's coffin. If the mother died first, the baby was placed either in her arms or next to her feet.[79] While the burial was performed by the men's sacred society of gravediggers, the women would have washed and readied infant girls who had died at birth alongside their mothers. Burial records and tombstone epitaphs indicate that death in childbirth was not an irregular occurrence, so the women of the hevrah kaddisha were exposed to these practices as a matter of course. These examples add context to the Rendsburg women's takkanot that made provisions for women who were too sensitive to perform certain duties: "When a woman has a sensitive nature that makes it impossible for her to attend to the dead, then she can exchange her shift for another."[80] Jewish communities' elevation of the care of the dead into the highest spiritual service and the social status attained by those who served ensured that hevrot remained staffed by the respectable women and men of the community.

Material Culture of Women's Hevrot

Very few visual depictions of Jewish death rituals have survived from the early modern period.[81] The interest of early modern Jews in documenting aspects of their culture in material and visual form rarely extended to depictions of the

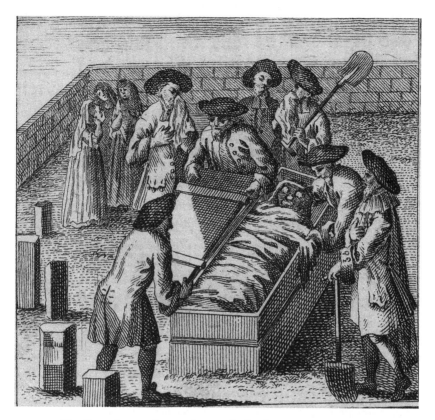

FIG. 2.5. The Gravediggers Society lowers the body into grave. Bodenschatz, *Kirchliche Verfassung*, 1749.

dead and their care. The few exceptions, as well as the Christian Hebraists' interest in Jewish rituals, allow us to see some contemporarily depicted settings and objects related to the work of the burial society.[82]

Some of the implements used by the burial society have survived, as, over the years, objects used in the sacred duties of the society would be treated in ways that transcended their utilitarian purpose. Objects that could have been made from cheaper materials were crafted in silver with dedicatory inscriptions. A precious few of these items are preserved in collections; some of these objects were dedicated by women.[83] Given the large number of ritual objects dedicated by pious women of Ashkenaz, there is every reason to believe that far more of them existed than have survived.

Women's hevrot had numerous material objects associated with their work. They had to have on hand, at least, linen for several shrouds, thread, needles, scissors, knives, and other implements needed for cutting and sewing the shrouds and for tearing their own and the mourners' clothing. In addition, they sewed the small bags to fill with soil from the Holy Land.[84] They combed the hair of the deceased with a special comb, cleaned their nails with a special pick, and cut away soiled clothing and bandages. They needed a board on which they poured water over the dead to perform the ritual purification and many pieces of rag to dry and clean the dead. They had at least one charity box, and maybe several, in which they collected donations from women in the women's section of the synagogue and on the streets during the time of a funeral.

That each society needed its tools at hand and close by in order to facilitate the earliest appropriate burial can be seen from a stray line in a *pesak din* (rabbinic judgment) rendered to the communities of Hamburg and Altona by R. Meshullam Zalman Mireles (ca. 1620–1706) on the division of financial responsibility over cemeteries and burial: "The implements of burial should be owned by each community separately to bury their dead; there should be no partnership in this."[85] It is possible that the gabbete stored these items in her home or that they were kept in the location in which women sewed.

In addition to the implements they used, the women (and men) of the burial society needed water for the purification rite. In Mannheim, Rebecca Sinzheim erected a fountain on the grounds of the cemetery to be used for purifications. While her husband was among the patrons who rebuilt Mannheim after the Nine Years' War (1688–1697), Rebecca sponsored the construction of the fountain, an item that was critical to the work performed by the burial society to which she belonged. To ensure the functionality and longevity of her gift, she instructed her children to "take heed that in case something is damaged, it is repaired as soon as possible."[86]

Manuals for Women

The duties of the burial society required extensive knowledge, and manuals and handbooks printed in Yiddish during this period prescribed detailed guidelines for them. Authors of compilations of instructions, customs, rituals, and prayers to offer while preparing the dead often added specific sections in Yiddish vernacular to be studied and read by women in the burial society. Some of these manuals were explicitly directed at female readers, seeking to empower them to properly perform their sacred duties. *Sha'ar Shimon*, published in the late eighteenth century as an adaptation of an earlier work, explicitly referred to female readers: "Part Two, encompassing all the laws pertaining

FIG. 2.6. Alms box of women's burial society, inscribed with names of each *gabba'it* and the female donor, Altona, 1854.

to those performing the sacred duty of lovingkindness in the Ashkenazi vernacular, and all the prayers said by women at the [side of] the dying in the Ashkenazi vernacular, and all the laws pertaining thereto clearly explained."[87] A compendium published in Berlin in 1750 was also intended for both men's and women's use. The author/editor appended a medieval text about mourning rites written by Nachmanides and *Kitzur ma'avar yabbok*, an abridged form of an early modern death manual composed in Prague.[88] He affixed copies of the bylaws of the men's and women's societies and, at the end of the volume, a prayer to be recited by the women's hevrah.[89] Even more striking is the special 1740 edition of the manual *Refu'ot ha-nefesh*, published in Altona at the women's initiative. The second part, written entirely in Yiddish and absent from earlier editions, was published for the "righteous women."[90] While not all of these instructions were carried out in practice, and certainly not in every community, the manuals nevertheless included contemporary recommendations and can, therefore, provide additional details about the women's work, especially when corroborated with other local sources.[91] Each of these texts adds to our knowledge of the ways women sought support within the society and were integrated as a group within the community structure.

The handbook *Sha'ar Shimon* included a song for the women to sing "in a mournful tune" at the side of a woman who was dying.[92] A Yiddish *tkhine* (supplicatory prayer) was recited by the members of the society as they tended to the body after death.[93] *Refu'ot ha-nefesh* similarly referred to the somber songs and prayers that accompanied the women's hevrah kaddisha during its sacred duties.[94] Prayers and music were part of the rhythm of other women's sororities as well. A Yiddish tkhine to be recited when the women visited the sick was printed for the women's society in Berlin and appended to their bylaws.[95]

Refu'ot ha-nefesh also taught the women to place a feather next to the dying person's mouth to check whether the feather stirred; this was to determine the moment of death.[96] Establishing the moment of death was critical for conducting the prescribed rites at the correct times: when to sing, when to lift the deceased from the bed onto a mound of straw, and when to begin sewing shrouds. How to ascertain the precise moment of death was a contested issue in the eighteenth century. Three decades after the publication of *Refu'ot ha-nefesh*, Jacob Emden and Moses Mendelssohn intervened when an edict issued by the Duke of Mecklenburg-Schwerin forbade early burial, lest someone mistakenly be assumed dead and erroneously interred alive.[97]

While the Altona-Hamburg community opted to print a Yiddish instruction manual to help the women correctly identify the moment of death, Prague's burial society acted differently. In 1769, the men's society claimed that since the women were not well-versed in the laws, they could not accurately determine the moment of death. Deciding "not to permit the women to serve as authorities" on this matter, they mandated that an elder or shamash from the men's society supervise; without his permission, the women could not lift the deceased from her bed to the straw "according to their own judgment."[98]

Organization of the Hevrot

The women's takkanot provide a lens into the inner workings of the women's hevrah kaddisha and how they managed their complex work, sometimes at a moment's notice. The structure of pious societies mirrored that of the kehillah, and men's and women's societies were organized in a similar fashion. The women's society was led by a gabba'ah (Hebrew) or a gabbete (Yiddish); the terms used differ from region to region.[99] These same terms were used for various officials entrusted with overseeing charitable funds, the maintenance of the synagogue, and pious societies. In parallel to men's confraternities, women's societies typically appointed at least two gabbetes, or more, depending on the size of the community. Each gabbete would serve for several months, rotating with a colleague over the course of the year. The gabbete oversaw the work and the finances of the society and was responsible for enforcing the society's bylaws. Typically, several other women (sometimes referred to as deputies) aided the gabbetes in determining financial penalties levied on members who violated the regulations.[100] The presence of the gabbete was deemed essential to the various tasks undertaken by the burial society, and she made decisions as to when and how tasks were performed within each shift.[101] Special instructions governed what to do if a woman had to miss her shift because she was not home or otherwise could not attend.[102] Since experience and knowledge were prerequisites for leading the society, the gabbetes seem to have been appointed rather than elected. In Mainz, the three women who assisted the gabbetes were selected by lottery in a process that mirrored election procedures in some communities.[103]

If a member was unable to attend the meeting, she was to send her vote in writing to the hevrah. The emphasis on a judicious and inclusive process highlights both the prestige associated with joining and how critical it was to achieve consensus about new members. A fair admission process was essential for working side by side amicably when preparing friends and neighbors for burial, sometimes in the dead of night. In Rendsburg, the entry fee shifted over time; the takkanot were emended and alternatively list one Reichsthaler and six Schilling as the initiation fee. The gabbetes set the rate of the entry fee for wealthier women as they saw fit.[104] The bylaws also stipulated fines for any woman who failed to attend the shift to which she had been assigned if she did not secure a replacement; women who engaged in physical or verbal violence toward another member of the hevrah were also fined. Additional yearly dues were levied to secure funding for the annual festive meal.[105]

Women who were not members of the burial society also contributed money to the society's coffer. Their donations to the hevrah kaddisha did not only cover the expenses of the society; in Rendsburg, the women used the funds in their treasury to provide financial assistance to mourners whose indigence rendered prohibitive the costs associated with mourning and burial rituals.[106] A memorial book from Prague includes a long list of names of women who had contributed to the burial society.[107] The pinkas of the men's hevrah kaddisha from Prague similarly attests to the women's constant and successful fundraising, alleging that the women "stand there from morning until evening, every heart melts, and every knee weakens from the uproar, large and small."[108] The men's description of their attempt to curtail women's collections in the public sphere reveals the latter's unwavering dedication to raising funds for the burial society.

Hierarchy and Status

Offenses against the honor of a member were treated very seriously, as in the larger community, and a breach of protocol or communal morals could result in fines and/or dismissal from the confraternity. A member who left had to advance the dues so that the coffers of the hevrah would not suffer.[109] In addition to the induction of members, societies enacted their internal hierarchies during the fulfillment of their stated mission, giving priority to members with seniority and positions of honor to members with high social status. Some men's societies staged elaborate processions or festive meals, which further enhanced their visibility.[110] Some commissioned commemorative printed or manuscript works to codify their regulations or their membership lists.

The burial society of Prague commissioned annual glass tumblers decorated with images of the hevrah and a series of paintings to immortalize their work. At least two tumblers preserved in the Jewish Museum in Prague include images of the women's society, one from 1783/4 and the other from 1787.[111] The society commissioned tumblers every year or every few years. On each of the two tumblers, the women's society was recognized, depicted with the women standing alone, clutching in their hands what might be linen cloths for purification or small sacks with earth from the Holy Land. Collectively, the societies provided community members with a second stage for enacting honor and status within the community, and its collegiality was greatly prized (see plate 35).

Women, too, viewed membership in these exclusive societies as an honor. Particularly in larger communities, they deliberated over accepting new members, instituted hierarchical structures, and honored their own work with a festive meal. In Mainz, members who had served in the society longer were given precedence in laying the body on the straw, performing the purification rite, and dressing the dead.[112] Taking part in the sacred work of the society was an important outlet for the spiritual devotion of pious women. The Mainz sorority regulations promised that "all of the women would merit" participating as long as they did so in an orderly fashion.[113] In Prague, if a member came too late to take part in dressing the dead in her shroud, the latecomer would nevertheless be honored with sewing a few last stitches in the shroud, thereby allowing her to partake in the holy deed.[114]

A manuscript from Copenhagen, penned in 1730 by Mordekhai ben Hirsch Hamel Hartig, a scribe, as well as the shamash of the men's burial society, illustrates how women's societies used rituals to mark their prestige. According to the ornate title page, the manuscript was used "on the day of the annual feast of the *hevrah kaddisha gemilat hasadim ve-ohave hesed*."[115] Each paragraph of the penitential prayer was arranged according to the Hebrew alphabet. The final page of the manuscript includes a *mi-sheberakh* (special blessing) for the women in the burial society. Publicly blessing the women was an essential part of the annual festivities. The manuscript specifically named ten women, with both their Jewish and vernacular names listed. Among those who were individually recognized were the sexton/scribe's sister, Hendel (Hanne Nathan); his wife, Ester bat Hayim; and the rabbi's wife, Hayke bar Michael Halevy (Johanna Wolff). Following this list of names, the text continues by blessing "all the other women of the sacred society, who faithfully performed the duties of the society; they acted with lovingkindness to the living, [by] visiting them during their illnesses, and with truth to the dead, purifying and dressing them in holiness and purity after their deaths."[116] The prayer for the women's burial society was recited in exchange for charity "pledged on their behalf by their husbands." A second unadorned manuscript composed by Hartig in that same year for the annual feast also includes the penitential song, yet not the blessing of the women.[117] The existence of two similar manuscripts, only one of which refers to women, suggests that the ornate manuscript may have been commissioned for use by the women at their own annual feast. At the very least, the women were publicly acknowledged and blessed at the men's feast.[118] Both the material form of the ornate manuscript and the oral recitation of the blessing at the annual rites of the burial society served to honor the women's piety.

Public recognition of women's burial societies could also be granted at burial. In Amsterdam, one of the two women's burial societies turned to the community leaders in 1767, requesting that the community allocate to them a special row in the Muiderberg cemetery, in which all the members of the women's hevrah could be buried side by side. The same privilege, they explained, had been granted to the men's burial society.[119] Just one week prior to the women's request, in an effort to raise money, the community had levied a new tax on the women's society.[120] The hevrah assented and paid the additional sum, then leveraged their monetary support of the kehillah in order to demand a joint burial plot for the women's hevrah kaddisha. The community leaders acquiesced to the women's request, thereby granting them an eternal marker of the status and solidarity that the burial society had provided them during their lifetimes.[121]

Men's and Women's Hevrot: Cooperation or Competition?

In some Jewish communities, the women's hevrot were well integrated into the work of the community at large, while in others, the men's hevrot saw the women's as completely subject to its oversight and suppressed any move toward autonomy. Perhaps the best example of cooperation between women's and men's societies and the communal leadership can be found in Berlin, where a formal women's society dates back to at least 1745.[122] Two men's confraternities worked alongside one another in Berlin. The *bikur holim* hevrah supported the local poor; supervised care for the sick and the foreign poor in the local hekdesh (hospice); visited the sick until the onset of death; and distributed charity and arranged for Torah study in memory of a deceased community member.[123] The *gemilut hasadim* society tended to purification and burial rites.[124] Women's societies in Berlin performed parallel tasks, although as was the case in all other communities, only the men buried the dead, while only the women sewed the shrouds.

The independence of the Berlin women's societies is evident from the duties of the seven gabbetes who headed them. Three groups of female leaders oversaw the societies. They managed the various coffers and issued receipts for donations to the women's collection and for services rendered. The women directly administered the finances and kept the books, and this, too, required collaborating with the (male) communal leadership, as the latter paid for some of the services provided by the sororities, particularly for the care of parturients in the hospice.[125] The constant coordination between the men and the women was undoubtedly facilitated by the familial relations between them. The gabbetes were themselves the wives and widows of the *alufim* and *ketzinim* (communal notables).[126] One of the gabbetes, Sarah, was married to the gabbay of the men's burial society, Isaiah Hollander. Gela, another gabbete, was married to the gabbay of the men's bikur holim society.[127] That society's elites were the leaders and members of both the men's and women's hevrot is a reminder of the great dignity that was associated with caring for the sick and the dead in Jewish communities.

In late eighteenth-century Amsterdam, the communal leaders cooperated with the women's society to ensure that they had enough funding to undertake their sacred work. In Amsterdam, one society tended to the dead, and another, the *hevrah kaddisha agudat nashim*, also known as *hevrat takhrikhin*, sewed shrouds for the poor.[128] In 1784, the sorority was no longer able to sustain its activities due to lack of funds. Therefore, the communal leaders added the women's society to the list of beneficiaries to whom those being called to the Torah could donate weekly, thereby actively encouraging and supporting the women's work in a public communal forum.[129] In Rendsburg as well, the rabbi explicitly praised the women's work: "Therefore, it is worthwhile in the case of such a great mitzvah, to confirm and uphold and encourage in every manner of encouragement, to strengthen their words so that not even one iota should fall by the wayside."[130] The rabbi's full support of the women's burial society was manifested in the takkanot.

In Prague, by contrast, the men's hevrah became increasingly perturbed by what it saw as the growing autonomy of the women's hevrah, which the men initially referred to in 1692 as "disorder."[131] Home to one of the earliest and most developed cultures of hevrah kaddisha, Prague was also home to some of the most notably literate women of the period.[132] The public piety of the women's burial society, its industriousness and manifest success, resulted in an indignant and condescending rebuke from the men's society in subsequent years. "Whereas we have seen an uproar in the 'House of Israel': these are the women of [the society of] lovingkindness, in all the matters in which they are involved, when they assemble as a death approaches."[133] With these words written in 1739/40, the men's burial society in Prague opened an attack on the parallel women's burial society that ultimately resulted in a takeover of the women's society. Read against the grain, the "uproar" the men describe provides a window into the women's devotion, pious labor, and dedication to raising charitable funds. Tasked with sewing burial garments, the women of Prague developed multiple enterprises to raise money for their society. They sold linen (the fabric used for shrouds), as well as eyeglasses: older women used the glasses to continue sewing and embroidering once their eyesight began to fail.[134] Showing industry and entrepreneurial spirit, the women began to stock extra shrouds to be used in the event of need; extras could be sold, and the proceeds could further the charitable aims of the society.[135]

The men's society, however, declared all such commerce prohibited to them going forward, revealing the tensions that simmered beneath a harmonious façade in which men and women supposedly worked in parallel to bury the dead. Bylaws from Prague, enacted by the men and inscribed in their logbook, gave voice to the tug of war over women's responsibility and autonomy. The men's society saw the women as completely subordinate to their own hevrah and complained that the women were not sufficiently selective in their membership: "Anyone who wishes to seize the name comes and gets it,[136] the debased alongside the dignified."[137] The men "warned the women involved in the [sacred society of] lovingkindness with mighty admonitions, and we threatened them with critical words,"[138] decrying the women's practice of accumulating premade shrouds. The men demanded to purchase the excess shrouds from the women, seizing control not only of the garments but of their sale, ruling "that it is forever prohibited for the women to engage in commerce with shrouds."[139] The men angrily ordered the abrupt suppression of any initiative on the part of the women to expand their good works beyond the narrow parameters assigned to them, and they granted the women only the space to tend to the female dead and to collect minimal amounts of charity. Given the ubiquity of a charity coffer in the series of illustrations of the men's society in Prague, one wonders if a subtle rivalry over charity collections motivated the men to curtail the women's fundraising efforts. They appointed (what was likely) a new slate of pious women to serve in the women's society, presumably dismissing those whom they found objectionable.[140]

As a result of the coup against the women's burial society, the men appropriated the sale of shrouds, although the women labored to sew the garments. An entry from a different logbook, dated approximately twelve years later, indicates that the men's burial society faced its own struggles with an undeniably immense and difficult task. R. Yissakhar Maldstein had been tasked with keeping track of the income and expenses associated with the sale of shrouds. At a meeting in January 1752, the leaders of the burial society decided to appoint

R. Moshe Weibler as his "helpmate, to lighten his accounting burden," ironically using the biblical phrase referring to Eve as Adam's partner despite the fact that the men retained sole control over the finances.[141] A third man was later appointed to assist with the sales and the recordkeeping, as the task was deemed so onerous. The men, moreover, decided to maintain stores of linen along with ready-made shrouds, instituting the very same practice they had disparaged when done by the women. Although the men retained control over the accounting and recordkeeping for the sale of shrouds, a woman was kept on hand to sew shrouds as needed.[142] This conflict adds great depth to the image of women sewing shrouds in the courtyard of the Kloyz shul in the Prague murals. What appears to be closely coordinated work was often brimming with tension. Dating to 1780, the image may well depict male oversight and control over what was once the autonomous domain of women.

Whether praised or criticized in the texts that have survived, the women's diligence and dedication to their sacred duties remain unmistakable throughout the burial society materials. The bylaws, song cycles, prayers, and other texts of the women's societies usher us into a world of the burial hevrot and pious sororities, in which women employed space, time, tools, and knowledge to perform a service that could not be done without them. We cannot know the long-term outcome of the attempt to suppress them in the Prague encounter. The texts taken together attest to the fierce devotion and multiple skill sets (craft, administrative, business enterprise, recordkeeping), beyond the households they ran and the children they raised, of early modern Jewish women.

3

Honor and Shame, Center and Periphery

MALKA, PESSCHE, and Serke, three women from the Jewish burial society, entered a prison cell in Hamburg on Sunday night, February 3 [21 Shevat], 1793. It was the night before local authorities were scheduled to execute Devorah Traub, a member of Hamburg's Jewish community, after she had been found guilty of poisoning her mother-in-law and her sister-in-law.[1] Eight days prior, Jewish communal officials had approached "the judge, the syndic Amsinck, for an audience and requested from him that they wish to send one *lamdan* (scholar), so that she could die as a Jew."[2] Amsinck acquiesced, and two men from the burial society came to study Torah with Devorah and to recite with her the *viduy* (confessional prayer before death). Next, the three women came to the room in which Devorah was held, and, in a departure from their usual duties, they purified the condemned woman's body while she was still alive: "The woman Dverl [diminutive of Devorah] allowed herself to be purified by the women of the Holy Society of Undertakers, namely the *gabba'it* Malka, wife of Elia Wiener, and my mother-in-law, Mrs. Pessche, wife of my father-in-law, R. Leyzer the bursar, and my wife, Mrs. Serke, daughter of R. Leyzer, the bursar.[3] They dressed her in a new garment of shrouds, and [she] accepted it all with love."[4]

The next day, clad in the white shrouds in which the three women had dressed her, Devorah was executed by sword in Hamburg's public square, where she was then buried in a shallow grave. The following Saturday night, under the cover of darkness between 10:00 p.m. and 5:00 a.m., seven men from the Jewish gravediggers' society exhumed her body, with the judge's permission; they then reinterred her a few days later in the Dammtor cemetery, where Jews deemed dishonorable or marginal by the community were buried.[5]

Devorah's public execution, preserved in both the municipal archives and in the pinkas of the gravediggers, undoubtedly brought shame to the Jewish community. Nevertheless, the rabbinic judge, the parnassim, and members of the women and men's hevrot—the highest echelon of Jewish leadership—negotiated and endeavored to ensure her a proper Jewish burial.[6] Many Jewish women fell outside the protective security of the favored classes of householders. Some of these women were temporarily ostracized, while others were excluded forcefully and permanently by the community. In some cases, such as Devorah's, they were pushed, literally, to the outer boundaries of communal space. This was a symbolic expression of the larger community's bidding them to remain shunned. However, it is precisely in the least visible spaces that some Jewish women in the most miserable circumstances were able to find their places and even their voices. Many of the most vulnerable women left few traces of their existence, and it is only thanks to the voluminous records of the early modern period that glimpses of their lives emerge. Women who were subject to sanctions by the community left traces in various sources: records of public denunciations, banishment, removal of membership rights in the community, burial on the sidelines of the cemetery, and Jewish court records. Other women belonged to no organized community yet appear occasionally in Jewish and non-Jewish records, allowing us brief and incomplete access to otherwise unknown lives. These "women on the margins"[7] must be considered alongside the more "respectable" community members. Much of the evidence gathered in this book pertains to the ba'alot bayit, the more visible class of women who headed households and fulfilled vital functions within their communities. This chapter is concerned with women who fell beyond the charmed circle of Jewish women at the center of their communities. Nashim hagunot (respectable women) constituted the ideal types in early modern Jewish society. Married or widowed, of upright morality, they had access to various types of capital—financial, moral, educational, or professional. Women who fell beyond the limits of respectability, either through their own actions or due to the status into which they were born or cast, also appear scattered throughout our sources. Some of the women proved to be proactive and resilient under insuperably difficult circumstances.

There were various degrees of dishonor and respectability; the boundaries were always very fluid. Communities stigmatized some women within their society for their actions through public shaming. A Jewish community regulation prohibited householders from making matches with people who had acquired a "bad reputation."[8] Other women more firmly outside the circle of community membership nevertheless flitted into and out of communal institutions, such as the hekdesh, a combination of hostel and infirmary; others worked in Jewish homes. Even the Jewish women on the far fringe of polite society had the power to affect Jewish communities, if only by association. The structure of early modern European society, in which Jewish rights and actions were tied to the larger kehillah, effectively connected vestigial Jews with central Jewish communities. The institutions that Foucault and other theorists have identified as solidifying the boundaries against outcasts had not matured in early modern Jewish communities. There were yet no shelters for abused women, no homes for pregnant outcasts or their children, and no welfare system responsible for all the poor and the homeless. The community tried to help those who had fallen on hard times, but many were beyond its reach or ability to assist. The hekdesh came closest to a welfare institution, but it could hardly house all society's fallen, destitute, disabled, mad, and criminal.

Honor and Shame in Communal Spaces

Premodern Jewish society had many ways of communicating who belonged within its circle of prestige—and who did not. One of the recurrent themes in Glikl of Hameln's memoir was the refrain of *oysher ve-khovod* (wealth and honor). While she began her life as an illustrious woman in Hamburg, at the end of her life, Glikl witnessed an auction of all her belongings on the street after her second husband had squandered their fortunes. "I was a woman who lived in greatest esteem beside my pious husband.... With his death it all vanished: my wealth, my honor... and I weep over this."[9] While Glikl remained in the center of the community, her lament over her lost assets included bemoaning the dishonorable position in which she found herself.

Concepts of honor and respectability were tied to probity in business, sexual modesty and fidelity in women, piety in religious circles, and loyalty to family and community. Money could buy honor, but only up to a point. Without a reputation for integrity, wealth could backfire against the rich. The conceptions of honor overlapped between men and women in some areas, while they were gendered differently in others. Thousands of entries over hundreds of years inscribed in memorial books, incised on tombstones, and written in rabbinic responsa paid tribute to the virtues of the honorable ba'alot bayit: their modesty, their piety, their good deeds, and the ideal households they ran. Honor was valued as a currency; the community often imposed shaming sanctions when a woman's actions or her circumstances debased it.

Jewish women could enact dramas of honor and shame in a variety of spaces. These included the public marketplace, communal spaces such as the synagogue, including its women's section, benevolent societies, venues of celebration, and more. Sumptuary ordinances intended to limit women's celebrations of life cycle rituals sanctioned both men and women for any violation of the takkanot. Men were precluded from performing public rituals, while "any woman who violates the takkanot will be publicly named/shamed in the synagogue, and the kahal cannot free her from this penalty."[10] The equation of public shaming with men being banned from performing synagogue rituals highlights the place that both men and women in the community occupied, a standing that could be revoked permanently or temporarily as a consequence.

The currency of honor and shame circulated so intensely in early modern Europe that many disputes arose over real or perceived slights. Arguments that involved insulting honor often led to violence. In Altona, an entire overflowing logbook devoted to the collection and tabulation of income from fines was primarily concerned with collecting penalties over petty insults, brawls, quarrels, and other unfriendly encounters.[11] This collection of small notices regarding minor incidents is significant precisely because traces of similar low-grade violence are most susceptible to disappearing over time. Discussions of interpersonal violence in the early modern period usually focus on statistics of murder because those are the only incidents that can be tracked through sources and multiple jurisdictions across time. Unlike homicide, which criminal courts prosecuted, leaving a web of written records, lower-level assaults tended to leave far fewer written traces.

A recurring verbal brawl between the daughter of Isaac and a man (possibly a relative) named Abraham in a sixteenth-century southern German village made its way before Rabbi Isaac mi-See. Though both were on notice of excommunication if they persisted in public quarrels, the two nevertheless got into a public shouting match in Yiddish; she cursed Abraham and called his father a murderer. Although she denied it, others heard them call one another rude and stubborn (*azus ponim hotzuf*); Abraham, incensed that she had falsely accused his deceased father, retaliated by calling her a harlot (*zonah*).[12] In 1693, the kahal of Altona deemed Kresle bat David the guilty party for provoking her husband's violence. First, Kresle insolently challenged a decision of the kahal by raising her voice and interrupting the prayers in the synagogue.[13] The kahal accused her of "causing her husband to lie in wait when people were exiting the synagogue, and he stabbed the ... lay leader R. Moshe ... with a knife." As a punishment for the public insult to the authority of the kahal and for causing her husband to commit violence against one of its members, Kresle would be relegated forever to a distant bench in the back of the synagogue.

> She may not benefit from the kahal in any way whatsoever; she may not attend a *se'udat mitzvah* (festive meal) forever; when she dies, she may not be buried in our cemetery in Altona; her burial and purification will not be performed for her as is customary; everything will only be performed by the community's servants. And a tombstone should not be erected for her, and she may not be inscribed into the Memorbuch. If she violates even one of these conditions, she must pay a fine of four Reichsthaler each time she violates. The parnas of the month must order the shamash to denounce her under *herem* (excommunication); on the Shabbat that is to come, they will announce in the synagogue concerning her and her punishment in detail.[14]

Remarkably, the kahal held Kresle solely accountable for the violence committed by her husband. Perhaps because she had violated the sanctity of the synagogue first with her outburst, the kahal meted out to Kresle the entire penalty of distancing and public shame in all the spaces where communal honor could be displayed. The exceptions to her ban are also noteworthy: Kresle was not barred from attending the synagogue altogether, and she could trespass the injunction upon payment of a fine. These exceptions to the ban highlight the uneven application of penalties to members of different classes within the kehillah.

In Altona, 1766, Judah, son of Nathan, maligned the wife of Itzik Bahur, calling her a whore. The kahal required him to pay a fine and to apologize publicly to her in the synagogue.[15] The need to apologize for public shaming is manifest in an earlier synagogue announcement in Altona from 1729, proclaimed after someone maligned the newly married Mehrel, wife of David Segal, by sending written notices that slandered her reputation. The rabbis and parnassim insisted that the instigator be excommunicated "until he comes before the communal leaders and the eminent rabbi and confesses and is punished." They further insisted that anyone who continued to spread these rumors face punishment and excommunication. The spread of written slander did not escape their notice: "Also, under penalty of excommunication, whoever wrote [to people in] other locations about these slanderous lies is obligated to recall these writings, and to write that it is all lies, and that evil enemies spread embarrassing rumors."[16] The leadership insisted that anyone who continued to publish these falsehoods be fined the hefty sum of one hundred Reichsthaler.

Many disputes began in some difference of opinion over scarce resources or a petty misunderstanding and then degenerated into insults and name-calling. Such insults tended to be gendered, with men often having their integrity impugned, while women were called sexually promiscuous. In one notable instance, two Jewish women in Hamburg were accused within their own community of practicing witchcraft. As the community thought of them as respectable women, the notice in the pinkas of publicly announced decrees defended their honor:

> Hear ye, holy congregation, we hereby notify in the name of the leaders of the community: that since a vile rumor has circulated about two *kosher* [upstanding] elderly women, Sara, wife of R. Hayim Metz and Fegilche wife of Judah Schalt Setzer, and they were suspected of, heaven forbid, being *makhshefot* [witches]: fortunate are those who are suspected and found innocent. We let it be known that the rumors are lies upon lies; there is no substance to them. From this day forward, it may not be mentioned, to speak of such things about these women. "For there is no magic in Jacob" [Num. 23:23], and if anyone is found strengthening the rumor and spreading such talk about these women, they will be punished with execrations and fines as libellers.... Announced on Tues. 3 Sivan [1732] in the synagogue at Hamburg.[17]

This announcement came to exonerate the women from the charge and restore them to their respectable places within the community. The announcement specifies that they were elderly, a common demographic for accusations of witchcraft. What their fate might have been had the charge been sustained is not made clear, and we have found no parallel cases.

In such instances, the remedy imposed by the kahal was to assuage a public insult with a public retraction or apology. The fines were not paid to the victim but to the kahal's coffers, and some of them were forwarded to the political authorities (in Altona, to the king of Denmark). The fine was, therefore, not a means of monetary compensation for lost personal honor but for violating the standards and decorum of the public sphere. An apology in public, a humiliation for the offender, was the kahal's means of restoring a reputation that had been damaged in public and exacting embarrassment for the shame inflicted by the perpetrator.

Women and Violence within Communal Spaces

Insults to one's honor could often lead to blows; interpersonal violence of many types arose in the pages of community records. Violence could occur between spouses, parents and children, or people who were unrelated. Our sources often use the term for assault from the Hebrew root *le-hakkot*. As it covers a wide range of injury, from a slap or punch to all-out physical battery, and undoubtedly to sexual assaults of various types that were not outright rapes, we often cannot tell whether physical violence was sexual in nature. Several cases of sexual harassment of Jewish women by Jewish and non-Jewish men confirm that transgressions and crimes of a sexual nature took place within the context of work and the community.[18] Such misconduct was always an assertion of power and desire to inflict humiliation.

In communities for which records of petty assaults and unspecified attacks survive, there is ample evidence that coming to blows was a common occurrence. The terse entries do not yield as rich a picture as we would like, but certain patterns emerge: there were plenty of physical encounters between unrelated men and women, both married and single. Thus, the man who appears in the Altona records as "Mordekhai ben Aaron in the mikveh" (apparently, he lived in the building that housed a mikveh, along with other tenants) was the subject of an outcry "by a woman from a foreign land" who stayed in that house, that he *hikkah* (assaulted) her for "absolutely no reason." A week later, the woman returned, "screaming to high heaven" that the same man was harassing her and had assaulted her again.[19] The nature of the assault is unclear, as is the question of whether Mordekhai singled out this woman as vulnerable because she was foreign and did not have a local support network.

When local women or girls claimed to have been attacked, it was often the father or husband who lodged a complaint. When on *Hoshanah Rabbah* (end of Sukkot holiday) in Altona, 1767, the wife of Hayim, son of Abraham Cohen, told her husband that one of the men had assaulted her, it was the husband, Hayim, who lodged a complaint against Abraham, son of Mikhel Gumpreich, for the assault against her. The text does not specify what prompted the assault or what type it was. The perpetrator was let off with a warning not to repeat his behavior.[20] Presumably, an attack against the dignity of a wife was seen as harming her husband as well. In the spring of 1768, the daughter of an Altona community member, R. Lazi, was assaulted. The type of assault is maddeningly unspecified, but whether physical or sexual, it did enough damage to warrant the ministrations of a doctor.[21] The Altona community council levied a fine of two Reichsthaler against Zekel, son of Isaac Almisharen (Elmshorn), for committing the assault, as well as an additional six Reichsthaler to pay for the physician's services. Notably, the entry mentions that Lazi was a member of the community; the perpetrator, presumably, was not.

Certain groups within Jewish society were renowned for their tendency toward violent behavior: slaughterers and butchers, undertakers and gravediggers, and thieves appear in various sources as committing assaults on community members. There do not appear to be similar professions among women associated with physical assault, but that is not to argue that women were less inclined to commit such acts. In one of the earliest sets of ordinances of the kehillah in Altona, married men were held financially liable to pay fines if their wives were found guilty of quarrel or assault: "A woman who is fined because of a quarrel or assault, her husband is the one who is obliged to pay."[22] It is unclear whether the author of the regulations believed that men controlled their wives' emotions or the household purse strings. In any case, such prescriptive regulations left much to be desired; communities improvised as new complications arose. When, several years later, Ulk, wife of the parnas Nathan, got into a quarrel with her husband, his colleagues the parnassim rallied around him and fined her thirty-nine quarter-Reichsthaler, "which fine she must pay from her own pocket."[23] Unlike other entries in this terse logbook, this one was signed by all the parnassim.

On Shabbat (*Parashat Ki tavo*) in 1767, as a result of a quarrel between Yuzpil Melammed and Meir ben Leyb and his wife, Meir's wife "threw a large stone at Yuzpil; and this stone is literally large enough to kill, and her intentions are counted as deeds."[24] Jewish women were involved in physical violence as victims and as perpetrators. In this case, the wife of Meir threw an object, rather than attacking with her bare hands, deploying a gesture more common to women.[25] Stories or images of women committing violent acts, such as Yael killing Sisera or Judith severing the head of Holofernes, appeared in popular books owned by or addressed to early modern Jewish women (see plate 8). While a highly stylized image would not likely lead a woman to follow suit, it did send a subtle message: highly admired women occasionally had to act violently. In Altona, 1767, a dispute that began between two men apparently spilled over to their wives. The wife of Feivush ben Leyb "did a bad deed and removed the covering from the head of the wife of Lipman the Butcher. This is not the way Jewish women should behave! Therefore, Feivush's wife must return the cap to the wife of Lipman, and, if not, she will get a sentence from the kahal. Despite this, the wife of Feivush did not pay heed to the warning, and she did not return the cap."[26] Acts of physical aggression often followed verbal contretemps as an escalation of the dispute. Did the regularity with which they occurred indicate the absence of sufficient venues for adjudicating petty disputes? Altona had one of the most active small-claims courts for adjudication of disputes, yet in the heat of the moment, many people allowed themselves to express their anger or contempt in ways that disrupted communal and personal harmony. By editorializing about the ideal behavior of respectable Jewish women, the kahal articulated its ideal versus the women's transgressions.

Sexual Morality and Illegitimate Pregnancies

Women's reputations were often linked to their sexual morality. Official communal policy stringently punished women whose sexual affairs outside of marriage had been undeniably confirmed by pregnancy. The physical evidence of their dishonor exacted consequences different from those imposed on their male partners, who often sought to escape culpability and often succeeded. The simple fact that only women's bodies could become pregnant could easily derail a young woman's life, even if she had been the victim of unwanted advances. We can chart a rough course of changing communal concerns over women's virtue in the early modern period. An ordinance from early seventeenth-century Prague thundered:

> On the subject of prostitutes, from this day forward, they may not be retained as wetnurses. Let them all leave our holy community, the eve of Rosh hodesh Heshvan 372 [Nov. 1612]. From this day forward, no more of them will be found in our community. Masters of the house who would violate this by keeping a prostitute in the house will be fined ten gold *hagirim* (ducats) for charity . . . if a prostitute is still found there, let the law be applied: let her immediately be arrested by the police and expelled from our holy community, and let her never return. And let the people see it and know it.[27]

"Zonah," a biblical term of opprobrium for a harlot, was used in early modern takkanot to designate any woman pregnant out of wedlock, regardless of the circumstances under which the pregnancy occurred; it did not refer to a professional sex worker. Stripping a member of her or his rights in the community was a way for the community to guard its honor by expelling the violator. A late seventeenth-century ordinance from Altona proclaimed that: "Anyone who has acquired a bad name in the matter of sexual mores, the kahal should investigate well. If their suspicions are confirmed, they [community leaders] have permission to punish the individual, and his membership in the community of Altona and Hamburg will be lost. The shamash should repeat this decree annually."[28] With ordinances like these, the community codified its notion that honor stood at the core of its hierarchy of values. Members who debased their honor would lose their precious membership in the community. As we have emphasized, the definition of honor was deeply gendered, and punishment often fell disproportionately on women. Each community had its own way of shaming women who had become pregnant out of wedlock. In seventeenth-century Frankfurt, a zonah was to be expelled after her pregnancy was discovered; in Metz, both the man and woman were to have their membership revoked; in Amsterdam, an illegitimately born son could not be circumcised in the main synagogues.[29]

A woman's reputation could be tarnished for years after youthful folly. In 1777, when the daughter of Yeshayah the butcher died in the Altona hekdesh, the community deliberated about where to bury her: "In truth, she had a disgraced reputation; however, because this was in her youth, and the kahal had pity on her, she was buried in the cemetery in Altona, and her relatives paid four Reichsthaler for the plot."[30] While the communal leaders ultimately pitied her and allowed her to be buried in the main cemetery rather than in Dammtor (the cemetery for those on the margins), as she had apparently mended her ways, they still recalled her sullied reputation from years earlier.

Both Christian and Jewish societies dealt particularly harshly with married women who committed adultery. The sanctions were so severe that such cases tended to be few, even if they left a strong mark on the sources. Of course, if such affairs remained completely hidden, there would be no way to know about them.[31] The chief rabbi of Altona accused a visiting woman of adultery: "Today a man passed through here called Eliyah bar Mendel, and the Chief Rabbi Yeshayah, said that his wife, who is also here, is a married woman [to someone else] . . . she is called Teibche bat R. Jacob; her husband [who was separated from her several years] . . . said that during that time she had an illegitimate child from another man."[32] This case would have *halakhic* (Jewish legal) implications, as children born to a married woman and a man not her husband would have been *mamzerim* (bastards who were not permitted to marry according to Jewish law). Surprisingly, the pinkas does not mention any follow-up on the case.

Single women, particularly those who had few options to marry respectably, often fell prey to the wiles of men who promised marriage after sexual liaisons without any intention of following through. Not all women, even young ones, fell prey to designing men. Teenage girls had a degree of agency, and some sought to advance their careers or gratify their own sexual needs by having relations with available men. By the eighteenth century, women from various social strata brought paternity suits before rabbinic, communal, and even imperial courts. In 1773, the wife of Haym Hollender in Altona came before the communal leaders, complaining that "Man'che, son of Moshe Cleve, committed an abominable act, defiling her virgin daughter, who became pregnant illegitimately, and she gave birth and told the midwife at the time of the birth that she was impregnated by him and none other. The parnas of the month decided that at the meeting next Thursday, Mr. Man should take an oath, with an object, between the prayers *ashre* and *u-va le-zion* that he is innocent from her [claims]."[33] Early modern Jews regarded taking an oath as an extremely serious act; most men would not have taken one lightly. Willingness to deny paternity under oath was sufficient to exonerate a man accused of illegitimately fathering a child. If he was found to be the child's father, he would be held responsible for the woman's delivery expenses and for the child's welfare. In this instance, the claim was brought before the lay leaders by the girl's mother, who sought to involve the midwife and thereby strengthen the paternity claim.[34] In other instances, men who had gotten their single partners pregnant were determined to marry them despite the strictures of the kahal against such liaisons. When the kahal heard that Aaron bar Shimon Hildesheim married the very pregnant "zonah" Serkhe, daughter of Mikhel Wagner, and, moreover, that the ceremony had been performed by a "vagrant," the kahal hired guardsmen to throw Aaron into jail, and he was put into herem. The kahal ruled that another man who was involved in the matter was to confess at the *Almemor* (pulpit) in public for aiding the sinners and beg forgiveness for his trespass. This case is unusual in that the kahal initially leveled penalties against the man rather than primarily against the woman, not for fathering an illegitimate child but for marrying without the sanction of the community. Ultimately, they were both banned with the full force of the communal ban.[35]

In some cases of illegitimate pregnancies, Jewish and Christian authorities collaborated with one another. Rabbi Shmuel Halevi was consulted on a case brought before the rabbinical court in Würzburg in the seventeenth century, in which a single woman who was engaged to one man became pregnant; she claimed her fiancé was the father, which he denied. Someone, likely the girl's family, notified the Christian authorities, who jailed the fiancé and demanded that the local rabbis come and marry the couple. Despite denying paternity, her fiancé married the woman in order to escape additional jail time although he refused to seclude himself with her as a means to avoid consummating the marriage. Halevi was asked whether the marriage could be annulled or whether a bill of divorce must be issued, as the man was adamant that he would not remain married to her.[36] The plea of the girl's family to the political authorities and their insistence that the man marry her demonstrates how Jews approached both Jewish and non-Jewish courts to achieve a particular outcome.[37]

Female community members or their daughters who found themselves pregnant out of wedlock were shamed publicly and inscribed as "zonot" in communal records. In November 1662, an entry in the pinkas of Frankfurt reported that "the widow Gitle Reisz zur Heb committed an abomination in Israel, to sleep with adulterers, and she prostituted herself until she became pregnant out of wedlock and gave birth to a male. She embarrassed her entire family; our entire sacred community, as well, became a mockery and subject of gossip in the mouths of people." The scribe here noted that Gitle's pregnancy (the terms "adultery" and "prostitution" are common exaggerations and are not necessarily to be taken literally) dishonored not only her family but also reflected poorly on the honor of the entire Jewish community. It had become the talk of the town and perhaps a subject of mockery in the eyes of the Christians as well.[38]

> Therefore, the council has ordered that the widow above-named will not have membership in our community; even when she marries ... regardless of who it may be, that man as well will not hold membership. In addition, she may not step foot into our community for the next three years, and no one may extend hospitality to her even for one night. After that, when she comes here, she may not wear the Shabbat cloak at all, and she may not enter the synagogue except for the new women's section. If she attends another synagogue, the neighbors may not sit near her in their places ... and she cannot receive any religious honors in our synagogue, such as godparenting and the like. This is how she will conduct herself forever. This matter will be announced in the synagogue on the meeting day. Sunday evening, 15 Kislev, [5]423 to the small counting [Nov. 16, 1662].[39]

Gitle was deprived of her membership in the Jewish community of Frankfurt, a coveted right, for life, and banned from the community for three years. Should she decide to return thereafter, signs of her disgrace would be applied on the stages of communal honor, such as her synagogue seat assignment, and on her body, as she would not be allowed to dress in the manner to which women of her station would have been accustomed.[40]

Although the community imposed public humiliation upon Gitle over the long term, the community showed more flexibility in practice than it did in the ordinances intended to deter such behavior in the first place. Women of a certain status often had a road back into the center of communal life after they faced the consequences of their dishonor. Specific policies varied according to class, circumstance, local practice, and membership in the community. In eighteenth-century Amsterdam, Heyman Samuels's communal membership was revoked when he impregnated his fiancée before their wedding. After the couple repented and donated a hefty sum of 250 Gulden to charity, their membership was reinstated. Their daughter, born just months after the wedding, was never granted membership, though she had done nothing to lose her communal status other than being born.[41] This case led to a new ordinance, which permitted any couple who married when the bride was already pregnant to reinstate their revoked communal membership in exchange for a donation of five hundred Gulden.[42] These flexible policies, which permitted a wealthy couple to reclaim their status and reputation after having been shamed and ostracized, likely derived from an increase in the number of premarital liaisons in the eighteenth century.

The frequency of premarital pregnancies is attested to also in the first folios of a new pinkas listing the customs of the Altona community. Itzik Lelov, the shamash, noted, "Here in Altona it is the custom, if the bride is a zonah, then one does not write [in the marriage contract] 'this virgin' but 'this one' alone; one does not write 'as was mandated to you by the Torah' but 'as was mandated by the rabbis,' and only 100 zuz as one writes in the contract of a widow."[43] The casual way in which the shamash listed this practice among other religious and local customs signifies that the matter of brides coming to the altar pregnant, or having given birth previously out of wedlock, had become so routine as to merely merit a note on the reformulation of clauses in wedding contracts.

Lay leaders, in particular, began to replace earlier concerns about sinfulness and tainted virtue with notions of community reputation and cost to the communal treasury. This concern with the budgetary consequences of illicit sexual activity, rather than with notions of modesty and virtue, overturned long-standing preoccupation with female virginity in Jewish sources. In the transition from girlhood to womanhood, no aspect of a young woman's body was freighted with more symbolic significance than her status as a virgin. Biblical sources, elaborated on by rabbinic law, and the centrality of virginity at the core of the Christian narrative (as well as in Islamic society), propelled the matter of a girl/woman's evidence of virginity at marriage as a symbol of purity and innocence, a family's honor, and a marriage contract's value.[44] By the early modern period, the rhetoric of rabbinic and communal texts continued to elevate virginity as the ideal bodily state of unmarried girls preparing to enter a marriage. Yet, in many of these texts, their primary anxiety over the practical consequences for the community came to replace the concern over virginity.

This attitude was reflected in two separate cases brought before Rabbi Yair Hayim Bacharach. In each, a male fiancé discovered that his wife-to-be had engaged in premarital sex, although that liaison did not result in pregnancy. In the first instance, a young man had sexual intercourse with his fiancée and discovered that she was not a virgin. He, therefore, no longer wanted to marry her. The young woman admitted that she had had relations previously but asserted that since her fiancé had had relations with her prior to the wedding ceremony, it was clear that marrying a virgin was not critical for him. Bacharach cited her as claiming "since I am not pregnant, what does it matter to you [*ma ekhpat lekha*]? If you hadn't done this [had premarital relations with me], none of this would have been known to you until after the wedding ceremony."[45] What is important here is the woman's exposing the hypocrisy of her fiancé's position, as well as her assigning a utilitarian value to her virginity. She did not become pregnant from her earlier sexual encounter, so that earlier act should now be inconsequential. In the same responsum, Bacharach considered another query along the same lines. By employing the same language for each bride to be—"What does it matter to you?"—Bacharach implied that he was describing an attitude rather than verbatim language, indicating a shift in outlook toward virginity over time.

Sometimes, leaders and rabbis stretched the boundaries of respectable behavior for couples (as opposed to single women) who found themselves in untoward situations, allowing them to marry. When it was revealed that a married man had impregnated his wife's sister before his marriage, Rabbi Judah Mehler was asked whether the man must divorce his wife. He recommended against divorce, noting that neither sister would be able to marry otherwise, given the scandal.[46] In another case, Rabbi Ezekiel Katzenellenbogen was asked about a widower who had been engaged to a woman who had become pregnant by another man during the engagement. The widower was barred from marrying his fiancée because she was deemed *meneket havero* (a woman nursing another man's baby). After the baby had been sent to a wetnurse, the widower inquired if he might marry her despite her infidelity, for he would not have another opportunity to wed.[47] Marriage provided these men and women with stable circumstances to ensure that they would not require financial support from the community.

The most frequent (or documented) cases of blatant sexual transgression of communal mores happened with those who never held coveted membership in the community and who could not reintegrate into respectable circles. In 1716, the triple community's leaders issued an ordinance with the approval of the chief rabbi: "If a maidservant, regardless of whether she had been a virgin or not, becomes pregnant illegitimately, the triple community will not spend one penny on it, regardless of what might happen, which cannot be written down on paper."[48] This ordinance, issued by the federation of three communities, Hamburg, Altona, and Wandsbek, identified the female population most liable to become pregnant out of wedlock: female servants. It spelled out the consequence that the kahal feared most: the financial burden such a child would impose. It anticipated such occurrences as likely to be frequent and threatened such dire consequences that they could not spell them out explicitly. In fact, communal records allow ample understanding of possible unspeakable consequences. The (usually young) women could die in childbirth for lack of shelter and assistance. They could turn to prostitution or conversion in their desperation. Their children could die of malnutrition or exposure.[49] Children given to Christian wetnurses could be adopted and raised Christian.[50] The community's overstretched budgets could not take such consequences into account. The ordinance, and many like it, is remarkable as well for what it omitted. It does not seek to know who fathered the child and imposes no consequences on the malefactor.

An ordinance from Halberstadt (1741) illuminates another nexus of entwinement between the "fallen" young women and the communal center: "A wanton woman who gave birth, the members of our kehillah may not employ her as a maidservant, even without pay; however, to nurse the children of our kehillah, it is permitted."[51] While denouncing the maidservants who became pregnant while single and ordering their expulsion from the community, this ordinance (in contrast to the one we cited earlier from Prague) explicitly exempted those who were willing to serve as wetnurses in the community. Wetnurses supplied a critically needed service to Jewish communities. Christian pastors strongly discouraged Christian women from serving the needs of Jewish employers in this intimate way. In an age without baby formula, children who could not be nursed by their mothers due to illness or death were in mortal danger without a hired wetnurse.[52] The loophole permitting pregnant single women to later serve as wetnurses suggests yet another instance in which women on the economic margins were intimately entangled with the mainstream; these wetnurses contracted with the ba'ale bayit of the community, resided among them, and nourished their children.

Despite the vital need for their services, wetnurses who had been termed "zonot" officially remained on the fringes of the community and were deemed unworthy of communal support. Community legislators warned that even wetnurses who bore children of their own would not be supported by the community: "As noted in the old pinkas ha-kahal, p. 123, if a man or woman hires a wetnurse or a maidservant who has a child, whether legitimate or illegitimate, the mother of the child must pay [its expenses] from her own pocket, regardless of what is required for her child. If the child's mother cannot afford to pay, then the one who hired her is obliged to pay, such that no monetary damage, not even a penny, accrues to the kahal on its [the child's] account."[53]

Infanticide

Unlike the crime of "fornication," for which punishment often depended on the class and status of the accused, infanticide, the deliberate killing of a baby to hide the fact of its existence, was one of the preeminent fears in early modern society. Many women who became pregnant out of wedlock were desperate to hide their pregnancies, the births, and the babies that resulted due to the associated shame.[54] In addition, since many men were highly mobile and often away for long periods of time, women who became pregnant while their husbands were absent were caught in a difficult bind. Some claimed late or premature birth, and midwives sometimes colluded with them. Others tried to hide the pregnancy; infanticide was one of the prevalent concerns of religious and secular authorities in the early modern period. The Carolina, the sixteenth-century Roman Law code introduced into the Holy Roman Empire, assumed that mothers who hid their pregnancies, or the childbirths that eventuated in "stillbirths" or babies found dead, were ipso facto guilty of infanticide. These were judged as crimes of the highest order.

Maria Boes has observed for Frankfurt in the late sixteenth through seventeenth centuries that no woman sentenced for infanticide was ever given a reduction in the severity of her sentence, usually a gruesome death.[55] One of the reasons that Jewish communal sources record few cases of infanticide is that they were not investigated or dealt with through the Jewish community. Like other capital crimes, these were judged by local or imperial forces. Boes described and analyzed a case in the Frankfurt records of criminal trials of a

Jewish maidservant, "Judin" Bölle, from 1695. Found lying next to a razor in a pool of her blood, in the house of Simon Moses, her Jewish employer, Bölle claimed she had been stabbed by an intruder while trying to bar him from entry into the house. When she was found, three days later, to have given birth to a dead child, the investigation turned from one in which she had been the victim to one in which she was the perpetrator. No evidence could be found to prove she had intentionally killed the child. She was convicted of killing herself out of shame over her pregnancy and was buried under the gallows with other criminals. The Jewish community did not claim her body.[56] The details of the excruciating case highlight the fact that municipal personnel investigated both the original presumed attack and the subsequent possible infanticide. Both as a victim of violent crime and as a perpetrator, the Jewish maidservant left the oversight of the Jewish community and entered the purview of the local municipal prosecutorial forces.

Women, Crime, and Shame

Early modern Jews committed various crimes against persons and property; sometimes, they were suspected and accused falsely. It is difficult to know the "truth" in any individual case. Despised minorities were, and still often are, the first suspects when a crime is committed. Jewish women could play several roles in configurations of early modern criminality. Perhaps the most common scenario was of women who took active roles trying to defend husbands accused of crimes. When a number of Jewish men were accused and incarcerated in Höxter in 1648, their wives chose two women to represent all of them to lodge a complaint with the *Vogt* (bailiff) in Corvey.[57] This showed that the women (rather than the communities) took primary responsibility for advocating for their imprisoned spouses, and they were able to organize themselves to petition in the most efficient way. In a different example, Miriam, daughter of R. Ber Sha"tz of Moisling, appeared in a letter written to one of the wealthy Jews of Schwerin in 1745. The letter describes her as a deeply distressed woman who came howling that her husband had been imprisoned; he sat in darkness in prison irons in the city of Kystra and was being physically abused. The letter writer asked for further information: if her words were true, he would advocate for her and help with several Reichsthaler to see if the husband could be freed. In the margins, the letter writer added: "However, if he himself had been found to have stolen, we withdraw from this case."[58]

Jewish Women in Criminal Bands

The Jewish criminal underclass, by design elusive and poorly documented, is particularly opaque when it comes to identifying women who fell into this class by birth, marriage, or inclination. Some Jewish criminals organized themselves into bands of thieves whose work was methodical, often taking advantage of their knowledge of the back roads and isolated houses to mark their prey. They communicated in Yiddish; this both marked them as other and protected their secrets.[59] These groups were often related by kinship and sometimes included wives and daughters who traveled with their menfolk. Most of our knowledge of these groups comes from prosecutorial records. A close reading of interrogations that were preserved (some printed and disseminated) demonstrates that, in these cases, prosecutors were determined to find the Jews collectively guilty and may have conjured conspiracies where none existed. So, while these sources must be used with extreme caution, we can still extract something from them. One of the lessons is that Jewish women were often active, or at least accused of assisting, in criminal acts.

The prosecution of an alleged ring of Jewish thieves based around Coburg (a town in southern Germany) in the early eighteenth century provides a case in point.[60] The court arrested the primary suspects, among them a Mendel Carben, along with his wife, Rosina, also known as Reiss, and their fifteen-year-old son, Isaac—whose presence (and torture) in the prison was intended to soften the suspect into confessing—as well as Hayum Moyses, along with his wife, Lea.[61] Some of the background information they provided the court sheds light on the trajectories of these very marginal Jewish lives. Lea claimed to have been born in Amsterdam and to have been raised by *fremden Leute* (foreigners); her husband said she "served" in the home of Portuguese Jews. She did not know her parents. Her husband, Hayum, was from the village of Treuchtlingen in the Duchy of Ansbach. When they failed to acquire *Schutz* (legal protection) there, they migrated to Altona. Hayum claimed that his father had eight sons from four wives. Beyond the theft, Hayum was accused of having been baptized, as well as having served as a soldier who deserted.

Rosina was forty years old, born in Reichensachsen near Frankfurt am Main. Her mother, Freudige, died before she knew her, and she did not get along with her father's wife, Scheben. She claimed that her husband dealt in horses during the summer and slaughtered animals during the winter. She had a chest in her home, but it was unsealed and contained laundry. Upon hearing the screams of her teenage son as he was tortured, Rosina was the first of the suspects to break and confess to what the court wanted to hear: a packet of stolen goods had passed through her home and had been hidden in that chest.[62]

The several-hundred-page dossier on this alleged ring of thieves allows for insights into how the local judicial system viewed these Jewish outlaws, as well as for some glimpses into their lives. Many of the characters were born into very difficult circumstances. They had unstable family situations, they were put into positions of service in which they could be exploited, and/or they had no rights of residence anywhere. They were highly mobile, moving through small villages, some so small that they didn't appear on maps, to larger cities where they could hope for some respite, charity, or work before being pressured to move on. The interrogator suspected that Lea was born Christian, which she denied. Regardless, his assumptions that rootless Jews crossed religious lines more easily, that they claimed to have lived in ungated port cities with substantial Jewish populations such as Amsterdam and Altona, and that the upstanding residents of these cities (including their Jewish residents) feared and loathed the constant stream of the unmoored, tell us something about the routes and roots of this class. Despite their legal and tangible disconnect from formal Jewish communities, there remained a link between this band and mainstream Jews. An anonymous "upstanding" Jewish husband and wife from nearby Cassel served as informants to the court on various aspects of Jewish life. The respectable wife opined to the court that "it would be good if these thieving Jews in Hessen would be *zerstöhret* (destroyed) because they ruin the region, and no honest man can tolerate them."[63] With these words, the upstanding Jewish woman sought to distinguish herself from her Jewish criminal sisters and brothers, allying herself with authorities seeking to maintain peace and order. Any perceived connection between the Jewish communities and Jewish criminals could potentially upset the stability of communities that had staked their toleration on the perception of their honorability.

Four women swept up in a criminal trial in the Schleswig-Holstein region in Flensburg (ca. 1765)—Sara, Ester, Thobe, and Hanna—do not fit neatly into many of the patterns we have seen for "respectable women," either.[64] For one thing, they had no fixed place to live. Each of them moved from spending weeks in one inn to days in rented rooms to the guest houses of larger Jewish communities. "Sara herself testified that before she came to the Lustig's inn, 'Blue Lamb,' she stayed eight days in the hut of a soldier's wife in New Street, as she had done the previous summer."[65] This movement allowed many different local residents, mostly non-Jewish, to observe them closely and offer testimony regarding their lifestyle. Sara was the wife of the accused ringleader, Nathan David, who was her second husband. Described as large and strong in appearance, she was over twenty years his senior. The couple led a peripatetic life, often moving separately between lodgings and rented rooms in private homes.[66] During the years prior to the trial in 1765, Sara gave birth to three children, all of whom died in infancy. One witness testified that Sara "placed the dead child wrapped in rags in the back of a carriage and travelled to Friedrichstadt or Rendsburg—he did not remember which—to bury it."[67] No midwife or other assistants to the birth were mentioned. One witness said that Sara took in sewing and laundry, while another claimed she farmed the work out and did not pay the wages she owed. Eventually, the couple were told to leave the region and never return. Sara was found to have engaged in thievery herself and was expelled from Rendsburg. The prosecution tried hard to build a picture of an incorrigible band of thieves, all of corrupt character. When Nathan was arrested and incarcerated in 1759 and subsequently sentenced to hard labor, Sara, like other women who had organized themselves to fight such charges, came to help defend him.[68]

Nathan's half sister, Ester, was also involved in the family business. Around twenty years old at the time of the trial and engaged to be married to Alexander (Süsskind) Berend, she stayed in town near the prison for two years when her fiancé was arrested along with Nathan. Questioned about her livelihood, Ester described a life of trading very small articles and borrowing and lending old clothes. One witness noted that Ester, frequently on the move, traveled "always on foot and alone."[69] When Ester appeared in Rendsburg in a silk headpiece, she was immediately stopped for questioning as to where she had obtained such an expensive article of clothing. She averred that she paid for everything promptly, including the food she ate. Asked about a particular item that she had not declared, Ester replied "that these items were written down on the slip of paper, and anyone can see that." Asked whether she could read the paper, she replied that she could not. So how did she know what was written there? Because [the person she borrowed it from] always wrote things on the slip of paper.[70]

Thobe, Nathan David and Ester's mother, appears also to have dabbled in the family business at times. Her first husband, father of Nathan, had died years earlier. After his death, the community supported Thobe as a widow and permitted her to attend the synagogue. Eventually, she married again and lost this support. Ester was her daughter from her second marriage. She crafted *Spitzen* (head coverings), which her husband sold, along with eyeglasses and other small household items. Her crafts, Nathan testified, had allowed him to regain his footing after an earlier imprisonment, as she gave him between four and six Reichsthalers worth of caps, which he sold for a small profit to buy other wares. Together with her second husband, now deceased, Thobe engaged in very petty trading, borrowing small sums against sundry items and redeeming them when possible. When they left their lodgings in Weding after a long stay, a small balance remained on their bill that they could not meet. As they had absolutely no cash, they gave their host/innkeeper a note of exchange, purporting to be from their son, Nathan David, with some Hebrew writing, as well as a pair of rings, which turned out to be brass.[71] Another witness testified that, three years earlier, Thobe had pawned several small articles with him, such as a green velvet armlet (a sleeve-covering fashionable in the day) and some white handkerchiefs; she later redeemed them. In the latter part of the trial, Nathan testified that his mother had passed away during the previous year; however, he did not know where she died or was buried. He later heard that she died in Meuslingen.

Hannah, wife of another of the incarcerated suspects, was also significantly older (sixteen years) than her husband, Phillip Salomons. Salomons was a ritual slaughterer and she a widow with two children when they married. Soon after, Phillip gave up his trade and began the wandering life. She sometimes joined him on the road but was left mostly to fend for herself. Hannah tried to stay near market towns where Jews congregated, presumably to trade. Braunschweig, Hannover, Celle, and Hamburg were among the cities she listed as stations in her life, including over a year in the last-named, where Phillip stayed as well. Her two children with him both died young. She claimed to know nothing of his family, including whether his parents were still alive, nor of his activities. Yet, while he was imprisoned, she sent him letters. Questioned about her circumstances, her husband noted that she mostly survived on alms from her co-religionists, as he could barely eke out a living. The previous summer, she lay ill and was very weak; she hoped some community would have pity on her and grant her subsistence. With some of her last energies, she wrote a petition to the Danish king to free her husband. Her husband likewise petitioned for his freedom, mentioning that he heard that she could no longer see or speak. Three years later, he noted that he had stopped hearing of her completely two years earlier and that he presumed she must have died then.[72]

The women of the Flensburg trial lived at the very precipice of existence, occasionally appearing in view of the Jewish community when they solicited charity or in brushes with the law. They married Jewish partners but dwelled among the non-Jews in the countryside. Their family lives were structured unconventionally, yet with bonds of affection despite the separations in age and distance. They lived from hand to mouth, using their meager resources to subsist. Neglect, exposure, and malnourishment doomed their young children. Their lives and deaths left faint traces in our sources, in stark contrast to the well-documented lives of the ba'alot bayit. It is noteworthy, however, that while they were not bound to any community by right or privilege, their Jewish identity was enough to allow for alms, food, and support from the kehillot.

Dina Jacob was the wife of an alleged Jewish smuggling ringleader operating in the tumultuous years immediately following the French Revolution.[73] Dina lived on the periphery of provincial French society, on the border of revolutionary France and the Netherlands. Her husband stood accused of various crimes, and the prosecution called on her to testify to his whereabouts during their commission. To the astonishment of the prosecutor, Dina displayed "fantastic knowledge of the geography of crime and brigandage."[74] She spun exaggerated tales that clearly played into the eagerness of the prosecution to see a vast Jewish criminal conspiracy plundering the countryside. Richard Cobb concluded that she had inflated the importance of her husband, turning him into the leader of a vast gang of smugglers, pirates, fencers, and robbers when he was actually no more than a petty thief. Her family members were impoverished Ashkenazi Jews; she had traveled with them extensively and was familiar with every byway, waterway, and shelter over an extensive territory. But the data she accumulated, Cobb concluded, would have been known to many wandering Jews of that time and class. Every itinerant Jewish man and woman had to know which addresses were safe for shelter.

Some aspects of Dina's life illuminate other features of her class. Dina had one or more children with her Christian paramour, presumably while her husband was busy committing his crimes. Another Jewish man, slightly figuring in her testimony, was married to a Christian woman, while he had another non-Jewish woman as mistress and worked with Jewish accomplices.[75] Given that these Jews had very little contact with or oversight by communal authorities of any kind, the strict boundaries between religions fell away.[76] So did the family ideals of the community.

The Itinerant Poor

Richard Cobb coined the phrase "geography of mistrust" to characterize the relationship between the well-anchored and often well-to-do inhabitants of a city and the many types of poor, disheveled, unstable people on the road who gravitated toward cities. Miri Rubin likewise studied the newcomers to cities and their reception at the hands of the urban establishments in late medieval Europe.[77] Women stood at every node of these loose networks. Poor pregnant women somehow made their way to the hekdesh in larger and smaller communities. There, they received food, shelter, and postpartum care for several weeks; their other children, if they had any, were also given care.[78] Vital records of midwives, mohalim, and the burial society point to the support that poor women, children, and some men received in the hekdesh.[79] In one pinkas mohel from a small German village, the mohel records circumcising the sons of *arhei parhei*, a derogatory term for vagrants. "I circumcised the child Abraham bar Eliezer, [the father being] one vagrant who was housed [here]."[80] This was a baby born in the hekdesh whose mother would have received postnatal care there. Charity donated by individual established community members or their confraternities paid for the needs of these poorest and most unrooted Jewish families. Despite the disparaging term for the baby's father, one of the village's foremost members served as *sandek*, an honor akin to godfather.

Poorer women in cities often rented out quarters to drifters for a short term, which many ordinances of Jewish communities prohibited. An announcement made in Hamburg in 1728 ordered: "For some time, 'foreign people' [nonresident Jews] have been drawn here and wish to remain; some desire to have a room. These people weigh heavily on our community. Therefore we warn with a great threat that the 'guests' must leave before the coming New Year [less than two weeks' notice], particularly because our community received an order from the authorities [the Hamburg Senate?] that no one may go begging from door to door, and . . . this would result in great danger to our community."[81] Hamburg, like other cities, had outlawed vagrant beggars, and the Jewish community followed suit.[82] Large swaths of Jewish people, particularly the unhoused in rural areas, lived out much of their lives completely severed from the discipline of community, entering the historical record only through their seeking of alms from established Jewish communities. Far too many of them left no trace. Yet, within the few records that survive, we glimpse something of the texture of their difficult lives.

Many women who married and moved, or orphaned children, found themselves far from their natal families and at the mercy of men who mistreated them. Jordan Katz recounted the story of a young, orphaned girl, Ester Salomon, from the village of Norbach [Forbach] near Metz. Placed in the home of an uncle who abused her, Ester fled to a Christian neighbor for protection. When the uncle demanded the girl's return, a local official advised the neighbor to refuse, as he had evaluated the situation and deemed it unsafe for Ester. The neighbor eventually remanded Ester to a convent, causing a ruckus that reached the Jewish community of Metz.[83]

Another horrific case of abuse of a young girl occurred in the center of Altona-Hamburg-Wandsbek. In 1690/91, Samuel ben Leyb Altona "committed an evil deed [*ma'aseh ra*], 'holding' a young girl, the illegitimate daughter of his wife's sister . . . for several years in Altona. He proceeded to compound this evil by subsequently sending the girl away with vagrants." The sequence of events is unclear from the record, but apparently, the girl was found wandering the countryside, perhaps abandoned after being harmed in a field. She was then brought to Hildesheim. This community apparently sent her back to Hamburg, where she was refused entry. "A note was hung on her neck, which communicated mockery and an embarrassment to the kehillah. Also, letters were written to the kahal [of Altona], insulting and shaming."[84] The scribe recorded this sordid tale of a young girl, an illegitimate child, singled out for abuse at the hands of many parties because she was vulnerable and had no honorable standing in the community. The scribe does not mention any efforts made to care for the child. Rather, the entry emphasized the communal honor, damaged publicly by the unscrupulous Samuel ben Leyb. Because he brought shame onto the community, he would be barred from communal honors for a decade. He was not fined at the time because he had no resources, but the door was left open for a subsequent leadership to punish him financially. Rather than frame the episode as one in which the paramount concern was for a (sexually) abused girl, the community focused its concerns on its own honor and shame.

In 1671, in Frankfurt, a three-and-a-half-year-old girl was discovered wandering the city streets. Found by a beggar at a gate not far from the Jewish ghetto, she was brought to the city council, who interviewed the various men and women who encountered her. Ultimately, she was identified as Jewish and taken in by the parnassim.[85] The ease with which a poor Jewish child could be abandoned and the ultimate responsibility that the community bore for the child, if only at the behest of the city, points once again to the connection between center and periphery.

In 1766, a woman who had fallen desperately ill in the environs of the small northern Jewish community of Aurich arrived in the port city of Altona on a boat. An entry in the logbook of the communal scribe tells us what happened next:

A man has come from Friesland with a woman from Aurich; the woman was very ill and still on the ship.[86] The Jewish community of Aurich sent the man . . . with the ill woman in order that she should remain in our hekdesh. But this cannot be done at all, to allow her into the hekdesh. After this, the man went and brought the woman from the ship and left her on the street and made a desecration of God's name (*hilul Hashem*) among the masses, and he also went to Lord Boyer to inform against us (*la'asot mesirah*). At this point, the kahal [of Altona] had no choice and allowed her to enter the hekdesh.[87]

The timing in this case may be a clue to the context for this incident, as Aurich had recently issued a decree expelling vagabonds, beggars, and wandering Jews.[88] This Jewish woman, who was not a resident of Altona and who did not appear to have any resources of her own, was transported to the open city so that she could be cared for in its hekdesh. Both the Jews of Aurich and the Christians of Altona presumed that the Jewish community of Altona should assume responsibility for the sick woman, although the community itself had become deeply concerned about the rising number of passersby who imposed on its generosity. Had her guardian not appealed both to the non-Jewish public and to the local non-Jewish authorities, she may very well have languished on the boat or somewhere in the fields until she died. By leaving her on the open street for passersby to see her miserable condition, the guardian shamed the Altona Jewish community into action. The exposure of her neediness, her body lying in the street, was a shame that reflected back onto the Jewish community.

The woman from Aurich became homeless through no fault of her own and sought to be treated as a respected traveler who would receive care from a Jewish community not too far away from her hometown. The Altona Jewish community initially denied her that care, presumably because poor laws and available resources restricted the degree of support the community could extend to vagrants and because of the cultural suspicion of foreigners that shaped both Jewish and Christian attitudes toward the poor. Her travel to Altona, however, highlights that people without community protection frequently came into contact with Jewish communities and their institutions. Ultimately, the issue of shame and scandal for the Jewish community in the eyes of the Christians forced it to care for this stranger.

This chapter has demonstrated that social honor and shame, center and periphery, existed in a tightly intertwined relationship in Jewish communities. Gendered bonds of dependency lay in the mutual need between employers and servants, parents and wetnurses, and producers of goods and their itinerant peddlers. Marginality or shame inhered in a number of categories that did not always overlap. Economic standing, legal entanglements, sexual honor, and religious affiliation defined status and belonging in early modern Jewish life. These boundaries were not rigidly enforced. Through actions or changed circumstances, a woman's status could shift. Honor could turn into shame, poverty to success, moral rectitude to scandal, often in highly gendered ways, demonstrating the fluidity of categories that seemed so certain in the prescriptive records.

4

Jewish Women and Print Culture

AT THE dawn of the seventeenth century, Yaakov Heilprun published a short treatise entitled *Dinim ve-seder* (Laws and Order), an abridged Yiddish version of R. Moshe Isserles's *Torat ha-hatat*, a legal work about Jewish dietary practices that had appeared in print a few decades earlier.[1] The pocket-size booklet, eight folios long, highlighted the potential afforded by increased literacy. Heilprun intended to teach the reader "how one should soak, salt, and porge meat, everything correctly explained so that every woman and girl who has recently learned to read can understand and learn."[2] Heilprun explained that these laws were critical for ba'alot bayit "because [the women] are at home while the men go to work, leaving the women to cook."[3] The text offers detailed instructions for ridding chicken and beef of blood, including laws concerning the pots used in the process. Heilprun marketed his text by claiming that translating the laws into Yiddish would "allow some people to learn as well as the rabbis . . . and then, one wouldn't have to pay a *rebbe*" to teach them the laws.[4] Heilprun thereby recognized the power of print in democratizing knowledge, and the access that printing in the vernacular provided to male and female readers.

Heilprun dedicated his text to Mosqita, an eight-year-old girl who was his student. Heilprun explained that despite her tender age, Mosqita was gifted; she knew more than many women who were far older than she. Mosqita could read and write in Yiddish and Italian.[5] She had even helped Heilprun edit one of his books, "better than some men" could have done.[6] Heilprun praised her learned father, her pious mother, and her learned sisters. The women in Mosqita's family were all rebbetzins (wives of rabbis) and Heilprun wrote that "we can only wait that you will be a rebbetzin one day, God willing."[7]

Mosqita's elite family likely supported Heilprun's work while he taught their daughter. Heilprun's other publications were also written for women and dedicated to female patrons.[8] Heilprun's successful employment as a translator of Jewish works into vernacular languages specifically for a female audience emphasizes the widespread demand for and availability of reading material for Jewish women, even ones as young as Mosqita. The invention of movable type by Johannes Gutenberg in the late fifteenth century and the subsequent proliferation of printed materials directly affected the lives of Jewish women.[9] Scholars have yet to appreciate, for Jewish culture writ large and for the early modern Jewish book, the profound implications of including women in the circle of Jewish literacy on a vast scale. This chapter argues that the intensification and expansion of literacy and writing in the early modern period was one of the driving forces that drew women into greater participation in the religious, economic, intellectual, and communal life of their time and place. Yiddish translators and printers opened domains of the law and Jewish lore that had been mostly closed off to average women, allowing many more to partake of the spiritual, religious, and ritual life of their communities (see plate 9).[10]

Jewish Women and Their Libraries

When his daughter Serlina was twenty-one years old (ca. 1553), Menahem (Mendlin) Katz, an Ashkenazi Jew in northern Italy, commissioned a rich miscellany in Yiddish for her.[11] This manuscript, consisting of 274 folios, has been rightly referred to as a woman's library within one binding.[12] Beginning with a compendium of *minhagim* (customs) following the Jewish calendar year, the manuscript included many religious and literary texts. The religious texts include a *froyen buchleyn* (women's small book), mostly about the "women's mitzvot," particularly the separation of hallah, a small piece of dough removed while preparing dough for bread, and candlelighting. It included biblical and other texts to follow in the synagogue, such as the five *megillot* (biblical scrolls, including the books of Ruth and Esther), and chapters of Psalms. A second section included Yiddish tales, bilingual versions of poems, songs, riddles, and other small compositions.[13] Notably, significant parts of Serlina's manuscript assume access to other books or manuscripts, indicating that the ba'alat bayit was expected to own several other texts.[14] For example, the book of customs assumes that the user had a separate volume containing the *selihot* (penitential prayers); it merely lists the titles of each prayer to be said at a certain time.[15] While most of these instructions would be useful to both men and women, certain portions of the customs were specifically directed to women, such as, "Every woman should be warned about" kneading the dough and removing the requisite portion of the hallah on Passover eve.[16]

Serlina's manuscript was well used. On the final folio of one section, her father recorded her birth in Nissan, 1532, in Venice. Decades later, in 1561, her husband Mordekhai wrote that on the very day she gave birth to a son, Serlina died in childbirth before her twenty-ninth birthday. He included the epitaph that he commissioned for her, noting that she was a peacemaker, all praised her goodness, she was charitable, and she said her set prayers, daytime and night. He added that she merited to be buried next to two children who had predeceased her: a son, Menahem, and a daughter, Hindele.[17] Serlina's compendium is one of several manuscripts written for individual Jewish women in the sixteenth and seventeenth centuries, some commissioned by themselves.

Not all manuscripts commissioned for women were religious in nature. Even as the availability of printed works expanded, women commissioned manuscripts that reflected their particular needs or desires. Shmuel Bak of Rovere (Italy) collected and wrote a compendium of around 120 *mayses* (tales) for his aunt Limet while he visited with her in Innsbruck (Austria) in 1596.[18] He blessed her to read it "for a thousand good years." Their familial and cultural connections traversed borders, a reminder that readers consumed Hebrew and Yiddish books across widely dispersed locations not limited by political boundaries. Another early example of Yiddish tales written for a woman comes in a manuscript called in Yiddish *Widuwilt*, an adaptation of King Arthur's Court tales.[19] Written apparently during the first half of the sixteenth century, likely in northern Italy, its scribe was Sheftl of Kojetín (Goitein), Moravia. It was written for a woman who proudly inscribed her ownership: "This book *Widuwilt* is mine, Brendlen, to long life, wife of the noble and learned Mr. Yekutiel Katz, may the Lord guard him, ben Moshe Yaakov, of blessed memory, from Venice."[20]

In 1579, a woman named Perlen, wife of Wolf Levi, commissioned from Anshel Levi, a scribe who had emigrated from German lands to Italy, a Yiddish compendium that included seventy-three tales mostly based on talmudic stories, a midrash on *Ethics of the Fathers,* and a poem on the binding of Isaac.[21] In his detailed colophon, the scribe praised Perlen and revealed something about his business. His tributes to his patron approximated the pious behaviors that were common in epitaphs and other descriptions of women of the time. Perlen separated hallah, lit the Shabbat candles, and "in a very refined and quiet manner, went on time to her ritual immersion."[22] She attended morning and evening prayer services. He noted as well that her time passed in *leyen und shrayben* (reading and writing). Regrettably, we do not know what Perlen read or wrote. But, perhaps most significantly, Anshel described himself as a "poor scribe, serving all pious women."[23] In the late sixteenth century, a scribe who could copy Yiddish texts fluently set himself up as a scribe for women. This description bespeaks a demand for such services from other women of Perlen's station, as well as the growing sense that women, particularly heads of household, required texts and were willing to pay for them.

Not long after the introduction of print, early modern Jews assumed that Ashkenazi women would (should) own copies of certain crucial texts. This extended beyond manuscripts to printed texts. The aforementioned Yaakov Heilprun, who translated texts for women and dedicated one to his young student Mosqita, was also employed by his wealthier relative, Roza, wife of Nehemiah Luzzatto. She employed him to print manuscripts of interest to women, to teach her daughters, and to provide them with appropriate educational materials.[24] This is another example of a female patron, male educational and scribal "servant," and the production of texts. Heilprun translated from Hebrew into Yiddish the book *Orekh yomim* "for the sake of pious and respectable women. Those who read it and follow its advice will merit children who study Torah and do good deeds and will live a long time."[25] Just as Anshel the scribe praised his patron Perlen, Heilprun lauded his patron: "A missive to the intelligent and endowed with good character, lovely in appearance and in her deeds, Mrs. Roza, may she live, wife of the *katzin* (notable) Nehemiah Luzzatto in the community of Venice, from me, your servant and cousin."[26] Roza's relationship with books went far beyond the publication of one book. She signed her name as owner inside a fifteenth-century parchment siddur (prayer book) with Yiddish instructions.

Perlen and Roza's commissions touch upon another aspect of women and texts in this period. Some women provided the necessary funding to scribes, authors, or printers so that a particular text could be printed. Some, such as Roza, specifically sought to support the publication of volumes for other women. These women were then acknowledged and commemorated as patrons in the printed texts.[27] This is yet another example of the intense significance with which commemorating a person or an event in writing was perceived in this period. By supporting the publication of a book, individual men and women ensured that they would be remembered in its pages.

The involvement of women in print continued into the eighteenth century. Bella (née Horowitz) Hazan published a story about the history of the Davidic dynasty in 1705.[28] In addition, together with Rachel (née Rausnitz) Poriat (alt. Porges) of Prague, Bella "brought books to print," publishing a story of how Jews initially came to settle in Prague. Like those of many other Yiddish books in the early modern period, the title page was written in rhyme and addressed to both men and women. It urged them not to worry about spending "a bit of money" on a lovely story that would gladden their hearts.[29] Bella and Rachel's names alone appear on the title page. Their precise role in bringing the booklet to press remains unclear; they may have been editors and patrons of the text. The standard opening confirms their familiarity with the world of Yiddish print and early modern marketing.

The dramatic tale involves ruses and thefts, which culminate in the emperor's inviting a young, wise Jewish man named Gumprecht to reside in Prague.[30] A starring role in the tale is played by Gumprecht's unnamed fiancée, who courageously outwits the emperor's duplicitous advisor, protecting Gumprecht's life and her own honor. It is perhaps no surprise that a woman stands at the center of this foundation tale, along with her fiancé, as two elite women from Prague—a city in which Jewish women were particularly active in literary production—brought it to press. More striking, perhaps, is the tale's assumption that women read as a matter of course. After Gumprecht had been duped by the emperor's advisor, he quickly penned letters, first to his future father-in-law and then to his fiancée, beseeching in turn that they come to his aid. Whereas his future father-in-law demurred, explaining that he was "a *lamdan* (Torah scholar) and a pious Jew who sits over his books day and night," inexperienced at speaking before the king, his fiancée (who also had no experience speaking with emperors) acted differently upon reading the letter.[31] She took decisive action, made haste to Prague, laid a trap for the advisor, and thereby saved Gumprecht. The casual mention of a woman's receiving letters underscores the degree to which reading and correspondence had become the norm among many Jewish women by the early eighteenth century.

The arc of women's ownership of books followed that of the Yiddish-speaking population. Northern Italy remained a center for Yiddish writing and print until approximately the mid-seventeenth century, by which time Ashkenazi Jews there had basically traded Yiddish for Italian. In the seventeenth century, Moses Poriat, originally from Prague, relocated to Jerusalem, later serving as a charity collector for the holy city among European Jews. He instructed European Jews wishing to move to the Land of Israel regarding which books were worth bringing along on their journey. He listed several Hebrew books, including the Bible, liturgical, and legal texts, which men were to carry along with them. Simultaneously, he advised women to bring a different list of Yiddish books. These included a Bible (likely the *Tsene u-rene*), a prayer book, *tkhines* ("supplications," sing. *tkhine*, discussed below), and other vernacular literature. The list suggests that these texts, unavailable in the Holy

Land, were essential to a woman's library.³² Rabbi Sheftel Horowitz advised in his ethical will, "You, my daughters and daughters-in-law, read the Bible regularly in the Ashkenazi language [Yiddish], as well as the book *Lev tov* [The book] *Emek ha-bracha* writes (par. 22): 'A pregnant woman should continuously pray for sons who are Torah scholars.'"³³ Noteworthy here is Horowitz's casual assumption that the women in his (rabbinic) household had access to a variety of books that they would read or refer to on a regular basis.³⁴

Glikl of Hameln wrote her memoir with her own library of reading uppermost in her mind. She instructed her readers to investigate the Bible for themselves.³⁵ The first passages in her book contain a biblical verse (in an erroneous citation); she sprinkled such verses throughout her work in the original and in Yiddish translation. She read books of morals, such as *Yesh nohlin, Lev tov,* and *Brantshpigel*.³⁶ After recounting one particularly complex tale, copied from a Yiddish collection, Glikl noted: "I found this story in a book by a distinguished man."³⁷ In addition to her library of Jewish books, Glikl called upon her reading of stories by and about non-Jews: "It may be a story told by heathens."³⁸

The Market for Women's Books

As Poriat's gendered lists indicate, Jewish women formed a discrete market for books.³⁹ Scholarship about women in early modern Europe has long noted the impact of women as consumers of books, but it generally leaves Jewish women out of this discussion. After the sixteenth century, Jewish women more commonly owned printed books than manuscripts, with the notable exception of the revival of a luxury manuscript tradition in the eighteenth century. Writers and publishers ceaselessly pitched their books to women. Printers were entrepreneurs and sought to advertise their books to the largest possible market. They positioned many works as suitable for men and for women, thus explicitly including women in the circle of piety, learning, or adventure in the books they printed. A prayer book printed in Venice (1599) advertised this inclusivity on its title page: "Siddur for the whole year in Hebrew and in Yiddish, the like of which you have never seen. Nothing is missing, as men and women can see."⁴⁰ In 1660, Nathan Nata Hanover, famed for his account of the massacres of Polish Jews in 1648/49, published a handbook for conversation and travel that listed words in four languages (Hebrew, German, Latin, and Italian). The book was organized in parallel columns around thematic clusters. He printed all the languages in Hebrew letters. *Safah berurah (Book of Clear Language)* could be extremely useful for those self-motivated to learn a new language, and women were first on the list of Hanover's promotion of the book on its title page: "It is useful for women and men, old and even older, boys and young men, teachers and merchants, as well as for the simple folk who travel everywhere."[41] These small but telling examples demonstrate how the circle of literacy broadened to the point at which printers of entire categories of texts explicitly invited women to become their readers.

Although both men and women throughout the Yiddish-speaking world could read these books, certain categories of texts, such as ethical/homiletical works, came to be perceived as gendered female. Moses Henochs Yerushalmi Altschuler, the author of *Brantshpigel*, a sixteenth-century homiletical book in Yiddish, explained that the choice to publish in Yiddish reflected his desire to provide "women and men who are like women" with access to the book's contents.[42] Altschuler thus defined male readers who preferred the vernacular Yiddish over the scholarly Hebrew as being "like women," gendering Yiddish writing as feminine.[43]

Many of the women involved in printing Hebrew or Yiddish books, from the print house floor to the wealthiest patrons, advertised their presence as a signal to other women. Women's ownership of books and manuscripts, or books containing dedications to women, demonstrate the value of books as treasured possessions, pious objects, and, in the case of those with elaborate bindings or decorative programs, conspicuous markers of status.[44] Some of the most lavishly decorated of the central European school of illuminated manuscripts were written for or dedicated to women.[45]

Even if a professional scribe or publisher did not address a work specifically to them, women often marked the books they owned. For example, a copy of *Melitz yosher* (1688) bears the inscription, "This book, *Melitz yosher*, belongs to Mindele, rebbetzin (rabbi's wife), in Amsterdam."[46] A 1706 copy of *Brantshpigel* bears the handwritten inscription, "This book belongs to W[idow] Rivkah, wife of Samuel Hayim Neugass of blessed memory." Rivkah wrote the inscription first in square letters in Hebrew, followed by cursive in Yiddish.[47] Women sometimes used their small books to mark milestones in their lives, as men often did with Bibles or other important volumes.

The books that women owned and read increased their participation in religious and spiritual endeavors. The miscellanea that enfolded entire libraries into one volume provide evidence that women did not separate their bookshelves (even if only imaginary) into religious versus ordinary materials. We consider them separately here, focusing on religious texts in this chapter and on literary and ordinary writing in the next, to make the argument that literacy

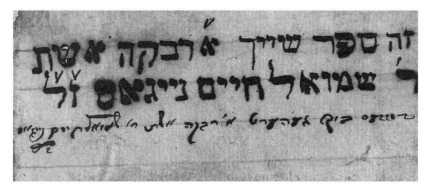

FIG. 4.1. Ownership inscription by Rivka Neugass in *Brantshpigel*, Frankfurt, 1706.

raised participation in both spheres, the synagogue and sacred, as well as the daily and ordinary.

Women's Religious Books and Ritual Participation

Translations of the Bible into Yiddish long preceded print. They were not intended for women exclusively, although women soon became their most ardent readers and students. One translation of the Bible into Yiddish from the late fifteenth to early sixteenth centuries was copied for the scribe's "dear sister," to whom he apologized for any errors.[48] From the first printing of the *Tsene u-rene*, a Yiddish adaptation and expansion of the biblical text (first printed in 1590), it became the runaway favorite of Ashkenazi women, often referred to as the women's Bible.[49] While the first printings have apparently succumbed to the ravages of time, it was subsequently reprinted hundreds of times, with variations promoted by editors and publishers according to the time and circumstances. The title of the work itself indicated that it was directed at a female readership,[50] and its inclusion on lists of works for Jewish women demonstrates that while men read it, too, Jewish women took possession of *Tsene u-rene* as with perhaps no other Yiddish title. Other popular works based on biblical narratives include the epic poems *Shmuel bukh* (*Book of Samuel*) and *Melokhim bukh* (*Book of Kings*), with the former, based on medieval traditions, being performed, as well as read, to a melody that became popular throughout Ashkenaz.[51] One copyist of *Shmuel bukh* from the late fifteenth century, Liva (Loewe) of Regensburg, thanked his good patron, a woman named Freidlin, wishing that she use and read it in good health.[52]

Works that guided women in prayer formed a significant category in the library and marketplace. Siddurim, *mahzorim* (holiday prayer books), and tkhines guided Jewish women in their interactions with God in the synagogue and at home. Most prayer books, whether for daily use, Shabbat, or holidays, contained text in Hebrew. Only the instructions in "translated" siddurim were in the vernacular Yiddish or other hybrid Jewish languages. They often instructed the user tersely: "Here one stands; here one weeps; here one bows; one says this passage three times."[53] While not all prayer books with vernacular language were intended exclusively for women, many included women directly in their target readership. The scribe Menahem Oldendorf completed a manuscript mahzor for a woman named Hannelein in Mestre in 1504. The end contains a special set of selihot.[54] A *Seder ma'amadot* (verses and prayers to be said on a daily rotation) with Yiddish translation, printed in Verona, 1594, made its primary market clear: "Women and also many men who cannot understand the Holy Tongue may recite it from here."[55] These written works addressing women signal their engagement in prayer; any vernacular instructions facilitated their involvement in rituals.

Tkhines (supplications), on the other hand, were less formal prayers that women could utter at special moments not covered in the formal synagogue services, such as immersion in a ritual bath or childbirth. In Hebrew or in the vernacular, Jewish women had always maintained oral traditions of prayers. (The biblical Hannah served as a model and seal of approval for this tradition.) Notably, no collections of tkhines have survived prior to the printed editions. Thus, print served to establish and disseminate these prayers particular to women's life cycle events and rituals in a more uniform fashion. The rise of printed collections of tkhines marks an example of texts designed exclusively for female consumption.[56] The publication of tkhines facilitated their circulation among a wide group of women and fostered piety through the reading of texts. Both men and women could write these prayers. Perhaps most famous among the female authors was the Polish female rabbinic scholar Sarah Rebecca Rachel Leah Horowitz (ca. 1715–1795), whose volume of tkhines was accompanied by her own introductions in Hebrew and Aramaic.[57] Jewish women throughout the Yiddish-speaking world consumed her work.

Chava Weissler, the preeminent scholar of tkhines, argues that there were significant differences between texts authored by men and by women. For example, male religious texts urged women to light candles in order to drive away the darkness that Eve brought into the world, whereas texts written by women did not include this explanation for candlelighting.[58] Several illuminated manuscripts commissioned specifically for women similarly omitted any discussion of women's sin. Instead, they emphasized that women must light candles at the proper time since "the primary reason our sages told us to light candles is to promote a peaceful home."[59] One text expanded on how women should light candles when they left to attend synagogue services, further emphasizing that women's synagogue attendance was normal and intersected with their domestic religious duties. The texts of these tkhines permit entry into the world of women's piety. The specific prayers and tkhines included in these works differ from one another and from prayers preserved in other printed materials, such as the tkhines included in Rabbi Benjamin Slonik's *Seder mitzvot nashim* (*Order of Women's Commandments*). Some manuscripts included kabbalistic prayers, while others did not; some referenced popular beliefs about Lilith; some referred to women as God's daughters, highlighting feminine aspects of piety rather than negative associations of women with Eve and sin.[60] Female authors of tkhines shaped these prayers to their own sensibility, and male authors who hoped to attract female customers sometimes followed suit.

Additional genres of early modern religious books were created and marketed exclusively to women. Among these, the *mitzvot nashim/froyen buchleyn* genre focused on the three special precepts of women's observance that were the domain of the ba'alat bayit: the separation of a small piece of dough when baking bread, known as "separating hallah"; lighting candles on Shabbat and festivals; and the laws of menstrual purity, including immersion in a ritual bath, or mikveh. This genre was immensely popular among women; variations of its texts, stand-alone or as part of miscellanea, were printed or handwritten, copied, and circulated within Ashkenazi society throughout the early modern period.[61] When the scribe Kalonymus bar Shimon completed a miscellany (Venice, 1554), he included "the laws of hallah and candle lighting" alongside the other contents of the manuscript. Beyond the specific contents for women, he included women explicitly in various places—for example, "May he redeem us, men as well as women."[62]

The proliferation of such handbooks demonstrates how quickly printed materials provided women greater access to these laws. In the fifteenth century, Rabbi Jacob Molin (d. 1427) had strongly warned against composing a handbook to teach men and women the laws of menstrual purity. Mothers were to pass on these traditions to their daughters, mimetically, within the home. If questions arose, they should pose them to rabbinic authorities.[63] In sharp contrast to Molin, sixteenth-century rabbi Benjamin Slonik indicated that his edition of *Seder mitzvot nashim* could be useful for women who were embarrassed to share their specific questions about menstrual purity with rabbis.[64] He even specified that a woman could erroneously determine herself to be menstrually impure, making "a mistake because she had not read books."[65] Slonik's text proved very popular: five printed editions appeared between 1577 and 1627, with an additional volume comprising excerpts from this text printed in Prague in 1629. Four Italian adaptations were published between 1616 and 1711.[66] The volume's success attests to the new ways in which halakhic knowledge became accessible through print and to the acceptance of print as a suitable medium for such transfer by contemporary elites.[67] The popularity of books addressed to women is evident from a set of data from 1595. When the Jews in Mantua were forced to register all their books and manuscripts with the church censor, books concerning women's commandments represented the single largest genre among all the Yiddish manuscripts.[68]

Another genre, the *bensherl*, a small booklet comprising a variety of blessings, was first printed with parallel Yiddish translations of the prayers in the late sixteenth century; the earliest extant edition is from 1600. The prayers, rites, and songs written or printed on their leaves were all performed in the space of the home and could be used by any family member.[69] Many were dedicated specifically to women. The 1600 edition included prayers that would be recited daily, such as birkat ha-mazon, blessings on food and spices, and *keriyat shema al ha-mitah* (the prayer recited before going to bed). Some versions included songs and prayers spanning the course of the calendar year. The texts of Shabbat songs, the Passover *seder* (ceremonial meal), and the Hanukkah candlelighting service appeared in Hebrew and Yiddish translations, as did the rites of *kapparot, sefirat ha-omer,* and *eruv tavshilin*.[70] While these books were available for family use, editors addressed female readers explicitly. The colophon and title page of the 1600 edition turned to the "pious and dear women," who, they claimed, would now be able to understand the prayers they recited.[71] Thus, while both men and women could and did use the bensherl, these small books were printed and reprinted with the stated goal of making such prayers and blessings accessible to women and girls.[72] The genre remained popular well into the nineteenth century.[73] Jewish law did not mandate women's participation in these rituals. The creation of texts that boasted of their ability to promote women's comprehension of the prayers, however, indicates that women's participation in these family rituals was both a current practice and a desirable outcome. Visual depictions of ba'alot bayit sitting at the family table with their own books confirm the presence of women with their own texts as a matter of course.

While printed bensherls captured a broad market, the genre emerged in manuscript form alongside the print during the mid-eighteenth-century revival of Hebrew manuscript culture. These beautifully illuminated manuscripts often contained the same contents as the printed bensherl: birkat ha-mazon, other blessings, and the prayer recited immediately before bed.[74] Some manuscripts included sefirat ha-omer (the ritual for counting the days between Passover and Shavu'ot) and/or tkhines for the three women's commandments. Various manuscripts explicitly refer by name to the female commissioner and owner of the manuscript. Fradlina, daughter of Yekutiel of Venice, noted that she acquired her manuscript *Minhogim* (Customs) in 1550.[75] The Yiddish instructions addressed her in a direct and user-friendly way: "Here I will write for you our customs regarding selihot."[76] Fradche, the wife of Moses Gundersheim, owned a volume commissioned in 1725; the *ketzinah* (notable woman) Bella of Frankfurt owned a 1736 birkat ha-mazon created in Mannheim; Hindle, the wife of Meir of Vienna, owned a manuscript of blessings and prayers from 1743; and the ketzinah Breindl, wife of Jaeckl from Fürth, possessed a *seder berakhot* (order of blessings; pl. *sidre berakhot*) from 1793.[77] Some manuscripts were commissioned for brides. A manuscript made in Vienna, 1725, featuring the work of two artists, was commissioned for the "eminent single woman," presumably as a gift for her upcoming wedding.[78] The title page of a 1747 manuscript from Vienna indicates that it was a wedding gift; the lavish and detailed images of women performing the three women's commandments, as well as other rituals, suggest it was for the bride's use. A 1741 manuscript, likely a wedding gift for a bride, given the illuminated depictions of women bathing and immersing ritually, includes the claim that it was unrivaled by anything available in print.[79]

A small intervention in the standard text in a 1728 Grace after Meals provides an even more striking sign of female readership. The traditional prayer refers to the "covenant that you [God] sealed on our bodies," referring to circumcision. A hand inserted in Yiddish that "this [phrase] *is not* recited by women and girls."[80] Feivush Yoel of Minden, a small community in northern Germany, gave this manuscript to his bride, Esther, daughter of Nathan Eisenstadt.

These manuscripts were luxury items written by noted scribes/illustrators such as Jacob Sofer ben Judah Leyb of Berlin and Aaron Wolf Herlingen.[81] Although the printed bensherl comprised some of the same prayers and often far surpassed the decorated manuscripts in terms of the content included, these manuscripts were prized primarily for their beauty and value. The rich images detail women's participation in a wide range of rituals, such as the women's commandments and the recitation of keriyat shema al ha-mitah, *tashlikh*, and

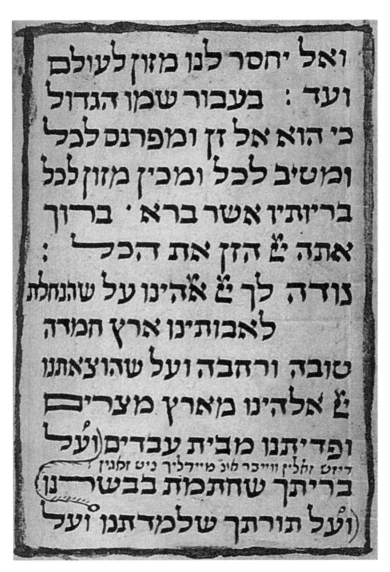

FIG. 4.2. At the phrase "And the bond You incised in our flesh," an interpolation reads: "*dizes zollen vayber un maydlakh nit zogen* (this should not be said by women and girls)." *Seder berakhot*, 1728.

FIG. 4.3. Praying the Shema while nursing a baby. *Seder birkat ha-mazon*, 1720.

mayim aharonim.[82] In addition, tkhines accompanying some of these rituals were included in the ornate manuscripts. In one manuscript, a woman separating hallah was to pray for herself, her husband, and her child. When immersing in the ritual bath, the reader would pray for a healthy pregnancy and for the birth of a learned son or pious daughter.[83] These personal requests recited by women are a window into their rites of piety.

Many of the illuminated prayer manuscripts prepared for women in the eighteenth century include images of a woman seated on her bed, holding a prayer book while reciting keriyat shema immediately before sleep. In one manuscript, the traditional prayer opens with an additional request for forgiveness and includes instructions for reciting the prayer such that one falls asleep without uttering any other speech. The accompanying illustration includes a woman at her table in her nightcap, with a prayer book in front of her, while her husband waits in the bed.[84] Whereas one sixteenth-century responsum deals with the question of why women were not required to recite the bedtime prayer, these commissioned manuscripts suggest that by the eighteenth century, elite women recited this prayer with devotion and even pride.[85] Many of the sidre berakhot manuscripts portray a woman sitting on her bed, sometimes with a baby at her breast or in a nearby cradle, praying while holding a small book.

These images suggest that women used these manuscripts for the recitation of the Shema prayer at bedtime.[86] In some manuscripts, the standard bedtime prayer expanded into a wider ritual performance, in which kabbalistic elements, additional prayers, prayers for safe travels, or kissing the *mezuzah* were added.[87] The new rituals in little prayer books that emerged in the eighteenth century may reflect a form of nighttime piety that was already practiced, and it may have further encouraged women to recite these prayers before retiring to bed. Although manuscripts of this caliber were owned by only a small number of elite women, others circulated by the hundreds in print. They usher us into the material, religious, and literary world of women in private moments as their days were done. With the little booklets in hand that spoke directly to them, women felt greater ownership and a sense of participation in rituals of daily life.

Depicting Women's Ritual Lives

The colorful, lavish illustrations in these luxury manuscripts are not the sole images that portray women's ritual lives. Sifre minhagim (books of customs), first composed in the thirteenth century, typically prescribed the correct sequence for prayers and outlined other customs. The genre flourished in response to both the ruptures and migrations of the fourteenth and fifteenth centuries.[88] During the early modern period, the genre expanded once again in both print and manuscript. Printed editions of medieval custom books, such as those compiled by Isaac of Tyrnau, were printed multiple times, accompanied by illustrations. Many such editions were translated into Yiddish, and both the vernacular language and the medium of print widened the audience for these texts.[89]

Most printed Yiddish custom books followed the liturgical or calendrical cycle, setting men as the central consumers of and actors within these texts. Most versions include an explicit passage explaining the different ritual requirements demanded of men and women according to Jewish law, noting that women were exempted from positive time-bound commandments.[90] Yet the illustrations accompanying these books portray women even when the texts did not make specific note of their presence. In one such example, a mother, father, two daughters, and two sons were all present at the *havdalah* ceremony (the ritual blessings that conclude Shabbat). The father and sons played a more active role, as they, not the mother and daughters, held the wine, aromatic spices, and candle over which blessings were recited.[91] One northern Italian Yiddish manuscript custom book from the sixteenth century depicts women counting the omer between Passover and Shavu'ot.[92] Significantly, the woman counting the omer does not look toward the communal calendar on the wall behind her. She triumphantly holds up her own copy of an omer calendar, in a rare instance of a woman being depicted as owning a Jewish calendar in this period. The decision to depict women in widely diffused printed custom books underscores the ubiquity of their engagement in a broad range of rituals. The illustrated printed vernacular volumes, in particular, also modeled women's participation in these rituals for additional readers and suggests that not only men consulted these Yiddish custom books.

Singing in Script and Print

Printed versions of popular, contemporary *lider* (songs) capture women's participation in group rituals. In the early modern period, popular ballads were printed as single-leaf broadsides and various song cycles collected into pamphlets or books. Some included musical notations; others contained instructions for singing to popular tunes, while yet others just contained the lyrics. The surviving evidence of this musical textual culture exists in many languages and vernaculars, including Yiddish and Hebrew. Women sang on many occasions of life cycle events in private homes, in women's communal settings, and in the women's section of the synagogue when ritually appropriate. While braiding a bride's hair, ritually washing a deceased neighbor, and celebrating Jewish holidays, women came together in song. Some of the lyrics cannot be traced to specific authors; some are clear borrowings from the larger non-Jewish culture, while others had named authors and particular Jewish meaning. A very few of these songs can be traced specifically to the authorship of Jewish women. The scarcity of songs explicitly written by women hardly does justice to the power of songs to inculcate verses, ideas, events, values, and emotions in the women who sang and transmitted them. Like other aspects of Jewish culture accessible to women of most classes and locations, these songs transcended explicit literacy and bound women together in a shared set of values and references.

Toybe (bas Leyb Pitzker) Pan composed a historical *lid* commemorating a plague in the ghetto of Prague, likely written in the late seventeenth century.[93] Pan's references to other works familiar to women "in the language of tkhines" and to the tune of "*adir ayom ve-nora*"[94] assumes women's familiarity with the special prayers recited privately by individuals in Yiddish, as well as those recited in synagogue. The refrain, *Foter kenig*, a Yiddish translation of a Hebrew prayer, "Our father, our king," would have been familiar to the men and women who attended synagogue. Kathryn Hellerstein argues that this song breaks new ground by merging male communal prayer with women's private tkhines and suggests that the community may have recited this song together. Whether recited by women or by both women and men, the song highlights female authorship as well as the broader involvement of women in group song and prayer.

Toybe Pan was not alone among Prague women who authored songs.[95] Rivkah Tiktiner, discussed extensively in the next chapter, composed a lid for the Simhat Torah festival in sixteenth-century Prague; Sorel, daughter of Jacob, composed a lid in honor of the Torah; Schöndele composed a song about the Ten Commandments; and Bella Hazan composed a song for the New Year.[96] Bella Hazan and Rachel Poriat also appended a different lid to their tale about Gumprecht and his fiancée in Prague, although their role in its production remains opaque.[97] These songs often survive in a single copy, testimony to a lost world of melody and sound, of words and their meanings, which women cherished. Of the many ephemeral genres we discuss, songs were perhaps the most evanescent. Nevertheless, through the texts that survive, we can catch some small drifts of the sounds of women singing for pleasure, for consolation, or for memorialization.[98]

Education of Jewish Girls

The books directed at women and girls and the expectation that women would own certain books in their libraries assumes a basic level of literacy among them. The eight-year-old Mosqita to whom Yaakov Heilprun dedicated his book on preparing kosher meat stands out as an exceptionally talented daughter of a rabbinic family. The level of Yiddish and Italian reading and writing that she acquired may not have been typical, and yet, texts in Yiddish were clearly marketed to both women and girls. Despite this, some of the most striking silences in our sources concern the communal education of Jewish girls. The western and central European Jewish communities whose records

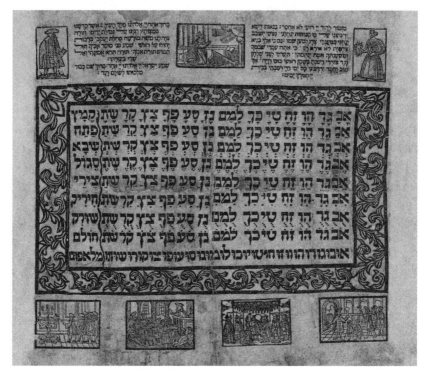

FIG. 4.4. Aleph-Bet Chart. Note woman on top right. Frankfurt, 1730.

and texts inform every discussion in this book contain few traces of the ways in which girls were educated. This stands in stark contrast to the education of boys, which communities saw as their religious obligation. Communal regulations and some records allow us to see how *melamdim* (teachers, mostly for boys; sing. *melamed*) were hired, how parents paid or were taxed for tuition, and how the teachers themselves were organized.[99] Despite the general silence, various glimmers stand out from the sources, differing from one community to another and even from one household to another. We know from memoirs and essays that girls did attend elementary classes in some places, such as Altona-Hamburg and many parts of eastern and central Europe. Glikl mentioned off-handedly, "I was about ten years old (ca. 1656)—when the Swede went to war. . . . I cannot write much news about it since I was a child and had to sit in *heder*."[100] Beyond these rather casual references, Glikl tells us nothing about the formal education she received—who taught her, for how long, which subjects were taught, and how.

In some communities, children were educated in the homes of teachers. The regulations of the Jewish community in the town of Wied-Runkel (in the south German state of Hesse) included several bylaws concerning education. These bylaws were renewed multiple times between the 1730s and 1780s. "Tuition for children who go to school will be calculated [as follows]: an "*aleph-beys*" child [one beginning instruction in reading the alphabet], whether a young boy or girl, half an hour. A young boy who studies Bible, and certainly Mishnah or Talmud, a full hour. This is the case unless there is a different, older tradition in place."[101]

These regulations further stated that parents who wished to hire private tutors for their children would be allowed to do so, but they also must pay the tax for education to the community.[102] The Ashkenazi pattern dominant in many communities had wealthy parents providing private tutors for their children, while only the poor sent their children to school. Regulations from communities in Moravia emphasized that girls' classes needed to be held in separate spaces from those of boys, even if girls were studying separately with the wife of the melamed.[103] Takkanot from Nikolsburg (Mikulov in Czech, in southern Moravia)[104] mandating that boys and girls be educated in separate spaces and with separate teachers reveal the existence of some formal education for girls in eastern and central Europe. Families that could afford to hire an in-residence private tutor often had brothers and sisters of young ages educated side-by-side at home.

For many girls, regardless of whether they acquired literacy as young children in school, informal education took place in the home. Rivkah Tiktiner emphasized the importance of a mother teaching her daughters, as that would set the tone for the household and the children to come:

> The mother, who can be found in the home at all times, is responsible for supervising her children, and she can accomplish many good things. She can study with them and teach them every nuance . . . she should sit next to her children/sons and speak with them on Torah matters and not idle matters. . . . Now I will speak about educating girls. The rabbis said, "A first-born daughter is a good sign for sons, for she can assist the mother with the education of the children who come after. . . . Every woman should try to educate her children into productive deeds . . . and not think, 'Why must my daughter work, I have enough money?' Since no one knows what the future may bring, as our own eyes can see . . . she should become accustomed as well to welcome guests . . . and not be lazy and idle."[105]

In his *Brantshpigel*, Moshe Altshuler similarly asserted that mothers were particularly obligated to see to their children's education.[106]

Despite these positive opinions about the importance of educating women so that they could in turn teach the next generation, various figures in the early modern period voiced reservations about formal schooling for girls, even young ones, in proximity to boys and men. In his book *Yosif ometz*, Juspe Hahn (d. 1637) voiced reservations, citing the medieval *Sefer Hasidim* on the subject of a young, unmarried man's educating girls, "even if their father stood there to chaperone," lest something untoward occur.[107] Jacob Emden objected strenuously to the social ease arising from women bringing their children (sons or daughters) to the place of the teacher, which could lead to improper socializing and worse. He railed against the practice of bringing young girls into the home or space of male teachers, "even bachelors," without paying heed. "Instead, they should be brought before an *ishah beki'ah* (experienced woman) or be taught in their parents' home but not among the boys, who accustom them to sin."[108] Emden's strident critique identified education of girls as a source of potential lapses in morality between adults and of potential sexual abuse of young children, both boys and girls. He pitted his own recommendations against the prevalent practice in his time. Reading his comments, we can deduce that many people in Hamburg-Altona where he lived were sending their young Jewish daughters to the homes of *melamdim* to be educated.

As a result of girls' uneven access to schooling during the early modern period and the sporadic mentions of girls' education, measuring girls' literacy is a fraught project. Girls also acquired literacy through alternative means, such as embroidery. They learned to embroider letters, numbers, and words on samplers, which became popular among Christian upper- and middle-class girls from the mid-seventeenth century onward.[109] The sampler taught young girls basic embroidery that could be used within the household or even for more elaborate creations, such as synagogue textiles and wimpels, the Torah binders dedicated at a boy's birth. But no less important were the reading and crafting of letters, which granted the girls literacy. As Susan Frye has shown, Christian girls in early modern England also sewed "Hebrew" samplers, which depicted biblical heroines from the Old Testament.[110] We have no way of knowing whether Jewish girls similarly sewed this type of sampler, which would have provided them with yet another avenue of access to biblical stories. As the popularity of such samplers grew, it is entirely possible that they did.

Although we can make few positive assumptions about the education of Jewish girls through the early modern period, we know one thing to be true:

FIG. 4.5. Sampler fashioned by a girl named Zirle. The top line is the aleph-bet. The second line reads: "The young girl Zirle, daughter of R. Berle, may God protect him." See plate 10.

levels of literacy and writing were growing throughout the period. From the beautiful samplers and wimpels with Hebrew lettering that women sewed to the contracts they wrote and signed, from their vibrant presence in the epistolary exchanges of the time, the lists they kept, and the many books addressed to them, we know that Jewish women were reading and writing. Across the class and cultural spectrum, from wealthy to average and even poor women and girls, familiarity with the vernacular Yiddish written word and with printed works aimed at them had a decisive impact on their daily lives.

In 1749, Isaac Wetzlar wrote a programmatic treatise urging a complete overhaul of the system of elementary education in the Ashkenazi realm. The changes he urged in his *Libes briv* extended to both young women and men, in Hebrew and Yiddish, in Jewish and secular subjects. His appeal built upon two sources: earlier internal Jewish calls for educational reform (mostly for young men), going back to the sixteenth-century Rabbi Judah Loewe of Prague,[111] as well as contemporary German pietist circles.[112] A manuscript copy of *Libes briv* from 1777 made for a woman of standing in her community shows that his plea for a more robust curriculum found readers in elite circles of Ashkenazi women.[113]

Access to Jewish Learning

Several broad circles of women had exceptional access to learning. We highlight them because of the proliferation factor: one woman's access often meant an extension to many others in the form of teaching or preaching to them, reading to them, writing for them, and sponsoring printed works for other women. Daughters of wealthy families, such as those of the northern Italian Ashkenazi elite, central European court Jews, and successful merchants everywhere, would be schooled in Jewish literature and lore, as well as in languages and possibly sciences beyond the Jewish curriculum. Several women pursued Jewish scribal arts. In 1603, Foigele bat Avraham Kalimani was the scribe of a memorial book, which she "wrote for the honor of God, and the honor of the holy community, the synagogue of the notables, the esteemed rabbi, Isaac Luzzato, and his grandson, the honorable Rabbi Nehemiah Luzzato."[114] Nehemiah Luzzato's wife, Roza, was one of the patronesses of Yaakov Heilprun's Yiddish translations, pointing to an Ashkenazi community in which a circle of women avidly read, commissioned, and patronized book publications and even served as scribes.

Similarly, Sara, daughter of David Oppenheim, a wealthy and influential member of a seventeenth-century court Jewish family also deeply committed to Jewish learning in the seventeenth century, wrote her own Esther scroll. Sara's Esther scroll prompted rabbinic discussion about whether a scroll that would be otherwise acceptable could be considered ritually kosher if written by a woman.[115] The rabbanit Hannah of Frankfurt (d. 1712), daughter and wife of a Torah scholar, was remembered for having "sat for twenty-two years in the bet midrash, and used her strength before upright students and scholars, reading and teaching them all of her days."[116]

Another set of women and girls who had access to certain levels of literacy were those involved in the printing trade.[117] Estellina Conat was the first woman to have her name as the "writer" of a Hebrew book. In the new print technology, terms for arranging the type did not yet exist; she typeset the book, supervising a young male assistant. Her husband, Abraham Conat, opened the first press to print Hebrew books in Italy. Abraham Habermann lists dozens of girls and women who worked in printshops, particularly as typesetters; their slender fingers made picking letters out of letterboxes easier. Widows of printshop owners often took over the enterprise upon the death of their husbands, a pattern common in the larger European print business. Women engaged in every aspect of book production and sale form another circle of Jewish women who attained some level of Jewish literacy.[118]

From the later decades of the eighteenth century, Jewish girls from wealthy families increasingly received tutoring or formal schooling in non-Jewish languages and learning outside the Jewish community, giving them a high degree of literacy beyond Hebrew or Yiddish. Some of these women combined their wealth and cultural capital to host famous salons that attracted a mingled crowd of Christians and Jews.[119] One Christian observer from Hamburg noted in 1798, "Private instruction is extremely expensive, and some fathers pay more for private tutors than all other household expenses combined. The wealthy Jew pays his tutor more than a prince does. The expense can rise to 800–1500 Mark."[120] The education that some of these women received is evident in their later writing. Rahel Levin Varnhagen's correspondence and her diary and Dorothea Mendelssohn's novel, *Florentin*, were respectively written at the end of the period we analyze, but they reflect the robust education these elite women received in their younger years, during the last decades of the eighteenth century. Esther Gad (ca. 1767–1833), granddaughter of Rabbi Jonathan Eybeschutz, wrote poems and treatises supporting women's intellectual activities and literary expression. She also publicly supported the Königliche Wilhelmsschule, a school for Jews in her native Breslau based on modern Enlightenment values, composing a poem on the occasion of its opening.[121] The

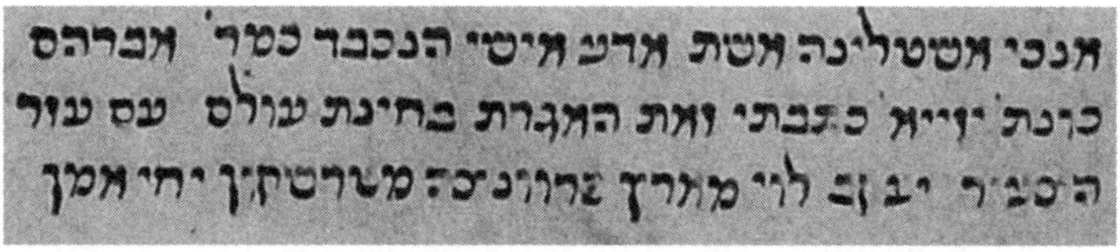

אנכי אסטלינה אשת אדני ויטי הנכבד כמר' אברהם
כ'נת יזייא ס'בבתי ואת המגרת בחינת עולם עם עזר
הב'ר' י'ב ן'ב לוי מארץ פרוונסה מטרטשקין יחי אמן

FIG. 4.6. Colophon by Estellina Conat, first Jewish woman who wrote her own colophon in a Hebrew printed book, Yedaia Penini's *Behinat Olam* [printed (between 1476 and 1480)]. "I, Estellina, wife of my lord, my husband, the respected R. Abraham Conat, have *written* this treatise *Behinat olam*, with the help of the young man Jacob Levi, from the land of Provence, from Tarrascon. May he live, Amen."

salonnières represent one direction in which elite Jewish women took their learning: for the most part, out of Judaism altogether.[122] Others, such as Madame Chaile Kaulla (see chapter 6), parlayed their training and acumen into strong economic entrepreneurship and support of Jewish communal institutions.

Another broad circle of learning among women could be found in rabbinic families. These families tended to have substantial Jewish libraries at their disposal, reverence for learning and the written word, and a presumption that girls who would become rabbis' wives would need to know various fields of Jewish law and lore in order to take respected places within the community. Dating back to medieval Europe, learning among women in rabbinic circles was taken for granted to some extent and praised by family members.[123]

In the sixteenth century, Rabbi Eliezer Eilburg wrote about his mother, within a family circle of sagacious elders, male and female: "In particular, my mother and teacher, garland on my head, was praised for all the intellectual qualities, in good deeds, as well as in Torah study. She offered her prayers early in the morning and late at night.... She excelled in matters of kabbalah, and for my sins, she perished on the way to Safed in the Holy Land."[124]

Rabbi Yair Hayim Bacharach (d. 1702) named his book of rabbinic responsa *Havot Yair* in memory of his grandmother Havah, herself the granddaughter of the Maharal of Prague. The entry for her in the memorial book of Worms noted both her learning and the many rabbis in her immediate family: her husband, father, grandfather, and two brothers were all renowned rabbinic scholars.[125] In his introduction, Bacharach extolled his grandmother's wisdom and knowledge, specifically referring to her as a learned reader and writer: "She had a *Midrash rabbah* without translation, and she studied it according to her capacity and intelligence.... She ... commented on mahzorim and selihot, as well as on Rashi's commentary to the Bible and the twenty-four [biblical books] as well as the *targumim* (Aramaic biblical homiletic paraphrases) and external books. Several times when the rabbinic titans of the generation struggled [with the meaning], she came and extended her quill and excelled in writing in the clearest language."[126] While it was not unusual for women raised in rabbinic households to have access to a greater range of books and an education that exceeded that of their peers, the scope of works mentioned by Bacharach indicates that his grandmother had access to and familiarity with a rich library of printed books. Moreover, Havah's reading brought her to comment and write, and her writing was consulted by others.

Rabbi Pinhas Katzenellenbogen's (1691–1767) memoir, *Yesh manhilin*, allows us entry into the mindset of the elite rabbinic circles of Ashkenazi Europe. His father had served as rabbi in several smaller southern German cities or villages, while he preferred the intellectual stimulation of the larger cities of Bohemia.[127] Katzenellenbogen's life trajectory is representative of the peripatetic lifestyle of an Ashkenazi rabbinic class that studied and occupied rabbinic positions across Ashkenazi communities in Europe. The rabbinic families married into one another, strengthening their scholarly and professional networks. Katzenellenbogen's extensive and meandering memoir allows us to glean something about the place of Jewish women in learned rabbinic culture. The two attributes Katzenellenbogen praised most highly in women were piety and learning. Young scholars sought and boasted about having learned women within their family circle. He referred to the women in his family with great affection and high honorifics: "The Lord put before me a second match, a tender dove, a pure and intelligent learned woman, a woman of valor, with fear of God and spiritually whole, that would be your mother, the modest and dear rabbanit, Marat Elik, may she live."[128] His memoir contains many episodes in which he recounts the participation of women in his circle in learned discussions.

Katzenellenbogen was not alone in seeing the women of his family as critical partners. Rabbi Judah Mehler (b. 1609) began the autobiographical introduction to his collection of sermons with "all that had happened to me from the day I became a person, namely, the day I took a wife, for he who has no wife is not called a full person."[129] Describing his wife as "whom my soul loved, the one that was lost to me, namely, the wife God had intended for me," he explained that after having met her in Hanau, "my soul lived, because he who is without a wife is as one without life."[130]

The centrality of the ba'alat bayit to the household in this period was not only captured by the written word but driven by it. Print culture created a cycle of reading and writing, ranging from elite rabbinic women, such as Havah Bacharach; women involved in print, such as Estellina Conat and the young girl Mosqita; scribes, such as Foigele Kalimani and Sara Oppenheim; and women of different strata who inscribed personal milestones or evidence of ownership in the books they cherished. The books printed for and owned by women and girls reveal the wide range of texts they consumed and the rich access they acquired to Jewish culture, learning, and ritual.

5
Ordinary and Literary Writing

> My beloved husband, great scholar, R. Ber, may the Lord guard him: I inform you of my health and that of our daughter, and I likewise hope that in all your 248 limbs, nothing is amiss. . . . I will not linger now, for I am tired of writing Hebrew for humble women like myself. . . .
>
> From your loving wife, Bella, daughter of Mar Jacob Peril Hefter of blessed memory of the holy community of Prague.[1]
> (November, 1674)

WHEN SHE wrote this letter, Bella Perlhefter (ca. 1650–1710) lived in Schnaittach, a village in southern Germany. Her prominent family had originated in Vienna; after the expulsion of its Jews in 1670, the family moved to Prague. As a reader and writer, Bella exemplifies the ever growing number of Jewish women who had the means and opportunity to dip their quills into their inkwells and write for themselves and others (see plate 11). The writings they left behind often survived by chance; many of them did not see the light of print in their author's lifetimes and some not until modern times. Reading inspired more Jewish women to write, if only for ordinary tasks. From business accounts to laundry lists, from recipes to tickets for attendance at a ritual bath, writing and reading went far beyond the covers of a book. The rich variety of women's writing across genres grants us access to otherwise obscure aspects of their lives, from daily chores and tasks to family relations, personal emotions, and religious reflections. It includes religious rituals, texts, and even consideration of the afterlife. This chapter begins by surveying women's ephemeral writing, including letters and the ordinary writing that accompanied

FIG. 5.1. Esther scroll depicting Esther as a contemporary woman at her writing table holding a quill. Prague, c. 1700.

them in their daily lives. We then turn to three exceptional women who adopted literary writing as a way to leave a permanent mark.

Bella wrote in an ornate and flowery Hebrew in her surviving letters; even those she wrote to her husband, Ber Eybeschutz Perlhefter, sound stilted and formal. She knew that they were not completely private, as her husband worked in the atelier of Christian Hebraist scholar Johann Christoph Wagenseil, a collector of epistolography, among other ephemeral Jewish writing. Knowing that her husband's employer and others in his circle might read her letters as examples of Jewish letter writing may have contributed to keeping her language far more literary than if she had dashed off a letter knowing it would be private. Bella alluded to her skill as a writerly stylist by referring to her "writing Hebrew for humble women like myself."[2] In fact, the women she wrote for would not have been like her, or they would not have needed her services. Bella's move from an urban to a rural setting bore a consequence that

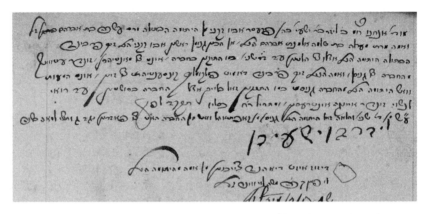

FIG. 5.2. An orphan's mother's signature, represented here by a circle: "This is the mark of her hand." *Pinkas hevrah kaddisha ma'asim tovim be-Amsterdam*, c. 1764.

she mentions incidentally. She assisted rural women, who had less mastery of the formal aspects of letter writing, in sending effective and well-written missives. This illustrates one of the arguments of this chapter: reading and writing had a ripple effect, extending far more broadly than the single individuals we trace. Literacy was contagious. Regardless of whether their learning occurred because they belonged to one advantaged circle or another, women shared their passion for the written word.

As a woman from an elite family in Vienna and Prague, Bella, a ba'alat bayit, would have had access to a higher level of instruction and exposure to reading and writing than did many Jewish women of her time. She held the advantage of belonging to the class of women whose Jewish literacy and writing abilities rose to the high levels. Bella noted that she held a position in the women's hevrah kaddisha (burial society) in Prague, for which reading and writing were essential.[3] Women born into well-to-do families, belonging to rabbinic families, and/or living in larger urban Jewish enclaves tended to have more access to formal and informal instruction in reading and writing than did other women. In the early modern period, even women who could not write their names were enveloped by the textual culture; their identity and status are documented through the marks they left in lieu of signatures. One pinkas of an Amsterdam benevolent society devoted to raising and dowering orphaned girls includes many signatures of widowed mothers who were paid for the expenses their daughters had incurred. If they could not write their names, they signed either with a circle or by copying letters that had been faintly outlined for them.[4] Women like these, who were deeply aware of and affected by written texts and records, would have benefited from Bella's skills and mastery.

Letters

One of the most important ways women's own words were preserved was through the letters they wrote. No written genre captures glimpses of daily life with the textured detail and minute observations as well as personal letters. Unlike treatises intending to share teachings and ideas, letters often addressed the most mundane and ephemeral aspects of life. Women and men of diverse classes, of course, wrote letters, and in many registers; they cover a vast range of human activities. Yiddish letters were often shared with a circle of family, friends, and neighbors hungry for news from afar. When Henele, daughter of Avraham ha-Levi Heller, wrote to her sister, Bona, and Bona's husband, Simon Wolf Auerbach, she addressed the letter also to three couples, all children of her sister.[5] The siblings were meant to share the letter once each had read it. This practice was so common that writers needed special strategies or secret codes to keep parts of letters away from prying eyes. In personal correspondence, we can follow the workings of family relationships on an ordinary basis: "Write to me how Tirzah gets along with her husband, as I heard that they are living badly together, and it makes me sad. I hope it's a lie."[6] Free from the tension of the courthouse, we see the way small business transactions were arranged, marriage bargains struck, and friendships cemented or betrayed. We see people anxious for political news: "Write me about some new things."[7] People hungered for news of their families, their communities, of markets and wares, births and deaths. Jews were highly mobile, and families were often separated for long periods of time. Personal letters were the glue that maintained close connections between husbands and wives, parents and children, kin and friends, although they may have lived far apart. In the early modern period, as literacy spread, letter writing became accessible to almost all layers of Jewish society. No more the province of the most learned or men of commerce, letters were written and received by women in significant numbers. Older letters served as models for copying.[8] Model letters that were copied and circulated helped shape a literary standard for letter writing; eventually, some of these collections were printed as letter-writing manuals in Hebrew, Yiddish, or other vernaculars. As time passed, women's letters became more elaborate, more literary, and more self-conscious. When Bella Perlhefter apologized for her "poor" writing in a linguistically ornate Hebrew letter, she testified to her sense that her letters were being judged for their literary qualities rather than based on their content alone.[9]

Privacy and Openness in Letters

Even if most people wrote their own letters, we cannot assume that most letters contained open and frank communication.[10] Some closed with a note of regret because they did not have enough time to write before the messenger was leaving: "I'll write more another time, for the woman who is standing here with me is hurrying to leave."[11] Not only did writers shape their letters literarily, but they also kept in mind that others might get hold of them. Despite the multiple warnings and imprecations against opening mail addressed to another, writers expressed unease at revealing certain things "in the field."[12] Messengers could prove unreliable, and during hostilities between rulers, packets of letters were frequently intercepted. Writers adopted many strategies to keep their private information from falling into the wrong hands. Schönchen bat Shlomo in Hamburg wrote to her husband in Copenhagen, "When you want to write something important to me, insert a *tsettelchen* (small slip) into my letter, that I can show my letter to everyone."[13] This indicates that Schönchen expected that she would show the letter her husband had written to a circle of relatives and acquaintances eager to read the latest news; asking him to slip a small private note within the regular letter was her strategy to keep their private communications between themselves. Leah bas Judah wanted to share additional things with her husband, but she did not feel comfortable "writing everything across the land."[14] Zekhariah (Mendel) ben Benjamin wrote to his sister, Bela, "Dear sister, know that I lost the key to our secret language, and I would like to have it back. Therefore ... send it with a known person, as one cannot write everything across the field, particularly in the circumstances that prevail in the region now; I'll write again, God willing, when I get the secret language."[15] In one letter, instead of referring to diamonds, the correspondents referred to onions.[16] Both their formulaic nature and the high chance of a letter's being read by someone other than the addressee contribute to making these sources slippery. That said, letters provide unparalleled access to aspects of women's lives we would not otherwise see.

Kosher Ponim

One striking example of the failed hope of keeping a letter secret comes in the form of a sixteenth-century Yiddish letter buried within a rabbinic responsum. A husband's discovery in his wife's locked letter box led us to what might be the oldest surviving Yiddish love letter. When the distraught husband suspected his wife of being unfaithful to him, he opened her private box and found there a trove of correspondence between the paramours. Unable to decide whether they constituted absolute proof of infidelity or simply the correspondence of would-be lovers who could never find the privacy to consummate their desire, the husband turned to the local rabbinic decisor, R. Isaac mi-See. His query includes excerpts from the correspondence he found in his wife's box as evidence for the rabbi:

> "Know this, that my entire happiness would be to be together with you, *kosher ponim* (pure face)...."[17] When I awoke... I nearly tore my hair out, that I did not merit to be with you then and had to take leave of you, with your snow-white hands...." Also in that letter, in these words: "I understood well that which you had written at your desk." In addition, he wrote in another letter, and these were his words: "Know my [manuscript torn] and joy that I began [to read] your letter, and my whole heart was [manuscript torn] overjoyed."[18]

While the rabbi did not find sufficient grounds for divorce (which would have been mandated by Jewish law if the woman's infidelity were proven), the poorly preserved manuscript of this rabbi's responsa preserves evidence of another kind: a young Jewish woman in sixteenth-century southern Germany wrote Yiddish letters that beguiled her suitor. Together with the text of the correspondence itself, letters like these allow us to reconstruct some of the material reality of women's letter writing. Even literate people would need separate instruction in writing; a letter-writing woman would have had to know at least the rudimentary forms of the genre, such as greeting, body, and closing formulas. Women needed a surface for writing, such as a table or desk; these often served to hold writing implements and boxes of various sizes. Some letter-writing manuals taught women how to position themselves properly at a desk to write comfortably.[19] The desk would typically contain paper of the right size and shape; sandpaper or a pot of sand for blotting; another pot for ink, purchased or made; and, possibly, a seal, sealing wax, and implements to melt the wax. The same goose that was slaughtered for food in the kitchen might be the source of feathers for quills, and most writers needed to know how to use a sharp knife to shape the nib.

The sixteenth-century woman wrote her love letters at a table or desk; clearly, she had the material and intellectual tools to do so, and she saved her lover's correspondence in a box of precious and private things that she thought secure. Small decorated boxes that sat on Jewish women's desks, containing jewels, keys, letters, and other treasured possessions, have survived from the sixteenth century from the very region where our lovers' correspondence originated.[20]

Special boxes were also made to be portable writing desks for literate women and men who wrote letters or kept records. Chröndel Schlössinger (d. 1732) of Vienna had a *Schreibkasten* (writing box) among her effects sealed for probate.[21] Judith Oppenheim's inventory had three *Schreibkästel* listed among her various effects. She also had one gilded *Dintenfassl* (inkwell) and one white one.[22] Many writing boxes had gendered features so that those carried or owned by women could also contain sewing implements and buttons alongside quills, nibs, assorted inks, seals, sealing wax, a melting spoon, and a travel burner for melting the wax.[23] Those for men might contain shaving equipment alongside the writing implements and in one example from the Jewish Museum, a carved box apparently created originally to hold correspondence also contained circumcision equipment.[24] Given the popularity of such boxes in the early modern period, as Laura Micciche has argued, it would be natural for people to assume that these boxes were personal spaces for guarding correspondence or other items that they hoped could remain private. This proved the undoing of the sixteenth-century would-be lovers in the aforementioned responsum of Isaac mi-See. The female partner kept letters from her suitor in her private box, a space she wrongly assumed would keep them hidden from prying eyes.

Letters as Windows on Emotions

Letters are one of few genres in which women expressed their emotions: grief and sorrow upon hearing of the loss of a loved one, anxiety and fear upon hearing of wars and natural disasters. Brayne, daughter of Samuel Fürst, living in Hamburg, wrote to her husband, Meyer Segal, in Copenhagen, "Here at home, we are very alarmed; today we were told that all of Copenhagen, God forbid, has burned down. In my grief, I cannot write."[25] Leah bas Judah in Hamburg or Altona, writing to her husband Abraham in Copenhagen (1678), expressed the rage and bitterness of her close friend: "Sarah has asked me to write you to find out why the fool [her husband] does not write ... she is very anxious, and the stupid man causes her much grief. If he does not know how to treat a woman, he should not have married one."[26]

A set of letters from Reichla, daughter of Judah Leyb of Lissa, a widowed mother living in Amsterdam, shows another side of letter writing: women could manipulate emotions in letters as the circumstances demanded. In some letters, Reichla expressed her frustration and bitterness that life dealt her a harsh hand. She sent some books to a trusted associate, R. Aaron, a scribe and learned man in London. He received the books but failed to send her the money. Now, she wrote, she was in dire need of it, as she had been unable to earn anything through the entire winter. The tone of her letter was resentful and plaintive. She complained that she was old and destitute and had been forced to nurse sick people at night. Nobody seemed to care for her anymore, not even her children in London. They did not write at all, and there was nobody to help her out in these difficult days. For these reasons, Reichla strongly appealed to R. Aaron to remember her old age and widowhood and to send her immediately the money she so desperately required. The letter ended with the usual greetings to R. Aaron's wife and their children.

But in another letter to the same correspondent, Reichla adopted a different tone entirely. Here she acted as mother and agent for her unmarried son, and the wheedling tone of her previous letter turned to one of exasperation with R. Aaron's handling of the matter: "I am really angry at you, that you write to me that I [prospective groom's mother] should give more than he [prospective bride's father]."[27] Reichla reacted indignantly to the suggestion that she provide a higher sum (fifty pounds sterling) toward the match than the bride's family (forty pounds). She said she would agree to the match for her son only if the other party would commit to one hundred pounds. After all, her son was not without means and was quite capable of earning a proper living; he had no reason to be ashamed of his family, either. In Amsterdam, he could easily get a dowry of five hundred guilders, but, as he was already in London, let him marry there and save the cost of coming home. Ultimately, she leaves the decision with her son, Mendle. "Let him do what he likes. He knows the girl, and she knows him."[28]

Above all, letters exuded love and longing for close family living great distances apart. Meyer ben Moshe in Copenhagen wrote to his wife, Brayne, in Hamburg, "After you have happily given birth, write to me all the details."[29] The latter, in particular—a sense that a spouse abroad meant a daily dose of anxiety for the safety and health of a life partner—can be found in many letters. Women expressed the added resentment of the burden of running a household and business and educating and rearing children mostly on their own. As Bella Perlhefter wrote from Schnaittach to her husband Ber in Altdorf, "Know that your beautiful daughter, may she live—you would not recognize her if you saw her."[30]

Private letters from the early modern period have been preserved in various ways. In some cases, they were confiscated during military hostilities or from messengers taken captive and ended up in a government archive without having reached their destination. The Prague, Copenhagen, and London letter collections appear to have been saved that way. Christian Hebraists of the early modern period began to collect Jewish letters for scholarly and pedagogical purposes. Johannes Buxtorf printed one hundred model letters in his *Institutio epistolaris hebraica* (1610).[31] As the title advertised, all the letters were in Hebrew—not even one in Yiddish—and not one was written by or addressed to a woman. Olav Gerhard Tychsen, Hebraist and Orientalist, collected hundreds of Jewish, mostly Yiddish, letters, now in Rostock.[32] Johann Wagenseil in Altdorf, by contrast, collected many types of letters, Hebrew and Yiddish, written by Christians, Jews, and converts, among them women and men of various stations. Wagenseil was interested in Jewish epistolarity, and he collected but never printed a rich variety of Jewish letters, including those of the Perlhefters.[33] The curated collections of the scholars differed in purpose and tone from the random collections of intercepted letters. In the aggregate, these sources of Jewish women's letters provide glimpses into the daily lives of ordinary women that are unmatched in any other source. Yiddish collections of letters have attracted the attention of scholars for some time for the light they shed on Jewish business and kinship networks. They have yet to be appreciated fully for the ways in which they can enlarge our knowledge of Jewish women's lives. Even the highly literate exchange between Bella Perhlhefter and Wagenseil includes snippets of the daily sale of household commodities:

> Therefore, I have come instead of my husband to inquire after his [Wagenseil's] welfare and the well-being of all the members of his household, and to inform him that here in this village, there is a farmer who has good wheat, that is, one sheaf for eight-and-a-half gold coins. Therefore, if my lord wishes to purchase wheat, please inform us through the villager who brings you my letter, and then we will send the local farmer with his wheat to the house of my lord, and you can purchase according to your desire. Yesterday,

I sent you veal, tender and good, weighing 15 1/2 liter; in German, 15 1/2 pounds, at one half-liter for three Kreuzer, and, indeed, yesterday I received the payment for the above-mentioned veal.[34]

Letters in Matchmaking and Courtship

The expense and difficulty of travel turned letter writing into one of the important channels of communication for matchmakers and prospective parents; after a betrothal, it allowed the bride and groom to express their mutual affection and plan their future. As marriage was the central institution in Jewish family life, the role of letters in conveying the virtues of a prospective bride and groom cannot be overstated. While matchmakers described prospective rabbinic grooms in terms of their scholarly prowess and future mercantile grooms in terms of their commercial prospects, matchmaking letter writers more often described brides (beyond their all-important dowries) based on their personal virtues and qualities.

Rabbi Judah Leyb of Lissa, then residing in London, attempted to encourage a match for an orphaned (but wealthy) woman from his community to Moshe ben Feivish, who resided in Dublin. He wrote to the matchmaker, R. Aaron the scribe: "The young woman Henna showed me a letter in your own hand, [saying] that you are a good friend, and you advised her to get engaged to R. Moshe ben Feivish.... She opined to me that she will rely on you because she is certain that you would not mislead an orphan despite the trickery of matchmaking. Therefore, do your best to bring the match to completion."[35] The amount of her dowry followed, along with the logistical details: Henna was willing to send security if the prospective groom was willing to come in person; he described how to complete the match if the groom could not come. Since the groom was in Dublin, she also needed to know before sealing the deal whether Moshe wanted to live there or come to her in London. Rabbi Judah Leyb's description of the prospective bride emphasized not only her wealth but her good name, her wisdom, and her knowledge: "For she has a good name in the congregation as extremely rich, full of wisdom and knowledge. No one in the whole congregation has spoken other than good of her all the time since she has been here."[36] The rabbi mentions another interesting point: he wrote the letter at the request and upon the initiative of the woman. The letter closes with the writer sending regards to R. Aaron (the matchmaker in Dublin) and to his wife and family from the woman, Henna. The letter was apparently written over time because, as a postscript, she asked that the prospective groom nevertheless come to London, where she was, so that they could see one another, to make the *kenas[mahl]* (meal to celebrate the betrothal) right there and get married two weeks later. She promised to provide additional things beyond the monetary dowry.

In another Yiddish letter from the early eighteenth century, Judah ben Menachem of Rotterdam requested R. Aaron's (in London) cooperation in a match between his stepdaughter, the virgin Hendle, and Isaac, son of the widow Sarah, wife of the late R. Itsik. He spoke in high terms of his stepdaughter, Hendle, who was a brave maiden, conspicuous for her good deeds and "particularly for her beauty, of which I have not seen the like in the whole of our congregation, and also well learned." He asked R. Aaron to take up the matter with the other party and to write to him fully "by the first post."[37] Both of these letters of proposal demonstrate that the parties esteemed learning as a valuable quality in the prospective bride.

Once a match was agreed upon, epistolary exchanges were a primary means for the new couple to discuss their future and express their emotions for one another. The Wagenseil collection contains examples of such letters, predicated on an understanding that the couple would be exchanging letters during the entire period of engagement.[38] They discuss their living arrangements and the gifts they will exchange: "Please prepare yourself to make a feast and merriment for my father and the [five] young men I will bring with me, and I will pay half the [costs of] the meal, as it is customary among Jews to arrange the wedding [costs] between both parties, and for the musicians and all the people needed to serve, I will pay from my pocket.... Regarding the place of settlement, I've already written several times that I will only live here in the place where I know the military and can trade and do business with them."[39] This very small sample represents two notable aspects of Yiddish letters: Women were just as likely as men to be the writers, and they did not hesitate to assert their voices when warranted in the conduct of family affairs.

Ordinary and Ephemeral Writing

Women did not only write across space to communicate with others; they integrated writing throughout the course of their daily lives. Women who managed complex households learned to keep numerous accounts and balance a budget. Household books contained steady reminders of tasks to be completed on schedule: household help had to be hired and paid at regular intervals, careful accounts of the purchases of food and dry goods kept, and

PLATE 1. The stages in women's and men's lives, from cradle (on left) to grave (on right). Woman visiting grave, bottom left, holds a prayer book. *Selihot*, Gravediggers Society, Frankfurt, 1740.

PLATE 2. The *ba'alat bayit* lights Shabbat or holiday candles in her home. *Seder birkat ha-mazon*, Nikolsburg, 1728.

PLATE 3. Women stand at the doorway to the men's section of the synagogue for a circumcision, Prague. *Dine u-tefillot ha-shayakhim le-brit milah*, 1728.

PLATE 4. Embroidered circumcision pillow, 1614. The Hebrew inscription mentions Jacob, son of Simon Ulmo, and his wife Breinle of the Ulmo-Günzburg family. Note the image at bottom center featuring a *sandeket/ba'alat brit* (godmother), as well as figures playing a board game.

PLATE 5. Midwife and her assistants. Harrison Miscellany, Corfu, c. 1720.

PLATE 6. Men and women preparing burial shrouds, burial society Prague, late eighteenth century.

PLATE 7. Burial society plaque, Florence, 1776, depicting the purification of the deceased.

PLATE 8. Judith with Holofernes' head and bloody body. *Seder birkat ha-mazon*, 1736.

PLATE 9. Woman participates in the Passover seder with book in hand. *Siddur minhag* Ashkenaz, fifteenth century. A later ownership inscription, 1551, indicates purchase from the dowry of the widow of R. Eliyah Halfan, Venice.

PLATE 10. Detail, sampler fashioned by a girl named Zirle. The top line is the aleph-bet. The second line reads: "The young girl Zirle, daughter of R. Berle, may God protect him."

PLATE 11. Esther and Mordekhai at a writing table. Each holds a quill and book. Esther scroll, eighteenth century.

PLATE 12. Jewish woman and her maidservant preparing the hallah. *Seder birkat ha-mazon*, 1746–47.

PLATE 13. Newly bereaved woman. *Seder birkat ha-mazon*. Nikolsburg, 1728.

the myriad personal expenses of family members and dependents all had to be balanced against available funds.[40] While no Jewish "house book" on a grand scale survives from the early modern period (so far as we know), even poor women had debts to repay and kept notes of all types to keep track of obligations. These writings were always intended to be ephemeral, yet several types of written lists survive that indicate reliance on writing for some of women's mundane chores. One category is lists or books of laundry, often used to keep track of items that were given out to wash.[41] From the northern Italian Yiddish-speaking cultural realm, two sets of writing about laundry have survived. One lists laundry items (in eight different lists) on the blank folios that precede the opening pages of a minhagim (customs) and prayer miscellany. The manuscript itself was written in the mid-sixteenth century by a scribe. Although no owner's name is present, the inclusion of various instructions for women at the end of the manuscript, the instructions given throughout, and the laundry lists all indicate that it was written for and owned by a woman.[42] The manuscript was meant to guide a woman through the Jewish calendar year, and it included general knowledge about the Hebrew calendar cycle, supplementary text and instructions for prayer services, and some tales, almost all about religious figures. The fact that the owner used the blank pages for a completely mundane household management task, keeping track of items she gave to be washed, tells us about the relationship between women's reading and writing and the folly of trying to untangle the different genres and planes on which these occurred.

A completely different type of laundry management tool can be found in another mid-sixteenth-century Yiddish manuscript. A proper laundry book, it opens with two folios of instructions for washing laundry.[43] While it contains a direct address to women readers—"Come close, women, so that I can tell you"—it was commissioned by a man named Shaye Kviler. It contains rhymed instructions by one Shvarts Kalman on how to prepare and treat the laundry: "*Ver do vil makhen ein gute vesh, der muz achten dos er hot gute esh*—Whoever wants to do a good wash, must be sure to have good ash [one of the ingredients in soap making]."[44] He exhorts women to use lots of water and the best soap; cleanliness will bring the messiah! The outstanding feature of this manuscript is its technical device: each folio is marked for one item of linen or clothing, and each contains an elaborate volvelle with numbers; at the center, a parchment hand tied onto the page can be spun to the number of items desired each time. The Jewish art historian Mordechai Narkiss has already pointed out the similarities between the device on a niello casket from the fifteenth century, made

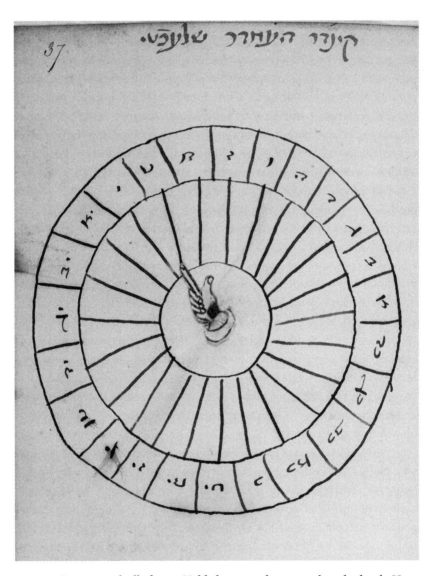

FIG. 5.3. Rotating volvelle from a Yiddish sixteenth-century laundry book, *Ver do vil makhn ayn gute vesh*. The header on this folio reads: "*kinder hemder shlechte* (bad/used children's shirts)."

for an Italian Jewish woman, and the devices found in this manuscript.[45] The editors of *Yiddish in Italia* presume that the author of the manuscript may have commissioned the scribe to make multiple copies of this model, as he addressed women in general rather than one specific woman. Yet another Yiddish book devoted to the management of laundry has survived from the late eighteenth or early nineteenth century. This *vesh bikhel* (small Yiddish alphabetized laundry book) was made as a gift for a Jewish woman, Netti Winter of Tešetice, Moravia. Each page names a different laundry item, with a numbered grid for easy marking. Thus, for example, "underpants, underfrock, white underfrock, bedcover, seat cover, *tzitzit* and women's (and men's) shirts" each formed page headings for the letter *aleph* in the booklet.[46] Laundry lists can seem like the very best example of ephemeral writing, destined to be used and discarded, of absolutely no value to anyone beyond the user and her immediate household needs. They perfectly exemplify the way in which textualization penetrated the most mundane aspects of women's lives.

Another type of list or booklet that drew women into reading and writing amid household life was the recipe book, intended to teach and collect methods of medical remedies, cosmetics, and food preparation. Such books have been compiled in many cultures since antiquity. By the early modern period, models of cooking compendia were available in manuscript form and, from the early age of print, in printed form, throughout Europe.[47] A compendium "library in one volume," owned (at one point) by Tserle bat Gelche, exemplifies the type of collection of nonnarrative written material that women as well as men valued. The volume includes all types of medical remedies, including for headaches, toothaches, and obstetrical conditions. It contains cosmetic recipes "to make old skin look fresh and new," a recipe for "good shoe polish that shines and does not stain," fabric dyes for many colors, and recipes for food and alcoholic drinks.[48]

Jewish cookbooks were distinguished not only by their being written in a Jewish script and language but also for their attention to the requirements of kosher cooking. Some cookbooks marked each recipe as dairy (*halav*), meat (*basar*), or neither (*kosher*): "A list of foods in this book of the type prepared neither with butter nor with schmaltz (animal fat) are *kosher*."[49] Each also was labeled by the method of preparation: cooking or baking. Entire categories of foods, such as shellfish and pork products, inherently unkosher, were, of course, absent from Jewish collections. A later manuscript Jewish cookbook from Prague lists 111 recipes in Yiddish in its table of contents; some recipes highlight that a strudel or dish was dairy, showing the intricacies of running a

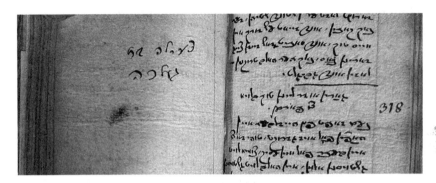

FIG. 5.4. Signature of Tserle bat Gelkhe, *Sefer segulot u-refu'ot*.

kosher home.[50] Whether they were preparing dairy meals for the Shavuot festival, or foods without even a trace of leavened goods for Passover, women and their piety were ever-present in the family kitchen.

Women baked hallot, special bread for Shabbat and holidays, and they prepared an array of traditional dishes for various holidays. As literacy grew, so did shopping lists, inventories of kitchen supplies, and written recipes to remind women how to prepare various foods. Over the course of the early modern period, various aspects of the household grew more specialized, and the written forms for these tasks expanded as well. Women learned some skills by mimesis, but greater access to writing and literacy expanded the range of dishes that they could prepare and share. Christian women's cookbooks were compiled and even printed from the sixteenth century.[51]

Life cycle events also required preparing special foods. Reyzel, daughter of Hanokh Hammershlag of Prague, wrote a letter to her brother Aaron, sharing that, "Mother also wanted to write to you; she just made a *reschige* [a large cake baked in honor of a circumcision]."[52] The mother had been selected to serve as *gevatterin* (godmother) and was, therefore, expected to bake an elaborate cake to mark the honor granted to her.

The traces of women's writing for ephemeral household matters underscore the argument we make about the textualization of many details of daily life. Women made lists of ordinary chores, of recipes, and remedies; officials took inventories and wills. Professional women recorded their transactions, whether in commerce, midwifery and medicine, or sorority-related expenses and resolutions.[53] Women embroidered pillows and wimpels for special occasions, and girls sewed samplers that proclaimed their identities, written in needle and thread rather than a stylus.

Often, the evidence for women's writing is circumstantial—during a transaction not intended to highlight the role of a woman's writing, that fact will nevertheless become visible. In a sixteenth-century responsum, Rabbi Judah Mehler ruled on the proper spelling of a woman's name on a *get* (bill of divorce)—a document that famously must be precise in every minute detail—that the way a woman signed her name determined how it must appear on the *get*. Even if the rabbinic decisors generally ruled that a Yiddish name should be written with the plene spelling that corresponded more closely to how the name was pronounced, in the case of Gelkhin bat Shmuel, "I arranged the *get* and it is written Gelkh'n and not Gelkhin with a *yud*. Although according to the decisors one should write with a *yud*, the woman signed herself, and as she wrote to me her signature Gelkh'n without *yud*, one goes according to her signature."[54]

We think of these surviving writings as tips of an iceberg whose true dimensions we might never know. We try not to make the argument *ex silencio*; on the contrary, we build on the surviving works and evidence that we have. Of all the women who wrote, three stand out as exceptional authors of full-length works: Rivkah Tiktiner of Prague (d. 1605), Glikl bas Judah Leyb (of Hameln, d. 1724), and her near-contemporary, Bella Perlhefter of Vienna/Prague/Schnaittach (d. 1710). For every Glikl bas Judah Leyb there may have been other memoirists; for every Rivkah Tiktiner, other writers of ethical works for women; for every Bella Perlhefter, other women who wrote literary letters and anthologies. We explore their writings below, focusing on two themes: the unique female perspective in their work and their desire, common also to male authors of their time, to leave a permanent mark through their literary contribution.

Rivkah Tiktiner

Rivkah bat Meir Tiktiner of Prague wrote a stand-alone Yiddish book of morals, *Meneket Rivkah*.[55] Such literature abounded in the sixteenth and seventeenth centuries in the vernacular; Rivkah's is the first known work in the genre by a woman. While it was not printed in her lifetime, it is important to note that the man who brought it to print addressed women directly and saw it as a book exclusively addressing women's piety. The printer's evaluation, that a significant market of women readers existed, is no less significant than the fact of a female Jewish writer. His introduction, in rhymed lines, was common in many Yiddish books, but unlike them, it contained no appeal "to men who were like women": "Listen, dear, esteemed, pious women. Take a look at this Yiddish book, and read it so that one shall place one's trust in G-d . . . and in all one's deeds rely on him."⁵⁶ He assumed that the readers "have known the respected woman who conceived and wrote this book, the *rabbanit* [here: learned woman] and darshanit Mrs. Rivkah of blessed memory."⁵⁷ Despite the fact that she had passed away five years earlier, he expected that many women had heard of Rivkah and that sufficient numbers of them would want to buy her book. He did not credit himself, moreover, with taking her notes and shaping them into a book. She apparently left a manuscript ready to be printed. He remarked on the pioneering nature of this undertaking: "Who has ever heard or seen such a novelty; has it ever happened in countless years, that a woman has written something of her own accord? She has read numerous verses and midrashim.... It shows that a woman can also compose words of ethical instruction and good biblical interpretation as well as many men.... She was brief and did not lengthen her words."⁵⁸ Tiktiner's writing illuminates several aspects of the relationship between women and literacy. Perhaps the most important is the distinctive woman's perspective and voice within her writing. From the title she chose, *Meneket Rivkah*, meaning "Rebecca's Nursemaid," to her perspective throughout the book, her writing reflects a woman's point of view.⁵⁹

In some respects, Tiktiner's book of morals, *Meneket Rivkah*, reads like a standard work addressed to women, emphasizing the importance of domestic duties and child-rearing and their religious significance for women. Claiming, for example, that a woman could earn heavenly merit by cooking meals for a scholar, she highlighted the proper roles delineated for women and the value of such domestic devotion. These handbooks, like some of the moral teachings contained in the *Brantshpigel* and *Lev tov*, prescribed behavior for women and sought to direct their religious observance.⁶⁰ Similar handbooks were composed by Catholics and Protestants to teach the running of a pious and holy household.⁶¹ Yet, similar to the tkhines composed by women, Tiktiner's lessons revealed her own sensibility as a woman. Von Rohden notes that virtually every Yiddish morality book blamed Eve for bringing mortality onto humankind and put the onus of repentance and punishment on all (Jewish) women. This makes Rivkah Tiktiner all the more conspicuous for refusing to see women in those terms. Rather than seeing the burden and pains of women, such as in childbearing, as punitive, she saw them as paths to righteousness.⁶² Similarly, von Rohden notes, in discussing creation, Tiktiner asks: "Why did He use the language of *binyan*, which means 'to build,' in reference to the woman, and in reference to the man, He uses the word *va-yitzer*, which means, in Yiddish, 'He created'? It seems to me that the essence of building lies with the woman."⁶³ Von Rohden argues that Rivkah championed women's responsibility for their own actions and strongly advocated that they read for themselves works of *mussar* (ethics) in Yiddish to become knowledgeable. This positive stance toward moral literature aimed at women "is completely unusual in moral literature of the sixteenth century."[64]

In addition to her book on morality for women, Rivkah Tiktiner authored a *Simhas toyre lid* (song for the celebration of the completion of the Torah cycle) that was printed at least three times.[65] Its refrain is a simple "Halleluyah," while the stanzas form rhymed couplets in Yiddish. The first stanzas complete a Hebrew alphabetical acrostic; the remainder of the song spells out Rivkah's name, "Rivkah daughter of our Rabbi Meir of blessed memory," in the Hebrew acrostic scheme.[66] Through this convention, Rivkah linked the song to her own authorship, much as Bella Perlhefter was to do in the introduction to her book *Be'er sheva*, discussed below. Rivkah's song touched on redemptive prophetic tropes, such as the eternal reign of the one God and the ultimate redemption of Israel. Her *lid* included women "pregnant and in childbed," as well as virgins. While Rivkah herself referenced the book of Isaiah, her song alludes to verses in Jeremiah 31, as the chapter contains well-known references to the matriarch Rachel, who would be consoled for her children's travails.[67] So far, the evidence regarding Rivkah's maternal status is conflicting. On the one hand, the memorial entry for her in the Altneushul memorial book mentions only her husband as sponsor of the entry; most entries contained names of children if they survived the parent. On the other hand, Rivkah mentioned the wish to see offspring follow the path of good deeds.[68] Without further evidence, it is difficult to know for sure whether Rivkah had children or whether they survived her. Regardless, Rivkah was a trailblazing figure who found a way into the hearts of Jewish women of her day through her preaching and teaching. Her book allows a glimpse of the novel path she forged as the writer of a moral handbook by and for women.

Glikl bas Judah Leyb

Glikl bas Judah Leyb (of Hameln, 1646–1724) remains one of the best-known premodern Jewish women writers. Her account of her life survived within her family in two manuscript copies. Glikl wrote to fill an absence in her life, that of her husband and life partner, Hayim Goldschmidt (Hamel), who died suddenly in the prime of his life. Glikl wrote a work of intentional literary ambitions, with chapters laid out in advance and myriad references to literature she had absorbed from reading Jewish and non-Jewish sources. She peppered her memoir with biblical, rabbinic, and narrative allusions to a host of other sources. Glikl interwove in her account the whole range of Yiddish literature, from classics such as the *Tsene u-rene* to lesser-known story collections translated directly into Yiddish from the German vernacular. Yet, utilizing these sources to create an account of a Jewish woman's life had no precedent, and Glikl herself had no vocabulary for the genre she created, calling it "*dos vos ikh shreyb* (that which I'm writing)."[69] Glikl addressed her writing to her family circle. It is, on one level, a justification, to her children of her and her husband's efforts to grow and preserve the family's good reputation and financial well-being, though she ended her life in relative poverty. The title page of the full copy that survives attests that her son, Moses Hamel, copied this manuscript "letter for letter" from Glikl's original.[70] Beyond the family, Glikl was well aware that inspirational women's writing was often circulated and copied, even if it was not printed. While praising the capability and piety of Pessele, wife of Model Dayyan, Glikl wrote, "It was astonishing to read her will. . . . Anyone wishing to read her will can still find it at her children's; surely they never threw it away."[71] Thus, Glikl inadvertently tells us that she read the last will and testament of another woman in her community (Hamburg), that it was remarkable, and that the family members preserved it to read for themselves and circulate to others. A later appreciative reader of Glikl's memoir penned in the flyleaf: "This is a book for every person //—whoever can read it // should sit over it day and night."[72] In the entire premodern period, there are many "ego-documents" by Jewish women—personal letters, wills, ethical treatises—but no other entire life story by a Jewish woman remains. This does not mean that Glikl was the only writer of such a work (there are several by Jewish men from this period), only that hers was the only one fortunate enough to survive.

Many scholars have sought to extrapolate specifics about women's lives from her diary.[73] Glikl's memoir reflected her woman's perspective on every page. Perhaps no passage displays this more powerfully than her recollection of the arrival of Sabbatai Tzvi, who claimed to be the messiah, at the synagogue in Hamburg. Glikl opened her recollection of those events in Hamburg with the birth of her daughter:

> In the meantime, I gave birth to my daughter Matte. She was a beautiful child, as shall be recounted presently. At that time people were starting to talk about Sabbatai Tzvi. . . .[74]

Glikl's account of the events of the messianic movement in Hamburg is the only female testimony to it:

I recall how young and old alike all over the world began repenting of their sins . . . it cannot be described. . . . Lord of the universe, we were hoping that you, compassionate God, would have mercy on Israel, your wretched people, and redeem us. We hoped for this . . . as a woman on the birthstool, in great labor and anguish, expects that after all her pain and suffering, she will rejoice in her child. But after all her pain and suffering, nothing came but wind.[75]

Glikl ended the chapter by recounting the sorrowful death of Matte at a tender age.[76] In Glikl's female perspective, the "birthpangs of the messiah," a common rabbinic locution, signified the relationship between the anguish of a mother who loses a beautiful child and the disappointment of a people who lose their dream of redemption. Her perspective is unique in all the literature about the movement of Sabbatai Tzvi.

Bella Perlhefter

While Glikl is the best-known female Ashkenazi Jewish writer of the early modern period on account of her rich and extraordinary memoir, Bella Perlhefter has been unjustly neglected as a writer who ranged over several genres. Bella's skills as a wordsmith survive her in other genres beyond the few letters that Wagenseil preserved. She conceived, wrote the introduction to, and likely coauthored the first encyclopedic work on Jewish thought in Yiddish: on Jewish history and destiny, interspersed with doses of midrash, mysticism, and moralism. She titled the work *Be'er sheva* (*Seven Wells*); each of the seven chapters was named for one of her children who did not live to adulthood. This remarkable work did not reach print until modern times, despite its author's intentions, as at least one of the manuscripts was prepared for print. Despite its great length, several manuscript copies have survived, and there is evidence of more lost copies.[77]

The detailed acrostic poem that Bella included in the opening of the volume assertively argued for her authorial voice within the whole volume, not only in the introduction, which was manifestly hers. While it is impossible to reconstruct exactly which passages in the work are the products of her pen—and many of them bear the marks of her husband, Ber—various passages indicate that she had a strong role in selecting and preparing some of the material for inclusion. She referred to the book as "*unzers bukh* (*our* book)" numerous times in the introduction.[78] In this introduction, Bella made it clear that she

FIG. 5.5. Bella and Ber Perlhefter prepared this manuscript, *Be'er sheva*, for printing.

considered herself a serious and professional writer. She compared writers to visual artists whose work is disparaged by those who cannot begin to approach their level. "An esteemed book writer, if they appear to have written the most artful book—often, a boastful person, a self-important person, or an enemy comes along and belittles it—even though they have no idea how to write even one page, let alone understand the books.... Therefore, no writer should take the mockers to heart; they should go ahead and write for the sake of heaven."[79] As a woman with serious aspirations to writerly success, Bella surely faced her share of scorn, but she resolved to rise above the doubters.

Bella chose to inscribe her name in the introduction to the book in the form of a *lid* which she composed: "Just as they [Moses and King Solomon] wrote a song of praise upon completing their books ... we too prepared a divine song in honor of God and in honor of our godly book. Within the song, the entire core meaning of the book can be perceived. The opening of each stanza of the song is a letter of [my] name, *Bella bat ha-katzin rabi Yaakov Perlhefter.*"[80] Bella recommended that the song be sung to the tune of the "Pragerish-Shvedishe" *lid*, presumably one her contemporaries knew well. This detailed opening poem contains a distillation of the contents of the entire encyclopedic work. In this way, Bella inscribed her name and ownership over the entire book, showing her deep familiarity with all its contents from the very outset of the work. This raises the question of the working relationship between Bella and Ber over the course of their writing and reworking of the monumental compendium *Be'er sheva*; for a portion of the time, she was in Schnaittach and Prague while he was in Altdorf.

Nathanael Riemer has identified three separate recensions of the manuscript, some with significant differences, and has reconstructed the order in which they likely were composed. The last version survives incomplete; it bears the signs of preparation for imminent print.[81] Several things are clear from the text: Bella alone, in her own first-person voice, wrote the acrostic and the introduction to the book. Bella was the animating force behind the composition of this monumental encyclopedic work that bears the stamp of Ber's kabbalistic interests and his midrashic and rabbinic scholarship. A complete accounting of all the book's literary sources has yet to be undertaken.[82] It is difficult to say with certainty that any particular rabbinic, midrashic, or kabbalistic passage reflects a woman's sensibility, but it is equally difficult to argue that some passages would not appeal to the experiences of Jewish women. One such passage based on the Zohar (pericope *Shelah*) is an extensive discussion about Jewish women's chambers in the world to come. The framing of the passage depicts Rabbi Shimon bar Yohai (a central figure long considered the principal author of the Zohar) as providing souls who appeared to him the answers to several questions. The first question is, "What type of chambers do women have in Paradise? Since they do not study Torah, I am doubtful whether they will have chambers as good as the men."[83] After considerable back and forth about whether these divine secrets can be revealed, permission was granted:

> There are six chambers for women, and they are joyous and wide and broad. Inside the first chamber there is a multitude of women[84] who atoned for their sins in this world, who never saw *gehenom* (hell).[85] The woman Serah bat Asher presides over them. Three times a day, a voice from heaven rings out, "Prepare to honor the soul of Joseph the Righteous [son of the biblical Jacob], which is about to appear." As soon as Serah hears this, she goes forth with her women [to greet him] up until the curtain of their chamber, and she moves with her women toward him, and she says: "Blessed is the day that I arrived and brought my grandfather Jacob the message that Joseph is still alive in Egypt. Then my grandfather Jacob said to me, 'You should also live, as he is living.' Thus, I came to *Gan Eden* (paradise) alive and merited to have such honor." After this, she goes back with her women and closes their curtain and begins, with her women, to sing praises before God.[86]

The passage continues similarly to describe additional chambers headed by other female biblical figures, including the matriarchs; Bitya, daughter of Pharaoh; and Yokheved, mother of Moses. Hundreds and thousands of Jewish women's souls congregated in each chamber. These unblemished souls had completed their suffering on earth and gone straight to their heavenly reward. The descriptions of their spiritual joys are remarkable for two reasons: first, they are directly parallel to the descriptions of the men's chambers in the world to come,[87] and second, the description of a space where women congregated and could proceed only up to the curtain dividing them from the next sacred space would have been familiar to Bella's contemporaries. It described the experience of many Jewish women in their section of the synagogue.

One of the manuscript versions of *Be'er sheva* describes the women who entered Gan Eden directly, without suffering gehenom. These women suffered in this world and nevertheless remained pious. Their direct road to heaven was ensured because of the losses they had already endured. Bella includes in this category women who had lost the children they had borne. Another category of women who attained Gan Eden were those who had not suffered but who consoled mourners and prayed with devotion.[88] The theme of bereaved mothers and their merit in the world to come unmistakably bears on Bella's personal experience.

The second question posed by the souls to Rabbi Shimon bar Yohai was about the nature of an echo: when a person cried out or pounded, a voice responded to it; what was its source? This answer would have resonated with Bella and with women more broadly as well: "Know that there are three *kolot* (sounds) that will not be lost in the world. The first sound is when a person dies, and the soul takes leave of the body, the person gives a cry or a sigh. This sound sweeps across the world from one end to the other end and cannot find a place to settle in the heavens, as they let through only the sound of prayer and Torah study; therefore, the sound conceals itself in a crevice of a rock or in an arch." Bella, a member of the hevrah kaddisha, was deeply familiar with the sounds of death and undoubtedly shaped the text.

"The other sound is that of a woman in childbirth: when she has the child, she gives a pitiful cry that also sweeps the world from one end to the other. It, too, remains in the crevices of a rock or in an archway."[89] While the source of this reply may be rabbinic or kabbalistic, the experiences it describes, as well as the desire that no such excruciating pain be allowed to vanish without leaving any impression, can be closely identified with Bella's experiences and those of so many women like her. Conventional wisdom taught that the only sound that could penetrate the heavens was prayer and Torah study. Through the excerpts cited here, Bella asserted that other forms of aural devotion also had a place: the cries of pain that accompanied a new soul into the world and the sounds made by the soul leaving the world. These sounds would have been familiar to Bella from her own experience of childbirth and from her work in the burial society.

Bella's introduction to *Be'er sheva* also opens a small window into the difficult exchange between a husband and wife and the different ways they expressed their grief. Concerning the deaths of their seven children, she wrote, "He [Ber] consoles me that I should not take this grief to heart, because no person lives on earth without suffering, some greater and some smaller, so I am not alone. He cites many midrashim and *gmoros* (Talmud excerpts), and as I feel a small trace of consolation in my heart, I beg him to write down these words of comfort, so that others who have been similarly afflicted can find some fulfillment in this book."[90] Ber replied to Bella's pleading, saying he was working on more important books in *loshn koydesh* (Hebrew; lit. "holy tongue"); she listed each of them carefully, with a brief description.[91] "Still, I spoke and pleaded with him every single day until I wore him down. I said to him, 'There is no difference how one does a meritorious public service, whether in *loshn koydesh* or in *teytsh* (Yiddish),' and through my many words he acquiesced to this book."[92]

Ber ultimately consented to Bella's plea to write "for me" the book in the Yiddish vernacular to serve a broad readership as a spiritual guide and consolation. He also agreed to Bella's suggestion to divide it into seven sections, each to serve as a memorial to one of "my" seven children who died, each named for the name by which "my" children were called. Bella's use of the possessive expressed her insistence that her grief for her children was far more intense than Ber's and that while he had many other books with his name embedded in the titles, this one was "hers."[93] Through the book, she maintained, their children's seven souls would be elevated through the seven layers of Gan Eden, and the title words meaning "seven wells" signified the seven graves that would become living wellsprings.[94] By naming each section after a child, they would have, Bella wrote, a greater presence in posterity through the book than if the children had lived.

Writing for Posterity

The fact that great personal losses—the deaths of Bella's children and Glikl's melancholic widowhood—compelled these two women to write emphasizes the solemnity and gravity with which recording, writing, and creating literary works were viewed in this period. While Glikl addressed her memoir to her children and even attempted to defend her life decisions to them, Bella Perlhefter and Rivkah Tiktiner saw in their written works a means of leaving a mark on the world beyond biological descendants. Both Bella and Rivkah prepared their manuscripts to be printed, a sign that it was not the composition of the work but the readership it would attract that was the true object of their writing. This is the first time we see Jewish women writing in this way. The three Ashkenazi women whose writing we highlight here knew that they were breaking barriers in their own time. Each felt that there was no precedent for their literary work. Personal and particular circumstances, such as widowhood, loss of children, and childlessness, drove each of these women to leave a permanent mark on their world through their writing.

While these three women are extraordinary and stand out for the scope of their written work, their engagement with writing was anything but exceptional. The world of women's reading and writing spanned the religious and the ordinary, lofty ideas, and worn-down objects. In addition, in their use of writing as a response to sorrow and as monuments to their posthumous memory, these Jewish female writers demonstrated their familiarity with the conventions of their age, as Christian women, too, created consolations for the departure of loved ones and shaped a picture of their lives for posterity.[95] While neither Glikl nor Bella's work was printed in their lifetimes, each consumed printed works that helped shape their religious and writerly imaginations.[96] As with their wills and personal letters, Glikl and her contemporaries wrote prose for the family circle and expected their words to be read by others and to live after them.

6

Dynamic Households

AN ORNATE title page of a 1740 *selihot* (penitential prayers) manuscript from Frankfurt's gravediggers' confraternity depicts at its center a pyramid on which a woman and a man stand side-by-side on ascending and descending steps. Each stair symbolizes a stage of life, from the cradle at the left to the graves on the right; such visual representations were common across eighteenth-century Europe.[1] In this image, children at play transform into youths, then married couples, and then elderly men and women grasping walking sticks. Their clothing, headgear, and accessories change to mark their journey through time. The depiction of a man and woman side-by-side in each stage, with marriage at the apex, reflects the centrality to the Jewish community of the family unit and of the creation of new households.

Households, rather than nuclear families, formed the bedrock of communities, of cities, and of the countryside. As Heide Wunder put it, "Women and men attained their self-reference and sense of self-worth . . . from their integration into household, generational unit, work . . . honor and piety and a life after death."[2] Yet, the idyllic picture of a couple going through life in tandem portrayed in this manuscript illustration differed from reality, in which households varied greatly in composition and size, forming and regrouping over people's lifetimes. Households continuously evolved through births and deaths, marriages, divorces, and remarriages, and the travel that brought individuals into one home and out of another. Such dynamic households were not unique to Jews; across Europe, household formation and configuration varied over time.[3]

The communal shaping of family and household dynamics directly impacted women's lives. Their economic, marital, and social circumstances mattered greatly in terms of the lives they could lead and the roles they could play in society. The cycle of fortunes could rupture household rhythms in a moment.

FIG. 6.1. The stages in women and men's lives, from cradle (on left) to grave (on right). Woman visiting grave, bottom left, holds a prayer book. *Selihot*, Gravediggers Society, Frankfurt, 1740. See plate 1.

In the face of forces that were larger than any one individual, women navigated the complexities of shifts within their households on multiple fronts.

Few of our records provide a running narrative of women within their households, yet one source, the product of a woman's pen, presents a woman's view of the household. Though taken from a genre that we rarely cite as evidentiary—a prescriptive manual on household management for pious women—Rivkah Tiktiner's *Meneket Rivkah* articulated the vision of a woman as the epicenter of the household: "A woman is responsible for everything: for her husband, for her children, and for her servants"[4] (see plate 12). In an age when men were thought to have "ruled" over idealized households like small heads of state,[5] Rivkah articulated her woman's truth: Jewish men were often on the road for long periods, and even if they lived at home, they often spent most of their days outside the house, for religious services, economic transactions, and civic engagement. Women were the true axes around which the household members rotated. For Rivkah, this was both a religious and practical matter. By placing women at the center of the family, she viewed them as the pivot around which God's will unfolded in this world. Following Rivkah's centering of women, we will trace women's experiences within the dynamic household, discussing, on the one hand, how their lives were shaped by their shifting roles and, on the other, the active role they took in navigating these changes.

Forming New Households in the Community

Jewish communities viewed every newlywed couple as potential ba'ale bayit, official community members. Therefore, they heavily regulated the formal steps involved in securing a match for a local young man or woman. Since parents sought to confer rights of communal membership on their children upon marriage, the community took a strong interest in overseeing marriage. This enabled them to restrict membership to those who would not burden the community financially and would become upstanding, taxpaying members down the road.

Honorable members conducted the process of marriage—the creation of households—from matchmaking, finances, and settlement rights to setting the date of the wedding celebration and its guest list, in complete conjunction with communal regulations and its leaders' oversight.[6] *Shadkhanim* (professional matchmakers; sing. *shadkhan*) often secured matches between young people, although individual men and women also played this role more informally. Joseph La Grange sued his brother-in-law, Feivush, claiming that Feivush had promised to pay him a matchmaker's fee if he helped Feivush secure a match. Feivush, however, denied that they had reached such a deal and claimed that Joseph's help "was due to kinship with his brother-in-law, and therefore, he owed him nothing."[7] Individuals demanding compensation for their role in pairing couples led to communities regulating matchmaking payments. In Bamberg, "anyone who opened their mouth to discuss a *shiddukh* (match) without actually doing anything, nevertheless tried to demand compensation, and this diminished the opportunity of the true matchmaker who worked on this day in and day out."[8] Regulations as to how matchmakers were to be paid, how to resolve disputes that might arise between the matchmaker and the family for whom they had secured a match, and how to navigate cases in which more than one matchmaker demanded compensation were common across communities.

Once parents secured a match and wished to announce an engagement formally, negotiation between communal leaders and the parents of the couple became far more intense. To wed, the couple was required to obtain a *hatarat kiddushin* (communal license to marry), issued by the lay leaders of the community. This requirement was standard practice in both rural and urban Jewish communities across western and central Europe.[9] Typically, the parents of the groom paid the fee, *hatarah gelt*, for acquiring the marriage permit. The communities barred rabbis from officiating at marriage ceremonies in cases in which a family had failed to secure such permission. These paper permission slips could also serve as proof, in some cases, of communal or rabbinic approval of a marriage. In one case in Altona, a hatarat kiddushin from fifty years earlier was brought before a rabbi in 1868. A local widower had betrothed a certain young woman, "recognizing that she would be a good mother to his children." He then found out that her mother had given birth to a child out of wedlock more than half a century before, although she had later married and had children, among them his intended bride. The rabbi ruled that he could marry the girl, relying also on the mother's hatarat kiddushin: "I saw this *hatarah* in the handwriting of the chief rabbi, and it says that the chief rabbi, who was renowned and prominent, knew of the case, that this man's wife had given birth when she was single."[10] The slip of paper served as evidence that the community and the rabbi had approved of the mother's marriage despite a previous pregnancy half a century prior.

Early modern Jewish communities granted permission to wed only once the parents of the bride and groom had paid all outstanding debts to their coffers, including yet-to-be-fulfilled pledges to charity.[11] In late eighteenth-century

Fürth, it was required that "any community member ... who wishes to betroth a son or daughter or to inscribe them as community members, must first report to the parnas of the month.... He must have first secured, via the communal notaries, an authorization from the tax collectors. Without this, it is not permitted to write the premarital agreement."[12] Betrothal was a juncture at which the community wielded leverage over families to pay outstanding taxes. Weddings were costly affairs, and communities could not count on being paid by a family that had taken on additional debt to marry off a child. The logbook of Altona's shamash includes names of various couples who had paid their debts and would thus be permitted to marry. The widowed Yente Wagner agreed to pay a debt of fifty Reichsthaler to the tax collectors. She paid half before the formal betrothal of her daughter; the other half was to be paid before the wedding ceremony. With this commitment and initial payment, she secured permission to formally betroth her daughter to R. Yuzpa ben Itzik.[13]

Once families obtained permission to marry, they drew up *tena'im rishonim* (premarital agreements).[14] Many communities regulated the financial agreements between families as well, granting formal communal membership only to those young couples who had access to a large sum of money from the dowry and other parental gifts. Christian policies in early modern European cities similarly granted citizenship only to economically stable couples and encouraged those who could not pay the requisite fees to leave the city.[15] The Jewish communities could not afford to welcome additional households that were too poor to pay taxes and thus would need to subsist on communal welfare. In seventeenth-century Worms, a family that was marrying off its first child to a member of a local family needed to pay one hundred Reichsthaler (a weighty sum) to acquire *hazakah*, or *hezkat kahal* (communal membership) for the couple. The couple was required to have an additional two hundred Reichsthaler at their disposal after all the wedding expenses. Anyone marrying a foreign Jew (from outside Worms) was required to have a four hundred Reichsthaler surplus.[16] Should local children fall on hard times, both sets of parents could step in; a foreign match was less secure and required more cash up front.

When parents wished to marry off additional children, the community expected an even larger amount to ensure that the couple would be financially stable, despite the parents' having paid for weddings and premarital gifts for multiple children.[17] The Jewish community of eighteenth-century Fürth legislated a far more detailed set of requirements for premarital wedding gifts "so that there would not be any poor or indigent in our midst."[18] The communal ordinances linked every imaginable permutation of a match to a requisite sum that would entitle the couple to membership: marrying someone single; widowed, with or without children; or someone local, foreign, or orphaned. Since every Jewish householder, moreover, was required to own his own home in Fürth, the community placed a premium on every additional child who wished to marry. Differential rates were provided for up to five marrying children, and any additional marriages beyond five were priced at the rates set for the fifth child.[19] Unless parents ordered differently in a will, the eldest child was entitled to marry first, with the lowest amount of money required. Communal regulations stipulated, however, that siblings could agree among themselves to allow a younger sibling to marry first at a lower cost.[20] Furthermore, unless a parent stipulated otherwise in a last will and testament, the right to communal membership was granted first to boys. Even if they had older sisters, male children were given the right to marry and attain communal membership at the lower rate.[21] Given the myriad permutations of how much money each couple was required to bring into a marriage, which depended on a bride and groom's sex, their birth order within their family of origin, their membership status, and previous marital statuses, communal officials recorded each newly married couple's status in a specially designated logbook.[22]

In Fürth, regulations mandated that the groom would take an oath in the synagogue prior to the wedding. With his hand on the open Ark where the Torah scrolls were stored, he was to swear regarding the amount of money that he and his bride had at their disposal.[23] After the premarital agreement had been signed, a deposit was usually placed in the hands of communal officials, typically nine months before the wedding (assuming the engagement period was that long), to ensure that future debts would be paid.[24] Early modern communities regarded oaths with great severity; some locals were able to avoid taking the oath based on their own recognizance.[25] The stringent regulations and the insistence on an oath were intended to protect the community as much as possible from admitting as members couples that would end up living dependent on charity.

Yet these regulations also had (perhaps unintended) consequences for families who wished to secure matches for their children. In Bamberg, families paid matchmakers a percentage of the dowry, which encouraged them to focus their efforts on the wealthier families in the community.[26] The high costs associated with marriage meant that families of more modest means would have more difficulty marrying off several children. While in Catholic communities, younger siblings could enter a convent or monastery, this was not a possibility in Jewish families. For that reason, communities granted to parents who were marrying off a child a deduction in their tax assessments, excluding the dowry and premarital gifts from the calculation of their net worth.[27] It is no wonder that dowering brides was among the most popular functions of charitable societies.[28]

These regulations also affected parents' choices of spouses for their children. Finances were a powerful force in dictating whether parents and matchmakers would seek out a local or foreign match. Less money was required as a deposit for a local match, rendering such matches particularly attractive for middle-class families or those marrying off more than one child in quick succession. Marrying a widower with children from his first marriage might seem a good opportunity, given that such a groom would likely be strongly motivated to find a stepmother for his young children. Yet, in Fürth, a larger deposit (one thousand Gulden for a widower and eight hundred for a widow) was required to ensure that the children from the first marriage would be adequately cared for by the family.[29] Another financial consideration was the matchmaker's fee, since matchmakers received higher payments for matches across greater distances, for which they incurred additional expenses and invested greater efforts.[30]

Matchmakers and anxious parents considered the reputation of a foreign match's family as another critical factor. The flurry of letters exchanged in anticipation of a match testifies to the trepidation some felt when securing a match across borders. When Hayim Hamel traveled to Amsterdam and betrothed their daughter, Esther, Glikl wrote that she had "received letters from every which way warning us against the match, since the young man had many faults. But less than a day later, I received a letter from my husband saying he had arranged the betrothal . . . it is easy to imagine how I felt and what kind of happiness this match brought me. . . . [Hayim] returned a week later, expecting a joyous welcome from me . . . in fact he found quite the opposite. I greeted him in low spirits, barely able to open my mouth."[31] Glikl wrote a letter to Yachet, the proposed groom's mother, sharing her concerns. She insisted that if the rumors about the prospective groom, Moshe, were true, Yachet should refrain from sending him to meet his intended bride, "for we will not defraud our daughter in such a terrible way." Yachet replied "angrily." Although the tensions were eventually resolved, and the couple happily married, "much time was frittered away in an aggravating exchange of letters."[32]

Communal officials insisted on verifying a foreign match's reputation as well. In Friedberg, "no one from our community has permission to marry his daughter to a foreigner who will [through the marriage] obtain membership in our community, if the groom is not known, or if he hasn't lived in Ashkenaz

FIG. 6.2. Wedding invitation of Eizik and Rivla bat Zimla written on preprinted form. Copenhagen, 1784.

for the past three years, so that one can determine whether he comports himself appropriately. If it is known that he has not behaved appropriately, for example, that he was in one of the famous groups of bandits, or other rumors of wrongdoing, he may not acquire membership here, whether he is single or a widower."[33] Communal interest in new members extended beyond the financial to include questions of respectability and honor, which were central communal values expected of any ba'al or ba'alat bayit.

Families typically made matches with others of the same class or, in some cases, between the rabbinic elite and wealthy families. Children of court Jews typically married one another, creating ties of family and trade that stretched across Europe.[34] Glikl's eldest daughter, Tzipor, for example, married the son of R. Elia Cleve, a prominent court Jew. Yachet, the mother of Moshe Krumbach, who would later marry Glikl's daughter, Esther, despite the angry letter exchange mentioned above, was herself the daughter of Elia Cleve; the two families had a double bond through marriage.

There were, nevertheless, cases in which spouses married across classes. In 1738, in Berlin, communal leaders decided that no manservant could contract to marry a local girl unless he had been out of service (and out of Berlin) for three consecutive years prior. While the underlying motivation of the leaders is not clear, the ordinance mentions that some communal members contracted marriages for their daughters with manservants without the requisite three-year waiting period. They also took their future sons-in-law into their homes under the guise of service once they had agreed upon the future marriage. The community leaders strictly prohibited such arrangements for the future, under penalty of an extremely hefty fine of five hundred Reichsthaler.[35] Given the high number of singles in Berlin (discussed further below), parents' desires to betroth their daughters may have surpassed their wish to marry them to someone of the same class.

Several cases attest to parental disapproval of such marriages. In Worms, the only daughter of a wealthy man fell ill, and no caretaker was available. Her father struck a deal with a handsome young servant, who asked for her hand in marriage in exchange for the care he would provide her. Her father agreed, and the young man nursed her back to health; she, in turn, cared for the young man when he became ill. Her father, however, reneged on his agreement, withdrawing his permission for them to marry. Despite his refusal to furnish the couple with a dowry, his daughter's "soul was tied to his [the servant's], and she loved him very much," and she married the young man against her father's will. Although the responsum that discussed this case employed biblical language to describe the depths of her feelings, and we do not hear the daughter's voice directly, her decision "to stand in her faith against the will of her father" spoke almost as loudly as her words would have.[36] Rabbi Judah Mehler reported another case in which a young man, under the pseudonym Jacob, "fell in love with Rachel [pseudonym]. He said to his father, 'Take her for me [as a wife], because she is upright in my eyes.' Though he spoke with him [his father] every day, he did not heed his son's words." Jacob married Rachel, and his father was furious; the father turned to the Christian authorities, who required parental permission to wed, and demanded their help in coercing his son to abandon his wife without paying any divorce settlement.[37] The couple, however, wished to remain married. Mehler, who was consulted on the validity of the couple's union, excoriated anyone who thought that a Jewish marriage could be undone simply because it was not recognized by the non-Jewish authorities. In both cases, intense feelings between the young people led to marriage over the objections of their parents.

Age at Marriage and the Household

Age at marriage is one of the most significant demographic factors influencing the lives of women. The younger a woman at the time of her marriage, the less control she could exert over the choice of marriage partner. Based on his research in Marburg's archives, Gerald Soliday argued that in the period between 1620 and 1800, Jewish men typically did not marry before they were twenty-five, and women did not marry before they were twenty-three in that small community.[38] Glikl of Hameln, however, married at fourteen. This could be a question of class or a regional difference.

Most of the data we have concerning age at marriage comes from the late eighteenth century when cities and states began to demand that Jews record life cycle events. We do not know whether this late eighteenth-century data is typical for the entire early modern period, as much of the data we have from earlier centuries comes from the personal examples of members of the elite, such as Glikl. The ages at marriage for Jewish men and women were similar in Metz and Berlin in the late eighteenth century. In Metz, between 1740 and 1789, most men were between twenty-three and twenty-nine years old at their first marriage, while women in those years were between seventeen and twenty-four years old.[39] In Berlin, the mean age at marriage was twenty-four for women and thirty-one for men; the median age, which provides a slightly different perspective, was twenty-seven for men and twenty-two for women between 1759 and 1770 and twenty-nine for men and twenty-two for women for two consecutive decades between 1771 and 1790.[40] One reason the median differs from the mean is that children of families from higher classes and children of families who held higher legal status married at earlier ages.[41]

The wider the gap between men's and women's ages at marriage, the greater the erosion of a woman's status within the marriage, as well as her place in her in-laws' household.[42] The trend of men marrying slightly later than women in the eighteenth century seems to have been common in both urban and rural settings. In the village of Steinbiedersdorf in Lorraine, more boys than girls lived at home in 1785 precisely because men married later than women. Similarly, in the nearby county of Kreichingen, out of sixty-eight Jewish households, there were one hundred boys and eighty-five girls (a 54:46 ratio) because men stayed at home longer as they married later in life.[43]

Once married, some couples started independent households immediately, such as the daughter of Avraham Italiener, whose home was furnished with gifts from her family and from the family of her husband, Moses Heilbut.[44] Others resided for a few years with either the groom's or bride's parents under terms agreed upon before the wedding. Communal policies regulated both types of households. In Fürth, the parents of a bride who betrothed their daughter to a Torah scholar who would study full time for several years rather than work for income committed to pay for the couple's food and living expenses for two years, ensuring that the new couple would not need support from communal coffers.[45]

Age at marriage and the finances of the household impacted the number of children a woman might have. This may have intersected with class, as wealthier girls tended to wed earlier. Glikl, who wed at fourteen, had fourteen children, twelve of whom lived until adulthood. Her husband, Hayim Hamel, was one of nine children. In his memoirs, Jacob Emden mentions families of ten and eleven children.[46] Malka, the wife of Asher of Reichshofen, by contrast, had three children, one of whom died in infancy.[47] Myriad additional factors, including infertility or a husband's frequent travel, influenced the number of children in a family. Anecdotal data gleaned from memoirs is not reflective of greater trends, and much remains unknown, such as the use of birth control in early modern Jewish communities. Even the data preserved about Jewish families by political authorities is incomplete when it comes to children, as sometimes, the lists contained only male children.[48] The same is true of records from mohalim, who recorded only the boys they had circumcised. Midwives' records include the births of baby boys and girls but do not always lend themselves to reconstructing

FIG. 6.3. Wedding procession. Schudt, *Neue Franckfurter Jüdische Kleiderordnung*, 1716.

the number of children born to a couple; sometimes, midwives recorded only the father's name.[49] Data from Halberstadt from 1699 includes 321 children born to eighty-seven families. There were 118 households; 74.3 percent of them included children. The average number of children per household was 3.7 (the median number is 4).[50] Raising the children and seeing to their daily needs was a mother's job: Rachel, daughter of Moshe Kunstatt of Mainz, was praised for "raising her children to do what was good and upright . . . she merited to see from them grandchildren who studied Torah."[51]

Death and the Disruption of Households

In the summer of 1761, Abraham Italiener brought a lawsuit against his son-in-law, Moses Heilbut, before the Jewish civil court in Altona.[52] Looming over the proceedings but never named in the document was the presence and absence of Abraham's daughter, who had been married to Moses for a brief time before she and, presumably, her child perished during or following a difficult childbirth. What followed her death can be viewed as the reversal of the process that went into building the couple's home, a step-by-step disassembly of the human relationships, financial entanglements, and embedding of objects within their quarters that collectively had created a new family within a new home—a household. Just as the first tentative contacts between families involved a negotiation about dowries and finances, the final severing of the relationship between *mehutanim* (families related indirectly through marriage) came about by reference to laws and traditions embedded contractually in their betrothal agreements that vouchsafed a family's investment if the woman should die within the first or second year after marriage.

Premodern dowries were often large, constituting a substantial share of a father's wealth, as dowries served as a mechanism for a daughter to inherit part of her father's estate. Jewish law originally dictated that a husband inherited from his wife, including the dowry that she had brought into the marriage. If that had remained the case, the husband of a young woman who died childless soon after marrying would retain control over her dowry, leaving the bride's family bereft of a child as well as a significant portion of their assets. Accordingly, in medieval Europe, Rabbi Jacob Tam (d. 1171) enacted an ordinance to allow a father whose daughter died within the first year of marriage to repossess the dowry from her husband.[53] Various permutations of this ordinance were accepted in northern France, the Rhineland, Provence, and other Ashkenazi communities.[54] Some versions stipulated that the dowry would revert to the bride's family within two years after the wedding, some allowed the father to retract only half of the dowry, and some permitted fathers of grooms who had passed away in the first or second year of marriage to reclaim what they had given to the young couple.[55] The span of time early in a marriage delimiting the return of the dowry came to be called *shenot ha-hazarah* (years of return). Early modern Ashkenazi communities often continued these traditions.[56] Individual rabbis cited these ordinances in cases when a young bride or groom died, and the eighteenth-century rabbinical court in Frankfurt reported that it abided by the ordinance adopted by the medieval Rhineland communities.[57]

Because his daughter had died within the second year of marriage, Italiener was entitled only to half of what he had given as dowry, and Moses Heilbut agreed to return that amount to him, as they stipulated in their *tena'im aharonim* (an agreement signed just after the marriage was contracted). The division of the dowry into halves, along with a tax that the bride's father prepaid, seemed straightforward; these amounts were uncontested. But Italiener listed many of the additional gifts and expenses he had bestowed upon his daughter, and he insisted that they, too, be considered returnable property. Italiener enumerated the furniture he had bought for the couple, as well as every item of housewares, down to the pots, spoons, and salt dishes, the bed and its linens, items of clothing and jewelry—a young woman's household condensed into a list of things and their value. In the face of this list, Moses Heilbut hired a *mursheh* (litigator) and sought, in return, to deduct expenses related to marrying and caring for the young woman from the amount he was to return to his father-in-law. While the bride's family was likely responsible for the lion's share of the wedding expenses, some of the expenses listed by Heilbut were borne by the groom's side. The groom's family hired the jesters that performed at the wedding and paid obligatory fees to communal functionaries, among them the communal license to wed, or hatarat kiddushin.[58] Heilbut also claimed every medical expense related to the childbirth and illness of his young wife. Down to the Schilling, he listed the cost of a physician, a hen, and a female aide to attend his wife. During the period of the birth, he paid the apothecary and an aide. Continuing illness incurred additional payments to R. Gershon, the physician; R. Tzadok, the barber-surgeon; the wife of Ziskind, the midwife; and additional Jewish and gentile midwives. During her parturition, he paid for a maidservant for four weeks; food for the expanded household; Klerche, the attendant; medicine; and the pharmacist. The young man had spared no expense in trying to save his wife's life. He also itemized the charity he paid for her during her pregnancy and after her death to elevate her soul, as well as every Mark and Schilling he laid out for her burial expenses. Now that it was over, he asked that these costs be deducted from his share of the dowry to be repaid.[59]

Many aspects of this detailed legal case echo throughout the early modern period in various sources, as family members ravaged by a death soon after a joyous nuptial event sought to salvage what they could.[60] Rabbinic responsa literature was filled with variations on this claim. Seventeenth-century Rabbi Judah Mehler's responsa collection contained several questions about various aspects of the "years of return" ordinance: "What is the practice regarding gifts given to the bride, known as *Einwurf*?" If a young bride died during the thirteenth month of their marriage, and it was a leap year, did this count as dying within the first or the second year?[61] If a woman died in the second year of her marriage, and her entire estate had to be returned, may her heirs retain the amount the husband had given to charity out of the dowry?[62] The rabbinical court in Metz likewise heard numerous cases regarding the years of return. If charity money was used to fund the bride's dowry, to whom did the dowry return if the woman died? A man who married a woman, thinking she was a virgin, only to find out she was not, demanded that the wife's father renounce his right to the dowry if she died.[63]

Heilbut's demonstration of having spared no expense for the care of his wife is echoed in the Frankfurt Memorbuch entry for "the *yoledet* (birthing woman), modest, pleasant, and delicate, the noblewoman Bella, daughter of the well-known noble Shlomo Zalman Kulpe ... Her eyes cast down while her heart soared, to endure the pains of childbirth with absolute love. To deter the [divine] rage and save her, her husband spared nothing; he went forth to abolish the evil decree, but in one day [or, on Sunday], the decree was decided: she was to go to the world of everlasting light."[64] Memorbücher and tombstones record many women torn away in childbirth, anecdotal evidence about the devastation wreaked by maternal deaths. To be sure, young people died of causes other than childbirth, and the years of return applied to men as well. The rate of maternal mortality, and mortality at younger ages in general in the early modern period, meant that households were constantly undergoing reconfiguration.

Reconstructing the Household

The nucleus of a family was often rearranged after a rupture (see plate 13). From his cramped stall in the Jewish marketplace of Prague in 1619, kosher butcher Baruch Reiniger wrote a letter to his son-in-law, Falk, and his daughter, Sarel, with some good news: "Traune is a bride, thank God." The groom was a relative of the family, and he had "something of a share" in a house, a place on the Tandel market, and a stall in the butcher market. Baruch lamented that the dowry he had had to settle on Traune exceeded what he would be able to give; he would remain in debt to the groom for half the amount. Moreover, he noted in passing, Traune would take on the duty of raising the groom's young children.[65] This final detail, brushed aside as a matter of course in the letter, is one of the most common aspects of early modern household formation, yet it is often taken so much for granted that it is easily overlooked. No matter which partner was the biological parent, in blended families, the hands-on responsibility for childcare fell on women. Here, we focus on the effect of disruption of the family and household on women and young children.

Breaks in continuity often fell more harshly on some parties than on others. As a rule, poor people, male and female, experienced more pressure to remarry if one spouse died. Poor men who could not otherwise afford childcare would seek a wife to care for their young children as soon as possible, while poor widows needed the presence of even a poor wage earner to cover the necessities of life to continue to care for their children. Wealthier men and women could afford to hire household help and choose to remarry when it suited them. When such reconfigurations worked seamlessly, they left minimal impressions on the records beyond registrations of the marriages. Glikl lived amicably with her husband for some thirty years. Her fame leaves the misimpression that her long and fecund marriage was typical in her time and place. But Glikl herself was raised in a home that had been constructed of multiple marriages. She recalled, "When my late father married my mother, he was a widower. For over fifteen years he had been married. He and his first wife had no children, then she died . . . and after her death my father married my mother. She was an orphan, poor thing . . . poverty stricken . . . fatherless with her pious, devout mother . . . whom I knew."[66] But there is one more wrinkle to Glikl's story: while her father and his first wife had no children during their fifteen-year marriage, she had been married previously and brought along her daughter from that marriage when she wed Glikl's father. This daughter was raised by Glikl's father as his own. Glikl described her great admiration for this older stepsister. Here was a case in which two unrelated daughters attained bonds of affection as sisters, and the families blended seamlessly. Variations on such configurations abounded in this period.

Young children were sometimes the most vulnerable because of their lack of agency to determine anything about the contours of their lives once their original families had been dismantled. Wealthier parents or the *bet din* (rabbinical court) appointed *apotropsim* (guardians) over their children's estates, sometimes to guard them from step-relatives. With funds to cover their expenses, a family member or friend could usually be found to care for such orphans. Women served as the primary day-to-day caregivers of orphans in their own homes.

An anonymous memoirist who left an account of his youthful years in Bohemia and Moravia, primarily in small countryside villages, allows us to see the traumatic effect of reconstructed families up close.[67] Born circa 1668, he recalled his mother and grandmother in idyllic terms. The young man described his mother's strength and resourcefulness under difficult circumstances; she had died when he was four years old. His recollection affords us a child's view of his ordeal when his father married a young girl who had neither the experience nor maturity to nurture him. He did not describe her as evil, only as "a young girl who did not know how to raise us young boys with proper cleanliness so that we were often ill."[68] She was unprepared to mother stepchildren and was then burdened by giving birth to her own children annually. The boy attributed his survival to the occasional ministrations of his grandmother and her daughters. Until his mid-adolescence, the boy's life was ruled by extreme neglect: he couldn't learn, he was virtually illiterate (until many years later), and he was unclothed; at age eleven, he still went around almost naked, without pants or shoes. In 1681, as plague swept through the region, he attributed his own near death to the filth, lice, and malnutrition he had suffered for years. By marrying a young girl, widowers with children could avoid taking on the burden of a widow's children. The memoir makes clear that they sometimes did so at the peril of their existing children's well-being.

Fostering or adopting a child or children was the most common way of constructing a family beyond the nuclear model. Most often, this meant accepting the children of a spouse born in an earlier marriage. Engagement and marriage contracts could stipulate the extent to which a partner was responsible for the spouse's children. "Meir [Weil] is obligated to pay for the upkeep of his wife's younger daughter, per his duty in the tena'im, and the elder [daughter] until age 15 and not longer."[69] Itzik Hess of Püttlingen agreed to foster two of the orphans left behind by Michael of Barschingen. He would assume full responsibility for two of the children, chosen by lottery.[70] The rest of the children would presumably remain with the widow. The feelings of the siblings about being separated into different households by means of a lottery are not mentioned in the source. Similar scenarios requiring children to be fostered also played out when children were abandoned by a parent. When Yuspa Mali fled his creditors and left his wife Gutche penniless, her relatives took in two of her children to feed and care for at no charge to her. Still burdened with many other children, including very small ones, she approached the rabbinical court for assistance. They decided that an additional one of her children must be kept in the home (and at the expense) of her father-in-law (the child's grandfather), while other relatives of the husband would be liable for additional support to her. Thus, the siblings of one family were scattered among at least three different homes, even though both parents were living.[71] While in some cases, estates or family members contributed to the cost of fostering children, the community contributed in other ways. When R. Judah Halberstadt decided to pull his foster son from a certain teacher's class, the kahal sent a reprimand: "R. Judah has no say in this matter and cannot make any such decisions for his foster son, for he did not pay the salary of the *melamed* (teacher); the Talmud Torah [charity fund] paid tuition for the boy."[72]

Communal membership was among the many issues that arose in blended families. In Fürth, where the price of hazakah was increasingly expensive for each subsequent child, the question of how to deal with half-siblings from first and second marriages was particularly acute. Communal regulations directed that in cases in which the widow or widower and the new spouse were local, the children from each marriage be granted the right of membership. Thus, the eldest child from each respective union was considered a firstborn and could obtain hazakah at the lowest cost. When a third child from either marriage wished to obtain hazakah, he did so at the standard cost for a third child. When locals married foreigners, the rules were more complex.[73] In communal regulations, women had less discretion than men in determining which of their children would receive official membership. Whereas a man with children from more than one wife "was permitted to grant hazakah to whichever child he wished," a woman was obligated to ensure that the sons from her first marriage received this status.[74]

Marital Strife and Divorce

Death was not the only cause of familial rupture. Marital strife, which sometimes ended in divorce, caused disruption in Jewish households that reverberated into the broader community. In October 1782, a recently married woman, Yetche, came before the Frankfurt rabbinical court complaining that she did not wish to live "according to the laws of Jewish men and women" with Abraham, the man she had married. She could not stand to be with him sexually because of the repellent things she had found on his body. Her claim, *ma'is alay* (he is repugnant to me), was one of the standard reasons for ending a marriage in rabbinic law.[75] She claimed *mezonot* (support) from him, as he had hidden his flaws from her. Abraham rejected Yetche's claim, noting that she hadn't found him repugnant at first. He argued that she only came to regret the marriage later and was using repugnance as a pretext to leave it, so he did not owe her support. The case is noteworthy in several respects: neither party had a father, so each represented himself or herself, speaking directly before the court. They signed an arbitration agreement to follow the court's ruling. The court ruled that as long as they remained married, if she did not live with him as man and wife, she would be categorized as a "rebellious wife," and no support would be accorded to her. Should she change her mind and agree to live with him, he would then owe her support. However, she could not be coerced to live with him.[76] The court did not force a reconciliation; it left the door open for any outcome.

The dispute between Abraham and Yetche was one of myriad marital quarrels and spats documented in court, rabbinic, and communal records. Altona's records testify to cases in which the tension between husband and wife rose to the level of public gossip. Thus, Bonfe[t], son of Shlomo, was written in the *daf issur* (prohibition page) on the order of the kahal "because of the quarrel he had with his wife."⁷⁷ Married couples would not appear before the rabbinic courts for petty squabbles. Matters might proceed to adjudication by the judges only when the marriage seemed under threat to the couple or to their neighbors. In virtually all cases, the rabbinic court would try to mediate a solution. "Meir Weil and his wife came before the bet din because of various arguments and quarrels between them. Meir contended that his wife caused all the quarrels, and his wife said it was he."⁷⁸

A similar mediation plan by the Jewish civil court in Altona for another couple centered on the spouses' unease at leaving a parental space or being visited by unwanted in-laws.

> Regarding the marital conflict between husband and wife, Bonafet bar Ber Frankfurt and his wife, Dossia bat Jacob bar Itzik, after they poured out their complaints and quarrels at length before us, in order to mediate peace between them, we find: that Bonafet ... should rent an apartment to live with his wife here in Altona, and the rent should be paid by Jacob [Dossia's father] from his own funds, and the apartment should be in the home of an upright man who is not related to Bonafet nor to his wife; and if it is impossible to find such an apartment, they should rent where there are Jewish neighbors near the house, and Bonafet should live there with his wife until her lying-in period is over, that is, a full four weeks after she has given birth. After that, he can choose to return to his house in Hamburg, and his wife can accompany him. But he does not have to move his furniture to Altona at all. During this time, the man and his wife should conduct themselves with love and affection and peace, and not incite quarrels with one another; rather, they should behave like other upright Jewish men and women. And if quarrels should break out between them, the neighbors should clarify who began and caused the conflict, and the law shall follow.⁷⁹

The rabbinical court in Metz ruled similarly in the case of the aforementioned Meir Weil: "Regarding the quarrels and fights between them, from now on, the neighbors will be relied upon to testify which [partner] was the cause."⁸⁰ Marital discord was a source of disquiet for the entire neighborhood, and Jewish courts imposed a burden of responsibility on neighbors to monitor households at risk of imploding. The first case mentioned above, that of Yetche and Abraham from Frankfurt, ended in a court-granted divorce about two years later, in 1784.⁸¹ The courts strove for reconciliation where possible and only arranged divorce when the marriage was considered unredeemable. Once it became clear that the marriage could not be saved, the rabbinical court record reflected the process of dismantling the household in reverse order to that with which it had been built.[82] Abraham was to return Yetche's dowry to her, with deductions for a small advance she had requested and received. Abraham was also to return to her the sixth of an inner house, with all the paperwork appertaining to it. Regarding their Einwurf, Abraham kept the silver vessels from his relatives, which were in his possession; the money that she received as Einwurf, she kept. She was to return the gifts he gave her: a golden chain and a silver box. Yetche was permitted to keep the clothing he had commissioned for her, a *Schurz* (silk overgarment) and the outfit she made of chintz; however, its value, five Gulden, was deducted from the dowry, as was the income she collected for renting out the premises. She also had to return all the furniture and housewares, according to a list certified by the court scribe. Yetche was responsible for the costs of filing the divorce papers, perhaps because she had initiated the process. Each was required to pay the other party what they owed and return to the court within thirty days of receipt of the ruling or face fines.

Divorces among Jews of early modern Europe rippled beyond a couple to their parents, offspring, neighbors, and the entire community. They left both parties in worse financial shape and often in lower standing than they previously had been. They undid the many layers of time and effort that went into constructing a household, dismantling it into pieces that never quite equaled the sum of the original. In many communities, the breaking apart of the household also caused the physical distancing of members of the couple. The eighteenth-century regulations of Fürth ordained: "When a man gives a *get* (bill of divorce) to a woman, only one of them may live here, either the divorcer [male] or divorcée [female], and the two may not hold membership in our community [simultaneously], ever. . . . Before the divorce is finalized, they should agree who will remain, and who will leave. If they already have children, none of them may add the children that will be born to the man or to the woman in their second marriage to their membership; they do not get a new status as head of household."[83] From this regulation, we see that in Fürth, a divorce meant the permanent dislocation of one of the partners, even if they were parents of young children. This would negate the possibility of a joint custody arrangement in which both parents could easily remain within physical proximity to their children. The ordinance addressed the concern for the disruption of community harmony that the presence of both divorced parties could engender. The takkanot express the expectation that each of the parties would marry again. There is no distinction between the remarriage chances of the man or the woman, as this would depend on multiple individual circumstances.

Until the sixteenth century, Jewish marriages were unique in western Europe in that they could be ended with divorce. Since late antiquity, the Catholic Church had taught that marriage was (like baptism) an indelible sacrament. Adultery was a sin, but it could not undo a marriage. Sometimes husbands and wives could separate their bed and board, but they would still be legally married in the eyes of the church and could never contract another marriage. Only death could end a marriage. Annulments, rarely obtained, declared a marriage retroactively invalid, leaving problems such as the existence of offspring never fully resolved. Jewish communities always permitted divorce as biblically sanctioned (Deut. 24:1–4), and permission for divorce even played a role in the Jewish-Christian polemic. Jews took pride in their ideal of affectionate marriage, enabled by the possibility of ending dead marriages, while Christians viewed celibacy as an ideal and the notion of contracting a second or third marriage while a first spouse was alive as a sign of Jewish carnality. Scrutiny of local records, wherever available, shows that the frequency of divorces within Jewish populations varied over time.[84] In the mid-fifteenth century, Rabbi Seligman of Bingen raised an alarm about the frequency with which divorces were being granted. He noted with chagrin that one or both spouses were already arranging their next marriages before their first one had run its course. "We decree ... that no one should propose a match while a woman is still with her husband, regardless of whether he is ill, or she is ill, or she plans to divorce soon anyway."[85] Under no circumstances, Bingen continued, should anyone agree to preside over a marriage of recently divorced people until at least three months had elapsed since the divorce. Israel Yuval attempted to test Bingen's perception; based on the available evidence, he argued that Bingen's understanding was correct: small, urban, western Jewish communities had a very high rate of divorces.[86]

Historians of Protestantism note that while Luther and other reformers no longer considered marriage a sacrament, it remained a pillar of society for them, not to be lightly put asunder.[87] Once they dethroned celibacy as theidealstate, it seemed cruel to force people to live in dead marriages. Yet, as Jeffrey Watt has argued, it took centuries after the rise of Protestantism for divorce to be commonly granted for grounds such as incompatibility.[88] Based on the rabbinical court records, Jewish couples appealed for divorce on a somewhat wider basis of complaints. The need for Jews who married to obtain residence permits caused economic stress and the related complaint that one partner was absent from the home for long periods. In a case before the Metz rabbinical court, Rivkah complained that her husband, Moshe, failed to obtain a legal residence permit for them, forcing them to wander in very reduced circumstances. "She should not be obligated to wander from village to village and from city to city, for there is great danger in that life."[89] Rivkah sought employment as a domestic servant to keep body and soul together; Moshe objected, as this would result in her living away from him. In another instance of a woman's coming before the court in distressed financial circumstances, the bet din of Metz took up the case of Malkah, wife of Meir Charry. She complained that Meir did not earn enough to support her; she had already brought him before the court earlier, but he did not follow their ruling even in part. Due to her distress, she fell ill, and her father had to pay an attendant and other medical expenses; she now requested permission to return to her father's house in order to sustain herself. Malkah requested that she be allowed to take with her on the road the bed she had been forced to purchase herself, a reminder that certain furnishings were central to a concept of home. The court interviewed many people, including the attendant, all of whom attested that Meir could not afford the basic bread and water to keep her alive, let alone medical care, so the court permitted Malkah to return to her father's home.[90]

Interfering family members, perhaps a universal potential source of tension, appear in Jewish records numerous times. They constituted a key source of friction in multigenerational households or even in families that did not share the same home. Jewish court records contain numerous examples of such intra-family conflict. Thus, the Jewish civil court in Altona ruled:

> Abraham bar David Shohet must live with his wife according to the laws of Moses and Israel, only she must undertake upon oath that she will not go to her mother, nor may her mother come to her. We also warned her that if she violates this oath she will leave the marriage [be divorced] and forfeit her ketubbah (marriage contract), as is the case with one who violates the norms. He, likewise, may not go to his father, nor his father to him, and if Abraham refuses to live with his wife, he must pay her support in accordance with the court's order.[91]

Spouses accused one another of improper behavior, from adultery to wantonness to theft of items, money, or loan contracts from the marital home. Such cases required resolution of the underlying charge, as well as the indignant countercharge of defamation of character if the accusations were disproven.[92]

Another cause for divorce was the conversion to Christianity of one partner. Women sometimes threatened conversion as the only means of exit from a terrible marriage, while men who converted often received custody of their children as a church and state policy.[93] Men who converted without their wives and wished to remarry in Catholic lands were obliged by church law to grant a Jewish divorce to their wives, as Catholicism recognized that Jews were bound by the Old Testament laws concerning divorce. When an Alsatian Jew, born Borach Levi in Hagenau, converted to Christianity with his two daughters, his wife refused to follow. The French Catholic Church would not allow him to marry without divorcing his Jewish wife.[94] The Jewish Museum in Prague preserves a letter from 1760 that mocked a *get* (Jewish divorce contract), written in Hebrew and signed and sealed by two witnesses:

> Since the Lord awakened my spirit to enter under the wings of the Divine Presence with full faith / In the Messiah, Jesus of Nazareth; however, Liba'le, daughter of Meir, who was my wife / Remains in her obstinacy refusing to follow me into the life of the world to come, therefore I will / Go with you [more leniently] than the strictures of the law, since according to our law I am not obliged to give you a *get* / As according to our faith, if a woman does not wish to follow her husband in this matter, the husband can take a woman according to his desire; however, within the strictures of the law, as above-mentioned, / Take your *get* and go from my house to another man according to the Law of Moses, not in any other manner.[95]

This parody was not a valid divorce document according to Jewish law, which required adherence to meticulous guidelines. It highlights the predicament of women whose husbands had converted, leaving them trapped in marriages from which many could not obtain release.[96] In Protestant lands, or when this Catholic doctrine did not apply, women whose husbands converted to Christianity formed a particular subset of abandoned wives.

In 1648, Hindche, the daughter of the parnas R. Itzik Katz of Frankfurt, hired R. Mendlin Mainz to track down and secure a bill of divorce from her converted husband, Moshe Kassel. The terms of the agreement highlight her precarious situation: she agreed to pay him two hundred Gulden regardless of whether he was successful, "even if he were to spend the money for naught, for a completely hopeless situation."[97] She also agreed to pay the emissary for any damages he incurred as he advocated on her behalf. Obtaining a *get* from a convert could be perilous in terms of interacting with powers of church and state; it could also prove fruitless if the husband had left the region or if he refused to free his wife from the bonds of marriage according to Jewish law.[98]

A comparison to the list of causes of marital disputes from the medieval Ashkenazi world shows that many of these root causes of marital conflict remained constant over time.[99] The range of disputes that come to light in records of Jewish courts and rabbinic responsa demonstrates that despite the protection afforded to women through their marriage contracts, human nature and external circumstances succeeded in causing marriages to fail and households to be undone.

In an interesting divergence from Jewish law, Protestant courts considered not only adultery but also desertion to be a sufficient reason to end a marriage. Desertion or prolonged absence could provoke "a substitute death certificate" for the missing spouse in the form of permission for the abandoned spouse to remarry.[100] But Jewish law required definitive evidence of the husband's death; hence, a deserted woman whose husband had not furnished her with a bill of divorce remained chained to her marriage. The status of an *agunah* (lit., "chained woman") had no parallel in Christian society. Noa Shashar has treated different types of agunot extensively, demonstrating how desertion and violent deaths in which no body could be identified left some Jewish women chained to marriages with little to no hope of freedom to remarry.[101] Unlike women whose husbands left them through death or desertion without closure, wives of converts knew exactly where their husbands stood. They faced relentless pressure from the sponsors of the convert to join him; without a *get*, they remained chained to their converted husband. A small (but halakhically notable) number of women were caught up in another permutation of this severe dilemma: Jewish widows who had no children were bound to a levir, a brother of the dead man who was obliged to perform *yibum* or *halitzah* (levirate marriage or formal release from such a marriage) with his brother's widow. If the levir had converted to Christianity, this presented serious difficulties; rabbis endeavored to find solutions. Needless to say, these deliberations and consultations took time, while women remained suspended with a blocked marital status and a marginal position within the community.[102]

Jewish communities in the early modern period generally did not record divorces as part of any vital statistics they accumulated. Yet, they became more involved in the process of granting divorces, as numerous ordinances testify. Thus, the Ashkenazi community of Amsterdam ordered: "No one may grant a divorce without the permission of the lay leaders. Whoever does so will be banned and must pay a ten Reichsthaler fine; the witnesses will be banned as well."[103] In some small rural communities, by contrast, basic religious needs were served by periodic visits from the rabbi of a large Jewish community. In cases of emergency, however, such as the need to write a divorce contract for an apostate who might change his mind or leave town, local scribes, such as Asher of Reichshofen, who had no training in the matter, wrote the document: "Although I had never witnessed the giving of a *get,* not to mention written one, I gathered my strength and wrote two *gittin.*"[104] Aware that he did not know the proper procedure, Asher nevertheless composed several bills of divorce, learning only after the fact from the visiting rabbi how to craft one in accordance with Jewish law. The lack of a cadre of trained professionals does not seem to have been a factor when people needed a divorce.

Communal records often noted the divorced status of women while rarely doing so for men. We have seen parallel treatment of widows but rarely widowers, and, crucially, ba'ale bayit but not their female counterparts. An exception to the general absence of such statistics appears in a pinkas from Frankfurt, which details the marriages, divorces, and remarriages of the official members of the community from 1750 to 1820.[105] The structure of the record demonstrates how communities defined women's lives by their relationships to male relatives. The pinkas notes only divorcées, making no mention of the number of men in the community who divorced. In the Frankfurt list, thirty-one women were listed in a separate category as divorcées. While four of those divorces are undated, the rest took place between 1771 and 1805. Eight of the thirty-one women remarried in Frankfurt, sometimes to men who had not been previously married. This indicates that divorce for women was not considered an onerous stigma in the community. The degree to which public shame attached to the status of divorce often influenced the rate of divorce. That divorced women remarried in their own community, often to men who were not divorced, tells us that less of a badge of shame was attached to this status. It should be noted that there may have been many more remarriages than the Frankfurt community records indicate, as many of these marriages and divorces took place outside the city in smaller communities.

Remarriage

Frankfurt's pinkas also includes a list of men who married multiple times, after either divorce or the death of a spouse. Second and even third marriages were not uncommon. In late eighteenth-century Frankfurt, 131 men married a second time; the pinkas does not mention whether they were divorced or widowers. Of those, seventy-five married women who had never been married previously, fifteen married widows, and the remainder of the second marriages remain unclear because the notary used imprecise terminology.[106] Of the 131 men marrying for a second time, fourteen married a relative, often the sister of the dead wife, a niece, or a grandniece. Twelve of these women had never been married previously; two are unspecified. Moreover, there were fourteen men who married a third time.[107] Of the fourteen men who married three times, nine married a woman who was previously unmarried (of these nine, only one was a relative), one married a divorcée, two married widows, and two married women listed as ishah (woman), with no other specification.

The high rate (over 50 percent) of men in a second marriage who married previously unmarried women is suggestive of the number of women who were single and desired to be married. It also may suggest that many men were reluctant to marry women who came with children from a previous marriage. Additionally, women who had been previously married, whether divorced or widowed, had certain Jewish legal constraints to remarriage. They had to wait a minimum of three months to determine whether there was a pregnancy from the previous marriage; if they had recently borne a child, that waiting period stretched to twenty-four months in many cases so that the mother could nurse her child without causing the new husband jealousy.

Domestic Violence and Abuse

Women often moved after marriage to the domicile of their husband's family; indeed, some communities mandated that women could not carry rights to communal membership once they had married.[108] Those who enjoyed a close relationship with influential family members could generally rely on their protection in the event a spouse or guardian abused them. Accounts of extreme spousal abuse are very rare because the abused woman often fell under the control of her abusive husband. One detailed account survives in the rabbinic responsa of Rabbi Judah Mehler:

> Query from a distance, from a large and pious Jewish community:[109] Word has spread in the community, an unceasing murmur, concerning a woman, abandoned and rejected, depressed and dejected,[110] separated from her husband....[111] The beginning of his corruption came about because he was enraged[112] that she did not heed [his request] to rob and steal from her

father's house. He regularly quarreled with her until, several times, he locked her outside the door of his sleeping quarters in the most freezing weather, and she was forced to stand outside[113] all night long; in addition to multiple abuses, curses, and debasements with which he insulted, cursed, and debased her and her father and her mother.... He secluded himself with single and also married Jewish women, as well as with daughters of the uncircumcised [non-Jews].... Ultimately, she became pregnant by him, and when the time came to give birth, he took the key to the house [and locked her out], and she feared for her life, as he threatened her that he would not call a midwife for her, and he did not permit entry to his house even to her mother. As a result of this great pressure, she was forced to flee for her life and the life of her unborn child to her mother's home, in order to save her life and the life of her child.[114]

The woman in this case, referred to by the pseudonym "Rachel," desperately sought freedom from her husband, referred to by the pseudonym "Shimon." According to Jewish law, a man cannot be coerced to give his wife a bill of divorce. Rachel turned to Mehler, asking that he rule on whether the specifics of her husband's abusive behavior nevertheless obligated him to grant her a divorce. Rachel made no financial claims on her husband despite having brought many assets into the marriage; she asked only for a divorce, even promising not to remarry. Rachel's dossier included many affidavits attesting to multiple violations of their marriage, and Mehler ultimately granted her request. Even a ruling in her favor, however, could not actually force Shimon's hand in granting a divorce. Some of the words in Mehler's responsum present Rachel in the first-person voice. Since she included many documents that already had been notarized, it is difficult to know the extent to which her words were mediated. Regardless, it is clear that Rachel left no stone unturned in seeking to free herself from the shackles of her abusive husband.

It is extremely unusual to find a description of spousal abuse in the words of the woman herself. Robert Liberles found a description of domestic violence in a private letter from a married woman whose husband beat her and whose family abandoned her.[115] The woman, an orphan, wrote to her uncle, her closest relative, describing how her previous confidence had been betrayed and her call for help had turned her husband even more brutally against her:

My "dear husband" came home from his mother's home that evening with the story. I was certain that he was going to kill me, God forbid, and he beat me, unfortunate human being that I am, on the head, so that I practically lost all my senses and blood gushed from my nose. . . . Thus he began saying, "You want to shame me and report what happens to the public? Now you will know what it is to [be] hit and what a bad life is; until today it was nothing yet, and now you have made it much worse; now I have nothing to lose, because people already know, and I have already been slandered. . . ." When he sees that there is no one to protect me, he thinks that he can simply do anything.[116]

Undoubtedly, cases such as these represented the tip of an iceberg whose depth cannot be known and measured. While wife beating was strongly condemned by Ashkenazi rabbis in this period, the prescriptive sources cannot tell us what transpired between spouses behind closed doors. Community forums tried to find ways to make peace between warring or quarreling spouses. But when women were isolated from their families and communities, they could be subjected to years of torment and abuse.

Single Women

The frequent construction and reconstruction of households and the deep involvement of the community in regulating, overseeing, and keeping the peace in households highlight the centrality of families and marriage within the Jewish community. Yet the privilege to marry was deeply intertwined with financial status, municipal law, and population control. In many locations in western and central Europe, marriage laws restricted the number of Jews who were permitted to wed. The policies enacted by political authorities to limit and control their Jewish populations often led to internal communal ordinances that shaped membership standards in the community. Already in sixteenth-century Frankfurt, daughters of Frankfurt community members could not extend hezkat kahal to their husbands.[117] The 1616 privilege issued to Frankfurt's Jews, which regulated Jewish life until the beginning of the nineteenth century, limited the number of marriages per year to twelve couples.[118] The city levied a special municipal tax to fund a city fountain on these couples, rendering marriage both limited and even more costly than in other communities.[119] In the early seventeenth century, seven Jewish couples (foreign men and local women) married without permission and later sought retroactive approval from the Christian authorities, who denied their request.[120]

In Bohemia and Moravia, the political authorities similarly issued strict regulations limiting Jews' rights to marry. These restrictions differentiated between male and female children, as well as between the eldest child in a family and the younger siblings. Limiting the number of couples that could marry led individuals to migrate elsewhere within and outside Moravia.[121] Eighteenth-century policies in Prussia similarly restricted the Jews' right to expand the number of households. Beginning in 1720, not one Jewish family from beyond the Cleves territories won the right of permanent residence. From the Seven Years' War (1756–1763) until the end of the century, only eight cases in which *Schutzjuden* (protected Jewish families) won the right for more than one son to marry and remain in the region are documented, a number that included three brothers from the same family. Sometimes, a firstborn would cede the right to marry to a sibling. The competition for permission to marry was so fierce that a late eighteenth-century regional meeting sought to limit Jewish male servants as potential competitors of local men who sought to marry local daughters and widows with settlement rights.[122] Restrictions on Jewish marriage only started to ease in the late eighteenth century, when nation-states began to understand that population growth stimulated their economies.[123]

When, as was often the case, families were not able to acquire permission for more than one son to marry, the death of the father caused the unmarried siblings to wander the region until the authorities expelled them. Others got married outside of the area and then were hit with enormous fines. After Leiser Moses of Duisberg did so, he subsequently attempted suicide "out of poverty and sorrow."[124] A sympathetic magistrate assessed that Leiser would have preferred to do without his wife and children rather than to have paid the hefty penalty imposed for conducting an outside marriage, surmising that given the high cost of a license, Leiser would not even have opted to purchase one had he been able to afford to do so. Many women who were not able to marry lived with their parents or brothers their whole lives. Others became servants.[125]

Quotas on the number of Jewish households in Swabia likewise led Jewish girls to seek employment as maidservants because maidservants could join an existing household, thereby residing in the community without violating the quota.[126] Thus, the caps on the Jewish population more broadly and the specific restrictions governing marriage reinforced one another. These factors, as well as the high costs associated with marriage, meant that many men and women remained single. Out of 114 families in Cleves in 1787, there were fifty-two single Jewish rural "children" aged twenty to thirty, as well as a fifty-one-, fifty-five-, and sixty-two-year-old.[127]

These restrictive policies, coupled with the high costs of marriage, meant that singles comprised a significant percentage of the Jewish community. A stream of young servants, both male and female, rotated in and out of early modern Jewish households. Records tallying the Jewish population, which became more common as political authorities sought to control their populations in the eighteenth century, allow us to provide some quantitative data, although such lists lack personal details. In 1699, in Halberstadt, there were ninety such servants.[128] More women than men entered domestic service, a trend that also was common among contemporary Christians.[129]

Female Jewish servants, who may have entered service as early as ten years of age, were ubiquitous in Jewish households in both the city and the countryside.[130] Cooks, nannies, maids, and laundresses lived with the families they served. Young men also entered service. Slightly older youths who had already finished their studies served as melamdim (schoolteachers or tutors), seeking to earn enough income to allow them to marry. They, too, lived with their employers; even married melamdim, who left their wives behind, joined local households. In 1709, over five hundred servants and teachers (almost 18 percent of the total Jewish population) lived in Frankfurt's Judengasse.

Prescriptive literature urged ba'ale bayit to see to the physical and spiritual well-being of servants as members of the households. Handbooks written by male authors urged the ba'al bayit to see to it that the servants prayed and recited Grace after Meals and that female servants were adequately chaperoned and not left unsupervised with men.[131] Rivkah Tiktiner's *Meneket Rivkah*, by contrast, emphasized that the supervision of the transient members of the household often fell to the ba'alat bayit, the female head of household. Communal records of all kinds confirm the fact of nonfamily members sharing a domicile.[132] They note the systems by which yeshivah students were "distributed" to families and servants quartered, hired, and paid. But Rivkah's view extended beyond the fact to the *texture* of these relationships. She argued that women were responsible for all the people who resided in their households as much as for their own children.

Rivkah evinced real passion in her advice to women who oversaw female servants.[133] She reminded them that the entire comportment of their servants was their responsibility. She was particularly upset about stories that circulated concerning maidservants (in some cases, they were Christian, as was common in parts of central and eastern Europe) whose ba'alot bayit did not properly supervise them in their cooking duties, resulting in serious violations of the kosher laws in their kitchens. They mixed up the meat and milk implements, rendering them *treyf* (nonkosher):

> I must write yet about something I have seen . . . with Christian maids in *Reyser Land* [Ruthenia]. I have observed this great impurity: On Friday night, after everyone has gone to sleep, she washed the dishes in a basin used for dairy. Her mistress also kept cows, and would rinse off the dishes in the milk basin. Then I also saw that they slaughtered geese, and the Christian maid took the heads and put them in the basin for dairy products and poured hot water over them. I told this to her mistress who answered, "I don't believe it—she's served here for many years."[134]

Rivkah expected women to attend to every detail of the training of household members, relatives, servants, and transient visitors alike.

Yitta bat Falk was a single woman born in mid-eighteenth-century Fredericia, a small town in Denmark. Traveling approximately 250 kilometers south to Altona to seek employment as a maidservant, she found a position and lodging in the home of Esriel and Ella Brill, where she likely took care of their six children, five of whom died young, between 1780 and 1802.[135] Esriel was an influential and wealthy communal member, listed as a parnas in communal records.[136] When Ella Brill died in 1792, Yitta's assistance in helping raise the children became essential. We do not know when Yitta began to work for the Brills, but there is no doubt that she was prominent both in carrying out daily household duties and in familial affections. Yitta's attachment to her employer's family is manifest in her 1794 will, in which she bequeathed to Heitze Brill, Esriel's daughter, many different swaths of fabric, as well as a purse and the ducats it contained. Yitta singled out Heitze for tending to her during her illness. Yitta also selected Esriel as an executor of her last will and testament.[137]

Yitta may have been saving the material goods she bequeathed, among them clothes to be worn and bed/household linens for her trousseau; that many of them were colored red may have been an expression of her individual taste.[138] Noteworthy as well are the chests in which she stored her possessions, common in many inventories and testaments of the period. They would have been particularly imperative for a transient employee who might have had to change locations on short notice.[139]

Yitta died on Tuesday, 21 Shevat [February 10, 1795], just under two months from the date on which her will was recorded. Although she may have accumulated goods and savings in the hopes of building her own family, her life and death as a single woman underscores that marriage was a goal that not every woman could attain. It entailed significant expenses that made it unaffordable for many women. Marriage required a substantial dowry, tax payments to the community and to relevant political authorities, as well as proof that a couple (or their parents) could sustain themselves financially rather than become a burden to the community by relying on its charity.[140]

Not all single men and women entered service. Those who did not typically lived in a household together with other family members, as we saw above in the Cleves region; in Marburg, too, single adults often lived with their relatives.[141] Although some single Christian women lived independently in boarding houses, we have yet to find a similar pattern for Jews. In Frankfurt, when Lippman Rofe and his wife sued her mother over the living space they had inherited, the married couple secured a room for themselves in the older woman's home, as well as another room to be occupied by Lippman's unmarried sister.[142] Yuzpa and Leah Hindele Trier resided in his ancestral home along with Leah's three unmarried sisters; when Leah's sister Hindche became betrothed, the couple attempted to sort out the expenses she owed them for rental and repairs.[143] They did not hold Hindche responsible for these expenses while she remained single.

Since single men and women were not considered heads of their own households, they do not appear on lists of taxpayers or in other formal communal records. Yet they comprised a significant enough segment of the population to warrant specific mention in various regulations about clothing, leisure, and prayer. They were also recognized as having amassed a degree of wealth. A blessing recited in eighteenth-century Fürth praised both married and single men and women who donated on the eves of Shabbatot and holidays to support the poor.[144] In the mid-eighteenth century, the Berlin community calculated a special tax rate for single men and women who traded independently of their parents. Their tax rate was lower because they were not considered heads of their own households, yet the need to determine an assessment rate for singles indicates that they constituted a relevant demographic from a tax perspective.[145] A few decades later, in 1787, a dispute arose in Berlin between the burial society and the communal leaders: "Regarding the tax that was levied on childless people at the time of their death, as was written on [date omitted] 1768, whether the intention was to include unmarried single men and single women [never married], or whether it intends only married people, for it was not made explicit in that writing, we have determined that within the category of childless people noted in the ordinance, single [never-married] men and women are included."[146] The drive to include singles who had never married in the tax suggests that they were a substantial part of the population and that some had accumulated a reasonable degree of wealth.

Some single women owned their own property, as was the case with the Goldenes Einhorn house in late eighteenth-century Frankfurt. Two unmarried sisters owned half of the house. One (unnamed) sister had sold her quarter house while still single; after marrying Kalman Stiebel, she and her new husband rented that same quarter house from the purchaser. Kalman, however, came before the rabbinical court, claiming that "the half of the house [originally owned by the two sisters] was not suitable" for the couple and his sister-in-law, Matla, to share. He urged Matla to sublet her quarter of the house to them. Although Matla agreed to sublet most of the space to her sister and her husband, she insisted that one unheated room remain hers to use. She also retained access to the heated room and to the shared kitchen.[147] Not only did Matla and her sister have ownership in the house, but Matla retained independence within the shared household.

Despite their numbers and their property, singles were treated as having lower status than married individuals by certain Jewish communal forums; contemporary Christian society treated unmarried individuals similarly.[148] Communal memorial books excluded most single men and women, although exceptions were made for some singles from elite families.[149] An undated entry in the Fürth Kloyz Memorbuch from the end of the eighteenth century memorialized Gnendl, the single daughter of Judle Wertheim, a communal deputy.[150] Her father's donation and standing sanctioned the inscription of her name despite her marital status.

While communal records lack many individual details of singles, disruptions such as death rendered them visible, particularly in the epitaphs marking their graves. Wealthy and elite families similarly spared no expense when memorializing their single daughters on gravestones. Many were praised for honoring their parents, as was Hava bat Aharon Flasche, who "was flawless in her fear of God, and in good qualities and virtues, and was especially careful with the commandment of honoring parents."[151] The lineage of some girls was noted in an arc above their tombstones, highlighting the potential they had possessed as marriage partners. For example, the grave of a young woman named Hava was marked with five generations of her ancestors, highlighting her pedigree.[152]

Epitaphs emphasize the centrality of marital status as part of a woman's identity. Thus, a betrothed young woman who had died before her wedding was referred to as a *kallah* (bride). Golche bat Gumpel Neumark of Altona-

Hamburg (d. 1711) was remembered as having reached the age of marriage.[153] The tomb of Esther bat Salman Bensheim of Worms (d. 1740) was inscribed with the phrase "her marriage will take place in the Garden of Eden."[154] These references highlight the cultural importance of marriage, acknowledging the unreached potential of these women. In one extraordinary case, Hindle bat Meierl of Schmalkalden died in 1750, the day before she was to have been married. Her epitaph noted that "the joy was turned to agony and sadness for the whole family."[155] Her gravestone was elaborately designed, with both the epitaph and ornamentation placed on both sides of the stone. This headstone had a unique feature, uncommon to most Jewish tombstones: an etched portrait of Hindle enclosed in an oval. Above the oval was a crown, likely a reference to the crown worn by brides. The grave thereby marked the family's loss for future visitors to the burial grounds. By contrast, a woman who remained single, such as Haike, daughter of Moshe David Pollack, was referred to as "the elderly maiden" on her 1790 tombstone despite her advanced age.[156] The single women who resided with their extended family members or with their employers confirm the complexity of the Jewish household.

Women confronted multiple circumstances over their lifetimes as their roles within a household shifted over time. Most early modern Jewish households were not congruent with the nuclear family, as they typically included older and younger extended relatives, boarders, servants, and blended families.[157] These households, led by their ba'ale and ba'alot bayit, constituted the foundational units of Jewish communities.

7

Economic Agents

EDEL, THE divorced daughter of Meir Wetzlar, lived in Frankfurt with her infant son. In 1651, she formally contracted to bequeath 1,500 Reichsthaler to her brother Judah upon her death, but only under certain conditions. Judah was to inherit from Edel only if her young son and heir did not survive her. Edel further stipulated that if she were to remarry, "R. Judah may not stop her from giving whatever she wished to that man [her future husband], and R. Judah could not collect [his debt from this contract] other than from that which she had not given to her husband [under the terms of the marriage]." Any children born from that future marriage would inherit all her holdings, including "real estate, movable goods, debts, collateral, silver, gold, and cash," and Judah and his heirs would have no legal right to contest her bequests; their birth nullified this agreement.[1] Edel thereby ensured that her assets would remain in the hands of her family of origin, perhaps shielding it from any claims by her ex-husband. Yet she simultaneously provided for her young son and set her sights on the possibility of remarriage and additional children. She thereby guarded her rights to retain her financial holdings (and her appeal as a spouse) for any future husband and ensuing heirs. Even as a divorced woman in the seventeenth century, Edel wielded economic agency; the terms of her contract with her brother Judah highlight the close link between women's access to property and their marital status.

Edel's financial transaction is one of many recorded in the seventeenth century by Frankfurt's *ne'emanim* (Jewish notaries). These officials maintained a logbook of every *kinyan sudar* (acquisition) contracted between ba'ale and ba'alot bayit (community members) over the course of thirty years. Each acquisition included a brief description that was then initialed by the notaries; a column on the right side of the notaries' initials was designated for marking a transaction as closed or a loan as paid. A few examples provide a sense of the range of activities in which women engaged at different stages in their lives. In 1648, the bride Esther committed to pay her half brother, Yishay Oppenheim, one thousand Reichsthaler, a sum derived from the inheritance left by their mother, before her death. The agreement legally bound her husband as well and was inserted into the premarital contract between Esther and her future groom.[2] The married Teltzen waived the sum of two hundred Reichsthaler promised to her by her husband, R. Mosel, at the time of their wedding, annulling the agreement and granting him full ownership of the sum in 1648.[3] A similar volume covering several years of economic exchanges in Worms documents a rental agreement from 1656, overseen by Krinchen, who rented out a house she owned jointly with her brother, Jacob, from Amsterdam, to a doctor, Hirtz Segal. Tamar, Krinchen's widowed neighbor, gifted a share of a house in Worms and three synagogue seats in the Judengasse to her single daughter Gitlen in 1657; she also transferred to Gitlen a loan of 130 Reichsthaler owed to her by her other neighbors.[4] These examples are representative of hundreds of additional women's transactions in the records; they bought, sold, gifted, rented, and purchased real estate and commodities on large or tiny scales.

This chapter explores the rich array of archival materials, including contracts, Jewish notarial records, and court cases that document a far wider range of Jewish women's economic agency than is visible for women in earlier centuries. Women appear throughout as actively supporting their families, whether with other family members or as individual entrepreneurs. They labored, invested familial assets, and protected themselves against threats to those assets in Jewish and non-Jewish courts. Developments such as print and the rise in women's reading and writing allowed some better-educated Jewish women to adopt new professions, working in print shops, as writers, or as teachers. Other women maintained financial ledgers, drafted contracts, and corresponded about their business, demonstrating that their literacy extended to financial and commercial dealings as well (see plate 14).

In the medieval period, rabbinic responsa, financial and tax documents, and charitable bequests demonstrated that Ashkenazi Jewish women actively engaged in the economy.[5] Widows who headed their own households constituted the most visible group of medieval female entrepreneurs, but several genres of sources establish the active role that married women played in family economies.[6]

Many of these patterns persisted into the sixteenth and seventeenth centuries. The richness of the communal archives of the early modern period yields a wealth of new information about a far broader range of women. The early

FIG. 7.1. Early printed image of Jewish moneylending prominently features husband and wife in their home. Folz, *Die Rechnung*, Nürnberg, ca. 1490/91.

modern sources deal with women from all economic echelons, and they record details of the economic activities not only of widows but of married and single women as well. Some contracts and court proceedings include richly detailed accounts of women's economic activities, while in other cases, a passing phrase refers to a woman's profession, such as the widowed mother of "Itzik, the guard at the gates" in Berlin in 1723. Itzik appears on a list of salaried officials in the Berlin Jewish community, which ruled that he, "together with his widowed mother, should have a salary of one-and-a-half Reichsthaler."[7] Gatekeepers were typically employed to identify and keep out foreign Jewish poor (municipal laws generally banned foreigners of all faiths from begging in cities).[8] It is unusual to find a female guard, and the record does not even provide her name. Through this fleeting reference, we learn that Itzik's mother, who likely interviewed or inspected female travelers to Berlin, served as a guard along with her son.

Recordkeeping and Women's Economic Lives

The level of detail that is available for women of so many different Jewish communities, both urban and rural, is a result of the rich culture of recordkeeping in communities and court systems. It was during this period that Jewish and Christian men and women maintained detailed economic ledgers.[9] In a late eighteenth-century court case in which Bunla, a maidservant in Frankfurt, demanded back pay from her late employer Schonle's estate, the court examined Schonle's logbooks. Schonle's heirs conceded that "the salary payments for the maidservant were recorded in the deceased woman's ledger for all of the seasons during which she was in service, but from last summer going forward, no payments were recorded in the logbook."[10] By the eighteenth century, a woman's logbook of payments was unremarkable, deemed a reliable and perhaps expected source by the court. As economic agents, many Jewish women mastered some degree of financial literacy.

The wide range of financial records kept by individuals, households, and the Jewish community reveals details about women's lives, families, and finances. Jewish communal authorities carefully preserved copies of marital and business contracts, records of sales, purchases, loans and debts, summaries of acquisitions, inventories, and copies of individual wills. Overseen and signed by scribes or notaries, communal officials or the relevant parties consulted the documents in the event of a legal dispute.[11] Hundreds of women are listed by name in these records. The communal archive from the small village of Schnaittach contains a small sheet of paper recording a tena'im aharonim (marital financial agreement) between Moshe ben Nathan and Pessche bat Zekle, signed and witnessed after the couple wed. The bride's father furnished his daughter with a dowry, clothing for Shabbat and holidays (including scarves and wraps), and a bed; her grandfather promised to bequeath part of his home to her after his death. The groom agreed to furnish her with the necessary clothing and jewelry. The document also stipulated specific terms for dividing the property upon dissolution of the marriage by death or divorce.[12] The agreement ushers us into the home of a newlywed couple, complete with the understanding of who brought each of the assets into the marriage.

This is one of many similar agreements preserved in the archives. A Jewish letter kept in the files of Christian Hebraist Johann Wagenseil similarly lists the Shabbat finery, wedding ring, and cash that the writer's sister was to receive from her betrothed; her family was accountable for the dowry, her scarves and wraps, a bed, and a *sivlonot* belt (a silver belt gifted to the groom or bride).[13] Although Moshe and Pessche were from Schnaittach, and this second unnamed bride was marrying a young man from Lwów (Lvov) in Poland, the similarities between the financial arrangements are unmistakable.[14] They are likely due to the proliferation of prepared agreements upon which individuals could base their own contracts. Given the expectation that all transactions would be formally documented and preserved, uniformity of the texts for the same type of contract was critical. Similarly, templates for the gifts and sums furnished by the bride's and groom's families before and after a marriage, marriage contracts, formulas for divorce ceremonies, and models for economic agreements and for wills were composed, circulated, and later printed.

Rabbi Shmuel Halevi's printed volume of contract templates, *Nahalat shivah* (1667), facilitated women's access to property by standardizing certain legal mechanisms that ensured women's inheritances, since under strict Torah and rabbinic law, only sons inherited. One such mechanism, *shetar hatzi helek zakhar* (a promissory note allocating one-half of a male's portion to daughters), was developed in the late medieval period. This contract indebted a father to his daughter immediately before his death. The debt could be forgiven only if her brother gave her one-half of the portion, or sometimes more, allotted to him from the estate.[15] Dissemination by print rendered this mechanism standard practice by the seventeenth century.[16] Halevi's printed volume popularized this and other formulas; contracts, wills, and court cases indicate that they were widely employed across Jewish communities.

Another set of documents critical for documenting women's economic agency are the decisions and dossiers of court cases recording how women defended their rights and property. Although this period was by no means the first in which Jewish women pursued justice in court, hundreds of cases involving early modern Jewish women were preserved in a wide variety of courts: rabbinic and lay Jewish courts, as well as municipal, regional, and imperial non-Jewish courts.[17] Several developments in law during the early modern period render women's presence in court far more visible. The resurgence of Roman law permitted women to appear personally before the court in Europe. As jurists integrated that corpus into other bodies of law in continental Europe, women appeared as plaintiffs and defendants in multiple non-Jewish courts. Law was a key element in early modern state building, and the documents associated with that process, whether court records or other bureaucratic paperwork, reveal the depths of women's involvement in legal systems. Jewish men and women appeared frequently before the two imperial courts in the Holy Roman Empire; most of these cases dealt with credit and loans.[18] Verena Kasper-Marienberg has shown that 108 cases brought before the *Reichshofrat* during the eighteenth century involved Jewish women, and about half of these were initiated by them.[19]

Women also appeared before both rabbinic and lay Jewish courts. About 40 percent of parties appearing before the rabbinical court in late eighteenth-century Metz were women, and they initiated a quarter of the suits.[20] In the course of 1,458 cases brought before the Jewish civil small claims court in Altona from 1768 to 1771, approximately 14.5 percent of those who appeared were women, sometimes alone and sometimes in partnerships with others (men and/or women) who do not appear to be related to them.[21] These courts recognized that women acted on their own, appeared often before the courts, and, in many cases, represented themselves. In addition, as Jewish and non-Jewish courts interacted with one another, they litigated and discussed issues of Jewish and local law and their impact on women's property rights.[22]

Women, Jewish Law, and Property

In addition to income they earned by their labor, early modern women typically acquired money and property upon pivotal life cycle events: marriage, the dissolution of marriage upon divorce or death, and the death of a parent.[23] Thus, a woman's marital status significantly impacted her claim to property. As Jay Berkovitz's foundational work on eighteenth-century Metz has established, both Jewish law and local custom determined women's access to property.[24]

Dowry at marriage was one point in the conventional life cycle of Jewish women and girls that involved the transfer of significant family assets.[25] Dowries in early modern Europe were notoriously expensive, sometimes unaffordable, even for many middle-class women in both Christian and Jewish communities.[26] Single women entered domestic service to earn money toward their dowries, individual benefactors and pious confraternities established funds to dower brides, and parents would sometimes travel to different Jewish communities seeking to solicit funds on their own.[27] While men were more frequently tasked with collecting charity, a seventeenth-century responsum of Rabbi Judah Mehler tells of "one woman who traveled from city to city, like an itinerant transient. [When] she arrived at a place where Jews resided ... she told the city inhabitants that she was traveling from place to place to collect [funds] from individuals, to raise and collect the sums to dower her daughter, who was betrothed to a young man."[28] We only learn of this woman's initiative because she fell ill and died while on her mission. The unnamed community, home to a small number of Jews, turned to Mehler to ask whether they might take the cash she had collected, which they found stowed in her bag, to cover some of the costs of her burial. Even that "was not sufficient to cover the cost of her burial, shrouds, and other funerary needs; only approximately half of the expense, more or less."[29] The woman's satchel didn't contain the standard letter carried by beggars, "specifically those who collected to dower poor brides," indicating that she embarked on this journey on her own initiative, without a note from a rabbi or communal leader vouching for her integrity.

Unforeseen economic circumstances could make it impossible for a bride's family to fulfill the terms of the premarital agreement they had reached with the groom. In 1723, Moses ben David Shurelim wrote a letter to his future son-in-law, Moses of Worms, apologizing that he had not been able to amass the sum promised as dowry; the time of the wedding as stipulated in the premarital contract had already passed. The groom agreed to an extension, asking that his future father-in-law deposit the dowry thirty days before the newly scheduled wedding date, which was standard practice.[30] In addition, he asked for collateral of one hundred Reichsthaler to be held by a third party as security toward the dowry. Should the new wedding date pass, the groom would take this sum and be free to marry another.[31] In a similar case in eighteenth-century Metz, the groom's father was distraught that the bride's father was unable to pay the promised dowry of eight hundred livres on time, and he sought to call off his son's wedding. Unlike the case in Worms, where the parties reached an agreement on their own, this case was brought before the rabbinical court. Since the bride's father expected to conclude a financial transaction that would yield most of the promised sum, the court achieved a settlement: they postponed the wedding and slightly reduced the amount of the dowry.[32] There was far more at stake in this case than the net amount of the dowry. Communal ordinances from Metz (1769) decreed that women who had brought higher dowries into their marriages could own up to six newly made dresses of the finest silks and fabrics and could cover their hair in the neighborhood with colored linen mantillas. Women with lower dowries were permitted only four or five new dresses, depending on their wealth, and the fabrics used to fashion their dresses were less expensive. Silks, elaborate headgear, and a greater number of newly made dresses visibly marked wealthier women as belonging to a higher social stratum.[33]

Fathers and mothers who were financially able often arranged their estates creatively to guarantee their daughters enough funds to wed. Many parents wrote wills and other contracts with specific terms that did not accord with talmudic law in order to ensure that their daughters received a share of the estate along with their brothers. Glikl of Hameln mentions that she and her sister, Elkele, had each been given promissory notes entitling them to a portion of their father's inheritance (the aforementioned shetar hatzi helek zakhar). Her husband, Hayim, and her wealthy brother-in-law, Joseph Stadthagen, opted to forgo their respective wives' claims on their father's estate in order to leave her widowed mother and the other orphaned children with additional assets.[34]

Sinai ben Yaakov of Worms employed a similar tactic to provide for his daughters in 1657. He bequeathed only ten Reichsthaler to his sons "so that the biblical precept of inheritance would not be cancelled" and stipulated that immediately prior to his death, his two daughters would inherit items of far greater value: all his books and real estate. Should either of his daughters predecease his sons, his sons were to inherit their sisters' portions; should the daughters marry prior to their father's death, the sons were to be their father's sole heirs since each daughter would have received her respective portion in the form of a dowry.[35] Similarly, Hirsch Oppenheim of Hamburg stated explicitly in his will (1777) that the dowry granted to his married daughter be considered a portion of her inheritance equal to those of her unmarried siblings.[36] Regarding the question of whether rabbinic courts honored such written wills, Berkovitz notes that by the late eighteenth century, the Metz rabbinic court tended to respect written wills even if they were not in conformity with halakhic guidelines.[37]

Mothers, too, sought to leave their daughters with financial means. In 1656, the widowed rabbanit Mehrle of Worms divided her movable property among her sons and her young and unmarried daughter "together, in equal amounts." Special stipulations about the family home ensured that she would provide for her daughter. Mehrle owned half of a house and bequeathed one-quarter to her sons and one-quarter to her daughter. She ordered that if one or both of her two sons were to adopt formal residency in Worms, that son was to pay his sister fifty Reichsthaler for her quarter of the house. If neither son resided in Worms, the entire half of the house would belong to Mehrle's daughter alone.[38] Similarly, in 1753, Fromet, the wife of Elia Levi in Metz, wrote and rewrote her will three times, allocating funds for her brother-in-law to hire a caretaker for her disabled daughter, Kilche.[39]

Legal strategies that granted property to daughters were not always appreciated by male heirs, and brothers did challenge their sisters' claims on estates.[40] In one seventeenth-century example, two brothers sought to invalidate the document providing for their sister, claiming the witness's signature could not be authenticated, as he had since moved to Poland.[41] In another case, when a newly widowed husband sought to procure his dead wife's share of the estate for his newborn baby, her brothers protested that the funds were intended solely for her and not for her progeny.[42] In a late eighteenth-century case from Metz, Rachel and Salomon Alphen challenged her father Samuel Lévi's will on appeal to the non-Jewish French Parlement following a ruling from the rabbinical court. Using discrepancies between his Hebrew and his French will, Rachel and Salomon invoked both French and Jewish law before the Parlement, arguing that she and her children should inherit. This case highlights how Jews could leverage the complex intersection between local and Jewish law to shape the outcome of a case.[43]

Provisions under French law led Merlé Spir-Levi to write a will in 1739 in which she disinherited her husband, Jacob Worms, claiming he had already squandered the money and property that she had brought into their marriage. Her powerful brother, a parnas in Metz, championed her position. Her husband turned to the Parlement, enraged that his wife had written a will that contravened Jewish law to exclude him.[44] In a second case from Metz, Magdeleine Cahen sought to exclude her dowry and additional property that she had inherited from her father from becoming joint marital property. The parnassim, including her guardian, urged her not to do so and excommunicated her. Magdeleine approached the Parlement, claiming that such excommunications prevented the French bailiwick from implementing its decisions. The Parlement forced the community to overturn her excommunication.[45] The numerous cases brought before various courts document the legal efforts invoked by women (and their relatives) to protect their property.

The court in Metz also recognized women's testimony in the context of a property dispute. Part of the conflict that had erupted between Yatkhe, the widow of Wolf Trani, and the executors of her husband's estate was contested ownership over certain pieces of jewelry. To determine whether said items belonged to Yatkhe or to the estate, the rabbinical court ruled that if Yatkhe had worn a specific item prior to her husband's death, that jewelry could be considered hers. The court recognized that women would be more likely to know what jewelry Yatkhe had worn, and it wrote: "The aforementioned determination can even be [executed] by women, and whatever is impossible to determine does not belong to her." Ultimately, the court based its decision upon women's testimony: "And following our decision, it became apparent, based on the testimony of several women who had seen and identified that the two aforementioned pairs of earrings, and the two aforementioned pearl collars and the aforementioned golden chain, had been on the body of the widow during her husband's lifetime. All of the aforementioned jewelry that was determined by women to have been on her body, as mentioned above, belong to the aforementioned widow."[46] Women's knowledge of and familiarity with Yatkhe's accessories were the deciding factors in the case; their testimony determined the outcome of the legal proceedings.

Any inheritance they may have received, gifts upon betrothal, and dowry settled upon their marriage constituted the cornerstones of women's assets. Women's wills testify to the diverse range of property they could control: the material goods they prized, the clothing they cherished and passed on to beloved heirs, the houses and synagogue seats in their possession, and the money that they bequeathed to charity and relatives. Martha Howell has analyzed two types of communal approaches to marital assets. In the first, a "communal property regime," the law merged and treated all the properties of a husband and wife as one unit, and the survivor generally inherited the joint estate. The second type was a "separate property regime," in which each party guarded the assets it brought into the marriage separately, making the disposition of those assets far more complicated when one partner died.[47] Jews of early modern Europe inherited a combination of approaches. According to Jewish law, one portion of the dowry was placed under the husband's control and management but would revert to his wife in its original value upon dissolution of the marriage, despite any loss that the husband may have incurred. A second portion remained in the wife's name, but any income produced from these joint assets belonged to the husband.[48] Thus, in 1768 in Altona, a communal official reported, "I was sent by the collector Leyb Hausen to the wife of R. Meir Wagner to tell her that: Whereas her husband is written on the page of non-compliers because he did not pay the fine and did not heed the mandatory injunction, therefore, the collectors will send for and notify the non-Jewish authority, to take the security from her home."[49] When Meir failed to pay the required fine, security was taken from *his wife's* home. This case underlines that a married woman's economic fortunes were dependent on her husband's. It also exemplifies another conspicuous facet of Jewish family life in the early modern period: women who became single as a result of death or abandonment were a familiar "type."[50] Meir's whereabouts were unknown, yet death was far from the only thing that took husbands away. Commerce, begging, and employment opportunities in distant places kept many Jewish men far from their homes and their wives. Abandoned women often ended up at the bottom of the economic ladder, desperate to keep their homes warm and their children fed.

Every Jewish woman was entitled by her ketubbah (marriage contract) to a certain sum upon her husband's death or dissolution of the marriage if she was not at fault. Rabbi Isaac mi-See, who served in several southern German towns, explained that in sixteenth-century Germany, each region had its own custom as to the amount a woman would receive. "Each region has a custom for the value of the marriage contracts; for example, in the region of Swabia,

Franconia until Koblenz, all of the virgins received 600; in Regensburg, it is 1200."[51] He relied on these norms to make financial determinations in cases in which a marriage contract, or other relevant information, was unavailable.

In practice, the disposition of a family's wealth could be quite complicated, especially since multiple sequential marriages were not uncommon, and neither were divorces. Leyb Essa gave his daughter Esther, born to his first wife, all her deceased mother's clothing and associated kerchiefs and scarves in 1657. He also gave her half of a house he owned in Worms, all without prejudice to his second wife's marriage contract; he alone was financially liable to his daughter.[52] When Fromet, the daughter of Moshe Wallerstein, was betrothed in 1657, her stepfather Hayim assumed responsibility for paying her dowry and splitting the wedding expenses with the groom's family; her brothers, however, undertook the assessment of her net worth.[53] Each of these steps added a layer of complication, but they also provide something of a gift to historians, for it is at these complex junctures—when ketubbah or other support payments were at stake, when written testaments and wills were contested, when inventories were taken of property, and litigation over them ensued—that written documents illuminate economic aspects of women's lives. One eighteenth-century Jewish man, after disposing of various obligations in his will, wrote that he left the remainder of all he had to his wife as a gift in his lifetime "so that my wife would not have to make a list, an accounting, or an inventory" for any debtor or heir, effectively leaving her all of his property.[54] Husbands concerned about providing for their widows might also increase the sum due to their wives under the marriage contract, thereby leaving them with a greater share of the family's wealth. Hirtz Segal, the doctor in Worms who had rented a home from Krinchen and her brother, did so for his wife in 1657, promising her one thousand Reichsthaler upon dissolution of their marriage.[55] The marriage contract was essential for protecting a widow's rights. Without the marriage contract in hand, officials could not accurately oversee the payments due to a widow from the estate. Therefore, when a marriage contract was lost, it was critical to replace it, as Meir ben Eliezer of Worms did after his wife's ketubbah was lost in 1656.[56]

Despite such precautions, a woman might nevertheless be unable to recoup the sum promised in her marriage contract due to debts and losses incurred by her husband's estate. Already in the Middle Ages, wives were demoted to secondary creditor status to facilitate men's borrowing money; otherwise, individuals might be loath to lend money, fearing they would not be repaid when the borrower's wife staked her claim on the estate. By the seventeenth century, a formal legal mechanism referred to by the Hebrew acronym *be'ohev* was established and widely employed in contracts to alleviate this concern.[57] By appending this term to a contract, the parties indicated that the debt and liability in the contract were assumed by both wife and husband, rendering the wife an active partner in the transaction and, thus, contractually responsible for the debt. This mechanism was essential in the early modern economy, in which wives worked alongside their husbands.

Legal forms of joint accountability paralleled German municipal laws that compelled "market women" (women who worked regularly) to assume responsibility for their husbands' debts.[58] In Frankfurt, in addition to the be'ohev formula, a 1627 communal ordinance mandated that "women are obligated to pay, together with their husbands, when he has legally transacted (by kinyan sudar). However, if the woman had previously come before the appointed witnesses and explicitly said that they should not make any contract nor accept any legal acquisition performed by her husband without her knowledge," then the woman would not be liable for the husband's debt.[59] In a striking parallel to the city laws in Frankfurt obligating market women to pay their husbands' debts, Jewish women who worked regularly were deemed responsible for their husbands' debts by default. Yet some Jewish women took the extra step of appearing before the communal notaries to shield their assets from lenders. Three folios in the seventeenth-century Jewish notaries' logbook list well over one hundred women who appeared before the notaries to exclude their property from their spouse's holdings, thus protecting it from any legal claims.[60] While most women appeared before the notaries themselves, some did so with the assistance of male relatives. The women's wishes, however, were essential to the process. In 1653, Hirz Oppenheim appeared before the Jewish notaries on behalf of his two daughters, Yacht and Hindchen. The notaries logged: "We have yet to independently solicit the opinions of his two aforementioned daughters." An additional note indicates that the notaries followed up: "After this, I asked them, Hindchen and Yacht."[61] Women and their families of origin worked together to safeguard the family wealth, as did Edel, the divorcée mentioned above, who sought to ensure that if anything happened to her and her son, her property would revert to her brother.

In many cases, however, contractual formulas such as be'ohev decreased the amount available to a newly widowed woman, since they ensured that other creditors were paid back before she was able to collect what had been promised to her under the terms of her marriage contract. A depreciated estate left one seventeenth-century widow with no funds to cover the amount promised her. All that remained were the synagogue seats owned by her husband, which the local charity collector sought to acquire against her husband's debts to the community. In this case, Rabbi Judah Mehler ruled that the wife, rather than the community, was the primary creditor.[62] Similarly, in the eighteenth century, Bela bat Moshe of Metz approached the communal leaders, explaining, "My husband of blessed memory owed me 1,100 Reichstaler, as is indicated in the contract that I have from him, and his entire estate was insufficient to pay me the aforementioned debt of 1,100 Reichstaler." Although her husband, Meir, had given a synagogue seat to their son, Avraham, Bela insisted that "it can be argued in court that my heirs and I should divide the seats, that is to say, that my husband of blessed memory did not have the right to bequeath the aforementioned seat [to my son] as a gift, for it all belongs to me as per the bill of debt of 1,100 Reichstaler."[63] Bela then gifted the seat (and an additional seat she owned) to her son in perpetuity, leveraging the economic claim she had against her husband's estate as an opportunity to formally register that her husband had failed to support her as promised.

While Bela had funds of her own, exemplifying a widow who achieved economic independence and success, others fell into penury. Gender formed the most significant dividing line between early modern people, but class came a close second. Jewish women's professions and the degree of financial stability they possessed varied considerably across the socioeconomic spectrum. Women held in common aspects of their living conditions, depending on their class status and, in many ways, regardless of religion. The greater access they had to wealth, the greater access women had to education, to networks of kinship and commerce, and to material comforts, living space, and decent nutrition for themselves and their families. Economic conditions within families also rose and fell for reasons both personal and circumstantial. Glikl famously bemoaned her situation after her second husband, Cerf Levy, lost both their fortunes; similar misfortune met other families of court Jews. When a fire raged through Frankfurt in 1711, destroying the homes in the Judengasse, over a quarter of the community's Jews received financial relief and charity.[64]

A 1790 letter from Anna Levinstret, originally of Dresden, to Isaac Herschel, her late husband's business associate in London, claims that the latter had in his possession goods belonging to Anna's husband. These included "two bundles of pearls, two diamond rings, and two large books." Anna had left Dresden for Vienna, renting space with her three sons, and urgently requested the goods, as she was in dire straits.[65]

Rivkah Hindele, widow of Avraham Mannheim, penned another Yiddish letter tucked into the Jewish communal archive of Worms in 1722. Rivkah was living in the village of Kirrweiler, some forty-six kilometers from Worms. She wrote to the communal leaders of Worms to claim a sum of money she was owed so that she would not become "a burden" on the community in her old age.[66] Like Anna Levinstret, who wrote from Germany to London to secure belongings to which she laid claim, Rivkah Hindele wrote to the Worms leaders from her home in Kirrweiler, navigating the routine economic relations between city and countryside. Although the distance between Worms and Kirrweiler may have posed a physical challenge for an elderly woman, it did not prevent her from voicing her claim.

Some widows faced the additional peril of losing their homes since Jewish law entitled them only to their own property and to the sum agreed to in their marriage contract. Men who owned houses frequently passed them directly to their children, who could take ownership of the home, leaving the widow bereft of spouse and home. Such cases could be especially fraught when the heirs to the home were the women's stepchildren, who could take possession of the home and oust their stepmother. In Metz in 1769, the community enacted a decree that would permit widows to remain in the family home unless and until they remarried, regardless of whether their marriage contract specified that right.[67] This marked a change from the medieval period when widows often struggled to remain in their homes after the death of a spouse.[68] Policies in other early modern communities were more akin to those of the Middle Ages than to those in eighteenth-century Metz in that they did not automatically accord widows the right to remain in their homes. In eighteenth-century Frankfurt, cases between widows and children litigated the widow's right of residence, ownership, and financial responsibilities in what had been her family home.[69] Multiple examples of widows renting rooms survive in communal records; these cases likely reflect widows who moved out of the family home to the benefit of their husband's heirs. For example, Bella, the widow of Mechel Speyer of Hamburg, lived alone in a single room in the house of another community member in the late eighteenth century.[70] The widow Rechle rented rooms from Ber Rindskopf of Frankfurt, agreeing in 1764 to pay for some of the household repairs.[71] In other places, husbands sought to arrange matters before they died to avoid a legal dispute. In 1657, Tevlin of Worms granted his wife Gitlen a lien on part of a house he owned in Worms, guaranteeing that she could reside there in her widowhood.[72] In exchange, she promised that the entirety of his estate would revert uncontested to his heirs, other than the wedding ring he had given her.[73] These different cases emphasize that Jewish women's property rights varied by time and by location, impacted by both Jewish law and local practice.

Jewish Women and Commerce

The structures governing dowries and marriage contracts gave women an interest in the family's economic health from the start of their marriages. Many ba'alot bayit started out in commerce as adjuncts to businesses that their husbands ran, sometimes with money they had brought into the marriage as dowry. Jewish involvement in commerce and lending was particularly common because restrictions precluded Jewish men and women from various types of work, guild membership, and most programs of university study.

The role of Jewish women in business can be measured on two levels, as Michael Toch has argued: the "formal" one, which appears in records and can be easily measured, and the far larger "informal" one, which does not appear in the written records, but in which Jewish women participated as part of their family businesses on an everyday basis.[74] Recent research on Christian women has also challenged the thesis that women's work declined throughout the early modern period, pointing instead to the myriad ways women were involved in work despite regulations prohibiting their labor.[75] Commercial documents generally privileged husbands as the legal heads of the family unit; their lone signatures on contracts might totally obscure the participation of (and the obligations assumed by) their wives.[76] Yet other sources show us how deeply involved women were in their families' business, not only when they became widowed but in all stages of life, daily. Frau Schoenlin, writing a letter from Sofia to her son, Eliezer Lippman in Trieste, described the challenges her family encountered in the Ottoman Empire, where they had traveled from southern Germany. Her son-in-law had difficulty obtaining work, and Schoenlin recounted that water carrying, which was arduous, and spinning wool, which was considered women's work, were inappropriate for him. Moving on to Sofia, he secured work as a teacher and a ritual slaughterer while earning additional sums for reading the Torah in the synagogue; Schoenlin found work as a midwife.[77] In matters small and large, spanning management of funds, letters of credit, and every conceivable commodity, women participated knowledgeably, often on their own.

In her memoirs, Glikl of Hameln recounted her involvement in her husband Hayim's business even before his death. In recalling her and her husband's unsuccessful early business relationship with their nephew, R. Yudah Berlin (better known later as court Jew Jost Liebmann), she noted that they articulated their concerns to Reb Yudah and stipulated that they would only enter into a business agreement with him if there were a written contract detailing all their conditions. Glikl wrote, "So I said to my husband, of blessed memory: 'We can try it for a year. When I get a chance I will draft a short agreement and show it to you to see how you like it.' That night I sat by myself to draft an agreement."[78] Glikl casually mentioned this small detail in her larger tale of the relationship, as though drafting contractual agreements with business partners was a regular part of her work in the family business. Similarly, Hevle Kann of Frankfurt (d. 1784) maintained her family's account books, as is attested in the communal memorial book: "She was intelligent, and skilled in writing and language and sums, to bring them before knowledgeable men."[79] A partner to her husband Leyb, she was literate in reading and mathematics and may have been conversant in German in addition to the Yiddish she would have spoken and read. Hevle's father, Todros Stern, and her husband, Leyb Kann, served as communal charity collectors in Frankfurt's Judengasse in addition to managing their own financial affairs. Hevle likely acquired her skills from a domestic apprenticeship, having observed the business and communal recordkeeping in her home; she later kept the family business records herself.

Still, much of the evidence of women's skills as entrepreneurs and partners surfaced when husbands died, and their widows took over, sometimes seamlessly. Brendele, resident of "zum Hirsch," in Frankfurt am Main, can serve as a typical case. To collect the funds owed to her deceased husband, Anselm (d. 1541), she played court systems against one another, pursuing her cases for over twenty years until her debtors paid. She then appeared in the records as conducting business independently.[80] Because many Jews were involved at some point in lending money at diverse levels, the pursuit of the capital tied up in debt was an important aspect of solvency, and considerable diplomacy was involved in compelling debtors, often in far-flung jurisdictions, to repay loans. Jewish widows across this period appear repeatedly in the records, acting to protect themselves in this way.

Regulations from late seventeenth-century Bamberg reflected the strong expectation that widows would work. The community taxed a nonworking widow at half the rate at which it taxed a man, and it exempted widows from all other communal fees. "However, if she [the widow] engages in commerce ... she is as one of the locals in all respects, except for the 'head of household' tax, for which she is still assessed at half."[81] Similar regulations existed in late eighteenth-century Alsace.[82] Communal memorial books praise women such as Marat Esther of Mainz, "who sustained herself throughout her widowhood by the fruit of her own labor."[83]

Two inventories of widows from Altona in 1809 open the doors of their respective homes, revealing the commerce they conducted there in the years before their deaths. The widow Hendele had among her possessions a sewing cushion; she also had a reckoning weight to weigh merchandise. Liebche, the widow of Mendel Eschwege, had no children; "her home was filled with iron implements, with which she conducted commerce."[84] These few words on a list of household possessions allow us to enter, if only a bit, the spaces in which these widows lived and worked, earning their living in commerce.

Widowed women also served as guarantors of loans taken out by family members. In 1774, Bella Pflegerin served as guarantor when her son-in-law, Solomon Kronberg, wished to purchase goods on credit from Ber Rindskopf, who did not know Solomon well. When Solomon defaulted, Ber pursued his claim against Bella in court; Bella paid the sum back in two installments.[85]

Surviving court and communal records are similarly skewed toward illuminating the activity of widowed women, obscuring the large number of married women whose role in their family economies was sizable. Evidence of married women's activities can, nevertheless, be found in some cases brought before both Jewish and Christian courts, in which the women appeared as parties. Sara of Rosheim was called to testify before Strasbourg's municipal court in the sixteenth century in a case involving loans and the sale of wine. While her son, Abraham, offered to appear in her stead because she was ill, the city magistrates adjourned the court date, wishing to hear from his widowed mother, Sara, directly.[86] In Metz, Tertzkhe, a married woman with children, approached the rabbinical court with her financial difficulties. Her husband, Wolf, had left for Paris, abandoning her and her children. He had arranged a marriage for his daughter, Reizle, at some point before leaving. Tertzkhe found herself unable to pay the agreed-upon sum as stipulated in the premarital contract. She appealed to the court, asking that the charity from a relative's will be used to provide her daughter with the funds necessary for a dowry. The court agreed, provided that she would be responsible for paying the tuition of the ten students who had previously been supported by that fund. They granted Tertzkhe a period of two years after the dowry had been given to her daughter to do so.[87] The married Anna Goldschneiderin of Prague battled the Christian Georg Reichel von Reichelsburg in non-Jewish courts over debts he owed her for several years starting in 1617; the litigation went all the way to an imperial court.[88]

Other traces of the activities of ba'alot bayit are mentioned in the records of communal notaries. On 21 Sivan 1748, the married Sprintz legally contracted to rent one-quarter of zum Appelbaum, her house in Frankfurt's Judengasse, to Jozbel Mans. The annual rental fee was eight Reichsthaler, three of which would be paid to the community as tax. Jozbel was also responsible for any repairs and for the municipal tax payment. Only ten months later did Sprintz's husband, Hayim, surface in the written record. "He was pleased with all aspects of the above [contract]" and recorded an advance payment made by Jozbel toward future rent.[89] Records such as these demonstrate that women were active in their family economies, whether lending, selling, renting, or representing the family's interests in court; they functioned much like married Christian women, who were empowered as "critical business partners."[90] The Jewish custom of requiring both husband and wife to be present during the tax assessment oath, normative in both large urban communities such as Worms and Frankfurt and small villages such as Runkel (a town in Hesse), shows that women were partners, deemed responsible for honestly and accurately reporting on their familial income and debt.[91]

Single women were also involved in lending and business, as seen in several eighteenth-century sources. A communal ordinance from Berlin in 1745 established the tax rate for "single men or single women, sons and daughters of community members, who trade in money that belongs either to them or their living parents."[92] Cases from late eighteenth-century Metz indicate that single women did, indeed, lend money to their relatives and neighbors, taking material goods as collateral against the loan. Nena, the daughter of Meir Wilstatt, sent a representative to the rabbinical court, asking for an appraisal of the [unspecified] cloth robe and skirt, the silk robe and skirt, and the men's silk robe she held from her sister as surety for a loan of twelve Louis d'or. Her sister, Reizche, had thirty days to repay her, or the clothing would revert to Nena.[93] Another single woman, Tipche, acting through her brother, Mordekhai, lent thirty livres to a married woman, Breinle. She, too, requested an appraisal of two golden crosses and a French book with silver clasps that she held as collateral.[94] The court provided the requested appraisals, approving the condition that Nena and Tipche would become the rightful owners of the goods if they were not repaid within a month. The court fully recognized these single women as lenders, suggesting that it was not uncommon for single women to have access to money of their own and to lend it.

Jewish women in rural areas were also involved in credit, providing small loans to both villagers and city dwellers. In seventeenth-century Swabia, Jewish men and women in Pfersee lent money to the burghers in Augsburg, a major city from which Jews had been expelled. Jews who resided in further outlying areas lent money to village peasants.[95] Similarly, in the rural Jewish communities of Alsace, Jews lent money both to urban burghers in nearby Strasbourg and to villagers in the countryside.[96] In the Swabian countryside, women such as Merle Ulman took simple items as pawns for small loans. The bedding, cloth, and garments that she and her husband took as collateral were unremarkable, recorded without any distinctive features or adornments. These small-scale loans were more typical in rural areas where poor Jews lent money to poor Christians than in urban ones. The modest size of rural markets led Jewish men to travel from village to village, leaving their wives to handle the local business. This arrangement rendered married women critical to the family's earnings; ten Jewish businesswomen appear in the records from the small town of Pfersee from 1800 to 1820.[97] In the village of Steinbiedersdorf in France, men whose wives were disabled sought relief from local government authorities because their wives could not work. As one man wrote, he was "inundated with children, and for a long time I have with me my weak and disabled wife, who has never been able to lend me a helping hand in any way."[98] This, too, speaks to the central role women played in the rural economy, as it was expected that wives would work. When a woman could not work, the family's finances were imperiled.

Urban commerce often entailed considerable travel, skills at negotiation, and deep knowledge of the prices and quality of commodities. Unlike their female coreligionists in eastern Europe, who stayed at home while their husbands traveled, Jewish women in western cities often accompanied their husbands on the road.[99] Women traveled to local markets and international fairs, where they were immersed in buying and selling, settling debts, and tending to networks of social and economic credit.[100] Glikl of Hameln recounts having visited the Leipzig fair, and her name appears on the pages of the fair register.

During her first husband's lifetime, her widowhood, and her second, unhappy marriage, Glikl was a sharp businesswoman who traveled and recorded many of her deals in her memoirs. She further recalled that Esther Hildesheim, one of Altona's first residents, was also "skilled at business," always attending the annual fair in Kiel.[101] Similarly, Gertraud Munk of Vienna, a married independent businesswoman, was granted an imperial travel pass to facilitate her travel to Poland, Hungary, and the court in Regensburg.[102]

The large number of responsa and regulations regarding the propriety of women appearing in public spaces and on the road shows that conflicts of values arose between notions of female modesty and the need for Jewish

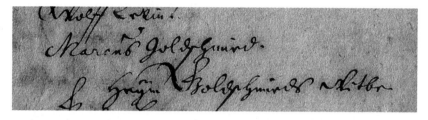

FIG. 7.2. Glikl of Hameln visits the Leipzig fair in 1692 for the first time since being widowed. She is listed as Haym Goldschmidt's widow.

women's mobility.[103] One seventeenth-century responsum highlights this conflict. Two men and two women traveled together from Frankfurt to Worms. Lacking the necessary travel permits, the women engaged in subterfuge and pretended to be the wife and daughter of their male companions. His suspicion roused due to the discrepancy in age between the men and women, the border guard said: "I don't believe you; how could this older woman be the wife of such a young man, and a daughter so old be the other man's daughter? Let each one of you swear to your identity, or else kiss the women full on the mouth, [demonstrating that] this is his wife and daughter."[104] Extramarital sexual contact, let alone in public, would have been unthinkable conduct for the pious Jewish travelers. Flustered, they bribed the guard and moved on; their story brings to the fore the tension between travel and gendered norms of propriety.

Despite these tensions, countless examples place women in markets, on the road, or at court. Glikl recounts several occasions on which she traveled on the mail train, which became common sometime after her marriage to Hayim in 1657.[105] The frequency of women's travel is evident also from a letter discouraging women from traveling during a pandemic: "Also, they do not permit anybody from Vienna to enter; people who arrived here were forced to stay in the cemetery for three days, and afterwards they were simply expelled under penalty of 500 Gulden."[106]

Women's travel could be perilous, particularly at night, as we learn from an anecdote Glikl shared about her husband. "Deeply worried" about her traveling at night, Hayim insisted that she change out of her "good traveling clothing to don old rags."[107] When their companion, Meir, mocked his concern, insulting Glikl's looks, Hayim was enraged. His fears lest she be attacked as a well-dressed woman while traveling at night highlight how gender and class rendered the road all the more hazardous, particularly in the dark.

Court Jews

Foremost among all the women involved in business and commerce were the wives of court Jews and a handful of Jewish women who were appointed court Jews in their own right.[108] In the seventeenth century, as the figure of the court Jew became prominent, husbands supplied provisions for nobles and their courts, while their wives often did the same for women of the court. These women wielded informal power as key players through whom alliances could be forged. Marriages between the children of wealthy court Jews and daughters of the economic elite with rising rabbinic figures cemented ties between elite families and forged networks spanning Europe.[109] As scholars of Christian court networks have shown, the women of the court, such as female patrons, ladies-in-waiting, and women who more broadly shaped reputations and opinions, held great influence over worldly events.[110] Court Jewish women similarly held the power to sway opinions, and communal sources praised them for their actions on behalf of the Jewish community. Miriam Sara, the wife of the court factor of Brandenburg, Elias Gomperz of Cleves (and mother-in-law of Glikl's daughter, Tzipor), exemplified this power. The Cleves memorial book notes: "She was wise and taught the nation with her agreeable words; she strengthened our faith and responded to accusations before the courts of the land, wisely and with reason, and with her pleasant words, she advised and reaped revenue from the lords of the land and the emperor."[111] Miriam undoubtedly continued to wield both wealth and influence after her husband's death. Rivkah Brendele of Mainz, the wife of the charity collector Wolf Offenbach, similarly "interceded on behalf of the poor and incarcerated before the Christian authorities, to help and exempt them from taxes, as she was able. She also provided her wise counsel to whomever sought her out."[112] Other female court Jews, such as Talze, the daughter of David Oppenheim and wife of Ber Cleves, were recognized for the advice they provided to their husbands: "She was so wise that her husband was confident in her that she would frequently provide him with wise and principled counsel."[113]

While women were not accepted in these roles without constraint, they were nevertheless active. In one notable case, a married woman in the eighteenth century, Madame Chaile [Karoline] Kaulla (b. 1737), served as court factor for the Hohenzollern in Hechingen and later for the Duke of Württemburg as the head of her own firm. Kaulla was the eldest daughter of Raphael, the court factor in Donauechingen and Hechingen (see plate 15). Educated in German by a Christian teacher hired by her father, she began to work alongside her father, as the eldest among her brothers was eleven years her junior. When her father died in 1760, she was twenty-one years old, and she took on the business herself, joined only in later years by her brother. In 1768, Madame Kaulla was officially named the court factor; she provided horses, jewels, silver, and other goods to the court.[114] Her prosperity and success are visibly displayed in her ornate blue-and-gold-patterned china coffee set, adorned with Hebrew phrases, which she commissioned for her home (see plate 16).

In 1803, Madame Kaulla and her brother transformed a house that had belonged to their father into a *kloyz* (study hall) in Hechingen; this is another example of a wealthy woman's participation in the male world of Torah study through financial support. Upon her death in 1809, her sons hired Moshe ben Hayim Dispek to compose a eulogy for their mother, which he did, writing twenty-eight folios in Hebrew. Bemoaning the loss, he wrote, "Who will now honor those who study the Torah of God as the righteous Kaulla did?"[115] Dispek further compared her to the biblical Shunamite woman who served as financial benefactor to the prophet Elisha. By likening her to a biblical woman, Dispek sought to fit Chaile Kaulla into a traditional pattern; in reality, her actions and independence as court factor far exceeded this framework.[116] His comparison is belied by her tombstone, which recognized her singularity, praising her "wisdom and counsel" as surpassing that of an honored man.[117] The monograms on her coffee set emphatically recognized her singular status and the title and position that she, rather than her husband, held. Presumably, at her instruction, the monogram refers to her husband Akiva as "the notable Akiva," using an abbreviation signifying status within the Jewish community. She inscribed her own with "Madame Kaulla von Hechingen," a title reserved for court factors alone.

Other court Jewish women worked and donated together with their husbands. Miriam and Leyb Sinzheim were court Jews who resided in Vienna; Leyb was the son of Rebecca and Hayim Sinzheim of Mannheim, and Miriam was a granddaughter of Samuel Oppenheim, a famed financier of the emperor. In 1720, they built the Rashi study hall in Worms, and they were jointly remembered in the communal memorial book used at the prayer service in the study hall.[118] In 1738, Leyb began a letter to one of the communal leaders of Worms about furnishing the study hall with appropriate amounts of wood in winter and summer months. In mid-letter, Leyb abruptly stopped writing; Miriam's seamless continuation of his words is evident only from the new hand that takes up the letter in the middle of the line. Miriam explains that she took over the correspondence because her husband "was busy with great burdens."[119]

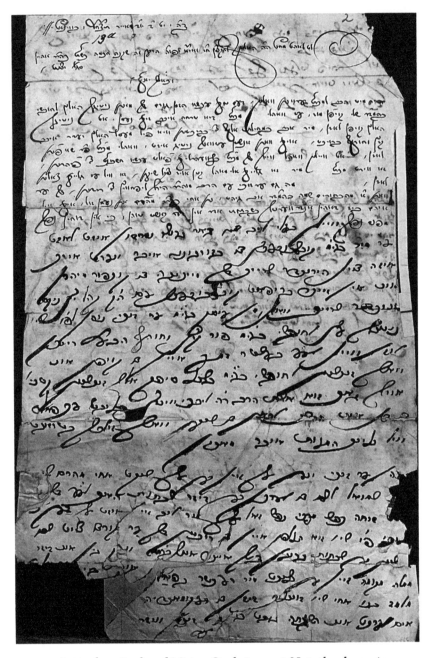

FIG. 7.3. Letter from Leyb and Miriam Sinzheim, 1738. Note the change in handwriting where Miriam took over.

Her ability to jump in at a moment's notice speaks to her involvement as a partner to her husband in finances and charity.

Women in the Household Economy

While many Jewish families, including both husbands and wives, were engaged in credit or commerce, others were jointly involved in the household economy by practicing a profession. The model of family members engaged in a profession with labor divided along gendered lines was common among contemporary Christians. Both Jewish and Christian women enjoyed far less access to funds than their male counterparts and had even fewer options for employment. Some types of work were gendered female, and these jobs typically paid lower wages. Others were based within the family, with women and men assigned those elements of labor deemed socially appropriate.

Several colophons record the labor of women in Jewish print houses, often alongside their husbands and fathers. We recall that Estellina Conat, the wife of Abraham Conat, a printer in Mantua and Ferrara in the late fifteenth century, recorded that it was she who arranged the printing of a Hebrew book based on an exemplar.[120] Such labor did not always necessitate understanding the text, as being able to recognize the Hebrew letters was sufficient for copying their arrangement on the page.[121] In one Yiddish book, the colophon includes a Yiddish statement by Ella, daughter of a printer in Dessau, excusing any mistakes one might find by explaining that she was merely nine years old.[122] Her much younger sister Gele (they had eight other siblings) also worked in her father's shop, where she composed a poem appended to a prayer book printed in 1710 when she was just under twelve: "This beautiful new prayer from the beginning to the end: I have set all the letters with my own hand."[123] Each continued to work in print in later years. Similarly, Rivkah and Reichel, the daughters of a printer in Wilmersdorf, worked in their father's print shop. Having acquired these skills, Reichel went on to work in print shops in Sulzbach and Fürth.[124] The colophon in a *mahzor* printed in Lublin in 1567 similarly records that the printers' families participated in the production of the text. The wives arranged the letters, and the sons dealt with the ink.[125] This division of labor reflects the structure of premodern economies, in which families worked together at a particular craft, often with a gendered division of labor. The print shop created a new space in which men and women worked side by side; it also brought women into more immediate contact with letters and literacy.

Married couples (and families) worked as employees in the Jewish hospice in Vienna and as workers in the cemetery and hospice in Frankfurt.[126] These latter positions, held by the laboring poor, provided indigent families with employment and residence. Like the aforementioned Itzik, who served as a guard with his widowed mother, these communal employees worked side by side, tending respectively to men and women.

In rural areas, Jewish women often pursued opportunities that arose in the countryside (see plate 17). Some made and sold dairy products. Some of their husbands were cattle merchants, and the wives also looked after the stables.[127] Poor urban women were also involved in making dairy products, as reported in a seventeenth-century responsum from Worms referring to Jewish women who sold chicks and chickens in the marketplace. When one chick jumped into a pail of milk in the marketplace and drowned, we learn also of "the wives of the poor, who woke early every day and left the Jewish street with small buckets with handles to milk the cows in Christian homes, before the cows went out to graze, and they would sell their wares in the Judengasse."[128] In eastern Frisia, Jewish women are listed in the tax records as pursuing a number of livelihoods. In the census of 1707/08, Samuel Uri's wife dealt in tobacco and lent money. Simon Nathan's wife traded in both of those commodities and also worked as a slaughterer. Isaac Josephs married a widow who dealt in horses and worked as a slaughterer.[129] Rural women adapted to their circumstances and showed initiative and self-reliance in earning their sustenance.

Domestic Service

Eking out a living as a poor Jew was not easy, and young, single Jewish girls and women of more limited means sought work in service. Without the salaries they earned as servants, they could not possibly amass enough money for a dowry. They would then be unable to wed in the competitive marriage market, for which a dowry was a prerequisite. In a 1713 letter from Amsterdam, Judah ben Isaac Kat"z wrote to R. Aaron, a scribe in London, seeking employment for his daughter as a maidservant:

> Because my situation is bad, there is nothing more to earn here.... My [daughter] Breinche has greatly in mind to travel to England; here there is no way of making a living. Most people don't have maidservants because it is such bad times. Those who used to have two maidservants keep only one, and the salary is not big, so it could add up to nothing. If ... you come

across, among your people, a good employment for her, please inform me. Not that I would have her dependent on you, heaven forbid. She is hardworking and knows needlework.[130]

Breinche's sole chance to marry rested on the opportunity of employment in London. Many other girls, particularly from rural areas, sought employment as maidservants in larger Jewish communities, where they could work for several years, putting together a nest egg with which they might secure a match. Larger communities held out the promise of employment, while it was difficult, barely possible, to secure work in the few Jewish homes in smaller, rural communities. Although in Swabia, single women could find work (and lodging) as servants, in Steinbiedersdorf in Lorraine, Jewish maidservants were few and far between.[131] By contrast, archival lists from 1703 in Frankfurt record approximately four hundred girls who were employed as maids, nannies, and cooks; only four were local.[132]

Most maidservants were single. Servant girls resided in the homes of their employers. Writing in the seventeenth century, Juspe Hahn urged employers to give their servants flexible time when their families came to visit.[133] In his native Frankfurt, only single women were to be hired as maidservants, and anyone who wished to employ a married maidservant had to pay a fine to the community.[134] This ensured jobs for single women who traveled to Frankfurt's bustling community seeking work and removed the threat of an extramarital affair between a married female servant and the men of the household. Out of the aforementioned four hundred maidservants who worked in Frankfurt in 1703 and 1709, only one was married; another, whose marital status is not mentioned, had a child.[135] Communal leaders sought to regulate maidservants' chastity by forcing pregnant maidservants to leave the community.[136] In seventeenth-century Altona, additional financial stipends of ten or twenty Mark were offered by the community to betrothed maidservants who had worked for at least three years in the community and had remained chaste.[137] In the early eighteenth century, any employer who hired a maidservant with children, "whether legitimate or illegitimate," had to assume financial responsibility for the maidservant's children.[138] This ensured that the community did not have to assume responsibility for additional poor.

Ensconced in the rhythm of the household, maidservants were privy to family secrets. In eighteenth-century Steinbiedersdorf, the married Perle Levy summarily dismissed her maidservant Sarle after three-and-a-half years of service. In a letter drafted on Sarle's behalf, Sarle explained her predicament:

"Today, as Shabbat was about to begin, Levy treated me with remarkable words of abuse and curses and threw me out of her house, saying I would have to leave that same Shabbat."[139] Sarle's dismissal was likely linked to her discovery of the extramarital pregnancy of her employer, Perle.

Girls secured the potential for social mobility by earning a living in service. Sorle, a woman who had been employed in Frankfurt during the late eighteenth century as a (widowed?) maidservant, amassed an estate of over one thousand Gulden, which she provisioned for her daughter Raizla and for the future marriages of her four grandchildren.[140] In eighteenth-century Altona, community member Falk ben Lazi sought permission to wed a non-native maidservant and made the relevant arrangements with the communal leaders. As there is no evidence she was pregnant at the time, it may have been a rare marriage based on affection across class lines.[141] Not all cases ended this way. Maidservants often became pregnant, and once their condition was visible, the communities frequently banished them. In one query brought before Rabbi Jacob Reischer, a widower had impregnated his maidservant, who hailed from a nearby village. According to her, "he seduced her and had relations with her in order to make her his betrothed. When she became pregnant from him, he told her to go to her father's house, and he set a time to write up the premarital agreement. But when she departed to her father's house ... he turned his back on her and came to these lands and betrothed himself to another virgin, betraying the one he had seduced."[142] Though the rabbis forbade him to marry his second betrothed, he did so in contravention of their warnings.[143]

Disputes between maidservants and their employers provide more details about their work. In a sixteenth-century case brought before Rabbi Isaac mi-See, a maidservant was tasked with bringing laundry back and forth from the house to be washed. When a garment was lost, her employer claimed that the maidservant should be held liable, as she had left the garment in the street; moreover, "the mistress had asked the maidservant whether she had brought the washing vessel back to the house, and she answered in the affirmative." The maidservant countered, "It was true; she believed she had returned everything to the house, and she still believed that to be the case. If [the garment] was lost later, what did that have to do with her? It could have gotten lost in the house, or before she had brought [the clean laundry] back."[144] Mi-See ruled that the employer could not charge the maidservant for the lost garment.

In later centuries, the work of maidservants became more differentiated. Some were designated laundresses, cooks, or nannies, while others sewed and cleaned. In late seventeenth-century Frankfurt, some (presumably wealthier) households employed more than one maidservant, with one designated as cook and the other as nanny, while, in other homes, one maidservant might have performed all the household chores.[145] Among their other duties, maidservants in seventeenth-century Frankfurt were responsible for preparing *hallot* (special bread for Shabbat and holidays) along with their mistresses, heating the food on holidays while the ba'alat bayit was in synagogue, and fetching the pots from the communal oven on Shabbat morning.[146]

Already in the late seventeenth century, several paragraphs in communal ordinances dealt specifically with the hiring, firing, and working conditions of maidservants.[147] Maidservants were typically hired for the summer or winter season. In Altona, communal ordinances stipulated that servants were free to hire themselves out to any householder they pleased, but each party must give at least four weeks' notice before the season ended if they wished to part ways. A later hand added to the regulations:

> Even prior to the four weeks, one who hires a maidservant [away from a current employer] must notify the father or the current employer of the girl, via the shamash or other reliable agent, that he had given *meydel geld* [a maidservant's fee as a binder]. This small sum was given to confirm the existence of an arrangement with the new employer. If within eight days of notification of his will to the householder or to the father of the maidservant, she wished to remain with her first employer, she may do so. After eight days, the binder could not be revoked.[148]

The ordinance demonstrates the involvement of communal officials in the domestic servant employment business. By the eighteenth century, Jewish women in some communities ran the equivalent of agencies for placing Jewish domestic servants in homes.[149] This streamlined the hiring process, and it points to a new profession adopted by early modern women.

The late eighteenth-century Jewish civil court in Altona refers to detailed and thorough regulations governing domestic service. Though they are no longer extant (and the court itself did not have a copy), these regulations promulgated by the Jewish community were modeled on local German regulations and became communal norms.[150] The cases litigated before that court allow us to piece together the intricate regulations and customs that governed the relationship between employers and domestic servants. The Altona court ordered Samuel Posner to pay his maidservant the entire wage for the seasons she worked for him, but he was permitted to deduct the expenses he paid for her stay at the hekdesh (hospice) during her illness, as well as additional costs she incurred during said illness (presumably doctor fees and/or medicine), "because this is the community regulation."[151]

In another type of case, the court ruled that an employer who had evicted a maidservant from his home before the contractual term of employment ended, "contrary to the community regulations," must forward the entire amount of the contract to the court. If the maidservant managed to find other employment, the amount of her new salary would be deducted from the amount held by the court; if not, the court would award the entire sum to her.[152] This case was one of many in which the communal court acted as guarantor for the specific sums owed to litigants. Maidservants, many of whom were migrants from the countryside, would be likely to end up on the community charity rolls if they did not find steady employment. By protecting the contractual rights of the servants, the community protected its own interests as well.[153]

Maidservants were also provided with clothing. When the aforementioned Perle Levy of Steinbiedersdorf fired her maid Sarle, Sarle sued her former mistress, demanding her wages and clothes. Perle, in turn, accused Sarle of stealing gloves, caps, towels, and ribbons. Sarle demanded that Perle return her new shoes, while Perle insisted that Sarle was only entitled to new shoes once her old ones had been worn through.[154] In a case before Frankfurt's rabbinical court between a maidservant and her employer's father-in-law, the unnamed maidservant demanded that her employer's estate pay her unpaid wages and provide her with "shoes and a frock, as was customary." Hired for the summer season, she was to be provided with these items as well as a salary and board. The court ordered the estate to pay the maidservant specific sums until she found new employment.[155]

It was not only individuals who hired maidservants. The burial society of Worms hired a young, single woman to wash the dishes at their annual festive dinner.[156] Images from such banquets in Prague prominently depict the elaborate dishes used by the society. Perhaps this girl also worked at other communal celebrations since pious societies rented out their dishes for larger life cycle celebrations.[157] A brief mention of female servants who aided Frankfurt's charity collectors indicates that the charity society, too, employed young female assistants. While their tasks are not mentioned, it is possible that the assistants helped wash and sort clothing from the dead, which was sometimes donated to them.[158] Communal hospices also employed poorer women, who served as nurses and caretakers; they likely also were responsible for cooking meals and laundering linens.[159]

Gendered Labor

Among the folios of a logbook of circumcisions, we find a reference to a boy born in 1763 to Hayim, the son of Hayale Schneiderin (seamstress).[160] No more information about Hayale is included, but other sources shed light on the profession and on the sewing circles in which women would socialize and design objects for the home and the synagogue. Domestic tasks, such as cleaning, sewing, and preparing food, were gendered female, and women were typically employed in these fields. The skills necessary to sew and embroider blankets, shrouds, clothing, and ritual items for the synagogue provided women not only with income (and heavenly merit) but with agency and pride in the beautiful objects they crafted.[161] Multiple women were recognized for their dexterity in needlework, particularly, but not solely, in the textiles they prepared for the synagogue. In 1766, two married women from the village of Bionville in Lorraine were reported to the Christian authorities for knitting, as they had done so on Sunday when mass was being recited in the Catholic church; this was prohibited on the Christian holy day.[162]

Other women earned money in related fields. In a query to Rabbi Judah Mehler from Emmerich, a German city not far from the Dutch border, a woman named Hanna Glaub "travels from place to place and from country to country and sells thread, now [for] more than twelve years."[163] Hanna came to Mehler's attention after her young son revealed that she had purchased new wares and surreptitiously sold linen thread, which posed a problem under Jewish law, as linen and wool could not be used in the same garment. Hanna's travels remind us that mobility was not limited to women of commerce and credit. Even simpler professions might bring a woman to travel (and trickery) for her livelihood.

Glikl and her mother worked on the side producing fine fabrics, such as lace, and luxury garments, such as silk stockings; ordinary women were involved in the creation, upkeep, and reuse of garments until they fell apart.[164] In an age when fabric was not yet mass-produced, bolts of cloth represented capital, and clothes were among the most valuable items people possessed. Coats and overclothes often appear in litigation as security for loans and as items for auction or sale.[165] The sale of secondhand clothing was popular among both Jewish men and women. A contract from 1747 between three parties, among them two married couples from Worms, records their partnership arrangements. Each party provided cash up front that was used to purchase clothing for resale and to rent a room for their operation, if necessary.

They agreed to maintain a logbook of each garment's purchase and resale price. Among the women's tasks was to try to obtain old clothing for free in order to offer them for resale.[166] Similarly, the widow Rösel, who lived in Haus Sperber in Frankfurt's Judengasse, also dealt in secondhand clothing; some of her other neighbors did the same. Centuries later, archaeologists discovered thimbles and needles outside their homes.[167]

Other women in Frankfurt's Judengasse earned a living through further types of labor gendered as female. The poor widow Spiegelin supported herself and her young children by preparing thirty to fifty pounds of coffee each Thursday evening, which she would distribute to customers over Shabbat.[168] A woman depicted in an illustrated *Me'ah berakhot* (ca. 1740) sold pastries, presumably homemade, to a variety of customers (see plate 18). Other women opened eateries in their homes, which fed locals (among them the poor) and foreign guests and travelers.[169] An anonymous memoir penned by a young boy from Moravia credits his mother with showing ingenuity after war had stripped their home completely bare: "My mother ... prepared by herself to maintain her household by the work of her hands and the fruits of her labor; to make barley liquor in a copper beaker that is customary in these places and it is heavy labor. Thus, she succeeded and earned while my father, may he live, sat and studied Torah."[170] As a result of good fortune, the father eventually obtained a liquor license and a large distillery, and he prospered.

Klerche of Altona sold meat. Court records refer to her as "the butcher, Klerche," when she took a loan from Abraham ben Isaac and left as pledge various items, including a small stool/chair and one small chest.[171] Later in the court logbook, she is referred to as "the widowed butcher, Klerche," indicating that her work as a butcher began while she was married and continued after the death of her husband.[172] In Bionville, the widow of David continued to work as a butcher along with her children after her husband's death.[173] Hayke bat Yeshayah, the single daughter of a seventeenth-century butcher, was paid her share of her father's business when two brothers purchased his butcher's license in Altona.[174] Since her father was still living, her financial interest in his business suggests that she, too, played a role in the family profession.

Poor women, among them widows, supported themselves through a variety of jobs deemed women's work. They took in laundry from better-off households and repaired or dyed clothing.[175] Some married (and more unmarried) Jewish women served for pay as wetnurses, one of the lowest rungs on the economic scale that could still provide sustenance for a poor woman's family.[176] Women who served as wetnurses could either take infants into their homes or live in the homes of their employers if they were not nearby. If they had never been married, they had obviously become pregnant as single women; in many cases, they had to leave their own babies in order to earn enough for subsistence. Despite the moral outrage of communal leaders, maidservants who became pregnant on the job could then earn an even higher salary as wetnurses. Communities were loath to allow married women to serve as wetnurses because that could lead to adulterous relationships with employers.[177] A case before the Metz rabbinical court in 1777 demonstrates some of the tensions within a marriage caused by this profession. Meir Weil came before the court to demand from his wife the salary she had earned from her employer, Yohanan Levi. Mrs. Weil had earned five Reichsthaler per month wetnursing the Levis' baby, and Meir claimed the entire salary under the legal principe that all the profits from a wife's handiwork belonged to her husband. Levi readily paid the sum before the bet din, and the wife handed most of it to Meir. Beyond that, Levi requested that Weil's wife remain in his home until after Sukkot (it was then mid-summer, so for approximately two months). During that time, he would nourish her at his table (at his own expense) because the doctor had warned that if she remained in the home with her husband Meir, lack of proper nutrition and stress from their constant fighting would cause her milk to be inadequate for the child. The wife argued that Meir could not stop her from remaining in the home of Yohanan until after Sukkot. The bet din ruled that she might remain within the Levi household all day until after Sukkot but not overnight.[178] The salary for wetnursing would belong to her alone from then on, according to the additional legal principle that a wife may declare that she will not be supported by her husband and would not give him the proceeds of her handiwork.[179] The case highlights the tensions that beset mothers in dire financial straits who could nurse other people's babies for money. Employers of wetnurses were willing to feed and house them to guarantee adequate milk for their own children, a benefit that many employers were too pressed to allow other types of servants. This special treatment could cause strain and resentment within the woman's marriage.

Other women's professions, such as working as nurses for parturients, also required travel and residence away from their own homes. In Fürth, widowed nurses were permitted to apply for a permit from the communal leaders, but a married woman had to seek approval from her husband as well. "[She] must first report to communal officials upon her arrival, and they may authorize her employment only after [receiving] a letter of consent from her husband, under the condition that she return home for at least one full month every six months.

One cannot authorize her employment without a letter from her husband, or when her husband is not at home; this cannot be approved under any circumstances."[180] Regulations such as these remind us that working women bore an extra burden. While married men were employed by communities as teachers for years at a time (with no requirement that their wives grant permission), married nurses were vetted by the community and were expected to return home more frequently.[181] Given men's travel (and, sometimes, their subsequent abandonment of their families), these restrictions encumbered poorer women who could not easily find work on which they were dependent.

Women's Professional Endeavors

Women worked for compensation in skilled professions beyond commercial ventures, with some supporting their families with the money they earned. Most notable among female professions was midwifery. From their earliest regulations in the early modern period, Jewish communities hired midwives as community professionals and granted community membership, a prized privilege, to them and their families. Like some merchant women, midwives were trained recordkeepers whose writings are only now being evaluated as a resource for women's and communal history.[182] Some midwives had extensive knowledge of medicine and healing that went beyond the immediate field of midwifery, as is evident from descriptions on epitaphs and in memorial books. Fromet, the daughter of Menahem of Frankfurt, served as a midwife: "She sat for days at the bedside of parturients and [other] ill individuals close to death, both the poor and the wealthy, and engaged in medicines and remedies by herself." The entry noted that she advised anyone who approached her about "matters of health, or cures for bruises and wounds."[183] Other women were noted for medical knowledge rather than midwifery. A double tombstone in Worms's Heiliger Sand cemetery commemorated the lay leader Ber Oppenheim and his wife, Talzen. Both were praised for their charitable donations, but Talzen was also remembered for "being swift [in supplying] the ill with medicines and recovery."[184]

A different kind of literacy was required for teaching. The 1599 epitaph in the Worms cemetery for Bella, wife of Itzik Hainsdorf, praises her "for teaching children, young and small."[185] A few sources refer to female teachers, including R. Jacob Emden's memoir, in which he recommends educating girls by "sending them to learn with a knowledgeable female teacher."[186] Moravian ordinances mention that the wives of male teachers were to instruct girls, including in "women's skills," in a separate area of their homes.[187] Perhaps this is a reference to handiwork. As scholarship on embroidery in Christian communities demonstrates, this, too, was a form of literacy, as girls could learn letters by embroidering texts on samplers.[188]

By the eighteenth century, several women used their literacy and the emerging system of mail to provide a service for money. Bella Perlhefter, who wrote that she penned letters for women such as herself, does not specify whether she received payment for her work. To her husband, she complained, "I am tired of writing Hebrew for humble women like myself," which sounds like she worked at it for compensation.[189] Rivkah, daughter of the judge Josel Rindskopf of Fulda, performed similar work in eighteenth-century Frankfurt. Her epitaph credits her with wielding "the pen of a scribe, with letters of greeting to gladden her father and sons, and travelers . . . she was known as a mother to the foreign youths."[190] It is not clear whether Rivkah was compensated for the letters she composed for young men studying in Frankfurt, but her epitaph speaks to her erudition, literacy, and skill.

Sarel bat Moshe ran a mail courier business with her husband, Leyb Sarel Gutmans. He was a Prague merchant who was staying in Vienna while she lived in Prague. Together, they organized a mail (and money order) service between the Jews of the two cities. A messenger he hired in Vienna took letters written to various people to Sarel in Prague. She delivered them to the recipients and collected replies to the letters, as well, which she sent back to her husband in the same way. As she transacted, Sarel kept a record of each item and obligation.

She sent the list as an inventory with the packet of letters; presumably, she kept a copy for herself, but that is not known. In her letter to her husband, Sarel described how their business worked: "Today, Friday, 14 Kislev, the messenger came with the break of dawn and brought us all the letters [she describes everyone's joy, as they hadn't had any for a long while]. . . . As you sent along a small note [regarding to whom the letters should go and what funds the people should pay or forward], I will send you in return a small note on the side: all those who have given, who have received letters; and those who responded, having sent letters."[191] Some of the letters in this packet demonstrated how their system worked from the customer's end. One man wrote to his parents, "I am giving this letter to the messenger, and I just received your letter from same messenger."[192] Another customer writes, "Leyb Sarel Gutmans' wife came and showed me a letter from her husband, in which he writes that he gave ten Gulden to R. Salman, may he live, and she should collect it here from

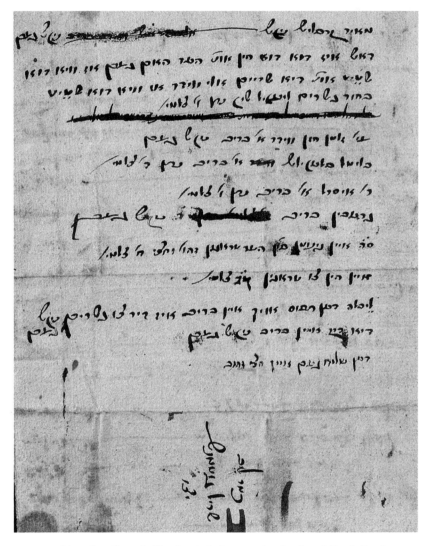

FIG. 7.4. List of mail carried by Sarel. At bottom, her husband, Leyb Sarel Gutmans, is the addressee.

David." Thus, Sarel went to collect payments following the instructions and on the strength of her husband's note. He conducted the same type of transaction on the other end, with her record or letter as proof.[193] They maintained a strict rule—they did not run a parcel service. A groom writing to his father-in-law noted that he would have liked to send his bride a small gift, but "the messenger did not want to carry it."[194] Their business allowed people to circulate funds by using their letters as small letters of credit sent along with their personal letters. But they did not accept parcels, which would have been a different type of business altogether and fraught with other risks.

When her husband requested her advice on whether to remain in Copenhagen or return to Hamburg, Sarel advised that the situation was dire for the rich people, let alone those with fewer resources. Her acknowledgment of the impact class and shifting fortunes had on the ability to earn a livelihood speaks to her immersion in the daily rhythm of the economy; she complained about all the taxes and expenses she had where she was located at the time.[195]

Sarel's work reinforces the thesis of this book: literacy provided early modern women with new opportunities. New jobs, such as those of letter writers, postmasters, and typesetters, reflected women's growing literacy in early modern Europe. Similarly, a greater number of women were involved in contract drafting and recordkeeping for business and home, including those who opened employment agencies or eateries or lent money. Their own documents and the records of courts and communities render them visible across class and profession.

From court Jews to laundresses, Jewish women were profoundly immersed in economic life and crucial to securing their families' well-being. The wide range of work undertaken by Jewish women underscores how critical class and, concomitantly, education were in shaping women's lives. Living in a city or in a small town or village was another factor affecting profession although it did not play as great a role as did class since work brought some Jewish women from the countryside to the city. While gender and marital status governed women's access to property and the degree of independence they could wield, class and wealth determined the opportunities open to any individual woman. Women of different classes worked in different fields, and the power and resources they had at their disposal differed immensely. Yet, both poor maidservants who insisted on compensation and wealthy businesswomen who secured family assets appeared in court to defend their assets, however abundant or meager. That the voices of both are preserved is a legacy of the culture of recordkeeping in early modern Europe.

8

Material Worlds

IN 1790, on Tuesday, 24 Adar, at five o'clock in the afternoon, two men entered the quarters of Zanvil Hahn, recently deceased, and his widow, Breindel. This Altona home belonged to David Cohen; the couple lived in a rented room. Their modest belongings could be found in two storage spaces: a linen chest, described as "below" in the room, and an entire box "above." Normally, the death in the community of a person with any property provoked the sealing of their living quarters and the taking of an inventory. Relatives and other creditors would be notified, and the estate's assets and debts would be tallied. If the debts exceeded the assets, the officials would arrange an auction of the belongings of the deceased, down to the smallest things, to settle the estate. Wealthy men and those who had the foresight to organize their affairs often requested in their wills that their wives be exempt from the inventory process, which required two officials of the community to search every nook of the home and take inventory of all the contents. Breindel interceded with the officials and intervened in the process. She needed to use her personal clothing, underwear, and bed linens while the estate was being settled. The officials recorded: "We handed over to the woman Breindel, *le-gufah* (for her personal use), 7 women's shirts, 4 bed sheets, 2 napkins, 2 colorful [items of] bedding, a few additional whites for her personal use, 2 nightcaps, and 2 pieces of headgear."[1]

While interventions such as Breindel's were not the norm, they were also not completely exceptional. Some widows requested financial support from the estate during the probate period; others requested the use of necessary or significant items.[2] Breindel's case exemplifies one of our arguments throughout this book: the culture of recordkeeping and of women's reading and writing, especially of inventories and lists, reveal aspects of women's lives in new detail in the early modern period. These sources allow us to begin to fill in a picture of women inside their homes, the possessions they prized within them, and how they chose to present themselves when they went out. While many of our sources date from the second half of the eighteenth century, some date to earlier in the period, and collectively, they allow us to envision the spatial and material circumstances of Jewish women's lives. Breindel's request provides one small example of the ways in which women interacted with the community and their families over their use of material belongings. The wealthiest ba'alot bayit and the poorest maidservants needed, used, and counted on these objects with which they functioned in the world.

From the tubs in which midwives washed babies at birth to the female shrouds that enfolded women in their eternal rest, particular objects served, clothed, protected, and adorned women. Vessels, furnishings, clothing, and religious articles carried multiple meanings for those who owned and used them (see plate 19).[3] We aim to view the material articles within their historical contexts and to understand their multiple functions as they circulated through society to illuminate the lives of early modern Jewish women. Among the categories of material objects we include are clothing, beds and linens, household furnishings, kitchen implements, and ritual objects used in the home. Even with the greater availability of merchandise on the markets, most items were handcrafted, and people did not regard them as "disposable."[4] The poor coveted even trifles such as a handkerchief or a tin spoon. In the days before disposable tissues, diapers, and sanitary pads, a good stock of textile scraps and kerchiefs, napkins, and the like was essential for women's personal hygiene. Beyond items for ordinary use, which women employed regardless of who they were, Jewish women had additional requirements for running a kosher kitchen and for seeing to special holiday needs, those of Passover in particular.

This chapter is organized into two principal parts. We begin with a brief introduction to the broad array of sources in a variety of genres—textual, material, and visual—from which we draw a sense of the physical objects that early modern Jewish women owned and employed to furnish their surroundings. These sources offer glimpses of women at different stages of their life cycles, across socioeconomic classes, and spanning western-central Ashkenazi cultural spaces. We then view clusters of material objects, from those found within the home to those that clothed women's bodies, assessing them to try to answer some of the questions we raise.

Inventories and Lists

Inventories that cataloged the belongings within individual households form rich textual sources for accessing the material culture of Jewish society in the late medieval and early modern periods. Such inventories, taken at various junctures, form the backbone of the work of historians such as Daniel Smail for fifteenth-century Lucca and Marseilles, Renata Ago for seventeenth-century Rome, and Daniel Roche for the material culture of early modern France.[5] While the inventories Smail worked on were mostly drawn up in the owners' lifetimes in order to settle debts, the Jewish inventories we rely on were mostly created upon the death of a householder. Merry Wiesner noted, "An inventory of property and household goods was usually taken on all deaths, whether the person was married or single, male or female, young or old. It did not matter if there was no dispute between the heirs or if there were no heirs at all. Nor did the size of the estate matter; inventories are recorded for servants who lived in one room and who owned nothing more than old clothing."[6] Wiesner's comments are true of Jewish property records as well. Inventories drawn up to inform the division of property after death often comprised lists of objects in detail, as did some last wills and testaments. In the event of property disputes, such as those over inheritance, divorce, or debtor-creditor, an accounting had to be given for every item.

Jewish communal officials in the "Altona community in Hamburg" kept a running record of inventories that the community oversaw, and a volume of the inventory records has survived.[7] Inventories assembled in the volume by J. Taglicht from the records pertaining to Jews in the Archive of the Imperial District Court for Civil Matters in Vienna provide us with another important collection containing lists of specific objects, thus shedding light on the material belongings of Jewish men and women.[8] These eighteenth-century records, in Vienna, overseen by non-Jewish officials and, in Hamburg, by Jewish communal officials, allow us to see up close the process of taking inventory, as well as to get a sense of the items that the officials and heirs deemed to possess value. In Hamburg, upon being notified of a death, the community immediately sent at least two ne'emanim (notaries) to seal the property.[9] This meant affixing a strong padlock on each of the trunks or containers that held all a person's valuables, or to the entrance to the dwelling.[10] Despite these precautions, relatives of the deceased could abscond with some of the valuables. When Baila, widow of Ephraim Goldziher, passed away, her creditors clamored to be paid. Some of her possessions were sold at auction and the remainder given to her nephew to guard until they could be evaluated. When the nephew refused to return the items, the community sued him in rabbinical court.[11] Because officials performed inventories even on the paltriest estates, inventories grant us access to the homes of both rich and poor women, including the itinerants in the hekdesh (hospice). Baila, widow of Mikhel Speyer, lived in a rented room in the home of Mendel Fasselburg. None of her relatives lived nearby. The charity collector paid for the expenses of her burial; her possessions were sold at auction to cover the costs.[12] When Breyna, widow of R. Shmuel Renir, died, one daughter, Merle, still lived with her. The woman was indigent and received a stipend from charity funds. The daughter showed the officials everything she had left behind: furniture and housewares—four old chairs, five old linen curtains, an old bench, several small lamps, an old bedstead with several pieces of bedding, an old cupboard containing a fur coat or jacket, and an old silk frock. There was nothing else, according to the daughter. They also owed the landlord retroactive rent on their room, and the owner would not consent to have anything removed until the rent was settled.[13] This brief inventory appears to be that of a widow who once may have owned nice clothes (silk and fur) but had descended into poverty and onto the charity rolls; she died with an estate in arrears.[14]

The legal tussle over the meager estate of a family of hekdesh women in Vienna may teach us not to take every statement made by the heirs at face value.[15] When, in June 1780, Malka died in the hekdesh where she worked, she left a living son and a daughter, Zierl, married and residing in Eisenstadt. The hekdesh attendant testified that she had left nothing behind. This would not ordinarily have aroused any suspicion, but Malka's death left a surprise in its wake: Zierl's daughter, Malka's granddaughter, Mindl, had been studying for conversion with a pastor in Währing. She let it be known that Malka, in fact, had left behind a modest estate and had, according to her witnesses, bequeathed it all to her. The estate consisted of items of tin, copper, brass, underwear, and clothing. Mindl claimed that there were two gold-adorned caps whose points had already been shorn by Solomon Wiener (Malka's son) before the funeral; the son also took a gold cup. According to the confession of Mindl and her advocate before the city judge, she and her son also had broken into a chest and taken things out, thrown the bedding over the wall, and dragged it beyond the *Stadel* (outbuilding) of these houses. Adding together all the effects Mindl counted, Malka had left a modest estate of thirty-eight Gulden. Malka's two children affirmed that there were no other effects.[16] The story does throw into question some of the testimonies of people's dying "with no effects" left behind. Perhaps the inventory and probate process constituted a greater burden than many poor could bear for a small number of items.

The paucity of items of material worth left by Malka, a widow down on her fortunes, can be compared to the impressive list of fine and expensive objects left by Judith Oppenheimer (1671–1738) in Vienna.[17] Judith had been married to an imperial court agent from a family of vast wealth and influence, and she had managed the estate and carried on the business for close to eighteen years after her husband's death. A default on a loan to the imperial court left her estate in deficit. Despite the dozens of objects of silver, fine imported porcelain, expensive bolts of gold and silver lace, silk stockings, and gloves in her personal wardrobe, Judith's inventory was something of a mirage. Court agents such as Judith, who lent and borrowed great sums, needed to project the impression of great prosperity. But their position as Jews left them always in a state of precarity, with little recourse when a royal borrower decided to default. Judith's opulent surroundings concealed an estate in dire deficit.

Several of our sources refer to a specific type of women's death that mandated the taking of an inventory. As we recall, Avraham Italiener, a noted community leader in Altona (d. 1785), took his son-in-law, the butcher Moses Heilbut, to the local Jewish court after his daughter died in childbirth. The court had retained a detailed record of the inventory of their wedding gifts and belongings, so that their household could be unraveled.[18] The list, drafted as claim and counterclaim, preserved a hint of the live proceedings and conveyed a sense of the oral arguments that each item occasioned. Thus, while the butcher agreed to return various amounts and items, he balked at others. When presented with a table that Italiener claimed to have bought the couple, Heilbut responded curtly, "That never ever happened."[19] The court retained the responses of the son-in-law regarding each of the items. Some, he asserted, had broken or disappeared, while the best clothing and jewelry were his own gifts to his bride and had never been part of the dowry or wedding gifts. Perhaps an inventory of the bride's belongings, as well as gifts to the couple, accompanied the woman into her marriage. Her father would then have used it to recover as much as he could after his daughter died. Of the house and tablewares, two silver goblets, a silver salt cellar, four silver spoons, and a silver sugar tong were the most expensive gifts, followed by eighteen tin plates, a lamp, eight leather chairs, and a kettle. The woman's personal effects, such as her bed, her clothing, and her jewelry, were listed separately. A separate list of linens was noted but not preserved in the court record. Even after her death, the objects a woman brought with her to create her home were tallied and appraised.

The value of a list of gifts to a couple upon their wedding in the cases noted above casts a new light on another type of written list: that of wedding gifts. When Rivkah and Eliezer married in Amsterdam in 1773, a list of the gifts they received was produced for them; each giver was noted alongside an amount or gift item.[20] The list itself, introduced by a paean to the couple in embellished scribal hand and adorned with colorful, embossed endpapers, may have been a gift. The main categories of gifts were cash in various amounts and several currencies,[21] housewares, and books.[22] The register listed gifts of closest relatives (e.g., a grandmother of the bride and of the groom, father of the bride, and stepfather of the groom) with the largest gifts first, followed by the rest in seemingly random order. The houseware items included both utilitarian (a porcelain milk pitcher and tray, two silver candlesticks) and decorative objects, including one gold and many silver spoons, coffee cups and plates, a dozen porcelain chocolate cups with an undertray, and a Japanese (style?) tray, all indicative of a higher class and of Amsterdam's status as a commercial entrepôt.[23] The list leaves us with many questions about the gift-giving habits of donors and recipients, but it also provides us with a precious glimpse into the ways young couples furnished their homes as they started out in life—and into the practice of elevating the written record itself into a decorated memento and valued object.

Records from rabbinical courts included detailed inventories of estates that were being adjudicated. When Gutle, widow of Bendit Schammes, sued her brother-in-law to allow her to access the items in her household that her husband had left for her use until she died or remarried, Rabbi Gundersheim, who presided over the Frankfurt bet din, included in his diary of court cases a detailed list of the items. This list included the ordinary contents of a home and the daily furnishings and implements that Gutle used on a regular basis. In addition, Gutle had provided the court with a second list of more valuable silver objects. As the government had seized these items from the estate, she asked her brother-in-law to provide replacements in silver. Four silver knives, forks and spoons, a silver "*bar*" [?], silver candlesticks, three silver goblets, a silver salt cellar, a silver soup ladle, a silver ring, a silver *besamim* (spice) box, a silver *haroset* dish for the Passover seder, and a silver saltwater dish for Passover.[24] The court did not preserve a copy of the will from Gutle's husband. The estate was far more complex than the material objects alone. Nevertheless, the careful inventory of every item, including old cloths and tin spoons, allows us to build a picture of what belongings a woman would have needed to preside over her household. Without the meticulous recordkeeping mandated by the community and carried out by the head of the rabbinical court, such detail would be lost to us.

While each list does convey a sense of valuables that belonged to a woman, a registry by nature obscures a great deal as well. It doesn't tell us how the objects were used; how often they were used; where they were stored, displayed, or hidden; or which were cherished and which neglected. The lists do tell us about the types of objects associated with women that were considered valuable: table settings that demonstrated economic status, as well as clothing and accessories made from the best available materials and bedecked with objects made of precious metals.

Sumptuary ordinances form another source pertaining to Jewish material culture. Many communities regulated festivities such as circumcisions and marriage parties, limiting the number of guests and even which dishes could be served. Most particularly, such laws related to the way women dressed outside their homes. As with all prescriptive texts, sumptuary regulations must be used with caution—they reflect the sensibility of those (men) who drew up the rules more than those of the affected women.[25] Such ordinances were widespread throughout early modern Europe, and Jewish community regulations stipulating aspects of dress, for men and for women, often tracked these ordinances.[26] Most guidelines pertained to women's garments and their embellishment. Takkanot from Metz in 1769, for example, opened the section of sumptuary laws with the announcement: "What pertains to women's ornamentation will be as follows."[27] Even without further amplification, this preamble establishes that the primary concern of the sumptuary regulations concerned the choices women could make. The ordinances allowed various displays of wealth on the bodies of women, depending on aspects of their status: their husband's *erekh* (assessed worth), their marital status (single above twelve years old versus married), and their membership status (locals versus maidservants who were not from local families). Within each category women could display certain luxuries, with those of the lower-valued families limited to the greatest degree. The regulations differentiated between styles and materials that could be worn within the Jewish quarter and those forbidden outside of it.

Sumptuary laws were specific to the locale and the fashions of the times. They abound in rich detail and differ from one set of rules to another. We cite excerpts from the Metz regulations only as exemplary: "Women whose husbands' worth is 15,000 crowns and above may not walk on the ramparts ... or other strolling spots, or to synagogue, with mantillas of muslin, gauze, toile, or silk, but they may wear mantillas of toile finette (a light linen), or printed cloth, or other textiles that are not silk, gauze, muslin, or toile. However, within the Jewish street, they may wear mantillas of any textile they wish, including muslin, silk, etc."[28] Women whose family incomes were lower were forbidden to have these luxury items made anew for them, although older versions they already owned could be worn. The regulations dictated how many dresses brides could commission and what materials they could wear, depending on the size of their dowries; they were not permitted to accept such outfits as gifts. Maidservants who were not of local families "were prohibited from wearing any silk clothing, even on Shabbat and holidays."[29] A list of other garments and textiles follows, with the stern warning that any violation of these ordinances would result in the immediate dismissal of the servant, who would not be allowed to remain in the community even one more night. Since servants often inherited hand-me-downs from their female housemistresses, such regulations were intended to mark social class. All the regulations would be enforced by a committee of overseers, who would collect fines for violations and exempt no one from the applicable rules.[30]

Sumptuary regulations tell us a great deal about the ideal order of society in the eyes of the legislators and rather less about what women actually wore or what they thought of such controls over their choices. The first time such regulations were drawn up, they may well have reflected current fashions; if they were repeated over decades, they no longer reflected anything but the legal-scribal profession's devotion to copying old rules. If not rigorously enforced, the rules would have been exercises in rhetoric rather than effective means of policing society. Nevertheless, they impart a great deal about the self-image and social consciousness of Jews in particular times and places and how these perceptions were projected onto Jewish women specifically. The ordinances were designed to maintain strict boundaries between social ranks, to curtail conspicuous consumption, to minimize resentment of Jewish financial success in Christian eyes, and to uphold community standards of modesty.

That women prized certain objects and outfits can be ascertained by other written sources from the early modern period: women's letters and their wills. In a letter from 1619, Friedel, daughter of Israel Hammerschlag, wrote to Mirel, daughter of Israel ben Shalom Auerbach:

> I want to let you know that I completed my assignment, and I had the cloak made, according to the best and nicest way possible in the world. It is

lined, with 10 ells double damask, each ell 2.5 *schok* (Mark); 2.5 Mark for cords, 2 Mark for linen, velvet for the border at 10 Mark for 2 ells; 1 Mark for silk, and the tailor's wage, 2 Mark. Therefore, do not do anything, but send me more money, that I can send it with Abner Henokh Schik in Poland, that he can buy a nice *spigel* [?] otter fur.[31]

Even at the elite level, sourcing an outfit required managing an international network of sources, not to mention the skilled labor to put it together. Sarah, widow of Meir Stern, left her wedding ring to her granddaughter, Frumet, along with a white embroidered silk jacket and coat and a blue mohair jacket. She left all her clothing and jewelry to particular individuals, but her household goods, "furniture and housewares of brass, lead and copper, wood and bedding and the remaining vessels of silver and gold," she asked to be sold and the proceeds divided among her heirs. By selecting the most meaningful of her belongings to bestow on individuals she cared about, she also showed which possessions held no sentimental value for her.[32] The maidservant Yitta of Fredericia left to the daughter of her employer, who nursed her through her illness, her most treasured item, a gold purse with two birds embroidered on it.[33] Pessche, widow of Juzpa Mentzer (Altona, 1794), left a specific outfit to each of her nieces; her rings and earrings to a good friend, the wife of Gedaliah; and a choice of the remaining clothing to her maidservant. She asked the executor to distribute her remaining effects as he saw fit. This is an example of women's assigning particular items that held meaning while generally leaving those they valued less.[34]

Images

Beyond textual sources of all types, visual depictions of Jews in books, printed and manuscript, convey a wealth of information about the material objects in a Jewish home and the clothing Jews wore. Jewish books depicted women in a variety of clothing and domestic settings. Illustrated customs books, calendar books, haggadot, megillot, and sidre berakhot were often directed at women as readers and users. Elaborate illustrated manuscripts would sometimes depict a woman's actual home, implements, and wardrobe. The printed works of Christian Hebraists are rich with visual and textual material often drawn from life by specially commissioned artists. Hebraists' depictions of Jewish ritual life in minute detail were "polemical ethnographies," which attempted to broaden medieval polemic from the world of biblical prooftexts to that of the domestic and daily life of Jews, but they also included descriptions and images based on scenes witnessed by the author or illustrator.[35] While no single image can be relied on to convey historically accurate information, in the aggregate, the illustrations provide a visual sense of domestic interiors and personal dress beyond the words of texts. Their presence signals the expansion of the Christian polemical gaze to include Jewish women. Most of the woodcut illustrations in the works of converts from Judaism Johannes Pfefferkorn and Antonius Margaritha depicted Jewish women as they performed rituals. By the eighteenth century, some polemical ethnographies, such as the Jugendres edition of Kirchner's *Jüdisches Ceremoniel* (1724) and Bodenschatz's *Kirchliche Verfassung* (1748/9), featured elaborate engravings of scenes of Jewish life, its spaces, and its customs. While the motives of the Christians who wrote these ethnographies differed, their emphasis on domestic ritual pulled Jewish women and their observances into the center of their accounts and included Jewish women in their engravings.

Material Objects

Collections of tangible material objects in private hands and in museum collections (documented in catalogs, on paper, and online) form a significant source for understanding material culture. Each surviving object from Jewish life in the early modern period is a small miracle. By their nature, everyday objects, such as kitchenware, clothing, and domestic furnishings, were used until they wore out; then, they were taken apart and repurposed or discarded. Luxury items and objects intended for ritual use are an exception to this rule; they tend to dominate most collections. In addition to wear and tear over time, Jewish objects were sometimes subjected to purposeful destruction, so every remaining article is a treasured survivor but one whose endurance was somewhat dependent on happenstance. We cannot, therefore, regard material objects as universally representative samples. When they are available, physical objects can teach us about the feel, the look, and the workmanship of items that we could not know from simply seeing a depiction or reading a description of it. We have tried to include (two-dimensional representations of) three-dimensional objects wherever relevant and possible.

Objects served several different functions simultaneously. These included their utilitarian function, their economic value (both in monetary value and as a professional instrument), and their value as display objects to signal class or pietistic-devotional virtues. A silver salt cellar was a practical vessel for holding a substance that needed a container on the table; at the same time, it represented monetary value in that it could be appraised and sold or left as security for a loan. It also signaled social status when displayed on a family table. In similar fashion, implements for making coffee, tea, and chocolate became wildly popular by the eighteenth century and could be found in many Jewish homes. For some Jewish women they represented tools for earning extra income, while others simply enjoyed them as part of their daily routines.[36] For wealthy women like Madame Kaulla, they represented the ultimate display of luxury (see plate 16). By reverse token, when an object in the home was there purely for commercial purposes, only that dimension defined it. When Baila, widow of Meir Traub, died, the inventory of her possessions listed many items in great detail, but twelve separate objects were listed as *mashkonot* (securities), and only their monetary value was noted. The type of object was irrelevant to the value of her inventory.

We view these categories through various lenses beyond their functions. How does gender work with regard to inanimate objects? How do objects associated with Jewish women differ from those associated with Jewish men? Men might have been the legal owners of items that are clearly gendered female, such as women's clothes, and vice versa (the latter particularly in the case of widows). An inventory of a man's books included an old "women's prayer book."[37] Perhaps nothing conveys this more pointedly than the case in which the court ordered the shamash to compensate a newly widowed woman for the clothing that had been removed from her dead husband. The community had allotted the clothing taken from the dead as part of the compensation of the guards hired by the community. She was apparently unprepared to lose these clothes and sued for compensation.[38] Thus, association and use were not always congruent with ownership.

Religiously specific devotional objects obviously were not the same for Jewish as for Christian women. But we can ask whether Jewish and Christian women owned similar numbers of such objects. How did the home and its contents differ for Jewish women in villages and those in urban settings? Can we account for change over time? Which objects faded into disuse, and which became more necessary in the period from the sixteenth to the eighteenth centuries? How did objects in Jewish homes differ across national borders? We cannot answer all these questions in full yet; this chapter attempts to address some of them.

The Space Within: Jewish Homes

"At Prage many Familyes of Jewes lived packed together in one litle house, which makes not only their howses but their streetes to be very filthy, and theire Citty to be like a Dunghill."[39] This description by an English visitor to Prague in 1592 echoes similar impressions of urban Jewish ghettos, from Venice to Prague to Frankfurt, throughout the early modern period. Jews who lived in enclosed urban ghettos coped with intensely crowded houses, limited to spaces that could not expand by law, even as the Jewish population grew by leaps and bounds. In this regard, their living conditions differed manifestly from those of their urban Christian neighbors. Jewish living quarters and family arrangements varied greatly from one place to another and between classes in any given location—and they depended on the often highly regulated conditions for Jewish residence. We see the acquisition and placement of material objects in their dwellings as the means by which Jewish women turned their houses (or rooms) into homes.

In Frankfurt, the *Judengasse* (Jewish street) was 330 meters long, with incredibly narrow houses. The number of households living in one building continued to grow over a period of three centuries, until, eventually, the lane housed over three thousand Jews.[40] When no new houses could be added, the Jews added spaces by dividing homes. In some cases, multiple unrelated families—three, four, or five most often (but up to nine in some cases!)—shared cramped houses. In the Wetterhahn house, two widows, Rösle Schwarzschild and the (unnamed) mother of Yuzpa Wetterhahn, swapped the upstairs and downstairs sections every three years, using a lottery system to determine who started in which apartment. Sharing spaces in this manner often led to conflicts, as it did when Rösle's brother inherited his sister's share of the house and quarreled with Yuzpa over the terms of the lottery in a dispute that the rabbinical court eventually adjudicated.

Among the terms stipulated in the Wetterhahn dispute was the use of the cellar and of the uppermost floor of the house. Both these spaces were particularly important on the Jewish holidays of Sukkot (Tabernacles) and Passover. Many German homes had a roof from which shingles could be removed, allowing residents to place branches on the square crossbeams to construct a sukkah (temporary structure) in what was normally a room in their home. Access to the upper floors during the fall months was an advantage. Similarly, storage in the cellar could be critical for business or for Passover. Therefore, the court stipulated that the cellar and the sukkah were to be shared by both parties during the holidays.⁴¹ Jewish women and men had to negotiate how to share these spaces in a divided house. In one Frankfurt home, shared by the Schotten and Hain families, a dispute over space led to an agreement that while the Schotten parents, who resided upstairs, could access the Hain home to make their way to the toilets at night, "as was customary," their children and their servants would have to use the toilets in the cellar.⁴²

Similarly, in Prague, while the statistics for the Jewish population vary, all agree that conditions were extremely cramped, and living space was scarce and expensive.⁴³ Disasters such as fires or plagues hit each of these ghettos very hard. Privacy of almost any type was impossible to obtain under such conditions. This crowding contributed to the grounds for lapses in sexual morality, particularly for servants who often slept in whatever spaces were available, just as it explains the search for privacy.

Jews living in rural villages faced very different conditions. While there might still be limitations on where they could reside and whether they could own property, the quarters were not as cramped as in the cities. Seventeenth-century memoirist Asher of Reichshofen recalled:

> The home that I built and acquired . . . I built three things within it: first, a small room to set aside time for Torah study and prayer, and to put my books in, that I bought with my own money. . . . Second, a small oven ready to bake matzot, and in this year, 1631, for the first time I fulfilled my wish, according to the custom of the [medieval rabbi] Roke'ah, I baked three matzot on Passover eve. . . . I warm up the same small oven every Friday to bake hallot . . . and to store the *hamin* [hot dish; Yid. "cholent"] for Shabbat. Third, a small bathhouse behind the oven of the *bet ha-horef* (heated room) for many reasons, the chief one being the bestial custom here, that the uncircumcised together with their wives go into one [bathing] room, and the circumcised with their wives [bathe] among the uncircumcised and their wives. I was zealous for God's honor and built myself one room in my home to enjoy on *erev Shabbat* (Shabbat Eve), or if I need it for bleeding, or a woman when she wears her whites, and the like, to be ready at all times.⁴⁴

Asher's lively memoir of Jewish life in the Alsatian countryside and some additional details about his dwelling places allow us to sense the isolation, in contrast to urban crowding, that attended the life of some Jews in rural settings. The anonymous Bohemian memoirist of the seventeenth century described the terror of entering the forests that surrounded the villages, where brigands and murderers waited to assault passers-by.⁴⁵

In her picture of the village of Steinbiedersdorf, Claudia Ulbrich provides another close look at early modern Jewish life beyond the cities.[46] To the chagrin of Christian clergymen, Jews rented not only entire houses from Christians but also individual rooms within their homes.[47] Ulbrich argues that the small Jewish rural upper class set itself apart from both the Jewish lower class and from Christians. In 1775, Jews owned almost 10 percent of the houses in the village, although they were 18 percent of the population. But even that ownership by Jews was not evenly distributed. The handful of wealthy families each owned more than one house; only a third of the Jews owned or partially owned any dwelling. Some rural Jewish women did have opportunities to access land on which to grow food or animals. One Jewish woman obtained a seigneurial garden at auction; others produced food by leasing or getting permission to use neighboring garden plots.[48] Despite living in a village surrounded by space, their actual living conditions were strained. A map of the layout of one Christian-owned house, that of Louis Keller, shows that he rented it out to four or five Jewish families, who lived in very cramped conditions.[49]

The conditions governing the domestic spaces in which Jewish women conducted their lives affected every aspect of their life arrangements, yet the sources are particularly reticent about matters such as available space and the layout of homes and rooms. A visitation record from Worms, dated July 1610, documents the number of rooms in each of the 103 homes on the curved lane of Worms's Judengasse in the seventeenth century. Many houses had cellars and courtyards; all had a combination of heated and unheated rooms. The largest house, zum Reisen, home to four households (a couple and their three married sons and grandchildren), comprised five heated rooms, eleven unheated rooms of varying sizes, two cellars, a courtyard, a stable, and three distinct kitchens.[50] Most houses were far more modest. Rifka and Hayim lived with their young son, Sinai, in a house with two heated rooms, four unheated rooms, a courtyard, and the vaulted cellar in which they likely stored wine; it was home also to Hayim's widowed mother and to his sister, who had once been married to Hirsch, resident of the neighboring house, zum Gulden Roth. Another poor Jew lodged with the extended family as well. Rifka, as ba'alat bayit, was responsible for managing the entirety of her household, including her nuclear family, her husband's extended family, and the boarder.[51] Multiple families might share one or two heated rooms, and not every home had a separate kitchen. In the zu Meisen house, Simon, his wife, and their young daughters, Hanna and Lea, lived alongside David, Sprintz, and their four young children, Gutge, Reitz, Koppel, and Baer. Another Jew, the son-in-law of a different neighbor, along with his two daughters and a poor Jewish boy, lived there as well. Perhaps the eight children played together in the two heated rooms and five unheated rooms; they shared the single kitchen and perhaps also the cellar.[52]

Such multigenerational living was common among Christians as well and was practiced in different forms, with one or more married children living with their parents, depending on the locale.[53] In the small Franconian village of Schnaittach, homes shared by more than one household could be found among both Jews and Christians. To give one example, in 1610, the Jewish community of Schnaittach purchased the house abutting the synagogue for use by the *Schulklopfer*, the man tasked with knocking on doors and shutters to call his neighbors for prayer. Over the years, the house was shared by more than one family. In 1727, for example, Mendla Levi and Koppel Schmul lived there with their respective families. Thirteen years later, Koppel's widow remained in the home together with Mendla's family and with Wolf Berl Levi.[54]

In Metz's larger Jewish quarter, lotteries like those conducted in Frankfurt dictated the terms of dividing homes. The widow Taub owned half a house along with her brother-in-law, Mordekhai; she resided in the home, as did other tenants, among them the elderly Fradche. The other half was jointly owned by two other parties. The four owners decided how to divide the space by holding a lottery every six years. The rabbinical court also weighed in on who would bear the cost of home renovations.[55] The agreement reached by the parties stipulated who had access to the warm rooms, to the oven, to the kitchen, and to the rooms facing the courtyard. That this house was rented out to tenants in addition to its being home for the four owners underscores the complexity inherent in these living spaces, as well as the relative frequency of change within the home. People moved in and out of rooms and of houses on a regular, and even on an established, agreed-upon, basis.

Not surprisingly, communal records include many references to renting out rooms in homes, a process in which women were intimately involved, both as tenants and landlords. In a seventeenth-century case, Frankfurt's leaders permitted R. Feivush to rent rooms "to a woman without children."[56] It is unclear if she was a single woman, a married woman, or a widow, but she seems to have lived alone. Women also rented rooms to boarders to earn money. In Steinbiedersdorf in Lorraine, widows rented out rooms to neighbors, as fewer than one-third of the Jews owned houses. This was another important distinction between Jews and Christians in the village, as 80 percent of Christians had some type of house ownership.⁵⁷ Only wealthy Jews had enough rooms for different functions, as the 1757 inventory of Jacob Cahen's rural home shows. There were separate rooms for various functions, such as a kitchen, a washroom, and a parlor room (front room). This is the only document to give us a sense of the flow of rooms in the home and the arrangement of objects within the rooms. There were nine spaces, headed by a main room that served multiple functions, down to some small storage spaces that we would think of today more as closets than as rooms. Of the rooms, five contained beds, but none of the rooms contained *only* beds. The largest room, with three beds, also served as the dining and Shabbat room, presumably because it was well-heated. Some of the other rooms contained pawned objects. The inventory lists many curtains, tablecloths, canopies/curtains for beds, and a blue-covered sofa, demonstrating how textiles of all types had made their way into rural homes. The kitchen contained many dishes (including up to thirty plates), table settings, and vessels of all sorts, as well as provisions, including coffee and tea, sugar and wine, jams, and pickles. Two goats in the barn presumably provided milk and possibly meat. Despite the rather lengthy list, Ulbrich notes, much has been omitted from this inventory, including any books or Jewish ritual items, tubs, buckets, and chickens. These were presumably there, but perhaps they were not valuable for the purposes of auction in a rural area.⁵⁸

In certain areas within southern German lands, including villages in Swabia and the city of Fürth in Franconia, acquiring or building a house was a prerequisite to obtaining protected status. Wealthier court Jews could afford to build homes and typically have capital left over, while less well-off Jews did not necessarily have assets beyond their physical home and the wares they traded. A shift in fortunes thus significantly affected the household. Simon and Merle Ulman of Pfersee, a village outside Augsburg, accumulated increasing debt over the course of the late seventeenth and early eighteenth centuries. To repay their debts, they were forced to sell their only asset, the home in which they lived; the sale, in turn, endangered their status as protected Jews. Eventually, their son-in-law, Siegmund Bacharach, who lived in another village, bailed them out. Their salvation, however, came with a catch. As part of the agreement to assist his in-laws, Siegmund insisted that his deceased sister's elderly and infirm husband live with them.⁵⁹

Siegmund was not alone in seeking a home for his elderly relative. Older adults frequently sought rooms within the homes of family members or of other families. Reizche, a notable woman from Lippstadt, turned to Rabbi Judah Mehler in the seventeenth century with a query about creating an *eruv*, a Jewish legal mechanism to enable carrying from one home to another on Shabbat. She shared her home with her son-in-law (and, presumably, with her daughter), but each household had its own private rooms, as well as separate entrances. In his answer, Mehler noted that, despite the separate spaces, they did not lock the doors between the homes at night, and they frequented one another's homes regularly. In addition, Reizche's son-in-law was financially responsible for her welfare.[60] This particular family's living arrangements provided each household with a degree of privacy, although they were clearly intermingled in financial and daily matters. Widows were compelled to rent out rooms frequently, especially when their children inherited the houses in which they had lived.

In Metz, Rivkah May and her children remained without any assets when "her husband [Koppel] abandoned her and her household in sorrow and sighing [Isa. 35:10]." The rabbinical court, to which she turned, noted that she already had exhausted the funds she had to support her family; she had nothing left to sustain them "other than the portion of a house in which she currently resided."[61] Renting out part of a home was not unusual; Rivkah needed the permission of the rabbinical court because the house did not technically belong to her but, rather, to her husband. Since he had abandoned her, the court granted her permission to rent out space in the house for a period of two years.

Home Furnishings

At a minimum, depending on the size of the household, people needed beds to sleep on, access to a hearth, kitchen, and dining implements, a table to eat on, chairs to sit on, linens for beds and table, and various articles for storage. Beds for married couples featured prominent drapery that could be drawn shut. Thickly curtained marital beds were not merely the style; they were a necessity for obtaining a modicum of privacy. Mothers who could afford it put their babies to sleep in cradles; they needed outfits to clothe their babies, clothes as their children grew, and, once they reached their teens, the beginnings of a trousseau for girls.

In illustrations from the early modern period, some homes were depicted with bare walls, while others featured walls decorated with symmetrical patterns or mirrors and paintings hanging on the wall. Some inventories mention mirrors or portraits, but it is unclear if they were freestanding or affixed to a wall.[62]

Homes needed sources of light—glazed panes for windows, ceiling fixtures, and candle holders for the nighttime and over Shabbat. Heat usually came from the hearth, and wood for kindling was a necessity in wintertime. Poorer Jews, who could not afford all these items, would sometimes receive from the charity collector clothing and other necessities that had belonged to deceased community members.[63] In the late eighteenth century, Jewish communities in cities such as Frankfurt established confraternities charged with providing firewood to the poor.[64]

Perhaps because of the restrictions on space and the cramped conditions that many urban settings imposed on Jewish living quarters, Jewish women attempted to brighten those spaces visually, through color, and even olfactorily, by displaying flowers and using perfumes. Juspe Hahn of Frankfurt wrote of "those who create a pleasant aroma in their homes, especially in the summer, with lilies or roses."[65] Many of the textiles, both clothing and housewares, that women bought, sewed, and wore, and with which they furnished their homes, were described and depicted visually as teeming with color. The inventory of Jacob Cahen's house in Steinbiedersdorf noted three feather beds, each with striped and plain covers, an oak bed with striped blue-and-yellow curtains, and, in a windowless room, a bed with "blue-yellow" trimmed curtains; an adjoining back room contained six chairs covered in yellow and a table with yellow wax cloth. The blue and yellow color scheme was broken only in an upper front room, which held four red curtains.[66] Bright colors and patterns, such as stripes and paisleys, may have served as an antidote to darkness and drabness in places where Jews lived under severe space regulation, notably in ghettos like those of Frankfurt and Prague, which travelers always described as dark and cramped.

Storage

Given the general lack of space in Jewish living areas, storage spaces and receptacles for storing objects were often valued independently of their contents. In rural settings, stalls, shacks, haylofts, stables, cellars, and attics served to store provisions and valuables. In urban settings, such spaces were scarcer, and attics and basements often became living spaces. Either way, receptacles were common and crucial for keeping possessions safe and accounted for. These ranged from elite jewelry boxes of great artistry to trunks that held trousseaus or maidservants' belongings to baskets for bread and produce. Inventories and wills included many storage receptacles in their lists of items. These include, in one inventory logbook, a *tevah* (trunk); a *kist* or *kistel* (chest); a *shank* or *shenklche* (small chests); a *schatel* (or *schachtel*, box); and a *coffret*

FIG. 8.1. Maidservant gathers vegetables. Note the simple clothing and the pouch. *Birkat ha-mazon*, 1725.

(small lockbox).[67] Some were listed as specialized for a particular purpose or adorned, for example, "a linen chest with animals, a small chest for glass with animals."[68] A *contoir* (writing desk), commode (covered desk), *kis* (pocket/purse), *nartik* (men's purse), and *zak* (sack) all made appearances in the inventories.[69] In some cases, inventories listed only the sealed containers without their contents.

Many of the itinerant working poor, such as domestic servants, carried all their possessions in trunks. If their employers suspected them of theft, they searched these containers; servants carried them to their next place of employment or to the hekdesh if they became ill.[70] The woman of the house often locked the closets holding linens, the boxes guarding tableware, and the pantries where food was stored to deter theft. We can often identify the woman of the house by the cluster of keys hanging from her waist. Women carried purses or handbags, and their clothes were often made with ample pockets.[71]

In the Kitchen

While women may not have owned all the objects associated with food preparation, all evidence points to the kitchen (or the hearth, where there was no separate room) as the realm of the woman of the household. In the early modern period, women performed or oversaw most domestic duties, regardless of whether they ran additional enterprises or worked outside their homes. Paul Wilhelm Hirsch, a convert from Judaism, averred in his polemical ethnography *Megalleh tekuphoth* (1717), "Since the men are not occupied with running the household or the kitchen, it falls solely on the women. They know best how great a supply of food and drink they have on hand."[72] It is important to remember that many homes, particularly those on the lower rungs of the socioeconomic ladder, did not have a separate space for a kitchen, and of those that had an elaborate hearth over which to cook, most did not have an oven in which to bake. In the houses on Frankfurt's Judengasse, a small stove or oven would have been tucked into the landing of the stairwell so that the smoke could vent from the window.[73] An illustration from a mid-seventeenth-century *sefer evronot* (Jewish calendar manual) depicts a book-lined room in which two scholars are studying. It contains one table, one chair, and a set of kitchen implements hanging on one wall, including a kettle, teapot, tea strainer, a towel, and several cruets. The opposite wall has a shelf holding six "sets" of tableware, each consisting of one plate and one drinking mug. Two hanging candelabras and the richly leaded windowpane show that this was by no means a poor dwelling, yet the dishes are displayed in the same room as the books.[74] In Renata Ago's sample of inventories from seventeenth-century Rome, approximately a quarter of the women owned plates, bowls, or other vessels for eating; only one-third of the sample owned any serving implements, such as serving spoons or knives. As there was no mass manufacturing, we cannot assume that people owned and used dishes and kitchenware in the early modern period in the same manner as they do today. Moreover, it is unclear which items in the household were necessarily owned by the woman. The only implements that women distinctively owned in Ago's inventories were the large cauldrons, prized items that could be used for laundry as well as cooking.[75]

The kitchen was a space where differences of use distinguished the material surroundings and objects of Jewish women from those of Christian women of similar class. Spoons might look identical in Jewish and Christian kitchens, but kosher laws required spoons differentiated for dairy or meat use; keeping them clearly identified and separated was part of a Jewish woman's role. After

FIG. 8.2. Woman putting up the Shabbat stew. She sets the smaller dish into the larger cauldron: "*zi zetst shalet.*" Yiddish *minhogim* manuscript, sixteenth century.

the passing of Baila, widow of Meir Traub, the inventory of her possessions included eight meat spoons with one soup ladle and five dairy spoons with a soup ladle.[76] Running a kosher kitchen was more complicated and more expensive than running the same level of kitchen in a Christian home. Christian Hebraist Johann Jacob Schudt remarked on how much more expensive it was for a woman of limited means to run a kosher kitchen: "They [the Jews] also have two saltshakers, one for meat and the other for dairy, and these are also marked [to designate each as meat or dairy]. They also require separate pots, spoons, plates, and forks, as well as separate storage that allows [them] to mark everything as either meat or dairy."[77]

The subsequent depiction by Schudt lets us know that even poor Jewish households had a tablecloth, and even women in poor households were punctilious about keeping everything in their kitchens separated and/or doubled so the meat and dairy implements were not mixed up.

> The poor have only one tablecloth, and they use one side for meat and the other side for dairy, and it is a big sin to eat [both meat and dairy] from the same side [of the tablecloth]. So as not to err, they mark the tablecloth in Hebrew characters, and it is customary to write *basar* (meat) on one end of the tablecloth for meat, or *halav* (dairy) for dairy. There are pious poor people who launder the tablecloth after having a meat meal before they eat a dairy meal.... They [the Jews] also have two saltshakers, one for meat and the other for dairy, and these are also marked [as meat or dairy].[78]

A household needed to invest not only in separate sets of pots and tableware but also in kosher meat, cheese, and wine. Matzah and other foodstuffs were regulated and presumably far more expensive to buy. Concerning matzah, Kirchner said, "The rich Jews help the poor from their own [allocations], so that they [the poor] could also eat 'easter-cakes [matzah]' as required by law."[79] Records that detail the flour and matzot given to the poor through communal charity can be found in a variety of communities, both large and small.[80]

Few households owned enough dishes and silverware to serve large numbers of people on festive occasions. Even with limitations on the number of guests permitted at various celebrations, most families did not own sufficient cooking and serving vessels and dishes to host a celebration such as a wedding or circumcision. In at least three instances, in Worms, Altona, and Schnaittach, communal bodies or their representatives rented out pewter dishes and large vessels as a means of serving the community as well as earning a return on their investment in the dishes.[81] In Worms, the burial society owned serving platters, large pots, and frying pans for cooking, plus several sizes of plates and spoons.[82] The gabbay (administrator) of the society kept them in his house; he had the responsibility of maintaining and collecting rent for them.[83] In eighteenth-century Altona, one shamash of the community kept a running tally of dishes he rented inside his personal copy of a community record book. He inscribed on the flyleaf, "Before Pesach, 1755: R. Joseph Haag, 16 plates, 4 trays, 1 kettle; R. Gershon the physician, 8 plates, 8 spoons, 2 trays, one kettle."[84] These stockpiles of dishes could be lent or rented when a family made a festive meal, reducing the need for each individual to own dishes that they would rarely use. It is not clear whether he ran this additional business for personal or communal gain.

If owning numerous and labeled sets of kitchenware distinguished Jewish homes from Christian, material objects in Jewish homes also varied according to the physical layout of the home and neighborhood. Some cooking pots belonging to Jewish women from urban communities identify their owners by name in Hebrew words inscribed on the pot itself. Gutin of Frankfurt, wife of Hirtz Popert, daughter of Moses zur Leiter, owned a brass pot on which the family name, the year of its creation (1580), and a small image of a ladder (a play on the family's house name) appear in Hebrew on the outside of the pot.[85] A similar two-handled bronze pot with two names inscribed, Alexander, son of Aaron, and Saraleh, daughter of Moshe, survives from early eighteenth-century Frankfurt (1708) (see plate 20). These inscriptions made their pots identifiable when women stored and retrieved them in a communal oven over Shabbat. Johann Jacob Schudt, the Christian ethnographer of Frankfurt Jewry, described how "every Friday, they place their pots and pans, which are marked with Hebrew letters on them, so that the food gets cooked and remains warm.

On Shabbat they take it out."[86] Each pot evokes the procession of women and maidservants walking to the communal oven where they had stored the Shabbat food to have a warm dish to feed their families.[87] Similarly, in nearby seventeenth-century Friedberg, then an important imperial city in the south of Germany, the Jewish community appointed a salaried official over the "*shalet* oven," the Shabbat oven where Jews brought their cholent to heat overnight.[88]

This personalization and its accompanying scenario would not have been necessary in rural settings, where most Jews had ovens in their homes and often were too thinly dispersed to share one. We recall that, in the early seventeenth century, Asher of Reichshofen installed a small oven in which to bake household foods on a regular basis. In 1759, when Ahron Cahen installed a new coal-fired baking oven in his house, his household members discarded the embers before the fire was fully extinguished, as they were inexperienced with this type of oven. As a result, the entire house burned down, and he was barely able to save his business papers.[89]

Ritual Items

Candlesticks serve as an example of a household item that had a ritual function in a Jewish household; they were gendered female, as they symbolized one of the three mitzvot associated closely with women in traditional rabbinic culture. Lighting Shabbat and holiday candles was an iconic and significant mitzvah for every Jewish household, one that usually fell to the ba'alat bayit. "Friday evenings, in wintertime between four and five o'clock, in summertime between six and seven o'clock, as Shabbat enters, they put away all money, the wife covers the table in white, takes three candles, lights them, holds her hands above them, and says the blessing."[90] In the descriptions and illustrations of Jewish custom books and Christian Hebraists' ethnographies, Jewish women were often depicted as lighting either a candelabra or candlesticks, and the objects appear very often in inventories, wills, and wedding gift lists. The number of lights varied according to family and custom. The eighteenth-century Frankfurt author Joseph Kosman noted his familiarity with a pair of candlesticks or with candelabras of six, eight, ten, or even more branches.[91] Both an eight-branched candelabra and a single candlestick are recorded among the bequests of women in eighteenth-century Metz.[92] Some women sewed hallah covers for their Shabbat tables and special matzah covers and hand towels for the seder service. When the parnas Yechiel Wallich had his effects sealed on the eve of Passover, 1789, his wife, Teibche, received a red silk seder cover with pockets, among other effects, presumably to use that same evening for the seder.[93]

In some cases, ordinary household items served ritual purposes. A ritual aimed at women during the *tekufah* (change of season) called for them to place an iron implement within a vessel of water to keep it from being tainted at that liminal time. An illustration for the ritual shows a sewing needle, which exemplifies the iron implement most women would have had at hand.[94]

As with other items, function and use could diverge from ownership. A silver besamim box (spice container) made in mid-sixteenth-century Frankfurt was inscribed with the name "Rekhlah, daughter of Eliezer Dayan, in 1650/51." The havdalah ceremony that concluded Shabbat during which this was used was usually conducted by the male head of household, so the besamim box would be gendered male. Yet, this one was clearly owned by a woman. Similarly, the *kiddush* cup that held the wine to be blessed in honor of Shabbat and holidays was used by the male head of household but could be owned by a woman. Such was the case with the widow of a chief rabbi who requested that this item from her deceased husband's effects be given to her immediately.[95] This one object held sentimental, ceremonial, and economic value; the same was true of other ritual and functional Shabbat and holiday vessels, including those used only on Passover or to decorate the sukkah. A Passover kiddush cup from late eighteenth- or early nineteenth-century Germany depicts a man and a woman at the seder table, each holding a cup and a haggadah. Either one of them (or both) could have owned the cup.

Venturing out: Jewish Women's Attire

On the most basic level, clothing of all types provides warmth and covers the human body. Beyond that, clothing signaled multiple sets of identity. The garments people wore could signify gender, religion, region, occupation, and class. In the early modern period, Jewish women and men in many parts of Europe were obliged to wear distinctive signs on their outer garments. Government legislation often dictated particular signs for groups they deemed marginal, including various colored hats and badges for Jews, prostitutes, and lepers. In the sixteenth century, Habsburg Emperor Ferdinand I ordained that a circular yellow ring badge must be worn on Jews' outer garments.

In 1670, Emperor Leopold ordered all the Jews of Prague to wear a prominent yellow or greenish linen ruff. The pleated collar that had been all the rage

FIG. 8.3. Jewish woman from Worms, depicted wearing contemporary garb with a compulsory yellow badge. *Thesaurus Picturarum*, ca. 1600. See plate 21.

FIG. 8.4. Jewish bride wears the *sivlonot* belt and lace cape, usually gifts of the groom. The women beside her each wear a "Jewish ruff," a coerced sign of Jewishness. Boener, "Eine Jüdische Braut," 1705.

during the Renaissance had, by then, become a relic and a sign of ridicule. In 1691, this decree was extended to all Jews in Bohemia, and it remained in effect until 1745, when Empress Maria Theresia expelled the Jews from Prague. Jewish women were included in legislation about wearing the "Jews' collar," and depictions from the period preserve this sign of difference.[96] Jewish clothing items per se did not always differ from Christians', but modesty rules, Shabbat and holiday garments, and other attire were different for women in each religious sector. Jewish women, as did men, refrained from garments made of *sha'atnez* (a forbidden mixture of wool and linen).[97] The wearing of special occasion outfits for celebrations and holidays also marked Jewish women as distinct from their neighbors.[98]

Ulinka Rublack has argued that the circulation of printed fashion illustrations intensified the demand for various looks and disseminated new styles of dress far more quickly than in the age before print. Even if the clothing on figures in Jewish books was not the main focus of the work, they still conveyed images of how people could dress and likely became part of a circle of influence. Such illustrations made people more conscious of their sartorial choices and helped those with limited means to use craftsmanship and ingenuity in

FIG. 8.5. Sivlonot belt. Frankfurt, late seventeenth century.

creating beautiful and expensive-looking effects.[99] Both men and women adorned their clothing according to the fashions of the day and locale. They incorporated buttons, ribbons, lace, fur, feathers, metallic threads (including gold and silver), sashes, and buckles into items of clothing and headgear, heightening their aesthetic effect. Some of the most decorative and expensive items of clothing or jewelry were created around celebrations, particularly weddings, and items such as rings and belts, made of precious metals and gems, were commonly given as gifts to brides. As noted earlier, sumptuary laws to regulate these items appear repeatedly throughout this period, in Jewish and non-Jewish regulations.[100] The regulations often bemoaned the rapidly changing fashions that caused women in particular to buy the latest baubles, head coverings, and even beauty marks.[101] Yet the merchant lay leaders who decried the frivolousness of these items bought and sold them in large lots as part of their mercantile commerce.

By the seventeenth and eighteenth centuries, most women bought manufactured cloth rather than spinning their own. Textiles for their clothing ranged from expensive imported silks, velvets, and brocades to plain wool, linen, and cotton. The material, the colors available for dyeing, and the needlework used to embroider and embellish mirrored the class of the wearer. Young girls learned basic techniques and sewed samplers that taught them stitchery and showed off their literacy. Sixteen-year-old Bremel, of a very poor family in the village of Steinbiedersdorf, "sought to earn a meager livelihood by sewing, spinning, and working."[102] Women who were nimble with the needle and thread could employ many techniques to refine the look of their garments, and if there was economic need, they could sew for others. The archaeology of the Frankfurt ghetto yielded many treasures, perhaps none so moving as the humble sewing equipment that survived the ravages of time. So many Jews earned their livelihoods in the secondhand clothing trade, the Judengasse Museum notes, that it is no wonder buttons, scissors, and thimbles were found when the area was dug up.

Women needed underwear and hose, separate outfits for daily and Shabbat or festive occasions, and outerwear such as cloaks to shield them from inclement weather. Women wore house robes when they were in childbed and nightclothes to sleep. Almost every woman, married or single, wore headgear of some sort. Like other fashions, these varied from place to place and changed to suit the occasion. Shoes, gloves, a handbag, and similar accessories completed the outfit. Given the handmade nature of most of these items, they were cared for, laundered, repaired, and eventually recycled if possible.

Books

Books form another category of objects that deeply touched the lives of Jewish women in the early modern period. We have discussed women as readers and writers of books; here, we want to emphasize books as material objects that women owned, received as gifts, or commissioned or wrote for themselves. Books were objects that announced piety, learning, a profession, the availability of leisure time, or the pursuit of practical knowledge or advice. Some women's books were adorned externally, while others bore rich illustrations for the private gratification of the owner. A beautifully bound devotional book expressed both a woman's piety and her social status, as poignantly illustrated by an entry in a pinkas from Worms (8 Nissan 1656). Sarlen, wife of the parnas Zalman Oppenheim of Worms, deeded to her brother Lemel as an absolute gift, a fur (an expensive item of clothing) and a siddur (prayer book) bound in silver.[103] Lemel would retain complete ownership of these items. Sarlen conditioned her gift on his lending her the items, the cloak to wear and the siddur to carry and use in the synagogue on festival days for the rest of her life. Her fancier dress and ornate siddur would sanctify the day, allow her to

FIG. 8.6. Ornate silver *siddur* cover, inscribed with: "Yeta, daughter of the honorable Samson, may he live many good days." Germany, 1794.

pray, and signal her social status to others (see plate 22, plate 23). Yentela, the widow of Moses Taub, also arranged for the use of several books from her husband's estate, including prayer books for the holidays and a Yiddish Bible.[104] These cases exemplify the multiple meanings Jewish women ascribed to objects, particularly to books. More broadly, the multiplication of texts, lists, and visual images relevant to Jewish life in the early modern period enable us to enter the material world created by Jewish women.

9

Last Words

FEARING THAT her end had come, Rebecca, daughter of Abraham Halfon, wife of Hayim Sinzheim, resident of Mannheim, dictated her last wishes to two male adult witnesses on December 4, 1713. This was, at least, the second iteration of her last testament, as she specifically mentioned an earlier will that she now asked her son to destroy and invalidate if it should be found. The final will, written in Yiddish, was preserved in a copy made by her offspring, possibly commissioned from a professional scribe, in March 1720.[1] Rebecca requested that her children read the will annually on the anniversary of her death (hence a copy made seven years after the original): "Remember what becomes of us people in the end and do good where you can; I will not be among you any more to remind you; remember your mother and how things went with her, that she was alive, and where she ultimately went. Give me the pleasure, preserve this will, each one of you, as a remembrance, read it every anniversary when you observe my yahrzeit, and when you have read it, confess your sins, and after that, let a quorum study each yahrzeit and say *kaddish* (mourner's prayer) when this study is completed."[2] Penned with elaborate care and bound in leather, it was intended to last as a keepsake and memorial within the family.[3]

The preservation of a matriarch's will and its circulation within the family circle is mentioned by Glikl in her memoir. She recalled reading the will of her contemporary, Pessele, wife of Model Dayyan; her children "surely never threw it away."[4] The testimony from Rebecca and from Glikl allows us to see another aspect of women's wills in the early modern period: the will as embodying the essence of a woman's voice, a form of writing that both women and their children valued, copied, read, and circulated.[5]

Rebecca's will, like all the Jewish wills we reviewed, of men and of women, can also be seen in part as an ethical will, expressing the concern of the

FIG. 9.1. The ornate title page of Rebecca Sinzheim's will, copied by her son, 1720.

individual for their soul in the afterlife and for their offspring in this life.[6] Thus, Rebecca wrote: "Do not be the cause that my soul, heaven forbid, should suffer on your account; dearest children, help, help that you don't miss attending synagogue. Do not chatter in shul; recite kaddish for me diligently; live together without strife with one another; also do not be in conflict with anyone else; treat your beloved father with respect; seek to help each other. Also my dear daughters and dear sons-in-law, comport yourselves to the highest standard; those who can study all day should study, and those who cannot should support scholars [of Torah]."[7] Her exhortations for proper behavior extended to the next generation as well; she exhorted her daughters and daughters-in-law, "Don't let my grandchildren go around looking sloppy, keep them well-bred, they should study and go to synagogue every day."[8]

Excerpts such as these capture what was significant to Rebecca. Yet, as probated and archived documents written according to formulaic legal specifications, often mediated by a lawyer and/or notary, wills, by definition, offer a very limited picture of individuals' lives. Given their prescribed language and the intervention of other parties in their creation, can women's wills even be considered the words or writings of the testators? We argue, following the suggestion of Federica Francesconi, that women can be considered coauthors of their wills.[9] The formulaic portions of wills are easily recognizable when one reviews a corpus of testaments composed in a similar place and time, while the individual wishes and life trajectories that shine through were based on women's own words.

Testamentary writing contains precious witness to aspects of the lives of the testators. Last wills and testaments performed multiple labors: they served as legal instruments and final spiritual reckonings. Wills drew a line under the sum total of economic activity and material holdings of a testator at a particular moment. The apportionment of responsibilities, of desirable assets, of guardianship of minors, and executorship of the estate allow us to see the close links of a person's affective ties. Clusters of wills often allow us to trace networked kinship ties of Jewish men and women and the ways they strategized to keep their assets in the hands of their trusted circles. Each of these aspects, which we cover in this chapter, is highly significant for forming a clearer sense of women's lives. Most wills drawn up by women (both Jewish and non-Jewish) from the early modern period were made by widows, and a smaller percentage by single women.[10] The collections we cover here, mostly from the eighteenth century, allow us to discuss the last estates (or lack thereof) of women, such as single women, maidservants, and the poor, who seldom appear in other sources. They allow us additional glimpses into the lives of well-known ba'alot bayit, such as Rebecca. Wills of married and widowed ba'alot bayit, as well as those of their husbands, reiterate that women were equal partners or more in many marriages and family economies.

Legal Aspects

Some Jewish testators made their wills in accordance with Jewish law (or at least nodded to it); others conformed to the prevailing laws of the land, and each differed according to the needs of the particular context.[11] The conditions of Jewish life in a specific place and time were reflected in the legal documents Jews produced, including wills. Thus, the study of wills can also become a study of the ways in which legal norms were adapted by Jews to suit the needs of their times and the legal customs and restrictions of their place.

Jay Berkovitz has analyzed extensively the issues confronting Jewish women as testators, as heirs, as guardians, and as wives of guardians; the latter might be liable if their husbands were found negligent in tending to the heirs' investments. He discussed the halakhic instruments devised to circumvent some of the difficulties that arose from the rabbinic guarantee of safeguarding certain women's property, such as that promised in the ketubbah (marriage contract) or that which was separated from marital property. Despite their limitations, wills allow us additional insight into how these arrangements played out over the course of a Jewish woman's life, alongside affective and social aspects of their lives that would not be known from other sources.[12]

Rebecca of Mannheim's *tzava'ah* (will) allows us to read a testament that was something of an anomaly: that of a ba'alat bayit who predeceased her husband. Rebecca expressed unease at the prospect that her husband, surviving her, might object to some of her allocations, as they might have exceeded her legal claims within the marital property. She nevertheless defended her right to spend on these spiritual matters, as she had been exceedingly frugal throughout her lifetime: "I never exceeded that which . . . was due from my beloved husband, as did other women [of my status], in the manner of all the women who had clothing made and spent a great deal. . . . That which I was stingy about, I put back [into the household]."[13] She beseeched her husband not to "strike her out of his heart" after her death and threatened terrible punishments if he should ignore her requests.

Preserving Last Wishes

In some places, almost all wills were preserved for an entire population, while, in others, those that survived did so seemingly arbitrarily.[14] Economic class had a great deal to do with survival of wills: the wealthy often had extensive property, encumbered in complicated ways, with loans and debts outstanding. Because many parties had an interest in the condition of the estate, such wills tended to be probated and then copied multiple times. Notaries could be paid to reproduce them. Jews sometimes made one notarized copy, translated into the vernacular to be probated by the state, and another in a Jewish language, which prioritized spiritual care of the soul, at least formulaically, over the distribution of earthly property.[15] When complications arose, entire legal dossiers or pinkassim could be devoted to the resolution of one estate.[16] The very poor, with few possessions, often left no will.

We have consulted various sources, including both individual wills and collections, as well as inventories made upon the death of women. One set of wills we use as the basis for our discussion comes from a communal logbook: copies of documents pertaining to the joint financial and communal interests of the Jewish communities in Hamburg and Altona. Each will in the volume notes the city in which it was made, as the notaries who wrote and signed these copies were by this time jointly appointed to serve in both communities.[17] We do not claim that the small number of wills we examine here are representative of anything beyond themselves. The wills included in the Altona-Hamburg volume were those of Ashkenazi Jewish men and women who had left bequests for communal charities or communally directed funds, and thus they represent far from a broad sample. Yet even this small sample is instructive regarding the variation between wills and the possibilities of individual expression in this formulaic genre. The wills are of two types. Some had been prepared years before the death of the testator, and the original, sealed in a packet, had been left in the hands of a trusted agent, often the shamash of the community, to be delivered to the parnas of the month upon the person's death, when the will would be read and executed. The scribe indicated those wills by the words "copy of the will" in the heading. Others, which opened with the words *zikhron edut* (record of testimony), are essentially testimonies of the communal notaries who, summoned to the bedside of a person who had fallen gravely ill, recorded their final wishes.[18] The wills contain an element of intertextuality—some widows referred to terms of their late husbands' wills; others refer to outstanding *shetare hov* (loan documents; sing. *shetar hov*), kept elsewhere or, perhaps, with the original will document; and several refer to the personal account books of individuals.

Women made seventeen of 137 wills copied into the Altona-Hamburg logbook from the years 1759 to 1810. At least two of those were the wills of single women who never married; an additional one was the will of an unmarried maidservant. All the rest of the women had been married and were widows by the time they made their wills. Scribal conventions indicated in a word the standing of a woman within the community. While most women were identified by their first names and their fathers' and husbands' names, many of the wealthy women with testaments in this collection are referred to as *ha-ishah ha-hashuvah* (the significant woman), *ha-ishah ha-yekarah* (the dear woman), or *ha-ishah ha-gevirah* (the noble woman), by the communal scribes. Yutche, a woman who was left in "miserable circumstances," is simply *ha-ishah* (the woman).[19]

In order to understand the position of the widows, we must first review some of the wills left by men who predeceased their wives. The eminent physician, scholar, and entrepreneur Mordechai Gumpel Shnaber wrote a will that contained generous provisions for his wife. A year later, close to the time of his death, he rewrote the will to be even more favorable to her. In the first recension, he opened the will with a paean to his wife: "My modest spouse M. [Marat] Fradche ... was pleasant to me in all her affairs, a God-fearing woman who is to be praised ... my love for her is unbounded. ... I decided to reward the fruits of her labor and repay her goodness."[20] Shnaber added to his original marriage contract another significant amount, which together came to the sum of two thousand Reichsthaler, which, he stipulated, should be paid before any other claim on the estate. He requested that she be exempt from having to take the "widow's oath" regarding her marriage contract.[21] He left to her all the durable goods in his home, including clothing, linens, bedding, and jewelry of gold, silver, and gems. In a later addition to his will, made on his deathbed, Shnaber appointed his wife executor of his entire estate; this comprised all his business dealings, including his "pharmacy."[22]

A will such as Shnaber's, in which the husband predeceased his wife and left her not only financially secure but also in a position to take over all their joint and his individual affairs, left widowed women in some cases with significant wealth to distribute and considerable power over their heirs. In many cases, they also attest to a ba'alat bayit's involvement in family enterprises even before her husband's death. When Herzl Khue (Kuh) died in Vienna in 1771, his wife, Malca Judith, was pregnant with their ninth child. His estate left virtually no cash but, rather, many letters of credit and outstanding debts—a highly complex commercial enterprise. He ordered that Malca Judith be his universal heir and take over his entire business. "She should carry on with all transactions as she sees fit, as she directs, disposes, and pleases. It is known throughout the world that she is capable and able to continue to direct the business, and she has sufficient knowledge of all of it."[23] This was not only the case with men of commerce. The chief rabbi of Altona-Hamburg-Wandsbek, David Berlin (d. 1771), left everything he had to his wife, the "modest, stately, learned rabbanit Tzirel," as an outright gift in his lifetime. He trusted "her pure heart, for she has great yearning for our children . . . and she will do the right thing with my estate . . . to see to the good of her children."[24] By reverse token, Hirsch Oppenheim left his "modest spouse" with a modest bequest: her marriage contract and its supplement, the betrothal gifts and wedding ring he bought her, and anything she brought with her into the marriage that was rightfully hers. Beyond that, "nothing should be accorded to her, for I cannot allow it, as I have many children. . . . It would be good if my spouse had mercy on the children and treated them beyond the letter of the law, for she knows how hard I tried to support her and the children honorably."[25] Women's varied circumstances after the deaths of their husbands were often reflected in both the spouses' and their own wills.

Care of the Soul

In the early modern period in Europe, Jews and Christians, women and men, saw the making of a will as the spiritual preparation for death. In that respect, wills illuminate the spiritual priorities of the individual and the communities to which they belonged. Rebecca of Mannheim's will included passages renouncing any evil thoughts contradicting her Jewish faith that she might have on her deathbed. Such clauses were also typical of Christian wills in this period, an illustration of cross-cultural influences embedded in seemingly separate spheres.

Many testators, male and female, made bequests that were intended to benefit their souls from the moment they began their journey from this world. Hendel, wife of Nathan, left a sum of two hundred Reichsthaler courant with the treasurer of Altona's Jewish community, to be held in escrow in the event she died intestate, to be used "for a good deed to benefit my soul upon my death."[26] As soon as she found time to write a will, those funds were redirected toward more specific ends and were to be returned "immediately upon my death."

The idea of giving a sum equivalent to the value of the letters in one's name appears frequently in wills, assuring that the charity would benefit that specific person's soul. Pessche, wife of Moses Hamm, requested, "Between the time of my death and my burial, the parnas R. Hirsch Halle and my grandson, Yehudah, should distribute to local and distant poor an amount equivalent to the numerical value of my name, Pessche [which equals] 240, in eight-shilling pieces, 235 Mark courant. After the seven days [of mourning] have passed, once again a sum in the amount of my name should be distributed to the poor, 470 Mark courant."[27] Hendel, wife of Nathan, similarly requested "redemption according to my name," without spelling it out.[28] Rebecca of Mannheim paid particular attention to the care of her body immediately after her death, as she was a member of a burial society and knew the procedures well. She requested that the very first thing done upon her death, "while I am still lying on the straw," be the distribution of alms in an amount corresponding to the value of letters in her Hebrew name, Rivkah. The sum of the letters in her name equaled 307, the same, she helpfully added, as the Hebrew letters *shin zayin*, which stand for *shikhvat zera*, a biblical term for semen. The association may derive from a kabbalistic custom, known to have been practiced in Mannheim, that sought at the time of the funeral to neutralize the negative power of seed that had been spilled from the deceased.[29] This amount should be multiplied by eighteen *peshitim* (cents), the numerical equivalent of the word "live."[30]

Testators typically prescribed a series of donations throughout the mourning period and on the anniversary of their deaths. Rebecca, for example, instructed, "On the day that the seven-day mourning period ends, from the money that I saved from spending on my body in order to help my soul, 20 Reichsthaler should be taken and used to clothe local poor orphans, who lack clothing."[31] Pessche Hamm stipulated that charity in various forms go to the poor of the community, so long as they were deemed honorable poor:

> On my first yahrzeit, 64 Mark courant should be distributed from my estate to poor people who are related, from my side as well as my husband's, and the closer kin get priority. Also on that day, my estate shall distribute charity for *hakhnasat kallah* (dowering poor brides) to two orphans of our community, ten Reichstaler each toward their dowry. And should, on this day, more than two orphan brides be found, a lottery should be made among them on that day, and whichever one wins the lottery, wins . . . but see to it that they should be honorable orphans, daughters of good people.[32]

She also stipulated that wax for the synagogue lamps lit at prayer times should be donated for one full year. While the amounts and specifics vary from will to will, the overall tenor of Pessche's will accords with those of women of her station, and the charitable beneficiaries can be found in many of the wills from this time and place. Most of the women in the Altona-Hamburg collection allotted funds for various charitable causes to benefit their souls. Many wills followed a template, and those models served as mirrors of the expectations for charitable and wealth distribution for women of mostly middle to higher economic class. The variations are what make them individual. Almost all the women who made wills, including the poorest (in this collection), had set aside money for the elevation of their souls. Sarah, wife of Ziskind Stern (Hamburg, 1771), noted, "Next to my shrouds, I set aside 150 Mark courant, for my children to distribute to the needy between my death and my burial."[33] Sarah prepared for her death by buying her own shrouds and setting alongside them death-related funds to be distributed to charity.[34]

Men and women shared some charitable causes, such as dowering poor brides and donating wax to illuminate the synagogue. Fromet, widow of Elia Levi of Metz, made elaborate plans in 1753 to ensure that her lamp be donated to the synagogue, and that it be lit on specific occasions for the elevation of her soul: "I give to the kahal as a gift before my death the silver lamp with eight silver arms that is in my estate, to hang in the old synagogue, and to be lit on Shabbat and holiday evenings. I give to the kahal, also as a gift before my death, the seat that belongs to me in the women's section downstairs. From the interest [on the sale] of my seat, the lamp should be lit at the aforementioned times."[35]

Women also donated funds toward causes that might seem particular to women's domains, such as fabric from their clothing to be refashioned into parokhot (textile ark coverings). Ritchel, widow of Moses, son of communal leader Ziskind Leidsdorf, donated textile interwoven with silver thread. She requested that her son-in-law see to it that a parokhet for the great synagogue in Altona be made from it.[36] Rebecca of Mannheim prescribed another way to recycle her garments for charity. Familiar with the ins and outs of shroud making, she explained to her children: "There will be pieces of linen found alongside my shrouds that, immediately after the seven-day mourning period, should be made into undershirts for the bride, and each poor bride should be given some pieces of it, those who still need it." She also instructed that they distribute "my everyday clothing and my linens [undergarments], that I wore on my own body . . . to my servants and to my children's domestic servants, to those who need it most." Her special Shabbat clothing was to "be distributed to the children of my poor brothers and sisters."[37]

Torah Study

More surprising is the extent to which women singled out institutions in the community that were gendered male, such as the kloyz (study hall). Pessche Hamm devoted a significant sum to support students who would pray and study Mishnah, another known source of elevation for the soul:

> After my burial, they should hire ten Torah students to pray the morning and evening prayer in my home. After the prayers, they should study a chapter of Mishnah in the proper order for my soul an entire year, and my grandson, R. Yehudah, should supervise that they learn with devotion. In return for that, they should be paid from my estate 12 Reichsthaler courant for each one, which comes to 360 Mark courant. Also, [they] ... should make a minyan in my house for 12 Reichsthaler courant. These twelve scholars, during the first year, should go on the eve of every new month to my grave to pray for my soul, for which each one will be paid a half Reichsthaler every eve of the New Month, which comes to 180 Mark courant.[38]

Pessche also allocated funds for the kloyzen of both Altona and Hamburg, although the preference for the kloyz of Altona, her own locale, is clear. "An eternal fund should be established by our kahal with capital of 1,100 Reichsthaler courant, giving off interest of 4 percent annually. An 'obligation' should be written to establish this.... My relative, parnas R. Hirsch Halle, and my grandson, R. Yehudah, should request [the profit] from the rabbinical court of our community, and should spend it as follows: to the kloyz in Altona, 12 Reichsthaler courant, and to the two kloyzen in Hamburg, 2 Reichsthaler to each, together 16 Reichsthaler courant."[39]

Hendel, wife of Nathan, made sure to include her favored communal official as a beneficiary of all her charitable bequests. She explicitly asked that R. Feivel, shamash of the rabbinical court, be among the ten scholars to be paid for learning and praying in the room where she died. She asked that Feivel be added to the scholars who learned for her in the kloyz, and she allocated funds to dower his daughter. Finally, she allocated more money for him to study a Torah lesson for her sake in his own home, "half an hour each day in the first year after my passing."[40]

Women's support for a kloyz was a consistent feature in their wills. The tombstone of Liba, wife of Issakhar Ber ha-Levi of Vienna, recalls the two synagogues that she supported financially, one of which was the kloyz.[41] Another unmarried woman from Mannheim, a daughter of the prestigious Reingarum family that had founded the local kloyz, "independently donated a certain sum before her death, to support Torah study."[42] Women who bequeathed funds to the kloyzen left their mark on additional communal records, including the memorial books used in the prayer quorum at these study halls. In 1726, Ella bat Binyamin of Fürth left a small sum to be invested by the community, and the interest was to be given annually to young men "studying in the bet midrash, in order to fulfill the precept, 'It is a tree of life to those who grasp [support] it.'"[43] The rebbetzin Bonla did the same just a few years later.[44] These were the early years of the Fürth Kloyz, which had been established in 1708. Men and women supported the kloyz with funds from their estates; the grandsons of one local rabbi pledged a sum in memory of their mother, Radis, in 1727, to support the new establishment.[45] The women's patronage was inscribed in the memorial book, and their names were read aloud as part of the liturgy in public recognition of their support.

Women from across the socioeconomic spectrum donated to kloyzen. The wealthiest among them established kloyzen, as did Shinkhen, daughter of the honorable Isaac Reiss, who "built a house in which words of Torah were heard at night as in the day . . . it was as lovely as the moon and as bright as the sun" and also had its own charity fund to support the poor.[46] Sarla, a rabbanit who was also the daughter of the court Jew Samson Wertheim, donated funds to open a bet midrash.[47] But less-well-off, and even unmarried, women supported kloyzen, too. Alongside her shrouds and the charity to be distributed immediately after her death, Sarah, wife of Ziskind Stern, "put there as well six Danish ducats for six scholars to study between the time of my death and my burial."[48] Sarah's will demonstrates that even women of limited means set aside money for distribution to charity and for Torah study for the elevation of their souls. Similarly, Yitta, a maidservant from Altona, donated money to the local kloyz in her testament, discussed at length below.[49]

Like the men of the community who donated money from their estates or their books to the kloyzen in Altona and/or Hamburg, women donated sums to ensure that men would learn in their memory after their death.[50] Not only did women often name the kloyz as a beneficiary institution, but they also sometimes specified individual scholars to study in their memory, as Pessche

Hamm did. Rebbeca of Mannheim even asked that a specific order of study be followed:

> My husband and beloved children should see to it that ten scholars should learn each day for one hour throughout the entire year. The content of their study should be, first and foremost: ten chapters of Psalms should be said from beginning to end; after that one chapter of the 24 books [of the Bible; Tanakh]; and, after that, at least three units of Mishnayot; after that, one page of Gemara; after that, a small passage from the Zohar. This should be paid by my husband from my money that is left after deducting the abovementioned 300 Gulden, and in case I have not left enough, I hope that my husband will have the good grace to pay the cost of such study from his own pocket.[51]

The very frequent bequests women made to the kloyzen allow us to see how invested women were in upholding Torah scholarship in their communities, and how entangled the gender lines of such institutions really were. Financial support of Torah scholarship enabled women to uphold communal institutions, even those in which they could not personally study.

Family Relationships

Many women's wills open a window into the complex family lives of ba'alot bayit, who sought to ensure that their relatives and loved ones would be cared for after they were no longer there to do so. Rebecca of Mannheim singled out, among her six children, her son Leyb: "I entreat my son, R. Leyb, may he live, whom God has granted a good heart from the cradle, [that] he should establish himself as a father and guardian to my nieces and nephews,[52] he should take care of them at all times, as much as possible; he should try to help them to the greatest extent possible, as though I were still here."[53] This guardianship assignment came in addition to the clothing and the dowries she had planned for them: "Three hundred Gulden should be set aside as an income-producing endowment to be used to dower several of my brothers' and sisters' children; fifty Gulden should be given [to each] until the principal and the interest is completely distributed."[54]

Pessche Hamm's will also singled out her granddaughter, Fegelschen, whom she raised after her son, Shimshon, died:

> My granddaughter, the girl Fegelschen, may she live, daughter of my son Shimshon of blessed memory, whom I raised in my home, I, and my

husband of blessed memory, gave her a *shetar matanah* [gift deed] in 1754, of 1,000 Reichsthaler L"d [*Louis d'or*, a currency]. We settled on her an outright gift of an additional 500 Reichsthaler L"d, such that this 1,500 Reichsthaler L"d should be given from my estate to a trusted man to invest, and she should enjoy the profits annually until she, with God's help, achieves an appropriate match; after that, her support should be drawn from this 500. If God grants me the merit to accompany her to the marriage canopy, then all of this is null and void, and she has no more claim on my estate [presumably because if Pessche were alive, she would provide a dowry].[55]

Pessche cross-referenced the will of her husband from 1754 repeatedly, as the bulk of the estate was disposed and detailed there. She assigned various amounts to other offspring and relatives. Her grandson, Yehudah, was to be the sole beneficiary of the remainder of the estate and all it entailed.

To a remarkable degree, beyond the charitable and pious grants, women of the communities of Hamburg and Altona left their entire estates to their families. This included not only direct offspring, such as children, children-in-law, and grandchildren, but sometimes also siblings and their offspring. Some women raised the grandchildren of their deceased children, and one included a girl she had raised "like a daughter" without specifying if there was a kinship bond. None of the Altona-Hamburg women's wills left anything to a "friend," although some singled out communal officials who had been helpful to them. Sarah, widow of Meir Stern, mentioned her maidservant by name: "All my ordinary daily clothing my sons should distribute to the poor, and my maidservant Tovah should take her share."[56] Ritschel, widow of Moses Leidsdorf, left five Reichsthaler to her maidservant, but she did not specify the servant's name.[57] In this regard, the will of Rebecca Mannheim provides a strong contrast, for in addition to providing for her family members, her and her children's domestic servants, and the poor, she left sums for her and her husband's friends:

> Regarding the friend of my beloved husband, no mention is necessary. May God allow him and you to remain in wealth, honor, and good health, and He should help you. Your relatives also have a portion in my clothing; also, the sum of 100 Gulden should be set aside for those friends, that is, 25 Gulden for each one for dowering [their daughters]. My dear, beloved son, R. Leyb, had read my old will, in which it had been mentioned that he should take a certain sum and invest it for profit to be given to my poor friend, and he had agreed to this.[58]

Rebecca praised Leyb and her other children for having already activated the fund in question, even before she had drafted this second and updated will.

Fromet, widow of Elia Levi, had been a member of the elite class in Metz. She wrote and rewrote her will at least three times. She had many concerns and beneficiaries and specified in her will that certain of her assets were to go to "my relatives specifically" rather than to those of her husband.[59] She specified two unmarried young girls and one woman as beneficiaries of her will, along with her maidservant. The latter was clearly a member of the household; she did not specify her relationship to the others. Primary among the beneficiaries was ensuring the continued care of her daughter, Kilche, who could not care for herself. In her will, she requested that her brother-in-law take Kilche into his home. The funds for this should be drawn from her estate, "to provide for all her needs, including food and clothing, anything in the world that she might require, since I know that the 600 livres that my husband of blessed memory left to my daughter, may she live, do not suffice."[60] In the event this was not possible, she asked that he oversee her care in another household setting. She allotted a significant sum so that Kilche would be attended to in the best possible way. While Fromet tasked her brother-in-law with oversight of her soon-to-be-orphaned daughter, she left unsaid that the daily tasks of caring for the motherless girl would fall on her brother-in-law's wife. If she were not willing or able to care for Kilche, Fromet hoped that a non-relative might be willing to adopt Kilche into their household if the expenses were paid. Upon her death in 1753, communal officials distributed the first tranche of her charity money, only to stop short when they realized that Fromet had bequeathed in her will far more than the value of her entire estate. At that point, her will came before the rabbinical court, and much of an entire pinkas was devoted to unraveling the complications that arose from her excessive bequests.[61] The rabbinical court ultimately decided that the daughter, Kilche, took priority over all other beneficiaries, as she was the legitimate heir of the estate.

Dolza Susman (née Wertheimer) reflected in her 1761 will the circumstances that her husband, Gershon, had described in his. Gershon Susman noted in his will that since his youth, many awful, distressing, and life-shortening heartbreaks had befallen him. In particular, he noted a hundredfold lottery loss, which overturned their great fortune into total financial ruin. From that time, he could not earn a living, and the household lived completely off Dolza's income. Equity, therefore, demanded that he protect her, and he listed the amounts she had brought into the marriage. He made her the universal heir of his estate and laid out how various creditors were to be paid after her interests were protected. In

Dolza's will, made a decade later (but only a Jewish will, as the state recorded her as intestate), she noted that her husband had, a decade earlier (1751), made an instrument to ensure her living standard, and since it was her earnings that bought everything in the house, he had nothing to dispose of. "All furnishings, which I bought with my money, should belong to my two daughters, Devora and Frumet (Veronica). When they marry, they should each get 1,000 fl. and the income from certain investments."[62]

Some women used their wills to settle scores. In one Viennese will, a father, Herz Löw Manasses, retaliated against his daughter for not doing his bidding: "My daughter, Miriam, wife of Moses Löw, sinned against me grievously; despite this, I will show her my paternal love and not disinherit her. She should get 200 Gulden."[63] This sum was far less than the other children got. Herz left money for his grandchildren from this daughter but stipulated that she was to have no part in it.

In her will (Hamburg, 1770), Yutche, daughter of Shlomo Nean-burg, the widow of Joseph Prager, expressed her bitterness at how she had been treated in her husband's will and detailed her plan to rectify her situation from beyond the grave. Joseph Prager had died in 1768 at age fifty-three after a life engaged in the pursuit of bitter polemics within the triple community.[64]

> It is well known that my late husband R. Joseph . . . left me in miserable circumstances. I did not receive even a small fraction of my ketubbah (marriage contract) and the *tosefta* (supplement to it) from his estate. Thus, my own estate is paltry and consists primarily of household goods. It seems to me . . . that the need is greater for a female, so that she should not sit until her hair turns white. . . . Therefore, it is my last will if God determines that I should die . . . that without any exception, small or large, everything will belong to my virgin [i.e., single] daughter, Fegelche. . . . She should give my son, Israel, household goods or books worth 50 Reichsthaler courant, which will serve as my inheritance to him. . . . God knows I did not do this to diminish my son. It distresses me greatly to have to write a will like this. The serpent tempted me, that my daughter should not sit [single] and come to great embarrassment.[65]

Yutche was not the only woman left in penury by the death of a husband, but not all of them suffered poverty until their deaths. Hendel, daughter of Abraham Curiel, widow of the charity collector Meir Levi, wrote:

> It is well known that when I moved from Altona to Hamburg, I was left in miserable circumstances.[66] I had to marry off children, which entailed both

dowries and support, alongside reversals in my business, such that I kept being reduced in circumstances. Nothing was left when I arrived in Hamburg, other than my household goods and the clothes on my body. . . . Then my two sons girded their loins to earn a living for us, including all the members of my household, and they supported us in great dignity . . . they paid off my debts as well. They did this for no reason other than my honor . . . and they called the business after my name, "Witwe (widow of) Meir Levi" even though it is known to all that my two sons were excellent businessmen.[67]

She, like Yutche, felt guilty about appearing to shortchange her other heirs, but she felt she owed the bulk of her estate to the two sons who had sustained her. Her personal clothing went to her daughters.

Klerche, widow of Moses Heilbut (Altona, 1773), daughter of Feivish Wagner, also recorded, "It is known to all and sundry that my late husband died without even leaving anything to cover my marriage contract." She, however, proved more adept than had Yutche at raising the family's financial status. "Only after my husband's death did God enlarge my boundaries, meaning that everything that is in my possession now, I earned after the death of my husband."[68] Klerche had gone into partnership with Joseph, one of her sons, and they divided all the profits from their business equally. They lent out money and received pawns as security. Due to the complicated nature of the possessions to be found in her home, she authorized only her son, Joseph, to take an inventory for the sake of the other children so that the pawn items and other wares meant for the business should be clearly separated from her personal effects. Beyond that, she stipulated that the estate should not be sealed by Jewish or non-Jewish court order, nor should any external party order a formal inventory to be taken. She left her role in the business to another son and divided her estate apart from the business so that the sons got double the portion of the daughters (who presumably had received dowries from her).

Sarah, widow of Meir Stern (and mother of a community bursar), was left in excellent circumstances by her late husband. "He ordered in his will that as long as I remain unmarried to another man, everything and all the business will be left in my hands, and the business was even continued under the name of the 'widow of Meir Yaakov Stern.' . . . I made matches for all my children, male and female, with dowries and support and the other expenses . . . and I carried on the commerce with great dignity for twenty-one years." Sarah wrote that the household was conducted "at great honor and expense," at times visible and, at others, hidden. "Any wise person," Sarah added, "would have realized that these things cost a huge fortune, and thus the cash was drained from my husband's estate, not to mention the yearly expenses and damages, expected and unexpected, so that my capital as well as the profits were greatly eroded." As in the case of Hendel Curiel Levi, discussed above, two of Sarah's sons gave her a loan to float the ship of her household and commerce so that she would not fall into shame and abasement.[69]

Even wealthy women left in good circumstances wanted to make sure that their share in posterity would not be seen as less than their husbands'. Hendel Curiel Levi insisted in her will that "my tombstone will be equal to that of my late husband in measurement, both in length and in width."[70] But just as women could try to rectify imbalances of power in their last wills, they also expressed their gratitude for honors or services that were meaningful to them. When she distributed her possessions, Hendel ordered that most of her jewels and expensive items, in gold, silver, or precious stone, be sold and the proceeds distributed to her grandchildren. She made one exception: "Except for my gold wedding ring, which will go as an outright gift to my grandson Leyb son of Yosef Wechsler, because I served as *sandeket* (godmother) for him."[71] It is unclear if she was his sandeket at his own brit in infancy or whether he asked her to serve as sandeket for his son. What is clear is that this was a very significant honor for her, binding her in a special way to this grandchild alone.

Sarah, widow of Ziskind, had copied a loan document proving that her son had given her a large loan, which she had yet to repay. As a result, she left her entire estate to that son, excluding all other children and grandchildren and prohibiting them from contesting the terms. As a result of her entire estate's going to one heir, she noted, "It is hardly necessary to say that my son Shlomo does not have to give an inventory or list of my estate to anyone; therefore, there is no need for the estate to be sealed, either by gentile or Jewish law."[72] Sarah, widow of Meir Stern, added several clauses that granted nominal amounts or gifts to other family members "*lifnim meshurat ha-din* (beyond what the law requires)." Thus, she left a sum "to my son-in-law, Moses, and his wife Dina . . . despite the fact that, according to the way of strictness, I shouldn't have given them a penny, as they received the royal treatment from me during my lifetime."[73]

One of the few widows to make a will (Altona, 1794) with no mention of children or descendants was Pessche, widow of Juzpa Mentzer, daughter of Michel Wagner.[74] Her will was structured such that she left the entirety of her assets to Gedaliah ben Gedaliah, to whom she owed a large debt of two thousand Reichsthaler. Pessche wrote that all her worldly assets she owed to him and to his wife, and no other debt might precede it. She referred to her husband's will, which explained why she had to take this loan and arrange her affairs as she did. Yet, despite her disposition of all she owned to Gedaliah, there followed a list of requests she made of Gedaliah (clearly all arranged in advance), including the usual charitable bequests, bequests to the three kloyzen, and many other listed items. Notably, Pessche owned, and already during her lifetime had donated to the Altona synagogue, a parokhet and a Torah scroll. It would be left to the kahal to decide whether to take possession of them or leave them in the hands of Gedaliah. She also left some items for the wife of her executor "over which he may have no interest." Perhaps a friendship with the wife explains her arrangement with the husband, Gedaliah. She left items and money to nieces and to her maidservant, and she arranged monthly payments for the upkeep of her sister in the hekdesh.[75]

Single Women's Wills

Single women wrote wills as well, which similarly shed light on their communal and familial ties. Sarah (Serke), "virgin" daughter of the late Aaron Austerlitz, requested that her will (1765, Altona) be recorded, although the text does not say that she was extremely ill. She set aside a sum for one learned nephew (a son of her brother) to say the kaddish for her: "Let him not take it lightly, for it will benefit my soul, and it is a mitzvah to do the bidding of the dead."[76] Other than that, she left all her worldly effects to the son of her sister. In contrast, Gitel, unmarried "virgin" daughter of Zanvil Heksher [Hoexter], recorded a will when she was in extremis. She allocated funds for the poor to be distributed during the period between her death and her burial and then immediately after her burial. She also designated a sum for her relative, Feivel, son of Shimon Heksher—fifty Reichsthaler courant—to say kaddish for her for an entire year after her death. She granted him a new outfit worth twelve Reichsthaler courant. Gitel recorded that she had given to the assessor Nathan Leidsdorf 1,100 Mark courant and then another tranche of 233 Mark for him to hold for her. She divided her money between her brother and her sister but then allocated all her articles, "all kinds of things" that were already in the home of her sister, Sheva, including fabric, a chest, and her silver bracelet, to her sister. She requested that the court penalize her brother if he decided to dispute those conditions.[77]

The Altona-Hamburg collection preserves one maidservant's will, as we discussed above: Yitta, daughter of Falk of Fredericia, who worked in the home of R. Ezriel Brill. Yitta made a will that followed many aspects of those of women in far higher stations, albeit with far more modest sums. Yitta expressed her faith in the absolute probity of her employer, into whose care she had entrusted all her accumulated wages and personal effects, as well as the execution of her will. She also asked that a sum be distributed to the poor between the time of her death and her burial, leaving twenty Mark courant for this purpose. She further instructed that "ten men will learn every thirtieth day for a full year after my death," setting aside ten Reichsthaler for this purpose. Another ten Reichsthaler were intended to pay for one scholar, who would learn Torah each day for a full year after her death. Forty Mark courant were left to light an eternal flame (likely in the synagogue) for one year after her death.[78] Out of the total cash she had saved, 500 Mark, she donated 383 Mark to charity.[79]

Yitta also donated the significant "sum of one hundred Mark Danish courant to contribute to a perpetual fund of the confraternity for caring for orphans, and for this, I request the rights from the confraternity that are standard for its members." Based on another contemporary will in the same collection, it seems she intended for the members of this confraternity to recite the kaddish prayer on her behalf. In addition, in exchange for a donation, the orphans and the rabbi who oversaw them were to recite Psalms before the burial and to escort the body from the deceased's home to the cemetery.[80] Yitta thereby ensured in her lifetime that her funeral would be paid for and that her soul would be prayed for, despite her distance from her siblings, who resided in Braunschweig, The Hague, and Fredericia.[81] She further earmarked funds from her estate to cover her burial costs and specifically requested to be buried in Altona's Koenigstrasse cemetery, which was normally limited to official members of the community. Yitta did not include the motive for her request in her testament, although her desire may indicate that she identified with the Altona community and wished to belong to it after death as well. Records of the burial society confirm that her wish was granted, and she was buried in the Koenigstrasse cemetery to the right of Mehrl, the wife of Hertz Levy.[82] The communal leaders may have granted Yitta's request because her relative, Mann of Fredericia, who also served as one of the executors of her will, served as a gabbay (officer) of the burial society.[83] This reinforces the observation that family connections, even more distant ones, were deeply influential in achieving status in the Jewish community.

Yitta's personal bequests speak of her ties to her family of origin, as well as to her close relationships within the Brill household. She set aside small amounts and effects for a sister, leaving the remainder of her estate, after all specific bequests, to be divided among her three brothers. She singled out her unmarried nieces, and her bequests of bolts of cloth indicate that she may have been saving for her own trousseau. "To the maiden Reitzche, daughter of my brother, M. Aaron, in Fredericia, two [bolts of] patterned cotton, as well as a brown taffeta garment; and for the maiden, Reitzche, daughter of my brother, M. Yaakov, in the Hague, the following should be given from my estate: 2 [bolts of] patterned cotton, a red garment of rustling silk fabric, also 6 bedlinens, 3 [bolts of] tulle, and 6 pair of wool stockings."[84]

She paid special attention to one of the daughters of her employer, Heitze, "as a reward for caring for me in my illness."[85] Yitta bequeathed to her "one purse of mine with two splashes of gold color, also 21 ducat pieces, and everything inside it; also 2 pillowcases . . . with trim; red cotton for curtains; also red cotton for bed linens; also nine measures of best brown cotton; also 2 [bolts of] patterned cotton that are in the chests."[86] While few of the women or men in this collection gave funds as tokens of friendship, Yitta remembered her co-servant, Henna, in a significant way, bequeathing to her "the sum of five Reichsthaler courant. Also, 3 [swaths of] patterned cotton [and] 2 red bottles/plates."[87] Yitta had a considerable estate for a maidservant, and her will demonstrates that careful husbanding of wages over what may have been many years, along with a good relationship with an employer, could leave some loyal servants with a substantial estate.

Dying Intestate

Compared to the wills we have examined, inventories recorded after death for settling an estate are even more laconic. Inventories are not wills, of course, so while they tell us something of the physical and economic circumstances of the dead, they are even less directly the words of women. Several inventories from Vienna were those of maidservants or other poor women who served the community, and, unlike Yitta, many died intestate and left very little of value. Zirl N. was a Jewish widow who served as a *Köchin* (cook) in the home of Loew Sinzheim.[88] She died in 1723, and while nothing was recorded in the inventory, her quarters were locked, indicating that some effects remained.[89] Freydle, *Kuchelweib* (kitchen maid) in the home of Loew Sinzheim (perhaps the replacement for the previous kitchen help), died intestate in November 1730. She died in the Jewish hospice near the cemetery, and as no lock was put on her quarters, presumably, she left no effects.[90] Helene Hainlin (her Jewish will was under the name Hendl Levin) was Köchin in the home of Moses Weissweiler and died a widow on April 12, 1749. She left a daughter, Ruechme Hainlin, married to Chaim Bior in Mattersdorf, Eisenstadt, and a fifteen-year-old son, Lazarus, also living in

Mattersdorf, by the "smiths." She was owed a year's pay of twenty-eight Gulden, and she owned a house in Tobitschau, Moravia, as well as clothing.[91] Fifteen years later, we find the woman who likely replaced her, Fögerle, described as a widow who served as "Köchin bey Weissweiler." Her effects were locked in Weissweiler's presence.[92] Another servant, Heyle, lived in the "Schmidlischen" house of Sara Oppenheimer, on the Rossau, where she worked as a *Kindesweib* (nanny). A lock was placed on her *Raysstrücherl* (travel trunk). She left two married daughters in Moravia but no will.[93] The widow Eva served in the home of Veronica Traiteurin and died leaving no effects; the widow Golde served as maidservant for the Arnsteiners and died in the hekdesh in 1778.[94] While several men who died poor and alone were said to have been living off alms, few women were named as beggars. Only Haya from Hungary (d. 1785) is listed as a *Bettlerin* (beggar) who had left her children behind in Hungary.[95] Without the written recordkeeping apparatus of the hekdesh, her life would have left no trace.

Wills and Communal Records

The wills of the servant Yitta and the other women mentioned here illustrate why communal officials included copies of individual bequests in their own administrative records. Many wealthier women left sums to be invested by the lay leaders; some, like Pessche Hamm, established a perpetual trust for the benefit of worthy scholarly institutions and needy brides. Even Yitta's more modest will required communal oversight: someone needed to negotiate her burial in Koenigstrasse and see to it that her bequests to the synagogue and the kloyz for the sake of her soul were carried out in accordance with her wishes. As in many of the other wills in the Altona-Hamburg collection, Pessche Hamm asked that a stiff penalty be levied against anyone who challenged the terms of the will. The fine against any challenger was to be distributed equally to the kehillah and to the non-Jewish poor.[96] Asking that fines or penalties be shared by a non-Jewish entity was another way to invoke its power to enforce the terms of the will. She requested that no Jewish court, whether rabbinic or lay, honor any challenge to the will. Michla, daughter of Nathan, widow of the scholar Meir Cohen, stated explicitly that her will was to be recorded, "signed and sealed, and given into the hands of those who will have a share in it." The original documents went to the heirs, and the community retained a copy for its records.[97]

The notarial aspects of Pessche's will, also typical of the others in this volume, are conspicuous as well. The signature and seal of the testator and her

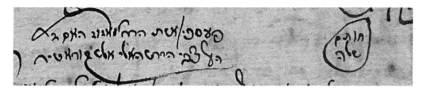

FIG. 9.2. The words in the circle on the right read "*hotam shelah*" (her seal), indicating Pessche Hamm's seal in the original document, 1763.

"curateur" are copied, and the seal indicated by a circle inscribed with the words "her seal."[98] This is significant for female testators, as it implies that they had their own seals. The communal officials attested to the accuracy of the copy and stated that the original remained in the hands of the primary heir, the grandson, R. Yehudah Hamm.

That some ba'alot bayit had their own seals reiterates the central role that they played in their families and in the economy. Sarah, widow of Meir Stern, kept a logbook of her profits, and she used it not just to record expenses and income but also to explain family entanglements that caused her to accumulate certain debts and obligations. She also kept a written list of the poor to whom she distributed funds, and she asked that her bequest continue to support them "according to the list written by my own hand."[99] Michla, widow of Nathan, ran a pawn shop in partnership with a male relative. "This is my portion from all my business, in commodities as well as in pawnbroking; and all my debt notes and 'obligations,' whether made orally or in writing, can be found in our pinkas."[100]

Women's wills firmly link them to other forms of written records. All types of financial accounts, a tally of the debts and profits over a lifetime, and items that bear monetary and emotional value undergird the economic aspects of last testaments. From women's wills, we learn that Jewish women kept not only pinkassim but also drafts of their wills, as Fromet of Metz and Rebecca of Mannheim did. Rebecca of Mannheim further requested that her funds be used to "inscribe her in the book of the dead" during the seven-day mourning period immediately after her death.[101] The voices of these women, preserved by their families and communities, served as models for other women, who were inspired to write their own wishes, attending to spiritual and material effects in the space of a few brief pages.

10

Bodies and Souls

WHEN THE doctor told those gathered around the sickbed of Hayim Hamel that there was nothing more he could do to save the patient's life, Hayim's wife, Glikl, came close to his bed and asked him, "My heart [my beloved], can I touch you? For I was *treyfe* (impure)." Hayim responded, "Heaven forbid, my child, it will not be long until you can immerse."[1] As the seventeenth-century memoirist recalled this last exchange with her life partner, she added, perhaps with a tinge of bitterness, that he did not live long enough for that to transpire. Glikl was referring to her state of menstrual impurity, one of several references in her memoir to her bodily state. The exchange opens a window into women's awareness of their bodies at various stages of their lives and the way these intersected with Jewish legal, ritual, communal, and personal life structures. While a comprehensive overview of every aspect of women's biological lives within the Jewish communities of early modern Europe would go well beyond the scope of this book, we choose several important inflection points. Our chapter focuses on women's biological processes, such as menstruation, pregnancy and childbirth, nursing, female illnesses, and old age. These aspects of being a woman in the early modern period were shaped by legal norms, communal ordinances, and social expectations, which rendered Jewish women distinct from their Christian peers and connected their shifting physical statuses to their religious lives. Even when our sources prescribe, rather than describe, behavior, we read against the grain to indicate how women navigated, understood, and experienced these physiological states. As such, we also explore female forms of piety that were tied to women's bodies, highlighting the connections between women's bodies and their souls.

FIG. 10.1. A woman immerses in the Ashkenazi mikvah in Amsterdam, built 1670/71. Caspar Philips, "Ritueel bad," Amsterdam, 1783.

Transmitting the Laws of Menstrual Purity

Biblical in origin and greatly elaborated over time by rabbinic law, laws and customs around menstrual purity had become a matter of general consensus in the early modern period, Glikl's time.[2] Observance of menstrual laws required knowledge of the basic patterns and obligations, calendrical and bodily awareness, and meticulous preparation for purification in the mikveh (ritual bath).[3] Full observance of these laws required an investment on the part of each individual woman, her husband, and the larger community.

When an early fifteenth-century rabbi, Hayim of Augsburg, proposed writing a work in Yiddish on the laws of menstruation, using language that would be accessible to most women and unlearned men, Rabbi Jacob Molin, one of the leading rabbinic authorities in Ashkenaz, erupted in anger: "I was greatly amazed that it should have occurred to you to compose a work in the language of Ashkenaz [Yiddish], as you plan. . . . People will glance at the works of great rabbis . . . and they will make practical legal rulings from such [popular] works. And now you have come, adding to all this . . . [a book] for the ignorant, and for women . . . in order to instruct them on the basis of your Yiddish work in matters of menstrual laws and stains . . . ?"[4] Instruction in the laws of menstrual purity was supposed to be orally transmitted by a mother or other learned woman to her daughter. If women erred, rabbis and their students should correct them.[5] In Ashkenazi halakha, women were to separate from any physical contact with their husbands from the time they saw menstrual blood (or on the date it was anticipated), through the days of menstruation, and then for seven "clean" days after menstruation had ceased. Similar constraints came into play after childbirth for a longer period. After a careful set of internal self-inspections, women immersed in a mikveh and their sexual lives could resume. While this might seem straightforward, every aspect of the laws was expanded over time. What was considered a normal or average menstrual cycle? Which type of stains were menstrual blood, and which came from another source? What constituted physical contact? Which of these guidelines could be flexible if a woman was having difficulty conceiving a child as a result of observing these laws?

For all such questions, women were expected to turn to rabbinic authorities through the mediation of the rabbi's wife or another wise woman. Rivkah Tiktiner refrained from discussing the laws of menstruation, saying, "I do not need to write much about this subject, because every woman knows well enough herself how she should conduct herself."[6] Frauke von Rohden argues that Rivkah deliberately avoided any detailed discussion of these laws to avoid encroaching on the authority of the rabbis and incurring their wrath. It took a distinguished rabbi, Benjamin Slonik of Poland-Lithuania, to publish in print a detailed guide to the halakhot of menstruation in Yiddish and addressed to women. Other manuscript and print works directed at women discussed or hinted at these laws, but the format tended to be brief and general.[7] Glikl's memoir and the responsa literature demonstrate that Jewish women took their own responsibility in these matters seriously, although how class, knowledge, and economic status affected their willingness and ability to monitor their menstrual cycles in the rabbinically prescribed way remains a question.

At Home

During the time a woman was considered a menstruant, Jewish law did not permit married couples to have sexual relations. Rabbinic law prohibited a long list of additional forms of physical closeness that married couples were to guard against during the time of *niddah* (menstrual impurity). These *harhakot* ("distancing" injunctions) prohibited any form of physical contact whatsoever; a menstruant and her husband were forbidden from sharing a bed, a seat, and dishes and passing items directly from hand to hand.[8] When Glikl made her request to her dying husband, she was asking about an embrace, nothing more.

Both Hayim and Glikl were aware of her menstrual status, and both were aware that even a touch was not permitted by the rabbinic rules until she immersed. Women, moreover, were expected to calculate the number of days in their average cycle and likewise refrain from physical contact when menstruation was expected. These distancing rules affected every aspect of a couple's marital life. Their physical and sexual life could resume only after the "clean" or "white" days were completed, and the woman immersed in a mikveh. The ongoing maintenance and construction of mikva'ot, the outpouring of guides for women's commandments, including precepts related to menstruation, and evidence from responsa testify to the ongoing observance of menstrual laws and customs by many Ashkenazi Jewish women. However, despite the availability of printed ephemera on so many other subjects, no calendar directed at women to aid in calculating their menstrual cycles appears to have been printed in the early modern period. Since such calculations were one of the foundational requirements of rabbinic menstrual observances, their absence sheds a degree of doubt as to how most women were able to observe this law punctiliously.

Women's observance of menstrual laws may have been partly motivated by fear. The Bible warned that sexual relations with a menstruating woman would result in the early death of the body and cutting off of the soul of both participants.[9] Some Jewish sources since late antiquity linked deficient observance of these laws to conception of a child with a physical "defect."[10] Jewish popular culture associated children born of menstruating women with spiritual and other imperfections.[11] Christian theologians had always debated the (negative) significance of menstruation; in the sixteenth century, it came to be linked with monstrous births.[12] By the late sixteenth century, in the writings of learned Jewish women such as Rivkah Tiktiner, the observance of the laws of menstruation provided evidence that women played a pivotal role in the creation of new life as partners with God and man. Rivkah's views provided a far more active and positive role for women's reproductive functions, elevating women beyond the authorities' view of them as passive or impure vessels.[13]

Menstruants in the Synagogue

One fine Monday morning in the synagogue courtyard of The Hague, "a tumult and fight" erupted toward the end of the prayer services. Merle bat Yitzhak Yaakov subsequently came before the kahal, complaining "bitterly and loudly" against two brothers, Susman and Yehudah, sons of Shalom Naarden. She accused the brothers of striking her with "great and cruel" blows to her backside; she showed the kahal a notarized testimony that she had drawn up to that effect before the (non-Jewish) notary on October 22, 1736. The kahal sent after the brothers numerous times to appear before them and apologize to Merle. This was due, the scribe of The Hague pinkas noted, not only to the disruption of public harmony but to the grave ritual violation that had occurred: they had touched a woman during her menstrual period.[14]

This episode is noteworthy for several reasons. It takes for granted that women were present during services at the synagogue on a weekday. Merle was apparently a well-connected ba'alat bayit, as no fewer than four communal officials had to recuse themselves from hearing her complaint due to their close kinship with her. The subject of the fight is not specified here, but it accords with numerous references in this period of disruptions to public order, including inside and on the premises of the synagogue. The reprimand of the brothers for touching a menstruant came as something of an afterthought to the complaint against the brothers, and it tells us that Merle (and presumably most other women of her time and place) attended synagogue during her menstrual state. It recalls a time, centuries earlier, when such attendance in the synagogue was deemed inappropriate, and pious women refrained from coming during their menses. Though he cited praise of the practice, of menstruants avoiding the synagogue, Rabbi Israel Isserlein (1390–1460), in his volume of response, *Terumat ha-deshen*, ruled ultimately that "this [practice was prompted by] enthusiasm and piety alone [and is therefore not required]."[15] In the sixteenth century, Rabbi Moses Isserles explicitly dismissed the opinions that discouraged Jewish women from attending synagogue during their menstrual state. In the voluminous ordinances issued by Jewish communities in western Ashkenazi lands, we have found no mention of this practice—on the contrary, women appear in our sources as regular synagogue attendees without limitations.

Menstruation and Privacy

Medieval rabbis were concerned that women wear white garments visible to all on the street during their menstrual state. Juspe Schammes was the sole voice in the early modern period who noted in passing that a woman wore a white skirt while menstrually impure (in the context of burying a woman who died in childbirth in that skirt).[16] To the degree this outward signaling was practiced in communities, this clothing would have explicitly marked women as being in the state of niddah. Similarly, women going to the mikveh were often visible to anyone on the same street, and women who did not attend the mikveh for more than a month were presumed to be pregnant. A woman's menstrual status could become the subject of community awareness, as in Merle's story. In another eighteenth-century case in Moravia, a woman was accused of an extramarital affair when she became pregnant around the time her husband died; community members knew on what dates she immersed and used that information to accuse her.[17]

Far more intrusive into women's bodily functions were the ritual laws around the menstrual cycle. This complex category of Jewish law, to which an entire talmudic tractate was dedicated, meant that many women could have no expectation of privacy around this bodily function. If a woman were in doubt concerning her menstrual status, she was to bring her stained undergarments to the rabbi's wife or directly to the rabbi to determine whether she was permitted to continue relations with her husband.[18] Hundreds of responsa regarding menstrual blood were written throughout the early modern period. Rabbis did not examine women directly; they relied on the women's own testimony, physical evidence, or the mediation of her husband or another woman. When a woman's night of immersion fell close to her *veset* (time she was expecting her period), the question presented to the rabbi was which took precedence—the obligation to immerse and have relations or the separation in anticipation of the onset of menstruation?[19] Another woman came before the same rabbi, reporting that she had an internal growth that caused her to bleed often. Ultimately, after consulting with a physician, the rabbi decided to take her own evaluation into account, "as the woman said that she knows the bleeding comes from her growth and is not menstrual blood."[20] Every one of the hundreds of questions regarding menstrual purity that were brought to rabbinic authorities also necessarily involved the woman in question intimately because the question dealt with her body and her sexual availability to her husband. The intricate details of these laws and their far-reaching impact on a couple's lives meant that rabbis frequently opined on individual cases. Since only the woman in question was privy to the details necessary for a legal ruling, such as the timing of her menstruation or the color of stains that she may have seen on her undergarments, women's bodies came under the frequent purview of rabbinic guidance, in a discourse which only they could initiate.

Our main point of access to how women experienced the various rites of menstrual purity comes through rabbinic decisions about ritual purity and communal regulation of ritual baths. In one example from early eighteenth-century Altona, Rabbi Ezekiel Katzenellenbogen described a woman who bled incessantly, apparently from an illness unrelated to her menses. He cited her own assessment that the blood was neither from sexual penetration nor from menstruation, "and it was appropriate to rule leniently." Moreover, she shared her frustration that "if they do not find her a lenient ruling, she would never become menstrually pure."[21] The responsum, therefore, captures the woman's emotional state, her weariness and vexation, for she did not go more than three days after her period without seeing blood.

Ritual Immersion

Women who were not suffering from regular or sporadic bleeding waited seven days after all blood had ceased and then immersed in a ritual bath at or after nightfall. The visit required intensive preparation by women. Women had to bathe, trim nails, unbraid their hair, and remove all makeup prior to immersing (see plate 24). Some wealthier women performed these tasks with the help of servants, as demonstrated in a sensational tragedy reported by Rabbi Pinhas Katzenellenbogen about Baila, the older sister of an acquaintance:

> It was her bad fortune, that the first time she went to prepare to purify herself for her husband after the wedding, a terrible thing happened, heaven forfend. She was sitting in her bath to wash herself, and she had a deaf maidservant. It was towards evening and one could not see well, the maidservant went out, and she was sitting inside the bath, and she took the boiling water from the fire and poured it into the bath, all over her head and her body, and she screamed, but the maidservant could not hear her, until she died and was burned from the boiling water, heaven forfend.[22]

Though highly irregular, this story highlights that women's immersion was not a solitary activity; other women assisted their employers and neighbors in washing and preparing their bodies for immersion (see plate 25).

Poorer women were reliant on charity for assistance in observing the rituals. Hindche Levi of Frankfurt supported the poor women in Frankfurt's ritual baths, where she "supplied them with aid and medicines from women's confraternities, so that they could observe their commandments."[23] Hindche likely provided white cloths, white undergarments, and combs that poor women would have needed in order to perform the ritual properly. It comes as no surprise that Hindche's pious acts were funded by women's confraternities; while the system of menstrual purity laws regulated both women's and men's sexual lives, they did so by regulating women's bodies. These laws set Jewish women apart from Jewish men and from Christian women, who did not immerse after menstruation, miscarriage, or childbirth. Thus, the practical necessities and implements needed to perform immersion were relevant to Jewish women alone.

The mikveh was a body of freshwater large enough to immerse an entire human body, with stringent rabbinic rules about its dimensions and water source. An open body of natural water could serve as a mikveh. Given practical and safety constraints regarding access to natural bodies of water (discussed below), mikva'ot have featured in the built environment of Jewish life since antiquity. Archaeologists have located quite a few medieval mikva'ot in Europe, such as those in Worms and Friedberg, which tended to be built deep underground.[24]

The expulsion of Jews from urban centers in the late medieval period and their resettlement, during the sixteenth century, in villages in which very few Jews resided, led to immersion in natural sources of water rather than in larger urban indoor ritual baths. Rabbi Isaac mi-See, who served rural Jewish communities, "was asked about a lone Jew" who resided in a certain village, "and his wife had nowhere to immerse other than the river."[25] A single family obviously did not have the means to construct an indoor ritual bath. Mi-See ruled leniently for this woman, but he stressed that wherever several families resided together, such as in Hechingen in Württemburg, it was incumbent upon the community to construct an indoor mikveh. One reason for this, mi-See stressed, was that heavy rains or snowfall would make it impossible for a woman to immerse in a river. Indeed, bodies of water in northern Europe could have been frozen in wintertime, and rabbis in medieval and early modern times discussed the question of whether heating the mikveh waters was permitted.[26] This offhand remark points to the difficulty women faced in immersing outside in frigid weather.

Immersing outdoors posed additional challenges. In another case, mi-See was asked about a "mikveh that was long and narrow, and its waters were shallow, and a woman had to strip completely naked and submerge herself in the ground if she wanted her entire body to be covered by the water at once," as was necessary for a halakhic immersion.[27] This particular query about an outdoor "ritual bath" highlights the woman's discomfort, as she contorted herself and placed her face on the earth to immerse. It also highlights her nudity, although that would have been the case even in an indoor mikveh. Outdoor immersion, however, posed additional dangers, as the ritual had to be performed at nightfall, and the sight of a naked woman immersing in the water could lead passersby to take advantage. Perhaps for that reason, another query came to mi-See as to the permissibility of immersing in a fountain comprising a vertical pipe through which spring water was diverted, enclosed in a wooden building.[28] Here, too, mi-See bemoaned the lack of proper indoor mikva'ot; yet, the trend of villagers lacking mikva'ot persisted in some areas until at least the eighteenth century.[29]

Even in cities, a polluted spring could lead to a problem in the mikveh, as happened in Amsterdam in the spring of 1760. "The women brought their complaints" before the communal leaders, who agreed to dig a new spring to connect to the mikveh.[30] Though ritual immersion affected both men's and women's sexual lives, only the immersing women could experience the physical conditions inside the mikva'ot.

In towns and villages in which there was neither a mikveh nor an appropriate source of water, women had to travel at night in order to immerse, contending with the dangers of the road. Mi-See was "asked about the women who were afraid of immersing at night . . . was it permissible for them to immerse in the daylight, and then refrain [from sexual contact] with their husbands until nightfall? . . . Would it be permitted to immerse in the daylight of the eighth day, so she would return to her home while it was still daylight?"[31] Mi-See insisted that women immerse on the eighth day, allowing them to do so close to nightfall.[32] In his bestselling Yiddish book about women's commandments, mi-See's contemporary, Benjamin Slonik, ruled similarly, noting, however, that a woman could immerse early if the location of the mikveh was dangerous for night immersion. In addition, if "the mikveh water was outside the town, and there is concern that the town will be locked, and that afterwards she will not be able to get into her house," she was permitted to immerse before nightfall.[33] Nighttime travel, particularly outside the city or town, posed dangers to all travelers, and especially to women.

Privacy was another concern, one often addressed in passing in rabbinic texts. A late eighteenth-century query about a ritual bath in Postelberg (today, Postoloprty) in Bohemia focused on the challenge of a mikveh inside a house in which alcohol was produced. The rabbis were concerned about the legal status of the water in the mikveh because non-Jewish workers would draw water from the bath in the course of their work; one wonders whether the women were not afraid of meeting workers there as they immersed in the nude at night.[34] Women's experiences come to us through the prism of rabbinic legal concerns, but the sources may be read against the grain to contemplate how women navigated the challenges of immersion at night, particularly in deserted areas.

In more densely populated rural and urban communities, formal indoor mikva'ot were available. In some communities, older medieval structures were used, while in others, women immersed either in newly built communal mikva'ot or in ritual baths located in private homes. Although these mikva'ot were safer, requiring women to travel through local streets rather than intercity roads or unfrequented riverbanks, they posed their own challenges. In the small town of Schnaittach, the mikveh was located underneath a trap door in the cantor's house. The cantor's wife was entrusted with overseeing immersion.[35] Although she could undress and place her clothing on a ledge in the underground cavern, the immersing woman would have her cycle of menstruation and sexual availability to her husband known to the cantor unless he left the house in the evening hours.

In larger communities, crowds could pose a challenge, as women immersed one at a time. In eighteenth-century Amsterdam, the lay leaders agreed to construct a new ritual bath intended only for foreign guests "because the number of female community members is rising, and also those of the many guests and residents, and one ritual bath is too small to contain them all."[36] Building a designated space for guests ensured that, at least in theory, ba'alot bayit had an exclusive mikveh and a shorter waiting time. Additional documentation in communal logbooks, however, suggests that, in practice, the process was not so smooth at first; it took over a month to distribute certificates proving communal membership.[37] This entry further suggests that women were required, at least technically, to bring identification to the ritual bath; perhaps some well-known women would have been admitted if they were familiar to the mikveh administrators.

Over the course of the early modern period, community leaders regulated women's immersion by setting fees. In Altona, a lower rate was set for poorer women who wished to immerse, whereas in 1734, in The Hague, twenty-five poor women were granted free access to the ritual bath.[38] Perhaps Hindche and the other women of Frankfurt also helped poor women of that community pay for their immersion. Communal leaders further regulated the mikva'ot by appointing women to oversee immersion and by designating certain ritual baths as the only ones in which women were permitted to immerse. This, too, impacted women, who lost a say over which ritual bath to attend. On two separate occasions in sixteenth-century Padua, women reported discomfort in immersing in the home of a family with which they were feuding.[39]

In communities with more than one bath, women might have had a preference regarding where they wished to immerse. In Altona-Hamburg-Wandsbek, immersion in the communal mikveh abutting the synagogue was mandated upon its construction in 1685. This decision was announced in the synagogue on Shabbat; by Saturday night, it was prohibited for women to immerse in the very ritual baths (located in private homes) that had been used just one day prior. The communal regulations do not preserve women's reactions to the new mandate, but one can infer from later records that some women preferred to continue to use the various mikva'ot they had frequented in prior months and years.[40] Almost fifty years later, communal announcements reflect that some women continued to immerse where they pleased. Rechle, the woman in charge of Altona's mikveh in 1733, reported that individuals continued to frequent the Hamburg mikveh. Perhaps tired of the lack of compliance, the communal leaders announced that women must still pay Rechle before they immersed, even if they were to immerse in Hamburg's mikva'ot.[41] Women's decisions as to how to perform these bodily rituals may sometimes be glimpsed by reading the communal sources against the grain.

Despite these readings, much of women's experiences remain inaccessible, as most of these texts were written by men. One responsum reveals the gap between rabbinic knowledge and women's practices. A woman approached Rabbi Yair Hayim Bacharach after having returned home from her immersion. It was her custom to immerse herself twice in the mikveh, and she was fearful that she had not been fully immersed in the water on her second immersion. Bacharach was in direct dialogue with the woman and questioned why she was accustomed to immerse twice; she reported having learned the custom from her mother. While Bacharach initially recommended that her husband annul her adoption of this practice, he later "became aware that several women were accustomed" to immerse twice, just as that woman had done.[42] His lack of familiarity with women's practices is but one hint of how much we cannot know. Bacharach then opted to explain why women immersed twice by referencing a rabbinic disagreement over whether one should recite the blessing before or after immersing in the water. The woman undoubtedly interpreted her own action in another light, as following the practice her mother had taught her.

A final aspect of women's immersion comprised the prayers she recited in the mikveh. Beyond the recitation of a Hebrew blessing over the immersion, contemporary custom and prayer books include additional prayers in an expanded ritual. The texts of these prayers demonstrate that immersion posed an opportunity for women to pray for good health, happy marriages, and children. In one Yiddish tkhine, the text beseeched God for a healthy pregnancy and for the birth of pious sons or daughters, perhaps lending insight into the hopes for the future that women prayed for as they immersed.[43]

Pregnancy

When Glikl was seven months pregnant with her ninth baby, she fell ill with "an outlandish fever." Concerned for his nauseated, sweating, and feverish wife, Hayim implored her to take a stroll outside, in the meantime hiring a chef to cook her a meal of delicacies "fit for a royal table." Glikl, however, could not handle the food: "The minute I came home and walked into the room where the food was, I was overcome by nausea, and I pleaded with them to remove either the food or me from the room."[44] Although Glikl delivered the baby easily, he contracted the illness and died fourteen days after his birth. This description of pregnancy's symptoms compounded by illness comes to us through Glikl's memoir, which stands out as an early modern Jewish woman's account of her own pregnancy.

Hayim's distress about Glikl's state was culturally normative among both Jews and Christians in early modern Germany. Ulinka Rublack has argued that Christian men played a role in their wives' pregnancies, endeavoring to ensure their well-being and to create the conditions for a smooth delivery. It was class, rather than religion, that most distinguished between women in pregnancy, as a poorer man of any faith would have been unable to procure food and medicine for his wife like Hayim did for Glikl. The physical experiences of pregnant Jewish and Christian women were likely quite similar across classes, as were many of the local customs and medical practices employed to protect them. Yet, religious law and rituals concerning pregnancy distinguished Jewish and Christian women.

Both Jews and Christians believed that having an environment free of strife was essential for a healthy pregnancy.[45] Juspe Hahn of Frankfurt cited earlier Jewish sources that taught that fighting in the house of a pregnant woman was dangerous to the fetus. Jewish communities also took upon themselves the responsibility of ensuring that pregnant women had all the food they needed or desired. In 1705, Schnaittach's communal leaders forbade the village's Jews from acquiring meat at nearby Hüttenbach if meat was available in Schnaittach. Although they ruled that anyone who consumed meat from Hüttenbach was like "one who had consumed the flesh of a pig," an exception was made for pregnant women and for the sick, who could get permission to circumvent the regulation and buy meat from Hüttenbach.[46] Contemporary Christians also believed that pregnant women should consume meat and even supplied it to women who were housed in the poorhouse (see plate 26).[47]

Glikl, too, believed that consuming the food one craved was essential to the baby's health. Though she recalls having "scoffed at hearing that women's cravings could be harmful," when she was pregnant with her son Yosef, she went out to the market area and saw a woman selling medlar fruit. Although she had intended to go back and purchase some, she had forgotten; when Yosef was born later that night, he was listless, covered with blotches, and refused to nurse. Glikl insisted on spreading medlar juice on Yosef's lips, despite others' laughter at her "nonsense." He responded, began to nurse, and the blotches went away, allowing him to be circumcised at the correct time (see plate 27).[48]

Rublack argues that the fear of harm to the baby led to better pre- and postnatal care among German Christian women, which in turn resulted in a relatively low number of women who died in childbirth.[49] Mary Lindemann did not find particularly high mortality rates for women in childbirth in eighteenth-century rural Germany.[50] Other statistical data do show relatively high maternal death rates, but a comparison between the Jewish and non-Jewish populations within a particular place and time has not (yet) been undertaken.[51] Very preliminary research shows that Jewish women had similar rates of maternal death. Frankfurt's burial records include only eleven women who died in childbirth over a sixty-five-year period between 1624 and 1680.[52]

Although the Mishnah taught that women died in childbirth for failing to observe the three women's commandments, no concrete trace of this condemnation appeared in the Memorbücher or on the tombstones memorializing women.[53] When Fromet, the wife of Lezer Oppenheim of Frankfurt, died in childbirth in 1712, Lezer commissioned a new memorial book for the community, after the old one had been destroyed in a fire in 1711, so that she (and many others) could be memorialized in its leaves.[54]

In his memoirs, Rabbi Pinhas Katzenellenbogen likewise highlighted the pain that an entire family suffered when a woman was lost to childbirth. He also exhibited the wishful thinking that certain strategies might help some men avoid this pain by not marrying women who would be susceptible to such dangers in the first place. He wondered why

> some women have great distress and others have it easy [in childbirth]. And I wondered if this was due to the *mazal* (astrological sign) of the woman, of the day or the time she was born. . . . Until I found in the book *Sefer toldot Adam* . . . "When the woman's palms are short, she will give birth in distress,

and this is because the sages have determined that the opening of the vagina is the same length as the measure of the length from a woman's middle finger tip to the end of her palm" ... some have narrow uteri, and they give birth in distress, and others have wide uteri, and they give birth with ease. What a wondrous sign this is, that you can tell from a woman's palms, if they are short, she will have distress at birth, and vice versa. ... I tried this with my first wife, who was modest and pious, Marat Sara Rechl, because her palms were short, as I measured hers against mine, and I knew she would have distress."[55]

Sara Rechl did have two difficult deliveries of her daughters, Yente and Beila. She had an even more difficult third labor, with a son who was born dead, and she herself then succumbed after one hundred days of pain. Katzenellenbogen attributed her death to the witchcraft of the non-Jewish midwife and noted, "I mourned her greatly because she was a good woman and modest and pious above all women."[56]

There is much to say about the misconceptions in this belief being passed around rabbinic circles about why some women were more likely than others to have more difficult childbirths. Yet, the unmistakable sentiment driving Katzenellenbogen was the heartbreak that he felt when losing a young wife, and later, a daughter as well. Since Katzenellenbogen's daughter had hands shorter than his wife's, he prepared his son-in-law to pray with extra devotion, and they both fasted and prayed. She gave birth a week before Yom Kippur and felt so strong that she announced her intention to fast even though it was not required. Yet, after Yom Kippur, on the night before the circumcision, she developed a fever, and she screamed in distress. When she recited the viduy (confessional prayer before death), she begged God to spare her, including "in the merit of the son I just bore." Despite the prayers, she succumbed just before her twenty-first birthday. Katzenellenbogen reported, "Our hearts and spirits were broken."[57]

When a birthing mother's life was in danger, both Catholics and Protestants privileged the life of the baby over that of the mother.[58] Jewish law, by contrast, ruled that saving the mother's life took priority. Rabbis wrote frequently of the amulets that they supplied to pregnant women to ensure their survival, along with the baby's. A detailed description of how amulets were to be applied appears in Katzenellenbogen's memoir: "The author gave him ... *shemot* (magical names) folded into a white linen cloth ... to be tied around the other side of the woman, in order that the package with the names be bound strongly onto her flesh, in order that it should not slip and fall from the belly. One must be exceedingly careful not to lay the names on too early, only at the exact time that the child is supposed to come out, and the midwife will know the exact time that it is necessary."[59] Katzenellenbogen's description highlights the ritual involvement of rabbis in ensuring safe deliveries, as well as the religious role assigned to midwives, who were also expected to be alert to the right moments to apply the formulas, amulets, and assorted kabbalistic, rabbinic, and folk healers' prescriptions and talismans to shield mother and newborn from malign forces.

One of the greatest rabbinic controversies in eighteenth-century Europe ignited over amulets prepared by Altona's chief rabbi, Jonathan Eybeschutz. In his book *Luhot edut*, Eybeschutz defended the efficacy of his amulets after Jacob Emden charged him with heretical Sabbatean tendencies due to these amulets. Eybeschutz claimed that whereas it had been alleged that "my amulets caused weakness in women, and that when the amulets had been removed, the plague lifted, all who come to my city gate know the opposite to be true." Claiming that when he came to Altona, deaths in childbirth had slowed, and God's wrath had been assuaged, he also printed an excerpt from the burial society pinkas of Metz, where he had served as chief rabbi prior to coming to Altona:

> Here is a copy from the pinkas of the burial society for good deeds ... and we saw, written in a valid hand, that from Tammuz [5]509 until the end of Elul [5]510, due to our great sins, 16 women died in childbirth. And from Tishrei [5]511, when the eminent rabbi, R. Jonathan [Eybeschutz], Chief Rabbi of the community of AH"W came here, until Tishrei [5]512, three women died in childbirth.[60]

Eybeschutz expected the written evidence from the burial society records to exculpate him and prove that his amulets were both dogmatically valid and practically effective. In a highly polemic booklet, Eybeschutz's nemesis, Jacob Emden, criticized him for entering the birthing chamber, where he was "walking among the women and running like an insane person among them." Emden further alleged that Eybeschutz and his son were present as his daughter-in-law gave birth, refusing to leave even as other women protested their presence.[61] Emden's polemical claim must be read with caution, yet it emphasizes the role of a rabbi in praying for a healthy delivery. The public debates over the amulets highlight how mothers in childbirth took center stage in this famous rabbinic and communal controversy.

Some Jewish birthing rituals closely paralleled rites celebrated by Christian women. Both Jewish and Christian women had a lying-in period of about six weeks after delivery, during which time a woman was not responsible for her household duties (see plate 28). In the Jewish community, her friends would visit, celebrating with food and drink; communal regulations granted the women special permission to play cards (see plate 29).[62] If a woman had given birth to a boy, a special ceremony was conducted in her home the night before the circumcision. In some communities, this occasion was marked by a festive meal with friends and neighbors, while in others, a select group of women gathered in the parturient's home to craft candles.[63] In Worms, the sandeket, the baby's godmother, would hand out cookies to the other women.[64] For a circumcision on Passover, when cookies were forbidden, the sandeket handed out almonds.[65] This paralleled "childbed-ale" parties and gatherings of neighbors and friends among Christian parturients, with food and wine to assist the new mother and to celebrate.[66] Notably, both Christian and Jewish leaders sought to curtail the number of participants in these female celebrations.

The Jewish women's lying-in period concluded with a formal ceremony called *Shabbat yetzi'at ha-yoledet*, in which the parturient officially returned to the synagogue. There, she presented the baby's wimpel (swaddling cloth) to the community to be used as a binder for the Torah scroll, and her husband would be honored with being called to the Torah. As Elisheva Baumgarten has shown, this ceremony paralleled, in many respects, the Christian post-birth ceremony of "churching," albeit with distinctions in the details of each rite.[67] The Jewish rite continued after services, with a social and communal aspect: a procession of women accompanied the new mother home. In Halberstadt, the parturient was accompanied by the sandeket, the wives of the mohalim, and midwives, in addition to family members, including her mother and mother-in-law; her sisters, her brothers' wives, and the wives of her husband's brothers; as well as her aunts and the aunts of her husband.[68] This highlights the communal nature of an individual life cycle event, although for this ceremony, too, communal leaders sought to limit the number of women to be invited as companions.

The return of the parturient woman to synagogue signified her return to a normal rhythm of household and communal duties. Fascinatingly, those women who attended synagogue during pregnancy received special mention in communal sources. "The esteemed and modest woman Marat Breinlin, the daughter of the *aluf* (community leader) Issachar Cohen from Hamburg, rose early in the morning and stayed late at night in the synagogue, to pray her prayers with awe, fear, trembling, and devotion, at all times, even in the days of her pregnancy."[69] Pregnancy was clearly perceived as a liminal time, somewhere between many women's normal routine of praying daily in synagogue and the postpartum period, when women were excused from communal and household duties. Women who attended synagogue, irrespective of this liminal stage and the physical hardship they may have incurred, were singled out for praise.

Nursing

Glikl's first childbirth took place in the winter season, eight days before her own mother gave birth. She lived then with her husband in her parents' home in Hamburg, as she was still a teenage girl, and she and her mother spent their mandated lying-in period together in the same room, the only heated room in the house, with their two babies and a maidservant.[70] Once she recovered, Glikl moved to her unheated bedroom upstairs, but her baby daughter remained in the heated room with her mother, her mother's baby, and the maidservant. Glikl noted that the maidservant brought her baby to her every evening after she had gone to bed so that she could nurse her for her night feeding. She recounted an amusing (in retrospect) tale of the confusion that ensued when the attendant brought each one the wrong baby to nurse.[71] The anecdote illuminates a number of aspects of maternal nursing of children. Later on, after she and her husband became wealthy and could easily have hired wetnurses, Glikl continued to nurse her children.

Women made the choice to breastfeed their children based on the knowledge and frameworks available to them. In the medical field, theories of how best to nourish infants abounded in early modern Europe. Into the early eighteenth century, progressive physicians who advocated mother's milk as most suitable for infants based their opinions primarily on classical theories of balancing humors, in which the mother's (menstrual) blood, which had nourished the fetus in utero, turned into milk after birth, so it was already "tested" on the child.[72] Midwives were often tasked with teaching new mothers how to nurse, and they were consulted when problems arose. It is unclear if women thought of breastfeeding as a contraceptive strategy. As nursing women generally did not menstruate, Jewish women who nursed and saw vaginal staining or bleeding constituted an anomaly from the perspective of Jewish law. They consulted rabbis to determine their status as menstrually pure or not. When the case of a nursing woman who saw a vaginal discharge came before

FIG. 10.2. Mother nursing baby in one hand while rocking the cradle of another. *Tikkune Shabbat*, eighteenth century.

seventeenth-century rabbi Judah Mehler, he solicited the opinions of *nashim zekenot* (wise women) and midwives, who opined that the drops came from a weakened uterus rather than as a result of menstruation.[73] The question came before the rabbi because the woman herself checked and was aware that her body was emitting conflicting signals. Beneath the layers of halakhic discourse, we can discern the body awareness of a woman who wanted to clarify her ritual status. We also get to see the other women around her, whose experience and expertise helped resolve her situation.

By the eighteenth century, rising concern about single women's pregnancies led some moralizers to condemn women who gave out their children to live with a wetnurse for the first months or years of life, theorizing that this encouraged indigent young women to get pregnant so that they could sustain themselves as wetnurses.[74] Such young women were regarded as morally inferior and, according to the prevalent theories of the time, could pass on their coarse and undesirable traits to wellborn children.[75] Thus, in a passing reference to a journey undertaken with some of her children to visit Hildesheim, where her in-laws lived, Glikl mentions that she was then nursing her son, Mordekhai, who was not yet one year old.[76] In traveling home from the magnificent wedding of her eldest daughter, Tzipor, Glikl became very seasick after rising to nurse her baby, Leyb, who could not be quieted by any other means.[77]

As noted earlier, Glikl described her recently born son, Yosef, as a sickly child who refused to nurse from her or take any other nourishment until she put a medlar to his mouth.[78] Glikl told the story to give substance to women's cravings during pregnancy, but it is also notable that every time she referred to feeding an infant, she was nursing the child herself. Glikl never discussed this as a choice; she simply mentioned it as a part of her life and a strand of her storytelling.

Glikl's acceptance of nursing as the proper duty of a mother to her child reflected the moralistic Jewish (and Christian) literature of her time. In her *Meneket Rivkah*, Rivkah Tiktiner admonished mothers:

> Every woman must apply great diligence and effort in raising her children. First, as soon as the child is born, she must watch over the child, and be careful not to give the child to anyone else for nursing. She herself should begin the next day, since as soon as the child tastes another, it will not want to suckle from the mother again. And then her milk will flow all of a sudden. There is no cure for that but to exercise [nursing] often. Some are so undutiful that they do not want to suffer any pain, and let the child be nursed by another woman.[79]

Rivkah painted women who did not want to suffer by nursing their own children as "undutiful," and she warned that they would never live down their shame. She also admonished women not to suckle from only one breast. Rivkah's admonitions implied that other voices upheld the practice of women's putting out their children to wetnurse, not out of biological need but, rather, so they could preserve their figures or attend to other work. Heide Wunder noted that this was more common in some upper-class circles and in some regions but not others.[80] A *kallah lid* (song sung by women preparing the bride) preserved from a later time reminded young women to weep for the suffering of their mothers who had nursed them, "carrying them under their hearts with great concern and pain."[81]

Other early modern Jewish prescriptive works single out Christian wetnurses as particularly unsuited to nurse a Jewish child. "The milk of a gentile wetnurse comes from the food she eats, which is treyfe; she blocks the heart of a child that drinks of her."[82] Other Yiddish moralistic works admonished women not to expose their breasts in public when they nursed their children, but Rivkah Tiktiner mentioned neither Christian wetnurses nor immodesty. She encouraged women to breastfeed their children because she believed it was in the best interests of the infants; and, more significantly, in the best interests of the mothers, as it would burnish a woman's good reputation.[83] Be that as it may, there were many instances in which the services of a wetnurse were urgently needed. No suitable substitute for mothers' milk existed in the early modern period, and infants left to other forms of nourishment would often die. When women died or became ill during or shortly after childbirth, or at any time in the first years of a child's life before weaning, the infant needed wetnursing to provide life-sustaining nutrition. This was the case everywhere, and eventually, Christian and Jewish communities accepted the reality by trying to regulate the profession of wetnursing rather than discourage it completely.

Jewish law provided another incentive for maintaining wetnurses for hire. Classical talmudic and medieval rabbinic sources through the sixteenth-century *Shulhan arukh* prohibited the remarriage of a pregnant or nursing woman who became widowed or divorced until her child was twenty-four months old.[84] The law constructed nursing his child as the contractual obligation of a woman to the father of the child and secondarily for the sake of the child's well-being. When Fradche, the maidservant in the home of the notable Netanel Augny, became visibly pregnant, she came before the bet din of Metz, seeking permission to marry the *na'ar mesharet* (young manservant) Itzik, who served in the same home alongside her. Fradche claimed that she had only ever had relations with Itzik and asked the court to issue a *hatarat nisu'in* (permit for the couple to marry). The court embarked on an investigation, questioning the young servants separately about the dates on which they had slept together and finding some inconsistency in one date. They also questioned another member of the household, a female servant who claimed that Fradche had admitted to her that she had had relations with a different man around the same time. Fradche refuted the testimony, but the damage was done. As a result of these discrepancies, the bet din refused to grant the permit to marry, ruling that Fradche was to be regarded as *me'uberet u-meneket havero* (one who was pregnant and [could be] nursing another man's child).[85] The court was faced with conflicting priorities. On the one hand, allowing the couple to marry would alleviate the likelihood that Fradche and her child would be ostracized, Fradche would be unable to secure further employment, and they would end up on the community's charity rolls. On the other hand, the court took very seriously the possibility that Fradche might not be carrying Itzik's child. By permitting a marriage while she was pregnant, they would be tolerating the possibility of Itzik's assuming paternity of a child he did not father. The ban against their marriage went beyond the period of her pregnancy and through the months (twenty-four) that she would/could be nursing her child. While it seems that the court acted stringently in this case, our interest lies in pointing out the seriousness with which the court took the question of me'uberet u-meneket havero. The court assumed that Fradche would nurse her own child, and it acted in accordance with talmudic law, although this would not necessarily be in the best interest of Fradche—or that of her unborn child.

This liminal halakhic status (me'uberet u-meneket havero) arose frequently in the halakhic literature of the early modern period, particularly in regions that were beset by war or plague that caused numerous deaths within short periods of time. Tamar Salmon-Mack has written extensively on the difficulties for women who were in precarious emotional and financial states with infant dependents, caught in the limbo of having to wait months or years before being permitted to marry.[86] This was true for widows and divorcées whose marriages had been perfectly respectable but who had had the misfortune to become single while potentially or actually pregnant. In the case of some women who became pregnant during the betrothal period, the Jewish court demanded oaths that they were pregnant from their fiancé rather than from another party so that the man should not be saddled with a child who was not his. When Baila, daughter of the late Yuzpil Katz of Augny, became pregnant during her betrothal period, she swore "a severe oath" that she had slept only with her fiancé, and he took a similar oath. Thus assured, the bet din allowed their marriage to proceed, albeit with some additional stipulations.[87] In contrast, three weeks after the marriage of Nene, daughter of Feivelman Rofe, and the Torah scholar Yonah Leyb Wilstadt, Yonah heard from others that she had been pregnant by another party since before their marriage. He separated from her immediately and asked the Jewish court for confirmation that the child was not his and that he owed it no support. The court issued a confirmation along with a statement: "Since she herself confessed that she will be nursing the child of another man, she is obligated to accept a divorce on the strength of her admission."[88] Although Nene had not committed adultery after her marriage, the fact of her pregnancy, rather than of her having had sexual relations before marriage, determined that Yonah was halakhically obligated to divorce her. He noted that he hated her for her deceit, so the legal act aligned with his emotional state.

Exceptions to the Jewish law could be granted only in cases in which the mother never nursed her child but handed it over immediately to a wetnurse or if the child died. Tamar Salmon-Mack has argued that this led to a tragic and paradoxical outcome. A woman who became widowed while pregnant and wished to remarry as soon as possible had to avoid ever nursing her child so that the infant would not become attached to her and refuse to nurse from another woman.[89] In times of war, plague, and other uncertainties, some women refused to nurse their own children for fear that if they became widowed, they would not be able to find another spouse for two years. Thus, a host of considerations, from the prevailing wisdom of women mentors to medical theories, economic status, and Jewish legal frameworks, guided the decisions women made regarding this elemental function in their maternal lives.

Miscarriages and Abortions

Communal records, custom books, and religious writings focus on communal and ritual aspects of pregnancy and nursing, but they are largely silent on their physical aspects, including miscarriage. One passing reference to miscarriage can be found in a letter from Hava Slave to her daughter and son-in-law: "Can you imagine what a time I've had, [as] I've had no letter for such a long time, and I knew that Bune was ill and Gertrud in childbed? . . . I nearly died, as I'd written, as I had a miscarriage with a son."[90] While such news may have been shared within the family circle, it may not have become public. In his discussion of the earlier aforementioned case, in which a woman who became pregnant proximate to her husband's death was suspected of conducting an affair, Rabbi Ezekiel Landau noted that the couple had been married for seven years without bearing children. The accused wife, however, maintained that unbeknownst to her gossiping neighbors, she had had two prior miscarriages.[91] Such occurrences were likely common but remain mostly obscured in the sources written largely by men.

A miscarriage in an unwanted, extramarital context appears in a rabbinic responsum. A single woman became pregnant out of wedlock and had come to a financial agreement with the father of her unborn child. She then miscarried, and only her mother, her brother, and the child's father knew she had been pregnant. Rabbi Ezekiel Katzenellenbogen was asked whether she would be able to wed a kohen, as she was no longer a virgin.[92] Implicit in the question was that the family secret not be revealed.[93] Although, normally, a pregnancy would have exposed a woman's premarital affair, whereas a man's complicity in such an affair could remain concealed, the woman's miscarriage freed her to try and hide her secret.

In another case of an unwanted pregnancy, a learned person turned to Rabbi Yair Hayim Bacharach about a woman who had become pregnant from an extramarital affair. He reported that, before detecting the pregnancy, she was already miserable and contrite: "After the deed, she repented and cried out day and night... in tears, and hit her head against the wall until blood would flow from her head. She told her husband and asked a rabbi to prescribe penance, [promising] to do whatever was demanded of her. But when she sensed she was pregnant from him [her lover]... she went to a sage and asked him if it was permitted to swallow a poisonous powder that would extricate the rotted seed that was inside her."[94] The woman's emotional state led her to seek permission to imbibe a substance that would abort the fetus. Her decision to consult with a rabbi, rather than to abort, is fascinating, as it reveals a desire to comport with religious norms in the wake of an affair and a pregnancy that contravened them. Both Bacharach and Rabbi Jacob Emden, who wrote about a similar question, noted the difficulty of this deliberation under Jewish law, which, on the one hand, allowed a mother to transgress dietary rules and Shabbat laws in order to save her baby but on the other, permitted saving the mother's life over that of the baby.[95] Neither rabbi, it must be noted, saw the woman in a positive light; whatever leniency they considered was because this baby was conceived in sin.[96] What stands out in the complicated reasoning offered in these two responsa is the broader difference between the Jewish position, which often prioritized the mother's well-being, and the Catholic and Lutheran positions, which prioritized the baby's welfare above the mother's. Whereas Protestant women in Württemberg were punished as criminals in cases of abortion, and some were suspected of abortion after having miscarried, no such suspicion fell on Jewish women who miscarried.[97] This woman even approached a rabbi about whether she might abort a fetus, and Bacharach and Emden disagreed over whether it was permissible in this extreme case. Just as women could derive pleasure from using their bodies in positive ways, such as attracting a good match, bearing and nursing children, and fulfilling the many mitzvot that depended on their bodies, many junctures in women's lives, including these cases, brought physical infirmity or emotional distress.

When Women's Health Faltered

It is difficult to find sufficient first-person descriptions of what women's bodies felt like to them when they believed something was amiss. This is partly because women turned first to other women—relatives, neighbors, and friends—for advice on remedies for what ailed them. Men mediated many medical consultations concerning women, and it is primarily their writing that has been preserved. As a result, many anecdotes about women's ailments in Jewish sources deal with vaginal blood or other complications that concerned issues of menstrual purity laws. These, rather than other cases, were preserved in rabbinic writings. For example, when a woman saw bloodstains that she believed may have been induced by coughing, Rabbi Isaac mi-See specified that it was essential to know whether the woman had pain upon internal inspection. While her concern about seeing vaginal blood brought her to consult a rabbi, the woman had previously consulted with "elderly women," who told her that the blood was from a burst vessel, a fact that was also relayed to the rabbi for his consideration.[98] Queries are also preserved from elderly menopausal women who, nevertheless, approached rabbis because they saw blood that could be considered impure under Jewish law. Rabbi Judah Mehler, for example, dealt with a case in which a woman "who had already stopped having womanly courses had an impure occurrence; she feels great discomfort and pain in her back and her belly" and saw blood in her urine.[99] Rabbi Ezekiel Landau consulted with a sixty-seven-year-old woman who had had a wax ring inserted into her body after experiencing a stomach illness in her youth. When she had a red discharge that left her unable to purify herself under Jewish law, she approached the rabbi. Local women who had assessed the problem believed that the redness was caused by the wax, which was disintegrating in her body after so many years. A non-Jewish doctor who had been consulted at first thought that it was flux, an overflow of blood or bodily fluids, and suggested that all of the woman's blood was flowing together out of her womb.[100] After he heard the women's opinion, however, he concurred that their assessment was certainly plausible.[101] Details about these illnesses reach us because of their impact on Jewish women's ritual status, and they emphasize this particular aspect of the illness.

Women would often send their husbands or other men to fetch a medical practitioner; these messengers often first transmitted their lists of symptoms. Even calling a midwife tended to be the future father's duty, and he would provide an account of the progress of labor. Some doctors kept records of their patients' symptoms and treatments, as did some rabbis in cases where medical and halakhic aspects of women's lives intersected. The Jewish midwives whose records have survived kept records of births they attended, but these contained few descriptions beyond the basic vital record, with rare exceptions. Barbara Duden's now classic account of the medical case records of Dr. Johann Storch, a women's doctor in eighteenth-century Eisenach, a south German village, allows us to assume certain general principles.[102] Among her observations, based on hundreds of cases over several decades, male doctors generally did not have access to women's private parts. Women in extreme pain or with extreme deformity would sometimes offer to show Storch the site, but this was rare. To inspect women's bodies, women practitioners were summoned. In his general practice, women, their husbands, or fathers, in person, described, orally or via written communication, what they felt or saw, and the doctor would prescribe accordingly.[103] A second important feature of the medical care of women was the truly vast array of types of medical, pharmaceutical, and/or magical practitioners accessible to women. Roy Porter has expanded on this by introducing the term "medical pluralism," and Nimrod Zinger has explored extensively how this worked for Jewish women in central and eastern Europe.[104] Zinger argues that various types of healers, religious and folk, circulated throughout the countryside, and their prescriptions crisscrossed the culture so that they cannot easily be separated into different categories.[105] Barbara Duden notes that the doctor often tailored his prescriptions to the patient's class. Thus, if the patient were well off, the compounds would require expense, effort, and a pharmacist's skills to produce. If the patient were poor, the recommended antidote would often be composed of materials likely to be found in the household. In addition, Duden notes the strong culture of self-treatment among women, particularly in rural areas. Women circulated myriad recipes to fix all types of female maladies. Academically trained medical doctors faced competition, Duden noted drily, not primarily from untrained barbers and folk healers but, rather, from mothers.[106] Suffering from menstrual discomfort, pregnancy, childbirth, parturition, and nursing were often known and temporary conditions, and women developed means of coping, often helping one another in individual and in organized form to get through the times when they could not meet all their usual responsibilities.

Because the doctor did not do internal examinations, pregnancy could not be confirmed or denied until time did its work.[107] Much of Storch's practice was based on a feeling that some fluids or substances that ought to have left the body were blocked from doing so (such as "retention" of menses), or various fluids or substances were extruded but did not seem healthy. The doctor remedied these conditions either by removing something from the body (bleeding or cupping) or supplying a prescription for something to be taken into the body.

Bleeding through leeches was also used to treat melancholia, a form of anomie or depression. Such treatment may have provided placebo relief. Jewish

FIG. 10.3. Woman being bled with leeches with accompanying blessing. *Birkat ha-mazon*, 1725.

calendars noted the best horoscopic times for such treatments, while abbreviated prayer books for Jewish women included scenes in which (upper-class) women can be seen receiving such treatment from a male doctor.[108] While these illustrations do not prove that these were common treatments, they would have familiarized women with this therapy. Slonik's handbook on women's commandments instructed women who had undergone bloodletting on how to prepare for immersion, given the scabs that had formed after the procedure; this was yet another intertwining of medical advice and ritual status.[109]

One extreme manifestation of despair was suicide. As Róisín Healy argued, historical scholarship has had a difficult time finding empirical records that confirm that a death was by suicide, tracing suicide's incidence over time and place, and, even for confirmed suicides, coming to understand the unfathomable motives.[110] If the evidence was not clear, families and communities would often go to great lengths to deny that the dead person had committed suicide. In Altona, in 1768, "Sarah, the widow of Hayim Kraut Kremer went to the bridge near the Elbe and fell into the water.[111] Later, on that same day, she was found in the water and had died in the water. The *av bet din* (chief rabbi) decided that she should be treated like any other dead person who dies in their bed; however, the communal leadership decided to bury her in Dammtor, and on Sunday, 15 Elul, she was buried near the Dammtor."[112] Sarah's burial in Dammtor, the cemetery reserved for non-community members and other marginal individuals, reflected the community's decision to ostracize her after her death, despite the rabbi's ruling that this questionable suicide be treated like an accidental drowning. There were other instances in which suicide was not ambiguous. One entry from 1764 in the record book of the Frankfurt cemetery still reverberates with the shock and horror felt by contemporaries at the double suicide of a Jewish woman and her fourteen-year-old son: "Regarding a deviant act, a matter for outcry and uproar such as [our ears] have never heard, and such things are not done, regarding a Jewish woman, heaven forfend, who committed an abomination in Israel, she and her son, that is to say, what Rizchen, wife of R. Meir Schiff, who hanged and strangled herself in the upper attic, on Sunday, 3 Kislev, and her son Shmuel, 14 years old, imitated her actions . . . and he descended from a high peak to the lowest pit, to the cellar, and hanged and strangled himself."[113] The sources do not say what drove the woman and her son to take their lives, apparently in two separate spaces within their home at the same time. The act is recorded as something that tore at the fabric of the community, as a "deviant act" and an "abomination." The community wished to express its distance from such acts by physically marking the graves in a way that made them stand out, ostensibly to keep anyone from being buried nearby after some time, but implicitly, as a warning to others.

Communal attitudes toward suicide were rooted in a broader cultural understanding of the proper way to deal with maladies and suffering. Duden argues that only in the eighteenth century did pain itself become a medical symptom rather than a spiritual affliction from above that was meant to be endured. Jewish communal Memorbücher indicate that managing pain was seen as a spiritual virtue well into the eighteenth century. These texts afford glimpses into women's illnesses through the lens of piety, without reference to the physical or psychological impact of these illnesses or to their treatment. The elderly Reitsche of Frankfurt "suffered for approximately three-quarters of a year, with great and bitter distress, and could not enter and leave [her home], and she took it all upon herself with love, until she died."[114] Although accepting one's physical pain was a trope in many entries, variations in the narrative give a sense of the diversity of women's illnesses. Rivkah Yacht Hirts (d. 1779) of Mainz suffered for a far longer period than did Reitsche, as she was "locked in her house for more than 18 years, and she suffered from bitter and difficult distress, and she accepted these with love and devotion for the sake of Heaven."[115]

These types of prolonged illnesses affected both the woman herself and all those who depended on her emotionally and financially. A private letter from a husband's perspective described his wife's debilitating condition:

> She lay on her bed and could not, in any way in the world, take even one step, for all her tendons and tissues were bunched up. If she needed to empty her bowels, she ... rolled across the earth like a snake, literally on her stomach. And all this befell her because of confusion, for she cut the strands of *koltunas*, and I spent what I spent, but no medicine in the world could cure her. She confessed her sins every hour before God and prayed for death to take her, heaven forbid. Only in the past year did her hair grow again, and she became a new person, thank God, without any medication, only she has curvature of her spine, such that she walks with a bent head like a man leaning on his cane.[116]

The writer of this letter, Shalom ben Moses, a scribe in the city of Eybenschütz, described his wife's illness, her matted strands of hair and misshapen limbs, which he refers to as "koltunas," a syndrome widely represented in medieval and early modern medical and halakhic literature. Seen today as an extreme result of malnutrition and poor hygiene systemically attacking the body, some physicians in Shalom's time believed the disease to be entwined with demonic forces. It was also thought that cutting the tangled mass of hair associated with the disease could lead to further extreme debility, as the letter writer believed. Names for the syndrome varied widely across regions; koltunas was one Eastern European designation. So closely was it identified with Eastern Europe that the medical literature fixed on *plica polonica* (Polish plait) as its medical term. Although both men and women could be afflicted by the syndrome, it tended to be gendered female. In halakhic literature, the matted hair posed a problem, forming a *hatzitzah* (barrier to full immersion in a mikveh). As cutting the matted plait was believed to be a great danger, halakhists tended to permit women to immerse without cutting it.[117]

While the foregoing examples describe the devastation of serious illness on individual families and homes, women at the margins of society—those who did not have family living nearby and were too poor to be able to provide shelter, nursing care, and medications for themselves—often relied on the local community and its institutions to take care of them. The community sought to balance the care it owed to its members with the high costs of tending to the ill. Juspe Schammes notes that community members were entitled to medical care and medications at the community's expense if they could not afford care themselves, and records of individuals receiving medications and the help of an aide can be found scattered in the community's charity records.[118] Community members who could afford to care for themselves or their loved ones were expected to pay for the care they received in communal institutions. Benjamin ben Leyb Furth paid the Berlin community five hundred Reichsthaler: "In exchange, his sick, single daughter will be taken into the hekdesh, where she will have lodging and food for five consecutive years without additional payment. The kahal will not be responsible for expenses related to nursing her or for her medications."[119] In this case, while the community provided the institution and care to house his unnamed daughter, Benjamin was expected to pay for her medications, nursing care, and her stay.

Communities also prayed for the ill, altering their names slightly in order to alter their fates. The Memorbuch from Alzey, a town in the Rhineland, specified, "The rabbi ascends and opens one of the doors of the Holy Ark, reciting the *mi-sheberakh* (prayer for divine blessing), first with the name that he held previously; then he recites another *mi-sheberakh* with the name he has been given now . . . and men and women are equal in this matter."[120] Prayers were recited aloud for both men and women, and special prayers were offered for a woman who was enduring a difficult childbirth.

Although the texts we have normally omit women's ages, some Memorbuch entries confirm that illness struck women of all ages. Rivkah Krasche died before her twenty-eighth birthday. A midwife in Mainz for several years prior to her death in 1796, she gave birth to a daughter a year after marrying and then "fell ill for a year and a half after giving birth to a daughter and [then] died. She suffered for the aforementioned period with terrible and great suffering and always gave thanks to God aloud with a whole heart."[121] By contrast, Rachel Leah, the daughter of Frankfurt rabbinical judge Itzik Hamel (d. 1798), "was weakened by great suffering at the end of her life, due to a fall in the street before [the early morning prayer] *shomrim la-boker*, and she suffered and accepted [this] with love."[122] We do not know how old Rachel Leah was, but she seems to have been older; younger women's tragic deaths were usually marked by a comment on their untimely passings.

Memorbücher entries note a few women who lived into their eighties and nineties. Shinche Ginzburg (d. 1740) was a widow in Mainz; "twenty-two years were added to her years," which was a reference to her reaching the age of ninety-two.[123] Her neighbor, Henle Mainz, lived until the age of ninety-eight.[124] Living so long was not the norm, and it led to the unusual notation of age at death. In a Memorbuch from the Fürth Kloyz, the "notable" woman Branete (née Katz) was remembered for passing away in Jerusalem at age ninety-three; clearly, news of her long life and demise far away had reached her hometown.[125] Klärchen bat Mosche of Altona died in 1685; born at the end of the sixteenth century, she lived ninety-six years.[126]

Old age could be accompanied by physical infirmity and vulnerability. We recall that Rebbetzin Yutel Reischer, wife of the notable eighteenth-century rabbi Jacob Reischer, was found murdered in her bed, the victim of a horrific and violent crime. Close to eighty, she was defenseless when faced by a young local woodchopper who entered her home and brutally killed her.[127] Some elderly women (and men) also faced mental deterioration. Pinhas Katzenellenbogen related a story he had heard from his elderly cousin Sarel of Prague about their great-grandmother Beila:

> More than 90 years old, and she was completely out of it, with no mental capacity, but the name of her son, R. P[inhas], was always in her mouth.... Not only this, but she made a crib, and she made a little bundle, and she put the bundle in the crib, and she rocked and carried the crib that is called *veg'k*, as is made for a very small infant, and she looked at it and called the bundle "Pinhas, Pinhas my son," and sometimes she took the bundle and lifted the sack of rags and hugged and kissed it as one does to babies.[128]

Although he did not witness her deterioration firsthand, Pinhas Katzenellenbogen is clearly describing the symptoms of dementia, in which his elderly great-grandmother confused a rag doll with her grown son. His description of her incapacity in old age, however, does not diminish whatsoever his appreciation for his ancestor, and he describes with pride how his grandfather, Pinhas Horowitz, would come to Prague once a year to honor his mother (see plate 30).

Rabbinic and communal texts provide us with a very specific window into how women's bodily experiences were shaped by Jewish law and ritual and how women's physical states and spiritual lives intersected. The Memorbuch entry of Hindche bat Aharon Bonn of Frankfurt (d. 1784) captures this clearly:

"She merited to live to an old age of more than 90 years. She was granted good all of the days of her youth, and then when she was over 40, she became blind, and she suffered terrible distress and was oppressed with great, hard, and bitter travails. She accepted these with love and devotion and further mortified her soul through fasting."[129] This entry contrasts Hindche's "good" younger years, in which she had sight, with the physical challenges she faced for approximately fifty years as a blind woman. Despite the hardships she faced after losing her sight, "her prayer routines were not altered; [she prayed] with awe, fear, tears, and supplication." By emphasizing Hindche's continued prayers even after she was no longer able to see the text and by highlighting the fasts she undertook despite her age and her physical condition, the Memorbuch reiterates that for early modern Jews, one's overall status was a reflection of both corporeal health and spiritual well-being.

Bodies and Souls

The deep connection between body and soul can be seen in the Frankfurt Memorbuch entries for Gitla, the daughter of Avraham Drach, who "mortified her soul with daily fasts, and . . . with limited food and drink," and for Hindchen, the daughter of Joseph Hanover, who "mortified her soul every day, including consecutive fasts from day to day."[130] Rainkhe, daughter of Hayim Gundersheim of Mainz, "sanctified herself and vowed not to consume meat on weekdays for several years, other than on days upon which fasting was forbidden."[131] Fasting as an act of piety was not limited to women, although, as Caroline Walker Bynum has argued, women's control over food lent special significance to female fasts.[132]

Leah Esther, daughter of Mordehai Yaffe, was praised for another spiritual act tied to women's bodies: "With regard to her garments, she did not insist on the honor to which she was due."[133] Similarly, Mehrle, daughter of Leyb Speyer from Mainz, "engaged in many deprivations, both regarding clothing and [other means] of demanding her due honor."[134] These fascinating entries praise women's more modest sartorial choices. Even the wives of ketzinim (elite community members), undoubtedly had greater restrictions on their choices than their non-Jewish social peers.[135] At the same time, these texts remind us that Jewish women were conscious of changing styles. Beyond the clothing they wore, women who could afford it applied various unguents, ointments, perfumes, and creams to their bodies, both to alleviate discomfort and to enhance the attractiveness of their bodies; they even applied beauty

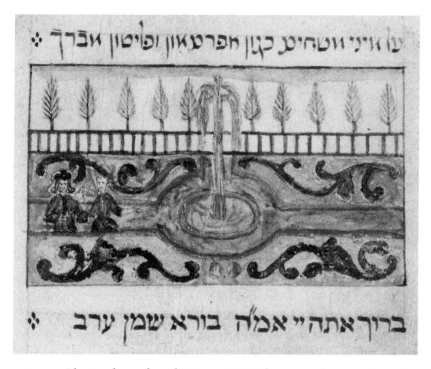

FIG. 10.4. Blessing for perfumed ointment. Note the man and woman dressed in finery, holding hands. *Birkat ha-mazon*, 1725.

marks. The luxury manuscript commissioned in 1725 for Fradche, wife of Moshe Gundersheim, depicts a perfumer surrounded by his wares, dozens of jars of oils and unguents, in many shapes, sizes, and colors, as well as *bore shemen arev* (a blessing for sweet-smelling oils). The illustration accompanying that unusual blessing depicts a man and woman holding hands, indicating that the purpose of the aromatic perfumes was to heighten the attraction between a woman and a man.[136] Such beauty products, along with the accessories that Jewish women wore in public, indicate a deep level of awareness and self-awareness of Jewish women's bodies. The blessing over the fragrant ointment was one of many rituals that linked the spiritual and the physical. Jewish women navigated religious, biological, and emotional challenges at every life stage. They did so with immense dedication to the law, fortitude in the face of suffering, and awareness of their bodies.

11

Custom and Ritual

WHEN HENDLEN, daughter of Wolf Oppenheim, gave birth to a son in seventeenth-century Worms, the *zakhar* celebration on Friday night, the *Wachnacht* meal the night before the circumcision, and the celebration of the circumcision itself occurred during the Sukkot holiday (Tabernacles), so the celebratory meals took place inside the sukkah (temporary structure). "The women, however, ate and rejoiced together with the new mother in the 'winter room' [the heated room in the house] rather than in the sukkah, and no one objected."[1] What is striking about this comment is that under normal circumstances, the women of Worms joined the men in the sukkah for family or communal festivities—despite the fact that Jewish law obligated men, but not women, to sit in the sukkah (see plate 31).

No celebration or solemn observance in the Jewish community took place without the participation of the women of the community in their homes, in the synagogues, and in public spaces. Yet, many contemporaneous sources omitted or greatly diminished the role of women in the pivotal observances of the Jewish calendar year. When the brothers Israel and Koppel, sons of Gumpel, decided to write and print a written record of the "customs of our community of Fürth," their section dedicated to the High Holy Days did not mention women at all.[2] They render in exquisite detail the holiday services as practiced in their synagogue, but by focusing only on synagogue practices, meaning services that were all led by men, the brothers completely omitted mention of the existence or participation of women in the holiday customs. We can contrast this to an earlier chronicler of his Jewish community's customs, Juspe Schammes of Worms.[3] Juspe frequently highlighted the customs of women, in one case on their own, in a separate segment he called *minhag nashim* (women's custom),[4] or in deliberate mentions of women's presence and roles in customs observed by the entire community. This difference cannot be attributed to the absence of women from the religious sphere in Fürth and their robust presence in Worms; rather, Juspe paid attention to spaces and rituals outside the main men's sanctuary as well.[5] Juspe's account is extraordinary in paying attention to so many aspects of women's religious activities, but it also highlights the invisibility of women in so many other sources. When we examine women's practices as described by Juspe, we do not argue that women in other cities and villages practiced in exactly the same way. Rather, we indicate that wherever Jewish communities observed a feast or fast day, women participated in their own fashion, often in ways that appeared prominent in their own time but went unrecorded for posterity.

From the many glimpses and references in various early modern sources, we argue here that many Jewish women structured their daily lives around religious practices in both domestic and communal rituals and that the Jewish calendar formed the timescape that shaped much of their lives. Each temporal unit—days, weeks, months, and years—was punctuated by rituals and obligations that collectively organized women's time, as it surely did men's. Of course, not all women followed all these practices, but when we see a certain activity repeated in many places for many different women, patterns begin to emerge. Religious rites shaped the rhythm of women's lives; they also created spaces and opportunities for them to gather and socialize.[6]

From Dawn to Dusk

Christian Hebraist Paul Christian Kirchner opened his polemical compendium of Jewish ritual with a near lyrical account of pious Jewish women awaking before daybreak to urge their husbands and sons to get to morning prayers on time.[7] What he did not capture was the direct relationship of many women to prayer, in some fashion, on a daily basis. Prayers and blessings in special siddurim, and in many tkhines collections, testify to the ongoing desire of women to reach out to God in prayer. More unexpected, perhaps, are the testimonies that some women attended synagogue on a daily basis.[8] An undated entry from the eighteenth-century memorial book in Büdesheim, a small village in the Palatinate region of the Rhine, memorialized Leah, the daughter of Moshe Amsterdam. Among many pious acts, "she went early in the morning and remained late in the synagogue, to pray with complete devotion."[9] Memorbücher across different communities laud women for several different elements of prayer: daily synagogue attendance, both morning and evening; recitation of the Psalms; and prayer with devotion. Faigel, the daughter of the venerable Yishai Oppenheim of Frankfurt, "went early and stayed late at the house of prayer, to pray to God who dwells in His residence, and the teaching of lovingkindness was on her lips,[10] in biblical and liturgical hymns and prayer; she discerned, understood, and knew how to sing sweet melodies to praise the Lord God, and she prayed with devotion."[11]

Although this Memorbuch entry cites biblical passages associated with women and therefore has a formulaic aspect, it celebrates Faigel for her devoted prayer, for her knowledge and familiarity with both the text and the tunes of the liturgy, and for her attendance at synagogue. Faigel was by no means unique in her regular presence in the synagogue. Maidservants often tended to the children and the home while their mistresses went to pray, and attendance at synagogue was a norm for many women in the community.[12]

Community records sometimes made special note of women's synagogue attendance in both fair and foul weather. Talze, the daughter of David Oppenheim in Cleves, "swiftly rose early and stayed late in the synagogue throughout her life, always, both in hot seasons and in cold seasons."[13] The Mainz Memorbuch includes multiple references to women's presence in the synagogue during the hot summer and cold winter months. Shifra Sara Hanle, the wife of Natan Hamel Segal of Mainz, was praised "for waking early for morning and evening prayers in summer and winter, and for praying with devotion, and for hearing the weekly [Torah] portion from the cantor each Shabbat."[14] The very next entry, for Gutle, daughter of Leyb Wetzlar, also praised her devoted prayer and her attendance at synagogue in summer and winter months. The repeated trope commending women's presence in the synagogue in all seasons underscores that this was a normative, accepted, and even expected form of women's piety. It was not only the standard morning and evening prayers that brought women to synagogue. Gitle, the daughter of the pious R. Yokel Metz of Frankfurt, "always went early and stayed late in the synagogue, and she poured out her soul in prayers and supplications, and in the praises and hymns of David, son of Jesse [Psalms]."[15] Glikl, too, described having attended synagogue before lunchtime in Metz, at which Psalms were recited in honor of the deceased—in this case, for Yachet, the mother of Glikl's son-in-law.[16]

Some Jewish women started and ended each day with daily prayer. Although they were not required by Jewish law to pray in a minyan (quorum), women were expected to pray daily.[17] Prayer books commissioned specifically for women or owned and prized by them highlight the significance and reverence associated with prayer, at the very least for women of a certain class. Many of the illuminated prayer manuscripts prepared for women in the eighteenth century include images of a woman seated on her bed, holding a prayer book while reciting keriyat shema, the prayer one recited immediately before sleep (see fig. 4.3, plate 19). In one manuscript, the traditional prayer opens with an additional plea for forgiveness and includes instructions for reciting the prayer such that one falls asleep without uttering any other speech. The accompanying illustration includes a woman at her table in her nightcap, with a prayer book in front of her, while her husband waits in bed.[18] Whereas one sixteenth-century responsum deals with the question of why women were not required to recite the bedtime prayer, these commissioned manuscripts suggest that by the eighteenth century, elite women recited this prayer as part of the nighttime ritual with devotion and even pride.[19]

From Candlelight to Starlight

Each day of the week contained its own order, punctuated by prayers, chores, and activities; the week culminated in Shabbat. Two out of the three "women's mitzvot" (commandments) relate directly to women's responsibility to infuse a home with the special spirit of Shabbat. Although women were obligated in a far greater number of commandments, lighting Shabbat candles, observing the laws of menstrual purity, and preparing hallot (special loaves for Shabbat and holidays; sing. *hallah*) properly were commandments seen as solely in women's domain. Several Memorbücher and tombstones in particular communities praised women for the care they took in fulfilling these obligations.[20] The hallah was prepared with a different recipe than the one used to prepare the bread that was consumed daily; in Frankfurt, Jews of different classes prepared these breads differently. Wealthy women baked their hallot "long and thick, adorned with many spices, so that they are pleasant to look at and to eat ... but the middle class are sparing and make a large cake, which is customary for Friday nights throughout Ashkenaz."[21] The commandment of hallah required that the woman remove a portion of dough after having recited the appropriate blessing, then burn and later discard that piece as a means to commemorate the bread that was used in the Temple. Several illuminated prayer books designed for women's use depict women removing the small portion of hallah. They include specific instructions for the proper ratios of eggs to flour and for removing and burning the dough. One such manuscript instructs the ba'alat bayit that while the maidservant could knead the dough, it was she who had to perform the commandment and remove the requisite amount from the loaf.[22] Another manuscript admonishes the woman of the house against giving the hallah to another who might not treat it with dignity.[23] These manuscripts also included Yiddish tkhines (supplicatory prayers) that were penned in this period to accompany this and other women's rites. Though formulaic, they offered women the opportunity to pray on a more personal level. One such tkhine asks God to allow the woman, her husband, and her children to merit blessings, including the return to Jerusalem.[24] In another manuscript, the tkhine sanctified the baking process in which the woman was engaged: "Send the angel in charge of baking and watch that it bakes completely and does not burn in honor of your holy Shabbat . . . hear my prayer."[25]

Composing new supplicatory prayers to accompany women's rites elevated the entire process of preparation and baking hallot by characterizing it as religiously meaningful. Writing these prayers and expanding the rituals further granted women the ability to interpret domestic tasks through the lens of religious piety. The hallot that women baked, then, were a significant mitzvah, but they also symbolized an entire range of foods that had to be prepared in advance of Shabbat or a holiday. A written culture began to grow around the preparation of kosher food in the home. One book of blessings listed an array of treats that Jewish women usually prepared to serve on Shabbat and holidays. Custom books, such as that of Juspe Hahn, included lists of many traditional holiday foods. Although he places the blessings and customs rather than the women at the center of his discussion, it was they who carefully prepared special cuisine and baked goods (see plate 32).[26] An illuminated book of blessings similarly notes, "the dishes for which it is not necessary to wash [hands, as for bread] include *vrimslakh* and *lokshen* [two types of noodles], *kreplakh* (dumplings), *kugel* (a savory pudding), *shalet* (the Shabbat stew, cholent)."[27] This list gives us some idea of the range of dishes with which Jewish women in this region were generally familiar. While some of the dishes were local fare that Christian women prepared in their homes, certain foods were prepared by Jewish women in a distinctive manner that adhered to the requirements of Jewish dietary laws; others were prepared specially for a particular holiday.

Just as "hallah" encompassed much more than the production of two loaves, lighting the Shabbat candles meant ushering a transcendent spirit into the home for the coming twenty-four hours. "It is a mitzvah for the woman to clean her hands and face for Shabbat before she lights; first she should put on her Shabbat clothes."[28] The washing and clothing here symbolized that women were setting aside quotidian concerns and entering a different, spiritual order of time. Special tkhines were also composed for this commandment.

FIG. 11.1. Woman preparing food. *Seder birkat ha-mazon*, 1751.

Some of the illuminated manuscripts commissioned for women included prayers for the woman and her household, stressing that a woman must light candles at the proper time since "the primary reason our sages told us to light candles is to promote a peaceful home."[29] The text further urged women to light candles when they were going to attend synagogue services, further emphasizing the normativity of women's synagogue attendance and its intersection with their domestic religious duties.

Women's practices related to the months and seasons are less discussed in our sources and perhaps were not as universally observed. Since medieval times, women in Ashkenaz observed the day (or two days) of Rosh hodesh, the beginning of the new Jewish month, by refraining from certain chores and observing a semi-holiday spirit. Several compilations of customs discuss the ways in which these days should be, or actually were, observed by women. Juspe Hahn writes in his *Yosif ometz*:

> It is the women's custom not to perform *melakhah* [certain chores] on Rosh hodesh; only the chores that must be done within the home, such as cooking and baking and the like [are permitted].... I merited to see in the manuscript of my grandfather, the pious R[abbi] Isaac Neuerlingen... in the sermons that he preached... that he warned of this, that women in his days had become lax about doing chores on Rosh hodesh.[30]

Similarly, a medieval custom related to the *tekufah* (turn of the seasons) is widely documented for the early modern period. This custom was based on the belief that waters left unguarded during the change of the seasons could become toxic if they were ingested. In the early modern period, this became primarily a women's custom. Synagogues warned their congregants repeatedly about the moment of the impending tekufah. As one Christian observer, Paul Wilhelm Hirsch, noted, "Since men are not occupied with running the household or the kitchen, it falls solely on the women."[31] Halakhic codes, Christian Hebraists, and an entire genre of sifre evronot (calendar manuals) described and warned about the dangers of this liminal period between the seasons. They urged women to guard all liquid in their kitchens or to apply an antidote of an iron implement to ward off the evil turn. After the eighteenth century, this custom, implemented mainly by women, mostly disappeared into oblivion.[32] It exemplifies the many aspects of women's ritual lives hidden from view today that figured prominently in early modern sources.

Annual Cycle

Women were central to every celebration of the holidays on the annual calendar cycle. In addition to communal observances, women prepared special foods that were customary for each holiday, such as dairy dishes for Shavu'ot and Passover recipes. On Hanukkah evenings, women refrained from doing chores while the candles were lit and read the story of Judith, a heroine from the Apocrypha whose story was printed in the early modern period and illustrated in books for women.[33] A Yiddish *minhogim* manuscript (book of customs) shows a man lighting the menorah "before he wishes to eat" the meal the ba'alat bayit prepared for Hanukkah.[34] The holiday of Purim provided opportunities for women to step out of their routines into a more playful mode. Women attended synagogue punctiliously on the Shabbat of Remembering

PLATE 14. Woman in commerce writes her accounts (there is no indication that she is Jewish). Note her quill, inkwell, and writing table, as well as the keys dangling behind her. Nicolaes Maes, *The Account Keeper*, 1656.

PLATE 15. Portrait of Madame Chaile Kaulla. The medallion on her necklace was a special mark of honor. Johann Baptist Seele, ca. 1804.

PLATE 16. Coffee set of Madame Kaulla, inscribed with her name and extolling the virtue of occasional coffee drinking. Nymphenburg, 1795.

PLATE 17. Jewish women sell vegetables at a stand. *Birkat ha-mazon*, 1725.

PLATE 18. Woman selling baked goods. Miniature *Me'ah berakhot*, c. 1740.

PLATE 19. Woman recites her bedtime prayers from a book beside her infant swaddled in its elaborately carved cradle. *Seder birkat ha-mazon*, 1746–47.

PLATE 20. Cooking pot inscribed with names of Alexander ben Aaron and Saraleh bat Moshe, Frankfurt am Main, 1708/9.

PLATE 21. Jewish woman from Worms depicted wearing contemporary garb with a compulsory yellow badge. *Thesaurus Picturarum*, ca. 1600.

PLATE 22. Jews in the synagogue plaza in Fürth, Germany, on the Sabbath. The woman on the right carries her *siddur*. Campe, "Der Samstag," c. 1800.

PLATE 23. This book "belongs to the esteemed woman Marat (Mrs.) Fradche wife of the notable R. Moses Gundersheim." Frontispiece, *Birkat ha-mazon*, 1725.

PLATE 24. Pre-immersion grooming. *Birkat ha-mazon*, 1741.

PLATE 25. Preparing for the mikveh at home. *Seder birkat ha-mazon*, 1736.

PLATE 26. Pregnant woman being served. Leipnik Haggadah, 1739.

PLATE 27. Praying the Shema while nursing a baby. *Seder birkat ha-mazon*, 1720.

PLATE 28. "Figure of the birthing mother in her bed and the women who swaddle and clean up the newborn." *Seder milah,* ca. sixteenth century.

PLATE 29. Women playing cards and socializing on *Rosh hodesh* (New Moon). Written for the bride Judith, daughter of the Primas, Benjamin Wolf Popper of Breznice. *Seder birkat ha-mazon*, Bohemia, 1755.

PLATE 30. Depiction of an elderly woman. Harrison Miscellany, Corfu, c. 1720.

PLATE 31. Men and women being served in a *sukkah*, depicted on a sukkah wall hanging from Germany, eighteenth century.

PLATE 32. *Shavu'ot* meal. Note the elaborately baked delicacies and greenery in honor of Shavu'ot. Yiddish *minhogim* manuscript, sixteenth century.

אן ראש השנה זאלן מן גיהט תשליך מאכין
זאגט מן דינה פסוקים:

מִי אֵל כָּמוֹךָ נֹשֵׂא עָוֹן וְעֹבֵר עַל פֶּשַׁע לִשְׁאֵרִית נַחֲלָתוֹ ׃ לֹא הֶחֱזִיק לָעַד אַפּוֹ כִּי חָפֵץ חֶסֶד הוּא ׃ יָשׁוּב יְרַחֲמֵנוּ יִכְבּוֹשׁ עֲוֹנוֹתֵינוּ ׃ וְתַשְׁלִיךְ בִּמְצֻלוֹת יָם כָּל חַטֹּאתָם ׃ תִּתֵּן אֱמֶת לְיַעֲקֹב חֶסֶד לְאַבְרָהָם אֲשֶׁר נִשְׁבַּעְתָּ לַאֲבֹתֵינוּ מִימֵי קֶדֶם ׃

PLATE 33. Four beautifully dressed women perform the *tashlikh* ceremony at the riverbank. *Seder birkat ha-mazon*, 1746–47.

PLATE 34. Order of the Passover seder with instructions in both Yiddish and Ladino. Note the woman participating in many of the frames. Leipnik Haggadah, 1739.

PLATE 35. Glass tumbler, Prague burial society, 1787. The *hevrah kaddisha* of Prague annually commissioned a tumbler to honor and commemorate its work. The one shown here illustrates the argument of this book: that women's work in the hevrah, and by extension in the community at large, was an integral part of life in the kehillah. When facing outward, the tumbler shows only the men in the hevrah; the women remain hidden unless one seeks them out.

FIG. 11.2. Woman trampling on Amalek and pelting him with stones. Yiddish *minhogim* manuscript, sixteenth century.

(Amalek) that preceded Purim.[35] On Purim itself, they flocked to hear the megillah (Esther scroll), dressed up in their finery. They dressed their daughters as Queen Esther or other masked and costumed figures and drank and ate at the festive Purim meal.[36] They prepared *mishloah manot* (special gifts of food for family and friends).[37] Details of the preparations for the Jewish holidays, major and minor, illuminate how ba'alot bayit upheld the core religious festivities across communities.

In this section, we focus on two pivotal seasons within the Jewish calendar year, the High Holy Days and Passover, to highlight the ways in which women observed and celebrated them. In each of these cases, the preparations for the holiday were complex and pervaded the atmosphere of the entire community with a special sensibility. The season known as *Yamim nora'im* (the High Holy

Days) began in late summer with the onset of the Hebrew month of Elul. In pious circles, the entire month was devoted to penitence and contemplation in preparation for the more intense season of atonement to follow. In most Ashkenazi communities, selihot (poetic prayers for forgiveness) were recited in special prayer services beginning on the Saturday night before Rosh Hashanah (or, if too few days remained, the prior week). Selihot were chanted in special melodies, offered in services that took place at midnight or very early in the morning. Selihot compilations prepared explicitly for women show that they (or some of them) participated in this midnight or very early special prayer.[38]

Women's attendance in the synagogue during the High Holy Days is confirmed in the famous early sixteenth-century woodcut images from the work of Johannes Pfefferkorn (1508), duplicated several decades later in Antonius Margaritha's book (1530).[39] The woodcuts illustrate women participating in and beyond the synagogue in various customs related to the High Holy Days. It is unclear whether these images reflect historical reality, although Pfefferkorn was raised a Jew, and Margaritha was raised in a rabbinic family.[40] The woodcuts depict women in the synagogue, some carrying babies in hand, behind a curtained-off partition. Although women are not the primary subject of the synagogue woodcuts, these illustrations provide offhand evidence that important rituals, such as the blessing by the kohanim (priests), blowing the shofar, and joining in the prayers, were important to Jewish women, who attended in their separate section of the synagogue, often holding their children.[41] These early sixteenth-century illustrations also depict women taking a robust role in other rituals of the atonement season: they go to the riverbanks for the custom of tashlikh; they immerse in a mikveh, and they twirl a hen overhead to symbolize the sacrifice of atonement for their own lives. A contemporaneous Yiddish manuscript from Italy confirms that many of these customs were observed by women. Women appear in the synagogue on Rosh Hashanah, seated at a separate table, some with their own prayer books, others without. The Yiddish manuscript also attests to the custom of women's bathing prior to immersing in a mikveh before the High Holy Days.[42] The idea of women's immersing as part of the preparation for Yom Kippur was contested by some medieval decisors, but R. Israel Isserlein (Maharil, d. 1427) wrote that all the members of the community above bar or bat mitzvah, men as well as women, immersed. He understood the custom as one of repentance rather than of bodily purity.[43] Many of these observances are confirmed by other collections of law and/or customs. While most custom collections do not point out the role of women in preparing the special foods eaten on Rosh

Hashanah, the Yiddish manuscript illustrates the table with women sitting prominently, an array of *simanim* (foods with symbolic meaning) and new fruits prominently displayed.[44] Juspe Schammes confirmed that women attended the Rosh Hashanah services in the seventeenth century. He noted that prior to the blowing of the shofar, the shamash stood near the door to the women's section and announced in Yiddish that everyone had to be quiet until the final *teki'ot* (shofar sounds).[45]

Tashlikh, a custom that originated in the medieval period, was performed on Rosh Hashanah if a body of water was close enough or during the week between Rosh Hashanah and Yom Kippur if it was distant. People gathered at the water's edge and threw crumbs to the fish, a symbolic expression of tossing away sins. The act was accompanied by a brief prayer to that effect. Although this custom arose during the medieval period, it was popularly embraced and found its way into all Ashkenazi books of customs. Multiple points of evidence indicate robust participation in this custom by women and men in the early modern period. The walk to the water, always depicted in the early modern period as separated by sex, provided women an opportunity to gather and enjoy the water's proximity at a time of year when the weather was generally favorable.[46] Both the German printed woodcuts and the Yiddish manuscript from Italy, as well as an early modern seder brakhot, depict women by themselves, performing tashlikh (see plate 33).[47]

Later, in the second half of the eighteenth century, the ordinances of the Fürth community (1770) indicated disapproval at the mingling of women and men as they assembled for tashlikh. "Tashlikh on Rosh Hashanah, how good it would be if the custom would be dropped for women and maidens. In any case, these should come to the water near the hekdesh prior to afternoon prayers, while the men and youths should go afterward. The supervisors should warn about this every Rosh Hashanah."[48]

Jews in many communities were accustomed to visit the graves of their relatives in the nearby cemetery and pray that they intercede for mercy. While some collections of customs mention only the men visiting the graves, both Christian Hebraists and other sifre minhagim specify that women visited the cemetery. Christian Hebraist Kirchner reported, "On Rosh Hashanah, women go to the cemetery to mourn and wail over their miserable condition on the graves of their relatives."[49] In the later eighteenth century, the Metz communal leaders ordained: "It is forbidden for women to go to the cemetery at the same time as men . . . particularly on the eve Rosh Hashanah and the eve of Yom Kippur, they may not go at all, but they may do so on the previous day."[50] In

FIG. 11.3. *Tashlikh*; women and children in top row. Margaritha, *Der gantz jüdisch Glaub*, Augsburg, 1530.

both cases, communal leaders in the eighteenth century sought to distance women from public spaces out of a heightened concern for community morality.

The culmination of the solemn portion of the High Holy Days was the fast day of Yom Kippur, the Day of Atonement. As it took place on the tenth day of the month of Tishre, the days leading up to it, including Rosh Hashanah, were known as the *Aseret yeme teshuvah* (Ten Days of Repentance). According to Jewish law, women who were not ill or recently delivered of a child were obligated to fast on Yom Kippur, and the evidence points to their full and robust participation in the synagogue services on Yom Kippur eve and day. Many stringencies in observance were practiced during this period. Jews who had not been careful about eating bread baked by non-Jews were exhorted to be stringent about it during these days.[51] That the baking of bread during this time fell to women, even if they usually purchased bread from a non-Jewish baker, can be seen by some additional customs related to baking included in the discussion by Juspe Kosman of Frankfurt: "Women have a custom of separating hallah on Yom Kippur eve. At the ritual meal eaten before the fast and after Yom Kippur, they eat the same cakes as [are] prepared for a holiday."[52] Beyond the preparation of special baked goods, women were in charge of preparing a robust meal before the fast to assist with the fasting to come, as well as a meal by which to break the fast; both generally were served by the women of the house. Pfefferkorn and Margaritha's works depict women overseeing the serving of the Yom Kippur eve meal. Candles were lit in the home before the meal, and Kosman urged women to light their Yom Kippur candles in the bedroom to remind them that marital relations were prohibited on Yom Kippur. Kosman exhorted women to "hurry to be ready while it is still daytime, as they, too, are obligated" to light candles in the synagogue after completing all their tasks at home. Those who prepared the candles for the synagogue should be sure to prepare very thick wicks so that the candles would burn for the entire holy day.[53]

Another custom that was widely performed by women as well as men before Yom Kippur was *kapparot* (atonements). Each person took a chicken, lifted it, and slowly rotated it around their heads as they asked God to accept the animal as a sacrifice instead of themselves. The chickens were then slaughtered and distributed to the poor; in some German-Jewish communities, the monetary value of the chicken was distributed. Women performed kapparot with hens, and pregnant women took an extra one for the life they bore inside them.[54]

The solemn days of repentance gave way to the joyful holiday of Sukkot when Jews built temporary structures in accordance with the requirements of Jewish law. For eight days, all meals were to be taken inside a sukkah (pl., sukkot). Christian Hebraists commissioned illustrations of sukkot from German lands in the early modern period. Some of the sukkot were ingeniously situated in the attics of homes or their courtyards. Many were elaborately decorated with local flora, wall hangings, and beautiful furnishings. Women were included in some of these depictions, often seated in the sukkah with their families.

The illustrations only hint at the additional labor involved: decorating the sukkah and setting the table for family meals, bringing every dish outside the

FIG. 11.4. Amsterdam Sephardi family celebrates Sukkot. Note the woman nursing her baby in the *sukkah*. Picart[d], *Historie générale*, Paris, 1741.

home into the sukkah and back for each meal of the eight-day holiday; these tasks inevitably fell to the ba'alot bayit, the women of the home. Many women attended the synagogue for the special holiday prayers, bearing their mahzorim (holiday prayer books). Juspe Schammes, recording the practices of the seventeenth-century community of Worms, describes the usage of etrogim (ritual citrons) in synagogue on the holiday: "He who purchased an etrog from the kahal sends it to his wife in the women's section at the conclusion of the Hallel prayer; she uses it first and then the other women, according to the order of their seats in the sanctuary. . . . the wives of those two [parnassim] who bought the etrogim get the etrog first, followed by the other women."[55]
In the communal ordinances issued by Fürth in 1770, men were forbidden to pass the etrog to the women's section, upon payment of a fine of the purchase

of wax for the synagogue.[56] The ordinance further specified that men might send the four species to their homes for their wives to make the blessing there rather than in a public space, such as the synagogue or its courtyard.[57] On the seventh day of Sukkot, Hoshanah Rabbah, it was customary to take *hoshanot* (branches of a willow tree) and beat them. In Worms, although it was sometimes difficult to obtain the correct plant, hoshanot were distributed to women as well as men, though this not was not halakhically mandatory.[58]

Perhaps the most surprising revelation in the descriptions of holiday celebrations in Worms by Juspe is his description of the separate and joyous celebrations by women on Simhat Torah. His detailed account is worth quoting at length:

> Between *minhah* (afternoon prayer) and *ma'ariv* (evening prayer), the women arrive in the best and finest clothing that they have. They arrive in the outer courtyard of the synagogue and in front of the outer entrance to the women's section. Most of the women, especially the unmarried ones, link hands; their leaders are the wives of the *hatan Torah* and the *hatan bereshit* (the men honored in the cycle of Torah reading that marked the holiday). They go around and around in a circle and sing *Yigdal* and other songs usually sung in honor of the bride and groom, all in honor of the Torah ... in the morning ... they have good fruits before them standing on a table, and they throw them to the young boys, who gather them with joy. The festive celebration that follows includes the rabbi and the rabbanit, almost the entire community, as they eat, drink wine, and celebrate the day around a large bonfire.[59]

This seventeenth-century portrayal of communal harmony and joy reflects the practices of many Ashkenazi communities on Simhat Torah. Many collections of customs illustrate, for example, the practice of throwing fresh fruits for the children, with both men and women tossing them to girls and boys. The exuberance manifested in this seventeenth-century description began to dissipate in the latter half of the eighteenth century due to fear that women's active presence in the synagogue would lead to immorality. Fürth ordinances of 1770 warned that "women who were not appropriate in the women's section on Simhat Torah, approaching lewdness" would be publicly branded as *hatzufot* (brazen women).[60] The nature of their transgression would, in fact, violate the boundaries of traditional standards of modesty. The ordinances accused the brazen women of going out to meet women who wanted to immerse themselves the previous day and coerce them to serve confections in the synagogue or in their homes on Simhat Torah.

Glikl of Hameln, then living in Metz, describes a ferocious brawl that broke out on Simhat Torah in the women's section of the synagogue: "On the holy day of Simhat Torah [1714] ... when all the Torah scrolls were raised aloft as is the custom. Even with seven Torah scrolls placed on the table, a fight broke out among the women, who started tearing the kerchiefs from one another's heads, woe is me, and stood bareheaded in the women's section. As a result the men in the men's section also started brawling and quarreling."[61] Glikl described a packed room filled with women and their egos, petty grievances overcoming the holiday spirit and causing the rabbi to flee the synagogue. She omitted the bothersome detail that one of the two initiators of the brawl was her stepdaughter, Hendele Levy. Hendele accused another woman "in a proud and impertinent tone that it was not suitable for her to stand in the posture in which she was standing and that she should hold herself in a different way."[62] Hendele's husband, Isaye Lambert, then quarreled with the husband of the second woman, Salomon Cahen, and the service unraveled quickly thereafter. Glikl attributed a later tragedy, a stampede that took the lives of six women in the same women's section, to the desecration of the holiday spirit that resulted from the quarrel.[63]

It is unclear how widespread women's celebrations were. Several of the Fürth ordinances appear to try to reverse customs that promoted women's presence in the public or communal sphere, and this is true of Simhat Torah. Read against the grain, and in the light of instructions to repeat these warnings annually, the ordinances pushed against what was apparently common practice. All the evidence, alongside much other documentary material related to women's seats in the synagogue, points to the importance early modern women attached not only to synagogue attendance but also to full-hearted participation in synagogue life within their own sphere.

Pesah Preparations

Perhaps the only other point on the Jewish calendar when a holiday pervaded an entire season is Passover and the weeks that preceded it. The preparations for Passover revolved around two primary axes: on the domestic front, the entire home had to be readied for Passover—a matter of weeks of labor that involved women on multiple levels. The entire season coincided, or rather collided, with the great spring fair in Frankfurt. This annual event was one that many Jewish men in mercantile life could not afford to miss, leaving their wives at home to shoulder the entire burden of Passover preparations.

On the communal level, the baking of matzot was one of the great obligations, requiring the highest available standards to ensure that no leavening would take place. The seder itself was the culmination of several weeks of labor, and it was followed by eight days of hosting festive meals for family and friends. On the Shabbat prior to Passover, called *Shabbat ha-gadol*, it was customary for the rabbi to deliver a discourse to the entire congregation; Juspe Kosman described men, women, and children flocking to hear the Shabbat ha-gadol sermon, during which the rabbi discussed the laws of *kashering* vessels (making ritually fit) for Passover and baking matzah.[64] If the second day of the holiday was Shabbat, the community would prepare an *eruv tavshilin* (a ceremonial legal mechanism that allowed them to prepare food for Shabbat on the holiday). This was the responsibility of the synagogue shamash, but if he forgot, he was to return to the house "with his wife" to make the eruv. This means that the woman played a role in this communal halakhic act.[65]

Illustrations of the production of matzot demonstrate that women were involved in virtually all its aspects. The grains for baking matzah were watched carefully so they would not become wet and inadvertently begin the process of fermentation. Similarly, the water that would be mixed into the ground grain, the only other ingredient in matzah, was drawn and left standing overnight to make sure that it was not roiling from its source but had come to "rest," a concept called *mayim she-lanu*. The early sixteenth-century Yiddish minhogim manuscript shows a woman at the center, flanked by two men, drawing water from a well. The caption says, "They are drawing water for the sake of the mitzvah."[66] A mid-seventeenth-century printed minhogim shows a woman carrying the "*mitzvos* water" for the matzot, something of a departure, as printed minhogim elided images of women in many cases.

Once the dough had been kneaded, often by women, women were directly involved in baking the matzot. An interesting contrast between the prescriptive depictions, which skew male, and the descriptive, which include women, can be seen when one compares the text written by a convert out of Judaism, Paul Christian Kirchner, and the editor who reissued his polemical ethnography with illustrations, Sebastian Jugendres. Kirchner's original text ascribed the entire grinding of grain and kneading of dough to men only. To women, he attributed only the separation of a small portion of the dough and burning it for hallah, a traditional woman's mitzvah. When writing about other tasks, he employed the passive voice; for example, the dough "is put" into forms so that it would retain its shape and would not run. The illustrations from live practice, commissioned by Jugendres, tell a different story. Women are kneading the

FIG. 11.5. Woman carries the "*mitzvos*" water as the man prepares to search for *hametz*. *Sefer Minhagim*, Amsterdam, 1662.

dough alongside men, and they are washing the indented circular forms to be reused for the next batch of matzah.[67] Kirchner noted that during the matzah baking, every implement had to be kept very clean to prevent *hametz* (leaven) from forming. Only the illustrations show the women washing the implements to ensure their purity. A Yiddish minhogim book printed in early eighteenth-century Frankfurt depicts women bringing the kneaded and shaped matzot in baskets on their heads to a man who placed them into the oven.

In the early sixteenth-century minhogim manuscript, the personification of Passover is a woman, holding aloft a round Passover matzah.[68] Matzah baking for an entire community was a collective enterprise. A count of every Jewish person who would need matzot was necessary. Kirchner discussed the number of matzot that would be needed for every member of the household, including servants. A communally kept distribution list of matzot from Altona demonstrates that ensuring each person was able to fulfill this religious precept

FIG. 11.6. Women bringing the kneaded and shaped *matzot* in baskets on their heads. Tyrnau, *Minhogim*, Frankfurt am Main, 1722–23.

was an obligation taken very seriously by the community. Matzot were provided to the poor as well.[69]

The readying of an entire home, and particularly the kitchen area, was another aspect of Passover preparation that fell almost entirely on the women of the house. Certain materials could not be kashered, and separate sets of Passover dishes had to be retrieved from their year-round storage spots. Metal implements could be kashered for Passover by immersing them in boiling water. A book of customs depicts a man and woman standing over the boiling cauldron. Bringing large cauldrons of water to the boiling point and immersing the dishes suitably was sometimes a communal activity supervised by the rabbi; in smaller settlements, women used the cauldrons on their hearths. Either way, the decisions as to which dishes they needed for the holiday and which could be stored away were those of the ba'alot bayit. Similarly, all foods that were hametz or unfit to be eaten during Passover had to be consumed before Passover, destroyed in a bonfire on Passover eve, or stored away and sold to a non-Jew until the end of the holiday. Kirchner described part of the end-of-Passover ritual in which Jews went to their non-Jewish neighbors to retrieve the keys to their storage rooms.[70] On the night before Passover, the ritual of *bedikat hametz* (inspecting the home to ensure that not a crumb of forbidden leavened food remained) took place. In many images of this ritual, the entire family, male and female heads of household with their offspring, are shown participating in the search.

Once the house was cleared of hametz, cooking the many special dishes for the two Passover sedarim, as well as for the entire family for eight days, commenced. The *tanur bet ha-horef* (main oven) had to be thoroughly cleaned and, according to Juspe Hahn, left fallow for three days before it could be used to

FIG. 11.7. Washing and *kashering* dishes for Passover. Leusden, *Philologus Hebræo-Mixtus*, Utrecht, 1699.

FIG. 11.8. Seder table. Woman on the right, seated next to child, gesturing. Prague Hagaddah, 1526.

cook for Passover.[71] If Passover eve fell on Shabbat, Hahn described a cholent made of matzah that people (presumably women) prepared; he discouraged the practice because the matzah pieces remained recognizable, which violated the prohibition against eating matzah on the eve of Pesah.

The seder itself has been the subject of a great many descriptions. It is the culmination of weeks of work, with the table finally laid with the best dishes and tableware. The table linens were either specially reserved for Pesah or newly laundered. Many women embroidered beautiful pieces of textile to adorn the table. The special foods had been procured in the marketplaces, the *maror* (bitter herbs) grated, and the accompanying *haroset* dip pounded. Juspe Hahn encouraged men to hurry home from evening services, "for if he tarries with kiddush and the seder, the children, women, and maidservants will fall asleep," as they had worked so hard to prepare.[72] The ba'al bayit, the head of household, sat on a reclining chair, called "the royal bed," according to one report, at the head of the table, and the ba'alat bayit often sat with him.[73] Many depictions of sedarim show the entire family encircling the table, with women often reading from their own haggadot (see plate 34).[74]

This reminds us that our sources portray primarily middle- and upper-class women who had the wherewithal to provide the holiday extras to their

FIG. 11.9. Ba'alat bayit holds her own haggadah and cup at the seder table. Offenbach Haggadah, 1795.

households. Individuals and communities made efforts to include the lonely, the poor, those in transit, and the unhoused in their circles. Some poor widows in Frankfurt, for example, ate their meals in the communal Garküche, an eatery that accepted pletten, communal charity vouchers, and provided holiday meals to the poor and to travelers.[75] What the holidays looked like from the vantage point of women who were not securely embedded in a community is a story that our sources largely do not divulge.

Women and Life Cycle Rituals

The women of the community also came together to celebrate life cycle rituals. Their involvement in these rites comes as no surprise, for marriages, divorces, and births could not occur without them. While, according to Jewish law, marriage and divorce are enacted, dominated, and initiated by men, women played a much more active role in life cycle rituals than was prescribed by law. Expanded celebrations and elaborate rituals provided ba'alot bayit and the girls in their families with a rich ritual life within their social circles. Their active participation in all life cycle rituals is most palpable through the synthesis of textual and visual materials. Read together, these sources highlight how women experienced the rites that marked the different stages of their lives through the songs they sang and the clothes they wore.

Women's expertise in life cycle customs came to light when Moshe Wachter's stepdaughter prepared to get married one spring Sunday in Worms. Normally, on the afternoon before the wedding, the bride went to the bathhouse, escorted by a procession of married and single women and by jesters. The women likely sang and danced as they accompanied her to and from the bathhouse; later that evening, the bride would immerse in the ritual bath. The shamash formally announced the procession as he called down the street of the Judengasse in Yiddish, *"zum Bad fuhren,"* alerting the entire community that the bride was being escorted to the bathhouse.[76] Yet, on this particular occasion, Rabbi Moses Samson Bacharach hesitated. Venturing that it was unseemly to hold such a procession on Shabbat, he also questioned whether the other rites held on the day before the wedding, specifically an exchange of gifts between the bride and the groom, could be held, as gift giving was normally forbidden on Shabbat. Yet, Bacharach originally came from farther east, and he wanted to rule in accordance with local tradition. He therefore turned to the elderly women of the community to ask whether, in previous years, those who married on Sunday had held these ceremonies on Shabbat. "They said it had always been that way, and that some of the current community members had had their weddings on Sunday, and the announcement *zum Bad fuhren* had been called out. When the rabbi heard this, and knew that it had been this way, he changed his mind and his will in the face of others' wishes."[77] Gifts were exchanged, and the call to the bathhouse was proclaimed on Shabbat afternoon in the Judengasse.

Bacharach opted to determine the local custom by asking the elderly women because women played a central role in this communal life cycle event, as in others. While most Jews in Worms wed on a Wednesday and performed the aforementioned rites on Tuesday, the elderly women remembered couples from among their friends and neighbors who had married on Sunday.[78] They had participated in the processions and the festivities and, therefore, served as guardians of communal knowledge and custom.

Life Cycle Rituals as Social Occasions

Women celebrated milestones alongside men (though separately from them) in indoor and outdoor communal spaces. They also held their own female rituals, which presented them with opportunities to socialize.[79] The Shabbat

Spinholz ceremony was one of many parties at which women gathered on their own to celebrate a bride and her impending nuptials.[80] The week before the wedding in particular was filled with a frenzy of different parties, all of which contributed to the expense, and many of which were single-sex gatherings. Some, like the procession to the bathhouse described above, included married women. Others, such as the *Suppe Mahl* (a meal celebrated seven days before the wedding), were limited to the bride and her single friends.[81]

Most prominent among the premarital festivities reserved for women alone was the hair braiding ceremony on the day of the wedding.[82] Our sources afford diverse glimpses into the ceremony, although none were written by any of the women who participated. Christian Hebraist Paul Christian Kirchner described how at midday of the wedding day, the bride's hair was braided by married women. Although he mocks the ceremony, claiming that the Jews "think they are following God's example, as He braided Eve's hair, sang before her, and danced with her in paradise," he claims to have "seen this ceremony once from beginning to end; I saw the women who braid, singing in *teutsch jüdischer* [Yiddish, lit. "German-Jewish"] language. The bride sits among them in veiled face and mourns her virginity, so strongly . . . but not truly, for at the turn of a moment they throw away the veil and laugh heartily, and how can it be otherwise, because true mourning must have an object."[83] Perhaps Kirchner or Jugendres, the artist who illustrated the second edition of his volume, did witness this women's ceremony, as they had attended so many other Jewish events in Fürth to illustrate the book. Juspe Schammes, who does not claim to have been at the ceremony, provides additional details that highlight the communal elements of the ceremony. As he did with the procession to the bathhouse, the shamash would call out, *die kallah flechten gehen* (the bride is going to have her hair braided). All the women would attend this ceremony, and both men and women were informed by the sexton's call that this final ceremony was to take place; in just a few hours' time, they would join the couple at the wedding ceremony. The communal nature of this ritual was emphasized by the first woman honored with braiding the bride's hair: not a relative or a friend but the rabbi's wife:

> The rabbanit, the rabbi's wife, comes first to the bride's house and starts with this commandment of braiding. This is the custom: all of the women come in jackets, those who are closer [in kinship] in a Shabbat jacket, and the others in a weekday jacket, and the bride sits on a chair, and on her lap is a large bowl, and, [using] it, they honor the bride; her relatives, and whoever

wants to, [gives] whatever she wants: this one a ring, and that one a silver spoon, and this one a scarf, and that one a coin, and this one whatever amount of money, and the like. They throw all this into the bowl, and everything is recorded on a note, and all of this is during the braiding. The women sing during the braiding, songs that are written for the bride and groom.[84]

This description by Juspe Schammes goes into great detail about the Einwurf (showering of bridal gifts). The gifts were "written down immediately in a note, so they could be remembered."[85] Such lists were particularly useful if the marriage were to be dissolved in the first two years, at which point the gifts would be returned to each family.

Kalleh lider, the genre of Yiddish songs sung at the hair braiding ceremony and other marital celebrations, also have been preserved both in manuscript and in print.[86] Some wedding songs were copied into the manuscript Menahem (Mendlin) Katz commissioned for his daughter Serlina in sixteenth-century Italy.[87] Some women sang kalleh lider, mentioning the women's commandments; others sang about true love. The concluding paragraph of one *lid* demonstrates the jovial and even risqué tones of these songs: "We sang this song with joy / To honor the groom and dear bride and other fine people / Come here now, the time has come / That the groom and bride must get to bed."[88] Although women likely sang this song at the wedding party before the community escorted the groom and bride home for bed, it nevertheless captures the merriment of the celebration, tinged also with jokes and anticipation of the couple's impending sexual union.[89] These songs and descriptions of celebration provide the sounds and atmosphere of women's joyous gatherings.[90]

Texts from custom books similarly show the central role played by women at communal nuptial gatherings. Juspe Schammes provides perhaps the richest narrative of pre- and postmarital celebrations in Worms, beginning with the announcement of the couple's engagement and continuing through the week after the wedding. Marriages were celebrated not only by the family but by the entire community, often in public communal spaces. In Worms, the formal engagement was usually made at the home of the rabbi and was followed by a festive meal hosted by the groom's family. Juspe Schammes is careful to note women's roles: in some cases, the bride, accompanied by her relatives and neighbors, walked to the home of the groom to wish his family a formal mazel tov.[91]

Local variations in marriage celebrations were pervasive among both Jews and Christians, particularly when it came to the many parties that were not binding according to Jewish law.[92] In sixteenth-century Italy, for example,

FIG. 11.10. Couples in marriage dance. The inscription below reads: "*di tantz zu der Breileft.*" Yiddish *minhogim* manuscript, sixteenth century.

two manuscripts depict mixed dancing as a feature of wedding parties. In Juspe Schammes's Worms, dancing took place outside the Braut Haus, the communal hall in which couples married, located next to the synagogue in the center of the Judengasse. Both women and men danced throughout the week of the wedding. Sometimes, their arrival was deliberately staggered according to marital status and gender, so both danced, but they did so separately. First, the bride and her friends held a procession to the Braut Haus. Later, they were joined by married women and, after that, by the groom and the men of the community. The alternating appearance of guests according to gender and marital status at this party symbolized the girlhood the bride was leaving and the life of a married woman she was entering.[93]

The singing, dancing, and processions of friends, family, and neighbors in the very heart of the Jewish street highlight the communal dimension of life cycle celebrations. In Worms, the entire week was filled with gatherings large and small in the homes of the couple, in the streets, and outside the Braut Haus. Some of these gatherings were single sex, providing occasions for the women and/or young girls of the community to celebrate alongside the bride, while the men celebrated along with the groom.[94] Others, such as the procession to the marriage canopy, where the rabbis oversaw the formal Jewish

FIG. 11.11. Groom hurls the glass against the *Treustein* before the bride. Kirchner, *Jüdisches Ceremoniel*, 1726.

legal ceremony, included both men and women. Kirchner explains that after the bride was veiled, "she is led to the synagogue door next to the groom where the ceremony will take place. Someone goes before her with two glasses of wine, over which the blessings will be said."[95] Both women and men can be seen in the images of the procession, of the official marriage ceremony, and of the groom's throwing a glass at the *Treustein*, a special stone on the synagogue exterior. The shattering of the glass symbolized the destruction of the Temples in Jerusalem and concluded the marriage ceremony.

Celebrating the Brit

The *brit* (circumcision ceremony), although a male ritual, provided ample opportunity for women to celebrate both with the community and on their own. The women washed the baby and dressed him, transporting him to and from his mother's side, as, in this region and period, the mother remained at home while the circumcision took place in the synagogue. The Jewish women of Worms demonstrated their deep commitment to this role when Taltze Blin gave birth on Wednesday, July 6, 1666. The following Sunday, the widow Faiglin, who lived in the Blin home, died of a contagious illness. This was quickly followed by the death of the baby's sister, who was buried on Tuesday. The family quarantined, and the rabbi, who had been selected as the mohel, refused to circumcise the baby. Juspe Schammes himself decided that the rite should not be delayed, and although all the other mohalim refused, he arranged for the baby to be brought out from his mother, "naked as he had been when he exited his mother's womb." Despite the danger, the women washed the baby outside of the home, dressing him as they would any other baby. After the circumcision, the women returned the baby to his mother, "for she was already bitterly crying for the baby, and also because the milk in her breasts was heavy, which caused her great pain. Thereupon, the women did as she wished and gave her the baby."[96]

One manuscript from Hamburg of customs for circumcisions noted, "Sometimes the women drink before they bring the baby to the synagogue."[97] This suggests a female celebration ritual when women performed final preparations for the baby and drank, likely to his and his mother's good health, before carrying him through the streets to the synagogue.

By transporting baby boys to and from synagogue for circumcision, women played an important role in the communal ritual. On the morning of the circumcision, they came to fetch the baby. To do so, Juspe Schammes explained, they left the synagogue services in the middle of morning prayer, as they already had been praying with the rest of the community. The wife of the *sandek* (the man who held the baby during circumcision), the wife of the mohel who would circumcise the baby, and several other women departed from the synagogue, setting out for the house of the parturient. "They prepare[d] everything the child would need" and then carried him to the women's section, where the sandeket passed him into the men's synagogue through the narrow door between the men's and women's sections.[98] The circumcision ceremony was one of the occasions on which the narrow door bridging the men's and women's sections of the synagogue was opened; the women could stand at the entrance and observe the ceremony, later retrieving the baby and carrying him home (see plate 3). While they did not enter the men's section where the actual circumcision was performed, they were present as observers and had a role to play in the ceremony.

In some instances, women's presence at a ceremony is made manifest only through visual materials, particularly those from Hebraist works. Although custom books in print and manuscript do not refer to women's presence at the *pidyon ha-ben* ceremony (the rite redeeming a first-born son), both parents appear at the center of the ceremony in Kirchner's volume.[99] Both texts and visual materials confirm women's active participation in many communal rites.

Women's Clothing

Women's experiences across life cycle events were affected by the clothing they wore to mark the occasion. Then, as now, attire demarcated status, whether socioeconomic or stage of life, and life cycle rituals leveraged costumes to broadcast symbolic meaning.[100] When a woman returned to the synagogue after giving birth, she arrived wearing shrouds over her clothing, which she then removed. This was a tangible symbol of her brush with death, the danger she had faced in childbirth, and her resumption of her normal routine.[101]

Mourners' clothing was used in two religious rites that disbanded marriages. Upon divorcing, both the husband and wife arrived at the ceremony wearing headgear designated for mourners: for men, a wide head covering that extended around the neck, and for women, a veil and special jacket.[102] A man who was performing halitzah with his sister-in-law wore the same mourning garb.[103] The halitzah ceremony was a rite performed when a man died childless. If the deceased husband had brothers, according to biblical law, one of the brothers, the *yabam* (levir), was obligated to marry the widow to maintain the legacy of the dead man. Though halitzah was not a divorce, it similarly severed the tie between two families.

Divorce, which could only be initiated by the husband, was performed in front of a rabbinic court. In Worms, the rabbi personally reviewed the bill of divorce issued by the husband and penned by the scribe. An old medieval tradition stipulated that the rabbis from the surrounding communities of Speyer and Mainz be notified.[104] Normally composed carefully, with names spelled precisely to ensure that it was clear whose marriage was being dissolved, the bill of divorce was thrown at the divorcée in what was sometimes a public ceremony.[105] The veiled woman who appears in the center of Hebraist Johannes Christoph Bodenschatz's depiction of divorce donned mourning garb as a symbol of the death of the union between the couple.[106]

One unusual and striking example from Worms brings the sartorial aspect of the ceremony into sharp relief. In 1640, an unnamed couple faced a dilemma: the husband was extremely ill, and he wished to conditionally divorce his wife so that if he died, she did not have to undergo halitzah.[107] Clearly, the

FIG. 11.12. *Halitzah* ceremony (enlarged detail). Woman garbed in mourning kneels at center. Kirchner, *Jüdisches Ceremoniel*, 1726.

couple was childless, and he had one or more brothers. The bill of divorce was issued, with a separate document indicating that the divorce was conditional upon this man's dying by a certain date. In this instance, however, the man who was "divorcing" his wife "was not wearing mourner's clothing and headgear; because of illness-induced weakness, he was sitting in his bed in his robe, without any clothing, and his wife was also standing in her clothing and scarf, without a [special] jacket, because of the emotional distress, lest he lose his mind, because they loved one another very much."[108] While this man wished to provide for his wife by protecting her from the halitzah ceremony, it was feared, nevertheless, that seeing her in mourners' garb would upset both parties. The visceral experience of wearing mourning garb was a central element of the divorce rite, one that, in this instance, was deemed too upsetting to a couple very much in love and not wishing to separate.

Even after this conditional divorce, the woman tended to her erstwhile husband, arranged his bed, and cooked for him. Yet, when he died a few months later, the conditional bill of divorce had expired. Ultimately, despite her husband's best intentions, she was forced to undergo the halitzah ritual. His desire to preemptively release her from that obligation could have stemmed from two motivations. First, a childless widow who did not undergo halitzah would remain chained to her brother-in-law; this could have devastating results if he lived far away, had converted to Christianity, or simply chose to extort her financially in exchange for granting her freedom.[109] Second, the halitzah ceremony may have been somewhat humiliating. A childless widow, already mourning her husband, came accompanied by several friends to a rabbinic court or a synagogue courtyard, veiled in her widow's garb.[110] Her brother-in-law, also wearing the long hat of the male mourner, donned a special shoe with extremely long shoelaces, which would be loosened by his sister-in-law. Juspe Schammes noted that he was to cut his toenails and scrub his feet the day before (see fig. 11.12).[111] After reciting formulaic statements that condemned him for not carrying on his brother's name, the woman loosened his shoe and spat at him. Like the divorce ceremony, this ceremony could be attended by a wider audience. While the couple may not have wished to wed, the public severance of this tie and the finality of the deceased's lineage just months after his death was likely painful to his widow and to his brother.

The symbolic meaning of mourning clothing was so great that one man turned to Rabbi Judah Mehler in the seventeenth century to inquire whether he should don mourning clothing when his son's fianceé died.[112] Though there was no formal tie, a meaningful relationship had been lost, and clothing was a means to convey that loss. In eighteenth-century Fürth, in-laws and grandparents also donned mourners' clothing, emphasizing the importance of the extended Jewish family and networks of kinship. Similarly, on the occasion of a wedding, celebratory Shabbat clothing was worn by a wide range of relatives, who were then visibly marked as more intimately linked to the happy couple than were other guests.[113]

Special clothing also could be used to convey other issues of status. In Metz, a virginal bride donned a special head covering for the Shabbat Spinholz party held on the Shabbat prior to her wedding. Widows celebrated the party without that headgear.[114] This was one of many symbolic distinctions that drew more and less subtle attention to a woman's sexual status before the couple's union was to take place. From Juspe Hahn of Frankfurt, we learn that in some communities, it was customary to recite a special blessing when the bride was a virgin.[115] Some parties were reserved for brides who were marrying for the first time. Such was the case with the *Mayen* celebration before the wedding day when the bride and groom were led with processions to the wedding hall, where participants pelted them with wheat as a symbol and blessing for fertility.[116] Remarrying widows did not hold this celebration. The ritual emphasis on virginity was echoed in material culture as well. Narrow glasses were used for the wedding of a virgin, while wider ones were used for a widow or divorcée, a material difference that jested about women's bodies and sexual pasts.[117] Such traditions and bawdy songs were common in Christian communities as well.[118]

Regulating Life Cycle Gatherings

Communal leaders sought to limit the scope of lavish weddings and other life cycle celebrations, issuing sumptuary laws (laws regulating conspicuous consumption) to limit guests and expenditures. These regulations were enacted both to ward off internal friction and to ensure that Jews did not arouse the ire of Christian neighbors and leaders. Sumptuary laws frequently highlight the ubiquitous presence of women at life cycle celebrations, as the laws sought to limit the number of male and female guests.[119] Communal leaders in Altona, for example, aimed to limit the circle of women who would send confections for a wedding or when a baby was born.[120] Read against the grain, these sources make clear that women also baked and sent a variety of sweets as a means to celebrate with one another.

These ordinances, though entirely prescriptive, document women's coming together on a variety of life cycle occasions. Regulations from Prague, for example, forbade all women other than a mother, sister, mother-in-law, and daughter-in-law (presumably of the parents) from attending a bar mitzvah celebration.[121] These same rules sought to limit which women would bake for a bride and groom. Perhaps most fascinating was the demand to limit women's presence in the synagogue on a variety of occasions: a bar mitzvah, an engagement, or the Shabbat before and after a wedding, as well as when a parturient returned to the synagogue for the first time.[122] "No women shall gather to wish 'mazel tov' on these occasions . . . for the cries of the women make it impossible to hear the Torah reading or to pray with devotion."[123] The ordinance sought to limit the list of attendees to close relatives. Instead, women could offer felicitations on the street or in the couple's homes. The rule further admonished that even those who gathered in homes to wish mazel tov "cannot send or distribute baked goods or other sweet foods, only coffee."[124] In Halberstadt, to curb the expense and levity at a party following a circumcision, communal leaders attempted to ban women from attending the ritual. A later regulation, however, confirms that this attempt was an abysmal failure. Halberstadt's women refused to be excluded from ceremonies: "That [older] takkanah that prohibited any women from attending any circumcision in our community has been rescinded in order to maintain truth and peace."[125] Its failure reiterates what is apparent from multiple texts and images: early modern Jewish women led robust ritual lives, celebrating both with other women and alongside the men of the community throughout the seasons of the year and the shifting rhythms of their lives. In these ordinances, the leaders acknowledged the limits of their attempts to curb women's celebrations and the fact that, despite their efforts, the women of the community were going to celebrate with one another.

Conclusion

EACH WEEK, Leah Hindchen Scheuer (d. 1773) furnished wine, oil, and flour to Frankfurt's poor and sick so that they could prepare for Shabbat. The sorority she oversaw also provided them with firewood. Born to an elite family in Frankfurt and married to one of its parnassim, Leah Hindchen led a life intimately bound together with the lives of Jews from all socioeconomic classes at all stages of life.[1] From her youth through her old age, she served as a midwife and a healer who distributed medicine to the poor for free. Tending to the sick and the deceased through her membership in the burial society, she also supported yeshivah students both financially and through her own hospitality.[2]

In many ways, Leah Hindchen is emblematic of women of her status. Her agency at home is firmly documented in communal records. A devoted mother to her two sons, she was remembered fondly for having served as a role model and teacher to her grandchildren.[3] Like other female entrepreneurs, from the lowly vagrants who sewed head coverings to the wealthy Madame Kaulla, Leah Hindchen also worked "with intelligence and wisdom" to support her family financially.[4]

No Jewish community functioned without its ba'alot bayit, who were community members in the fullest sense. Some, like Leah Hindchen, stand out as informal community leaders, deeply committed to and involved in the community and immersed in many of its essential ventures (see plate 35). Every community had at least one midwife and a women's burial society; in every kehillah, women helped establish and maintain communal institutions, including local yeshivot. Leah Hindchen's contributions were deeply entrenched in the daily needs of the community; she is even credited with helping converts to Judaism. "She served God and man night and day, gladdened to perform good deeds as one is to find precious treasure."[5] Most of the activities in which she was engaged were normative among female community members. Hundreds of women across early modern communities frequented synagogue day and night, summer and winter; they devotedly fashioned candles to light the synagogue and adopted penitential fasts as a pious practice, as she did. Many sought coveted memberships in women's sororities, working tirelessly in those communal roles that were accessible to women.

Although she left no writings of her own behind, Leah Hindchen was "renowned" for her medical knowledge and her piety, as well as for her Torah learning. "She was . . . a darshanit (public speaker) . . . occupied daily with the Bible and the commentaries of Rashi and others; she always guided her children and grandchildren in the proper path, and to open their hearts to scripture, Mishnah, and Gemara [Talmud]. She herself taught them Bible and brought them to fear of Heaven."[6]

Leah's mastery of these sources undoubtedly came from her mother, Miriam, the daughter of Rabbi Aaron Teomim of Worms and later of Kraków.[7] Celebrated as a rabbanit, Miriam was similarly remembered for having taught her five children to study the scriptures.[8] Not all women possessed the level of knowledge that Leah Hindchen did, but she was by no means unique, as evidenced by many nearly identical phrases in her and her mother's respective entries in Frankfurt's Memorbuch. They are among dozens of women from rabbinic families who were recognized and praised in communal records for having attained a high level of Jewish literacy. As she was a teacher of her own family members and of other women, moreover, Leah Hindchen's literacy filtered down to others, who benefited from her proficiency in Jewish sources and from her medical skills. What we have seen in the early modern period are three hundred years during which women were full partners in their own gendered way in the life of Jewish communities. Their robust and colorful participation in so many aspects of daily Jewish life, vividly captured on the leaves of communal logbooks and proudly etched on tombstones, has been almost completely ignored by scholars until now.

Women like Leah Hindchen, Glikl, and Bella Perlhefter lived in a deeply gendered society and were shaped, and constrained, by it in many ways. Their existence was intensely embodied. They and their contemporaries did not produce rabbinic literature or mystical texts; they could never be elected leaders of the general kahal. Rather than focus on a catalog of ways in which early modern Jewish women did not adhere to the male model of intellectual and institutional contributions, we advocate for a new model, one that views women as creative and enterprising actors in constituting a lively and thriving form of Jewish life that sustained European Jews for three centuries. That way of life was the kehillah, and we must take into account the gendered and general spheres in which women acted fully. The contours of the kehillah have been outlined here briefly and elsewhere in greater detail.[9] It was a fully traditional world, filled with creative passion for the Jewish religion and its lifeways. The kehillah allowed for self-expression by women in multiple forms. The evidence we have gathered here is only a surviving remnant of that multifarious world of text and textile, food and clothing, homes and hearths.

One cannot consider early modern Jewish women's lives without taking into account the ways in which the rise of print and recordkeeping changed their ability to participate in communal life. The crucial recordkeeping function of the kahal, so central for our book, ceased as the states took over these roles. Emancipatory changes arrived slowly over the course of the nineteenth century. Under the emancipatory arrangement, Jews owed their primary civic obligations to the state: they paid taxes directly as individuals rather than through the kehillah, and the state collected vital statistics and provided access to courts of justice. During this time, the structure of the kehillah eroded and, in some cases, shriveled into voluntary associations of Jews centered on synagogues and cultural centers. The price for this integration was the disappearance of a holistic Jewish life and culture that drew much from its own palette.[10]

These changes allowed Jews greater mobility as they migrated from village to urban settings, from economic margins to bourgeois prosperity, and from old world to new.[11] Opportunities opened for Jewish men as they attained citizenship and entered universities, liberal professions, and elite society. As Marion Kaplan has argued, these changes were experienced very differently by Jewish women.[12]

Our work has convinced us that the historical trajectory of Jewish women has been mischaracterized and misunderstood. Their narrative has been swept up in a teleological arc of modernity and Jewish history that does not accurately pertain to them. The dominant historiographic narrative of Jews, based primarily on the western Ashkenazi model of ghetto and emancipation, has long been criticized for omitting the eastern European and the Sephardi Jewish experiences.[13] The term "early modern" contributes to this confusion, as (despite protestations to the contrary) it assigns primacy to modernity, however defined, and it imprints the sixteenth through the eighteenth centuries with anticipatory character.[14] The world of women we have presented in *A Woman Is Responsible for Everything* does not fit this mold. The prevailing narrative ignores three centuries of creative and participatory roles for women within the Jewish community. We have argued that the kehillah must be seen as a critical framework for understanding early modern Jewish history and that women's experiences within it are an integral component of that history. The early modern period may very well have been the era in which Jewish women attained the greatest degree of Jewish literacy and communal agency until contemporary times.

ACKNOWLEDGMENTS

THIS BOOK was born in the archives. As we sat side-by-side, poring over communal records, working on our individual projects, an entire world of women leaped out at us from the worn brown folios. Our joint interest in and collaboration on Jewish women's history started years ago. In 2004, at Queens College CUNY in New York, we developed and co-taught a course on Jewish women in premodern times. Primary sources in English that we could read with our students were scarce, and we began mining material from our own research, translating texts to read and analyze in class. Searching through our respective files, we were struck by the vast array and tremendous depth of sources about Jewish women's lives we encountered in our research. As the years passed, we each pursued other projects, although we continued to note and transcribe additional materials about women's lives that we shared with one another.

During these two decades, our shared sense of discovery sustained our project through tumultuous periods in our lives. It bridged a transatlantic divide, family joys and sorrows, and professional projects and obligations. The strength of our interest sustained our research in the face of numerous other commitments, not to mention a global pandemic and catastrophic war. The joy of discovery inherent in the project inspired us to persevere through it all. But we could not have completed this project on our own. Many institutions, technological advances, and individuals made this book possible. We cannot do full justice to them all for fear of exceeding our word count, but our debt remains, and we hope the work itself justifies their generosity to us.

The lion's share of our textual sources was held at the Central Archives for the History of the Jewish People in Jerusalem. Visiting the reading room of the Central Archives was a unique experience, in many ways ideal for researchers who seek to delve deeply into communal records. The knowledge and generosity of the staff is unparalleled. Over the years, more than one director of the archives leaned over our shoulders as we leafed through the pages stored in file folders. Glancing at the pink call slip tucked into the file, they inquired about what we were reading and why. They, and the wonderful archivists who focus on the regions we study, subsequently suggested to us additional files that might be of interest, sometimes calling or writing to us after stumbling across an as-yet-uncataloged communal record of immense value to our project. The generosity of the staff who made materials accessible to us helped us render visible the many Jewish women whose traces are scattered across the archives' holdings. Special thanks to the current director, Yochai ben Ghedalia, and the former director, Hadassah Assouline, as well as Inka Arroyo Antezana, Denise Rein, Pnina Younger, Tami Sisel, and Eli ben Yosef.

We were also privileged to work in other archives and rare book collections both in New York and in Europe, benefiting there from the knowledge and dedication of archivists and librarians. Many of them shared our enthusiasm as we carefully opened fragile dossiers comprising communal correspondence or as we exclaimed in delight over a colorful image depicting Jewish women's lives. If our book was born in the archives, the archivists and librarians who reliably brought and reserved for us file after file, even when one of us visited an archive only for a few brief days, are its midwives. We thank David Kramer, Joseph J. and Dora Abbell Librarian; Havva Zellner, Director of Library Services; Naomi Steinberger, former Director of Library Services; Mordechai Schwartz, Ripp Schnitzer Librarian for Special Collections; Andrew Katz, Public Services Librarian; and Jerry Schwarzbard, former Librarian for Special Collections of the Library of the Jewish Theological Seminary, who gladly facilitated access to a wealth of treasures. Extra special thanks to Sharon Liberman Mintz, Curator of Jewish Art at the Library of the Jewish Theological Seminary and International Senior Specialist in Judaica, Sotheby's, who brought her vast knowledge of rare illuminated books to bear on our project to its immense benefit. Sharon found new visual treasures for our project and forged connections with owners and collectors we could never have encountered on our own.

Thanks to Dudi Benayem, Librarian of Judaica Manuscripts and Rare Books at Bar-Ilan University; Rahel Fronda, Hebrew and Judaica Deputy Curator at the Bodleian Libraries; Daniella F. Eisenstein, Director, and Alisha Meininghaus, Deputy Director, Jüdisches Museum Franken; Riki Grinberg, Head of Digital Projects and Special Collections, and Keren Barner, Digital Collection Publisher, at the Younes & Soraya Nazarian Library, University of Haifa; Anna Nizza-Caplan, Associate Curator at the Israel Museum; Roman Fischer and Michael Matthaus at the Institut für Stadtgeschichte Frankfurt;

Abigail Rapoport, Curator of Judaica at the Jewish Museum, New York; Daniel Polakovič and Tomáš Krákora at Jewish Museum Prague; Gerald Boennen at Stadtarchiv Worms; the archivists at the Lesesaal in Staatsarchiv Hamburg; and Andreas Lehnardt, Gutenberg University, Mainz.

The Center for Jewish History in New York, and particularly the librarians and archivists at the Leo Baeck Institute and YIVO Institute for Jewish Research, were always gracious in locating materials. Michelle Margolis, Norman E. Alexander Librarian of Jewish Studies at Columbia University Libraries, has cheered us on from the outset and provided invaluable assistance and suggestions, both through illustrations from the library's extensive collections and her work on the Footprints project. Thank you to the digital photography staff at Columbia Libraries, Brianna Gormly, Assistant Director for Preservation, Reformatting, and Metadata, Preservation Division; Andy Moore, David Ortiz, and Jeffrey M. Wayno, Collection Services Librarian, The Burke Library at Union Theological Seminary. Thank you to Hebrew Union College, whose former librarians, Yoram Bitton and Tina Weiss, assisted us in procuring materials.

From the outset, we have benefited from conversations, conferences, and consultations with colleagues and specialists, among them Elisheva Baumgarten, Jay Berkovitz, Neta Bodner, Lynn Broyde, Kimmy Caplan, Ted Fram, Emmanuel Friedheim, Judah Galinsky, Uriel Gellman, Felicitas Heimann-Jelinek, Verena Kasper-Marienberg, Jordan Katz, Michael Korey, Stefan Litt, Claudia Rosenzweig, Moshe Rosman, Pinchas Roth, Emile Schrijver, and Adina Yoffie. Thank you to our students Omer Ahituv, Racheli Berkovitz, Alessia Fontanella, Elisheva Friedlander, Tirtza Rimmel, Hannah Vorchheimer, and Shirel Yair. Menachem Butler has been a good friend and indefatigable supporter of our scholarship and of the academic Jewish enterprise more broadly. We thank our friends and colleagues of the Early Modern Workshop, whose gatherings and website highlighted the importance of new primary sources and became the first platform for some of our translations and interpretations. Our heartfelt gratitude goes to its past and current directors, Magda Teter, Francesca Bregoli, and Joshua Teplitsky.

We wish to acknowledge and applaud the libraries, archives, digitizers, and donors, some of whom remain anonymous, who made it possible for us and so many others to access their materials when we could not visit in person. William Gross, of Tel Aviv, generously shared access and images from his vast collection. The pioneering Institute for Microfilmed Hebrew Manuscripts at the National Library of Israel and its online counterpart, Ktiv, became a gateway to many felicitous discoveries. Thanks to Avraham David, Yisrael Dubitsky, Yitzchack (Chico) Gila, and Alexander Gordin for assistance beyond the call of duty. The Leo Baeck Institute's extraordinary decision to digitize its entire archive was a priceless gift to researchers; the Compact Memory and Yiddish book digitization project at Goethe University Frankfurt, the Braginsky Collection, and the Center for Jewish Art—all embody the highest values of creating accessible collections that can be studied and enjoyed around the world and around the clock. Recent scholarship highlights the creative decisions made by the digitizers; we salute those who remain unnamed but essential to the work of so many scholars.

As our work neared completion, we were fortunate beyond measure to have in Fred Appel, publisher at Princeton University Press, the consummate shepherd for our project. Fred immediately understood its significance. His guidance and counsel as the manuscript traversed the press's multiple stages proved extremely valuable. Two anonymous peer reviewers for the press read the manuscript closely and made multiple valuable suggestions for its improvement. James Collier, Elizabeth Byrd, Erin Davis, and Sherry Howard Salois helped guide a complicated manuscript from raw material to finished product.

A portion of this research was funded by the Israel Science Foundation, grant 1802/18 and grant 2170/23. Thanks to the Israel and Golda Koschitzky Department of Jewish History at Bar-Ilan for its support. Research funds from Columbia University, and the assistance of the Institute for Israel and Jewish Studies for logistical support contributed to the completion of this book. Thank you to Co-Director of Columbia's Institute for Israel and Jewish Studies, Rebecca Kobrin; Director of Administration, Julie Feldman; and Chris Bak-Coleman for your support, advice, and assistance. Some of the research that appears in this book draws on two articles that we coauthored: "Jewish Women in Early Modern Central Europe, 1500–1800," in Federica Francesconi and Rebecca Lynn Winer, editors, *Jewish Women's History From Antiquity to the Present* (Detroit: Wayne State University Press, 2021), 169–192, and "Sacred Sororities: Devotion and Death in Early Modern Jewish Communities," *Jewish History* 36 (2022): 297–336. All other relevant references to our respective previous scholarship may be found in the bibliography.

GLOSSARY

Ba'al bayit (pl., **ba'ale bayit**) Male head of household. Most common unit of communal membership.

Ba'alat bayit (pl., **ba'alot bayit**) Female head of household.

Etrog (pl., **etrogim**) Ritual citrons used on Sukkot holiday.

Gabbay (pl., **gabba'im**) Male official or administrator, often of synagogue and/or charitable fund or society.

Gabbete (pl., **Gabbetes**) (Hebrew variants: gabba'it/gabba'ot). Female official or administrator, often in the synagogue and/or of charitable fund or society.

Get (pl., **gittin**) Bill of divorce.

Hallah (pl., **hallot**) Twisted loaf of bread eaten on Sabbath. A small portion of the dough was burned as a remembrance of the Temple showbread.

Hevrah/hevrah kaddisha (pl., **hevrot**) Society, Sacred society.

Kahal Elected body of lay leaders of the community.

Kehillah (pl., **kehillot**) The Jewish community.

Ketubbah Marriage contract, which, among other clauses, stipulated a financial amount owed to a wife upon dissolution of the marriage by divorce or her husband's death.

M. (=**Marat**) Mrs.

Mahzor (pl., **mahzorim**) Holiday prayer book.

Megillah (pl., **megillot**) Biblical scrolls, including the books of Ruth and Esther.

Melamed (pl., **melamdim**) Schoolteacher or tutor.

Mikveh (pl., **mikva'ot**) Ritual bath required for married women to purify after menstruation.

Minhag (pl., **minhagim**) (Yiddish variants: minhog/minhogim). Custom. Sefer minhagim refers to a book of customs.

Mitzvah (pl., **mitzvot**) Commandments.

Niddah Jewish laws of menstrual purity.

Parnas (pl., **parnassim**) Lay leader of a Jewish community.

Parokhet (pl., **parokhot**) Textile covering for the Ark.

Pesah Passover holiday.

Pinkas (pl., **pinkassim**) Logbook/ledger, often of the community or its officials.

R. (=**Reb**) Mr.

Rosh hodesh New Moon.

Sandek (m.), **sandeket** (f.) Similar to a godparent, who held a newborn baby boy at the circumcision ceremony.

Selihot Penitential prayer.
Shabbat (pl., **Shabbatot**) Jewish Sabbath.
Shamash Communal scribe/notary/official.
Shavu'ot Jewish holiday celebrated seven weeks after Passover.
Siddur (pl., **siddurim**) Prayer books.
Sukkah (pl., **sukkot**) Temporary structure.
Sukkot Tabernacles, Jewish holiday during which meals are taken in the sukkah.
Takkanah (pl., **takkanot**) Communal ordinances and regulations.
Tkhine (pl., **tkhines**) Supplicatory prayers.

NOTES

Introduction

1. NLI, MS 4° 1092, fol. 173. Alt. sp. Trach.
2. MS 4° 1092, fol. 173. See also her tombstone, Horovitz, *Inschriften*, 202.
3. *Ele toldot* database: Rechle (30.XI.1727); Ber (10.I. 1752); Moshe (18.III.1750); Serle (21. III. 1759). The grandchildren are listed on the pages for Moshe and Serle's husband, Eliyah (26. XII. 1746). While Serle is listed as having had one son, this record seems incomplete, as Serle's son was buried next to his brother Leyb (25.V.1803). On Ber, see also ISG, MS H.15.36, 29.
4. See NLI, MS Heb. 2° 662, par. 280. For further information, CAHJP, P302-S1.2, par. 280, n. 108.
5. E. Reiner, "Aliyat 'ha-kehillah ha-gedolah.'"
6. Wunder, *He Is the Sun*, 192.
7. Ozment, *When Fathers Ruled*, 54–55; Wunder, *He Is the Sun*, 92, 191–92.
8. *Meneket Rivkah*, 106. Yiddish section, p. 223: "*es iz als ohn ihr gelegen*."
9. CAHJP, MS AHW 20, fol. 11a. We use the abbreviation "R." to mean *Reb*, a male title slightly more honorable than *kemar* (Mister). Rabbis are referred to as "Rabbi."
10. Raeff, "Well-Ordered Police State," 1221–43.
11. Raeff, "Well-Ordered Police State," 1226.
12. Litt, *Jüdische Gemeindestatuten* (Takkanot Worms, 1684), 98, par. 82.
13. Tal, *Ha-kehillah*, 125.
14. Tal, *Ha-kehillah*, 209.
15. Graupe, *Die Statuten*, vol. 2, 101–2.
16. Graupe, *Die Statuten*, vol. 2, 94–95.
17. NLI, MS Heb. 2° 662, par. 320, publ. in Litt, *Jüdische Gemeindestatuten* (Takkanot Frankfurt, 1764), 53–84.
18. Litt, *Jüdische Gemeindestatuten* (Takkanot Metz, 1769), 356–95; (Takkanot Fürth, 1770), 136–273.
19. Turniansky, "Old Yiddish Language and Literature," 3.
20. NLI, MS Heb. 2° 662, par. 410.
21. On reading aloud among lower classes and women, see Chartier, "Leisure," 103–120 (on reading), 33–38 (on music and exposure to text).
22. Braginsky, MS 344 (Vienna, 1725), fols. 26r–27r.
23. Throughout this book, when we refer to "Glikl" without any additional modifiers, it is to her that we are referring.

24. Our goal here is not to survey the evolution of women's history or gender studies but, rather, to stake out space for a forgotten chapter in Jewish history. Some of the pioneering works include Scott, "Gender: A Useful Category of Historical Analysis"; Lerner, *Creation of Patriarchy*; Bock, *Women in European History*.

25. For two examples from the study of early modern Europe, see Shepard, *Meanings of Manhood*; Wiesner-Hanks, *Gendered Temporalities*.

26. J. Katz, "Nisu'im ve-hayye ishut." We refer readers to the recent translation by Jonathan Karp in Karp and Trivellato, *Classic Essays*, 26–73.

27. Selma Stern's essay, "Woman of the Ghetto," is based almost completely on prescriptive sources.

28. J. Katz, *Tradition and Crisis*, transl. Cooperman.

29. See the various translations and introductions listed in Glikl, *Memoirs* (2019), 35; Roth, *Doña Gracia*; Harrán, *Sarra Copia Sullam*; Westwater, *Sara Copia Sullam*.

30. For a bibliography of medieval Jewish women, see Tallan, "Medieval Jewish Women." Elisheva Baumgarten's *Beyond the Elite* research project shed light on daily life in the Middle Ages. See, e.g., E. Baumgarten et al., *Jewish Daily Life*.

31. Goitein, in *A Mediterranean Society*, vol. 3, also dealt with issues of family.

32. The works by the authors listed here can be found in the bibliography.

33. Ruderman, *Early Modern Jewry*, 16. Ruderman reaffirms this position in a later article and explicitly states that while the topic of Jewish women is "significant," it is "less so" for a discussion of the early modern period because "the most significant changes in the status of Jewish women emerge in the modern, not the early modern era." Ruderman, "Looking Backward," 1097.

34. In her recent book on medieval Jewish women, Sarah Ifft Decker accepts that women's history is one of stasis, "continuity more than change. . . . Readers should not therefore assume that the lives of Jewish women looked drastically different from what we have seen . . . after the date of 1500, which is where for the sake of convenience, this book ends." Ifft Decker, *Jewish Women*, 117.

35. E. Baumgarten, *Biblical Women*, inventively leans on biblical commentary to extract lessons about the "daily lived experience" of Jewish women, since many non-elite Jews left no texts behind.

36. Wiesner-Hanks, *Women and Gender*; Rublack, *Gender in Early Modern German*; Ostovich and Sauer, *Reading Early Modern Women*.

37. Roper, *Holy Household*; Marshall, *Women in Reformation*; Harrington, *Reordering Marriage*; Karant-Nunn, *Reformation of Ritual*; Strasser, "Cloistering," 221–46; Diefendorf, *From Penitence to Charity*; Herzig, "Reformations," 32–47.

38. See, e.g., women's religious communities in Leonard, *Nails in the Wall*.

39. Rublack, introduction to *Gender in Early Modern German History*, 5.

40. Natalie Zemon Davis, *Women on the Margins*, saw Glikl as the ideal Jewish comparand to contemporary female Christian writers.

41. On the role of nuns in the state-building process, see Strasser, "Early Modern Nuns," 538–47.

Chapter One. Life in the Kehillah

1. Archives of the Jewish Museum in Prague, Pinkas synagogue collection, Pinkas of the Pinkas synagogue, 1601–1845, sine no.

2. On the structure of the Pinkas synagogue's women's galleries, see Krautheimer, *Bate knesset*, 168–72.

3. Archives of the Jewish Museum in Prague, Pinkas synagogue collection, Pinkas of the Pinkas synagogue, fol. 39r.

4. Baron, *Jewish Community*, vol. 2, 115.

5. Several scholars have pointed to Jewish women's communal roles. For Italian women, see Adelman, "Italian Jewish Women," 52–55. Keil, "Public Roles of Jewish Women," 324, argued that in fourteenth-century Regensburg, a woman served in a role equivalent to parnas. However, the documents suggest she was a wealthy widow with much economic clout but do not place her in a formal administrative or legislative role. See Bastian and Widemann, *Regensburger Urkundbuch*, vol. 2, 45, 66–67, 134–35, 275, 411–12. We similarly were unable to locate archival evidence to support a reference in Hakohen Fishman, *Sare ha-me'ah*, vol. 4, pt. 5, pp. 5–6, to a woman who signed a rabbinical contract in Amsterdam.

6. For a general overview see Hills, *Architecture and the Politics of Gender*.

7. For Poland, Rosman, "Jewish Women," 202–3.

8. For a recent discussion of women's sections in synagogues, particularly in Eastern Europe, see Levin, "Architecture of Gender"; Stiefel, *Jews and the Renaissance of Synagogue Architecture*, 7–60. The sources refer variously to women's sections as *ezrat nashim* and *bet knesset nashim*.

9. Kirchner, *Jüdisches Ceremoniel*, 106–7. The engravings by Sebastian Jugendres were based primarily on the synagogues in Fürth.

10. For medieval references, see Grossmann, *Pious and Rebellious*, 181–82. For later examples, see Zborowski and Herzog, *Life Is with People*, 54.

11. See Chovav, *Maidens*, 369–71. We do not agree with Chovav's interpretation of several epitaphs as referring to a firzogerin. We interpret all but one of these epitaphs as referring to women's prayer more broadly, in line with many similar entries in Memorbücher from a wide range of communities. Note also Chovav's discussion of women's prayers on Tishah be-Av (371–372). For a woman who may have been a firzogerin farther east, see Weissler, *Voices of the Matriarchs*, 197n24. Weissler interprets the word *dabranit* (speaker), found in a rabbinic approbation for Ellus bat Mordekhai of Slutsk's Yiddish translation of liturgy, as firzogerin.

12. Muneles, *Ketovot*, 214, tombstone no. 114. Cited also in Chovav, *Maidens*, 370.

13. Muneles, *Ketovot*, 16, tombstone no. 61.

14. JMP, MS 148.

15. Litt, *Protokollbuch*, 170, par. 69.

16. The mikveh in Friedberg was next to the synagogue.

17. Bodleian, MS Opp. 4° 953. The letter was published in Yaari, "Shene Kuntresim Me-Eretz Israel."

18. CAHJP, MS AHW 31.1a, fol. 11.

19. Litt, *Jüdische Gemeindestatuten* (Takkanot Halberstadt, 1741), 112, par. 16.

20. Litt, *Jüdische Gemeindestatuten* (Takkanot Metz, 1769), 394, par. 123.

21. See, e.g., Fram, *Window*, Appendix 5.

22. A similar dynamic may be seen in Prague regarding the women's burial society. See in this volume, chapter 3.

23. Litt, *Jüdische Gemeindestatuten* (Takkanot Fürth, 1770), 232, par. 325; 255, par. 420; 271, par. 503.

24. The charity logbook from eighteenth-century Worms accounts for funds collected in the coffers outside the men and women's sanctuaries. CAHJP, MS D-W03-662.

25. JMP, MS 113, fol. 30v.

26. Tal, *Ha-kehillah*, 172, par. 45.

27. Tal, *Ha-kehillah*, 172, par. 46.

28. Tal, *Ha-kehillah*, 166, par. 15.

29. Jerusalem, Karlin-Stolin, MS 41, fol. 117.

30. NLI, MS Heb. 4° 1092, fol. 249. The same was true of Christian women, who sewed vestments and made candles for parish churches. See French, *Good Women of the Parish*, 17–49.

31. Epidat database, wrm-1088.

32. Epidat database, wls-614. For additional examples from Amsterdam, see Tal, *Ha-kehillah*, 173, pars. 51–52.

33. Fashioning parokhot out of women's garments is a theme that recurs in responsa as well. R. Judah Mehler discussed whether one could craft a parokhet from a skirt that had been owned by a non-Jewish woman. Jerusalem, Karlin-Stolin, MS 41, fol. 158.

34. See JMP, MS 113, fol. 30v; JMP, MS. 89, fol. 24v; see also Greenblatt, *To Tell Their Children*, 66.

35. NLI, MS Heb. 4° 1092, fol. 163.

36. See, e.g., JTS, MS 8875, pars. 645, 753.

37. Meisl, *Pinkas kehillat Berlin*, 74, par. 14; similarly, 75 par. 3; NLI, MS Heb. 4° 928, fol. 15v.

38. CAHJP, MS AHW 14, par. 50.

39. On ritual baths in the medieval period, see Bodner "Romanesque."

40. D. Kaplan, "To Immerse Their Wives," 268–73.

41. CAHJP, MS AHW 20, fol. 20a.

42. Gemeente Amsterdam Stadsarchief, 1.1.1.1.1-4, Register van resoluties van Parnassim, 1, Protocol 1 (12 Tamus 5468–14 Ab 5497), 30 Jun 1708–11 Aug 1737, fol. 167.

43. Hildesheimer, *Pinkas kehillat Schnaittach*, 202.

44. See the discussion in CAHJP, MS AHW 14, par. 90. See also D. Kaplan, "To Immerse Their Wives," 259–63.

45. In the medieval period, escorting immersing women was not regulated, although at times midwives performed this task. See Baumgarten, *Mothers and Children*, 47.

46. Oliel-Grausz, "Communication and Community," 119.

47. CAHJP, MS AHW 85a, par. 339.

48. The seventeenth-century description of the ritual by Juspe Schammes of Worms indicates that female friends and neighbors, among them the rabbi's wife, accompanied the woman to the synagogue. See Schammes, *Minhagim de-k"k Warmaisa*, vol. 2, par. 288.

49. D. Kaplan, *Patrons and Their Poor*, 55–58.

50. French, *Good Women of the Parish*, 19–37. Note the discussion of pastors' wives, which parallels the above discussion of the wives of Jewish communal officials.

51. Schammes, *Minhagim de-k"k Warmaisa*, vol. 1, par. 186.

52. Schammes, *Minhagim de-k"k Warmaisa*, vol. 1, par. 186.

53. Schammes, *Minhagim de-k"k Warmaisa*, vol. 2, par. 284.

54. NLI MS Heb. 2° 662, par. 6.

55. Duckesz, *Hakhme AH"U*, 1.

56. See Kasper-Marienberg and Kaplan, "Nourishing," 25–26, on alternatives that developed in the eighteenth century, when some residents were loath to participate in the *pletten* system.

57. JTS, MS 8875, par. 442.

58. In Altona, the society for caring for orphans was founded in 1766. See CAHJP, MS AHW 17b, fol. 24. See also JTS, MS 10632, for another society for orphans in Amsterdam.

59. NLI, MS Heb. 4° 1092, fol. 493.

60. JTS, MS 8875, par. 606.

61. NLI, MS Heb. 4° 1092, fol. 542. For another example in which education is mentioned, see fol. 374.

62. Epidat database, ffb-45 (1709). The same is true for Shlomo ben Natan Meise (d. 1764), also of Frankfurt, who was noted as having raised orphans in his home and for marrying off a female orphan. Epidat database ffb-278 (1764).

63. J. Bloch, "Le testament," 146–60, based on a manuscript that we consulted in the original. See AIU, MS 423, fol. 5r.

64. Hayim's tombstone in Mannheim was one of a few preserved from the older Jewish cemetery, in which Jews were interred before 1842. The older cemetery was forcibly sold in 1938, and the bodies disinterred and reburied in a mass grave in the newer cemetery. Rebecca's tombstone seemingly did not survive. See Mannheim, Marchivum archives, grave number SGr-11.

65. Emden, *Divre emet*, 12r, par. 5.

66. Kasper-Marienberg and Kaplan, "Nourishing," 8.

67. ISG, MS Criminalia 609.

68. Berkovitz, *Protocols*, 449, no. 42.

69. CAHJP, MS D-Da1-437.

70. Yuval, "Hospices and Their Guests."

71. D. Kaplan, *Patrons and Their Poor*, 38–39, 78–79, 116–17.

72. In seventeenth-century Worms, archival documents refer to a separate men's and women's hospice. See Stadtarchiv Worms, MS 1 B 2024/16. In the eighteenth century, regulations refer to elderly men and women being housed in separate rooms. See CAHJP, MS AHW 25, fol 1a.

73. Administering to the sick was divided along gendered lines even in times of crisis and in makeshift institutions, as is apparent from a list of men and women who were employed to tend to the sick during the 1713 plague in Prague. See Teplitsky, "Order in Crisis."

74. NLI MS Heb. 2° 662, par. 83a.

75. D. Kaplan, *Patrons and their Poor*, 80–81.

76. CAHJP, MS AHW 25, fol. 3a, par. 14.

77. CAHJP, MS AHW 25, fols. 2–3a.

78. Taglicht, *Nachlässe*, 201, no. 163. Like many of the poor, he died "in the Jewish cemetery," which was apparently where the hekdesh was located.

79. Although the rooms in hospices were segregated by sex, this suggests that the attendants were familiar with multiple inhabitants.

80. This tradition carried on: see Taglicht, *Nachlässe*, 240, no. 247, in which locking the effects of a man dying in the hekdesh was done "in the presence of the *Krankenwarters Eheweib* (wife of the sick-care attendant)."

81. Taglicht, *Nachlässe*, 206, no. 173. He said the same for other poor who died there. See, e.g., Taglicht, *Nachlässe*, 207, no. 175.

82. Taglicht, *Nachlässe*, 214, no. 97.

83. On midwives, see also Zinger, *Ba'al ha-shem*, 73–83.

84. Carlebach, "Community, Authority," 8.

85. NLI MS Heb. 4° 1092, fol. 329.

86. *Sefer toldot Adam*, Yiddish takkanot (1745), pars. 10, 11.

87. See, e.g., the references to *hevrah bikkur holim* in Altona's hospice. CAHJP, MS AHW 25, fol. 1a.

88. *Sefer toldot Adam*, Yiddish takkanot (1745), par. 15.

89. CAHJP, MS AHW 10, fol. 21, par. 102.

90. Litt, *Jüdische Gemeindestatuten* (Takkanot Fürth, 1770), 201, pars. 209–10.

91. NLI MS Heb. 2° 662, par. 261.

92. Meisl, *Pinkas kehillat Berlin*, 296–97, par. 285.

93. Carlebach, "Community, Authority," 7.

94. NLI MS Heb. 2° 662, par. 540: an appeal of two doctors for an increase in salary in which they refer to the midwife's salary and benefits as well.

95. CAHJP, MS AHW 33a, 6b.

96. CAHJP, MS AHW 17a, fol. 56.

97. Some of the material on midwives appeared previously in Carlebach, "Community, Authority," 5–33.

98. Berkovitz, *Protocols*, 536, no. 146.

99. JTS, MS 10772, fols. 25v-26r.

100. J. R. Katz, "Jewish Midwives, Wise Women," 4.

101. Mi-See, *Shu"t yefe nof*, Yoreh de'ah, no. 92. On mi-See, see Zimmer, "Sefer yefe nof."

102. See J. R. Katz's analysis in "Jewish Midwives, Wise Women," 6–12.

103. Litt, *Pinkas, Kahal, and the Mediene*, 101–2, notes that these cases were recorded in a copy of the takkanot rather than in the main pinkas and suggests that the choice stemmed from the delicate nature of the issue. For similar cases in Italy, see Malkiel, "Woodstruck Deed."

104. Isserlein, *Sefer leket yosher*, pt. 2, 20. See also the discussion in Fram, *My Dear Daughter*, 83n230.

105. Jerusalem, Karlin-Stolin, MS 41, fol. 54r.

106. Fromet was the daughter of court Jew Ephraim Gumperz of Koblenz. See Löwenstein and Brann, "R. Juda Mehler II," 286.

107. Litt, *Protokollbuch*, 42. There is no additional information allowing us to identify their respective husbands. Our knowledge of rabbis in Friedberg begins in 1550. See Löwenstein, "Zur Geschichte der Juden in Friedberg."

108. Epidat database, wm-1223. This reference is to his first wife, whose own tombstone refers to her erudition. See Epidat database, wrm-1224. Bacharach remarried the widow of another rabbi, and they were married for three years before her death during a plague. See Epidat database, wrm-1252.

109. Bacharach's tombstone also refers to him as a darshan, but it is unlikely that the reference to her as darshanit derived solely from his position rather than hers.

110. See chapter 11.

111. Schammes, *Minhagim de-k"k Warmaisa*, vol. 1, par. 224.

112. CAHJP, MS D-Sc10-5ab, fol. 128v.

113. NLI MS Heb. 2°662, par. 305.

114. Stadtarchiv Worms, MS 1B 2024/19, fol. 26.

115. This factor figured in the debates over hiring a rabbi in the bishopric of Speyer. See Rosenthal, *Heimatgeschichte der badischen Juden*, 135–36.

116. CAHJP, MS AHW 20, fol. 10.

117. CAHJP, MS AHW 121–2, fol. 11. This court order was recorded in the main record and again on a small slip of paper inserted into the volume with additional details, fol. 294.

118. Gemeente Amsterdam Stadsarchief, Archieven van de Nederlands Israelitische Hoofdsynagoge van Amsterdam, Register van resoluties van Parnassim, 1, Protocol 1 (12 Tamus 5468–14 Ab 5497), 30 Jun 1708–11 Aug 1737, fol. 166.

119. The honor associated with serving as a lay leader was far greater in the seventeenth century. By the end of the eighteenth century, it was difficult to find volunteers to fill the position.

120. Schammes, *Minhagim de-k"k Warmaisa*, vol. 1, par. 66.

121. Litt, *Jüdische Gemeindestatuten* (Takkanot Metz, 1769), 381, par. 82.

122. NLI, MS Heb. 2° 662, par. 199, par. 202.

123. Hildesheimer, *Pinkas kehillat Schnaittach*, 166, par. 19.

124. CAHJP, MS AHW 85a, par. 189.

125. CAHJP, MS AHW 71, fol. 7.

126. Carlebach, "Community, Authority," 17–18.

127. Carlebach, "Community, Authority," 19–21. See J. R. Katz, *Jewish Midwives, Medicine*.

128. Strasbourg, Bibliothèque nationale et universitaire de Strasbourg, MS Strasbourg 4048.

129. CAHJP, MS AHW 63.

130. The Hebrew reads, "*Ani ha-ha-meyaledet*." She added an extra *heh* to perfect the calculations.

131. BR, Hs. Ros. 381, title page. A contemporary prayer to be recited by a husband whose wife was pregnant similarly beseeched: "May she give birth easily, like a hen." The husband also prayed that she "not give birth on the Shabbat, so people do not have to violate the Shabbat for her." BR, Hs. Ros. Pl-C-06.

132. Carlebach, "Community, Authority," 25.

Chapter Two. Sacred Societies

1. The Hebrew terms are *hesed* and *emet*. "Truth" refers to a selfless act of kindness that cannot be repaid because the recipient is deceased.

2. JTS, MS 8875, par. 589.

3. The number eighteen is rendered in Hebrew letters, creating a play on words, as the sentence reads, "the mother of all *living* beings" (see Gen. 3:20). The number eighteen additionally refers to the eighteen women who were members of the hevrah kaddisha in Mainz, a number that was symbolic, as it is the Hebrew numerical equivalent of the word "life."

4. Epidat database, hha-3972.

5. Jacob R. Marcus notes a Prague women's society from 1692. See Marcus, *Communal Sick Care*, 36. The earliest reference to a formal women's society that we have found is in a set of bylaws that began in 1692 and was updated each year. JMP, MS 422, par. 25.

6. CAHJP, MS GA-Rendsburg S-28-18, par. 1.

7. On medieval Spain, see Assis, "Welfare," 325–38. For early modern Italian confraternities, both Jewish and Christian, see Terpstra, *Politics*.

8. Goldberg, *Crossing*, 91–92. See also E. Horowitz, "Haburot," 224.

9. See, e.g., CAHJP, MF HM2 3827, which includes an account book and lists of new members and officials within the Prague men's burial society.

10. E. Horowitz, "Haburot," 237–38. For an example of the induction of a *ben yanik*, a young baby, into the Ferrara burial society, Haifa, MS 45, fol. 8r. Also in Horowitz, see page 226 for a discussion of rivalries between confraternities, and of regulations forbidding members to hold positions in more than one confraternity.

11. A. Unna, *Pinkas ha-takkanot*, 75, 95, 117.

12. See e.g., CAHJP, MS GA-Rendsburg S-28-9.

13. Wachtel, "Jewish Burial Societies," 217.

14. In some communities, one voluntary society performed all these functions; in others, they were differentiated into separate organizations (e.g., *bikur holim, kavranim, hevrah kaddisha gemilut hasadim*).

15. For an English translation, see I. G. Marcus, "Mothers," 33–45.

16. Fourteen women signed the founding takkanot of a society in Ferrara. See Ruderman, "Founding," 233–67. Beyond the list of signatures, the women are not mentioned in the article.

17. J. R. Marcus, *Communal Sick Care*, 135–45.

18. CAHJP, MS AHW 10, fol. 16a, par. 77.

19. Sulzbach, "Wohltätigkeitsverein," 263.

20. *Sefer toldot Adam*, Yiddish takkanot at the end of the volume, pars. 13–16.

21. NLI, MS 4° 1092, fol. 457.

22. NLI, MS 4° 1092, fol. 482.

23. Ulbrich, *Shulamit*, 191. See also Meyer, *La communauté juive*, 73.

24. Gemeente Amsterdam Stadstarchief, 1.1.2.2.1.25, Register van contributie voor een vrouwenvereniging.

25. The respective burial society logbooks from Rendsburg and Prague refer to the men's takkanot on parchment. See CAHJP, MS GA-Rendsburg, S-28-9, fol. 5r; JMP, MS 422, fol. 1.

26. Mainz, MS Nr. 22/III, fol. 1v-2r, par. 8. We thank Prof. Andreas Lehnardt for locating this document and making it accessible to us.

27. Francesconi, "Confraternal Community," 252.

28. The Frankfurt burial records were consulted after the fire in 1711 in order to reconstruct the Memorbuch. See NLI, MS 4° 1092, fol. 1.

29. CAHJP, MS AHW 16, fol. 254a.

30. The will, dated 5 Iyyar 1769, can be found in CAHJP, MS AHW 16, fol. 29a. Zwoleń is a small town east of Radom.

31. CAHJP, MS AHW 16.

32. CAHJP, MF HM2 4042, fols. 8, 17.

33. *Sefer toldot Adam*, Yiddish takkanot at the end of the volume, pars. 13–16.

34. JTS, MS 9835, fol. 11. She also left money to three men's hevrot: the gravediggers' society, the society of coffinmakers, and the men's society for purification rites. It is not clear whether these were donations or payment of expenses for her and her late husband's rites, shrouds, and burials.

35. CAHJP, MS GA-Rendsburg S-28-18, par. 4.

36. Mainz, MS Nr. 22/III, fol. 1v, par. 4.

37. Mainz, MS Nr. 22/III, fol. 1v, par. 2.

38. AIU, MS 423, fol. 3v.

39. AIU, MS 423, fol. 3v.

40. On the origin of the custom of burying the dead in simple white shrouds, see Wachtel, "Jewish Burial Societies," 215.

41. AIU, MS 423, fol. 4r.

42. CAHJP, MS AHW 71, fol. 2a.

43. JMP, MS 422, fol. 23, par. 5.

44. Schammes, *Minhagim de-k"k Warmaisa*, vol. 2, par. 248.

45. Mainz, MS Nr. 22/III, fol. 1v, par. 5; see also fol. 2r, par. 9.

46. JMP, MS 422, fol. 23, par. 5.

47. Schammes, *Minhagim de-k"k Warmaisa*, vol. 2, par. 248.

48. Frankfurter, *Sha'ar Shimon*, part 2, fol. 7v.

49. JMP, MS 422, fol. 23, par. 7.

50. AIU, MS 423, fol. 3v.

51. Larger communities had separate societies of *kavranim* (undertakers), who built the coffins and dug and filled the graves. See New York, Columbia University, MS General 320, for the regulations of the gravediggers' society in Altona.

52. Commentary by Schammes (to his own text), *Minhagim de-k"k Warmaisa*, vol. 2, par. 249, at page 100.

53. See, e.g., CAHJP, MS AHW 121–1, p. 35, par. 210, for when a widow was reimbursed for clothing held by the burial society.

54. Jitte, daughter of Matthias Gluckstadt, Testament. For her tombstone, see Epidat database, hha-4274.

55. CAHJP, MS GA-Rendsburg S-28-18, no. 1; insertion after no. 24.

56. For the men's bylaws, see CAHJP, MS GA-Rendsburg S-28–9, fol. 65v, no. 4.

57. JTS, MS 5396, fol. 346.

58. JTS, MS 5396, fol. 318.

59. The pultar was a sheet that covered the dead. See Jerusalem, Israel Museum, MS 180/073.

60. JTS, MS 5396, fol. 304.

61. JTS, MS 5396, fol. 287.

62. Glikl, *Zikhroynes* (2006), 146.

63. AIU, MS 423, fol. 4r-v.

64. Glikl, *Zikhroynes* (2006), 74. Glikl doesn't specify, but presumably this happened in Hamburg. Note that here, too, we see a circle of women sewing shrouds for the dead, but it is not clear whether they constituted a formal hevrah.

65. Mainz, MS Nr. 22/III, fol. 1v, par. 5.

66. Glikl, *Zikhroynes* (2006), 190.

67. JTS, MS 5396, fol. 91.

68. S. Halevi, *Nahalat shivah*, vol. 3, responsum 59.

69. JTS, MS 5396, fol. 312.

70. An additional reason provided for burying murder victims in their clothes was that it provoked heavenly sympathy and vengeance for their deaths. See S. Halevi, *Nahalat shivah*, vol. 3, responsum 59.

71. See *Nahalat shivah*, vol. 3, responsum 59, in which Halevi ruled that one should not dress women who had died in childbirth in the clothes in which they had died. Among other reasons, he cited R. Jacob Moellin (Maharil, d. 1427), who had noted that most women died of internal damage rather than of excessive bleeding outside the body.

72. Kirchheim, *Minhagot Warmaisa*, 315.

73. Schammes, *Minhagim de-k"k Warmaisa*, vol. 2, par. 249. For most women, this was a skirt worn during menstrual impurity. Juspe Schammes notes that for a wealthy woman, a new skirt of white wool might be sewn.

74. Kirchheim, *Minhagot Warmaisa*, 315.

75. The signatures on the Rendsburg takkanot indicate that almost all the members of the women's society were married or widowed. While they may not all have had children, it is likely that the majority of them did.

76. Frankfurter, *Sha'ar Shimon*, part 2, fol. 13v-14r.

77. See the description by the Polish rabbi Shabbetai Kohen, commentary on *Shulhan arukh, Yoreh de'ah*, no. 364, par. 11, who reports having seen this practice in many communities.

78. New York, Columbia University, MS General 320, fol. 3r, par. 10. On circumcision, see also A. Reiner, "Circumcision," 453–75.

79. New York, Columbia University, MS General 320, fol. 3r, par. 7.

80. CAHJP, MS GA-Rendsburg S-28-18, par. 12. A similar provision appears in the men's burial society takkanot.

81. Mintz, "Material Culture," 249–62.

82. See Deutsch, *Judaism*, 58–59, 64.

83. See, e.g., Israel Museum Jerusalem, 191/029, accession HF 0167.

84. Kirchner, *Jüdisches Ceremoniel*, 217, notes that "*Eheweiber*, married women, take a small clean linen sack, fill it with earth, and give it to the men to put under the head of the dead man." He noted that some Jews went to great trouble to obtain soil from the Holy Land. See also the above-referenced expense in the death of Hayim of Zwoleń.

85. Emden, *She'elat Yaavetz* (ed. Bergstein), vol. 3, 253.

86. AIU, MS 423, fol. 5r.

87. Frankfurter, *Sha'ar Shimon*, part 2, fol. 1r.

88. On *Ma'avar yabbok*, see Goldberg, *Crossing the Jabbok*.

89. *Sefer toldot Adam*.

90. *Refu'ot ha-nefesh*, part 2, title page. Our thanks to the Klau Library, Hebrew Union College Cincinnati, for making this rare edition available to us.

91. Bar Levav, "Amsterdam Way," 122.

92. Frankfurter, *Sha'ar Shimon*, part 2, fol. 2r.

93. Frankfurter, *Sha'ar Shimon*, part 2, fol. 7r.

94. *Refu'ot ha-nefesh*, part 2, fols. 2–6.

95. *Sefer toldot Adam*, unpaginated (final folio in volume).

96. *Refu'ot ha-nefesh*, part 2, fol. 8.

97. Panitz, "Modernity"; Silberstein, "Mendelssohn und Mecklenburg," 282–83.

98. JMP, MS 422, No. 74.

99. The Mainz takkanot, e.g., mention a *knell gabbete*, a term that was also used in nearby Worms to refer to the youngest and newest member of the society. See Mainz, MS Nr. 2, fol. 11. A. Unna, *Pinkas ha-takkanot*, 31; see also Schammes, *Minhagim de-k"k Warmaisa*, vol. 1, par. 424, where the term *knell gabbay* is used in a context outside the burial society.

100. See, e.g., CAHJP, MS GA-Rendsburg S-28-18, par. 18.

101. On the importance of the gabbay's work to the members of the hevrah, see New York, Columbia University, MS General 320, fol. 1r-v.

102. CAHJP, MS GA-Rendsburg S-28-18, par. 7.

103. On the Mainz takkanot, see Hausmann, "Die Statuten."

104. CAHJP, MS GA-Rendsburg S-28-18, par. 22.

105. CAHJP, MS GA-Rendsburg S-28-18, paragraph inserted between ordinances 24 and 25.

106. CAHJP, MS GA-Rendsburg S-28-18, par. 14.

107. JMP, MS 148.

108. JMP, MS 422, fol. 22.

109. See, e.g., CAHJP, MS GA-Rendsburg S-28-18, par. 21. This was similar to *abzug geld* (the sum exacted from members who left a community). In the eighteenth century, many hevrot complained that members left without paying the dues they owed. See CAHJP, MS AHW 121–1, p. 51, par. 495; p. 97a, par. 1354; p. 99, par. 1383.

110. See, e.g., E. Horowitz, "Processions," 231–47.

111. D. Altschuler, *Precious Legacy*, 162; Jewish Museum in Prague, inv. no. 063619.

112. Mainz, MS Nr. 22/III, fols. 1r-v, pars. 3, 4, 6.

113. Mainz, MS Nr. 22/III, fol. 1v, par. 6.

114. JMP, MS 422, fol. 22v, par. 8.

115. Copenhagen, Jewish Community of Copenhagen, MS 30, fol. 1.

116. Copenhagen, Jewish Community of Copenhagen, MS 30, fol. 6.

117. Copenhagen, Jewish Community of Copenhagen, MS 31.

118. If the ornate manuscript was intended for the women, it is possible that the men's society used the simple manuscript. It is also possible that the plain manuscript was a draft and that the ornate manuscript was used by the men, who nevertheless saw fit to bless their female counterparts at the annual feast.

119. Tal, *Ha-kehillah*, 143, no. 15.

120. Tal, *Ha-kehillah*, 143, no. 14.

121. On burial place as a reflection of status in early modern Europe more broadly, see Koslofsky, *Reformation*, 123–24; Cherryson, Crossland, and Tarlow, *Private Place*; Gonen, "Choosing," 87–104.

122. The takkanot that refer to the women are dated 1745, the latest date for the establishment of the women's hevrot. One of the hevrot is referred to as new in the text; it is therefore possible that the women's burial society existed before it was mentioned in the bylaws.

123. The bylaws are printed in *Sefer toldot Adam*, unpaginated. See *takkanot bikur holim*, pars. 12 and 25, for the services they performed after death.

124. For the pinkas of the Berlin gravediggers, see New York, Leo Baeck Institute, Jacob Jacobson collection AR 7002, Box 4, Folder I39. This logbook includes several sets of bylaws.

125. *Sefer toldot Adam*, Yiddish takkanot, pars. 10, 11.

126. *Sefer toldot Adam*, Yiddish takkanot, pars. 13–16, list the gabbetes by name and delineate their responsibilities.

127. *Sefer toldot Adam*, Yiddish takkanot, par. 15.

128. Tal, *Ha-kehillah*, 143–44, nos. 14–16.

129. Tal, *Ha-kehillah*, 143–44, no. 16.

130. CAHJP, MS GA-Rendsburg S-28-18, fol. 1v.

131. JMP, MS 422, no. 25.

132. E.g., Rivkah Tiktiner, Toybe Pan, and Bella Perlhefter all spent time in Prague. Another darshanit, Rivkah bat Shabbetai Horowitz, lived there as well.

133. JMP, MS 422, fol. 22.

134. JMP, MS 422, fol. 23, pars. 5–6. The Jewish women's sale of glasses (*brillen*) is parallel to Christian women selling eyeglasses. There are records of bequests of eyeglasses to convents, such as one pair of glasses preserved in a German cloister. See Wiesner-Hanks, "Adjusting," 28–31.

135. JMP, MS 422, fol. 22. The men note that the women "had already accumulated pre-made shrouds in significant quantity," and "they earn a huge profit, of which they claim to use the proceeds for charity for the poor or the sick." In Altona, the hekdesh sold shrouds for its benefit. CAHJP, MS AHW 16, fol. 3a.

136. Mishnah, Berakhot 2:8.

137. JMP, MS 422, fol. 22.

138. JMP, MS 422, fol. 22.

139. JMP, MS 422, fol. 22.

140. JMP, MS 422, fol. 23.

141. CAHJP, MF HM2 4042, fol. 6.

142. CAHJP, MF HM2 4042, fol. 42.

Chapter Three. Honor and Shame, Center and Periphery

1. For the case, Staatsarchiv Hamburg, 111–1 Cl. VII Lit. M e nr. 8 vol. 11. Devorah's husband, Zalman ben Meir Traub, is listed in the pinkas of Hamburg's Elbestrasse synagogue. CAHJP, MS AHW 30, p. 73 (original pagination). We plan a further study of this case.

2. Amsinck family members served as patrician leaders in Hamburg for centuries. This was likely Wilhelm Amsinck (1752–1831), later mayor of Hamburg and president of its Senate.

3. The text was written by Abraham, son of the late R. Meir Gerlitz, the shamash of the undertakers, whose wife and mother-in-law served in the burial society. Gabba'it is a variant of gabbete. R. Leizer was a *goveh* (bursar) for the community.

4. CAHJP, MS AHW 726, fols. 51–52.

5. Zürn, *Die Altonaer*.

6. The rabbinic judge was consulted on how she should be buried after her bloody execution.

7. Our use of the term "women on the margins" thus echoes Natalie Davis's title but intends something far more marginal.

8. Graupe, *Die Statuten*, vol. 2, p. 181, par. 106.

9. Glikl, *Zikhroynes* (2006), 228.

10. Y. T. Lewinsky, "Takkanot le-seudat ha-brit," 142.

11. CAHJP, MS AHW 15.

12. NLI, MS Heb. 4° 522; Mi-See, *Shu"t yefe nof, hoshen mishpat*, no. 79.

13. On *ikuv tefillah* (interruption of the prayer services) as an ancient and medieval strategy for obtaining redress, see Assaf, *Bate ha-din*, 25–29.

14. CAHJP, MS AHW 14, fol. 68, par. 161.

15. JTS, MS 10772, fol. 6b.

16. CAHJP, MS AHW 85a, par. 227.

17. CAHJP, MS AHW 85a, fol. 96a, par. 400.

18. See, e.g., the case of a man whose daughter was harassed by the Christian customer to whom they sold their wares. Bacharach, *Havot Yair*, no. 108. In another case, a cantor from Frankfurt was charged with inappropriate contact with women; various steps were taken to curb his abusive behavior over the years. See Fram, *Window*, 319–20, 455–46, Appendix 3; Kasper-Marienberg and Kaplan, "Nourishing," 27–28. An entry from an Eastern European record reminds us that the most vulnerable could also be subject to terrible abuse. The pinkas of the kahal of Mstislav in Belarus (covering 1760–1795) records in one faint line, "May it be remembered that the virgin girl Basha, daughter of [?] David, when she was a young girl of six years, was raped by a Jew, and as evidence we have affixed our signatures, Thursday 13 Nissan [1796]." New York, YIVO Institute, *Pinkas Mstislav chadash*, RG 87, folder 915, page 73087.

19. JTS, MS 10772, fol. 10a. The records indicate that, about two weeks later, the kahal granted the woman permission to take all her belongings and leave the lodging of Mordekhai, as she had left a security payment to cover her rent with the parnassim.

20. CAHJP, MS AHW 20, fol. 9a.

21. CAHJP, MS AHW 20, fol. 14b.

22. Graupe, *Die Statuten*, 2: 156, par. 114 (from 1675).

23. CAHJP, MS AHW 15, p. 33, par. 167 (from 1689). Fines in multiples of thirty-nine recalled the penalty of up to forty lashes meted out in biblical and rabbinic law.

24. CAHJP, MS AHW 20, fol. 9a.

25. Ruff, *Violence*.

26. JTS, MS 10772, fol. 93r.

27. Rivkind, "Kuntres," 345–52, cited and trans. in Goldberg, *Crossing*, 228. On the reference to wetnursing, see below in this chapter.

28. CAHJP, AHW 13, par. 112; Graupe, *Die Statuten*, vol. 2, 155 (from 1675).

29. Litt, *Jüdische Gemeindestatuten* (Takkanot Frankfurt, 1674/5), 64, par. 29; 370, par. 43; Tal, *Ha-kehillah*, 64, no. 85. For nineteenth-century policies that denied zonot who wished to marry many of the visible communal honors granted to brides, see Litt, *Jüdische Gemeindestatuten* (Takkanot Deutschkreuz, 1816), 441–442, par 44.

30. CAHJP, MS AHW 20, fol. 44.

31. For a case in which a woman was suspected of adultery, see E. Landau, *Noda be-Yehudah, Even ha-ezer*, no. 69.

32. CAHJP, MS AHW 20, fol. 9a.

33. CAHJP, MS AHW 17b, fol. 56.

34. For other cases before imperial and rabbinical courts, see Kasper-Marienberg, "Jewish Women." Berkovitz, *Law's Dominion*, 306–12, has counted thirty paternity suits brought before the Metz rabbinical court at the end of the eighteenth century.

35. CAHJP, MS AHW 20, fol. 44, 44a (1778).

36. S. Halevi, *Nahalat shivah*, vol. 3, responsum 19.

37. For an example of another illegitimate pregnancy in which Christian authorities summoned rabbis to administer oaths, see E. Landau, *Noda be-Yehuda, Even ha-ezer*, no. 24.

38. Compare this to the case of Perle Levy, a widow from rural Steinbiedersdorf, who became pregnant while engaged; her fiancé denied paternity. Her case demonstrated the threat of becoming the subject of village gossip and its concomitant loss of honor within her small community. Ulbrich, *Shulamit*, 204–5.

39. NLI MS Heb. 2° 662, no. 292.

40. In the eighteenth century, the Jewish community of the Hague ordered the expulsion of two sisters, one of whom had become pregnant out of wedlock, out of concern for the honor of the community. No inquiry into the paternity of the pregnancies was ordered. Litt, *Pinkas, Kahal, and the Mediene*, 69–70, 216. The language of the expulsion ordinance implicates them both in wanton behavior.

41. Tal, *Ha-kehillah*, 208, no. 6.

42. Tal, *Ha-kehillah*, 208, no. 388.

43. JTS, MS 10772, fol. 4r.

44. Deut. 22:13–21; E.g., BT *Ketubot* 7b–8a; Langer, "Jewish Celebration of Bridal Virginity," and the bibliography cited there, discusses evidence for a ceremony and blessing recited by Jews in late antiquity when a marriage was consummated and evidence of virginity produced.

45. Bacharach, *Havot Yair*, no. 211.

46. Jerusalem, Karlin-Stolin, MS 41, fol. 23v.

47. E. Katzenellenbogen, *Knesset Yehezkel*, no. 73.

48. CAHJP, MS AHW 9, fol. 36; cited in Graupe, *Die Statuten*, vol. 2, 138–39 (from 1716).

49. See the cases and sources cited in Carlebach, "Fallen Women."

50. The last concern is the subject of a lengthy responsum in Heksher, *Sh"ut Adne Paz*, no. 29. Although ostensibly addressed to a "distant community," it is likely to have emerged in his own community of Altona, whose identity he disguised.

51. CAHJP, MS D-Ha11-334, fol. 7v(1741), cited with slight variation in Litt, *Jüdische Gemeindestatuten* (Takkanot Halberstadt, 1741), 121, par. 19.

52. Salmon-Mack, *Tan-du*, 93–94.

53. Graupe, *Die Statuten*, vol. 2, 114 (cited from CAHJP, MS AHW 10). In CAHJP, MS AHW 9, which contains the same text, the takkanah is dated Sunday, 2 Heshvan [5]453 [1692]. The reference to an earlier set of ordinances is in the original, indicating multiple renewals of this ordinance over time.

54. Boes, "'Dishonourable' Youth."

55. Boes, *Crime and Punishment*, 137. See also Myers, *Death and a Maiden*, in which a woman was accused of infanticide even though an infant's body was never found.

56. Further details in Boes, *Crime and Punishment*, 172–77.

57. Ulbrich, *Shulamit*, 169n15.

58. "*Ishah keshat ruah*," CAHJP, MS AHW 33a, fol. 2a, dated 1745, unsigned.

59. The German thieves' cant, Rotwelsch or Gaunersprach, contained some elements of Yiddish.

60. Einert, *Entdeckter jüdischer Baldober*.

61. See Einert, *Entdeckter jüdischer Baldober*, 235, where a fifteen-year-old son is arrested, and 239 about the arrest of the wife of a suspect.

62. Einert, *Entdeckter jüdischer Baldober*, 248.

63. Einert, *Entdeckter jüdischer Baldober*, 230, par. 119: "es wäre gut, wann das Diebs-Juden-Volk in Hessen zerstöhret würde, weilen solches das Land ruinirte und kein ehrlicher Mann mehr bestehen könte."

64. Anders, *Sara, Ester*. Our information about the Flensburg trial is based on this source.

65. Anders, *Sara, Ester*, 43.

66. Anders, *Sara, Ester*, 40–41.

67. Anders, *Sara, Ester*, 47.

68. The term for the labor sentence, *Juden Esclaven*, needs further explanation.

69. Anders, *Sara, Ester*, 49: "*immer zu fusse und zwar alleine gegangen.*"

70. Anders, *Sara, Ester*, 50–51.

71. Anders, *Sara, Ester*, 53.

72. Anders, *Sara, Ester*, 55.

73. The information about Dina Jacob is based on Cobb, *Paris*, 142–93.

74. Cobb, *Paris*, 169.

75. Cobb, *Paris*, 173.

76. Mingling across religious boundaries at the lower end of the class spectrum in this period is noted by Endelman, *Jews*, 267–69; but compare Lowenstein, *Berlin Jewish Community*, 56–67.

77. M. Rubin, *Cities*.

78. CAHJP, MS D-W03-662, fols. 26, 54, 56, 62, 84; Hildesheimer, *Pinkas kehillat Schnaittach*, 196, par. 5.

79. On preference given to women and children, see D. Kaplan, *Patrons and Their Poor*, 115–20.

80. Ramat Gan, Bar-Ilan University, MS 846, fol. 15 of latter half of the manuscript.

81. CAHJP, MS AHW 85a, p. 48, par. 189.

82. D. Kaplan, *Patrons and Their Poor*, 110–13.

83. J. R. Katz, "'Judge and to Be Judged,'" 448.

84. CAHJP, MS AHW 14, fol. 66, par. 159.

85. ISG, MS Juden Akten 412.

86. It is unclear from this source whether they were a married couple.

87. JTS, MS 10772, fol. 54v (1766).

88. On the Jews of Aurich, see Anklam, *Judengemeinde in Aurich*; Reyer, *Juden in Aurich*. For the expulsion of vagrants, including specifically Jewish vagrants, see *Placaat*.

Chapter Four. Jewish Women and Print Culture

1. Heilprun, *Dinim ve-seder*. Isserles first published *Torat ha-hatat* in 1569. On *Torat ha-hatat*, see Fram, *Codification of Jewish Law*, 198–218.
2. Heilprun, *Dinim ve-seder*, fol. 1r.
3. Heilprun, *Dinim ve-seder*, fol. 3r.
4. Heilprun, *Dinim ve-seder*, fol. 3v.
5. He uses the term *galhes*, which probably means Italian but possibly refers to Latin.
6. Heilprun, *Dinim ve-seder*, fol. 2r.
7. Heilprun, *Dinim ve-seder*, fol. 2v.
8. See, e.g., his Italian translation of Benjamin Slonik's *Book of Women's Commandments*, dedicated to Bona, the wife of Lazero D'Italia, Jew of Mantua. Slonik, *Precetti da esser imparati dalle donne ebree*.
9. On the general impact of print in early modern Europe, see Eisenstein, *Printing Press*; Johns, *Nature of the Book*; Pettegree, *Book in the Renaissance*. Mayer, *Defus rishon*, 226–30, has argued that in the transition from manuscript to print culture, conceptions of Jewish knowledge shifted. Once perceived as orally transmissible and inherently available in human memory (and only incidentally embodied in material forms), knowledge came to be seen as embodied in the material form of books.
10. On the cultural implications of translation, see Idelson-Shein, *Between the Bridge*; Fram, *My Dear Daughter*.
11. Chava Turniansky paved the way in posing the questions that shape the topic of Jewish women's libraries. See her "Aron ha-sefarim," 185–204.
12. Bodleian, MS Canonici Or. 12. See Turniansky and Timm, *Yiddish in Italia*, 49–50, no. 47.
13. For further description of this miscellany, see Turniansky, "Aron ha-sefarim," 189.
14. Shtif, "Handwritten Yiddish Library," 141–50, 525–44.
15. Bodleian, MS Canonici Or. 12, fol. 6v. *Selihot* are sets of penitential poems recited in the weeks and days leading up to Yom Kippur. Women attended these solemn services in many Ashkenazi communities.
16. Bodleian, MS Canonici Or. 12, fol. 99r.
17. Bodleian, MS Canonici Or. 12, fol. 274v.
18. NLI, MS Heb. 8° 5245, fol. 117b. See Turniansky and Timm, *Yiddish in Italia*, 68, no. 65.
19. On the early Jewish King Arthur tales, see Leviant, *King Artus*; on the cross-cultural uses of the Arthurian tales in early modern Europe, Oehme, *Knight*.
20. Trinity College, MS Loewe 135, Shelfmark F.12.44, fol. 84v. Cited in Turniansky and Timm, *Yiddish in Italia*, 71, no. 68.
21. BnF, MS cod. héb. 589. Turniansky, "Aron ha-sefarim," 190. On the central place of the binding of Isaac in stories, poems, and the early modern Yiddish epic *Yudisher shtam*, see Roman and Schleifer, "Niggun akedah."
22. BnF, MS cod. héb. 589, fol. 134. "*Un gor veyn un gor shtille geyt zi zu tseyten t'villa.*"
23. BnF, MS cod. héb. 589, fol. 134. "*Der arim shreyber, diner aler vromen veyber.*"
24. On Roza and her patronage of Heilprun, see Turniansky, "Aron ha-sefarim," 190–91.
25. Heilprun, *Orekh yomim*, title page.
26. Turniansky, "Aron ha-sefarim," 190.

27. Habermann, *Nashim ivriot*, lists some two dozen Jewish women patrons of printed works in the early modern period, some individually and some within family groups.

28. Kayserling, *Die jüdische Frauen*, 153.

29. Bodleian, MS Opp. 8° 796, fol. 1a.

30. On this text, see Greenblatt, *To Tell Their Children*, 136–37; N. Rubin, "Agadah al sheloshah ve-arba'ah."

31. Bodleian, MS Opp. 8° 796, fol. 9r.

32. Poriat (Porges), *Darkhei Zion*, as cited in Ya'ari, *Masa'ot Eretz Israel*, 277. On Poriat, see Mor-Rozenson, *Ba-derekh mi-Yerushalayim*. On the immigration of Ashkenazi Jewish women to the Holy Land, see the example of Eliezer Eilburg's mother. Eilburg, *Ten Questions*, 62–63. J. Davis, "A German Jewish Woman Scholar."

33. S. Horowitz, *Yesh nohlin*, 45, par. 22.

34. For inscriptions by women who owned early modern printed books, see, e.g., Footprints no. 11535.

35. Glikl, *Memoirs* (2019), 41.

36. Glikl, *Memoirs* (2019), citing *Yesh nohlin* (Prague, 1615), at 47–50; *Lev tov*; *Brantshpigel* at 50.

37. Glikl, *Memoirs* (2019), 84. She calls the author "Prager." The work has never been identified; presumably, no copies have survived. See notes 100, 101 on evidence that Glikl copied her story directly from a Yiddish book.

38. Glikl, *Memoirs* (2019), 56.

39. N. Z. Davis, "Printing and the People," in *Society and Culture*, 189–226.

40. Turniansky and Timm, *Yiddish in Italia*, 14, no. 14. An almost verbatim boast can be found in Turniansky and Timm, *Yiddish in Italia*, 13, no. 13.

41. Hanover, *Safah berurah*. On this work, see Turniansky and Timm, *Yiddish in Italia*, 82, no. 76.

42. M. Altschuler, *Brantshpigel* (e.p. Kraków 1596; here, Basel 1602), fol. 12v. See also Weissler, *Voices of the Matriarchs*, 52.

43. On the gendering of Jewish languages, see Seidman, *Marriage Made in Heaven*.

44. We exclude here the many books that passed through women's hands as commodities, often as inheritances that they passed on to others. The rabbanit Ulkelin inherited from her father, R. Zimlin, a manuscript copy of the Jerusalem Talmud that became the basis for its printed edition. R. Zimlin migrated from Ashkenazi lands to Italy in the late fifteenth century. Mayer, *Defus rishon*, 53. For a later example, see Footprints no. 21217. This "footprint" of the anonymous compilation *Zikhron hurban ha-bayit* (Cremona, 1566) records that in 1711, the widowed Sheinkhe, daughter of Moses Abreschviller, gave it to Jonah b. David, her brother-in-law. It had belonged to her husband, Jonah's brother; she presented it to him as "a sign and keepsake." He signed his name and the record of this gift "lest someone come and claim it." If not for this inscription, we would never have known that it passed through her hands. Thanks to Joshua Teplitsky for this reference.

45. Among the many examples, see e.g., JTS, MS 9340, a year-round siddur copied and illuminated by Aryeh Judah Loeb ben Elhanan Katz of Trebitsch for Simon Wolf ben Daniel Moses Oppenheim of Worms and his wife, Vogel bat Moses Zunz of Frankfurt, in 1712–14.

46. Elyakim of Komarna, *Melitz yosher*.

47. *Mar'ah ha-sorefet ha-nikret bi-leshon Ashkenaz Brantshpigl* (Frankfurt, 1706), via Footprints no. 18325.

48. Parma, La Biblioteca Palatina, Palatina, MS 2510, fol. 249r. See also Turniansky and Timm, *Yiddish in Italia*, 5, no. 5. The manuscript contains a translation of two books of the Bible, as well as relevant *haftarot* (prophetic portions) and megillot.

49. On the *Tsene u-rene*, see Faierstein, *Ze'enah u-Re'enah*; Elbaum and Turniansky, "Tsene-rene."

50. The title is derived from Song of Songs 3:11, where it is addressed to "daughters of Zion."

51. Turniansky, "Old Yiddish Biblical Epics," 26–33. According to Turniansky, *Melokhim bukh* was printed first in 1543 and *Shmuel bukh* in 1544, both at the same printer in Augsburg. See also Fox and Lewis, *Many Pious Women*.

52. Staats- und Universitätsbibliothek Hamburg Carl von Ossietzky, MS cod. Heb. 313, fol. 165 (via Ktiv). Turniansky and Timm, *Yiddish in Italia*, 8, no. 8.

53. The formulation is from Turniansky, "Aron ha-sefarim," 191.

54. Turniansky and Timm, *Yiddish in Italia*, 12. London, British Library, Oriental and India Office Collections, MS Cod. Add 18695.

55. Turniansky and Timm, *Yiddish in Italia*, 21, no. 19.

56. Weissler, *Voices of the Matriarchs*, 66–148.

57. Rosman, "Lehiyot ishah," 415–43; Rosman, "Jewish Women," 193–216.

58. See, e.g., the tkhine in Amsterdam, BR, Hs. Ros. 500. Weissler, *Voices of the Matriarchs*, 66–74. See also Baumgarten, "'Like Adam and Eve,'" 51–53.

59. The Hebrew phrase is *shalom bayit*. Braginsky, MS 351, fol. 14v. For another example of a prayer for pious children, see BR, Hs. Ros. 500.

60. Baumgarten, "Like Adam and Eve," 44–61.

61. Turniansky and Timm, *Yiddish in Italia*, 32, no. 30. On the genre, see Romer-Segal, "Yiddish Works," 37–59; Fram, *My Dear Daughter*.

62. Bodleian, MS Canonici Or. 12, fol. 207r: "*Er zoll unz der lozn manen und viber.*"

63. Fram, *My Dear Daughter*, 12–15. Molin's interlocutor was Rabbi Hayim of Augsburg.

64. Fram, *My Dear Daughter*, 156.

65. Fram, *My Dear Daughter*, 228.

66. Fram, *My Dear Daughter*, xviii. See also Rosenzweig, "Women."

67. On resistance to print by some rabbis, see E. Reiner, "Ashkenazi Élite," 85–98.

68. Romer-Segal, "Yiddish Works," 40; Turniansky and Timm, *Yiddish in Italia*, 32, no. 30.

69. Turniansky, "Ha-bensherl," 51–52.

70. *Kapparot*: an atonement ceremony in which a chicken or the equivalent value was offered in place of the sinful person, usually performed before Yom Kippur. *Sefirat ha-omer*: a ceremonial countdown of the forty-nine days between Passover and Shavu'ot. *Eruv tavshilin*: a ceremony permitting preparation for the Shabbat when it is immediately preceded by a holiday.

71. *Seder birkat ha-mazon* (Basel, 1600). For a set of fascinating notations on the title page, see the copy digitized in the NLI, in which instructions for reworking the text for a second edition appear: https://www.nli.org.il/he/books/NNL_ALEPH990012839910205171/NLI.

72. *Birkat ha-mazon* (Frankfurt, 1712/13); *Birkat ha-mazon* (Frankfurt, 1726/27).

73. Turniansky, "Ha-bensherl," 69–92, provides a comprehensive list.

74. On the genre, see Sabar, "Illustrated Prayer Book," 205–19; Sabar, "Seder birkat ha-mazon," 455–72.

75. Turniansky and Timm, *Yiddish in Italia*, 41, no. 39. Staatsbibliothek zu Berlin, MS Or. Qu. 694. Two separate manuscripts are bound together in this volume. The first is Fradlina's. The Hebrew inscription attributed to her dating the manuscript to 1550 does not appear in the digitized scan on the SBB website.

76. Staatsbibliothek zu Berlin, MS Or. Qu. 694. The second book of customs (*minhogot*) bound in this manuscript has a censorship stamp dated 1609 and bears the inscription on folio 79r: "I am Hannah, daughter of Joseph Katz, zt"l, wife of Mr Zalman Peuz."

77. Braginsky, MS 328; JTS, MS 8230; JTS, MS 8252.

78. Braginsky, MS 344.

79. Braginsky, MS 351.

80. BR, Hs. Ros. 500.

81. On Jacob Sofer, see Fishof, *Jüdische Buchmalerei*, 192–95, 342–44; Schrijver, "'Be'otiyyot Amsterdam,'" 24–26.

82. *Tashlikh* is a ritual casting away of sins near a body of water; *mayim aharonim*, ritual washing of hands before saying Grace after Meals. The latter custom is depicted in Braginsky, MS 344, fol. 2r, in which women are sitting at table with men, and a woman holds the cup for the ritual.

83. BR, Hs. Ros. 500, fols. 30r, 34r-v.

84. Braginsky, MS 351, fol. 17.

85. Mi-See, *Shu"t yefe nof, Orah hayim*, no. 42.

86. Israel Museum, MS 180/006.

87. Braginsky, MS 217, fols. 17v-24v.

88. Mincer, "Increasing Reliance," 103–28.

89. J. Baumgarten, "Prayer, Ritual and Practice," 121–46; Raspe, "Minhag and Migration." See various editions in the bibliography.

90. See the discussion in Grossman, *Pious and Rebellious*, 178–80; E. Baumgarten, *Practicing Piety*, 138–71.

91. Bodleian, Bodleian Library, MS Opp. 4° 1006. See also chapter 11.

92. BnF, MS cod. héb. 586, fol. 10v. On the latter, see Wolfthal, *Picturing Yiddish*.

93. Turniansky, "Yiddish Song," 189–98; Hellerstein, *Question of Tradition*.

94. A variant indicates that the song was sung to the tune of the *akedah*. See Hellerstein, "Name in the Poem," 40.

95. See also Hellerstein's discussion of Royzl Fischl of Kraków, *Question of Tradition*, 35–39.

96. Kayserling, *Die jüdischen Frauen*, 154.

97. See Bodleian, MS Opp. 8° 796, fols. 12r-v; Kayserling, *Die jüdischen Frauen*, 154.

98. On the vast storehouses of Yiddish literature and ephemera of which no material traces have survived, see Turniansky, "Yiddish Language and Literature," 122.

99. See, e.g., regulations from Schnaittach in Hildesheimer, *Pinkas kehillat Schnaittach*, 169, par. 27; from Altona, CAHJP, MS AHW 10, par. 151, published also in Graupe, *Die Statuten*, vol. 2, 90; CAHJP, MS AHW 121–1, p. 30a, par. 106; p. 35a, par. 224, and throughout.

100. Glikl, *Zikhroynes* (2006), 54; for translation, see Glikl, *Memoirs* (2019), 61.

101. Wachstein, "A yiddishe kahal," 93, cited in Assaf, *Mekorot*, vol. 4, 84.

102. Wachstein, "A yiddishe kahal," no. 20.

103. Similarly, from Moravian takkanot, Assaf, *Mekorot*, vol. 1, 147, pars. 3–4. The original Yiddish manuscript was published in Güdemann, *Quellenschriften*, 276.

104. Assaf, *Mekorot*, vol. 1, 143, par. 19, cites Takkanot Nikolsburg as referring to girls studying with a melamed. For the Yiddish, see Güdemann, *Quellenschriften*, 259–60.

105. *Meneket Rivkah*, 266.

106. M. Altschuler, *Brantshpiegel* (Basel, 1602), 175–77, qtd. in Assaf, *Mekorot*, vol. 1, 59.

107. Hahn, *Yosif ometz: Seder limmud banim ketanim*, 284, no. 7. Known as Juspe Hahn after the name of his home in Frankfurt, his formal family name was Neuerlingen.

108. Emden, *Birat migdal oz*, 33.

109. Two Hebrew band samplers from nineteenth-century America can be found in the Smithsonian National Museum of American History: B. Lazarus sampler, 1843 (Accession number 293320); B. Hollunder, 1845 (accession number 2011.0040).

110. On literacy and samplers, see Frye, *Pens and Needles*, 126–35; on Hebrew samplers, 120–21.

111. Faierstein, *Libes Briv of Isaac Wetzlar*.

112. Aptrood and Voß, *Libes Briv*.

113. London, British Library, MS Or. 10668, title page: "This book was written for the notable [woman] extolled with every praise ... Marat Kimhe, may she live, wife of the notable and esteemed torah scholar, Mr Goetschlik P"b [Paderborn?]."

114. We thank Sharon Mintz for this reference. See JTS, MS 8869, fols. 11v-12r.

115. Teplitsky, *Prince of the Press*, 54, 225n132. Teplitsky cites three rabbinic discussions prompted by Sara's scroll. Charlotte Rothschild similarly copied a Passover haggadah in the mid-nineteenth century. Braginsky, MS 314.

116. NLI, MS 4° 1092, fol. 119.

117. For a suggestive analysis of categories of Jewish literacy, see Kanarfogel, "Levels of Literacy," 187–211.

118. University of Pennsylvania Library guide, "Jewish Women Printers," https://guides.library.upenn.edu/c.php?g=468836&p=3209418, cites a rich bibliography of sources on Jewish women and early Jewish printing.

119. Braun and Bilski, *Jewish Women*, date the salon phenomenon from 1780. On the Berlin salonières and their Jewish backgrounds, see Hertz, "Salonières," 97–108.

120. Grunwald, *Hamburgs deutsche Juden*, 58–59, quoting Niemann, "Die Ehre Hamburgischer Staats-Bürger."

121. On these women and others in their circle, see Naimark-Goldberg, *Enlightened Jewish Women*, 123–61. Gad was the daughter of Raphael Gad and Nissel Gad, née Eybeschutz.

122. Hertz, "Salonières," counted seven conversions out of eight eighteenth-century Berlin Jewish salon women. On the only one who remained a professing Jew, see Cypess and Sinkoff, *Sara Levy's World*.

123. On medieval Jewish women as writers and readers, see Baskin, "'May the Writer Be Strong,'" 9–28; Kogman-Appel, "Portrayals of Women," 525–63; Grossman, *Pious and Rebellious*, 162–69.

124. Eilburg, *Ten Questions*, 62–63.

125. NLI, MS 4° 656, fol. 29v. The expansive entry called her "*maskilah*" and "*melumedet u-beki'ah be-Tanakh ve-tirgumehem, u-midrash*" (a scholar and expert in biblical works and their targumim, as well as midrash).

126. Bacharach, introduction to *Havot Yair*.

127. His father served as Chief Rabbi in Ansbach and lived in the village of Schwabach; he left the German villages for the richer Torah life in the central European towns of Leipnik and Boskowitz; he spent time in Prague as well. Thus, he is illustrative of rabbis who were deeply familiar with both German and central European (Bohemian/Moravian) Jewish life.

128. P. Katzenellenbogen, *Yesh manhilin*, 99. Similarly, "my refined and clever/learned daughter, the widow Marat Rachel, may she live" (100); about a woman in the larger family circle: "the learned and wise rabbanit Baila" (114). He described learned women similarly throughout the memoir.

129. Schocken Institute for Jewish Research, MS 70057, fol. 4 (pencil pagination). See also P. Bloch, *Ein vielbegehrter Rabbiner des Rheingaues*.

130. Schocken Institute for Jewish Research, MS 70057, fol. 1.

Chapter Five. Ordinary and Literary Writing

1. Leipzig, UB Leipzig, MS B.H. 18, fol. 91r. Printed in Weinryb, "Historisches . . . Briefwechsel," 339–40, no. v. The letters have been digitized at AT-OeStA/HHStA HS W 1002.

2. Leipzig, UB Leipzig, MS B. H. 18, fol. 91r.

3. Bodleian, MS Opp. 148, fol. 1v. According to Riemer and Senkbeil, introduction to *Be'er Sheva*, xix, the Oxford MS is the final version of the manuscript and the only one written by Bella and Ber themselves.

4. JTS, MS 10632, fol. 7v.

5. Landau and Wachstein, *Jüdische privatbriefe*, 22, no. 6b.

6. Landau and Wachstein, *Jüdische privatbriefe*, 34.

7. Landau and Wachstein, *Jüdische privatbriefe*, 34: "*ven du shreybst, shreyb mir epes noyigkeyten*."

8. For examples of individual model letters, see Leipzig, UB Leipzig, MS BH 18, fols. 88r-v.

9. On model letter writing manuals in Yiddish and Hebrew in the early modern period, see the literature cited in Carlebach, "Letter into Text"; on early modern letter writing, see e.g., Daybell, *Material Letter*.

10. Diemling, "Privacy, Literacy."

11. Leipzig, UB Leipzig, MS BH 18, fol. 82r. Letter of Christian Zarfo, a convert, to Wagenseil.

12. On the repeated references on most sealed letters to the ban of R. Gershom against opening others' mail, see Landau and Wachstein, introduction to *Jüdische privatbriefe*, xxviii; Carlebach, "Letter into Text," 119–22. The responsum of Mehler, Jerusalem, Karlin-Stolin, MS 41, fol. 163r, discusses whether the ban must be explicitly written on the outside of a letter to render it prohibited to unaddressed readers.

13. Arnheim and Turniansky, *Yiddish Letters*, 86 and 28.

14. Arnheim and Turniansky, *Yiddish Letters*, 115 and 73.

15. Landau and Wachstein, *Jüdische privatbriefe*, 60.

16. Arnheim and Turniansky, *Yiddish Letters*, 54, no. 18.

17. "Kosher" and "treyf" signified "pure" and "impure" in Old Yiddish. See e.g., Glikl, *Zikhroynes* (2006), 366: "*Ikh bin treyfe gevesen.*"

18. NLI, MS Heb. 4° 522, fol. 115v.

19. Smith, "Women and the Materials of Writing," 18.

20. For an exquisite example of an embellished and decorated lockbox belonging to a Jewish woman in early sixteenth-century southern Germany, precisely the time and place of our letter writer, see Yosef Kaplan, *Posen Library*, 5: 626.

21. Taglicht, *Nachlässe*, 159, no. 88.

22. Taglicht, *Nachlässe*, 63; 69.

23. Micciche, "Portable Devices."

24. New York, Jewish Museum, JM 35–66.

25. Arnheim and Turniansky, *Yiddish Letters*, 69. In this case, the rumors were untrue.

26. Arnheim and Turniansky, *Yiddish Letters*, 73.

27. Maitlis, "London Yiddish Letters," 264, no. 5: "*Ikh bin recht broygez iber eykh, doz ir mir shreybt doz ikh zol mer geben az er.*"

28. Maitlis, "London Yiddish Letters," 162, dated 1713/14.

29. Arnheim and Turniansky, *Yiddish Letters*, 65–66.

30. Leipzig, UB Leipzig, MS B.H. 18, fol. 91r.

31. Buxtorf, *Institutio epistolaris hebraica*.

32. The Olav Tychsen Collection, University of Rostock, contains ca. six hundred Yiddish letters. According to Goldstein, "Jewish Communal Life," the collection contains no letters written by women and only five addressed to Jewish women. See discussion in Prager and Sabin Hill, "Yiddish Manuscripts," 105n53. For more on Tychsen and the Jews, see Leiman, "Two Cases"; Reichman, "What Became of Tychsen?"

33. Leipzig, UB Leipzig, MS B.H. 18; Carlebach, "Letters of Bella Perlhefter."

34. The original word for *Kreuzer* was *tselemer*, the Yiddish substitute for the currency whose name referred to a cross. Leipzig, UB Leipzig, MS B.H. 18, fol. 90r.

35. Maitlis, "London Yiddish Letters," 239, no. 1.

36. "*Den hot shem tov ba-kehillah, doz iz mekhtige gevirtiyut un hokhma ve-gam vissen.*"

37. Maitlis, "London Yiddish Letters," 162 (dated 1713/14).

38. Leipzig, UB Leipzig, MS B.H. 18, fol. 88r.

39. Leipzig, UB Leipzig, MS B.H. 18, fol. 88v.

40. For an annotated example of a household book from Hamburg, see Spalding and Spalding, *Account Books*.

41. A seventeenth-century single-leaf (from England) contains an (apparent) laundry list: "6 pair of slives; 6 cravats, 2 stocks; 4 servitours; 4 Napkins; 2 pairs of Ruffels; 4 shirts." University of St. Andrews blog, accessed Aug. 2, 2023.

42. AIU, MS Cod. H 9 A; Turniansky and Timm, *Yiddish in Italia*, 38, no. 36. The laundry lists appear on the blank folios before the beginning text; folios Ir-IIIv include eight laundry lists.

43. BnF, Gallica, MS Cod. héb. 1312. This manuscript is described extensively in Turniansky and Timm, *Yiddish in Italia*, 78–79, no. 73.

44. BnF, Gallica, MS Cod. héb. 1312, fol. 1r.

45. Narkiss, "Italian Niello Casket," 288–95.

46. JMP, MS 310.

47. Notaker, *Printed Cookbooks*.

48. JTS, MS 2709, *Segulot u-refu'ot*. Shoe polish, fol. 34v; unviable pregnancies, fol. 44r. The manuscript contains Hebrew prayers and verses for travelers, many Yiddish recipes, and some Latin words for herbs and medical terms.

49. JMP, MS 320, p. 47. Similarly, JMP, MS 294. Today, the neither-meat-nor-dairy recipes would be called *pareve*.

50. JMP, MS 324. This manuscript is dated as either from the late eighteenth or early nineteenth century.

51. For Christian women's cookbooks, see Kowalchuk, *Preserving on Paper*; Carlin, "Early Modern Culinary Texts."

52. Landau and Wachstein, *Jüdische privatbriefe*, 16–17, no. 5.

53. See, e.g., Glikl, *Zikhroynes* (2006), 204.

54. Jerusalem, Karlin-Stolin, MS 41, fol. 102v.

55. Tiktiner, *Meneket Rivkah*.

56. Tiktiner, *Meneket Rivkah*, 79.

57. "Ishah ha-hashuvah ha-rabbanit ha-darshanit Marat Rivkah." The term "rabbanit" often refers to a rabbi's wife, but there is no record of Rivkah's having been married to a rabbi, so we use the secondary translation, "learned woman."

58. Tiktiner, *Meneket Rivkah*, 80. The original phrase, "*dos eyn isha het oys ihren kup vos mekhaber gevesen*" (lit. "that a woman composed something out of her own head"), expresses the editor's sense of novelty at what he presented in print.

59. "Rivkah's nursemaid" (Gen. 35:8).

60. Chovav, *Maidens*, 225–30.

61. Bell, *How to Do It*.

62. von Rohden, introduction to Tiktiner, *Meneket Rivkah*, 33.

63. von Rohden, introduction to Tiktiner, *Meneket Rivkah*, 32, 95.

64. von Rohden, introduction to Tiktiner, *Meneket Rivkah*, 24. The extensive introduction to *Meneket Rivkah* by von Rohden contains much additional valuable analysis of Rivkah's pioneering status.

65. For the entire *lid* in its original, see Tiktiner, *Meneket Rivkah*, 283–85. The translation in Y. Kaplan, *Posen Library*, vol. 5, 350–51, crucially omits the word *betterins* after *kinder*, translating "pregnant women, children," rather than "pregnant women, parturients," as per Rivkah's text.

66. The Hebrew, beginning on line 45, reads "Rivkah bat Mhr"r Meir zt"l."

67. Jer. 31:7, 31:14–16.

68. For a discussion of the conflicting evidence, see von Rohden, introduction to *Meneket Rivkah*, 7.

69. Turniansky, introduction to Glikl, *Memoirs* (2019), 2. See the extended discussion there of Glikl's search for genre definition.

70. Universitätsbibliothek Frankfurt, MS Oct. 2, t.p., carries this attestation by Glikl's grandson, Hayim Hamel of Baiersdorf, from 1743.

71. Glikl, *Zikhroynes* (2006), 314; Glikl, *Memoirs* (2019), 177.

72. NLI MS Heb. 8° 4311, Flyleaf, fragment. "*Doz iz eyn bukh far yeder mensh; ver drinen leye kennen der zol yom vo-layla doriber sitzen.*"

73. See, e.g., Richarz, *Hamburger Kauffrau*.

74. Glikl, *Memoirs* (2019), 103.

75. Glikl, *Memoirs* (2019), 103.

76. Glikl, *Memoirs* (2019), 139–41.

77. Riemer and Senkbeil, introduction to *Be'er Sheva*, xvii-xix. This edition, while enormously useful, must be approached with several caveats. The Yiddish text contains numerous editing errors, and the manuscript on which it is based is a copy made in the late eighteenth century. No full manuscript has survived from an earlier date.

78. Riemer and Senkbeil, *Be'er Sheva*, 11.

79. Riemer and Senkbeil, *Be'er Sheva*, 10.

80. Riemer and Senkbeil, *Be'er Sheva*, 10. Like many women of this period, Bella held more tightly to her identity as her father's daughter than as the wife of her husband.

81. Bodleian, MS Opp. 148.

82. Bella explained that while the word *sheva* was spelled with an aleph in the Yiddish phonetic writing common at the time, "those who studied *dikduk*" (grammar and language arts) understand that the word *be'er* can be written with *ayin*, as the two are phonetically interchangeable in Yiddish, and moreover, that spelling encodes Ber's name in the title. Riemer and Senkbeil, *Be'er Sheva*, 9. Bella's note indicates that most women readers of the work would have encountered these words of biblical Hebrew origin only in their vernacular phonetic spelling.

83. Riemer and Senkbeil, *Be'er Sheva*, 91. The Zohar passages can be found in Parashat Shelah, ch. 25.

84. The words *alafim* (thousands) and *revavot* (myriad) can be found together in 1 Samuel, 18:6–9. The verses describe the joyful response of women's going forth to celebrate the victories of their king, Saul, and his general, David. Their song was (mis)interpreted by Saul as slighting him.

85. *Gehenom*, a term that can be loosely culturally compared to hell, was the place in the afterlife where people suffered for their sins. See also the discussion below.

86. Riemer and Senkbeil, *Be'er Sheva*, 93.

87. For a recent translation of the sections about the men's chambers, see Y. Kaplan, *Posen Library*, vol. 5, 660–61.

88. Bodleian, MS Opp. 148, fol. 43a.

89. Riemer and Senkbeil, *Be'er Sheva*, 95, lines 12–14.

90. Riemer and Senkbeil, *Be'er Sheva*, 7.

91. Bella listed four titles of Ber's works in progress: *Ali be'er*; *Me ha-be'er*; *Be'er la-hay ro'i*; and a *sefer evronot* that instructed how to make the Jewish calendar, titled *Be'er ha-golah*. Riemer and Senkbeil, *Be'er Sheva*, 7.

92. Riemer and Senkbeil, *Be'er Sheva*, 7.

93. Riemer and Senkbeil, *Be'er Sheva*, 7.

94. Riemer and Senkbeil, *Be'er Sheva*, 8.

95. Moore, "Quest for Consolation," 247–68; N. Z. Davis, *Women on the Margins*.

96. Turniansky, "Die Erzählungen," 121–48.

Chapter Six. Dynamic Households

1. See, e.g., the reproduction of an engraving by Christophe Bertello, *L'Échelle de la Vie Humaine*, Wellcome Collection 26361ii; another "ages of man" is represented in a step scheme, Wellcome Collection 26288i.

2. Wunder, *He Is the Sun*, 207. We have lightly edited her remarks.

3. Szoltysek, "Households," 313–41.

4. Tiktiner, *Meneket Rivkah*, 106.

5. Ozment, *When Fathers Ruled*.

6. On setting the wedding date, e.g., see Litt, *Jüdische Gemeindestatuten* (Takkanot Fürth, 1770), 165, par. 88.

7. Berkovitz, *Protocols*, 191, no. 24.

8. See Kaufmann, "Pinkas k"k Bamberg," 4–5, pars. 8 and 9; see also NLI, MS 2° 662, no. 277, par. 49; Litt, *Protokollbuch*, 173, pars. 78, 79.

9. See, e.g., the regulations from Alsace in Löwenstein, "Statuten," par. 17; Altona, in Graupe, *Die Statuten*, vol. 2, 96, 108; Düsseldorf, in Kaufmann, "Mekorot," 7–16, pars. 11–12; Litt, *Jüdische Gemeindestatuten* (Takkanot Fürth, 1770), 183, par. 82; Frankfurt, in NLI, MS 2° 662, no. 74; Schnaittach in Hildesheimer, *Pinkas kehillat Schnaittach*, 247, par. 60; *medinat Speyer*, in Ramat Gan, Bar-Ilan University, MS 803, fol. 1r-v, pars. 1–3.

10. Ettlinger, *Shu"t binyan Zion ha-hadashot*, no. 18. Both the widower and his future father-in-law were *kohanim* (of Jewish priestly descent), who were not permitted to wed women of questionable virtue.

11. D. Kaplan, *Patrons and Their Poor*, 65–66.

12. Litt, *Jüdische Gemeindestatuten* (Takkanot Fürth, 1770), 163, par. 82.

13. CAHJP, MS AHW 17a, fol. 65v. Multiple references to families' paying their debts so that they might betroth and marry off their children can be found in CAHJP, MS AHW 17a and 17b.

14. For examples of pre-marriage contracts see S. Halevi, *Nahalat shivah*, vol. 1, 83–157.

15. Roper, "'Going to Church,'" 86.

16. Litt, *Jüdische Gemeindestatuten* (Takkanot Worms, 1684), 95, pars. 58, 59.

17. Litt, *Jüdische Gemeindestatuten* (Takkanot Worms, 1684), 95, pars. 60–62.

18. Litt, *Jüdische Gemeindestatuten* (Takkanot Fürth, 1770), 165, par. 90.

19. Litt, *Jüdische Gemeindestatuten* (Takkanot Fürth, 1770), 166–168, par. 90.

20. Litt, *Jüdische Gemeindestatuten* (Takkanot Fürth, 1770), 174–175, par. 104.

21. Litt, *Jüdische Gemeindestatuten* (Takkanot Fürth, 1770), 174–175, par. 114.

22. Litt, *Jüdische Gemeindestatuten* (Takkanot Fürth, 1770), 168, par. 92.

23. Litt, *Jüdische Gemeindestatuten* (Takkanot Fürth, 1770), 170, par. 94. In the oath, the groom swore that the sum he had brought, as well as the sum his bride had brought, had been counted and that the sworn sum accounted for all debts and taxes due.

24. Litt, *Jüdische Gemeindestatuten* (Takkanot Fürth, 1770), 168–169, par. 93.

25. Litt, *Jüdische Gemeindestatuten* (Takkanot Fürth, 1770), 171–172, par. 97.

26. Kaufmann, "Pinkas k"k Bamberg," 5, par. 9.

27. See, e.g., Litt, *Protokollbuch*, 43, where dowry is exempt from certain taxpayer's assessments.

28. E. Horowitz, "Dowering," 347–71.

29. Litt, *Jüdische Gemeindestatuten* (Takkanot Fürth, 1770), 166, par. 90.

30. Kaufmann, "Pinkas k"k Bamberg," 5, par. 9.

31. Glikl, *Memoirs* (2019), 186.

32. Glikl, *Memoirs* (2019), 187.

33. Litt, *Protokollbuch*, 186, par. 176. Similarly, see Litt, *Jüdische Gemeindestatuten* (Takkanot Fürth, 1770), 163, par. 84.

34. Teplitsky, *Prince of the Press*, 83–84.

35. Meisl, *Pinkas kehillat Berlin*, 76, par. 81.

36. Bacharach, *Havot Yair*, no. 60.

37. Jerusalem, Karlin-Stolin, MS 41, fol. 23r.

38. Soliday, "Jews of Marburg," 506.

39. Meyer, *La communauté juive*, 228–33.

40. S. Lowenstein, *Berlin Jewish Community*, 174. On the median age at marriage, see Lowenstein, "Ashkenazic Jewry," 155–75.

41. S. Lowenstein further noted that the connection between early marriage and later conversion is an elite phenomenon; women from poorer families who converted often were not residents of Berlin.

42. Krakowski, *Coming of Age*, 120–28.

43. Ulbrich, *Shulamit*, 178–89.

44. CAHJP, MS AHW 121–1, p. 26a. See below for a detailed discussion of their household.

45. Litt, *Jüdische Gemeindestatuten* (Takkanot Fürth, 1770), 171, par. 97.

46. See the discussion in Berner, *In Their Own Way*, 47–48.

47. A. Halevi, *Memoiren*.

48. In one list from eighteenth-century Frankfurt, e.g., no male children under ten and no female children are included. See ISG, MS Juden Akten 17.

49. On midwives' records, see Carlebach, "Jewish Midwives."

50. Stern, *Der Preussische Staat*, vol. 1, part 2, 531–35. Berner calculated the mean number of children in Halberstadt as 2.7 per family, not taking into account households without children. Berner, *In their Own Way*, 47–48.

51. JTS, MS 8875, par. 645.

52. CAHJP, MS AHW 121–1, p. 26a.

53. Grossman, *Pious and Rebellious*, 150. For an English translation of the ordinance, see Finkelstein, *Jewish Self-Government*, 166–68. For a legal analysis of Rabbenu Tam's position and its roots, see A. Reiner, "Rabbenu Tam's Ordinance," 71–98.

54. Some medieval communities in eastern Germany and Austria rejected the ordinance. See Yahalom, "Dowry," 136–67.

55. There is a wide range of literature about the ordinance. For an overview, see Kupfer, *Teshuvot u-fesakim*, 316–24. For a recent treatment of the medieval ordinance and its spread, see Barzen, *Taqqanot Qehillot Sum*, 1: 239–47.

56. See extensive discussion of the various customs regarding the "years of return" in S. Halevi, *Nahalat shivah*, vol. 1, 183–91.

57. Jerusalem, Karlin-Stolin, MS 41, fol. 2r. For Frankfurt, see Fram, *Window*, no. 194, in which imperial authorities in Vienna inquire whether the Jewish community in Frankfurt had

adopted the medieval ordinance. See also no. 190 for a case that deals with a young bride who died in the second year of her marriage.

58. See Graupe, *Die Statuten*, vol. 2, 97, for fees paid to communal functionaries. The ordinances did not specify that these were to be paid by the groom's family. It may have been the common practice or one specific to this marriage.

59. Similar expenses are enumerated in talmudic and medieval sources. See Finkelstein, *Jewish Self-Government*, 160–68. See also Jerusalem, Karlin-Stolin, MS 41, fol. 124v, a responsum involving a husband who wished to deduct what he had spent on his wife's medical bills when she died in the first year of marriage without children. Her father, by contrast, insisted that his son-in-law was liable for these expenses.

60. Compare Fram, *Window*, 398–403.

61. Jerusalem, Karlin-Stolin, MS 41, fol. 2r.

62. Jerusalem, Karlin-Stolin, MS 41, fol. 10v. See also fol. 45r for a similar question.

63. Berkovitz, *Protocols*, 464, no. 62; 631–32, no. 265.

64. NLI, MS 4° 1092, fol. 161. Another Baila, daughter of R. Koppel Kohen in Frankfurt, was mourned for having died before she turned twenty years old. NLI, MS 4° 1092, fol. 165.

65. Landau and Wachstein, *Jüdische privatbriefe*, 35–36. The name "Reiniger" indicates that Baruch was a *menaker* (porger) who prepared meat to be ritually kosher after the *shohet* slaughtered it. It is unclear from the letter if Traune previously had been married or had children of her own. Baruch signed his letter in haste from the stall in the meat market. On the Tandelmarkt, see Miller, "Noisy and Noisome," 105–23.

66. Glikl, *Memoirs* (2019), 64.

67. Marx, "Autobiography."

68. Marx, "Autobiography," 277–78.

69. Berkovitz, *Protocols*, 413, no. 6.

70. Berkovitz, *Protocols*, 74, no. 36 (more on this case on pp. 145–46 and 612).

71. Berkovitz, *Protocols*, 405, no. 251; Berkovitz, *Law's Dominion*, 345, no. 159.

72. JTS, MS 10772, fol. 56v.

73. Litt, *Jüdische Gemeindestatuten* (Takkanot Fürth, 1770), 173–174, par. 112.

74. Litt, *Jüdische Gemeindestatuten* (Takkanot Fürth, 1770), 174, par. 114.

75. BT Ketubot 63b; Maimonides, *Mishneh Torah*, hilkhot ishut, 14:8 (*me'astihu*). Fram, *Window*, 323 (Oct. 2, 1782).

76. The decision accords with *Shulhan arukh*, *Even ha-ezer*, 77:3.

77. CAHJP, MS AHW 20, fol. 30b.

78. Berkovitz, *Protocols*, 412, no. 6.

79. CAHJP, MS AHW 121-1, p. 45a, par. 381, decision dated 18 Shevat 1769.

80. Berkovitz, *Protocols*, 413, no. 6.

81. Fram, *Window*, 377.

82. The extant court record notes that it is only a summary—a separate file of complaints, *kuntres ha-ta'anot*, had been deposited in the court.

83. Litt, *Jüdische Gemeindestatuten* (Takkanot Fürth, 1770), 175, par. 105.

84. Grossman, *Pious and Rebellious*, 231–52, contains a thorough overview of the available (mostly prescriptive) material from the medieval period in Europe.

85. Yuval, "Regulations," 190.

86. Yuval, "Regulations."

87. Bonfield, "Developments," 108–10.

88. Watt, "Impact," 134–36.

89. Berkovitz, *Protocols*, 652, no. 295.

90. Berkovitz, *Protocols*, 413–14, no. 8.

91. CAHJP, MS AHW 121–1, p. 41a, par. 329.

92. Berkovitz, *Law's Dominion*, 316–18.

93. Carlebach, *Divided Souls*, 35–36, 138–56.

94. Levi, *Recueil important*, n.p., cited in Carlebach, *Divided Souls*, 139.

95. Prague, Archives of the National Library of the Czech Republic, Censor and Reviewer of Jewish Books, Prints and Manuscripts, Prague, 1700–1842, Inv. No. 35, via JMP. Facsimile, JMP, PF 521.

96. For an example of a woman whose converted husband did grant her a bill of divorce, see Stadtarchiv Worms, MS 1B 2024/19.

97. CAHJP, MS D-Fr3-32, fol. 60.

98. See the case study by Evers, "Philipp Alexander and Crona David."

99. Grossman, *Pious and Rebellious*, 235.

100. Watt, "Impact," 131.

101. Shashar, *Gevarim*.

102. On the Jewish legal status of converts regarding dissolution of marriages in the medieval period, see Kanarfogel, *Brothers from Afar*.

103. Tal, *Ha-kehillah*, 64, no. 84.

104. A. Halevi, *Memoiren*, 40.

105. NLI, MS Heb. 8° 3212.

106. The rest are unspecified, often referred to as *ha-ishah* (the woman), or *zugato* (his spouse).

107. The pinkas did not list second marriages for some of these men, so the rate of second marriages would likely be slightly higher.

108. CAHJP, MS AHW 84a, fol. 11b: "From this day forward, the custom of the triple community [Altona-Hamburg-Wandsbek] will be that the female follows the male. The couple must hold membership in the community of the male."

109. To preserve the flow of the translation, we have inserted light interventions in punctuation and grammar throughout the text. The terms used to describe the community were culled from Ps. 48:3 and Isa. 1:21.

110. Isa. 54:6.

111. Here, the editors of the printed edition corrected the manuscript as per BT Rosh Hashanah 26a.

112. Esther 1:12.

113. It is not clear from the text whether Rachel was locked out of the house altogether or whether Shimon locked her out of the only heated room in the house during the winter.

114. Jerusalem, Karlin-Stolin, MS 41, fol. 24.

115. Liberles, "Family Life," 34–37.

116. Liberles, "Family Life," excerpts from p. 36.

117. ISG, MS Juden Akten 435, 7.

118. ISG, MS Juden Akten 3. Marriage restrictions were not placed on other religious minorities in Frankfurt—only on the Jews.

119. ISG, MS Juden Akten 973. More research is required to determine whether Jews married elsewhere to skirt this prohibition or whether they found ways to wed without permission.

120. ISG, MS Ratsprotokoll 1612, fol. 99r-v; MS BMB 182 (1613), fol. 328v.

121. Kahana, "Limitation," 203–6.

122. Baer, *Protokollbuch*, 58–59.

123. Kreager, "Early Modern Population Theory," 207–27.

124. Baer, *Protokollbuch*, 59n13.

125. Baer, *Protokollbuch*, 58–59.

126. Ullmann, "Poor Jewish Families," 111.

127. Baer, *Protokollbuch*, 59.

128. Stern, *Preussische Staat*, vol. 1, part 2, 531–35.

129. French, "Cock on the Hoop"; Johnson, "Politics."

130. This was the age for girls to enter service, according to the 1595 regulations from Krakow. See Balaban, "Die Krakauer Judengemeinde," 345.

131. Hahn, *Yosif ometz*, nos. 289–90, par. 6.

132. D. Kaplan, *Patrons and their Poor*, 81–84.

133. Tiktiner, *Meneket Rivkah*, 104.

134. Tiktiner, *Meneket Rivkah*, 105. See also 106 for an additional example in which a woman directed her Christian servant to light an oven and stuff the chickens on Yom Kippur. When admonished, the woman responded that "this is how she'd seen it done and how she'd always done it."

135. Heitze, mentioned in Yitta's will, married Samson Halberstadt and died at an old age in 1854. Epidat database, hha-4969. Hirsch died as a youth on 7 Iyyar 5540 [May 12, 1780]. Yoseph Bendit died on 11 Heshvan 5545 [October 26, 1784]. Two unnamed sons also died, one on 16 Heshvan 5552 [October 16, 1791], CAHJP, MS AHW 73, fol. 427; and the other on 2 Tishrei 5562 [September, 1801], AHW 73, fol. 480. Simon died on 10 Sivan 5562 [June 10, 1802]. See CAHJP, MS AHW 73, fols. 360, 389, 427, 480, 484. Marwedel, *Die Königlich privilegirte*, 734, n571.

136. The aforementioned burial records, beginning in 1792, refer to him as "parnas."

137. CAHJP, MS AHW 16, fol. 111a. For an extended discussion of Yitta's will, see chapter 9.

138. Smail, *Legal Plunder*, 35–45, noted (for late medieval Marseille) clothing and household textiles were expensive for most people; they often bought them in bulk and saved them for years, and they wore and reused individual items until they literally fell apart.

139. Smail and Shryock, "On Containers," 1–6, 49–51. For similar chests in contemporary Jewish inventories, CAHJP, MS AHW 71, fols. 4, 7a.

140. See, e.g., the ordinances of Friedberg: Litt, *Protokollbuch*, 186, pars. 174–75, which set a high bar for acquiring communal membership.

141. Soliday, "Jews of Marburg," 503, identifies four single individuals other than servants: two men and two women (one, an unwed mother).

142. Fram, *Window*, 308–11.

143. Fram, *Window*, 101–5.

144. Jüdisches Museum Franken, MS 1998.002, fol. 19v.
145. CAHJP, MS P35–79.
146. Meisl, *Pinkas kehillat Berlin*, no. 332.
147. Fram, *Window*, 391.
148. See Bennett and Froide, *Singlewomen*.
149. D. Kaplan, *Patrons and their Poor*, 151–53.
150. Jüdisches Museum Franken, MS 1998.002, fol 40v.
151. See, e.g., Epidat database, ffb-1061 (1772).
152. Epidat database, ffb-109 (1776).
153. Epidat database, hha-1445.
154. Epidat database, wrm-321.
155. Epidat database, smk-29. The language echoes Esther 9:22 in reverse.
156. Epidat database, hha-678.
157. D. Kaplan, *Patrons and their Poor*, 76–77. Friedrichs, "Jewish Household Structure."

Chapter Seven. Economic Agents

1. CAHJP, MS D-Fr3-32, fol. 169r.
2. CAHJP, MS D-Fr3-32, fol. 58v.
3. CAHJP, MS D-Fr3-32, fol. 57v.
4. CAHJP, MS D-Wo3-339, fol. 29.
5. See, e.g., Toch, "Jewish Women Entrepreneurs," 256; Keil, "Business Success"; Grossman, *Pious and Rebellious*, 117–21; Baumgarten, *Practicing Piety*, 103–71. On responsa as a historical source, see Soloveitchik, *Use of Responsa*.
6. Bartlet, "Three Jewish Businesswomen." One of the best-attested professions for medieval Jewish women is midwifery. See Baumgarten, "Ask the Midwives."
7. Meisl, *Pinkas kehillat Berlin*, p. 4, par. 9.
8. On gatekeeping in Berlin, see Bodian, "Jewish Entrepreneurs," 174–75.
9. See, e.g., the account books of one Christian family. Spalding and Spalding, *Account Books of the Reimarus Family*.
10. Fram, *Window*, 255, no. 121.
11. On the importance of notaries in early modern Europe, see Nussdorfer, *Brokers of Public Trust*. On the preference for a notarized document in a Jewish court, see Berkovitz, *Law's Dominion*, 178.
12. CAHJP, MS D-Sc10-28.
13. Leipzig, UB Leipzig, MS B.H. 18, fol. 85v.
14. The city passed into Austrian hands in 1772; it was then called Lemberg.
15. S. Halevi, *Nahalat shivah*, vol. 1, 457–88; Berkovitz, *Law's Dominion*, 171.
16. Berkovitz, *Law's Dominion*, 278–81.
17. For examples of women's cases before the rabbinical court in medieval Ashkenaz, see Furst, "Marriage before the Bench."
18. Baumann, "Jüdische Reichskammergerichtsprozesse."
19. Kasper-Marienberg, "Jewish Women," 179. On Jewish women before the imperial supreme court from the sixteenth century, see Menashe, "Imperial Supreme Court."

20. Berkovitz, *Law's Dominion*, 296.

21. These numbers, based on CAHJP, MS AHW 121–1, do not take into account multiple appearances by the same party over time. See Carlebach, "Big Stakes."

22. See, e.g., a question sent by the imperial court to the rabbinical court in Frankfurt about its marriage records. Fram, *Window*, 564–65 (Appendix 6).

23. Schneider, "Women before the Bench," 8–9.

24. Berkovitz, *Law's Dominion*, 283–331.

25. On the importance of the dowry and its impact on a girl's adolescence, see Krakowski, *Coming of Age*, 142–80.

26. Hughes, "From Brideprice to Dowry"; E. Horowitz, "Dowering."

27. D. Kaplan, *Patrons and their Poor*, 37–38. On solicitations, see Friedman, "Letters of Recommendation."

28. Jerusalem, Karlin-Stolin, MS 41, fol. 94r.

29. The question at stake was whether the community could redirect money designated for dowering the daughter to another charitable purpose.

30. Berkovitz, *Law's Dominion*, 295.

31. CAHJP, MS D-Wo3-548.

32. Berkovitz, *Protocols*, 979, no. 649. See also Berkovitz, *Law's Dominion*, 294–96.

33. Litt, *Jüdische Gemeindestatuten* (Takkanot Metz, 1769), 358–361, pars. 5–8.

34. Glikl, *Zikhroynes* (2006), 310–11.

35. CAHJP MS D-Wo 3–339, fol. 30.

36. Graupe, "Jewish Testaments," 29.

37. Berkovitz, *Law's Dominion*, 275–76.

38. CAHJP, MS D-Wo 3–339, fol. 31. Although Jews in Worms did not technically own their houses, which the Jewish community rented from the municipality, they retained the right to buy and sell as if they were the homeowners, so long as the rent was paid to the municipal government.

39. JTS, MS 9835, fol. 19. See chapter 9.

40. In addition to the examples described below, see Jerusalem, Karlin-Stolin, MS 41, fols. 65r, 190.

41. Jerusalem, Karlin-Stolin, MS 41, fol. 135.

42. Jerusalem, Karlin-Stolin, MS 41, fol. 188.

43. Berkovitz, *Law's Dominion*, 281–82. The appeal was brought before the Parlement in 1786.

44. Malino, "Resistance and Rebellion"; J. R. Katz, "'To Judge,'" 450–53.

45. Malino, "Resistance and Rebellion"; J. R. Katz, "'To Judge,'" 453–56.

46. Berkovitz, *Protocols*, 589–90, no. 208.

47. Howell, *Women, Production, and Patriarchy*, 9–20.

48. For a full discussion of the division of marital property, see Berkovitz, *Law's Dominion*, 294.

49. CAHJP, MS AHW 20, fol. 11a.

50. Shashar, *Gevarim*.

51. Mi-See, *Shu"t yefe nof*, no. 83. He does not include a currency; we assume he referred to Gulden.

52. CAHJP, MS D-Wo3-339, fol. 30.

53. CAHJP, MS D-W03-339, fol. 26.
54. Graupe, "Jewish Testaments," 13.
55. CAHJP, MS D-W03-339, fol. 29.
56. CAHJP, MS D-W03-339, fol. 28. Medieval and early modern responsa deal with the question of lost marriage contracts. See, e.g., a responsum by Rabbi Joseph Colon (Italy, fifteenth century), *She'elot u-teshuvot Maharik*, no. 72.
57. Berkovitz, *Law's Dominion*, 321–25. The mechanism Berkovitz describes was used frequently in Ashkenazi communities in northern Europe.
58. Wiesner, *Working Women*, 28.
59. NLI, MS Heb. 2° 662, no. 136.
60. CAHJP, MS D-Fr3-32, fols. 229r-230v.
61. CAHJP, MS D-Fr3-32, fol. 230r.
62. Jerusalem, Karlin-Stolin, MS 41, fol. 25v.
63. Kaufmann, "Mekorot . . . k"k Metz," 3–5.
64. D. Kaplan, *Patrons and their Poor*, 98–99.
65. Prager and Hill, "Yiddish Manuscripts," 90.
66. CAHJP, MS D-W03-401.
67. Litt, *Jüdische Gemeindestatuten* (Takkanot Metz, 1769), 375, no. 60.
68. Kalaora, "Jewish Widows' Homes."
69. See, e.g., Fram, *Window*, nos. 149, 150, 178.
70. CAHJP, MS AHW 71, fol. 7.
71. Fram, *Window*, no. 66.
72. Tevlin owned one-quarter of one house and two-thirds of another. While he placed a lien on the quarter house, he stipulated that it was within his rights to move the lien to the other home.
73. CAHJP, MS D-W03-339, fol. 22.
74. Toch, "Jewish Women Entrepreneurs," 256; D. Kaplan, "Women and Worth."
75. For earlier work that argued for a decline, see Wiesner, *Working Women*, 7; Howell, *Women, Production, and Patriarchy*. For a historiographic discussion and new approaches, see Bellavitis, *Women's Work and Rights*, 48–53.
76. Berkovitz, *Law's Dominion*, 328; Fram, *Window*, 35.
77. Ginsberg, "Private yiddishe briv," 342, letter V.
78. Glikl, *Memoirs* (2019), 126.
79. NLI, MS 4° 1092, fol. 577.
80. Toch, "Jewish Women Entrepreneurs," 258.
81. Kaufmann, "Pinkas k"k Bamberg."
82. *Eks[t]rakt mi-protokol shel ha-medinah*.
83. JTS, MS 8875, par. 460.
84. CAHJP, MS AHW 71, fol. 50.
85. Fram, *Window*, 117, no. 48.
86. D. Kaplan, *Beyond Expulsion*, 79.
87. Berkovitz, *Protocols*, 325, no. 147. Fram, *Window*, 35, argues that, in Frankfurt, married women were usually heard by the court through a representative or agent, although there were exceptions.

88. Staudinger, "Ungleichheiten als Chance?" 395–97.
89. CAHJP, MS D-Fr3-32, fol. 59v.
90. Dermineur, "Credit, Strategies, and Female Empowerment."
91. For Worms, see Schammes, *Minhagim de-k"k Warmaisa*, vol. 2, par. 280. For Frankfurt, see NLI, MS Heb. 2° 662, no. 8. For Runkel, see Wachstein, "A yiddishe kahal," at par. 3.
92. CAHJP, MS P35-79. Parameters for taxing orphaned males and females were also included.
93. Berkovitz, *Protocols*, 387–88, no. 224.
94. Berkovitz, *Protocols*, 67–68, no. 26.
95. Ullmann, "Poor Jewish Families," 95–96.
96. D. Kaplan, *Beyond Expulsion*.
97. Ullman, "Poor Jewish Families," 96–98.
98. Cited in Ulbrich, *Shulamit*, 195.
99. Halpern, *Pinkas va'ad arba aratzot*, no. 52 (for the year 1607); Dubnow, *Pinkas ha-medinah*, nos. 132, 259, 356.
100. For the Leipzig fair, see Freudenthal, *Leipziger Messgäste*; Markgraf, *Zur Geschichte der Juden*.
101. Glikl, *Zikhroynes* (2006), 62, 496.
102. Staudinger, "Ungleichheiten als Chance?" 394.
103. D. Kaplan, "'Because Our Wives Trade.'" See Fram, *My Dear Daughter*, 50, regarding a case in which a man in Poland sought to divorce his wife because she walked the streets and marketplaces.
104. Bacharach, *Havot Yair*, no. 182.
105. Glikl, *Zikhroynes* (2006), 110, 185. For other references to travel on the mail train, see 146, 304.
106. Kobler, *Letters*, vol. 2, 456–58.
107. Glikl, *Zikhroynes* (2006), 282.
108. On court Jewish women, esp. their use of the court system, see Evers, "Traces of Court Jewish Women."
109. Teplitsky, *Prince of the Press*, 83–84.
110. Wiesner-Hanks, *Women and Gender*, 277; Akkerman and Houben, *Politics of Female Households*.
111. NLI, MS 8° 2398, fol. 14.
112. JTS, MS 8875, par. 610. See also par. 613.
113. NLI, MS 8° 2398, fol. 45.
114. On Madame Kaulla, see G. Katz, *Die erste Unternehmerin*; Hebell, "Madame Kaulla"; Ries, "'Unter Königen.'"
115. Hamburg, Staats-und Universitätsbibliothek Hamburg Carl von Ossietzky, MS Cod. Levy 137, fol. 27.
116. This can be found throughout contemporary Memorbücher as well. See, e.g., the reference to Hendele Kann (d. 1784), mentioned above, who was compared to the biblical woman of valor in the context of her knowledge of sums, languages, and recordkeeping.
117. Her epitaph is published in Pinner, *Kitve yad*, 101.
118. NLI, MS Heb. 4° 656, fol. 3.

119. CAHJP, MS D-W03-372, fol. 1r.

120. Habermann, *Nashim ivriot*, 7.

121. Fram, *My Dear Daughter*, 54n88.

122. Habermann, *Nashim ivriot*, 13.

123. Hellerstein, *Question of Tradition*, 63–69. See also Turniansky, "Young Women in Early Modern Yiddish Literature."

124. Habermann, *Nashim ivriot*, 12–13.

125. Fram, *My Dear Daughter*, 54.

126. See Taglicht, *Nachlässe*, 201–7; NLI MS Heb. 2° 662, par 82.

127. Kronenberger, *Der jüdischen Vieh- und Pferdehändler*, 13; Ulbrich, *Shulamit*, 194.

128. Bacharach, *Havot Yair*, no. 198.

129. CAHJP, Inv. 1338.1, nos. 1–8. We have not found evidence of other women serving as *shohtot* (ritual slaughterers) in this region and period.

130. Maitlis, "London Yiddish Letters," vol. 2, 240, no. 2.

131. Ullmann, "Poor Jewish Families," 100–112; Ulbrich, *Shulamit*, 196.

132. ISG, MS Juden Akten 17.

133. Hahn, *Yosif ometz*, nos. 289–290, par. 6.

134. NLI, MS Heb. 2° 662, par. 320, no. 46.

135. See D. Kaplan, *Patrons and Their Poor*, 81. There were 348 maidservants in 1703 and 446 in 1709.

136. Litt, *Jüdische Gemeindestatuten* (Takkanot Frankfurt, 1674/5), 64, par. 29.

137. CAHJP, MS AHW 15, no. 145.

138. CAHJP, MS AHW 17b, fol. 53b.

139. Ulbrich, *Shulamit*, 204–5.

140. Fram, *Window*, no. 185.

141. CAHJP, MS AHW 17b, fol. 4b.

142. Reischer, *Shu"t shevut Yaakov*, pt. 3, no. 121.

143. E. Horowitz, "Between Masters and Maidservants."

144. Mi-See, NLI, MS Heb. 4° 522, *Shu"t yefe nof*, fols. 49–50.

145. ISG, MS Juden Akten 17.

146. Hahn, *Yosif ometz*, no. 826. For depictions of Jewish maids working, see Ries, "Jüdische Mägde."

147. Graupe, *Die Statuten*, 53, 67–69.

148. CAHJP, MS AHW 9, fol. 17, par. 95.

149. E.g., Meisl, *Pinkas kehillat Berlin*, 205–6, par. 205. Carlson, *Domestic Service*, 54n26, notes that over 100 women in Amsterdam acted as placement agents for maidservants, some part-time.

150. For examples of contemporaneous regulations in German lands, see Schröder, "Gesinderecht," 13–39.

151. CAHJP, MS AHW 121–1, p. 42a, par. 359.

152. CAHJP, MS AHW 121–1, p. 81, pars. 1075, 1076.

153. On the migrant status of many servants in Jewish communities in Germany, see Richarz, "Mägde, Migration und Mutterschaft." For the laboring poor, D. Kaplan, *Patrons and Their Poor*, 80–86.

154. Ulbrich, *Shulamit*, 206.
155. CAHJP, MS HM2 4447, fol. 21a.
156. A. Unna, *Pinkas ha-takkanot*, 75, 95, 117.
157. A. Unna, *Pinkas ha-takkanot*, 75, 95, 117.
158. NLI, MS Heb. 2° 662, no. 193.
159. NLI, MS Heb. 2° 662, no. 83a.
160. JTS, MS 3697, written by David ben Aryeh Leyb, ca. 1650–96.
161. See Jones and Stallybrass, *Renaissance Clothing*, 134–35.
162. Ulbrich, *Shulamit*, 194.
163. Jerusalem, Karlin-Stolin, MS 41, fol. 82.
164. Smail, index to *Legal Plunder*, s.v. clothing.
165. See, e.g., CAHJP, MS AHW 71, fol. 6.
166. CAHJP, MS D-W03-337.
167. Museum Judengasse.
168. Liberles, *Jews Welcome Coffee*, 71.
169. See, for example, ISG, MS Criminalia 609.
170. Marx, "Autobiography," 277.
171. CAHJP, MS AHW 121-1, p. 32, par. 142.
172. Compare CAHJP, MS AHW 121-1, p. 65a, par. 760 through fol. 71, par. 865.
173. Ulbrich, *Shulamit*, 195.
174. CAHJP, MS AHW 17b, fols. 3–4.

175. For repairing clothing, see Toch, "Jewish Women Entrepreneurs," 259, regarding Sara, wife of Isaac of Alsfeld (1529), who "used to sew shirts and collars for her customers." On rural women, see D. Kaplan, "Women and Worth."

176. Lindemann, *Patriots and Paupers*, 48. On Jewish wetnursing, see Salmon-Mack, *Tan-du*, 91–97.

177. On maidservants and wetnurses in Altona and Hamburg, see Carlebach, "Fallen Women."

178. The ruling may have been informed by the fact that the wife had two daughters from a previous marriage whom Meir was required to support until age fifteen, and one of the girls was close to that age. Leaving the daughters alone at home with their stepfather overnight would have created additional halakhic problems. If Berkovitz is correct in assuming that this Meir Weil is the same as Meir, son of Hertz Weil, who married Fogel, the widow of Itzik of Courcelle, the couple had quarreled before the court even prior to their marriage. See Berkovitz, *Protocols*, 168–69, no. 138.

179. Berkovitz, *Protocols*, 412–13, no. 6. The principle is "*eini nizonet ve-eini osah*" (I will not be supported, and I will not sustain).

180. Litt, *Jüdische Gemeindestatuten* (Takkanot Fürth, 1770), 201, par. 209.
181. CAHJP, MS AHW 10, par. 150, *published in* Graupe, *Die Statuten*, vol. 2, 90.
182. J. R. Katz, *Jewish Midwives, Medicine*.
183. NLI, MS Heb. 4° 1092, fol. 157 (1724).
184. Epidat database, wrm-1024.
185. Epidat database, wrm-1.
186. Emden, *Birat migdal oz*, 33.

187. Assaf, *Mekorot*, vol. 1, 147, par. 3. The Hebrew term is *melekhet nashim*.

188. Frye, *Pens and Needles*, 126–59.

189. Leipzig, UB Leipzig, MS B. H. 18, fol. 91r; Weinryb, "Historisches und Kulturhistorisches . . . Briefwechsel," 339–40, no. V.

190. Epidat database, ffb-4065 (1771).

191. Her list of mail and payments, in transliteration, appears in Landau and Wachstein, *Jüdische privatbriefe*, no. 47, pp. 97–98; pp. 59–60 in the Hebrew.

192. Landau and Wachstein, *Jüdische privatbriefe*, 43–44.

193. Landau and Wachstein, *Jüdische privatbriefe*, 53.

194. Landau and Wachstein, *Jüdische privatbriefe*, 41.

195. Landau and Wachstein, *Jüdische privatbriefe*, 94, no. 46.

Chapter Eight. Material Worlds

1. CAHJP, MS AHW 71, fol. 5.

2. An example of a widow requesting financial support from an estate can be found in CAHJP, MS AHW 121-2, fol. 11, and repeated almost verbatim on a small slip of paper inserted at folio 294. Similarly, Gutle, widow of Bendit Schammes in Frankfurt, demanded of her husband's estate a sum of five thousand Gulden, to be held in escrow until her halitzah was finalized. Among her claims was one for "her expenses to open the seal of the authorities so that she could remove some clothes." Fram, *Window*, 503 (at lines 14–15).

3. See Auslander, "Beyond Words," 1015–44.

4. The women we study lived for the most part in expanding economies by the eighteenth century; they often had opportunities not yet available to those of rural economies such as those described by Ogilvie, *Bitter Living*.

5. Smail, *Legal Plunder*; Ago, *Gusto*; Roche, *Culture of Clothing*.

6. Wiesner, *Working Women*, 143. For a Jewish woman's inventory, see Aust, "Was von einem Leben."

7. This community was a branch of the Ashkenazi community in Altona whose members resided in nearby Hamburg. CAHJP, MS AHW 71.

8. Taglicht, *Nachlässe*, based on the wills probated in the Archiv des K.K. Landesgerichtes in Zivilsachen.

9. See, e.g., CAHJP, MS AHW 71, fol. 2a: "Because R. Bendit [shamash] was in Altona, I summoned R. Zimle, may he live, to attend the sealing with me." One official served as "shamash and notary," while the other was "cantor and notary."

10. When R. Leyb Düsseldorf of Altona died in 1789, he left two separate chests with possessions, each fitted with a separate padlock. The shamash recorded that his daughters received for their personal use three *leichter* (silver lamps), four silver spoons, three blouses, and one table linen. The estate was unsealed several months later. CAHJP, MS AHW 71, fol. 2a.

11. CAHJP, MS AHW 71, fol. 6.

12. CAHJP, MS AHW 71, fol. 7.

13. CAHJP, MS AHW 71, fol. 10a. The term for her stipend in the source is *peras*.

14. Riello and Rublack, *Right to Dress*, 20, argue that by the mid-sixteenth century, advances in global commerce already made fabrics such as silk affordable and accessible to broad swaths of the population.
15. Riello, "'Things Seen and Unseen,'" 125–40.
16. Taglicht, *Nachlässe*, 239, no. 245.
17. D. Horowitz, "Domestic Interiors," 98–103.
18. Since she died childless within the first two years of marriage, it was customary for the families to disentangle their finances. This has been discussed in detail in chapter 6.
19. CAHJP, MS AHW 121–1, p. 26a. "*Lo hayu ha-devarim me-olam.*"
20. BR, Hs. Ros. 572.
21. Guineas, various Reichsthaler, ducats, and Gulden.
22. The books on the list were *Zera Berakh* (by Berekhya Berakh; an edition was printed in 1730), a Haggadah for Passover (no edition listed); *Bigde Aaron* (an edition was printed in 1711), and *Sefer tsemah David* (by David Gans, Prague, 1592).
23. See McCants, "Porcelain for the Poor," 316–41.
24. Fram, *Window*, 505–6.
25. Aust, "Covering," 5–21.
26. On sumptuary regulations in Europe, see Riello and Rublack, *Right to Dress*, 6. They note (8) that German principalities issued the greatest number of sumptuary regulations during this period. See also chapter 9.
27. Metz regulations of 1769. Original in JTS, MS 8136, cited here from the printed version in Stefan Litt, *Jüdische Gemeindestatuten* (Takkanot Metz, 1769), 359, par. 5.
28. Litt, *Jüdische Gemeindestatuten* (Takkanot Metz, 1769), 359, and translations of some terms ad loc.
29. Litt, *Jüdische Gemeindestatuten* (Takkanot Metz, 1769), 361. The more expensive fabrics, such as silk and cotton, also provided a more comfortable sensation to the wearer than did the coarser textiles used to make servants' garb.
30. Riello and Rublack, *Right to Dress*, 15, argue that the fines were a means of collecting a luxury tax, as the very wealthy could afford to flout the regulations and pay the fines. See 17, ad loc., for a parallel to the *ba'ale hashgahot* and *shomre takkanot*; in Florence, *birri* were appointed to patrol the streets and impose fines on violators of sumptuary laws.
31. Landau and Wachstein, *Jüdische privatbriefe*, 29, no. 10. On the familial links in this correspondence see Hödl, "Die Briefe"; J. Davis, "Concepts."
32. CAHJP, MS AHW 16, fols. 74a–75. Sarah's will is dated 3 Nissan 1782.
33. CAHJP, MS AHW 16, fol. 111a.
34. CAHJP, MS AHW 16, fol. 108.
35. Hsia, "Christian Ethnography," 223–35; Deutsch, "Polemical Ethnographies," 202–33.
36. Liberles, *Jews Welcome Coffee*, 71; Kahana, "Shabbat," 5–50.
37. "*Alte weibe tefillah,*" CAHJP, MS AHW 71, fol. 15.
38. CAHJP, MS AHW 121–1, p. 35, par. 210. See also the example of Sarlen, discussed below.
39. Fynes Moryson (1566–1630), based on a 2-month stay in Prague in 1592. Cited in Spicer, "Star of David," 218.

40. See chart and analysis in D. Kaplan, *Patrons and Their Poor*, 87. For parallels, see Teller, *Hayim be-tzavta*.

41. Fram, *Window*, 114–17.

42. Fram, *Window*, 171.

43. On Prague and Bohemian and Moravian Jewry, see, most recently, Kasper-Marienberg and Teplitsky, "Jews," 22–60.

44. Halevi, *Memoiren*, 32.

45. Marx, "Autobiography," 294.

46. Ulbrich, *Shulamit*, 166.

47. Ulbrich, *Shulamit*, 175.

48. Ulbrich, *Shulamit*, 181. In contrast to Asher's report on the mingling of the sexes in the baths, Ulbrich notes from several testimonies that separation of the sexes in religious matters, not just in synagogue seating but also in evening attendance, was seen as a distinguishing sign between Jews and Christians. Ulbrich, *Shulamit*, 189.

49. Ulbrich, *Shulamit*, 176, reproduces a map of the layout of the house and the spaces allocated to each family.

50. Worms, Stadtsarchiv Worms, MS 1 B 2024/11, fol. 2r.

51. Worms, Stadtarchiv Worms, MS 1 B 2024/11. Jewish households in Worms were typically multigenerational. Friedrichs, "Jewish Household Structure," 481–93.

52. Worms, Stadtarchiv Worms, MS 1 B 2024/11.

53. Szoltysek, "Households," 313–41.

54. Kroder and Kroder-Gumann, *Schnatticher Hauschronik*, 475.

55. Berkovitz, *Protocols*, 454, no. 48.

56. CAHJP, MS D-Fr3-32, fol. 76r.

57. Ulbrich, *Shulamit*, 176.

58. Ulbrich, *Shulamit*, 198–200.

59. Ullmann, "Poor Jewish Families," 106–9.

60. Jerusalem, Karlin-Stolin, MS 41, fol. 35v.

61. Berkovitz, *Protocols*, 631, no. 263.

62. CAHJP, MS AHW 71, fol. 7a, lists two portraits of the well-to-do (male) deceased, a large and a small one. CAHJP, MS AHW 71, fol. 12a, lists a mirror.

63. NLI, MS 2° 662, no. 193.

64. Sulzbach, "Wohltätigkeitsverein," 241–66.

65. Hahn, *Yosif ometz*, no. 442.

66. Ulbrich, *Shulamit*, 198–99.

67. CAHJP, MS AHW 71. *Tevah*, fols. 2a, 12; *kist* or *kistel*, fol. 3, 3a; *schatel*, fol. 3, 3a; *shank* or *shenklche*, fol. 3; *coffret*, fol. 4a.

68. CAHJP, MS AHW 71, fol. 3.

69. *Contoir*, CAHJP, MS AHW 71, fols. 7–7a. On the importance of containers of all types, see Smail, *Legal Plunder*, 32–35.

70. See, e.g., CAHJP, MS AHW 71, fol. 12, regarding a maidservant who fell ill and was sent to the hospice. Her employer gave a chest with her belongings to her brother-in-law.

71. See Fennetaux, "Women's Pockets." Note the purse hanging from the waist of the female mikveh attendant in Kirchner, *Jüdisches Ceremoniel*, ed. Jugendres (Nuremberg, 1724), copper-

plate 24, lower right. CAHJP, MS AHW 71, fol. 7, notes that a widow left behind a *kis* containing two Mark and twelve Schilling.

72. Hirsch, *Megalleh tekuphoth*, 27.

73. See a depiction of such a "stairwell kitchen" with oven in Kasper-Marienberg and Kaplan, "Nourishing," 306.

74. It is unclear if this was a depiction of a Jewish or Christian dwelling. Staatsbibliothek zu Berlin-Stiftung Preussischer Kulturbesitz, MS Or. Oct. 3150, fol. 78r. The image is reproduced in Carlebach, *Palaces*, 73.

75. Ago, *Gusto*, 95.

76. CAHJP, MS, AHW 71, fol. 5a.1, fol. 5a.

77. Schudt, *Jüdische Merckwürdigkeiten*, vol. 2, 364.

78. Schudt, *Jüdische Merckwürdigkeiten*, vol. 2, 364.

79. "Die reichen Juden helfen den Armen von den Ihrigen aus, damit sie nach dem Gesetz Oster-Kuchen essen können." Kirchner, *Jüdische Ceremoniel*, 87.

80. Hildesheimer, *Pinkas kehillat Schnaittach*, 158, par. 2; CAHJP, MS AHW 31b, a pinkas that recorded matzah distribution in the triple community.

81. For Schnaittach, Hildesheimer, *Pinkas kehillat Schnaittach*, 195–96, par. 2.

82. Presumably, serving spoons.

83. A. Unna, *Pinkas ha-takkanot*, 73, par. 36.

84. JTS, MS 10772, flyleaf.

85. Gutin's first name is not on the inscription; it can be found in S. Unna, *Gedenkbuch*, 18, no. 128. For Hirtz Popert's tombstone (d. 1625): Epidat database, ffb-960. The Hebrew letters for the year are cleverly configured to spell *shalet*, the food intended to be stored in the pot.

86. Schudt, *Jüdsiche Merckwürdigkeiten*, vol. 22, 76–77, cited and trans. in Kasper-Marienberg and Kaplan, "Nourishing," 318.

87. Kasper-Marienberg and Kaplan, "Nourishing," 304–9, contains several relevant descriptions of cooking arrangements within the Frankfurt Jewish ghetto.

88. JTS, MS 3684, SHF 1545:23–24, fol. 31b, printed in Litt, *Protokollbuch*, 54.

89. Halevi, *Memoiren*, 32; for Ahron Cahen, see Ulbrich, *Shulamit*, 202.

90. Kirchner, *Jüdisches Ceremoniel*, 79. Copperplate 3 (near p. 79) depicts a woman lighting candles on three separate candlesticks.

91. Kosman, *Noheg ka-tzon Yosef*, no. 154, attributed the Sephardi practice of lighting seven candles to the Lurianic custom of lighting one candle for each day of the week.

92. JTS, MS 8855 (= CAHJP HM2–5037), fols. 10, 19.

93. CAHJP, MS AHW 71, fol. 2a.

94. See Carlebach, *Palaces*, 162, Fig. 7.2.

95. CAHJP, MS AHW 20, fol. 9a. See also Gross Collection 017.001.007 (17).

96. Jakobovits, "Die Juden Abzeichen," 154–70; Carlebach, "Death," 25–26. On the imposition of earrings on northern Italian Jewish women as a sign of shame, see Hughes, "Distinguishing Signs," 3–59; Cassen, *Marking*, 90–101. Cassen notes some instances when Jewish women were exempt from wearing a particular Jewish hat because their regular headgear sufficiently distinguished them from Christian women (101).

97. See Hahn, *Yosif ometz*, 426, par. 2, where women specifically are mentioned.

98. Aust, "Noble Dress," 90–112.

99. In Riello and Rublack, "Right to Dress," 39–40, Rublack argues that works such as Hans Weigel's *Trachtenbuch* (Nuremberg, 1577) and Jost Amman's *Frauentrachtenbuch* (Frankfurt, 1586) showed thousands of people the possibilities for dress across sexes and classes in rich detail.

100. See Aust, "Covering."

101. The Metz takkanot, cited in Litt, *Jüdische Gemeindestatuten* (Takkanot Metz, 1769), 359, par. 5, specified the permitted size for *graines de beauté* (applied beauty marks).

102. Ulbrich, *Shulamit*, 167.

103. CAHJP, MS D-W03-339, fol. 3v.

104. Fram, *Window*, no. 138.

Chapter Nine. Last Words

1. The will was edited and printed by J. Bloch, "Le testament," 146–60. The Yiddish text begins on p. 154.

2. AIU, MS 423, fol. 4v.

3. AIU, MS 423, fol. 1r.

4. Glikl, *Zikhroynes* (2006), 314; *Memoirs* (2019), 177. See chapter 5.

5. Glikl's memoir remains difficult to classify. Certainly, it is in part an ethical will. It is also a memoir, a reckoning, a literary miscellany, and a collection of tales.

6. On the genre of ethical wills, see Abrahams, *Hebrew Ethical Wills*.

7. AIU, MS 423, fol. 4v.

8. AIU, MS 423, fol. 5v.

9. Francesconi, *Invisible Enlighteners*, 9, applies the concept of "coauthor" to the mediated voices of Modenese Jewish women whose minutes of the *So'ed holim* society were kept by a male scribe.

10. Moody, "Wills," 16–20.

11. In order to avoid the pitfalls of distributions that would violate biblical rules, many of the testators formulaically designated the inheritance as a "gift to be distributed one hour before my death." This classical solution was problematic in the eyes of some medieval decisors; nevertheless, it was widespread in the early modern wills. On similar practices, see Berkovitz, *Law's Dominion*, 275.

12. Berkovitz, *Law's Dominion*, 271. A will in Jewish law had similar weight to a testament in Roman law, in that it could override prevailing legal norms if it did not contravene Jewish law outright, and the document itself had integrity.

13. AIU, MS 423, fol. 3r.

14. Mirvis, *Jews of Eighteenth-Century Jamaica*, is a wonderful example of the history of a Jewish community whose wills were almost universally probated.

15. In the Jewish wills copied into CAHJP, MS AHW 16, the non-Jewish government was often invoked as enforcement for collecting fines, such as those threatened for anyone who contested the will. Sarah, widow of Meir Stern, asked that funds she allocated to dower her granddaughters be held at the "Hamburg Kammer" after a year had passed. Perhaps she did not trust the Jewish kahal to retain the proper records in the long term. CAHJP, MS AHW 16, fol. 75.

16. See, e.g., JTS, MS 9835, which is almost entirely devoted to the will made by Fromet, widow of Elia Levi, in Metz.

17. CAHJP, MS AHW 16. Four of the wills from that collection were published in Graupe, "Jewish Testaments," 9–33.

18. The will of Yitta the maidservant, discussed at length in chapter 6 and below, was something of a hybrid. It was written by the shamash while she was ill, and then sealed in the customary way until her death. CAHJP, MS AHW 16, fol. 111a.

19. In CAHJP, MS AHW 16, *ha-ishah ha-hashuvah* was used for Hendel, wife of Nathan (fol. 33); and Klerche, widow of Moshe Heilbut (fol. 48a); *ha-ishah ha-yekarah*, for Sarah, wife of Ziskind Stern, wife and daughter of a communal leader (fol. 45); for Michla, daughter of Nathan, widow of the scholar Meir Cohen, (fol. 51, 1773); for Hendel, daughter of Abraham Curiel, wife of charity gabbay Meir Levi (fol. 71, 1775); and Sarah, widow of Meir Stern, (fol. 74a, 1782); *ha-ishah ha-gevirah* was utilized for Michla, daughter of Nathan, widow of the scholar Meir Cohen (fol. 51, 1773). For Yutche, (fol 32a).

20. CAHJP, MS AHW 16, fol. 133a.

21. Regarding the widow's oath, see BT Gittin 34b–35a; Berkovitz, *Law's Dominion*, 323. Many husbands made similar requests that their widows be released from this oath. Such explicit requests were no guarantee that they would be respected in case of challenges, but they show how onerous the oath was considered for the widow.

22. CAHJP, MS AHW 16, fols 133a, 135. On Shnaber, see Graupe, "Mordechai Shnaber-Levison," 3–20.

23. Taglicht, *Nachlässe*, 215–18, no. 200. Citation at 218: "Es ist weltkundig dass sie hierzu capabl und fähig die Werke weiter zu dirigiren und hat von allem genugsam Information."

24. CAHJP, MS AHW 16, fol. 37a.

25. CAHJP, MS AHW 16, fol. 41a.

26. CAHJP, MS AHW 16, fol. 33.

27. CAHJP, MS AHW 16, fol. 4a. Her will is also published in Graupe, "Jewish Testaments," 24–26.

28. CAHJP, MS AHW 16, fol. 33.

29. See Benayahu, *Studies in Memory*. This custom is referred to in the will of Lemle Reingarum, the close associate of the Sinzheims. See Benayahu, 214, and the will of Reingarum, LBI Collection AR 11546.

30. AIU, MS 423, fol. 3v.

31. AIU, MS 423, fol. 3v.

32. On lottery as a means of choosing among equals and its religious overtones, see Fram, *Window*, 47. Pessche established a perpetual fund for dowering poor brides, closely modeled on the stipulations she made for the one on the first anniversary of her death. This perpetual fund, administered by the kahal, would have justified her will being included in the communal records. See CAHJP, MS AHW 71, fol. 2, for a list kept by the kahal of the winners of a similar annual dowry lottery established by a bequest.

33. CAHJP, MS AHW 16, fol. 75.

34. Sarah's purchase of a shroud for herself prior to her death mirrors something we saw above in the women's burial society in Prague: the preparation and sale of shrouds in advance of their immediate use.

35. JTS, MS 9835, fols. 11r-v, dated Rosh hodesh Av 513 (1753).

36. CAHJP, MS AHW 16, fol. 78a (1773).

37. AIU, MS 423, fol. 4r.

38. CAHJP, MS AHW 16, fol. 4a.

39. CAHJP, MS AHW 16, fol. 4a.

40. CAHJP, MS AHW 16, fol. 33.

41. Wachstein, *Inschriften*, 423, no. 560.

42. CAHJP, MS Memorbuch der Klaussynagoge Mannheim, Bd. 1, fol. 57.

43. Jüdisches Museum Franken, MS 1998.002, fol. 31r.

44. Jüdisches Museum Franken, MS 1998.002, fol. 31v.

45. Jüdisches Museum Franken, MS 1998.002, fol. 31r.

46. NLI, MS Heb. 4° 1092, fol. 139.

47. NLI, MS Heb. 4° 1092, fol. 159. For another reference to a woman who founded a bet midrash, see fol. 155.

48. CAHJP, MS AHW 16, fol. 75.

49. CAHJP, MS AHW 16, fol. 111a.

50. On donation of books, see CAHJP, MS AHW 16, fols. 133a, 136.

51. AIU, MS 423, fol. 4r.

52. Leyb and his wife, Miriam, were childless, which may be why she singled him out to become a father to her nieces and nephews.

53. AIU, MS 423, fol. 5r.

54. AIU, MS 423, fols. 3v-4r.

55. CAHJP, MS AHW 16, fol. 5.

56. CAHJP, MS AHW 16, fol. 74a (1782).

57. CAHJP, MS AHW 16, fol. 78a (1773).

58. AIU, MS 423, fol. 5r.

59. JTS, MS 9835, fols. 11r-v, dated Rosh hodesh Av 513 (1753), *"ha-kerovim sheli davka."*

60. JTS, MS 9835, fol. 19.

61. JTS, MS 9835, esp. fol. 11r-13v.

62. Taglicht, *Nachlässe*, 203–4, no. 170.

63. Taglicht, *Nachlässe*, 83.

64. Yosef Prager was a partisan of Jacob Emden's in the controversy against R. Jonathan Eybeschutz and the author of a massive anti-Sabbatian polemic, *Gahale esh*, which remains in manuscript until this day. On the work, see Oron, "Sefer gahale esh," 84 and 84n30.

65. CAHJP, MS AHW 16, fol 32a. The original Hebrew for small fraction is *sheminit she-besheminit*.

66. Hendel used the same term as Yutche.

67. CAHJP, MS AHW 16, fol. 71 (1775).

68. CAHJP MS AHW 16, fol. 48a.

69. CAHJP, MS AHW 16, fol. 74a. Sarah's will is dated 3 Nissan 1782. See a very similar situation in the inventory taken after the death of Baila, widow of the late Meir Traub, on 3 Nissan 1790. After listing her personal effects, the communal official listed twelve items as securities. He listed those items only by their value rather than by any description. CAHJP, MS AHW 71, fol. 5a.

70. CAHJP, MS AHW 16, fol. 33.

71. CAHJP, MS AHW 16, fol. 33a.

72. CAHJP, MS AHW 16, fol. 45 (1771). Several other testators (e.g., Klerche, widow of Moses Heilbut, and Michla, daughter of Nathan) similarly stipulated that their estate should not be sealed, and inventory should not be taken. This indicates that the sealing and inventory process was a financial and time burden on the heirs, and testators sought to protect their heirs from it.

73. CAHJP, MS AHW 16, fol. 75 (1782).

74. CAHJP, MS AHW 16, fol. 107v-108r. This will was written in a more professional hand, with markings from the non-Jewish will on the top of the page in German. Over time, this became a more common feature of the wills copied into this volume.

75. A parallel bequest for a sibling's care can be seen in Mordechai Shnaber's will, who asked that his brother be kept in the hekdesh. Graupe, "Mordechai Shnaber-Levison," 3–20.

76. CAHJP, MS AHW 16, fol. 40.

77. CAHJP, MS AHW 16, fol. 43 (1772).

78. CAHJP, MS AHW 16, fol. 111a. For additional discussion of Yitta's will, see chapter 6.

79. The total was 260 Mark and 41 Reichsthaler (= 123 Mark).

80. See CAHJP, MS AHW 16, fol. 66a. The Society for the Care of Orphans (*Megadle yetomim*) was founded in Altona in Elul of 5526 (1766). For printed founding regulations of this hevrah, see New York, Leo Baeck Institute, Jacob Jacobson Collection AR 7002 / MF 447 / MF 134, Box 6, Folder: II7.

81. An ordinance signed by Aaron b. Falk, Yitta's brother, who was likely a young student at the time, has been preserved in Copenhagen's Jewish communal archive. See CAHJP, MF HM 2300.

82. CAHJP, MS AHW 73, fol. 444. For similar dispensation given to a maidservant, Rivka, in exchange for payment, CAHJP, MS AHW 17b, fol. 12r.

83. See CAHJP, MS AHW 73, fol. 497. Mann died on 21 Tevet 5565 (Dec. 23, 1804) at an old (unspecified) age.

84. CAHJP, MS AHW 16, fol. 111a.

85. The Hebrew is unclear and may read *she-shamrah* (watched over) or *she-shimshah* (tended to). For another example of gifts bequeathed by maidservants to members of the household in which they served, see Francesconi, "And if I Could," 311–29.

86. CAHJP, MS AHW 16, fol. 111a.

87. CAHJP, MS AHW 16, fol. 111a.

88. This may well be Leyb, the son of Rebecca of Mannheim.

89. Taglicht, *Nachlässe*, 98, no. 35.

90. Taglicht, *Nachlässe*, 99, no. 38. She died "in dem Juden-freythof, in der Rossau." Taglicht notes that this was the hekdesh.

91. Taglicht, *Nachlässe*, 192, no. 139.

92. Taglicht, *Nachlässe*, 207, no. 174.

93. Taglicht, *Nachlässe*, 192, no. 140. Similarly, the widow Rachel, a nanny by Leidersdorfer, died in the hekdesh, leaving nothing behind. She had two children who lived in Kreuz. Taglicht, *Nachlässe*, 238, no. 242.

94. Taglicht, *Nachlässe*, 236, no. 237.

95. Taglicht, *Nachlässe*, 242, no. 254.

96. CAHJP, MS AHW 16, fol. 5.

97. CAHJP, MS AHW 16, fol. 51.

98. On the term "curateur," see Berkovitz, *Law's Dominion*, 207, 254.

99. CAHJP, MS AHW 16, fol. 75.

100. CAHJP, MS AHW 16, fol. 51.

101. AIU, MS 423, fol. 3v. The term she uses is *Sefer meytim*, an unusual locution for the Memorbuch; we have not found it used elsewhere. Normally, the book was called *hazkarat neshamot*.

Chapter Ten. Bodies and Souls

1. Glikl, *Zikhroynes* (2006). At 367n27, Turniansky argues that the comment about her state of impurity was made for the benefit of her future readers rather than directly to her husband. Other scholars disagree. See also Diemling, "*Den ikh bin*."

2. For a recent discussion of the development of the rabbinic approach to menstrual law, see Libson, *Law and Self Knowledge*, 64–97.

3. On an early modern manual of the laws of menstrual purity for women readers, see Fram, *My Dear Daughter*.

4. English cited from von Rohden, introduction to *Meneket Rivkah*, 25.

5. On the entire exchange, see Fram, *My Dear Daughter*, 12–15.

6. von Rohden, introduction to *Meneket Rivkah*, 26.

7. Fram, *My Dear Daughter*, 139–49, on this literature in the early modern period, and on Slonik generally.

8. The harhakot are mentioned in passing in the Talmud, BT Shabbat 13a-b, and were greatly elaborated by the medieval decisors.

9. Lev. 20:18.

10. Marienberg, *La Baraita de-Niddah*.

11. Marienberg, "Jews, Jesus, and Menstrual Blood," 1–10.

12. Niccoli, "Menstruum quasi monstruum," 413–34.

13. von Rohden, introduction to *Meneket Rivkah*, 32.

14. Litt, *Pinkas, Kahal, and the Mediene*, 210.

15. Isserlein, *Terumat ha-deshen, pesakim u-khtavim*, no. 132. Cited in translation by Baumgarten, *Practicing Piety*, 32.

16. Schammes, *Minhagim de-k"k Warmaisa*, vol. 2, par. 250.

17. Landau, *Noda be-Yehudah, Even ha-ezer*, no. 69.

18. For example, see Ashkenazi, *She'elot u-teshuvot Hakham Zvi*, no. 73.

19. Landau, *Noda be-Yehudah*, no. 33.

20. Landau, *Noda be-Yehudah*, no. 34. See also nos. 43–46, in which a woman's self-evaluation, evaluations of other women, and a physician's knowledge all play a role in determining the outcome of the response.

21. E. Katzenellenbogen, *Knesset Yehezkel*, no. 34.

22. P. Katzenellenbogen, *Yesh manhilin*, 243.

23. NLI, MS 4° 1092, fol. 623.

24. Fuchs, "Die Mikwen von Speyer," 60–69; Bodner, "Romanesque," 369–87.

25. Mi-See, *Shu"t yefe nof, Yoreh de'ah*, no. 113.

26. Marienberg, "Women, Men, and Cold Water," 1–37.

27. Mi-See, *Shu"t yefe nof, Yoreh de'ah*, no. 109.

28. Mi-See, *Shu"t yefe nof, Yoreh de'ah*, no. 114.

29. The eighteenth-century takkanot of the region around Speyer mandated the construction of mikva'ot in each settlement. See Ramat Gan, Bar-Ilan University, MS 803, fol. 5b.

30. Tal, *Ha-kehillah*, 159, no. 13.

31. Mi-See, *Shu"t yefe nof, Yoreh de'ah*, no. 107.

32. An exception was made for a woman whose immersion day fell on a Friday, as travel on Shabbat was prohibited.

33. Fram, *My Dear Daughter*, 190.

34. Jerusalem, Karlin-Stolin, MS 457.

35. Hildesheimer, *Pinkas kehillat Schnaittach*, 202.

36. Tal, *Ha-kehillah*, 159, no. 14. In later years, pipes were built to transport the spring water to both the communal and guest mikvehs. See Tal, 162, no. 25.

37. Tal, *Ha-kehillah*, 159, no. 15.

38. Litt, *Pinkas, Kahal, and the Mediene*, 167.

39. Carpi, *Pinkas Padua*, vol. 2, nos. 289, 296.

40. D. Kaplan, "'To Immerse their Wives,'" 257–79.

41. CAHJP, MS AHW 85a, fol. 108a.

42. Bacharach, *Havot Yair*, no. 181.

43. BR, Hs. Ros. 500, fol. 34r-v.

44. Glikl, *Memoirs* (2019), 192.

45. Rublack, "Pregnancy," 93–94.

46. Hildesheimer, *Pinkas kehillat Schnaittach*, 203.

47. Rublack, "Pregnancy," 89–90.

48. Glikl, *Memoirs* (2019), 189–91. A baby who was ill would not have been circumcised on the eighth day after birth.

49. Rublack, "Pregnancy," 97–98.

50. Lindemann, *Health and Healing*, 239.

51. B. M. Willmott Dobbie measured a maternal mortality rate in late medieval western England of 24.4 and 29.4 per 1,000 baptisms. Dobbie, "Attempt," 79–90.

52. S. Unna, *Gedenkbuch*. Because we do not have birth records from the community, it is not possible to ascertain the percentage of deaths in childbirth in relation to the number of births per year.

53. Mishnah, Shabbat 2:6.

54. NLI, MS Heb. 4° 1092. See the introductory colophon, which explains how Lezer commissioned the manuscript.

55. P. Katzenellenbogen, *Yesh manhilin*, 98.

56. P. Katzenellenbogen, *Yesh manhilin*, 99. Contrast this to Katzenellenbogen's description of his second wife's experience in childbirth (p. 109).

57. P. Katzenellenbogen, *Yesh manhilin*, 109–11 (citations from p. 111).

58. On cases brought against women in Germany, see Rublack, "Pregnancy," 90–93.

59. P. Katzenellenbogen, *Yesh manhillin*, 99–100, par. 24.

60. Eybeschutz, *Luhot edut*, 5r. The pinkas of the burial society of Metz does not indicate which women died in childbirth (although its members would have known by the names alone). See JTS, MS 5396, fols. 244–49.

61. Emden, *Bet Yehonatan ha-sofer*, 13a-b, nos. 22, 39. We thank Jordan Katz for this reference.

62. Carlebach, "Community, Authority," 12–13. Keeping company of parturients was only one of the occasions when communities permitted cardplaying by women. Another was on Rosh hodesh, celebrating the New Month, a minor holiday observed by Jewish women. On playing cards, see, e.g., Litt, *Jüdische Gemeindestatuten* (Takkanot Frankfurt, 1674/5), 67, par. 48.

63. See, e.g., Schammes, *Minhagim de k"k Warmaisa*, vol. 2, par. 239; Litt, *Jüdische Gemeindestatuten* (Takkanot Fürth, 1770), 268, par. 490.

64. On baked goods for the parturient, see also Baumgarten, *Mothers and Children*, 97.

65. Schammes, *Minhagim de-k"k Warmaisa*, vol. 2, par. 239.

66. Rublack, "Pregnancy," 101–3.

67. Baumgarten, *Mothers and Children*, 105–18.

68. Y. T. Lewinsky, "Takkanot le-seudat ha-brit," par. 3. For a similar reference, see takkanot Fürth in Litt, *Jüdische Gemeindestatuten* (Takkanot Fürth, 1770), 269, par. 492.

69. NLI, MS Heb. 4° 1092, fol. 128. For similar entries, see fols. 203, 207.

70. Glikl does not mention how long the "lying-in" period was. European customs mandated that a woman not leave her bed after childbirth for a period from two weeks to two months.

71. Glikl, *Zikhroynes* (2006), 134–35.

72. See, e.g., Hairston, "Economics of Milk," 187–212.

73. Jerusalem, Karlin-Stolin, MS 41, fol. 149.

74. Lindemann, "Love for Hire," 379.

75. On the belief that morals could be passed on through breastmilk, see Grieco and Corsini, *Historical Perspectives*, 27–28.

76. Glikl, *Zikhroynes* (2006), 262–63.

77. Glikl, *Zikhroynes* (2006), 276–77.

78. Glikl, *Zikhroynes* (2006), 345–47.

79. von Rohden, *Meneket Rivkah*, 154.

80. Wunder, *He Is the Sun*, 19. See, e.g., Spalding, *Account Books of the Reimarus Family*, vol. 2, 1253. This upper-middle-class family employed a wetnurse or nanny for seventeen years running, from 1730 to 1747.

81. "Bei der Mutter lass rinnen deine Augen, weil sie dich hat lassen saugen / Unter vielen Sorg und Schmerzen dich getragen unterm Herzen." Qtd. in Cohn and Kirschner, "Kallah-Lied," 154.

82. Cited in von Rohden, *Meneket Rivkah*, 155, from *Brantshpigel*, 137. See also *Meneket Rivkah*, 90, note at line 4.

83. Cited in von Rohden, *Meneket Rivkah*, 155, from *Eyn shayn froyenbukhleyn* and *Brantshpigel*.

84. For talmudic sources, see BT Yevamot 42a; BT Ketubot 60a-b; *Shulhan arukh, Orakh hayim*, 13, 11–12; on the medieval halakhic sources, Baumgarten, *Mothers and Children*, 117–53.

85. Berkovitz, *Protocols*, 889, no. 569.

86. Salmon-Mack, *Tan-du*.

87. Berkovitz, *Protocols*, 373, no. 205.

88. Berkovitz, *Protocols*, 856–57, no. 537.

89. Salmon-Mack, *Tan-du*, 95–99.

90. Landau and Wachstein, *Jüdische privatbriefe*, 27, no. 8a.

91. Landau, *Noda be-Yehudah*, *Even ha-ezer*, no. 69.

92. Single women who were not virgins and divorced women were not permitted to marry a kohen under Jewish law.

93. E. Katzenellenbogen, *Knesset Yehezkel*, no. 56.

94. Bacharach, *Havot Yair*, no. 31.

95. In this case, neither the baby nor the mother was in physical danger, but, in their deliberations, they cited these as well as talmudic sources over how to apply the death penalty to a pregnant woman.

96. Emden, *She'elat Ya'avetz*, pt. 1, no. 43.

97. Rublack, "Pregnancy," 90–93.

98. Mi-See, *Shu"t yefe nof*, *Yoreh de'ah*, no. 92.

99. Jerusalem, Karlin-Stolin, MS 41, fol. 98v.

100. Rublack, "Fluxes," 1–16; Stollberg, "'You Have No Good Blood,'" 63–82.

101. Landau, *Noda be-Yehudah*, *Yoreh de'ah*, no. 55.

102. Duden, *Woman Beneath*, mentions only two Jewish women patients, in passing, out of the entire ca. 1800 cases (80, 82).

103. Wetnurses constituted one of the significant exceptions to this rule. Their milk and breasts were not considered their own, as they had been contracted out, and the doctor could be asked to examine them directly in the event of trouble with milk or sores. Duden, *Woman Beneath*, 80, 85.

104. Porter, *Health for Sale*.

105. Zinger, "Who Knows What the Cause Is?," 134–35.

106. Duden, *Woman Beneath*, 75.

107. Duden, *Woman Beneath*, 160.

108. Braginsky, MS 344, fols. 14v-15r; Victoria and Albert Museum, MS 1868/513, fol. 15.

109. Fram, *My Dear Daughter*, 186. His discussion aimed at showing women how to ensure that the scabs did not constitute a hatzitzah.

110. See the comprehensive survey of scholarship on suicide in early modern western Europe in Healy, "Suicide," 903–19; Lind, *Selbstmord*.

111. The text refers to her as his wife, which is crossed out and emended to read "widow."

112. CAHJP, MS AHW 20, fol. 17.

113. S. Unna, *Gedenkbuch*, 484, no. 72, from 1764.

114. NLI, MS 4° 1092, fol. 578.

115. JTS, MS 8875, par. 919.

116. UB Leipzig, MS BH 18, fols. 93r-94v. Regarding the affliction described here, we are grateful to Jordan Katz for directing us to the literature on *plica polonica*.

117. For a full discussion of the syndrome, see Guesnet, "Demonic Entanglements"; Zinger, "'Unto their Assembly,'" 83–84. On immersion and the plait, see also Fram, *My Dear Daughter*, 184.

118. Schammes, *Minhagim de-k"k Warmaisa*, vol. 2, par. 284. See also a case in Altona in which an elderly woman named Tziper was provided with medical care and a non-Jewish aide. CAHJP, MS AHW 36a. See also D. Kaplan, *Patrons and Their Poor*, 70–74.

119. Meisl, *Pinkas kehillat Berlin*, 214, par. 217.

120. NLI, MS 4° 928, fol. 12.

121. JTS, MS 8875, par. 1083.

122. NLI, MS. 4° 1092, fol. 728.

123. JTS, MS 8875, par. 606. Ps. 90:10 refers to the typical age of human life as seventy years.

124. JTS, MS 8875, par. 598. The text notes that twenty-eight years were added to the years of her life.

125. Jüdisches Museum Franken, MS 1998.002, fol. 26v.

126. Epidat database, hha-3228.

127. JTS, MS 5396, fol. 287. See above in chapter 2.

128. P. Katzenellenbogen, *Yesh manhilin*, 228.

129. NLI, MS Heb. 4° 1092, fol. 575.

130. NLI, MS Heb. 4° 1092, fols. 114, 117. See also fol. 55, for Fagel, daughter of Natan Bose of Frankfurt, who was praised for synagogue attendance, devoted prayer, participation in the burial society, reciting the Psalms, and fasting.

131. JTS, MS 8875, par. 708. In the Hebrew: "*ve-kidsha atzmah ve-nazrah be-nezirut she-lo akhlah basar be-khamah shanim be-hol, im lo ba-yamim she-assur le-hit'anot bahem.*"

132. Bynum, *Holy Feast*. See also Baumgarten, *Practicing Piety*, 51–102, on medieval Jews and fasting.

133. JTS, MS 8875, par. 955.

134. JTS, MS 8875, par. 706.

135. In some communities, women of different socioeconomic statuses were permitted different types and numbers of dresses. Litt, *Jüdische Gemeindestatuten* (Takkanot Metz. 1769), 359–61.

136. Braginsky, MS 328, fol. 9v.

Chapter Eleven. Custom and Ritual

1. Commentary by Schammes (to his own text), *Minhagim de-k"k Warmaisa*, vol. 1, par. 171, at p. 203.

2. Bney Gumpel, *Sefer minhagim*.

3. Schammes, *Minhagim de-k"k Warmaisa*.

4. Schammes, *Minhagim de-k"k Warmaisa*, vol. 1, par. 220.

5. See, e.g., CAHJP, MS Fu1-534, a list of the synagogue seats owned and used by women in one of the Fürth synagogues.

6. Stollberg-Rilinger, "Function of Rituals," 359–73.

7. Kirchner, *Jüdisches Ceremoniel*, 1–2.

8. See also the references to a woman from Amsterdam who recited the kaddish prayer. Bacharach, *Havot Yair*, no. 222; Jerusalem, Karlin-Stolin, MS 41, fol. 76r.

9. NLI, MS Heb. 8° 2423, fol. 8v.

10. Hebr. *Torat hesed al leshonah*, from Proverbs 31, the "Woman of Valor."

11. NLI, MS Heb. 4° 1092, fol. 115.

12. Hahn, *Yosif ometz*, no. 826. Lists of synagogue seats similarly do not include maidservants as owners or users of seats.

13. NLI, MS Heb. 2398, fol. 45.

14. JTS, MS 8875, par. 1104.

15. NLI, Ms. Heb. 4° 1092, fol. 136.

16. Glikl, *Memoirs* (2019), 298, including n. 53, where Turniansky explains that Yachet had subsidized a daily afternoon recitation of Psalms.

17. Juspe Hahn of Frankfurt remarked that a head of household should ensure that even his domestic maidservants recite certain daily prayers. *Yosif ometz*, no. 284.

18. Braginsky, MS 351, fol. 17.

19. Mi-See, *Shu"t yefe nof, Orah hayim*, no. 42.

20. JTS, MS 8875, par. 786, 868. See also Epidat database, hha-3157 (1696); hha-3163 (1699); wrm-1010 (1749); Wachstein, *Inschriften*, 498, no. 644a; Marienberg, "Mystery on the Tombstones."

21. Hahn, *Yosif ometz*, no. 573. The author does not blame the middle class for being parsimonious, as one could only prepare for Shabbat based on the household's budget.

22. Braginsky, MS 351, fol. 13v.

23. Braginsky, MS 217, fol. 15v.

24. BR, Hs. Ros. 500, fol. 30r-v.

25. Braginsky, MS 351, fol. 13v.

26. Hahn, *Yosif ometz*, nos. 387–402.

27. Braginsky, MS 217, fol. 12v. Schalet (cholent), a stew cooked through Friday night so that there would be a hot meal on Shabbat day, was famously praised by Heinrich Heine as divine ambrosia. See his "Prinzessin Shabbat," in *Hebrew Melodies*, 12–15.

28. Braginsky, MS 351, fol. 14r.

29. The Hebrew phrase is *shalom bayit*. See Braginsky, MS 351, fol. 14v.

30. Hahn, *Yosif ometz*, 88, no. 682. See also Schammes, *Minhagim de-k"k Warmaisa*, vol. 1, par. 63, for a prescriptive admonition that women should refrain from certain chores on Rosh hodesh. Kirchner, *Jüdisches Ceremoniel*, 76, describes Rosh hodesh as a full holiday for women, on which they engaged in festive activities such as playing cards (see plate 29), and as a half-holiday for men.

31. Carlebach, *Palaces of Time*, 183, cited from Hirsch, *Megalleh tekufot* (1717).

32. On the medieval custom, see Baumgarten, "'Remember that Glorious Girl'"; for the early modern period, Carlebach, *Palaces of Time*, 160–88.

33. von Bernuth and Terry, "Shalom bar Abraham's Book of Judith," and other studies in the same volume.

34. BnF, MS cod. héb. 586, fol. 96r.

35. BnF, MS cod. héb. 586, fol. 106r, shows a woman trampling on the head of Amalek. Like Judith, this depiction shows strong women asserting their power in defense of their people.

36. BnF, MS cod. héb. 586, fol. 109v, depicts drinking on Purim with a woman shown guzzling wine straight from the pitcher. Schammes, *Minhagim de-k"k Warmaisa*, vol. 1, par. 218, describes the festivities in Worms with emphasis on the girls' participation, a rare reference.

37. Kosman, *Noheg ka-tzon Yosef*, 272.

38. See Turniansky and Timm, *Yiddish in Italia*, 12, no. 12.

39. Pfefferkorn, *Ich heyss ain büchlein*; Margaritha, *Der gantz jüdisch Glaub*.

40. Regarding Pfefferkorn's authorship, see Carlebach, *Divided Souls*, 178.

41. In his discussion of Purim, Schammes, *Minhagim de-k"k Warmaisa*, vol. 1, par. 137, confirms that women attended shofar-blowing in the synagogue in seventeenth-century Worms.

42. BnF, MS cod. héb. 586, fol. 93v.

43. Baumgarten, *Practicing Piety*, 36.

44. BnF, MS cod. héb. 586, fol. 90v.

45. Schammes, *Minhagim de k"k Warmaisa*, vol. 1, par. 137.

46. Both Pfefferkorn's and Margaritha's books included woodcuts of women and men, segregated by sex, performing the *tashlikh* ceremony. Freiman, "Tarbut ve-hevrah yehudit," argued that this medieval custom began as a way to gather at riverbanks during a long holiday and was gradually adopted by rabbinic authorities as an approved custom.

47. BnF, MS cod. héb. 586, fol. 121r, depicts one woman performing tashlikh (Yid., *zie makht tashlikh*).

48. Litt, *Jüdische Gemeindestatuten* (Takkanot Fürth, 1770), 262, par. 457.

49. Kirchner, *Jüdisches Ceremoniel*, 115.

50. Litt, *Jüdische Gemeindestatuten* (Takkanot Metz, 1769), 375, par. 62.

51. Kosman, *Noheg ka-tzon Yosef*, 273.

52. Kosman, *Noheg ka-tzon Yosef*, 273.

53. Kosman, *Noheg ka-tzon Yosef*, 278.

54. Kirchner, *Jüdisches Ceremoniel*, 117; Litt, *Jüdische Gemeindestatuten* (Takkanot Metz, 1769), 365, par. 22; Kosman, *Noheg ka-tzon Yosef*, 74b.

55. Schammes, *Minhagim de k"k Warmaisa*, vol. 1, par. 1.

56. Litt, *Jüdische Gemeindestatuten* (Takkanot Fürth, 1770), 262, par. 458.

57. See, further, Kaplan and Fram, "Four Species," 119.

58. Schammes, *Minhagim de-k"k Warmaisa*, vol. 1, par. 181.

59. Schammes, *Minhage k"k Warmaisa*, vol. 1, par. 187, 192. See also Kosman, *Noheg ka-tzon Yosef*, p. 413.

60. Litt, *Jüdische Gemeindestatuten* (Takkanot Fürth, 1770), 262, par. 459.

61. Glikl, *Zikhroynes* (2019), 310.

62. N. Z. Davis, *Women on the Margins*, 258n220.

63. See chapter 2.

64. Kosman, *Noheg ka-tzon Yosef*, p. 284, no. 2. Kosman criticized the presence of children but did not say how women would attend if they had young children at home.

65. Schammes, *Minhagim de-k"k Warmaisa*, vol. 1, par. 46.

66. BnF, MS cod. héb. 586, fol. 2r.

67. Kirchner, *Jüdisches Ceremoniel* (1734), 89a-90b.

68. BnF, MS cod. héb. 586, fol. 118v.

69. Kirchner, *Jüdisches Ceremoniel*, 89a; CAHJP, MS AHW 31b.

70. Kirchner, *Jüdisches Ceremoniel*, 90b.

71. Hahn, *Yosif ometz*, no. 795.

72. Hahn, *Yosif ometz*, no. 742.

73. Kirchner, *Jüdisches Ceremoniel*, 90b.

74. For another early sixteenth-century example, see BnF, MS cod. héb. 586, fol. 4r.

75. Jüdisches Museums Frankfurt am Main, Inv.nr.: B 1999/004. Hauptbuch. On Garküche, see Kasper-Marienberg and Kaplan, "Nourishing."

76. In contemporary Frankfurt, the announcement was made by the cantor, as is indicated in one 1628 contract. See NLI, MS Heb. 2° 662, no. 155.

77. Schammes, *Minhagim de-k"k Warmaisa*, vol. 2, par. 230.

78. On the timing of weddings, see Sperber, *Jewish Life Cycle*, 171–78.

79. Weissler, "Religion."

80. On Tuesday, as another example, the *Manis Mahl* was celebrated, respectively, by the groom and his friends and the bride and her friends. See Schammes, *Minhagim de-k"k Warmaisa*, vol. 2, par. 229. On the etymology, see Zimmer's annotations, 10n2.

81. Schammes, vol. 2, par. 227. For parallel single-sex celebrations in Christian communities, see Roper, "'Going to Church,'" 94.

82. For medieval precedents, see Davidovich-Eshed, "On Brides and Braids."

83. Kirchner, *Jüdisches Ceremoniel*, 178–79.

84. Schammes, *Minhagim de-k"k Warmaisa*, vol. 2, par. 231. The ceremony is mentioned briefly in printed Yiddish minhag books, for example that of Frankfurt (1707), 72.

85. Schammes, *Minhagim de-k"k Warmaisa*, vol. 2, par. 231. The word *Einwurf*, as used by Juspe, meant "tossing in" the gifts. See chapter 6, as well as BR, Hs. Ros. 572.

86. For early modern lider, Matut, *Dichtung*; Roman, "Be-nign Shmuel-bukh"; Amsterdam, BR, Hs. Ros. 106. Zimmer's annotations to Schammes, *Minhagim de-k"k Warmaisa*, vol. 2, par. 227, at p. 7n45, lists some of the wedding songs and where they are printed.

87. Bodleian, MS Canonici Or. 12.

88. Matut, *Dichtung*, 351–53.

89. Schammes noted that the couple was escorted to bed by men and women. See *Minhagim de-k"k Warmaisa*, vol. 2, par. 231. For parallel Christian practices, Roper, "'Going to Church,'" 90–92.

90. Matut, "Early Modern Yiddish." See chapter 10 for a discussion of women's gatherings at the bedside of a parturient.

91. Schammes, *Minhagim de-k"k Warmaisa*, vol. 2, par. 227. The sixteenth-century Yiddish minhogim manuscript, BN 586, fol. 113v, depicts the betrothal ceremony with the caption, "*Man entspost* [espouses] *an kallah*."

92. On some local differences, see D. Kaplan, "Courtship and Ritual."

93. Schammes, *Minhagim de-k"k Warmaisa*, vol. 2, par. 227. The women left the meal early as the men started Grace After Meals, allowing them to start dancing before the men arrived. This gendered timing was deliberate.

94. For parallel single-sex celebrations in Christian communities, see Roper, "'Going to Church,'" 94.

95. Kirchner, *Jüdisches Ceremoniel*, 178–79.

96. Schammes, *Minhagim de-k"k Warmaisa*, vol. 2, par. 245.

97. JTS, MS 3697 (*Sod Hashem ve-sharvit ha-zahav*), fol. 7r.

98. Schammes, *Minhagim de-k"k Warmaisa*, vol. 2, par. 240.

99. The engravings were made in the workshop of Johann Georg Puschner the Elder (1680–1749), by him or by his son (also called Johann Georg). Magnes Museum online, item no. 161764. The mother seems to be the only woman in the room.

100. Rublack, *Dressing Up*.

101. Schammes, *Minhagim de-k"k Warmaisa*, vol. 2, par. 288. On this ritual and Christian parallels, see also Baumgarten, *Mothers and Children*, 100–18.

102. Schammes, *Minhagim de-k"k Warmaisa*, vol. 2, par. 267.

103. Schammes, *Minhagim de-k"k Warmaisa*, vol. 2, par. 268.

104. Schammes, *Minhagim de-k"k Warmaisa*, vol. 2, par. 264.

105. Schammes, *Minhagim de-k"k Warmaisa*, vol. 2, par. 265, notes that anyone who wished to attend a divorce could do so; it was announced on the street by the sexton. For the standard bill of divorce, see S. Halevi, *Nahalat Shivah*, vol. 2, par. 45.

106. Bodenschatz, *Kirchliche Verfassung*, plate XIII, near p. 141.

107. See S. Halevi, *Nahalat shivah*, vol. 2, pars. 54–55.

108. Schammes, *Minhagim de-k"k Warmaisa*, vol. 2, par. 266. The fear that he would lose his mind was essential to the rite, as a man had to be of sound mind to issue a divorce.

109. For this reason, many couples signed a *shetar halitzah* upon marriage. These documents preemptively freed the wife from the obligation to marry each of her brothers-in-law. See S. Halevi, *Nahalat Shivah*, vol. 1, par. 22.

110. Schammes, *Minhagim de-k"k Warmaisa*, vol. 2, par. 267. Schammes reports that the rabbinical court of three selected an outdoor location for the ceremony a day prior and that the shamash announced the ceremony. The depictions by Christian Hebraists place the ceremony indoors, perhaps before the court or in a study.

111. Schammes, *Minhagim de-k"k Warmaisa*, vol. 2, par. 268.

112. Jerusalem, Karlin-Stolin, MS 41, fol. 137v.

113. Bney Gumpel, *Sefer minhagim*, no. 98.

114. Litt, *Jüdische Gemeindestatuten* (Takkanot Metz, 1769), 370, no. 40.

115. Hahn, *Yosif ometz*, 410, no. 8. See also Langer, "Birkat betulim."

116. For other references to this ceremony and an analysis of the possible etymological roots of its name, see Zimmer's annotation to Schammes, *Minhagim de-k"k Warmaisa*, vol. 2, par. 231, at pp. 20–21n5.

117. Tyrnau, *Minhogim* (1728–29), 65. See also Cohen and Horowitz, "In Search of the Sacred," 242–43.

118. Roper, "'Going to Church,'" 88–93.

119. For examples in communities large and small, see Wachstein, "Die Prager takkanos," 335–54; 478–79; and Wachstein, "A yiddishe kahal . . . Pinkas Runkel."

120. CAHJP, MS AHW 20, fol. 20.

121. Wachstein, "Die Prager takkanos," par. 1.

122. We have found no traces of rituals that celebrated girls' reaching legal maturity (bat mitzvah) in our sources.

123. Wachstein, "Die Prager takkanos," par. 2.

124. Wachstein, "Die Prager takkanos," par. 4.

125. Y. T. Lewinsky, "Takkanot le-seudat ha-brit," par. 3.

Conclusion

1. See *Ele toldot*, 13.IV.1773. For her father, *Ele toldot*, 23.III.1707; for her mother, *Ele toldot*, 8.I.1744.

2. NLI, MS 4°1092, fol. 482.

3. For her children, see the entry for her husband, Leyb Scheuer, in *Ele toldot*, 20.II.1777.

4. From her tombstone, in Horovitz, *Inschriften*, 390.

5. NLI, MS 4° 1092, fol. 482.

6. NLI, MS 4° 1092, fol. 482.

7. After being widowed, Miriam later married the chief rabbi of Mannheim.

8. See the Memorbuch entry for Miriam, NLI, MS 4°1092, fol. 268.

9. See, e.g., Grossman and Kaplan, *Kehal Yisrael*; Litt, *Pinkas, Kahal, and the Mediene*, 33–91; Carlebach, "Early Modern Jewish Community," 168–98.

10. Hundert, *Jews in Poland-Lithuania*, 159.

11. Carlebach, introduction to *Posen Library, Confronting Modernity*, xxxvii-xviii.

12. M. Kaplan, *Making of the Jewish Middle Class*.

13. Hundert, *Jews in Poland-Lithuania*; Y. Kaplan, "Jewish Amsterdam's Impact"; Hacker, "He-omnam," 165–80.

14. Rosman, *How Jewish*, 61–64; Hundert, *Jews in Poland-Lithuania*.

SELECTED BIBLIOGRAPHY

List of Abbreviations

AIU	Paris, Bibliothèque de l'Alliance Israélite Universelle
BnF	Paris, Bibliothèque nationale de France
Bodleian	Oxford, Bodleian Library
BR	Amsterdam, Bibliotheca Rosenthaliana, Allard Pierson, University of Amsterdam
Braginsky	Zurich, Braginsky Collection
BT	Babylonian Talmud
CAHJP	Jerusalem, Central Archives for the History of the Jewish People
ISG	Frankfurt, Institut für Stadtgeschichte
JMP	Prague, Jewish Museum in Prague
JTS	New York, The Library of the Jewish Theological Seminary
Ktiv	"Ktiv" project, The National Library of Israel
MF	Microfilm
NLI	Jerusalem, National Library of Israel
UB	Universitätsbibliothek

Primary Sources

Manuscripts and Archives

AMSTERDAM

Bibliotheca Rosenthaliana, Allard Pierson, University of Amsterdam, Hs. Ros. 106.
Bibliotheca Rosenthaliana, Allard Pierson, University of Amsterdam, Hs. Ros. 381.
Bibliotheca Rosenthaliana, Allard Pierson, University of Amsterdam, Hs. Ros. 500.
Bibliotheca Rosenthaliana, Allard Pierson, University of Amsterdam, Hs. Ros. 572.
Bibliotheca Rosenthaliana, Allard Pierson, University of Amsterdam, Hs. Ros. Pl-C-06.
Gemeente Amsterdam Stadstarchief, Archieven van de Nederlands Israelitische Hoofdsynagoge van Amsterdam, 1.1.1.1.1-4, MS Register van resoluties van Parnassim, 1708–1808, 1 Protocol 1.

Gemeente Amsterdam Stadstarchief, Archieven van de Nederlands Israelitische Hoofdsynagoge van Amsterdam, 1.1.2.2.1.25, Register van contributie voor een vrouwenvereniging, 18th century. [Pinkas *hevrah kaddisha pikuah nefesh*.]

BERLIN

Staatsbibliothek zu Berlin-Stiftung Preussischer Kulturbesitz, Berlin, MS Or. Oct. 3150. [*Sefer evronot*.]
Staatsbibliothek zu Berlin-Stiftung Preussischer Kulturbesitz, MS Or. Qu. 694.

CAMBRIDGE

Trinity College, MS Loewe 135.

COPENHAGEN

Det Kgl. Bibliothek, Cod. Sim. Heb. Add. 9.
Det Kgl. Bibliothek, Cod. Sim. Heb. Add. 10.
Det Kgl. Bibliothek, MS Cod. Heb. 32.
Jewish Community of Copenhagen, MS 30 (via Ktiv).
Jewish Community of Copenhagen, MS 31 (via Ktiv).

FRANKFURT

Goethe University, Universitätsbibliothek Christian Senckenberg, MS Oct. 2. [Glikl, *Zikhroynes*]
Institut für Stadtgeschichte, MS BMB 182.
Institut für Stadtgeschichte, MS Criminalia 609.
Institut für Stadtgeschichte, MS H.15.36, 29.
Institut für Stadtgeschichte, MS Juden Akten 3.
Institut für Stadtgeschichte, MS Juden Akten 17.
Institut für Stadtgeschichte, MS Juden Akten 412.
Institut für Stadtgeschichte, MS Juden Akten 435, 7.
Institut für Stadtgeschichte, MS Juden Akten 973.
Institut für Stadtgeschichte, MS Ratsprotokoll 1612.
Jüdisches Museums Frankfurt am Main, Inv.nr.: B 1999/004. Hauptbuch des Wohlfahrtsfonds und der Suppenküche der Jüdischen Gemeinde Frankfurt am Main: 1785–1804.

FÜRTH

Jüdisches Museum Franken, MS 1998.002 [Wiener Memorbuch der Fürther Klaus-Synagoge]

HAIFA

University of Haifa, MS 45. [*Pinkas gemilut hasadim be-kehillat Ferrara*]

HAMBURG

Staats- und Universitätsbibliothek Hamburg Carl von Ossietzky, MS Cod. Heb. 313 (via Ktiv).

Staats- und Universitätsbibliothek Hamburg Carl von Ossietzky, MS Cod. Levy 137 (via Ktiv).

Staatsarchiv Hamburg, 111–1 Cl. VII Lit. M e Nr. 8 Vol. 11.

JERUSALEM, CENTRAL ARCHIVES FOR THE HISTORY OF THE JEWISH PEOPLE

Central Archives for the History of the Jewish People, Inv. 1338.1, nos 1–8. Gerhard Ballin-Seesen, Jüdische Heiraten in Ostfriesland (1710–1719), Nach den Notizen in Staatsarchiv Aurich, Rep. IV B II r 1 (1962). [unpublished typescript]

Central Archives for the History of the Jewish People, MF HM 2300. [Fredericia misc.]

Central Archives for the History of the Jewish People, MF HM2 3827. [Prague, *hevrah kaddisha*]

Central Archives for the History of the Jewish People, MF HM2 4024. [Prague, *pinkas* Pinkas synagogue]

Central Archives for the History of the Jewish People, MF HM2 4042. [Prague, *pinkas hevrah kaddisha*]

Central Archives for the History of the Jewish People, MF HM2 4447.

Central Archives for the History of the Jewish People, MF HM2 5182. [Worms, *pinkas hevrah kaddisha*]

Central Archives for the History of the Jewish People, MS AHW 9.
Central Archives for the History of the Jewish People, MS AHW 10.
Central Archives for the History of the Jewish People, MS AHW 13.
Central Archives for the History of the Jewish People, MS AHW 14.
Central Archives for the History of the Jewish People, MS AHW 15.
Central Archives for the History of the Jewish People, MS AHW 16.
Central Archives for the History of the Jewish People, MS AHW 17a.
Central Archives for the History of the Jewish People, MS AHW 17b.
Central Archives for the History of the Jewish People, MS AHW 20.
Central Archives for the History of the Jewish People, MS AHW 25.
Central Archives for the History of the Jewish People, MS AHW 30.
Central Archives for the History of the Jewish People, MS AHW 31.1a.
Central Archives for the History of the Jewish People, MS AHW 31b (=CAHJP, MF HM2 6464a).
Central Archives for the History of the Jewish People, MS AHW 33a.
Central Archives for the History of the Jewish People, MS AHW 36a.

Central Archives for the History of the Jewish People, MS AHW 63.
Central Archives for the History of the Jewish People, MS AHW 71. [Our foliation follows the penciled pagination.]
Central Archives for the History of the Jewish People, MS AHW 73.
Central Archives for the History of the Jewish People, MS AHW 84a.
Central Archives for the History of the Jewish People, MS AHW 85a.
Central Archives for the History of the Jewish People, MS AHW 121–1.
Central Archives for the History of the Jewish People, MS AHW 121–2.
Central Archives for the History of the Jewish People, MS AHW 726.
Central Archives for the History of the Jewish People, MS D-Da1-437.
Central Archives for the History of the Jewish People, MS D-Fr3-32. [Frankfurt, *pinkas ne'emane kahal.*]
Central Archives for the History of the Jewish People, MS D-Ha11-296. [Halberstadt, *pinkas hazkarat neshamot.*]
Central Archives for the History of the Jewish People, MS D-Ha11-334. [*Takkanot Halberstadt.*]
Central Archives for the History of the Jewish People, MS D-Sc10-5ab. [Schnaittach, *pinkas kahal.*]
Central Archives for the History of the Jewish People, MS D-Sc10-28.
Central Archives for the History of the Jewish People, MS D-Wo3-337.
Central Archives for the History of the Jewish People, MS D-Wo3-339. [Worms, *pinkas iska'ot.*]
Central Archives for the History of the Jewish People, MS D-Wo3-372.
Central Archives for the History of the Jewish People, MS D-Wo3-401.
Central Archives for the History of the Jewish People, MS D-Wo 3–548.
Central Archives for the History of the Jewish People, MS D-Wo 3–662. [Worms, *pinkas gabba'im.*]
Central Archives for the History of the Jewish People, MS Ful-534.
Central Archives for the History of the Jewish People, MS GA-Rendsburg S-28-9. [Rendsburg, *pinkas hevrah kaddisha.*]
Central Archives for the History of the Jewish People, MS GA-Rendsburg S-28-18.
Central Archives for the History of the Jewish People, MS Memorbuch der Klaussynagoge Mannheim Bd 1.
Central Archives for the History of the Jewish People, MS P35–79.
Central Archives for the History of the Jewish People, P302-S1.2. [Aryeh Segall Private Collection, Annotations to Pinkas Frankfurt.]

JERUSALEM, COLLECTION OF THE GRAND RABBI OF KARLIN STOLIN, RABBI BARUCH SHOCHET

Karlin-Stolin, MS 41. Judah Mehler of Bingen. *She'elot u-teshuvot shevut Yehudah.* Vol. 3 (via Ktiv).
Karlin-Stolin, MS 457. *Iggeret el Shmuel Landau be-inyan mikveh mi-Maharam Heller* (via Ktiv).

JERUSALEM, ISRAEL MUSEUM

Israel Museum, MS 180/006. *Seder birkat ha-mazon, birkat ha-henenin, u-keriyat shema al ha-mitah.*

Israel Museum, MS 180/073. [Mannheim, *pinkas hevrah kaddisha*, 1804.]

JERUSALEM, NATIONAL LIBRARY OF ISRAEL

National Library of Israel, MS Heb. 2° 662. [Pinkas Frankfurt.]
National Library of Israel, MS Heb. 4° 522. [*She'elot u-teshuvot yefe nof le-Rav Isaac mi-See*, 1577.]
National Library of Israel, MS Heb. 4° 656. [Worms Memorbuch.]
National Library of Israel, MS Heb. 4° 928. [Alzey Memorbuch.] (via Ktiv)
National Library of Israel, MS Heb. 4°1092. [Frankfurt Memorbuch.]
National Library of Israel, MS Heb. 8° 2380. [*Sefer evronot.*]
National Library of Israel, MS Heb. 8° 2398. [Cleves Memorbuch]. (via Ktiv)
National Library of Israel, MS Heb. 8° 2423. [Büdesheim Memorbuch.] (via Ktiv)
National Library of Israel, MS Heb. 8° 3212. [Frankfurt, *pinkas ba'ale bayit.*]
National Library of Israel, MS Heb. 8° 4311. [Glikl, Memoirs.] (via Ktiv)
National Library of Israel, MS Heb. 8° 5245.

JERUSALEM, THE SCHOCKEN INSTITUTE FOR JEWISH RESEARCH

The Schocken Institute for Jewish Research, MS 70057. [Judah Mehler Reutlingen, 1609–1659. *Shevut Yehudah*. Our foliation follows penciled pagination.] (via Ktiv)

LEIPZIG

Universitätsbibliothek Leipzig, Wagenseil Collection, MS B.H. 18.

LONDON

British Library, MS Or. 10668.
British Library, Oriental and India Office Collections, Cod. Add 18695.
Victoria and Albert Museum, MSL 1868/513. [*Seder birkhat ha-mazon . . . ve shalosh mitsvot nashim.*]

MAINZ

Johannes Gutenberg-Universität Mainz, MS Nr. 2. [*Minhage hevrah kaddisha de-kavronim.*]
Johannes Gutenberg-Universität Mainz, MS Nr. 22/III. [*Hevrah kaddisha de-gemilut hasadim de-nashim.*]

MANNHEIM

Marchivum archives, Jüdischer Friedhof Database, grave number SGr-11. https://www.marchivum.de/de/recherche/datenbanken/juedischer-friedhof

NEW YORK

Columbia University, MS General 320. [*Pinkas ha-takkanot. Altona, kavranim.*]
Leo Baeck Institute, Jacob Jacobson Collection AR 7002, Box 4, Folder I39.
Leo Baeck Institute, Jacob Jacobson Collection AR 7002 / MF 447 / MF 134, Box 6, Folder: II7. [By-laws of the society for the care of orphans (*Takkanot hevrah yetomim*), photocopy of printed book, Hebrew, 1766.]
Leo Baeck Institute. Lemle Moses Reinganum Collection. AR 11546.
The Library of the Jewish Theological Seminary, MS 2709. [*Segulot u-refu'ot.*]
The Library of the Jewish Theological Seminary, MS 3684. [*Pinkas Friedberg.*]
The Library of the Jewish Theological Seminary, MS 3697. [*Sod Hashem ve-sharvit hazahav: likutei dinim ve-hanhagot u-tefilot ha-shayakhim le-brit ha-milah.* Hamburg, 1763.]
The Library of the Jewish Theological Seminary, MS 5396. [Metz, *pinkas hevrah kaddisha.*]
The Library of the Jewish Theological Seminary, MS 8136. [*Pinkas Metz.*]
The Library of the Jewish Theological Seminary, MS 8230.
The Library of the Jewish Theological Seminary, MS 8252. [*Seder berakhot.*]
The Library of the Jewish Theological Seminary, MS 8855 [=CAHJP MF HM2–5037, *Pinkas Metz im tzava'ot.*]
The Library of the Jewish Theological Seminary, MS 8869.
The Library of the Jewish Theological Seminary, MS 8875. [*Mainz Memorbuch.*]
The Library of the Jewish Theological Seminary, MS 9340.
The Library of the Jewish Theological Seminary, MS 9835. [*Pinkas Metz.*]
The Library of the Jewish Theological Seminary, MS 10632. [*Pinkas hevra kaddisha ma'asim tovim be-Amsterdam.*]
The Library of the Jewish Theological Seminary, MS 10772. [*Pinkas shamash Altona.*]
YIVO Institute. Tcherikower Archives, Simon Dubnow Papers, RG 87, folder 915. [*Pinkas Mstislav chadash.*]

OXFORD

Bodleian Library, MS Canonici Or. 12.
Bodleian Library, MS Opp. 4° 953.
Bodleian Library, MS Opp. 4° 1004. [*Sefer Minhagim*, Venice, 1600.]
Bodleian Library, MS Opp. 4° 1006. [*Sefer Minhagim*, Venice, 1593.]
Bodleian Library, MS Opp. 8° 796. [*Ayn shayn mayse.*]
Bodleian Library, MS Opp. 148. [*Be'er sheva.*]

PARIS

Bibliothèque de l'Alliance Israélite Universelle, MS Cod. H 9 A.
Bibliothèque de l'Alliance Israélite Universelle, MS 423.
Bibliothèque nationale de France, MS cod. héb. 586.
Bibliothèque nationale de France, MS cod. héb. 589.
Bibliothèque nationale de France, MS Cod. héb. 1312.

PARMA

La Biblioteca Palatina, MS 2510.
La Biblioteca Palatina, MS 2895.

PRAGUE

Archives of the Jewish Museum in Prague, Pinkas synagogue collection, Pinkas of the Pinkas synagogue, 1601–1845. Jewish Museum Prague, sine no. [microfilm at CAHJP, HM 4024].
Archives of the National Library of the Czech Republic, Censor and Reviewer of Jewish Books, Prints and Manuscripts, Prague, 1700–1842, Inv. No. 35, via Jewish Museum Prague. facsimile, JMP, PF 521.
Jewish Museum in Prague, MS 62. [*Kuntres beit knesset be-kehillat Steinitz.*]
Jewish Museum in Prague, MS 64. [*Kuntres beit knesset be-kehillat Kolin.*]
Jewish Museum in Prague, MS 89. [*Kuntres beit knesset ha-gavohah.*]
Jewish Museum in Prague, MS 113. [Altneuschul Memorbuch.]
Jewish Museum in Prague, MS 148.
Jewish Museum in Prague, MS 294.
Jewish Museum in Prague, MS 310.
Jewish Museum in Prague, MS 320.
Jewish Museum in Prague, MS 324.
Jewish Museum in Prague, MS 422.

RAMAT GAN

Bar-Ilan University, MS 803.
Bar-Ilan University, MS 846.

STRASBOURG

Bibliothèque nationale et universitaire de Strasbourg, MS Strasbourg 4048.

WORMS

Stadtarchiv Worms, MS 1B 2024/11.

Stadtarchiv Worms, MS 1B 2024/16.
Stadtarchiv Worms MS 1B 2024/19.

ZURICH

Braginsky Collection, 211. [*Haggadah shel Pesach*, Prague, 1526.]
Braginsky Collection, MS 217. [*Seder Birkat ha-mazon*, 1751.]
Braginsky Collection, MS 314.
Braginsky Collection, MS 328. [*Seder birkat ha-mazon*, 1725.]
Braginsky Collection, MS 344. [Vienna, 1725.]
Braginsky Collection, MS 351. [*Birkat ha-mazon*, 1741.]

Printed Primary Sources

Abrahams, Israel. *Hebrew Ethical Wills*. 2 vols. Philadelphia: Jewish Publication Society, 1926.

Altschuler, Moshe ben Hanokh. *Brantshpigel: Ir frome leit komt her*. Basel: Konrad Waldkirch, 1602.

Altschuler, Moshe ben Hanokh. *Brantshpigel: Ir frome leit komt her*. Prague: Gershon Katz, 1610.

Altschuler, Moshe ben Hanokh. *Mar'ah ha-sorefet ha-nikret be-leshon Ashkenaz Brantshpigel*. Frankfurt: Johannes Wust, 1706.

Anonymous. *Zikhron hurban ha-bayit*. Cremona, 1565–66.

Aptrood, Marion, and Rebekka Voß, eds. and trans. *Libes Briv (1748/49): Isaak Wetzlars pietistisches Erneuerungsprogramm des Judentums; Textedition, Übersetzung, Kommentar und historische Beiträge*. Hamburg: Buske, 2021.

Arnheim, Arthur, and Chava Turniansky. *Yiddish Letters from the Seventeenth Century World of Glikl Hamel*. Jerusalem: Magnes, 2020.

Asher Halevi. (see Halevi, Asher).

Ashkenazi, Tzvi Hirsch ben Jacob. *She'elot u-teshuvot Hakham Zvi*. Amsterdam, 1712.

Assaf, Simcha, ed. *Mekorot le-toldot ha-hinukh be-yisrael*. 4 vols. Tel Aviv: Dvir, 1925–42.

Bacharach, Yair Hayim. *Havot Yair*. Frankfurt am Main, 1699.

Baer, Yitzhak. [Fritz]. *Das Protokollbuch der Landjudenschaft des Herzogtums Kleve*. Erster Teil, Die Geschichte der Landjudenschaft des Herzogtums Kleve. Berlin, 1922.

Balaban, Majer. "Die Krakauer Judengemeinde und ihre Nachträge." *Jahrbuch der Jüdisch-Literarischen Gesellschaft* 10 (1912): 296–360.

Barzen, Rainer, ed. *Taqqanot Qehillot Sum: Die Rechtssatzungen der jüdischen Gemeinden Mainz, Worms und Speyer im hohen und späten Mittelalter*. Wiesbaden: Harrassowitz, 2019.

Bastian, Franz, and Josef Widemann, eds. *Regensburger Urkundbuch, 1371–1378*. 2 vols. Munich: C.H. Beck, 1956.

Baumgarten, Elisheva, Eyal Levinson, and Tzafrir Barzilay, eds. *Jewish Daily Life in Medieval Northern Europe, 1080–1350: A Sourcebook*. 2nd ed. Kalamazoo, MI: Medieval Institute Publications, 2022.

Berkovitz, Jay. *Protocols of Justice: The Pinkas of the Metz Rabbinic Court, 1771–1789*. [In Hebrew.] Leiden: Brill, 2014.

Birkat ha-mazon ke-minhag Ashkenaz u-Folin. Frankfurt: Aptrood/Gamburg, 1726–27.

Birkat ha-mazon le-sova ve-lo le-razon ke-minhag Ashkenaz u-Folin. Frankfurt, n.p., 1712–13.

Bloch, Joseph. "Le testament d'une femme juive au commencement du XVIIIe siècle." *Revue des études juives* 90 (1931): 146–60.

Bloch, Philippe. *Ein vielbegehrter Rabbiner des Rheingaues, Juda Mehler Reutlingen.* Breslau: A. Favorkes, 1916.

Bney Gumpel, Israel and Koppel. *Sefer minhagim de-kehilatenu.* Fürth: Hayim b. Zvi Hirsch, Schindelhof, 1766–67.

Bodenschatz, Johannes Christoph. *Kirchliche verfassung der heutigen Juden, sonderlich derer in Deutschland: In IV. haupt-theile abgefasset.* Strassburg und Leipzig: Joh. Friedr. Beckers nachgelassenen wittwe, 1748–[49].

Buxtorf, Johannes. *Johann Buxtorfii Institutio epistolaris hebraica: Cum epistolarum hebraicarum familiarium centuria, ex quibus ... quinquaginta punctis vocalibus animatæ, versione latina & notis illustratæ sunt.* Basel: Konrad Waldkirch, 1610.

Carlebach, Elisheva. "The Letters of Bella Perlhefter." Accessed January 20, 2025. https://research.library.fordham.edu/emw/emw2004/emw2004/11/.

Carlebach, Elisheva, ed. *The Posen Library of Jewish Culture and Civilization.* Vol. 6, *Confronting Modernity: 1750–1880.* New Haven, CT: Yale University Press and The Posen Library, 2019.

Carlin, Martha. "Early Modern Culinary Texts, 1500–1700." Accessed November 27, 2023. https://sites.uwm.edu/carlin/early-modern-culinary-texts-1500-1700/.

Carpi, Daniel, ed. *Pinkas va'ad kehillah kedoshah Padua.* Jerusalem: Ha-akademiah ha-le'umit ha-yisre'elit le-mada'im, 1973.

Colon, Joseph. *She'elot u-teshuvot Mahari"k.* New York: Y. Ze'ev, 1968.

Dubnow, Simon, ed. *Pinkas ha-medinah.* 2nd ed. Jerusalem: Ha-akademiyah ha-le'umit ha-yisraelit le-mada'im, 1968.

Eilburg, Eliezer. *The Ten Questions and Memoir of a Renaissance Skeptic.* Translated by Joseph Davis with Magdaléna Jánošiková. Cincinnati, OH: Hebrew Union College Press, 2020.

Einert, Paul N. *Entdeckter jüdischer Baldober: Oder Sachsen-Coburgische acta criminalia wider eine jüdische Diebs-und Rauber-band.* Coburg: Joh. Georg. Steinmarck, 1737.

Eks[t]rakt mi-protokol shel ha-medinah ... bi-devar takanot ha-kehilot Elsass. Strasbourg, 1777.

Elyakim of Komarna. *Melitz yosher/Tsene u-rene.* Amsterdam: Moses Kosman ben Elijah, 1688.

Emden, Jacob. *Bet Yehonatan ha-sofer.* Altona: s.p., 1763[?].

Emden, Jacob. *Birat migdal oz.* Zhitomir: Yitzhak Bakst, 1874.

Emden, Jacob. *Divre emet u-mishpat shalom.* Altona, 1776.

Emden, Jacob. *She'elat Ya'avetz.* Edited by Yaakov Bergstein. Monroe, NY: Keren Zikhron Moshe Yosef, 2017.

Emden, Jacob. *She'elat Ya'avetz.* Lemberg: Uri Dov Wolff Salat, 1882.

Ettlinger, Jacob. *She'elot u-teshuvot binyan Zion ha-hadashot.* Altona, 1868.

Eybeschutz, Jonathan. *Luhot edut.* Altona, 1755.

Faierstein, Morris, ed. and trans. *The Libes Briv of Isaac Wetzlar.* Atlanta, GA: Scholars Press, 1996.

Faierstein, Morris, ed. and trans. *Ze'enah u-Re'enah: A Critical Translation into English.* Berlin/Boston: De Gruyter, 2017.

Finkelstein, Louis. *Jewish Self-Government in the Middle Ages.* New York: Feldheim, 1964.

Fox, Harry and Justin Jaron Lewis. *Many Pious Women: Edition and Translation.* Berlin/Boston: De Gruyter, 2011.

Fram, Edward. *My Dear Daughter: Rabbi Benjamin Slonik and the Education of Jewish Women in Sixteenth-Century Poland*. Cincinnati, OH: Hebrew Union College Press, 2007.

Fram, Edward. *A Window on Their World: The Court Diaries of Rabbi Hayyim Gundersheim, Frankfurt am Main, 1773–1794*. Cincinnati, OH: Hebrew Union College Press, 2012.

Frankfurter, Shimon. *Sefer sha'ar Shimon*. Amsterdam, 1797.

Freudenthal, Max. *Leipziger Messgäste: Die jüdischen besucher der Leipziger messen in den jahren 1675 bis 1764*. Frankfurt am Main: J. Kauffmann, 1928.

Ginsberg, Dovid. "Private yiddishe briv fonem yor 1533." *Yivo Bletter* 8, nos. 3–4 (1938): 325–44.

Glikl of Hameln. *Glikl: Memoirs 1691–1719*. Edited by Chava Turniansky and translated by Sara Friedman. Waltham, MA: Brandeis University Press, 2019.

Glikl of Hameln. *Glikl: Zikhroynes, 1691–1719*. Edited by Chava Turniansky. Jerusalem: Merkaz Shazar, 2006.

Graupe, Heinz Moshe, ed. *Die Statuten der Drei Gemeinden Altona, Hamburg und Wandsbek*. Vols. 1–2. Hamburg: Hans Christians, 1973.

Graupe, Heinz Moshe. "Jewish Testaments from Altona and Hamburg (18th Century)." [In Hebrew.] *Michael: On the History of the Jews in the Diaspora* 2 (1973): 9–33.

Güdemann, Moritz. *Quellenschriften zur Geschichte des Unterrichts und der Erziehung bei den deutschen Juden: Von den ältesten Zeiten bis auf Mendelssohn*. Berlin: A. Hofmann, 1891.

Hahn Neuerlingen, Juspe. [Juspe Hahn]. *Yosif ometz*. Frankfurt am Main: Johann Kellner, 1723.

Halevi, Asher. *Die Memoiren des Ascher Levi aus Reichshofen*. Edited by Moshe Ginsburger. Berlin: Lamm, 1913.

Halevi, Shmuel. *Nahalat shivah ha-shalem*. 3 vols. Bnei Brak: Yehezkel Schwartz, 2019.

Halpern, Israel, ed. *Pinkas va'ad arba aratzot: Likkute takkanot, ketavim, u-reshumot*. Jerusalem: Mossad Bialik, 1945.

Hanover, Nathan Nata. *Safah berurah*. Prague: Sons of Yaakov Bak, 1660.

Heilprun, Yaakov. *Dinim ve-seder*. Venice: Giovanni de Gara, 1602.

Heilprun, Yaakov. *Orekh yomim*. Venice: Giovanni de Gara, 1599.

Heksher, Ephraim. *She'elot u-teshuvot adne paz*. Altona, 1743.

Hildesheimer, Meir, ed. *Pinkas kehillat Schnaittach*. Jerusalem: Mekize Nirdamim and Leo Baeck Institute, 1992.

Hirsch, Paul Wilhelm. *Megalleh tekuphoth*. Berlin, 1717.

Horovitz, Marcus, ed. *Inschriften des alten Friedhofs der israelitischen Gemeinde zu Frankfurt a. M*. Frankfurt am Main: J. Kaufmann, 1901.

Horowitz, David H. "Domestic Interiors of Two Viennese Jewish Elites." Early Modern Workshop: Jewish History Resources 2; Jews and Urban Space, University of Maryland, 2005, 98–103. https://research.library.fordham.edu/cgi/viewcontent.cgi?article=1031&context=emw.

Horowitz, Sheftel. *Yesh nohlin*. Amsterdam: Attias, 1701.

Isserlein, Israel. *Sefer leket yosher*. Parts 1–2. Berlin, 1903.

Isserlein, Israel. *Terumat ha-deshen*. Warsaw, 1882.

Isserles, Moses. *Mappah* to the *Shulhan arukh*. [any standard edition]

Jitte, daughter of Matthias Glückstadt. Testament. Altona, April 8, 1774. Translated by Richard S. Levy and edited in Key Documents of German-Jewish History. Accessed February 24, 2022. https://dx.doi.org/10.23691/jgo:source-42.en.v1.

Kaplan, Yosef, ed. *The Posen Library of Jewish Culture and Civilization.* Vol. 5, *The Early Modern Era.* New Haven: Yale University Press and The Posen Library, 2023.

Katzenellenbogen, Ezekiel. *She'elot u-teshuvot knesset Yehezkel.* Altona: n.p., 1732.

Katzenellenbogen, Pinhas. *Yesh manhilin,* edited by Yitzhak Feld. Jerusalem: Mekhon Hatam Sofer, 1986.

Katzenellenbogen, Pinhas. *Yesh manhilin* (excerpt). Translated by David E. Cohen. In *Posen Library of Jewish Culture and Civilization.* Vol. 6, *Confronting Modernity, 1750–1880,* edited by Elisheva Carlebach, 4–5. New Haven: Posen Library and Yale University Press, 2019.

Kaufmann, David. "Mekorot le-korot bnei yisrael: Mi-pinkassah ha-medinah shel k"k Metz." *Otzar ha-Sifrut* 3, no. 2 (1889–90): 3–7.

Kaufmann, David. "Mekorot le-korot bnei yisrael: Mi-pinkassei shel k"k Dusseldorf." *Otzar ha-Sifrut* 3, no. 2 (1889–90): 7–16.

Kaufmann, David. "Pinkas k"k Bamberg." *Kovets al Yad* 7 (1896/97): 1–46. (Based on MS Merzbacher.)

Kirchheim, Loewe. *Minhagot Warmaisa.* Jerusalem: Mifal Torat Hakhme Ashkenaz, 1987.

Kirchner, Paul Christian. *Jüdisches Ceremoniel.* Edited by Sebastian Jugendres. Nuremberg, 1724.

Kobler, Franz. *Letters of Jews through the Ages: From Biblical Times to the Middle of the Eighteenth Century.* 2 vols. New York: East and West Library, 1978.

Kohen, Shabbetai. Commentary to the *Shulhan arukh.* [any standard edition]

Kosman, Joseph. *Noheg ka-tzon Yosef.* Hanau, 1718.

Kupfer, Ephraim. *Teshuvot u-fesakim me'et Hakhme Ashkenaz ve-Tzarfat.* Jerusalem: Mekize Nirdamim, 1973.

Landau, Alfred, and Bernhard Wachstein, eds. *Jüdische privatbriefe aus dem jahre 1619: Nach den originalen des K. u. K. Haus-, hof- und staatsarchivs im auftrage der Historischen kommission der Israelitischen kultusgemeinde in Wien.* Vienna/Leipzig: W. Braumüller, 1911.

Landau, Ezekiel. *Noda be-Yehudah.* Prague: Moshe Katz and Israel Jeiteles, 1776.

Lewinsky, Avraham. "Takkanat ha-kehillah be-Hildesheim." *Ha-Eshkol* 6 (1902): 236–40.

Lewinsky, Yom Tov. "Takkanot le-seudat ha-brit de k"k Halberstadt, 1776." *Reshumot: Me'asef le-divre zikhronot ke-etnografia ule-folklor be-Yisrael,* n.s. 1 (1946): 142–50.

Litt, Stefan. *Jüdische Gemeindestatuten aus dem aschkenasischen Kulturraum 1650–1850.* Göttingen: Vandenhoeck & Ruprecht, 2014.

Litt, Stefan. *Pinkas, Kahal, and the Mediene: The Records of Dutch Ashkenazi Communities in the Eighteenth Century as Historical Sources.* Leiden/Boston: Brill, 2008.

Litt, Stefan, ed. *Protokollbuch und Statuten der Jüdischen Gemeinde Friedberg: (16.-18. Jahrhundert).* Friedberg: Bindernagel, 2003.

Löwenstein, Leopold. "Statuten des Landes Elsass." *Blätter für jüdische Geschichte und Litteratur* 2, no. 3 (1901): 18–22; 37–38.

Maitlis, Jacob. "London Yiddish Letters of the Early Eighteenth Century." *Journal of Jewish Studies* 6 (1955), no. 1: 153–65; no. 2: 237–52.

Malkiel, David. "The Woodstruck Deed." Early Modern Workshop: Jewish History Resources 3; Gender, Family and Social Structures. 2006. https://research.library.fordham.edu/cgi/viewcontent.cgi?article=1042&context=emw.

Margaritha, Antonius. *Der gantz jüdisch Glaub.* Augsburg: Heinrich Steyner, 1530.

Marwedel, Günter. *Die Königlich privilegirte Altonaer Adress-Comtoir-Nachrichten und die Juden in Altona*. Hamburg: Hans Christians, 1994.

Marx, Alexander. "A Seventeenth-Century Autobiography: A Picture of Jewish Life in Bohemia and Moravia." *Jewish Quarterly Review* 8, no. 3 (1918): 269–304.

Mehler, Judah, 1661–1751. See Jerusalem, Karlin-Stolin MS 41.

Meisl, Josef, ed. *Pinkas kehillat Berlin, 1723–1854*. Jerusalem: Reuven Mas, 1962.

Minhogim: oif taitsh . . . shabbat yamim tovim . . . Frankfurt am Main: Leyzer Florsheim, 1706–7.

Mi-See, Isaac. *She'elot u-teshuvot yefe nof le-rabbenu Yitzhak mi-See*. Edited by Avigdor Berger. Jerusalem: Makhon Yerushalayim, 1986.

Muneles, Otto. *Ketovot mi-beyt he-almin ha-yehudi he-atik be-Prag*. Jerusalem: Israel Academy of Sciences, 1988.

Oliel-Grausz, Evelyne. "Communication and Community: Multiplex Networks in the 18th-Century Sephardi Diaspora." Early Modern Workshop: Jewish History Resources 7; Jewish Community and Identity. https://research.library.fordham.edu/cgi/viewcontent.cgi?article=1098&context=emw.

Ostovich, Helen, and Elizabeth Sauer, eds. *Reading Early Modern Women: An Anthology of Texts in Manuscript and Print, 1550–1700*. New York: Routledge, 2004.

Pfefferkorn, Johannes. *Ich heyss ain büchlein der iuden peicht*. Augsburg: Jörgen Nadler, 1508.

Placaat: Tot Weeringe van Omzwervende Landlopers, Vagebonden et. in deze Provincie. 1765. NLI. Jerusalem, Valmadonna Trust, N13.

Poriat (Porges), Moses. *Darkhei Zion*. Frankfurt: n.p., 1650.

Refu'ot ha-nefesh. Altona: Aaron ben Eli Katz, 1740.

Reischer (Rzeszów), Jacob. *She'elot u-teshuvot shevut Yaakov*. 3 vols. Halle, 1709; Offenbach, 1719; Metz, 1789.

Riemer, Nathanael, and Sigrid Senkbeil, eds. *Be'er Sheva: An Edition of a Seventeenth Century Yiddish Encyclopedia by Beer and Bella Perlhefter*. Wiesbaden: Harrasowitz, 2011.

Rivkind, Isaac. "Kuntres Takkanot Prag: A Codex of Prague, 1611." [In Hebrew.] *Reshumot* 4 (1925): 345–52.

Schammes, Juspe Manzbach. *Minhagim de-k"k Warmaisa*. Edited by Benjamin Salomon Hamburger and Yitzhak (Eric) Zimmer. 2 vols. Jerusalem: Mifal Torat Hakhmei Ashkenaz, 1988.

Schudt, Johann Jacob. *Jüdische Merckwürdigkeiten: Vorstellende was sich Curieuses und Denckwürdiges in den neuern Zeiten bey einigen Jahrhunderten mit denen in alle IV Teile der Welt, sonderlich durch Teutschland, zerstreuten Juden zugetragen*. 4 vols. Frankfurt: Hocker, 1714.

Seder birkat ha-mazon: Di zemiros gedrukt in ivri un of taitch. Basel: Konrad von Waldkirch, 1600.

Sefer toldot Adam. Berlin: Aharon ben Moshe Rofe, 1750.

Slonik, Benjamin. *Precetti da esser imparati dalle donne ebree . . . composto per Rabbi Biniamim d'Harodono . . . tradotto . . . per Rabbi Giacob Halpron Hebreo*. Venice: Giacomo Sarzina, 1616.

Spalding, Almut, and Paul Spalding, eds. *The Account Books of the Reimarus Family of Hamburg, 1728–1780: Turf and Tailors, Books and Beer*. Leiden/Boston: Brill, 2015.

Steinhard, Gütgen, and Laur Herold. *Gütgen Steinhardin einer jungen jüdischen* . . . Nürnberg: G. F. Six, 1775.

Taglicht, J. *Nachlässe der Wiener Juden im 17. und 18. Jahrhundert: Ein Beitrag zur Finanz-, Wirtschafts- und Familiengeschichte des 17. und 18. Jahrhunderts.* Vienna-Leipzig: W. Braumüller, 1917.

Tal, Elhanan. *Ha-kehillah ha-ashkenazit be-Amsterdam ba-me'ah ha-shemoneh esreh.* Jerusalem: Merkaz Shazar, 2010.

Tiktiner, Rivkah bat Meir. (See von Rohden, Frauke.)

Tyrnau, Isaac. *Dize minhogim hoben mir tun druken nay mit vil verbessert un naye gemelder.* Amsterdam: Samuel ben Joseph Proops, 1727/8.

Tyrnau, Isaac. *Minhogim: Dize minhogim hoben mir tun druken . . . ke-seder noch ale minhogim geshtelt: Ashkenaz, Polin, Pihem, Mehren.* Amsterdam: Yitzhak di Kordova, 1722/23.

Tyrnau, Isaac. *Minhogim: Vi man zich noheg izt in Ashkenaz dos gantze yohr oikh Polin, Pihem Mehren . . . fil dinim . . . sheini naiei kupfr shtich.* Frankfurt am Main, 1728–29.

Tyrnau, Isaac. *Minhogim: vil hipsher den di ersten zeyn gevezin. . . .* Dyrenfurt: Bass, 1691–92.

Tyrnau, Isaac. *Minhogim: von ale minhogim in Ashkenaz durch daz gantze yohr . . .* Frankfurt: Juzpa Trier Kats, 1714–15.

Unna, Avigdor, ed. *Pinkas ha-takkanot ve-harishumim shel ha-hevrah kaddisha de-gemilut hasadim Warmaisa, 5476–5597.* Jerusalem: Mossad ha-Rav Kook, 1980.

Unna, Simon, ed. *Gedenkbuch der Frankfurter Juden: Nach aufzeichnungen der Beerdigungsbruderschaft hrsg. vom Komitee zur erhaltung und wiederherstellung der grabdenkmäler auf dem alten israelitischen friedhofe am Börneplatz zu Frankfurt am Main.* Frankfurt am Main: J. Kauffmann, 1914.

von Rohden, Frauke, ed. *Meneket Rivkah: A Manual of Wisdom and Piety.* Translated by Frauke von Rohden. Philadelphia: Jewish Publication Society, 2009.

Wachstein, Bernhard, ed. *Die Inschriften des Alten Judenfriedhofes in Wien.* Vienna: Wilhelm Braumüller, 1912.

Wachstein, Bernhard. "Die Prager takkanos fun 1767 kegen luksis." *YIVO Bleter* 1 (1931): 335–54.

Wachstein, Bernhard. "A yiddishe kahal in 18ten Jahrhundert: Pinkas Runkel." *YIVO Bleter* 6 (1934): 84–116.

Weinryb, Bernard. "A pekl briv in yidish fun 1588, Kroke-Prag" [A collection of Yiddish letters from 1588, Kraków-Prague]. *Historishe shriftn fun yivo* 2 (1937): 43–67.

Ya'ari, Avraham. *Masa'ot Eretz Israel shel olim yehudim me-yeme ha-benayim ve-ad le-reshit shivat Zion.* Tel Aviv: Moden, 1996.

Databases

Ele toldot database. Shlomo Ettlinger. Burial records of the Jewish community of Frankfurt am Main, 1241–1824. Leo Baeck Institute, New York, NY, AR 5241. [References are provided through the name of the deceased and the date of his or her burial.]

Epidat database. Salomon Ludwig Steinheim-Institut für deutsch-jüdische Geschichte an der Universität Duisburg-Essen. http://www.steinheim-institut.de/cgi-bin/epidat. [References are given using the identifier for each tombstone.]

Footprints database. Columbia University, New York, NY. https://footprints.ctl.columbia.edu/. [References are provided through the footprint number.]

Secondary Sources

Adelman, Howard. "Italian Jewish Women at Prayer." In *Judaism in Practice: From the Middle Ages through the Early Modern Period*, edited by Lawrence Fine, 52–60. Princeton: Princeton University Press, 2001.

Adelman, Howard. "Religious Practice among Italian Jewish Women." In *Judaism in Practice: From the Middle Ages through the Early Modern Period*, edited by Lawrence Fine, 203–209. Princeton: Princeton University Press, 2001.

Ago, Renata. *Gusto for Things: A History of Objects in Seventeenth-Century Rome*. Chicago: University of Chicago Press, 2013.

Akkerman, Nadine, and Birgit Houben, eds. *The Politics of Female Households: Ladies-in-Waiting across Early Modern Europe*. Leiden: Brill, 2014.

Altschuler, David. *The Precious Legacy: Judaic Treasures from the Czechoslovak State Collection*. New York: Summit Books, 1983.

Anders, Katrin. *Sara, Ester, Thobe und Hanna: Vier judische Frauen am Rande der Gesellschaft im 18. Jahrhundert; Ein mikrohistorische Studie unter Verwendung Flensburger Gerichtsakten*. Flensburg: Gesellschaft für Flensburger Stadtgeschichte, 1998.

Anklam, Karl. *Die Judengemeinde in Aurich*. Frankfurt am Main: J. Kauffmann, 1927.

Assaf, Simcha. *Bate ha-din ve-sidrehem ahare hatimat ha-Talmud*. Jerusalem: Sifriya Mishpatit, 1924.

Assis, Yom Tov. "Welfare and Mutual Aid in the Spanish Jewish Communities." In *Moreshet Sepharad: The Sephardi Legacy*, edited by Haim Beinart, 325–38. Jerusalem: Magnes, 1992.

Auslander, Leora. "Beyond Words." *American Historical Review* 110, no. 4 (2006): 1015–44.

Aust, Cornelia. "Covering the Female Jewish Body: Dress and Dress Regulations in Early Modern Ashkenaz." *Central Europe* 17, no. 1 (2019): 5–21.

Aust, Cornelia. "From Noble Dress to Jewish Attire: Jewish Appearances in the Polish-Lithuanian Commonwealth and the Holy Roman Empire." *European History Yearbook: Dress and Cultural Difference in Early Modern Europe* (2019): 90–112.

Aust, Cornelia. "'Was von einem Leben übrig bleibt'... Inventare jüdischer Frauen." In *Dingliche Gottesliebe: Die Materialität religiöser Emotionen in Christentum, Judentum und Islam*, edited by Ulrike Gleixner, 32–43. Wolfenbüttel: Herzog August Bibliothek, 2024.

Bar Levav, Avriel. "The Amsterdam Way of Death: R. Shimon Frankfurt's *Sefer Ha-Hayyim* (Book of Life), 1703." In *The Religious Cultures of Dutch Jewry*, edited by Yosef Kaplan and Dan Michman, 100–123. Leiden: Brill, 2017.

Bar Levav, Avriel. "The Ritualisation of Jewish Life and Death in the Early Modern Period." *Leo Baeck Institute Year Book* 47 (2002): 69–82.

Baron, Salo W. *The Jewish Community: Its History and Structure to the American Revolution*. 3 vols. Philadelphia: Jewish Publication Society, 1945.

Bartlet, Suzanne. "Three Jewish Businesswomen in Thirteenth-Century Winchester." *Jewish Culture and History* 3, no. 2 (2000): 31–54.

Baskin, Judith, ed. *Jewish Women in Historical Perspective*. Detroit, MI: Wayne State University Press, 1991.

Baskin, Judith. "'May the Writer Be Strong': Medieval Hebrew Manuscripts Copied by and for Women." *Nashim* 16 (2008): 9–28.

Baumann, Anette. "Jüdische Reichskammergerichtsprozesse aus den Reichsstädten Frankfurt und Hamburg: Eine quantitative Annäherung." *Zeitschrift für Historische Forschung* 39 (2007): 297–316.

Baumgarten, Elisheva. "Ask the Midwives: A Hebrew Manual on Midwifery from Medieval Germany." *Social History of Medicine* 32, no. 4 (2019): 712–33.

Baumgarten, Elisheva. *Biblical Women and Jewish Daily Life in the Middle Ages.* Philadelphia: University of Pennsylvania Press, 2022.

Baumgarten, Elisheva. "'Like Adam and Eve': Biblical Models and Jewish Daily Life in Medieval Christian Europe." *Irish Theological Quarterly* 83, no. 1 (2018): 44–61.

Baumgarten, Elisheva. *Mothers and Children: Jewish Family Life in Medieval Europe.* Princeton: Princeton University Press, 2004.

Baumgarten, Elisheva. *Practicing Piety in Medieval Ashkenaz: Men, Women, and Everyday Religious Observance.* Philadelphia: University of Pennsylvania Press, 2014.

Baumgarten, Elisheva. "'Remember that Glorious Girl': Jephthah's Daughter in Medieval Jewish Culture." *Jewish Quarterly Review* 97 (2007): 180–209.

Baumgarten, Jean. "Prayer, Ritual and Practice in Ashkenazic Jewish Society: The Tradition of Yiddish Custom Books in the Fifteenth to Eighteenth Centuries." *Studia Rosenthaliana* 36 (2002–03): 121–46.

Bell, Rudolph. *How to Do It: Guides to Good Living for Renaissance Italians.* Chicago: University of Chicago Press, 1999.

Bellavitis, Anna. *Women's Work and Rights in Early Modern Urban Europe.* Translated by Clelia Boscolo. Cham, Switzerland: Palgrave Macmillan, 2018.

Benayahu, Meir. *Studies in Memory of the Rishon le-Zion R. Yitzhak Nissim.* [In Hebrew.] Vol. 6. Jerusalem: Yad le-R. Yitzhak Nissim, 1985.

Bennett, Judith M., and Amy M. Froide, eds. *Singlewomen in the European Past, 1250–1800.* Philadelphia: University of Pennsylvania Press, 1999.

Berkovitz, Jay. *Law's Dominion: Jewish Community, Religion, and Family in Early Modern Metz.* Leiden: Brill, 2020.

Berner, Tali. *In Their Own Way: Children and Childhood in Early Modern Ashkenaz.* [In Hebrew.] Jerusalem: Merkaz Shazar, 2001.

Bock, Gisela. *Women in European History.* Oxford: Wiley-Blackwell, 2002.

Bodian, Miriam. "The Jewish Entrepreneurs in Berlin and the 'Civil Improvement of the Jews' in the 1780s and 1790s." [In Hebrew.] *Zion* 49, no. 2 (1984): 159–84.

Bodner, Neta, "Romanesque Beyond Christianity: Jewish Ritual Baths in Germany in the Twelfth and Thirteenth Centuries." *Jewish Studies Quarterly* 28, no. 4 (2021): 369–87.

Boes, Maria R. *Crime and Punishment in Early Modern Germany: Courts and Adjudicatory Practices in Frankfurt am Main, 1562–1696.* London/New York: Routledge, 2016.

Boes, Maria R. "'Dishonourable' Youth, Guilds, and the Changed World View of Sex, Illegitimacy, and Women in Late-Sixteenth-Century Germany." *Continuity and Change* 18, no. 3 (2003): 345–72.

Bonfield, Lloyd. "Developments in European Family Law." In *The History of the European Family.* Vol. 1, *Family Life in Early Modern Times, 1500–1789,* edited by David I. Kertzer and Marzio Barbagli, 87–124. New Haven: Yale University Press, 2001.

Braun, Emily, and Emily Bilski. *Jewish Women and their Salons: The Power of Conversation*. New York: The Jewish Museum/Yale University Press, 2005.

Bynum, Carolyn Walker. *Holy Feast and Holy Fast: The Religious Significance of Food to Medieval Women*. Berkeley: University of California Press, 1987.

Carlebach, Elisheva. "Big Stakes for Small Claims: An Early Modern Jewish Court between the Civil and the Rabbinic." In *A Jew in the Street: New Perspectives on European Jewish History*, edited by Jonathan Karp, James Loeffler, Howard Lupovitch, and Nancy Sinkoff, 121–46. Detroit, MI: Wayne State University Press, 2024.

Carlebach, Elisheva. "Community, Authority, and Jewish Midwives in Early Modern Europe." *Jewish Social Studies* 20, no. 2 (2014): 5–33.

Carlebach, Elisheva. "The Death of Simon Abeles: Jewish-Christian Tension in Seventeenth-Century Prague." Berman Memorial Lecture, Queens College, New York, NY, November, 2001.

Carlebach, Elisheva. *Divided Souls: Converts from Judaism in Germany, 1500–1750*. New Haven: Yale University Press, 2001.

Carlebach, Elisheva. "The Early Modern Jewish Community and Its Institutions." In *The Cambridge History of Judaism*. Vol. 7, *The Early Modern World, 1500–1815*, edited by Adam Sutcliffe and Jonathan Karp, 168–98. Cambridge: Cambridge University Press, 2017.

Carlebach, Elisheva. "Fallen Women and Fatherless Children: Jewish Domestic Servants in Eighteenth-Century Altona." *Jewish History* 24 (2010): 295–308.

Carlebach, Elisheva. "Letter into Text: Epistolarity, History, and Literature." In *Jewish Literature and History: An Interdisciplinary Conversation*, edited by Eliyana R. Adler and Sheila E. Jelen, 113–33. Bethesda: University Press of Maryland, 2008.

Carlebach, Elisheva. *Palaces of Time: Jewish Calendar and Culture in Early Modern Europe*. Cambridge, MA: Harvard University Press, 2011.

Carlson, Marybeth. *Domestic Service in a Changing City Economy: Rotterdam, 1680–1780*. Madison: University of Wisconsin Press, 1993.

Cassen, Flora. *Marking the Jews in Renaissance Italy: Politics, Religion, and the Power of Symbols*. Cambridge: Cambridge University Press, 2017.

Chartier, Roger. "Leisure and Sociability: Reading Aloud in Early Modern Europe." Translated by Carol Mossman. In *Urban Life in the Renaissance*, edited by Susan Zimmerman and Ronald F. E. Weissman, 102–20. Newark: University of Delaware, 1989.

Cherryson, Annia, Zoe Crossland, and Sarah Tarlow, eds. *A Fine and Private Place: Archaeology of Death and Burial in Post-Medieval Britain and Ireland*. Leicester: University of Leicester School of Archaeology and Ancient History, 2012.

Chovav, Yemima. *Maidens Love Thee: The Religious and Spiritual Life of Jewish Ashkenazic Women in the Early Modern Period*. [In Hebrew.] Jerusalem: Merkaz Dinur and Carmel, 2009.

Cobb, Richard. *Paris and its Provinces, 1792–1802*. London: Oxford, 1975.

Cohen, Esther, and Elliott Horowitz. "In Search of the Sacred: Jews, Christians, and Rituals of Marriage in the Later Middle Ages." *Journal of Medieval and Renaissance Studies* 20 (1990): 225–50.

Cohn, M., and E. Kirschner. "Kallah-Lied." *Mitteilungen der Gesellschaft für jüdische Volkskunde* 2, no. 8 (1901): 154.

Cypess, Rebecca, and Nancy Sinkoff, eds. *Sara Levy's World: Gender, Judaism and the Bach Tradition in Enlightenment Berlin*. Rochester, NY: University of Rochester Press, 2018.

Davidovich-Eshed, Avital. "On Brides and Braids: Brides' Hair and Virginity in Medieval Ashkenazi Wedding Customs." [In Hebrew.] *Zmanim* 118 (2012): 50–61.

Davis, Joseph. "Concepts of Family and Friendship in the 1619 Yiddish Letters of Prague Jews." *Judaica Bohemia* 49 (2014): 27–58.

Davis, Joseph. "A German Jewish Woman Scholar in the Early Sixteenth Century." In *Freedom and Responsibility: Exploring the Challenges of Jewish Continuity*, edited by Rela Mintz Geffen and Marsha Bryan Edelman, 101–10. New York: Ktav, 1998.

Davis, Natalie Zemon. *Society and Culture in Early Modern France*. Stanford, CA: Stanford University Press, 1975.

Davis, Natalie Zemon. *Women on the Margins: Three Seventeenth-Century Lives*. Cambridge, MA: Harvard University Press, 1997.

Daybell, James. *The Material Letter in Early Modern England: Manuscript Letters and the Culture and Practices of Letter-Writing, 1512–1635*. Houndmills: Palgrave Macmillan, 2012.

Dermineur, Elise. "Credit, Strategies, and Female Empowerment in Early Modern France." In *Women and Credit in Pre-Industrial Europe*, edited by Elise Dermineur, 253–80. Turnhout: Brepols, 2018.

Deutsch, Yaacov. *Judaism in Christian Eyes: Ethnographic Descriptions of Jews and Judaism in Early Modern Europe*. New York: Oxford University Press, 2012.

Deutsch, Yaacov. "Polemical Ethnographies: Descriptions of Yom Kippur in the Writings of Christian Hebraists and Jewish Converts to Christianity in Early Modern Europe." In *Hebraica Veritas? Christian Hebraists and the Study of Judaism in Early Modern Europe*, edited by Allison P. Coudert and Jeffrey Shoulson, 202–33. Philadelphia: University of Pennsylvania Press, 2004.

Diefendorf, Barbara B. *From Penitence to Charity: Pious Women and the Catholic Reformation in Paris*. Oxford: Oxford University Press, 2006.

Diemling, Maria. "*Den ikh bin treyfe gevezen*: Body Perceptions in Seventeenth-Century Jewish Autobiographical Texts." In *The Jewish Body: Corporeality, Society, and Identity in the Renaissance and Early Modern* Period, edited by Giuseppe Veltri and Maria Diemling, 93–125. Leiden/Boston: Brill, 2009.

Diemling, Maria. "Privacy, Literacy and Gender in Early Modern Jewish Letters from Prague (1619)." *Studia Judaica* 26, no. 2 (2023): 1–25.

Dobbie, B. M. Willmott. "An Attempt to Estimate the True Rate of Maternal Mortality, Sixteenth to Eighteenth Centuries." *Medical History* 26, no. 1 (1982): 79–90.

Duckesz, Eduard. *Hakhme AH"U*. Hamburg: Goldschmidt, 1908.

Duden, Barbara. *The Woman Beneath the Skin: A Doctor's Patients in Eighteenth-century Germany*. Translated by Thomas Dunlap. Cambridge, MA: Harvard University Press, 1991.

Eisenstein, Elizabeth L. *The Printing Press as an Agent of Change: Communications and Cultural Transformation*. Cambridge: Cambridge University Press, 1980.

Elbaum, Jacob, and Chava Turniansky. "Tsene-rene." In *YIVO Encyclopedia*, online.

Endelman, Todd. *The Jews of Georgian England, 1714–1830: Tradition and Change in a Liberal Society*. Philadelphia: Jewish Publication Society, 1979.

Evers, Renate. "Philipp Alexander and Crona David: A Conversion, Divorce, and Custody Case, Braunschweig, 1752/53." *Jewish Culture and History* 20, no. 2 (2019): 99–122.

Evers, Renate. "Traces of Court Jewish Women: Legal Case Studies." MA thesis, Columbia University, 2021.

Feiner, Shmuel. *The Jewish Eighteenth Century: A European Biography, 1700–1750*. Bloomington: Indiana University Press, 2022.

Fennetaux, Ariane. "Women's Pockets and the Construction of Privacy in the Long Eighteenth Century." *Eighteenth Century Fiction* 20, no. 3 (2008): 307–34.

Fishof, Iris. *Jüdische Buchmalerei in Hamburg und Altona: Zur Geschichte der Illumination hebräischer Handschriften im 18. Jahrhundert*. Edited by Andreas Brämer and translated from the Hebrew by Dina Herz and Smadar Rahveh-Klemke. Hamburg: H. Christians, 1999.

Fram, Edward. *The Codification of Jewish Law on the Cusp of Modernity*. Cambridge: Cambridge University Press, 2022.

Francesconi, Federica. "'And if I Could, I Would Leave Her More': Women's Voices, Emotions, and Objects from the Venetian Ghetto in the Seventeenth Century." In *From Catalonia to the Caribbean: The Sephardic Orbit from Medieval to Modern Times*, edited by Federica Francesconi, Stanley Mirvis, and Brian Smollet, 309–29. Leiden: Brill, 2018.

Francesconi, Federica. "Confraternal Community as a Vehicle for Jewish Female Agency in Eighteenth-Century Italy." In *Faith's Boundaries: Laity and Clergy in Early Modern Confraternities*, edited by Nicholas Terpstra, Adriano Prosperi, and Stefania Pastore, 251–71. Turnhout: Brepols, 2012.

Francesconi, Federica. *Invisible Enlighteners: The Jewish Merchants of Modena, from the Renaissance to the Emancipation*. Philadelphia: University of Pennsylvania Press, 2021.

Freiman, Eli. "Tarbut ve-hevrah yehudit be-Ashkenaz be-reshit ha-et ha-hadashah be-eynaim yehudiot ve-notzriot: Tarbut amamit ve-tarbut rabbanit." PhD diss., Hebrew University, 2007.

French, Katherine L. "The Cock on the Hoop: A Lodging House in Late Medieval London." Paper presented at the Sixteenth Century Studies Conference, Albuquerque, NM, November 1, 2018.

French, Katherine L. *The Good Women of the Parish: Gender and Religion after the Black Death*. Philadelphia: University of Pennsylvania Press, 2013.

Friedman, Menachem. "Letters of Recommendation for Jewish Mendicants: A Comment upon the Problem of Jewish Vagrancy in Eighteenth-Century Germany." [In Hebrew.] *Michael: On the History of the Jews in the Diaspora* (1973): 34–51.

Friedrichs, Christopher R. "Jewish Household Structure in an Early Modern Town: The Worms Ghetto Census of 1610." *History of the Family* 8, no. 4 (2003): 481–93.

Frye, Susan. *Pens and Needles: Women's Textualities in Early Modern England*. Philadelphia: University of Pennsylvania Press, 2010.

Fuchs, Stefanie. "Die Mikwen von Speyer und Worms: Aktueller Forschungsstand." In *Die jüdische Gemeinde von Erfurt und die SchUM-Gemeinden: Kulturelles Erbe und Vernetzung*, 60–69. Vol. 1. Jena and Quedlinburg: Bussert & Stadeler, 2012.

Furst, Rachel. "Marriage before the Bench: Divorce Law and Litigation Strategies in Thirteenth-Century Ashkenaz." *Jewish History* 31, nos. 1–2 (2017): 7–30.

Ginsburg, Dovid. "Private yiddishe briv funem yohr 1533." *Yivo Bletter* 13 (March–April 1938): 325–34.

Goitein, Shlomo Dov. *A Mediterranean Society*. Vol. 3, *The Family*. Berkeley: University of California Press, 2000.

Goldberg, Sylvie Anne. *Crossing the Jabbok: Illness and Death in Ashkenazi Judaism in Sixteenth- through Nineteenth-Century Prague*. Translated by Carol Cosman. Berkeley: University of California Press, 1997.

Goldstein, Lisa L. "Jewish Communal Life in the Duchy of Mecklenburg as Reflected in Correspondence, 1760–1769." Graduate Rabbinic Program diss., Hebrew Union College-Jewish Institute of Religion, New York, 1993.

Gonen, Amiram. "Choosing the Right Place of Rest: The Socio-Cultural Geography of a Jewish Cemetery in Jerusalem." In *Land and Community: Geography in Jewish Studies*, edited by Harold Brodsky, 87–104. Bethesda: University Press of Maryland, 1997.

Graupe, Heinz Moshe. "Mordechai Shnaber-Levison: The Life, Works and Thought of a Haskalah Outsider." *Leo Baeck Institute Year Book* 41 (1996): 3–20.

Greenblatt, Rachel. *To Tell Their Children: Jewish Communal Memory in Early Modern Prague*. Stanford, CA: Stanford University Press, 2014.

Grieco, Sara Matthews, and Carlo A. Corsini. *Historical Perspectives on Breastfeeding: Two Essays*. Florence: International Child Development Centre, 1991.

Grossman, Avraham. *Pious and Rebellious: Jewish Women in Medieval Europe*. Translated by Jonathan Chipman. Waltham, MA: Brandeis University Press, 2004.

Grossman, Avraham, and Yosef Kaplan, eds. *Kehal Yisrael: Ha-shilton ha-atzmi ha-yehudi le-dorotav*. Vol. 2, *Yeme ha-benayim ve-ha'et ha-hadashah ha-mukdemet*. Jerusalem: Merkaz Shazar, 2004.

Grunwald, Max. *Hamburgs deutsche Juden bis zur Auflösung der Dreigemeinden, 1811*. Hamburg: A. Janssen, 1904.

Guesnet, François. "Demonic Entanglements: Matted Hair in Medieval and Early Modern, Western and Eastern Ashkenaz." In *Monsters and Monstrosities in Jewish History from the Middle Ages to Modernity*, edited by Iris Idelson-Shein and Christian Wiese, 86–101. London/New York: Bloomsbury, 2019.

Habermann, Abraham Meir. *Nashim ivriot be-tor madpisot, mesadrot, motziot le-or, ve-tomkhot be-mehabrim*. Berlin: Reuven Maas, 1933.

Hacker, Joseph. "He-omnam 'et ha-hadashah ha-mukdemet' hi tekufah be-toldot Yisrael?" In *Avne derekh: Masot u-mehkarim be-historiah shel am Yisrael: Shai le-Tzvi (Kuti) Yekutiel*, edited by Immanuel Etkes, David Assaf, and Yoseph Kaplan, 165–80. Jerusalem: Merkaz Shazar, 2016.

Hairston, Julia. "The Economics of Milk and Blood in Alberti's *Libri della famiglia*: Maternal versus Wet-Nursing." In *Medieval and Renaissance Lactations: Images, Rhetorics, Practices*, edited by Jutta Gisela Sperling, 187–212. London: Routledge, 2013.

Hakohen Fishman, Yehuda Leib. *Sare ha-me'ah: Reshumim ve-zikhronot*. 6 vols. Jerusalem: Mossad ha-Rav Kook, 1942–1957.

Harrán, Don, ed. and trans. *Sarra Copia Sullam: Jewish Poet and Intellectual in Seventeenth-Century Venice*. Chicago: University of Chicago Press, 2009.

Harrington, Joel F. *Reordering Marriage and Society in Reformation Germany*. Cambridge: Cambridge University Press, 1995.

Hausmann, Ulrich. "Die Statuten der Mainzer Beerdigungsschwesternschaft, 1789." In *Aus den Bücherregalen: Entdeckungen in der Jüdischen Bibliothek Mainz, Ma'ayanot* 1, edited by Andreas Lehnardt, 85–99. Berlin: Andreas Lehnardt epubli, 2018.

Healy, Róisín. "Suicide in Early Modern and Modern Europe." *Historical Journal* 49, no. 3 (2006): 903–19.

Hebell, Kersten. "Madame Kaulla und ihr Clan: Das Kleinterritorium als individuelle Nische und ökonimisches Sprungbett." In *Hofjüden- ökonomie und Interkulturalität: Die jüdische Wirtschaftselite im 18. Jahrhundert*, edited by Rotraud Ries and Friedrich J. Battenberg, 332–48. Hamburg: Christians, 2002.

Heine, Heinrich. "Prinzessin Sabbat." In *Hebrew Melodies*, translated by Stephen Mitchell and Jack Prelutsky and illustrated by Mark Podwal, 12–15. University Park: Pennsylvania State University Press, 2019.

Hellerstein, Kathryn. "The Name in the Poem: Yiddish Women Poets." *Shofar* 20, no. 3 (2002): 32–52.

Hellerstein, Kathryn. *A Question of Tradition: Women Poets in Yiddish, 1586–1987*. Stanford, CA: Stanford University Press, 2014.

Hertz, Deborah. "Salonières and Literary Women in Late Eighteenth-Century Berlin." *New German Critique* 14 (1978): 97–108.

Herzig, Tamar. "Reformations, Nuns, and Nunneries in the Early Modern Era." [In Hebrew.] *Zmanim* 140 (2019): 32–47.

Hills, Helen. *Architecture and the Politics of Gender in Early Modern Europe*. Aldershot, Hants, England/Burlington, VT: Ashgate, 2003.

Hödl, Sabine. "Die Briefe von Prager an Wiener Juden (1619) als familienhistorische Quelle." In *Die jüdische Familie in Geschichte und Gegenwart*, edited by Sabine Hödl and Martha Keil, 51–79. Berlin/Bodenheim: Philo, 1999.

Horowitz, Elliott. "Between Masters and Maidservants in the Jewish Society of Europe in Late Medieval and Early Modern Times." In *Eros, erusin ve-issurim: Sexuality and the Family in History: Collected Essays*, edited by Israel Bartal and Isaiah Gafni, 193–211. [In Hebrew.] Jerusalem: Merkaz Shazar, 1998.

Horowitz, Elliott. "The Dowering of Brides in the Ghetto of Venice: Between Tradition and Change, Ideals and Reality." [In Hebrew.] *Tarbiz* 56, no. 1 (1987): 347–71.

Horowitz, Elliott. "Haburot be-Italia ba-me'ot ha-16-18: Dimui u-metziut." [Confraternities in Italy in the 16th–18th centuries: Image and reality]. In *Kehal Yisrael: Ha-shilton ha-atzmi ha-yehudi le-dorotav*, edited by Avraham Grossman and Yosef Kaplan. Vol. 2, 221–42. Jerusalem: Merkaz Shazar, 2004.

Horowitz, Elliott. "Processions, Piety, and Jewish Confraternities." In *The Jews of Early Modern Venice*, edited by Robert C. Davis and Benjamin Ravid, 231–47. Baltimore: Johns Hopkins University Press, 2001.

Howell, Martha C. *Women, Production, and Patriarchy in Late Medieval Cities*. Chicago: University of Chicago Press, 1986.

Hsia, Ronnie Po-Chia. "Christian Ethnography of Jews in Early Modern Germany." In *The Expulsion of the Jews: 1492 and After*, edited by Raymond B. Waddington and Arthur Williamson, 223–35. New York/London: Garland, 1994.

Hughes, Diane Owen. "Distinguishing Signs: Ear-Rings, Jews and Franciscan Rhetoric in the Italian Renaissance." *Past & Present* 112, no. 1 (1986): 3–59.

Hughes, Diane Owen. "From Brideprice to Dowry in Mediterranean Europe." *Journal of Family History* 3 (1978): 262–96.

Hundert, Gershon David. *Jews in Poland-Lithuania in the Eighteenth Century: A Genealogy of Modernity*. Berkeley: University of California Press, 2004.

Hyman, Paula. *Gender and Assimilation in Modern Jewish History: The Roles and Representation of Women*. Seattle: University of Washington Press, 1995.

Idelson-Shein, Iris. *Between the Bridge and the Barricade: Jewish Translation in Early Modern Europe*. Philadelphia: University of Pennsylvania Press, 2024.

Ifft Decker, Sarah. *Jewish Women in the Medieval World: 500–1500 CE*. New York: Routledge, 2022.

Jakobovits, Tobias. "Die Juden Abzeichen in Böhmen." *Jahrbuch der Gesellschaft für Geschichte der Juden in der Čechoslovakischen Republik* 3 (1931): 154–70.

Johns, Adrian. *The Nature of the Book: Print and Knowledge in the Making*. Chicago: University of Chicago Press, 2000.

Johnson, Carina. "The Politics of 'Count Stephan's House': Living Quarters, Hierarchy, and Familiarity in Early Modern Vienna." Paper presented at the Sixteenth Century Studies Conference, Albuquerque, NM, November 1, 2018.

Jones, Ann Rosalind, and Peter Stallybrass. *Renaissance Clothing and the Materials of Memory*. Cambridge: Cambridge University Press, 2000.

Kahana, J. Z. "Limitation of Jewish Marriages in Moravia." [In Hebrew.] *Zion* 8, no. 4 (1943): 203–06.

Kahana, Maoz. "Shabbat be-vet ha-kafe be-Prague." *Zion* 78, no. 1 (2013): 5–50.

Kalaora, Etelle. "Jewish Widows' Homes in Ashkenaz in the 12th and 13th Centuries." *Jewish Studies Quarterly*, 28, no. 3 (2021): 315–30.

Kanarfogel, Ephraim. *Brothers from Afar: Rabbinic Approaches to Apostasy and Reversion in Medieval Europe*. Detroit, MI: Wayne State University Press, 2020.

Kanarfogel, Ephraim. "Levels of Literacy in Ashkenaz and Sepharad as Reflected by the Recitation of Biblical Verse Found in the Liturgy." [In Hebrew.] In *Rishonim ve-ahronim: From Sages to Savants; Studies Presented to Avraham Grossman*, edited by Joseph R. Hacker, B. Z. Kedar, and Yosef Kaplan, 187–211. Jerusalem: Merkaz Shazar, 2010.

Kaplan, Debra. "'Because Our Wives Trade and Do Business with Our Goods': Gender, Work, and Jewish-Christian Relations." In *New Perspectives on Jewish-Christian Relations: In Honor of David Berger*, edited by Elisheva Carlebach and Jacob J. Schacter, 241–61. Leiden: Brill, 2012.

Kaplan, Debra. *Beyond Expulsion: Jews, Christians, and Reformation Strasbourg*. Stanford, CA: Stanford University Press, 2011.

Kaplan, Debra. "Courtship and Ritual." In *A Cultural History of Marriage in the Renaissance and Early Modern Age*, edited by Joanne Ferraro, 19–34. New York: Bloomsbury, 2019.

Kaplan, Debra. *The Patrons and Their Poor: Jewish Community and Public Charity in Early Modern Germany*. Philadelphia: University of Pennsylvania Press, 2020.

Kaplan, Debra. "'To Immerse Their Wives': Communal Identity and the 'Kahalishe' Mikveh of Altona." *AJS Review* 36, no. 2 (2012): 257–79.

Kaplan, Debra. "Women and Worth: Female Access to Property in Early Modern Urban Jewish Communities." *Leo Baeck Institute Year Book* 55, no. 1 (2010): 93–113.

Kaplan, Debra, and Edward Fram. "The Four Species in Pre-Modern Europe: Views from East and West." In *Be Fruitful: The Etrog in Jewish Art, Culture, and History*, edited by Warren

Klein, Sharon Liberman Mintz, and Joshua Teplitsky, 97–120. Jerusalem/New York: Mineged, 2022.

Kaplan, Marion. *The Making of the Jewish Middle Class: Women, Family, and Identity in Imperial Germany.* Oxford: Oxford University Press, 1995.

Kaplan, Yosef. "Jewish Amsterdam's Impact on Modern Jewish History." In *Schöpferische Momente des europäischen Judentums in der frühen Neuzeit,* edited by Michael Graetz, 19–62. Heidelberg: C. Winter, 2000.

Karant-Nunn, Susan C. *The Reformation of Ritual: An Interpretation of Early Modern Germany.* London: Routledge, 2007.

Karp, Jonathan, and Francesca Trivellato, eds. *Classic Essays on Jews in Early Modern Europe.* New York: Routledge, 2023.

Kasper-Marienberg, Verena. "Jewish Women at the Viennese Imperial Supreme Court: A Case Study from the Eighteenth Century." *Jewish Studies Quarterly* 21, no. 2 (2014): 176–92.

Kasper-Marienberg, Verena, and Debra Kaplan. "Nourishing a Community: Food, Hospitality, and Jewish Communal Spaces in Early Modern Frankfurt." *AJS Review* 45, no. 2 (2021): 302–33.

Kasper-Marienberg, Verena, and Joshua Teplitsky. "The Jews of Bohemian Lands in Early Modern Times." In *Prague and Beyond,* edited by Kateřina Čapková and Hillel Kieval, 22–60. Philadelphia: University of Pennsylvania Press, 2021.

Katz, Gabriele. *Die erste Unternehmerin Süddeutschlands und die reichste Frau ihrer Zeit: Madame Kaulla, 1739–1806.* Filderstadt: Markstein, 2006.

Katz, Jacob. "Nisu'im ve-hayye ishut be-motza'e yeme ha-benayim." *Zion* 10 (1944/5): 21–54. We refer readers to the recent translation by Jonathan Karp in Jonathan Karp and Francesca Trivellato, eds. *Classic Essays on Jews in Early Modern Europe,* 26–73. New York: Routledge, 2023.

Katz, Jacob. *Tradition and Crisis: Jewish Society at the End of the Middle Ages.* Translated by Bernard Dov Cooperman. New York: New York University Press, 1993.

Katz, Jordan R. *Jewish Midwives, Medicine, and the Boundaries of Knowledge in Early Modern Europe, 1650–1800.* PhD diss., Columbia University, 2020.

Katz, Jordan R. "Jewish Midwives, Wise Women, and the Construction of Medical-Halakhic Expertise in the Eighteenth Century." *Jewish Social Studies* 26, no. 2 (2021): 1–36.

Katz, Jordan R. "'To Judge and to Be Judged': Jewish Communal Autonomy in Metz and the Struggle for Sovereignty in Eighteenth-Century France." *Jewish Quarterly Review* 104, no. 3 (2014): 438–70.

Kayserling, Meyer. *Die jüdische Frauen in der Geschichte, Literatur und Kunst.* Leipzig: Brockhaus, 1879.

Keil, Martha. "Business Success and Tax Debts: Jewish Women in Late Medieval Austrian Towns." *Jewish Studies at the Central European University* 2 (2002): 103–23.

Keil, Martha. "Public Roles of Jewish Women in Fourteenth and Fifteenth-Century Ashkenaz: Business, Community, and Ritual." In *The Jews of Europe in the Middle Ages (Tenth to Fifteenth Centuries),* edited by Christoph Cluse, 317–30. Turnhout: Brepols, 2004.

Kogman-Appel, Katrin. "Portrayals of Women with Books: Female (Il)literacy in Medieval Jewish Culture." In *Reassessing the Roles of Women as "Makers" of Medieval Art and Architecture,* ed. Therese Martin. Vol. 2, 525–63. Leiden/Boston: Brill, 2012.

Koslofsky, Craig M. *The Reformation of the Dead: Death and Ritual in Early Modern Germany, 1450–1700*. New York: St. Martin's, 2000.

Kowalchuk, Kristine, ed. *Preserving on Paper: Seventeenth-Century Englishwomen's Receipt Books*. Toronto: University of Toronto Press, 2017.

Krakowski, Eve. *Coming of Age in Medieval Egypt: Female Adolescence, Jewish Law and Ordinary Culture*. Princeton: Princeton University Press, 2017.

Krautheimer, Richard. *Bate knesset bi-yeme ha-benayim*. Translated by Amos Goren. Jerusalem: Mossad Bialik, 1994.

Kreager, Philip. "Early Modern Population Theory: A Reassessment." *Population and Development Review* 17, no. 2 (1991): 207–27.

Kroder, Karl, and Birgit Kroder-Gumann. *Schnaittacher Hauschronik*. Nürnberg: Gesellschaft für Familienforschung in Franken, 2002.

Kronenberger, Friedrich L. *Der jüdischen Vieh- und Pferdehändler im Birkenfelder Land und in den Gemeinden des Hunsrücks*. Birkenfeld: Schriftenreihe der Kreisvolkshochschule Birkenfeld, 1983.

Langer, Ruth. "'Birkhat betulim': A Study of the Jewish Celebration of Bridal Virginity." *Proceedings of the American Academy for Jewish Research* 61 (1995): 53–94.

Leiman, Shnayer. "Two Cases of Non-Jews with Rabbinic Ordination: One Real and One Imaginary." Seforim Blog, November 16, 2006. https://seforimblog.com/2006/11/dr-leimans-post-two-cases-of-non-jews/?print=print.

Leonard, Amy. *Nails in the Wall: Catholic Nuns in Reformation Germany*. Chicago: University of Chicago Press, 2005.

Lerner, Gerda. *The Creation of Patriarchy*. New York: Oxford University Press, 1986.

Leviant, Curt. *King Artus: A Hebrew Arthurian Romance of 1279*. New York: Ktav, 1969.

Levin, Vladimir. "The Architecture of Gender: Women in the Eastern European Synagogue." *Jewish History* 35 (2021): 89–134.

Liberles, Robert. "Family Life." In *Jewish Daily Life in Germany, 1618–1945*, edited by Marion Kaplan, 24–46. Oxford: Oxford University Press, 2005.

Liberles, Robert. *Jews Welcome Coffee: Tradition and Innovation in Early Modern Germany*. Waltham, MA: Brandeis University Press, 2012.

Libson, Ayelet Hoffmann. *Law and Self-Knowledge in the Talmud*. Cambridge: Cambridge University Press, 2018.

Lind, Vera. *Selbstmord in der frühen Neuzeit: Diskurs, Lebenswelt und kultureller Wandel am Beispiel der Herzogtümer Schleswig und Holstein*. Göttingen: Vandenhoeck & Ruprecht, 1999.

Lindemann, Mary. *Health and Healing in Eighteenth-Century Germany*. Baltimore: Johns Hopkins University Press, 1996.

Lindemann, Mary. "Love for Hire: The Regulation of the Wet-Nursing Business in Eighteenth-Century Hamburg." *Journal of Family History* 6, no. 4 (1981): 347–442.

Lindemann, Mary. *Patriots and Paupers: Hamburg, 1712–1830*. Oxford: Oxford University Press, 1990.

Löwenstein, Leopold. "Zur Geschichte der Juden in Friedberg." *Blätter für jüdische Geschichte Friedberg und Literatur* 4 (1903): 13–20, 54–59, 81–86.

Löwenstein, Leopold, and Marcus Brann. "R. Juda Mehler II." *Monatsschrift für Geschichte und Wissenschaft des Judentums* 61 (1917): 285–92.

Lowenstein, Steven M. "Ashkenazic Jewry and the European Marriage Pattern: A Preliminary Survey of Jewish Marriage." *Jewish History* 8, nos. 1–2 (1994): 155–75.

Lowenstein, Steven M. *The Berlin Jewish Community: Enlightenment, Family and Crisis, 1770–1830*. Oxford: Oxford University Press, 1994.

Malino, Frances. "Resistance and Rebellion in Eighteenth-Century France." *Jewish Historical Studies* 30 (1987): 55–70.

Marcus, Ivan G. "Mothers, Martyrs, and Moneymakers: Some Jewish Women in Medieval Europe." *Conservative Judaism* 38, no. 3 (1986): 33–45.

Marcus, Jacob Rader. *Communal Sick Care in the German Ghetto*. Cincinnati, OH: Hebrew Union College Press, 1947.

Marienberg, Evyatar. "Jews, Jesus, and Menstrual Blood." *Transversal* 14 (2016): 1–10.

Marienberg, Evyatar, ed. *La Baraita de-niddah: Un texte juif pseudo-talmudique sur les lois religieuses relatives à la menstruation*. Turnhout: Brepols, 2012.

Marienberg, Evyatar. "A Mystery on the Tombstones, or: Menstruation in Early-Modern Ashkenazi Culture." *Women in Judaism* 3, no. 2 (2003): 1–2.

Marienberg, Evyatar. "Women, Men, and Cold Water: The Debate over the Heating of Jewish Ritual Baths from the Middle Ages to Our Own Time." [In Hebrew.] *Jewish Studies Internet Journal* 12 (2013): 1–37.

Markgraf, Richard. *Zur Geschichte der Juden auf den Messen in Leipzig von 1664–1839*. Bischofswerda: F. May, 1894.

Marshall, Sherrin, ed. *Women in Reformation and Counter-Reformation Europe: Public and Private Worlds*. Bloomington: Indiana University Press, 1989.

Matut, Diana. *Dichtung und Musik im frühneuzeitlichen Aschkenas: Ms. Opp. Add. 4° 136 der Bodleian Library, Oxford (das so genannte "Wallich"-Manuskript) und Ms. hebr. oct. 219 der Stadt- und Universitätsbibliothek, Frankfurt a. M.* Leiden: Brill, 2011.

Matut, Diana. "Early Modern Yiddish Wedding Songs: Synchronic and Diacronic Functions." In *The Oxford Handbook of Jewish Music Studies*, edited by Tina Frühauf, 512–30. Oxford: Oxford University Press, 2023.

Mayer, Yaakov. *Defus rishon: Mahadurat ha-Talmud ha-Yerushalmi, Venetsia, 1523, ve-reshit ha-defus ha-ivri*. Jerusalem: Magnes, 2022.

McCants, Anne E. "Porcelain for the Poor: The Material Culture of Tea and Coffee Consumption in Eighteenth-Century Amsterdam." In *Early Modern Things: Objects and Their Histories, 1500–1800*, edited by Paula Findlen, 316–41. London: Routledge, 2013.

Melammed, Renée Levine. *Heretics or Daughters of Israel? The Crypto-Jewish Women of Castile*. New York: Oxford University Press, 1999.

Menashe, Tamar. "The Imperial Supreme Court and Jews in Cross-Confessional Legal Cultures in Germany," 1495–1690. PhD diss., Columbia University, 2022.

Meyer, Pierre-André. *La communauté juive de Metz au XVIIIe siècle: Histoire et démographie*. Nancy: Presses universitaires de Nancy, 1993.

Micciche, Laura. "Writers Have Always Loved Portable Devices." *Atlantic*, August 18, 2018.

Miller, Michael L. "A Noisy and Noisome Place: The Jewish Tandelmarkt in Prague." *AJS Review* 43, no. 1 (2019): 105–23.

Mincer, Rachel Zohn. "The Increasing Reliance on Ritual Handbooks in Pre-Print Era Ashkenaz." *Jewish History* 31 (2017): 103–28.

Mintz, Sharon Liberman. "The Material Culture of Death in the Early Modern Jewish Community." *The Jurist* 59 (1999): 249–62.
Mirvis, Stanley. *The Jews of Eighteenth-Century Jamaica: A Testamentary History of a Diaspora in Transition*. New Haven: Yale University Press, 2020.
Moody, Charlotte. "The Wills of Women in Sixteenth-Century North Craven." *North Craven Heritage Trust Journal* (2019): 16–20.
Moore, Cornelia Niekus. "The Quest for Consolation and Amusement: Reading Habits of German Women in the Seventeenth Century." In *The Graph of Sex and the German Text: Gendered Culture in Early Modern Germany 1500–1700*, ed. Lynne Tatlock, 247–68. Leiden: Brill, 1994.
Mor-Rozenson, Yifat. *Ba-derekh mi-Yerushalayim le-Ashkenaz: Darkhei Zion le-Rav Moshe Porges u-kehal korim be-Ashkenaz ba-et ha-hadasha ha-mukdemet*. MA thesis equivalent, Bar-Ilan University, 2018.
Museum Judengasse. Accessed September 23, 2024. https://artsandculture.google.com/story/museum-judengasse-jewish-museum-frankfurt/tQUxqTh9mGztKQ?hl=en
Myers, William David. *Death and a Maiden: Infanticide and the Tragical History of Grethe Schmidt*. DeKalb: Northern Illinois University Press, 2012.
Naimark-Goldberg, Natalie. *Enlightened Jewish Women in Berlin*. [In Hebrew.] Jerusalem: Merkaz Shazar and Leo Baeck Institute, 2014.
Narkiss, Mordechai. "An Italian Niello Casket of the Fifteenth Century." *Journal of the Warburg and Courtauld Institutes* 21, nos. 3/4 (1958): 288–95.
Niccoli, Ottavia. "Menstruum quasi monstruum: Monstrous Births and Menstrual Taboos in the Sixteenth Century." In *Sex and Gender in Historical Perspective*, edited by Edward Muir and Guido Ruggiero and translated by Margaret Gallucci, with Mary M. Gallucci and Carole C. Gallucci, 413–34. Baltimore: Johns Hopkins University Press, 1990.
Niemann, D. *Die Ehre Hamburgischer Staats-Bürger ohne Unterschied der Nationen nebst einem Anhang: Herr D. Niemann gegen die Juden*. 2nd suppl. Altona, 1798.
Notaker, Henry. *Printed Cookbooks in Europe, 1470–1700: A Bibliography of Early Modern Culinary Literature*. Leiden: Brill, 2010.
Nussdorfer, Laurie. *Brokers of Public Trust: Notaries in Early Modern Rome*. Baltimore: Johns Hopkins University Press, 2009.
Oehme, Annegret. *The Knight without Boundaries: Yiddish and German Arthurian Wigalois Adaptations*. Leiden: Brill, 2022.
Ogilvie, Sheilagh. *A Bitter Living: Women, Markets and Social Capital in Early Modern Germany*. Oxford: Oxford University Press, 2003.
Oron, Michal. "Sefer gahale esh: Te'udah le-toldot ha-ma'avak ba-shabta'ut." In *Ha-halom ve-shivro: Ha-tenu'ah ha-shabta'it u-sheluhotehah, meshihiyut, shabta'ut u-frankism*, edited by Rachel Elior. Vol. 1, 73–92. Jerusalem: Jewish National and University Library, 2001.
Ozment, Steven. *When Fathers Ruled: Family Life in Reformation Europe*. Cambridge, MA: Harvard University Press, 1983.
Panitz, Michael Edward. "Modernity and Mortality: The Transformation of Central European Jewish Responses to Death," *1750–1850*. PhD diss., Jewish Theological Seminary, 1989.
Pettegree, Andrew. *The Book in the Renaissance*. New Haven: Yale University Press, 2010.
Pinner, Ephraim Moshe. *Kitve yad, sifre defus, kitve yad im ha'atakah, shemot ha-tzadikim ve-yeme mitatan*. Berlin, n.p., 1861.

Porter, Roy. *Health for Sale: Quackery in Early Modern England, 1660–1850*. Manchester: Manchester University Press, 1989.

Prager, Leonard, and Brad Sabin Hill. "Yiddish Manuscripts in the British Library." *British Library Journal* 21 (1995): 81–108.

Raeff, Marc. "The Well-Ordered Police State and the Development of Modernity in Seventeenth and Eighteenth Century Europe: An Attempt at a Comparative Approach." *American Historical Review* 80, no. 5 (1975): 1221–43.

Raspe, Lucia. "Minhag and Migration: Yiddish Custom Books from Sixteenth-Century Italy." In *Regional Identities and Cultures of Medieval Jews*, edited by Javier Castaño, Talya Fishman, and Ephraim Kanarfogel, 241–59. London: Littman Library of Jewish Civilization; Liverpool: Liverpool University Press, 2018.

Reichman, Edward. "What Became of Tychsen? The Non-Jewish 'Rabbi' and his 'Congregation' of Jewish Medical Students." Seforim Blog, November 1, 2020. https://seforimblog.com/2020/11/what-became-of-tychsen-the-non-jewish-rabbi-and-his-congregation-of-jewish-medical-students/.

Reiner, Avraham. "Circumcision of Stillbirth: Between Custom, Halakha, Geography and History." [In Hebrew.] *Zion* 79, no. 4 (2014): 453–75.

Reiner, Avraham. "Rabbenu Tam's Ordinance for the Return of the Dowry: Between Talmudic Exegesis and an Ordinance that Contradicts the Talmud." *Diné Israel* 33 (2019): 71–98.

Reiner, Elchanan. "Aliyat 'ha-kehillah ha-gedolah': Al shorshe ha-kehillah ha-yehudit ha-ironit be-Folin ba-et ha-hadashah ha-mukdemet." *Gal-Ed* 20 (2006): 13–37.

Reiner, Elchanan. "The Ashkenazi Élite at the Beginning of the Modern Era: Manuscript versus Printed Book." *Polin* 10 (1997): 85–98.

Reyer, Herbert, ed. *Die Juden in Aurich (ca. 1635–1940): Beiträge zu ihrer Geschichte*. Aurich: Ostfriesische Landschaft, 1992.

Richarz, Monika, ed. *Die Hamburger Kauffrau Glikl: Jüdische Existenz in der Frühen Neuzeit*. Hamburg: Hans Christians, 2001.

Richarz, Monika. "Mägde, Migration und Mutterschaft: Jüdische Frauen der Unterschicht im 18. Jahrhundert." *Aschkenas* 28, no. 1 (2018): 39–69.

Riello, Giorgio. "'Things Seen and Unseen': The Material Culture of Early Modern Inventories and their Representation of Domestic Interiors." In *Early Modern Things: Objects and Their Histories, 1500–1800*, edited by Paula Findlen, 125–50. 2nd ed. London: Routledge/New York: Taylor Francis, 2021.

Riello, Giorgio, and Ulinka Rublack, eds. *The Right to Dress: Sumptuary Laws in Global Perspective, c. 1200–1800*. Cambridge: Cambridge University Press, 2019.

Ries, Rotraud. "Jüdische Mägde vom 14. bis zum 18. Jahrhundert—Bilder, Stimmen, Positionen." In *Erforschen und Gestalten: Festschrift für Leonhard Scherg zum 80. Geburtstag*, edited by Gertrud Nöth, Monika Schaupp, and Michael Pulverich, 305–20. Marktheidenfeld: Historischer Verein Marktheidenfeld, 2024.

Ries, Rotraud. "'Unter Königen erwarb sie sich ein grossen Namen': Karrieren und Nachruhm der Unternehmerin Madame Kaulla (1739–1809)." *Aschkenas* 17 (2007): 405–30.

Roche, Daniel. *The Culture of Clothing: Dress and Fashion in the 'ancien régime'*. Translated by Jean Birrell. Cambridge: Cambridge University Press, 1994.

Roman, Oren. "Be-nign Shmuel-bukh: On the Melody (or Melodies) Mentioned in Old-Yiddish Epics." *Aschkenas* 25, no. 1 (2015): 145–60.

Roman, Oren, and Eliyahu Schleifer. "Niggun 'Akeda': A Traditional Melody Concerning the Binding of Isaac." *Yuval* 11 (2020). https://jewish-music.huji.ac.il/yuval/22902.

Romer-Segal, Agnes. "Yiddish Works on Women's Commandments in the Sixteenth Century." *Studies in Yiddish Literature and Folklore:* Research Projects of the Institute of Jewish Studies, Monograph Series 7 (1986): 37–59.

Roper, Lyndal. "'Going to Church and Street': Weddings in Reformation Augsburg." *Past & Present* 106 (1985): 62–101.

Roper, Lyndal. *The Holy Household: Women and Morals in Reformation Augsburg.* Oxford and New York: Clarendon Press and Oxford University Press, 1989.

Rosenthal, Berthold. *Heimatgeschichte der badischen Juden seit ihrem geschichtlichen Auftreten bis zur Gegenwart.* Baden: Konkordia, 1927.

Rosenzweig, Claudia. "Women: Instructions for Use; Slonik's *Seder mitzvot nashim* from Yiddish to Judeo-Italian." In *Rabbinical Literature in Yiddish and Judezmo,* edited by Katja Šmid and David M. Bunis, forthcoming.

Rosman, Moshe. *How Jewish Is Jewish History?* Oxford/Portland: Littmann Library of Jewish Civilization, 2007.

Rosman, Moshe. "Jewish Women in the Polish Lithuanian Commonwealth: From Facilitation to Participation." In *Jewish Women's History from Antiquity to the Present,* edited by Federica Francesconi and Rebecca Lynn Winer, 193–216. Detroit, MI: Wayne State University Press, 2021.

Rosman, Moshe. "Lehiyot ishah be-Folin-Lita be-reshit ha-et ha-hadashah." In *Kiyyum ve-shever: Yehudei Polin le-dorotehem,* edited by Israel Bartal and Israel Gutman. Vol. 2, 415–31. Jerusalem: Merkaz Shazar, 1987.

Roth, Cecil. *Doña Gracia of the House of Nasi.* Philadephia: Jewish Publication Society, 1948.

Rubin, Miri. *Cities of Strangers: Making Lives in Medieval Europe.* Cambridge: Cambridge University Press, 2020.

Rubin, Noga. "Agadah al sheloshah ve-arba'ah: Le-toldoteha shel masoret yehudit be-Prag ba-me'ah ha-sheva esreh." *Jerusalem Studies in Jewish Folklore* 29 (2015): 103–14.

Rublack, Ulinka. *Dressing Up: Cultural Identity in Renaissance Europe.* Oxford: Oxford University Press, 2011.

Rublack, Ulinka. "Fluxes: The Early Modern Body and the Emotions." *History Workshop Journal* 53 (2002): 1–16.

Rublack, Ulinka, ed. *Gender in Early Modern German History.* Cambridge: Cambridge University Press, 2002.

Rublack, Ulinka. "Pregnancy, Childbirth and the Female Body in Early Modern Germany." *Past & Present* 150 (Feb. 1996): 84–110.

Rublack, Ulinka. "The Right to Dress: Sartorial Politics in Germany, c. 1300–1750." In *The Right to Dress: Sumptuary Legislation in a Global Perspective, 1300–1900,* edited by Giorgio Riello and Ulinka Rublack, 37–73.

Ruderman, David B. *Early Modern Jewry: A New Cultural History.* Princeton: Princeton University Press, 2011.

Ruderman, David B. "The Founding of a Gemilut Hasadim Society in Ferrara in 1515." *AJS Review* 1 (1976): 233–67.

Ruderman, David B. "Looking Backward and Forward: Rethinking Jewish Modernity in the Light of Early Modernity." In *The Cambridge History of Judaism*. Vol. 7, *The Early Modern World, 1500–1815*, edited by Jonathan Karp and Adam Sutcliffe, 1089–1107. Cambridge: Cambridge University Press, 2018.

Ruff, Julius R. *Violence in Early Modern Europe*. New York: Cambridge University Press, 2001.

Sabar, Shalom. "The Illustrated Prayer Book of Reizele Binge of Fürth, 1737/38." In *A Crown for a King: Studies in Jewish Art, History and Archaeology in Memory of Stephen S. Kayser*, edited by Shalom Sabar, Steven Fine, and William M. Kramer, 205–19. Berkeley: Judah L. Magnes Judaica Museum, 2000.

Sabar, Shalom. "Seder birkat ha-mazon,Vina taf peh: Ketav ha-yad ha-metzuyar ha-mukdam be-yoter shel ha-sofer-oman Aron Wolf Schreiber Herlingen mi-Gewitch." In *Zekhor davar le-avdekha: Asufat ma'amarim le-zekher Dov Rappel*, edited by Shmuel Glick, 455–72. Jerusalem: Ha-merkaz le-hagut be-hinukh ha-yehudi al shem Dov Rappel, 2007.

Salmon-Mack, Tamar. *Tan-du: Al nisu'in u-mashberehem be-yahadut Polin-Lita, 1650–1800*. Tel Aviv: Ha-Kibbutz ha-meuhad, 2012.

Schneider, Zoë A. "Women before the Bench: Female Litigants in Early Modern Normandy." *French Historical Studies* 23 (2000): 1–32.

Schrijver, Emile G. L. "'Be'otiyyot Amsterdam': Eighteenth-Century Hebrew Manuscript Production in Central Europe; The Case of Jacob ben Judah Leib Shamas." *Quærendo* 20, no. 1 (1990): 24–26.

Schröder, Rainer. "Gesinderecht im 18. Jahrhundert." In *Gesinde im 18. Jahrhundert*, edited by Gotthardt Frühsorge, Rainer Gruenter, and Beatrix Freifrau Wolff Metternich, 13–40. Hamburg: F. Meiner, 1995.

Scott, Joan Wallach. "Gender: A Useful Category of Historical Analysis." *American Historical Review* 91, no. 5 (1986): 1053–75.

Seidman, Naomi. *A Marriage Made in Heaven: The Sexual Politics of Hebrew and Yiddish*. Berkeley: University of California Press, 1997.

Shashar, Noa. *Gevarim ne'elamim: Agunot ba-merhav ha-Ashkenazi, 1648–1850*. Jerusalem: Carmel, 2020.

Shepard, Alexandra. *Meanings of Manhood in Early Modern England*. Oxford: Oxford University Press, 2006.

Shtif, Nokhem. "A Handwritten Yiddish Library in a Jewish Home in Venice in the Mid-Sixteenth Century." [In Yiddish.] *Tsaytshrift* (Minsk) 1 (1926): 141–50; 2–3 (1928): 525–44.

Siegmund, Stefanie. *The Medici State and the Ghetto of Florence: The Construction of an Early Modern Jewish Community*. Stanford, CA: Stanford University Press, 2006.

Silberstein, Siegfried. "Mendelssohn und Mecklenburg." *Zeitschrift für die Geschichte der Juden in Deutschland* 1, no. 4 (1930): 275–90.

Smail, Daniel Lord. *Legal Plunder: Households and Debt Collection in Late Medieval Europe*. Cambridge, MA: Harvard University Press, 2016.

Smail, Daniel Lord, and Andrew Shryock. "On Containers: A Forum. Introduction and Concluding Remarks." *History and Anthropology* 29 (2018): 1–6; 49–51.

Smith, Helen. "Women and the Materials of Writing." In *Material Cultures of Early Modern Women's Writing*, edited by Patricia Pender and Rosalind Smith, 14–35. Houndmills: Palgrave Macmillan, 2014.

Soliday, Gerald. "The Jews of Early Modern Marburg, 1640s–1800: A Case Study in Family and Household Organization." *History of the Family* 8 (2003): 495–516.

Soloveitchik, Haym. *The Use of Responsa as an Historical Source*. [In Hebrew.] Jerusalem: Merkaz Shazar, 1991.

Sperber, Daniel. *The Jewish Life Cycle: Custom, Lore, and Iconography; Jewish Customs from the Cradle to the Grave*. Translated by Ed Levin. Ramat Gan: Bar-Ilan University Press, 2008.

Spicer, Joaneath. "The Star of David and Jewish Culture in Prague around 1600, Reflected in Drawings of Roelandt Savery and Paulus van Vianen." *Journal of the Walters Art Gallery* 54 (1996): 203–24.

Staudinger, Barbara. "Ungleichheiten als Chance? Hofjüdinnen als Kauffrauen." *Aschkenas* 17 (2007): 385–403.

Stern, Selma. *Der Preussische Staat und die Juden*. 4 vols. Berlin: C. A. Schwetschke, 1925.

Stern, Selma. "The Woman of the Ghetto, Part I." Translated in *Classic Essays on Jews in Early Modern Europe*, edited by Jonathan Karp and Francesca Trivellato, 74–84. New York: Routledge, 2023.

Stiefel, Barry L. *Jews and the Renaissance of Synagogue Architecture, 1450–1730*. London: Pickering and Chatto, 2014; Routledge, 2016.

Stollberg, Michael. "'You Have No Good Blood in Your Body': Oral Communication in Sixteenth-Century Physicians' Medical Practice." *Medical History* 59, no. 1 (2015): 63–82.

Stollberg-Rilinger, Barbara. "On the Function of Rituals in the Holy Roman Empire." In *The Holy Roman Empire, 1495–1806*, edited by R. J. W. Evans, Michael Schlaich, and Peter H. Wilson, 359–73. Oxford: Oxford University Press, 2011.

Strasser, Ulrike. "Cloistering Women's Past: Conflicting Accounts of Enclosure in a Seventeenth-Century Munich Nunnery." In *Gender in Early Modern German History*, edited by Ulinka Rublack, 221–46.

Strasser, Ulrike. "Early Modern Nuns and the Feminist Politics of Religion." *Journal of Religion* 84, no. 4 (2004): 529–54.

Sulzbach, Abraham. "Ein alter Frankfurter Wohltätigkeitsverein." *Jahrbuch der Jüdisch- literarischen Gesellschaft* 2 (1904): 241–66.

Szoltysek, Mikolaj. "Households and Family Systems in Early Modern Europe." In *The Oxford Handbook of Early Modern European History, 1350–1750*. Vol. 1, *Peoples and Place*, edited by Scott Hamish, 313–41. Oxford: Oxford University Press, 2014.

Tallan, Cheryl. "Medieval Jewish Women in History, Literature, Law, and Art: An Annotated Bibliography." Accessed December 4, 2024. https://the-orb.arlima.net/encyclop/religion/judaism/jew-wom.html.

Teller, Adam. *Hayyim be-tzavta: Ha-rova ha-yehudi shel Poznan be-mahazit ha-rishonah shel ha-me'ah ha-sheva-esreh*. Jerusalem: Magnes, 2003.

Teplitsky, Joshua. "Order in Crisis: Jewish Relief Workers during the Prague Plague of 1713." *Jewish Quarterly Review* 111, no. 3 (2021): 362–73.

Teplitsky, Joshua. *Prince of the Press: How One Collector Built History's Most Enduring and Remarkable Jewish Library*. New Haven: Yale University Press, 2019.

Terpstra, Nicholas, ed. *The Politics of Ritual Kinship; Confraternities and Social Order in Early Modern Italy*. Cambridge: Cambridge University Press, 2000.

Toch, Michael. "Jewish Women Entrepreneurs in the 16th and 17th Century: Economics and Family Structure." *Jahrbuch für Fränkische Landesforschung* 60 (2000): 254–62.

Turniansky, Chava. "Aron ha-sefarim shel ha-ishah be-Ashkenaz ba-et ha-hadasha ha-mukdemet." In *Mahshevet ha-sefer: mehkarim be-sifruyot yehudiot mugashim le-Avidov Lipsker*, edited by Yigal Schwartz, Lilach Netanel, Claudia Rosenzweig, and Rona Tausinger, 185–204. Ramat Gan: Bar-Ilan University Press, 2020.

Turniansky, Chava. "Die Erzählungen in Glikl Hamelns Werk und ihrer Quellen." In *Der Differenz auf der Spur: Frauen und Gender in Ashkenaz*, edited by Christiane E. Müller and Andrea Schatz, 121–48. Berlin: Metropol, 2004.

Turniansky, Chava. "Ha-bensherl ve-ha-zemirot be-Yiddish." *Alei Sefer: Studies in Bibliography and in the History of the Printed and the Digital Hebrew Book* 10 (1982): 51–92.

Turniansky, Chava. "Old Yiddish Language and Literature." *Shalvi/Hyman Encyclopedia of Jewish Women*. December 31, 1999. Jewish Women's Archive. https://jwa.org/encyclopedia/article/old-yiddish-language-and-literature

Turniansky, Chava. "On Old Yiddish Biblical Epics." *International Folklore Review* 8 (1991): 26–33.

Turniansky, Chava. "The Stories in the Memoirs of Glikl Hameln and their Sources." [In Hebrew.] *Jerusalem Studies in Jewish Folklore* 16 (1994): 41–65.

Turniansky, Chava. "Yiddish Language and Literature in the Early Modern Period and the Yiddish Historical Song." In *Report of the Oxford Centre for Hebrew and Jewish Studies, Academic Year 2011–2012* (Oxford, 2012): 119–24.

Turniansky, Chava. "Yiddish Song as Historical Source Material: Plague in the Judenstadt of Prague in 1713." In *Jewish History: Essays in Honour of Chimen Abramsky*, edited by Ada Rapoport-Albert and Steven J. Zipperstein, 189–98. London: P. Halban, 1988.

Turniansky, Chava. "Young Women in Early Modern Yiddish Literature." [In Hebrew.] *Massekhet* 12 (2016): 79–84.

Turniansky, Chava, and Erika Timm, with the collaboration of Claudia Rosenzweig. *Yiddish in Italia: Yiddish Manuscripts and Printed Books from the 15th to the 17th Century*. Milan: Associazione italiana amici dell'Università di Gerusalemme, 2003.

Ulbrich, Claudia. *Shulamit and Margarete: Power, Gender, and Religion in a Rural Society in Eighteenth-Century Europe*. Translated by William V. Dunlap. Leiden: Brill, 2004.

Ullmann, Sabine. "Poor Jewish Families in Early Modern Rural Swabia." *International Review of Social History* 45 (2000): 93–113.

University of Pennsylvania Library guide. "Jewish Women Printers." Accessed July 17, 2023. https://guides.library.upenn.edu/c.php?g=468836&p=3209418.

University of St. Andrews Special Collections Blog. Accessed July 17, 2023. special-collections.wp.st-andrews.ac.uk/2017/07/13/where-can-you-find-a-400-year-old-laundry-list-a-rhyming-love-note-and-a-fragment-from-the-king-james-bible/.

von Bernuth, Ruth, and Michael Terry. "Shalom bar Abraham's Book of Judith in Yiddish." In *The Sword of Judith: Judith Studies across the Disciplines*, edited by Kevin R. Brine, Elena Ciletti, and Henrike Lähnemann, 127–50. Cambridge: Open Book, 2010.

Wachtel, David. "Jewish Burial Societies: The Origins and Development of the Hevra Kaddisha." *The Jurist* 59 (1999): 214–22.

Watt, Jeffrey. "The Impact of the Reformation and Counter-Reformation." In *The History of the European Family*. Vol. 1, *Family Life in Early Modern Times, 1500–1789*, edited by David I. Kertzer and Marzio Barbagli, 123–52. New Haven: Yale University Press, 2001.

Weinryb, Bernard. "Historisches und Kulturhistorisches aus Wagenseils hebräischen Briefwechsel." *Monatsscrift für Geschichte und Wissenschaft des Judenthums*, n.s. 47 (1939): 325–41.

Weissler, Chava. "The Religion of Traditional Ashkenazic Women: Some Methodological Issues." *AJS Review* 12, no. 1 (1987): 73–94.

Weissler, Chava. *Voices of the Matriarchs: Listening to the Prayers of Early Modern Jewish Women*. Boston: Beacon, 1999.

Westwater, Lynn Lara. *Sara Copia Sullam: A Jewish Salonnière and the Press in Counter-Reformation Venice*. Toronto: University of Toronto Press, 2019.

Wiesner, Merry E. *Working Women in Renaissance Germany*. New Brunswick, NJ: Rutgers University Press, 1986.

Wiesner-Hanks, Merry E. "Adjusting Our Lenses to Make Gender Visible." *Early Modern Women* 12, no. 2 (2018): 3–32.

Wiesner-Hanks, Merry E., ed. *Gendered Temporalities in the Early Modern World*. Amsterdam: Amsterdam University Press, 2018.

Wiesner-Hanks, Merry E. *Women and Gender in Early Modern Europe*. Cambridge: Cambridge University Press, 2019.

Wolfthal, Diane. *Picturing Yiddish: Gender, Identity, and Memory in the Illustrated Yiddish Books of Renaissance Italy*. Leiden: Brill, 2004.

Wunder, Heide. *He Is the Sun, She Is the Moon: Women in Early Modern Germany*. Translated by Thomas Dunlap. Cambridge, MA: Harvard University Press, 1998.

Yaari, Avraham. "Shene Kuntresim Me-Eretz Israel." *Kiryat Sefer* 23, no. 2 (1947): 140–59.

Yahalom, Shalem. "The Dowry Return Edict of R. Tam in Medieval Europe." *European Journal of Jewish Studies* 12 (2018): 136–67.

Yuval, Israel. "Hospices and their Guests in Jewish Medieval Germany." *Proceedings of the Tenth World Congress of Jewish Studies* 10 (1989): 125–29.

Yuval, Israel. "Regulations against the Proliferation of Divorce in Fifteenth-Century Germany." [In Hebrew.] *Zion* 48, no. 2 (1983): 177–215.

Zborowski, Mark, and Elizabeth Herzog. *Life Is with People: The Culture of the Shtetl*. New York: Schocken, 1962.

Zimmer, Eric. "Sefer yefe nof le-R. Yitzhak mi-See: Ktav yad beyt ha-sefarim ha-leumi veha-universita'i Heb. 4°522." *Kiryat Sefer* 56, no. 3 (1981): 529–45.

Zinger, Nimrod. *Ba'al ha-shem ve-ha-rofe: Refu'ah u-magiah be-kerev yehude Germanyah be-reshit ha-et ha-hadashah*. Haifa: Haifa University Press, 2017.

Zinger, Nimrod. "'Unto Their Assembly, Mine Honor, Be Thou Not United': Tuviya Cohen and the Medical Marketplace in the Early Modern Period." *Korot* 20 (2009/10): 67–95.

Zinger, Nimrod. "'Who Knows What the Cause Is?' 'Natural' and 'Unnatural' Causes for Illness in the Writings of Ba'alei Shem, Doctors and Patients among German Jews in the Eighteenth Century." In *The Jewish Body: Corporeality, Society, and Identity in the Renaissance and Early Modern Period*, edited by Giusuppe Veltri and Maria Diemling, 127–55. Leiden/Boston: Brill, 2009.

Zürn, Gabriele. *Die Altonaer jüdische Gemeinde (1611–1873): Ritus und soziale Institutionen des Todes im Wandel*. Münster: Lit, 2001.

ILLUSTRATION CREDITS

Figures

1.1. Archives of the Jewish Museum in Prague (AJMP), Pinkas synagogue collection, Pinkas of the Pinkas synagogue, 1601–1845. Courtesy of Jewish Museum in Prague, fol. 20b, sine no. © Jewish Museum in Prague.

1.2. Paul Christian Kirchner, *Jüdisches Ceremoniel*, 1726, copperplate 7 (near p. 107). Courtesy of Columbia University Libraries.

2.1. Courtesy of The Younes & Soraya Nazarian Library, University of Haifa Digital Collections, University of Haifa, MS 45, fol. 3v.

2.2. Courtesy of Stadsarchief Amsterdam, Acc. 714, Inv. 25, p. 1.1.2.2.

2.3. Cycle of Paintings of the Burial Society of the Prague Jewish Community, *Sewing the Burial Shroud, 1770–1890*, oil on canvas. Courtesy of Jewish Museum in Prague, inv. no. 12.843/5. © Jewish Museum in Prague.

2.4. Burial society coach, Szarvas, Hungary, nineteenth century. Wood, carved and painted; felt. Courtesy of The Israel Museum Jerusalem, Purchase, the Charles and Lynn Schusterman Family Foundation, USA, through the Menorah organization. B96.0198 191/034 Photo © The Israel Museum Jerusalem, by Elie Posner.

2.5. Johannes Christoph Bodenschatz, *Kirchliche Verfassung*, vol. 4, Frankfurt, 1749, fig. XVII (near p. 179). Courtesy of Columbia University Libraries.

2.6. Alms box of women's burial society, inscribed with names of gabba'ot and the donor Pessche daughter of R. Mikhel Wagner. Altona, Germany, 1854. Pewter, silver-plated, engraved, and punched. Courtesy of The Israel Museum, Jerusalem. The Feuchtwanger Collection, purchased and donated by Baruch and Ruth Rappaport, Geneva Accession number: HF 0169 130/045 Photo © Israel Museum, Jerusalem, by Ofrit Rosenberg.

4.1. *Brantshpigel*, Frankfurt, 1706. Photograph courtesy of Jacob Djmal.

4.2. *Seder berakhot*, 1728. Courtesy of Bibliotheca Rosenthaliana, University of Amsterdam, MS 500, fol. 1v. Photography by Allard Pierson.

4.3. *Seder birkat ha-mazon*, 1720. Courtesy of Private Collection, Chicago.

4.4. Aleph-Bet Chart, Frankfurt, 1730. Courtesy of Columbia University Libraries, Plimpton Broadsides.

4.5. Sampler collection # HGF F 690. Courtesy of Jewish Museum, New York.

4.6. Jedaja ben Abraham Penini Bedersi, *Behinat Olam* (Mantova, Italy: Estellina Conat, ca. 1476–77). Courtesy of Biblioteca Palatina, Stampato De Rossi 595, c. 3r. By concession of the Ministry of Culture—Monumental Complex of the Pilotta, Palatine Library.

5.1. Esther scroll, Prague, c. 1700. Courtesy of Private Collection.

5.2. *Pinkas hevrah kaddisha ma'asim tovim be-Amsterdam.* Courtesy of Library of the Jewish Theological Seminary, MS 10632, fol. 7v.

5.3. *Wer do wil makhn ayn gute wesh.* Courtesy of Bibliothèque nationale de France, Département des Manuscrits, MS héb. 1312, fol. 37.

5.4. *Book of Healing and Charms.* Courtesy of Library of the Jewish Theological Seminary, MS 2709, fol. 71r.

5.5. *Be'er sheva.* Courtesy of The Bodleian Libraries, University of Oxford, MS Opp. 148, title page, Creative Commons license CC-BY-NC 4.0.

6.1. *Selihot,* Gravediggers Society, Frankfurt, 1740. Courtesy of Private Collection. Photography by Ardon Bar-Hama.

6.2. Wedding Invitation, 1784. Courtesy of The Royal Library, Copenhagen, Cod. Sim. Heb. Add. 10m.

6.3. Johann Jacob Schudt, *Neue Franckfurter Jüdische Kleiderordnung.* Frankfurt, 1716, title page. Courtesy of Leo Baeck Institute.

7.1. Hans Folz, *Die Rechnung Ruprecht Kolpergers.* Nürnberg: Hans Mair, ca. 1490/91. Courtesy of Bayerische Staatsbibliothek Collection. Licensed under CC BY-NC-SA 4.0, https://creativecommons.org/licenses/by-nc-sa/4.0/legalcode.

7.2. List of attendees at Leipzig's Michaelis fair in 1692. Courtesy of Sächsischen Staatsarchivs, 10024 Geheimer Rat Loc. 948311, fol. 119.

7.3. Letter, 1738. Courtesy of CAHJP, MS D-W03-372.

7.4. Epistolae judaeorum Pragensium, 1619. Courtesy of Österreichisches Staatsarchiv, OeSTA HHSTA HS W 1002, fol. 54v.

8.1. *Birkat ha-mazon,* 1725. Courtesy of Braginsky Collection, Zurich, MS 344, fol. 12r. Photography by Ardon Bar-Hama, Ra'anana, Israel.

8.2. *Recueil de coutumes et régles pour fixer les fêtes du calendrier hébreu.* Courtesy of Bibliothèque nationale de France, Département des Manuscrits, MS héb. 586, fol. 105v.

8.3. Marcus zum Lamm, *Thesaurus Picturarum,* ca. 1600. Courtesy of Technische Universität Darmstadt via Wikimedia.

8.4 Johann Alexander Boener, "Eine Jüdische Braut, wie sie in Procession," engraving from *Kurzer Bericht von dem Alterthum und Freyheiten des freyen Hof-Markts Fürth,* 1705. Courtesy of Thuringian University and State Library Jena, https://collections.thulb.uni-jena.de/. Licensed under CC BY-NC-SA 4.0, https://creativecommons.org/licenses/by-nc-sa/4.0/legalcode.

8.5. *Sivlonot* belt. Frankfurt, Germany. Late seventeenth century, buckle: before 1760. Silver, cast, engraved and pierced. L: 95; W: 5.8 cm. The Israel Museum Jerusalem. The Feuchtwanger Collection, purchased and donated by Baruch and Ruth Rappaport, Geneva Accession number: HF 0079 101/024. Photo © Israel Museum, Jerusalem, by Ofrit Rosenberg.

8.6. *Siddur* cover, Germany, 1794. Courtesy of Gross Family Collection, Tel Aviv. Image by Ardon Bar-Hama.

9.1. Rebecca Sinzheim's will. Courtesy of Bibliothèque et Archives de l'Alliance Israélite Universelle, MS 423, fol. 1.

9.2. Copy of a woman's seal. Courtesy of CAHJP, MS AHW 16, fol. 5.

10.1. Caspar Jacobsz Philips, "Ritueel bad van Asjkenazische Joden. Het bad der Hoogduitsche Jooden, te Amsterdam," Amsterdam 1783. Courtesy of Rijksmuseum, Amsterdam Collection.

10.2. *Tikkune Shabbat*, Vienna, ca. 1725. Courtesy of the collections of The British Library, MS Add. 8881, via Ktiv.

10.3. *Birkat ha-mazon*, 1725. Courtesy of Braginsky Collection, Zurich, MS 344, fol. 14v. Photography by Ardon Bar-Hama, Ra'anana, Israel.

10.4. *Birkat ha-mazon*, 1725. Courtesy of Braginsky Collection, Zurich, MS 328, fol. 12v. Photography by Ardon Bar-Hama, Ra'anana, Israel.

11.1. *Seder birkat ha-mazon*, 1751. Courtesy of Braginsky Collection, Zurich, MS 217, fol. 12v. Photography by Ardon Bar-Hama, Ra'anana, Israel.

11.2. *Recueil de coutumes et régles pour fixer les fêtes du calendrier hébreu*. Courtesy of Bibliothèque nationale de France, Département des Manuscrits, MS héb. 586, fol. 106r.

11.3. Antonius Margaritha, *Der gantz jüdisch Glaub*, Augsburg, 1530. Courtesy of Columbia University Libraries.

11.4. J. F. Bernard, Illustr. Bernard Picart[d], *Historie générale des cérémonies, moeurs, et coutumes religieuses de tous les peuple du monde*, Paris, 1741. Courtesy of Columbia University Libraries.

11.5. *Sefer Minhagim*, Amsterdam, 1662, p. 46b. Courtesy of Library of the Jewish Theological Seminary, BM700.I818 1662.

11.6. Isaak aus Tyrnau, *Minhogim: fun ale minhogim in Ashkenaz*. Frankfurt am Main: 1722–23. Digitized by the University Library JCS Frankfurt am Main, 2024: [urn:nbn:de:hebis:30:1–161718], 1526.

11.7. Johann Leusden, *Philologus Hebræo-Mixtus*, Utrecht, 1699 (near p. 186). Courtesy of National Library of Israel.

11.8. Seder table. Prague Hagaddah, 1526. Courtesy of Braginsky Collection, Zurich, 211. Photography by Ardon Bar-Hama, Ra'anana, Israel.

11.9. Offenbach Haggadah, 1795. Courtesy of Gross Family Collection, Tel Aviv. Image by Ardon Bar-Hama.

11.10. *Recueil de coutumes et régles pour fixer les fêtes du calendrier hébreu*. Courtesy of Bibliothèque nationale de France, Département des Manuscrits, MS héb. 586, fol. 113v.

11.11. Paul Christian Kirchner, *Jüdisches Ceremoniel*, 1726, copperplate 23 (near p. 185). Courtesy of Columbia University Libraries.

11.12. Paul Christian Kirchner, *Jüdisches Ceremoniel*, 1726, copperplate 26 (near p. 198). Courtesy of Columbia University Libraries.

Plates

1. *Selihot*, Gravediggers Society, Frankfurt, 1740. Courtesy of Private Collection. Photography by Ardon Bar-Hama.
2. *Seder birkat ha-mazon*. Nikolsburg, Czechoslovakia, 1728. Courtesy of The Royal Library, Copenhagen, Cod. Heb. 32, fol. 12r.
3. Aaron Herlingen, *Dine u-tefillot ha-shayakhim le-brit milah*, Women at the entrance from the women's to the men's section of the synagogue for a circumcision, 1728, ink on parchment. Courtesy of Jewish Museum in Prague, inv. no. 170565. © Jewish Museum in Prague.
4. Circumcision pillow, 1614. © Freiwilliger Museumsverein Basel. Courtesy of Jewish Museum of Switzerland.
5. Harrison Miscellany. Courtesy of Braginsky Collection, Zurich, MS 67, fol. 40. Photography by Ardon Bar-Hama, Ra'anana, Israel.
6. Cycle of Paintings of the Burial Society of the Prague Jewish Community, *Sewing the Burial Shroud, 1770–1890*, oil on canvas. Courtesy of Jewish Museum in Prague, inv. no. 12.843/5. © Jewish Museum in Prague.
7. Burial society, Florence, 1776, depicting the purification of the deceased. Handwritten; ink on paper and tempera on parchment Hebrew inscription listing names of burial society members. H: 84; W: 55 cm. Courtesy of The Israel Museum Jerusalem. Purchased through the Viktoria Witlin-Vinrica bequest. Accession number: B90.0108 177/148. Photo © Israel Museum, Jerusalem, by Zohar Shemesh.
8. *Seder birkat ha-mazon*, 1736. Courtesy of Library of the Jewish Theological Seminary, MS 4789, fol. 3r.
9. Courtesy of Biblioteca Palatina, MS 2895, fol. 235. By concession of the Ministry of Culture of Italy, Complesso monumentale della Pilotta, Biblioteca Palatina.
10. Sampler collection # HGF F 690. Courtesy of Jewish Museum, New York.
11. Esther scroll, eighteenth century. Courtesy of Leo Baeck Institute, Fürth Jewish Community Collection, AR 994 A.
12. Aaron Schreiber Herlingen, Miniature prayer book, 1746–47. Courtesy of Victoria and Albert Museum, London, MSL 1868 513, fol. 15b. © Victoria and Albert Museum, London.
13. *Seder birkat ha-mazon*. Nikolsburg, Czechoslovakia, 1728. Courtesy of The Royal Library, Copenhagen, Cod. Heb. 32, fol. 12r.
14. Nicolaes Maes, "The Account Keeper," 1656. Oil on canvas. Courtesy of Saint Louis Art Museum, accession no. 72:1950.
15. Madame Chaile Kaulla. Note her necklace, a special mark of honor. Johann Baptist Seele, "Portrait of Madame Kaulla," ca. 1804. Courtesy of Hohenzollern State Museum via Wikimedia.
16. Coffee set of Madame Kaulla. Nymphenburg, Germany, 1795. Porcelain, painted. Pottery mark: Nymphenburg, impressed. The Israel Museum, Jerusalem. Gift of Noemi Tedeschi-Blankett, Jerusalem, and Delia Tedeschi Gardella, Genoa, in memory of Bianca

and Vittorio Tedeschi, Genoa. B92.1539(a-d). The Feuchtwanger Collection, purchased and donated by Baruch and Ruth Rappaport, Geneva HF 0135. Photo © The Israel Museum, Jerusalem, by Yair Hovav.

17. *Birkat ha-mazon*, 1725. Courtesy of Braginsky Collection, Zurich, MS 328, fol. 11v. Photography by Ardon Bar-Hama, Ra'anana, Israel.

18. Wolf Leib Katz Poppers of Hildesheim, Miniature *Me'ah berakhot*, c. 1740. Courtesy of Private Collection.

19. Aaron Schreiber Herlingen, Miniature prayer book, 1746–47. Courtesy of Victoria and Albert Museum, London, MSL 1868 513, fol. 18a. © Victoria and Albert Museum, London.

20. Cooking Pot, Frankfurt am Main, 1708/9. Courtesy of Jewish Museum, New York. Purchase: Judaica Acquisitions Fund.

21. Marcus zum Lamm, *Thesaurus Picturarum*, ca. 1600. Courtesy of Technische Universität Darmstadt via Wikimedia.

22. Friedrich Campe, "Der Samstag," c. 1800. Courtesy of History and Art Collection / Alamy Stock Photo.

23. *Birkat ha-mazon*, 1725. Courtesy of Braginsky Collection, Zurich, MS 328, frontispiece. Photography by Ardon Bar-Hama, Ra'anana, Israel.

24. *Birkat ha-mazon*, 1741. Courtesy of Braginsky Collection, Zurich, MS 351, fol. 10v. Photography by Ardon Bar-Hama, Ra'anana, Israel.

25. *Seder birkat ha-mazon*, 1736. Courtesy of Library of the Jewish Theological Seminary, MS 4789, fol. 16r.

26. Leipnik Haggadah, 1739. Courtesy of Braginsky Collection, Zurich, MS 317, fol. 40b. Photography by Ardon Bar-Hama, Ra'anana, Israel.

27. *Seder birkat ha-mazon*, 1720. Courtesy of Private Collection, Chicago.

28. *Seder milah, dinehah, birkhotehah, u-piyutehah*, ca. sixteenth century. Courtesy of Wellcome Collection, MS Hebrew A3, fol. 8v.

29. *Seder birkat ha-mazon*, 1755. Courtesy of Private Collection. Photography by Ardon Bar-Hama.

30. Harrison Miscellany. Courtesy of Braginsky Collection, Zurich, MS 67, fol. 53. Photography by Ardon Bar-Hama, Ra'anana, Israel.

31. *Sukkah* wall hanging from eighteenth-century Germany. Courtesy of Library of the Jewish Theological Seminary, B (NS) FD 18.

32. *Recueil de coutumes et régles pour fixer les fêtes du calendrier hébreu*. Courtesy of Bibliothèque nationale de France, Département des Manuscrits, MS héb. 586, fol. 25v.

33. Aaron Schreiber Herlingen, Miniature prayer book, 1746–47. Courtesy of Victoria and Albert Museum, London, MSL 1868 513, fol. 54. © Victoria and Albert Museum, London.

34. Leipnik Haggadah, 1739. Courtesy of Braginsky Collection, Zurich, MS 317, fol. 2r. Photography by Ardon Bar-Hama, Ra'anana, Israel.

35. The Burial Society Cup, glass. Courtesy of Jewish Museum in Prague, inv. no. 063619. © Jewish Museum in Prague.

INDEX

abortion, 295–96
abuse, 90, 212; sexual, of children, 96–97, 119, 361n18; spousal, 76, 177–79, 212
Abzug geld, 359n109
adultery, 83, 85, 173, 175, 294, 361n31
agunot, 175, 195
Alsace, 201, 204. *See also* Hagenau; Rosheim
Altdorf, 134, 137
Altona, 43–44, 57, 65–66, 77–83, 91–92, 184, 195, 204, 216, 222, 279, 300, 303, 357n51, 376n108, 395n118; claims court in, 163, 169–70, 173, 191, 213; and maidservants, 182; and marriage, 4, 155–56, 226, 230; and midwives, 38–40, 211, 212–13; records from, 45, 53, 55, 57, 77, 80–81, 86, 224, 243, 288. *See also* Altona-Hamburg-Wandsbek
Altona-Hamburg-Wandsbek, 15, 25, 32, 34, 50, 62, 83, 97–98, 117, 119, 132; and communal institutions, 28–30, 36, 283, 322, 336, 353n58, 354n87, 357n51, 391n80; and illegitimate pregnancies, 83–84, 86, 88; inventories and wills from, 52–53, 55, 57, 202, 224, 256–70, 272. *See also* Altona; Hamburg
Altschuler, Moses Henochs Yerushalmi, 106
Alzey, 28, 30
Amsterdam, 6, 17, 27, 34, 44–45, 83, 86, 91–92, 106, 133, 158, 175, 210, 227, 351n5, 366n58, 382n149, 396n8; and *mikva'ot*, 29–30, 275, 282–83; and women's *hevrot*, 51–52, 70–71, 128; Sephardim in, 318
Aurich, 97–98

ba'ale bayit, 3, 154, 160, 176, 181, 186, 200, 325. *See also ba'alot bayit*
ba'alot bayit, 2, 4–5, 17–18, 34, 40, 44, 75–76, 89, 95, 100–101, 109, 110, 125, 128, 186, 202, 213, 223, 235, 244, 255, 257, 263, 273, 278, 283, 309, 312–13, 318, 323, 325, 326, 338
Bacharach, Moses Samson, 42, 327
Bacharach, Yair Hayim, 11, 87, 123, 284, 295–96, 354nn108–109. *See also Havot Yair*
Bamberg, 155, 157, 201
beauty products, 248, 304–5
Be'er sheva, 143, 145–49
Berlin, 37, 39, 51, 52, 54, 65–66, 70
bet din. *See* rabbinical court
Bingen, Seligman, 172
Bionville, 215–16
birkat ha-mazon, 9–10, 110–13, 181, 240, 299, 305, 311; in printed form as bensherl, 110–11
blended families, 60, 136, 158, 166–68, 185, 196, 199, 227, 320, 327, 383n178
Bodenschatz, Johannes Christoph, 63, 231, 333
Bohemia, 124, 179, 234, 247, 282
book of customs, 10, 12, 64, 114, 230, 244, 310–12, 315, 333; manuscripts of, 101, 111, 114–15, 134, 242, 295, 312–13, 321, 330; printed editions of, 115, 319, 322–23. *See also* Hahn, Juspe; *minhagim*; Schammes, Juspe Manzbach
book ownership, 8, 9, 101–14, 116, 121, 125, 137, 249–50
books (as material objects), 8–9, 193, 198, 203, 227, 232, 237, 249–51, 266

Brantshpigel, 105–7, 119, 142
Braunschweig, 94, 270
Büdesheim, 307
burial society: donations to, 24; leaders of, 47, 67–70; and manuals for, 64–67; and material culture, 62–64; members of women's society, 1, 50, 128, 149, 259, 338; and men's society, 70–73, 214, 243; records of, 51–54, 96, 183, 270, 288; tasks of, 48–50, 54–62, 73–75
bursar. See *goveh*

candlelighting, on Shabbat, 101–2, 108–10, 244, 309–11, 387n90; on Hanukkah, 312; on Yom Kippur, 317
candle making, 28, 31, 57, 289, 339, 352n30
cantor, 3, 23, 29, 283, 308, 361, 384n9, 398n76
caretakers for the sick, 30, 133, 160, 163, 165, 173, 214, 230. See also *hekdesh* attendants; postpartum care attendants
Catholics, 15–16, 48, 142, 157, 172, 174, 215, 287, 296
Celle, 94
cemetery workers, 210
charitable societies. See *hevrah*
charity, 25–27, 31–33, 52–53, 55, 64, 72, 155, 157, 165, 183, 209, 243, 302; as fine, 82, 86; and *hekdesh*, 36–37; to Kloyz, 261–63; and poor, 35, 92, 94, 94, 191, 206, 214, 225, 239, 280, 293, 302, 317, 323, 326, 338 (*see also* poverty); of Torah scrolls, 27, 269; for Torah study, 70, 168, 261–63; in wills, 195, 202, 259–61, 265–66, 270. See also *gabbay*; *gabbete*; *hevrah*; *pletten*
childbirth, 10, 108, 149, 274, 276, 281, 290, 293, 298, 302, 334; and amulets, 287–88; and circumcision, 37, 96, 132, 140; death during, 61–88–89, 102, 62, 163–66, 226, 286–88, 358n71, 393n52, 393n58, 394n60; and postpartum care, 38; records of, 45, 162, 215, 228, 243, 285–89, 306, 331–32, 336–37, 358n71, 393n48; and *sandeket* (godmother), 268, 289, 332

Christian Hebraists, 12, 23–24, 63, 127, 134, 189, 230–31, 242, 244, 307, 312, 315–17, 321, 328, 333. *See also entries under individual names*
Christians, 11–13, 40, 46, 92, 95–96, 151, 174, 188, 202, 204, 210, 219, 229, 235, 258, 277, 361n18, 362n37; authorities, 3, 84, 156, 161, 179, 206, 215; and comparative practices, 13, 35–36, 48–49, 83, 98, 119, 122, 140, 172, 175, 184, 191, 233, 236, 243, 247, 329, 336, 386n48, 399n81; maidservants and wetnurses, 88, 181–82, 292–93, 377n134; women, 15–16, 31, 151, 183, 200, 203, 209, 232, 241, 274, 280, 285–86, 289, 310, 350n40, 352n30, 360n134, 371n51, 387n96. *See also* Catholics; Christian Hebraists; conversion; Protestants; Reformation
Cleves, 180, 183, 206, 208
clothing, 28, 51, 69, 95, 152, 164, 164, 171, 183, 189, 192, 195–96, 203, 205, 214–16, 222–24, 226, 229–32, 239–40, 245–49, 255, 257, 259–61, 263–67, 272, 278, 283, 304, 310, 319, 340; armlets, 94; and burial, 61, 357n53, 358n71; and mourning, 51, 64, 333–35; responsibility for, 18, 32; and sumptuary laws, 7, 228–29, 248, 336, 385n26, 385n29, 385n30. *See also* head covering; laundry
Coburg, 91
communal membership. See *hezkat kahal*
communal regulations. See *takkanot*
Conat, Abraham, 123, 209
Conat, Estellina, 122–23, 125, 209
confraternity. See *hevrah*
conversion, 88, 134, 174–75, 231, 241, 321, 355, 368n122, 374n41, 376n96
Copenhagen, 17, 52, 69, 130, 132–34
Corvey, 90
court Jews, 18, 121, 160, 200, 206–9, 221, 237, 262, 354n106
court records, 4, 12, 17, 75, 84, 175, 187–91, 202, 267, 340; of lay Jewish courts, 43–45, 82; of municipal/imperial courts, 1, 15, 77, 224; of rabbinical courts, 227. *See also* lay Jewish court; rabbinical court
crime, 7, 17, 76, 80, 89, 90–95, 303

darshanit, 23, 42, 339, 354n109, 360n132
death, 1, 11, 26, 28, 36–37, 57–59, 66, 70–71, 74, 76, 88–89, 93, 129, 145, 149–50, 152, 172, 175–76, 180, 182–184, 186–87, 189–91, 199, 200, 202, 206, 207, 216, 218, 222, 277, 294, 295, 301–3, 335; maternal, 60–62, 88, 102, 163–69, 278, 286–88, 293, 333, 358n71, 393nn51–52, 394n60. *See also* burial society; childbirth; clothing; infanticide; inventories; shrouds; suicide; widows; wills
desks, 45, 131–32, 240
Dessau, 209
Dinim ve-seder, 100–101
divorce, 11, 16, 19, 85, 87, 131, 141, 152, 161, 169–78, 186, 189–91, 196, 224, 293–94, 326, 333–35
Donauechingen, 206
dowry, 133, 135–36, 156–58, 160, 163–66, 171, 183, 189, 191–96, 200, 202, 210, 226, 259, 264
Drach, Rechle, 1, 5, 17
Dresden, 198
Dublin, 135
Düsseldorf, 373n9

education, 33, 75, 116–25, 198, 221
embroidery, 72, 215, 244, 248–49, 325; of brit pillow, 28; of mappot, 27; of parokhet, 11, 27–28, 260, 352n33; of prayer shawls, 1, 28; and samplers, 12, 119–21, 219, 249; of Torah binder, 11, 119, 121, 289
Emden, Jacob, 66, 119, 162, 219, 288, 296, 390n64
Emmerich, 215
ethical works, 10, 105–6, 141–42, 144, 252. See also *Brantshpigl*; *Lev tov*
etrog, 44, 318. See also Sukkot
excommunication, 78, 84, 194
Eybenschütz, 301
Eybeschutz, Jonathan, 122, 288, 390n64
eyeglasses, 72, 93, 360n134

family relations, 123–25, 131–35, 143–44, 151, 152–79, 195–97, 199, 211–12, 225–26, 233–38, 252–55, 263–71, 273, 286–87, 289–90, 295, 302, 313, 321–25, 329–30, 335;

sister, 36, 69, 87, 97, 129–30, 177, 183–84, 189, 192–93, 203, 209, 235, 269–70, 336. *See also* blended families
fasting, 23, 287, 304, 207, 316–17, 339, 396n130
female authors, 23, 46, 108–9, 115, 116, 126, 141–51, 254
female butchers, slaughterers meat sellers, 7, 210, 216. *See also* (food: meat)
firzogerin, 23–25, 351n11
Flensburg, 92, 94
food, 93, 110, 131–32, 136, 162, 165, 240, 265, 285–86, 289, 292, 314–15, 340, 387n85; and baked goods and confections, 6, 140, 234, 241, 244, 309–10, 317, 319, 336; and charity, 1, 32, 37, 43, 51, 95–96, 302, 304; and cheese, 6, 242; and coffee, 6, 35, 207, 216, 232, 237, 336; and eateries, 34–35; and meat, 6–7, 36, 100, 116, 139, 216, 237, 285–86, 304; preparation of, 139–40, 182, 213, 215, 241–44, 310–313, 321–25, 336; sale of, 6–7, 81, 166, 216, 235
foreign Jews, 32, 35, 91–92, 96, 216, 283
France, 95, 164, 204, 224. *See also* Alsace; Bionville; Hagenau; Kreichingen; Lorraine; Metz; Paris; Steinbiedersdorf
Franconia, 29, 45, 196, 236–37. *See also* Fürth; Hüttenbach; Schnaittach; Schwabach
Frankfurt (am Main), 1, 7, 8, 31, 37–39, 83, 43–44, 50–51, 85, 89, 91, 97, 122, 201, 205, 210, 216, 218–19, 285–86, 300, 302–304, 308, 320, 335, 353n62, 356n28, 361n18, 365n45, 368n107, 375n64, 380n87, 396n130; and books, 111, 117, 152–53; and charity, 27, 28, 34, 36, 198, 280, 283, 338–39; and food, 309, 317, 322–23, 326; and houses, 183–4, 199, 202–203, 233–34, 236, 239, 241; maidservants in, 189, 211–14, 397n17; marriage and divorce in, 164–65, 169–70, 174, 176, 179, 186, 197, 377n118, 379n22, 384n2; material culture in, 227, 243–44, 248–49
Fredericia, 230, 269–71
Friedberg, 7, 24–25, 42, 158, 244, 281

Frisia, 210. *See also* Aurich; Emden
furniture, 12, 45, 110, 114, 127, 131–32, 164, 170–71, 173, 223, 225, 226–28, 230, 237–40, 266, 317
Fürth, 7, 26, 32, 38, 111, 168, 171, 183–84, 209, 217, 237, 262, 303, 328, 335, 351n9, 396n5; and holiday celebrations, 306–7, 315, 318–20; and marriage arrangements, 156–58, 162

gabbay, 20, 34, 71, 243, 270. *See also* charity; *hevrah*
gabbete, 19–21, 25, 31, 47, 55–56, 64–65, 67, 70–71, 74. *See also* charity; *hevrah*
Garküche, 34–35, 326
girls, 5, 13, 33, 40, 41, 80, 84, 86–87, 96–97, 100, 128, 155, 160, 167–68, 180, 184, 191, 210–14, 238, 249, 263–65, 290, 361n18; education of, 116–19, 121–23, 125, 218, 368n104; infant, 62, 162; in printing trade, 122; in rituals, 110–12, 319, 326, 330, 397n36, 400n122; sewing by, 12, 120, 140, 219, 249
Glikl 'of Hameln', 10, 13, 17, 76, 105, 117, 141, 143–45, 150–51, 198, 252, 274–77, 339; on pregnancy and nursing, 285–86, 290–92; and involvement in business, 200–201, 204–5, 215; and grandmother Mata, 32; and marriages, 157–58, 160–62, |167, 192, 206; and raising children; and synagogues, 308, 320; and stepsister, 60
Goldschmidt, Hayim. *See* Hamel, Hayim
Gomperz, Elias, 206
goveh, 53, 74, 267, 360n3
grandchild/ren, 1, 33, 163, 212, 235, 254, 264, 266, 268, 338–39, 349n3
grandfather, 123, 148, 168, 189, 303, 312
grandmother, 1, 32, 123–24, 167, 227
graves, 49, 57, 150, 152–53, 184–85, 300, 315; desecration of, 59–60. *See also* burial society; tombstones
Groningen, 46
Gutmans, Sarel, 18, 219–21

Hagenau, 17
Hahn, Juspe, 119, 211, 239, 285, 210, 312, 323, 325, 335
Halberstadt, 26, 88, 163, 181, 289, 386
Halevi, Asher (of Reichshofen), 162, 176, 234, 244
Halevi, Shmuel, 61, 84–85, 190, 358n70, 358n71
halitzah, 175, 333–35, 384n2, 400n109
hallah, 101–2, 109, 113, 309–10, 317, 321
Hamburg, 64, 74, 79, 94, 96, 122, 130–32, 170, 189, 193, 221, 224, 261–62, 266, 284, 289, 332, 360nn1–2, 388n15; communal institutions in, 29, 32–34; and Glikl, 76, 144, 290, 357n64; midwives in, 39–40, 45. *See also* Altona-Hamburg-Wandsbek
Hamel, Hayim, 143, 158, 162, 192, 200, 205, 274–277, 285
Hannover, 94
Hanover, Nathan Nata, 105–6
Hanukkah, 312; and Judith, 81, 312
harlot. *See zonah*
havdalah, 115, 245
Havot Yair, 123. *See also* Bacharach, Yair Hayim
hazakah. *See hezkat kahal*
Hazan (Horowitz), Bella, 103, 116
hazzante, 24–25. *See also firzogerin*
head coverings, 81, 93, 192, 248, 333, 335, 338
Hechingen, 206–7, 281
Heilbut, Moses, 162–65, 226
Heilprun, Yaakov, 100, 103, 116, 121
hekdesh, 32–33, 35–39, 46, 51, 70, 76, 83, 96–98, 213, 225, 240, 269, 272, 302, 315, 353n78, 353n80, 360n135, 391n75, 391n93
hekdesh attendants, 35–38, 46, 210, 225, 353nn79–80
herem. *See* excommunication
Herlingen, Aaron Wolf, 111
hevrah, 38, 47–73, 75, 128, 140. *See also* burial society
hezkat kahal, 3, 8, 35, 76, 83, 85–86, 154, 156–60, 168–69, 171, 177, 179, 218, 228, 233

Hirsch, Paul Wilhelm, 241, 312
hospitality, 33, 338; in eateries, 34–35, 216, 221; serving coffee, 216
household goods, 136, 202, 230, 266–67. *See also* furniture; kitchenware
houses, 29, 44, 80, 90, 91, 177–78, 183–85, 187, 193, 195–96, 199, 207, 212, 233–45, 261, 262, 266, 272, 282–83, 285, 301, 306, 321, 323, 332
Höxter, 90
Hungary, 58, 204, 272
Hüttenbach, 285

illegitimate pregnancies, 39–40, 82–89, 97, 211–12, 217, 293, 362n34, 362nn37–38, 362n40. See also *zonah*
Illness, 18, 30, 41, 54, 57, 69, 88, 165, 213–14, 230, 271, 274, 279, 285, 296–304; and melancholy, 150, 298; and Polish plait, 301
images of women, 9–12, 55, 58, 62–63, 68, 81, 110–11, 113–15, 127, 216, 230–31, 244, 246–47, 251, 305, 309, 314–15, 317, 321–23, 325, 330–31, 334, 337
immersion, 28, 30, 103, 108–9, 279–85, 299, 301, 393n32. See also *mikveh*
infanticide, 89–90
insult, 77, 79–80, 97, 178, 205
invention of print, 101
inventories, 11, 36, 45, 55, 132, 140, 182, 189, 196, 202, 219, 222, 224–27, 232, 237–42, 244, 256, 267–68, 271, 377n139
Isserlein, Israel, 41, 278, 314
Isserlein, Shondlein, 41–42
Isserles, Moses, 100, 278
Italiener, Avraham, 162–64, 226

Jacob, Dina, 95
Jerusalem, 25, 35, 104, 303, 310, 331
jewelry, 94, 164, 189, 194, 198–99, 226–27, 269, 230, 248, 257–58, 268. *See also* jewelry boxes; wedding ring
judge (rabbinical court), 4, 21–22, 44, 75, 170, 360n6. *See also* rabbinical court

Kabbalah, 48, 123
kahal, 3–4, 30, 39–40, 43, 50, 77–79, 81–84, 88–89, 97–98, 156, 168, 260–61, 269, 277–78, 302, 318, 339–40
Kalimani, Foigele, 121, 125
Katz, Serlina, 101–2
Katzenellenbogen, Ezekiel, 87, 279, 295, 297
Katzenellenbogen, Pinhas, 11, 124, 280, 286, 303
Kaulla, Chaile [Karoline], 18, 123, 206–7, 232, 338
kehillah, 2–5, 14–15, 17–18, 20–46, 51, 67, 70, 76, 78, 81, 88, 97, 272, 338, 340–41
Kehillat Ah"u. *See* Altona-Hamburg-Wandsbek
keriyat Shema, 110–11, 113–14, 309
ketubbah, 43, 86, 173, 195–96, 255, 266
Kirchner, Paul Christian, 23; and Hebraism, 12, 23–24, 63, 127, 134, 189, 230–31, 242, 244, 307, 312, 315–17, 321–24, 231, 242, 308, 315, 321–23, 328, 331, 333–34
Kirrweiler, 199
kitchenware, 164, 223, 226, 231, 241, 243, 323. *See also* pots
Koblenz, 42, 196, 354n106
Kosman, Juspe, 244, 317, 321, 387n91
Kraków, 339
Kreichingen, 162

laundress, 181, 212, 221. *See also* laundry
laundry, 9, 17, 93, 126, 137–39, 212, 216, 241
laundry books and lists, 9, 12, 126, 137–39, 370
lay Jewish courts, 82, 191, 213–14, 216
Leipzig, 204–5
leisure, 7, 183, 249; and games of chance, 7; and playing cards, 289
letters, 26, 39, 42, 90, 97, 104, 151, 160, 166, 174, 178–79, 189, 191–92, 198, 205, 207–8, 201–11, 217–21, 295, 301; Bella Perlhefter and, 127, 140–41, 145, 219, 369n1; collections of, 10, 134–35, 369n8; of credit, 200, 221, 257; love and courtship, 131–32, 135–36, 158; personal, 8–11, 94, 126–36, 229; in printing, 122, 209, 221; privacy in, 130, 369n12

letter writers, 126, 219
Levi, Perlen, 102–3
Lev tov, 105, 142
Libes briv, 121
Library, 101, 105, 108, 124, 139
lider, 10, 115–16, 143, 147, 292, 329
Liebmann, Jost, 200
living arrangements. *See* houses
London, 21, 133–36, 198–99, 210–11
Lorraine, 162, 211, 215, 236. *See also* Bionville; Kreichingen; Metz; Norbach, Steinbiedersdorf
Lublin, 53, 209
Luzzatto, Roza, 103, 121
Lwów (Lvov), 189

mahzor, 108, 124, 209, 318
maidservants, 3, 5, 18, 60, 165, 173, 180–82, 185, 223–24, 229–30, 234, 239–40, 280, 290, 308, 322, 325, 377n134, 382n153, 286n70, 391n82, 397n17; and extramarital pregnancy, 40, 88–90, 293; and terms of employment, 189, 210–14, 217, 221, 244, 382n149; and wills, 10, 255, 257, 260, 262, 264–65, 269, 271–72
mail carrier, 18, 219–20
Mainz, 28, 32–33, 47, 52, 54, 55, 60, 67, 69, 201, 206, 301–4, 308, 333
mamzer, 83
Mannheim, 64, 111, 262, 353n64; and Sinzheim family, 33, 55, 207, 252, 255, 258–60, 263–64, 273
Marburg, 161, 183
Margaritha, Antonius, 314, 316–17
marginal Jews, 74–76, 91, 99, 175, 300. *See also* criminals
marketplace, 77, 94, 166, 204–5, 223, 286, 325
market woman, 197
marriage, 12–13, 16, 33, 85, 129, 135, 152–63, 189–91, 204, 212, 228, 293–94, 326, 333; and assets, 195–99, 202, 226, 254, 265–67, 329; and celebrations, 330–31; and commerce, 200–203, 256; restrictions on, 179–81; and strife, 169–79, 217; and status, 44–45, 182–85, 192, 206. *See also* blended families; divorce; dowry; *ketubbah*; premarital contracts
matchmaking, 135–36, 154–55, 157–58
mayim aharonim, 113
Mehler, Judah, 11, 42, 87, 124, 141, 161, 165, 177–78, 191, 198, 215, 237–38, 291, 297, 335, 352n33
Melitz yosher, 106
Melokhim bukh, 107
memoirs, 8, 11, 124, 141, 162, 167–68, 216, 218, 234, 252, 274, 276, 285–87; and Glikl, 76, 105, 117, 143–45, 200, 204
Memorbuch, 5, 12, 28, 32, 60, 68, 76, 78, 143, 206–7, 262, 339, 392n101; and death in childbirth, 165–66, 286; and illness and pain, 300, 302–4; and prayer, 24, 307–9, 351n11; and sacred societies, 47, 51; and single women, 184; and women's knowledge, 121, 123, 201, 218
meneket havero, 87, 177, 292–94. *See also* nursing
Meneket Rivkah, 141–42, 154, 181, 292
menstrual purity. *See niddah*
menstruation, 11, 277–80, 290–91, 298
Metz, 5, 7, 26, 35, 40, 44, 83, 96–97, 161, 165, 170, 173, 190–94, 198–99, 202–3, 217, 226, 228, 236, 238, 288, 293, 315, 335, 362n34, 388n101; and Glikl, 320; and *hevrot*, 51, 52, 54, 56–61, 394n60; and women's bequests, 244, 260, 265, 273
mezuzah, 114
midwives, 5, 18, 89, 140, 165, 178, 200, 223, 287–91, 297, 302, 338, 352n45; as record keepers, 45–46, 96, 162–63, 218; and role in community, 27–41, 84
mikveh, 16–17, 21–22, 25, 26–30, 46, 113, 126, 275–84, 301, 314, 327–28; books and prayers for, 108–9, 113. *See also* immersion
mikveh attendants and managers, 28–31, 352n45
Mi-See, Isaac, 77, 131–32, 195, 212, 281–82, 297
mohel, 45, 62, 96, 162, 215, 330–32
Molin, Jacob, 109, 275, 366

Moravia, 5, 37, 52, 102, 118, 139, 167, 179–80, 216, 218, 272, 279, 369n127
Mosqita, 101–1, 103, 116, 125
murder, 34, 60–61, 77, 234, 303, 358n70. See also infanticide; suicide

Nahalat shivah, 61, 190
nannies, 181, 211, 212–13, 272, 391n93, 394n80
nashim hagunot and *nashim kesherot*, 40–41, 75
ne'emanim. See notaries
niddah, 41, 56, 110, 274–81, 290–91, 297, 309.
   See also menstruation
Nikolsburg (Mikulov), 118
Norbach (Forbach), 96
notaries, 107, 156, 177–78, 186–87, 189, 197, 202, 224, 254, 256, 272, 278
nursing, 88, 113, 286, 290–95, 296, 298, 318.
   See also *meneket havero*; wetnurses

oaths, 40, 44, 84, 157, 203, 257, 294
Oldendorf, Menachem, 108
Oppenheim, David, 121, 206
Oppenheim, Judith, 132, 226
Oppenheim, Samuel, 207
Oppenheim, Sara, 121, 125
Oppenheim, Talze, 206
Orekh yomim, 103
orphans, 40, 96, 128, 135, 157, 167–68, 178, 193, 265, 381n92; care and support for, 25, 33–34, 51, 259, 270, 353n58, 353n62

Padua, 283
Pan, Toybe (bas Leyb Pitzker), 116
Paris, 35, 202
parnas, 3–4, 7–8, 29–30, 33, 44, 75, 81, 97, 182, 194, 318; of the month, 78, 84, 156, 256
Passover, 101, 110–11, 115, 140, 223, 227, 233–34, 245, 289, 313, 320–26
paternity suit, 39–41, 84, 293. See also illegitimate pregnancy; *zonah*
penalties/fines: and Christian authorities, 180, 205, 272; in communal regulations, 7, 25–26, 30, 160, 176, 211, 318–19; individual cases of, 77–79, 81–82, 84, 97, 171, 195,
361n23; in sacred sororities, 52, 67.
   See also charity, as fine
Perlhefter, Bella, 17, 126–30, 134, 141, 143, 145–51, 166, 219, 339, 360n132. See also letters
Perlhefter, Ber Eybeschutz, 127, 134, 145–50, 219
Pesah. See Passover
Pfefferkorn, Johannes, 231, 314, 317
pinkas, 4–5, 8, 18, 29, 72, 75, 79, 81, 83, 85–86, 97, 176–77, 186, 189, 216, 239, 256, 278, 283, 339; of charity collectors, 25; and fines/penalties, 77; of the *kahal*, 8, 41, 89; of midwives, 45–46; of *mohalim*, 96, 215; of notaries, 197; of synagogues, 20–21; of sacred societies, 47–53, 59, 61, 68, 72, 75, 128, 288; of wills, 256, 265, 273
plague, 32, 56, 116, 168, 234, 288, 294–95, 354n108
pletten, 32, 326. See also charity
Poland, 44, 53, 189, 193, 204, 230, 276.
   See also Kraków; Lwów; Rzesów
Poriat, Moses, 104–5
Poriat, Rachel, 103, 116
postpartum care, 30, 37, 96, 217–18, 290; and attendants, 38
pots, 12, 100, 164, 213, 242–43
poverty, 46, 54, 76, 118, 121, 137, 156, 166–67, 204, 225–26, 235–36, 239–43, 249, 255, 264, 266, 271–73, 285–86; and begging, 188; and communal support for, 32, 34–39, 51, 70–71, 183, 214; and dowries, 50, 191; and illness, 298, 302; and immersion, 29, 280, 283; and itinerants, 95–99; and labor, 210–11, 216, 218; and maidservants, 221, 223. See also charity; *hekdesh*; marginal Jews
Prague, 17, 20–21, 66, 82, 88, 110, 121, 123, 134, 139–40, 147, 166, 174, 202, 219, 233–34, 239, 245, 247, 303, 325, 336, 369n127; and Bella Perlhefter, 126–28; and burial societies, 24, 49, 68–69, 71–73, 214, 389n34; and educated women, 23, 103–4, 116, 360n132; and Rivkah Tiktiner, 141–43; and women's bequests, 27–28, 52–53, 55–56, 68

prayer, 10, 20, 50–51, 57–58, 69, 73, 74, 84, 101–5, 123, 149, 183, 207, 209, 234, 236, 249–51, 260–62, 287, 290, 304, 307–11; and illness, 302; interruption of, 77, 277; and *kaddish*, 269–70; in manuscripts for women, 108–11, 113–14, 137; in synagogue, 22–25, 314–15, 318–19, 332; and women's rituals, 284; in Yiddish, 64–66, 116. See also *mahzor; siddur; selihot; tkhines*

pregnancy, 18, 40, 61, 76, 96, 143, 155, 165, 177–78, 257, 274, 279, 285–296, 298, 317; and prayer, 105, 113, 355n121. *See also* illegitimate pregnancy

premarital contracts, 4, 156, 164, 168, 187, 189, 192, 202, 212

print culture, 7–9, 14, 17, 100–125, 139, 340

printing: patrons of, 100–104, 106–7, 121; publishers, 103, 105, 107; typesetters, 122–23, 221

Protestants, 6, 15–16, 142, 173, 174–75, 287, 296

Provence, 123, 164

Prussia, 180

Purim, 42, 61, 312–13

rabbanit, 8, 41–44, 60, 100, 106, 122, 124, 142, 193, 258, 262, 303, 319, 328, 339, 365n44, 369n128, 371n57

rabbinical court, 44–45, 75, 84–85, 187–94, 225, 227–28, 261, 265, 272, 293–94, 333, 335, 379n22, 400n110; in Frankfurt, 164, 184, 233, 380n87; and marital strife, 167–73, 202, 217; in Metz, 35, 40–41, 236, 238

rebbetzin. See *rabbanit*

Reformation, 2, 16, 142, 172, 174–75, 287, 296. See also Christians

Regensberg, 107, 196, 204, 351n5

Reichensachsen, 91

Reischer (Rzeszów), Jacob, 59–60, 212

Reischer (Rzeszów), Yutel, 59–60, 303

Rendsburg, 47, 52, 54, 57, 62, 67–68, 71, 93

responsa, 4, 11, 41, 61, 76, 123, 131, 165, 175, 187, 204, 276–77, 279, 296, 352n33. *See also* entries under names of individual rabbis

Rhineland, 49, 52, 164, 302. *See also* Alzey; Mainz; Speyer; Worms

ritual bath. See *mikveh*

ritual items, 28, 215, 227, 223, 244–45; for burial, 63–64. *See also* embroidery; *siddur*

Rosheim, 202

Rosh Hashanah, 314–16. See also *tashlikh*

Rosh hodesh, 311–12, 394n62, 397n30

Runkel (in Hesse), 118, 203, 381n91

Ruthenia, 182

Schammes, Juspe Manzbach, shamash of Worms, 10, 56, 278, 302, 306–7, 315, 318–19, 328–30, 332, 335, 352n48, 358n73

Scheuer, Leah Hindchen, 51, 338–39

Schnaittach, 29, 45, 189, 236, 243, 283, 285; and Bella Perlhefter, 134, 141, 147

Schwabach, 369n127

Schwerin, 99; and Duke of Mecklenburg-Schwerin, 66

scribe, 27, 102–3, 106–9, 111, 133, 135, 137, 139, 176, 210, 252, 333; communal scribes, 3, 19, 97, 189, 256–57, 278; in court, 171; female scribes, 46, 121–22, 125, 219; of sacred societies, 61, 69

seder, 110, 227, 244–45, 321, 325–26. *See also* Passover

Seder mitzvot nashim, 109, 282, 299

Sefer minhagim. See book of customs

sefirat ha-omer, 110–11, 115

selihot, 101, 108, 111, 124, 152–53, 314

sexual violence, 80–85, 97, 361n18

Sha'ar Shimon, 62, 64, 66

Shabbat, 27, 42, 56, 61, 108–10, 115, 140, 183, 237–38, 260–61, 284, 289, 308–12, 321, 327–28, 338; and candle lighting, 102, 244–45; and clothing, 85, 189, 229, 247, 249, 335–36; and food preparation, 212–13, 216, 234, 242–44, 325; and prayers, 5, 10

shamash, 27, 39, 55–56, 67, 69, 78, 83, 86, 156, 232, 243, 256, 261, 315, 321, 327–28, 384n9, 389n18, 400n110. *See also* Schammes, Juspe Manzbach

shame, 17, 74–80, 85–86, 89–90, 97–99, 176, 179, 268, 292
Shavu'ot, 111, 115, 140, 312
shetar hatzi helek zakhar, 190, 192
shetar mukat etz, 41
Shmuel bukh, 107
shrouds, 1, 49, 51, 53–57, 59–64, 66, 69–74, 191, 215, 223, 260, 262, 333, 357n34, 360n135, 389n34
siddur, 8, 10, 103–5, 108, 113–14, 137, 209, 232, 249–51, 284, 299, 307, 309, 314
Sidre berakhot, 10, 111, 114, 230, 307
Simhat Torah, 31, 116, 319–20
single women, 7, 18, 80, 111, 136, 143, 157, 160, 177, 187–88, 224, 228, 249, 302, 327–28; and domestic service, 191, 210–11; and economic roles, 203, 214, 216–17; in households, 179–85; and pregnancy, 83–89, 155, 291, 294–95; and wills, 254–55, 257, 266, 269–71
Sinzheim, Hayim, 34
Sinzheim, Leyb, 34, 207–8, 271
Sinzheim, Miriam, 207–8
Sinzheim, Rebecca, 33, 55–56, 60, 64, 252–55, 258–60, 263–65, 273
slander, 77, 179
Slonik, Benjamin, 109–10, 276, 282, 299, 364n8
Sofer, Jacob ben Judah Leyb of Berlin, 111
Sofia, 200
songs, 10, 69, 101, 110, 115–16, 143, 147, 327; and funerals, 66, 73; and weddings, 292, 329, 336. See also *lider*
sorority. See *hevrah*
Speyer, 333; and Jews of bishopric, 355n115, 373n10
Steinbiedersdorf, 13, 162, 204, 214, 235, 239, 249, 362n38
step relationships. See blended families
storage, 222, 237–40, 242, 323; in chests, 91–92, 182, 216, 225, 239–40, 269, 271; in jewelry boxes, 132, 239; in pockets/purses, 182, 230, 240, 245, 271, 386n71
suicide, 180, 299–300

Sukkot, 44, 80, 217, 233, 306, 317–19. See also *etrog*
Sulzbach, 109
sumptuary laws, 7, 77, 228–30, 248, 337–37
Swabia, 180, 195, 203–4, 211, 237
synagogue, 3, 55, 67, 83, 101, 107–9, 116, 144, 157, 200, 228, 236, 254, 312, 330–33, 340; announcements in, 6, 30, 45, 77–78, 284; seats in, 20, 85, 187, 195, 197–98, 260, 318, 320, 386; women's attendance in, 1, 93, 213, 249, 277–78, 289–90, 306–8, 311, 314, 317–21, 335–36, 339, 396n130, 397n41; women's bequests to, 25–28, 119, 215, 260, 262, 269–70, 272; women's tasks in, 30–32, 46; women's section in, 16–17, 20–25, 42–43, 64, 115, 148, 351n8, 386n48

takkanot, 5–7, 21–22, 24–26, 28–30, 36, 38, 44–45, 77, 81–83, 88, 96, 118, 154–55, 157–58, 160, 164–65, 168–69, 171–72, 183, 192, 197, 200–201, 203–4, 213–14, 218–19, 228–29, 248, 274, 278, 284–85, 289, 315, 318–20, 336–37; of sacred societies, 47–50, 52, 54–57, 60–62, 66–69, 71–73. See also sumptuary laws
Tam, Jacob, 164
tashlikh, 111, 314–16
taxes, 221; collected by Jewish community, 3–5, 8, 39, 42, 70, 117–18, 154, 156, 158, 164, 183–84, 187, 196, 201, 203, 228, 373n27, 381n92; collected by non-Jewish authorities, 179–80, 183, 203, 206, 210, 340
tena'im. See premarital contracts
Tešetice, 139
theft, 91, 93, 95, 104, 173, 240
Tikkune shabbat, 291
Tiktiner, Rivkah, 3, 17, 23, 116, 118, 141–43, 150, 154, 181, 276, 277, 292
Tishah be-Av, 23–24, 351n11
tkhines, 10, 66, 108–9, 111, 113, 116, 142, 284, 307, 301
tombstone, 1, 12, 23–24, 33–34, 42, 47, 62, 78, 166, 184–85, 207, 218, 262, 268, 286, 309, 339
Torat ha-hatat, 100

Traub, Devorah, 74–76
travel, 2, 8, 39, 42, 105–6, 114, 152, 162, 200, 239, 326; and female travelers, 37, 61, 91, 93, 95, 98, 182, 188, 191, 204–5, 210–11, 215–19, 282–83, 291; and food, 34–35; and *hekdesh*, 37; and letters, 135, 158
Trieste, 200
triple community. *See* Altona-Hamburg-Wandsbek
Tsene u-rene, 104, 107, 144
tumblers (glass), 68
Tyrnau, Isaac of, 114, 323. *See also* (book of customs, printed editions of)
Tzvi, Sabbatai, 144–45

Vienna, 17, 36, 111, 126, 128, 132, 141, 198, 204–5, 207, 210, 219, 224, 226, 257, 262, 271, 374n57
violence, 58, 60, 68, 77–78, 80–81, 90, 175, 177–179
virginity, 41, 84, 86–88, 165, 212, 295, 328, 335–36

Wagenseil, Johann Christoph, 134, 136, 145, 189
Wandsbek. *See* Altona-Hamburg-Wandsbek
washing: in bathhouse, 234, 327–28; and fountain for burial, 64; in sink for prayer, 27. *See also mayim aharonim*
wedding, 30, 33, 42, 87, 136, 154, 156–57, 159, 165, 187, 196, 243, 291, 327–28, 330, 335–36; and gifts, 111, 171, 226–27, 243, 248; and wedding ring, 189, 199, 230, 258, 268; and songs, 10, 329. *See also* marriage
wetnurses, 82, 87–89, 98, 216–17, 290–94. *See also* nursing
Wetzlar, Isaac, 121
widows, 10, 18–19, 75, 85–87, 133, 136, 150, 300, 351n5, 354n108, 357n53, 369n128; and communal role, 42–45, 47, 71, 156, 158, 303, 358n75; as donors, 27, 54, 388n15; and economic role, 28–29, 36–37, 122, 166, 187–88, 193–94, 196–202, 205, 210, 212, 216–17, 271; and estates, 224, 232, 242, 245, 251, 254–257, 260, 264, 265–68, 273, 365n44, 384n2, 387n71, 390n69, 391n72; and family role, 33, 168, 175–77, 180, 230, 293–94, 333, 335–36, 362n38; and homes, 222, 225–27, 233, 235–36, 238, 242, 332; and poverty, 25, 93–94, 128–29, 326
Widuwilt, 102
Wied-Runkel. *See* Runkel
wills, 5, 8, 10, 33, 36–37, 53, 57, 60, 140, 144, 151, 157, 189–90, 224, 229, 239, 244, 252–73; ethical wills, 105; and inheritance for women, 192–96, 222
Wilmersdorf, 209
wise women, 41, 291. *See also nashim hagunot*
witches, 79, 287
women's commandments, 11, 110–11, 114, 280, 282, 286, 309. *See also Seder mitzvot nashim*
women's commerce, 140, 198, 200–209, 215, 248, 267–68
women's recordkeeping, 5, 8, 9, 29–30, 35, 37, 39, 46, 52–54, 70–71, 136–40, 189, 201, 215–16, 273
Worms, 6, 10, 27, 32, 35, 42, 44, 49, 123, 160, 187, 193, 198–99, 203, 205, 218, 246, 289, 249, 281, 306–7, 332–33, 339; and burial society, 55–57, 61–62, 214, 243; and holiday celebrations, 31, 318–19; and houses, 43, 196, 207, 235; and marriages, 156, 160, 192, 327, 329–30; and tombstones, 185, 218
Württemburg, 281, 296; and Duke, 206

Yom Kippur, 287, 314–17, 364n15, 366n70, 377n134
Yosif ometz, 119, 312

zonah, 77, 82–86, 89, 169, 361. *See also* illegitimate pregnancies

A NOTE ON THE TYPE

This book has been composed in Arno, an Old-style serif typeface in the classic Venetian tradition, designed by Robert Slimbach at Adobe.